THE BARBOUR
COLLECTION
OF CONNECTICUT TOWN
VITAL RECORDS

D1711615

THE BARBOUR COLLECTION
OF CONNECTICUT TOWN
VITAL RECORDS

BRANFORD 1644–1850

BRIDGEPORT 1821–1854

Compiled by

Lorraine Cook White

INTRODUCTION

As early as 1640 the Connecticut Court of Election ordered all magistrates to keep a record of the marriages they performed. In 1644 the registration of births and marriages became the official responsibility of town clerks and registrars, with deaths added to their duties in 1650. From 1660 until the close of the Revolutionary War these vital records of birth, marriage, and death were generally well kept, but then for a period of about two generations until the mid-nineteenth century, the faithful recording of vital records declined in some towns.

General Lucius Barnes Barbour was the Connecticut Examiner of Public Records from 1911 to 1934 and in that capacity directed a project in which the vital records kept by the towns up to about 1850 were copied and abstracted. Barbour previously had directed the publication of the Bolton and Vernon vital records for the Connecticut Historical Society. For this new project he hired several individuals who were experienced in copying old records and familiar with the old script.

Barbour presented the completed transcriptions of town vital records to the Connecticut State Library where the information was typed onto printed forms. The form sheets were then cut, producing twelve small slips from each sheet. The slips for most towns were then alphabetized and the information was then typed a second time on large sheets of rag paper, which were subsequently bound into separate volumes for each town. The slips for all towns were then interfiled, forming a statewide alphabetized slip index for most surviving town vital records.

The dates of coverage vary from town to town, and of course the records of some towns are more complete than others. There are many cases in which an entry may appear two or three times, apparently because that entry was entered by one or more persons. Altogether the entire Barbour Collection--one of the great genealogical manuscript collections and one of the last to be published--covers 137 towns and comprises 14,333 typed pages.

TABLE OF CONTENTS

ABBREVIATIONS

ae.------------age
b. ------------born, both
bd.------------buried
B. G.---------Burying Ground
d. ------------died, day, or daughter
decd.---------deceased
f.--------------father
h.--------------hour
J. P.-----------Justice of Peace
m.-------------married or month
res.------------resident
s.--------------son
st.-------------stillborn
w. ------------wife
wid.----------widow
wk.-----------week
y. ------------year

THE BARBOUR
COLLECTION
OF CONNECTICUT TOWN
VITAL RECORDS

BRANFORD VITAL RECORDS
1644 - 1850

	Vol.	Page
ABBOT, ABUT, ABUTT, Abegell, d. Robert, b. Oct. 2, [1650]	1	171
Abigail, [d. Joseph & Hannah], b. June 24, 1747	3	115
Beniamin, s. Robert, b. Jan. 10, [1653]	1	171
Beniamin, s. Robert, d. Mar. 27, 1654	1	170
Dani[e]ll, s. Robert, b. Feb. 12, 1654	1	172
Daniel, s. Stephen & Hannah, b. Jan. 4, 1725/6	3	59
David, s. Stephen & Hannah, b. Aug. 16, 1727	3	74
Hannah, m. Benjamin **BARNS**, 2d, b. of Branford, Dec. 7, 1727, by Rev. Sam[ue]ll Russell	3	65
Hannah, [d. Joseph & Hannah], b. Apr. 4, 1741	3	115
Hannah, m. Ebenezor **FRISBIE**, June 29, 1758, by Sam[ue]ll Barker, J. P.	3	152
Jemima, [d. Joseph & Hannah], b. Oct. 13, 1733	3	115
Jemima, d. Joseph & Hannah, b. Oct. 23, 1733	3	77
John, s. Robert, b. Apr. 20, 1652	1	171
Joseph, m. Hannah **MARKS**, b. of Branford, Apr. 14, 1730, by Jno. Russell, J. P.	3	70
Joseph, [s. Joseph & Hannah], b. Aug. 28, 1737	3	115
Lydia, [d. Joseph & Hannah], b. Feb. 14, 1739	3	115
Marie, m. John **ROBINS**, Nov. 4, 1659	1	173
Mary, d. Robert, b. Mar. 13, [16]57	1	172
Rebe[c]kah, [d. Joseph & Hannah], b. Jan. 18, 1744/5	3	115
Robert, d. Sept. 31 (sic), 1658	1	170
Stephen, m. Hannah **FRISBE**, b. of Branford, Jan. 6, 1724/5, by Rev. Sam[ue]ll Russell	3	59
Thankfull, d. Joseph & Hannah, b. Jan. 29, 1730/1	3	70
ADAME, George, m. wid. [ ] **BRADFEELD**, Sept. 5, 1657	1	173
ALLEN, ALLIN, [see also **ALLING**], Amelia, of New Haven, m. Abel **HOADLEY**, of Branford, [1839?], by Rev. Timothy P. Gillett	3	376
Anne, d. Sam[ue]ll & Anne, b. Apr. 12, 1760	3	161
Elisabeth, w. of Sam[ue]ll, d. June 27, 1753	3	133
Joseph, s. Sam[ue]ll & Anne, b. Nov. 18, 1757	3	146
Mary, d. Thomas & Phebe, b. Mar. 2, 1740/1	3	96
Mary, d. Samuel & Ann, b. Aug. 29, 1755	3	140
Mary, m. John **BARKER**, b. of Branford, Mar. 17, 1765, by Philemon Robbins	3	284
Sam[ue]ll, of Stratford, m. Elisabeth **ROSE**, of Branford, Jan. 23, 1748/9, by Rev. P. Robbins	3	120
Sam[ue]ll, s. Sam[ue]ll & Elisabeth, b. Aug. 10, 1750	3	120
Sam[ue]ll, m. Ann **FOOT**, b. of Branford, May 8, 1854, by		

1

	Vol.	Page
ALLEN, ALLIN, (cont.		
Rev. Philemon Robbins	3	136
Thomas, m. Phebe **WARDELL**, b. of Branford, Apr. 10, 1740,		
by Rev. Philemon Robbins	3	96
William, m. Jemima **FULLER**, b. of Branford, Dec. 17, 1739,		
by Jona[than] Arnold, Missionary	3	92
ALLING, [see also **ALLEN**], Phebe, of New Haven, m. Jonathan		
BYINTUN, of Branford, Jan. 10, 1753, by Jacob		
Hemingway	3	168
AMES, Augustus, s. Chloe **HOADLY**, b. Apr. 8, 1785	3	280
Augustus, s. Chloe **HOADLY**, b. Apr. 8, 1785	3	390
ANDREWS, Atwater, of Wallingford, m. Susan **PALMER**, of		
Branford, Mar. 27, 1831, by Edw[ar]d J. Ives	3	361
Betsey Hobart, d. Atwater & Susan, b. Feb. 24, 1838	TM3	238
George H., of Branford, m. Lydia **BASSETT**, of Hamden, May		
2, 1853, by (Episcopal Minister) in New York	TM3	172
George Hoadley, s. Atwater & Susan, b. June 11, 1832	3	365
Hiram, [s. Nicholas & Jerusha], b. Oct. 13, 1810	3	387
Nancy, d. Nicholas & Jerusha, b. July 26, 1815	3	410
Nancy, m. Charles **HOADLEY**, July 2, 1843, by Rev. Davis		
T. Shailer	TM3	156
Nicholas, m. Jerusha **HOPSON**, Sept. 24, 1807	3	387
Sarah, d. Nicholas & Jerusha, b. May 15, 1818	3	410
Uri, [s. Nicholas & Jerusha], b. Aug. 11, 1808	3	387
Uri, m. Susan **LINSLEY**, July 27, 1845, by Rev. Frederick		
Miller	TM3	160
APPALY, [see also **APPLE**], Almira, m. Truman **SHELDON**, May		
27, 1840	TM3	161
APPELL, [see under **APPLE**]		
APPLE, APPELL, [see also **APPALY**], Alonzo, m. Lois		
RUSSELL, Sept. 6, 1829, by J. A. Root	3	350
Apollos, of North Branford, m. Almira **COOK**, of Guilford,		
Apr. 8, 1827, by Rev. Timothy P. Gillett	3	343
Peter, m. Lois **BALDWIN**, b. of Branford, May 21, 1793, by		
Sam[ue]l Eells	3	263
Polly, d. [Peter & Lois], b. Mar. 27, 1794	3	263
Silvia, d. Peter & Lois, b. Apr. 29, 1796	3	269
ASHBAND, Mary, of Milford, m. John **WAY**, of Branford, Oct. 30,		
1718, by Rev. Jacob Hemingway, at East Haven	3	44
ASHER, Mariet, m. Kalep **COPES**, June 26, 1823, by Charles		
Atwater	3	423
ATWATER, Anne, [d. Rev. Jason & Anne], b. May 1, 1787; d.		
in a few hours	3	400
Anne, [d. Rev. Jason & Anne], b. Apr. 1, 1788; lived one day	3	400
Anne, [d. Rev. Jason & Anne], b. Sept. 15, 1792	3	400
Anne, wid. of Rev. Jason, m. Rev. Lynde **HUNTINGTON**,		
June 15, 1796	3	401
Hannah, of New Haven, m. Charles **BUTLER**, Nov. 6, 1771,		

	Vol.	Page
ATWATER, (cont.)		
by Jon[a]th[an] Edwards	3	292
Jason, Rev., m. Mrs. Anne **WILLIAMS**, b. of Branford, Dec.		
7, 1784, by Warham Williams	3	312
Jason, Rev., m. Anne **WILLIAMS**, Dec. 7, 1784	3	400
Jason, Rev., d. June 10, 1794, in the 36th y. of his age		
and 11th y. of his ministry	3	401
Mary, of Hamden, m. Davenport **WILLIAMS**, of Branford,		
Feb. 5, 1789, by Joshua Perry, in Hamden	3	260
Sophia, [d. Rev. Jason & Anne], b. Nov. 22, 1790; d. Mar.		
4, 1794	3	400
Sophia, [d. Rev. Jason & Anne], b. Mar. 12, 1794; d.		
in a few hours	3	401
----, s. [Rev. Jason & Anne], b. Sept. 22, 1785; d. soon	3	400
ATWOOD, Bennett, m. Harriet **COOK**, b. of Wallingford, Mar. 18,		
1849, by Rev. T. P. Gillett	TM3	163
AUGUR, AUGAR, AUGER, Abraham, ae 40, of Georgia, m. Ellen		
MORRIS, ae 25, July 28, 1850, by Rev. Lucius Atwater	TM3	167
Abraham, of Georgia, m. Ellen **MORRIS**, of Branford, July		
29, 1850, by Rev. Lucius Atwater	TM3	165
Dan[ie]l Page, s. John, Jr. & Dinah, b. Mar. 14, 1781	3	313
Edward Blak[e]slee, s. Peter & Chlorane, b. July 19, 1788	3	266
Har[r]iot, s. Peter & Chlorane, b. May 19, 1792 (Perhaps a		
daughter?)	3	266
Harvey, s. Peter & Chlorane, b. July 31, 1794	3	266
Jared, s. Jos[ep]h & Rebec[c]ah, b. Sept. 27, 1777	3	267
John, m. Rachel **BARNS**, b. of Branford, Jan. 5, 1743/4,		
by Rev. Jonath[an] Merick	3	113
John, s. John & Rachel, b. June 11, 1748	3	124
John, s. John & Rachel, b. June 19, 1748	3	158
John, 3rd, s. Joseph & Rebecca, b. May 26, 1776	3	267
John, Jr., m. Dinah **PAGE**, 2d, b. of Branford, Nov. 20, 1776,		
by Warham Williams	3	313
Joseph, s. John & Rachel, b. July 23, 1752	3	159
Joseph, m. Rebec[c]ah **BOILES**, b. of Branford, Feb. 20, 1775	3	267
Joseph, Jr., s. Joseph & Rebec[c]ah, b. June 4, 1779	3	267
Keturah, d. John & Rachel, b. June 17, 1746	3	113
Leveret, s. Peter & Chlorane, b. Dec. 4, 1784	3	266
Lorene, d. Peter & Chlorane, b. July 20, 1790	3	266
Lucinda, m. Andrew **GATES**, b. of Branford, Apr. 13, 1823,		
by Rev. Oliver Willson, of North Haven	3	422
Peter, s. John & Rachel, b. July 12, 1750	3	124
Peter, s. John & Rachel, b. July 12, 1750	3	159
Peter, m. Chlorane **BLAK[E]SLEE**, Feb. 19, 1784	3	266
Peter, s. Peter & Chlorane, b. Nov. 27, 1786	3	266
Phebe, d. John, Jr. & Dinah, b. Apr. 8, 1783	3	313
Puah, d. John & Rachel, b. May 1, 1755	3	159
Rachel, d. John & Rachel, b. Oct. 27, 1744	3	113

	Vol.	Page
AUGUR, AUGAR, AUGER, (cont.)		
Rachel, m. Nehemiah **ROGERS**, b. of Branford, Mar. 1, 1763,		
by Jon[a]th[an] Merick	3	190
Rebec[c]ah, d. Jos[ep]h & Rebec[c]ah, b. May 7, 1781; d.		
Oct. 25, 1795	3	267
Reuben, s. John, Jr. & Dinah, b. June 29, 1787	3	254
Rhoda, d. John, Jr. & Dinah, b. Aug. 5, 1777	3	313
Robart, s. John, Jr. & Dinah, b. July 9, 1785	3	313
We[a]lthy, d. John, Jr. & Dinah, b. Aug. 30, 1779	3	313
AUSTIN, William P., of Wallingford m. Eliza **BROCKWAY**, of		
Branford, Oct. 22, 1834, by Rev. Timothy P. Gillett	3	367
AVERILL, Betsey, [d. Daniel & Hannah], b. Sept. 30, 1802	3	286
Betsey, [d. Daniel & Hannah], d. Sept. 10, 1805	3	286
Betsey, [d. Chester & Sally], b. June 22, 1813	3	396
Betsey A., of Branford, m. Shubael **TILLOTSON**, of New		
Haven, Oct. 27, 1836, by Rev. Timothy P. Gillett	3	373
Charles Albert, s. Daniel & Jane, b. May 26, 1843, in		
Roxbury, Conn.	TM3	235
Chester, m. Sally **RUSSELL**, Mar. 8, 1809	3	396
Daniel, m. Hannah **TYLER**, Nov. 3, 1796	3	286
Daniel, [s. James & Amanda], b. July 9, 1840	TM3	236
Daniel, d. Aug. 5, 1842	TM3	304
Elvira E., m. Joseph **POND**, June 5, 1845, by Rev. Frederick		
Miller	TM3	160
Eunice, m. John **TYLER**, Jr., b. of Branford, July 23,		
1828, by Rev. Timothy P. Gillett	3	347
Eunice A., of Branford, m. Russell S. **GLADDING**, of		
Saybrook, Sept. 13, 1847, by Rev. A. C. Wheat	TM3	160
Frances Eliza d. Samuel, b. Nov. 7, 1835	TM3	229
George Marshal, [s. John & Almena], b. Oct. 12, 1838	TM3	237
Harriet, [d. Chester & Sally], b. Nov. 9, 1819	3	396
Harriett, m. Timothy **COOK**, b. of Branford, Oct. 11, 1849,		
by Rev. Timothy P. Gillett	TM3	164
Harriett, ae 32, m. Timothy **COOK**, ae 30, Oct. 11, 1849,		
by Rev. T. P. Gillett	TM3	167
Harriet Jennet, [d. John & Almena], b. Sept. 27, 1840	TM3	237
Henry W., s. Samuel & Myrta A., b. Feb. 21, 1851	TM3	244
Irene, [d. Daniel, Jr. & Abigail], b. Jan. 12, 1828	3	354
Irene, m. Henry **PALMER**, b. of Branford, Jan. 15, 1846,		
by Rev. Timothy P. Gillett	TM3	159
James, [s. Daniel & Hannah], b. June 30, 1807	3	286
Jane Maria, [d. Samuel], b. Aug. 27, 1838	TM3	229
Josaphine, [d. James & Amanda], b. Feb. 5, 1837	TM3	236
Lucy, [d. James & Amanda], b. Feb. 4, 1845	TM3	236
Lucy, d. James & Amanda, d. Nov. 1, 1845	TM3	307
Lucy, d. James & Amanda, b. May 14, 1849	TM3	241
Mary Ann, m. Jared **SHEPHERD**, Sept. 4, 1837, by Rev.		
David Baldwin	3	375

	Vol.	Page
AVERILL, (cont.)		
Mary Maria, [d. James & Amanda], b. Mar. 30, 1841	TM3	236
Polly, w. of David, d. July 30, 1833, ae 44 y.	3	366
Ralph, [s. Daniel, Jr. & Abigail], b. Dec. 2, 1817	3	354
Rowland Gilston, [s. John & Almena], b. May 3, 1843	TM3	237
Samuel, [s. Daniel, Jr. & Abigail], b. July 12, 1824	3	354
Samuel, m. Betsey **BLACKSTONE**, b. of Branford, Dec. 9, 1832, by Rev. T. P. Gillett	3	359
Samuel, m. Mariette **TYLER**, b. of Branford, May 9, 1843, by Rev. Timothy P. Gillett	TM3	156
Samuel, d. Dec. 21, 1850, ae 51 y.	TM3	310
Wallace F., s. Sam[ue]ll & Murta Ann, b. Aug. 5, 1847	TM3	239
William, [s. Daniel & Hannah], b. Feb. 16, 1805	3	286
William, m. Elisa **BLACKSTONE**, b. of Branford, Jan. 2, 1842, by Rev. Timothy P. Gillett	TM3	154
William Bassett, [s. James & Amanda], b. Jan. 4, 1835	TM3	236
William Bassett, s. James & Amanda, d. May 20, 1843	TM3	307
William Hoadley, [s. Daniel, Jr. & Abigail], b. July 10, 1821	3	354
AVERY, David, m. Thankful **LINSLEY**, Feb. 4, 1838, by Rev. David Baldwin	3	375
Nancy, of Branford, m. Reuel **HOADLEY**, of Scott, N. Y., Mar. 19, 1823, by Rev. Timothy P. Gillett	3	422
Nelson, s. [Thaddeus & Nancy], b. Mar. 19, 1811	3	393
Thaddeus, of Wallingford, m. Nancy **FRISBIE**, of Branford, Sept. 15, 1809	3	393
[BAILEY], BAYLEY, Caroline, of Greenfield, N. Y., m. Pharez **FRISBIE**, of Branford, Apr. 14, 1805, at Greenfield	3	396
Mary Eliza, d. Nath[anie]l & Desiah, b. Apr. 2, 1808	3	282
Nathaniel, m. Desire **ROBINSON**, July 6, 1807	3	282
Sally, d. Nathaniel & Deziah, b. Apr. 30, 1810	3	282
BAKER, Catharine, d. Jonathan & Mary, b. May 13, 1759	3	161
Elisabeth, d. Sam[ue]ll & Mercy, b. Mar. 17, 1733/4	3	94
Elisabeth, m. John **LINSLY**, Jr., b. of Branford, June 8, 1754, by Rev. Jon[a]th[an] Merick	3	137
Esther, d. Sam[ue]ll & Mercy, b. Mar. 27, 1727, [at Easthampton]	3	94
Esther, m. Sam[ue]ll **BARKER**, b. of Branford, Apr. 12, 1744, by Rev. Jonathan Mer[r]ick	3	102
Hannah, d. Sam[ue]ll & Mercy, b. Feb. 4, 1724/5, [at Easthampton]	3	94
Hannah, m. Timothy **BARKER**, b. of Branford, Aug. 9, 1744, by Rev. Jon[a]th[an] Merick	3	105
Jacob, s. Sam[ue]ll & Mercy, b. Feb. 11, 1731/2	3	94
Jacob, m. Thankful **FOOT**, b. of Branford, Dec. 7, 1749, by Rev. Jonath[a]n Mer[r]ick	3	124
Jacob, s. Jacob & Thankful, b. Oct. 11, 1750	3	124
Jacob, d. Oct. 31, 1751	3	124
Jonathan, s. Sam[ue]ll & Mercy, b. Nov. 10, 1736	3	94

	Vol.	Page

BAKER, (cont.)

Jonathan, m. Mary **BARKER**, b. of Branford, Sept. 27, 1758,
by Sam[ue]ll Barker, J. P.   3   153

Mary, d. Sam[ue]ll & Mercy, b. July 23, 1722, [at
Easthampton]   3   94

Mercy, w. of Sam[ue]ll, d. Aug. 25, 1749   3   125

Sam[ue]ll, s. Thomas, decd., of Easthampton, N. Y., m. Mercy
SKELLINX, d. Jacob, decd., of Easthampton, N. Y., Oct.
18, (1721), by Rev. Nath[anie]ll Hunting, of Easthampton   3   94

Sam[ue]ll, s. Sam[ue]ll & Mercy, b. Dec. 24, 1729   3   94

Sam[ue]ll, of Branford, m. Mrs. Martha **GOODSEL[L]**, of
New Haven, a wid., Jan. 24, 1749/50, by Deodate
Davenport, J. P.   3   125

Samuel, d. Aug. 16, 1767, in the 66th y. of his age   3   191

Thankful, w. of Jacob, d. Dec. 24, 1751   3   124

BALDWIN, Aaron, s. Israel & Dinah, b. Sept. 3, 1724   3   57

Aaron, m. Sarah **FRISBIE**, b. of Brandord, Nov. 30, 1748,
by Rev. Jonathan Mer[r]ick   3   117

Aaron, [twin with Moses], s. Aaron & Sarah, b. Dec. 17,
1749; d. Jan. 17, 1749/50   3   134

Aaron, s. Aaron & Sarah, b. Jan. 8, 1755   3   158

Aaron, d. Mar. 24, 1800   3   273

Abigail, d. John, Jr. & Eleanor, b. July 1, 1726   3   59

Abigail, m. Capt. William **HOADL[E]Y**, b. of Branford,
Dec. 19, 1739, by Rev. Philemon Robbins   3   150

Abigail, d. Noah & Rebecca, b. Dec. 15, 1749   3   120

Abigail, d. John, 3rd, & Abigail, b. Sept. 22, 1756   3   143

Abigail, d. Aaron & Sarah, b. Dec. 27, 1763   3   194

Abigail, m. Orchard **GUY**, Jr., b. of Branford, Aug. 20,
1767, by Philemon Robbins   3   195

Abigail, d. Ebenezer & Lydia, b. July 17, 1772   3   207

Abigail, twin with Elisabeth, d. George & Hannah, b.
Nov. 4, 1774   3   258

Abigail had d. Levina, b. Sept. 24, 1777   3   257

Abigail, wid., m. Bille **ROSE**, b. of Branford, Apr. 15,
1778, by Samuel Eells   3   264

Abigail, [d. Elihu & Abigail], b. July 5, 1780   3   255

Abigail, m. Jon[a]th[an] **TOWNER**, Jr., b. of Branford,
Mar. 10, 1782, by Sam[ue]ll Eells   3   274

Abigail, m. Capt. Jesse **LINSL[E]Y**, b. of Branford, Apr.
27, 1817, by Rev. Elijah Plumb   3   335

Aleaetta, [d. Samuel & Flora], b. Jan. 24, 1811   3   387

Alice C., d. George & Mary, b. May 17, 1851   TM3   244

Almond, [child of Samuel & Flora], b. Nov. 9, 1800   3   387

Ambros[e], s. John & Margery, b. Oct. 29, 1750   3   156

Ammi, s. Capt. Sam[ue]ll, 2d, & Leucy, b. Dec. 13, 1774   3   288

Ammi, s. Zaccheus & Hannah, b. Aug. 24, 1788   3   255

Ammi, m. Mercy **HOADLY**, Dec. 24, 1810   3   56

	Vol.	Page
BALDWIN, (cont.)		
Ame, d. John, Jr. & Eleanor, b. Oct. 12, 1724	3	56
Amy, m. Samuel **HOWD**, Feb. 14, 1754, by Philemon Robbins	3	139
Anson, s. Jonathan & Kaziah, b. July 9, 1794	3	264
Assinthy, [d.Israel & Elisabeth], b. Mar. 31, 1798	3	274
Augustus, s. Capt. Sam[ue]ll, 2d, & Leucy, b. May 20, 1782	3	288
Augustus, [s. John & Alithea], b. Apr. 20, 1784	3	273
Augustus, m. Sally **MONROE**, May 4, 1808, by Rev. Aaron Dutton, of Guilford	3	418
Augustus, of Deerfield, Mass., m. Betsey **GOODRICH**, of Branford, June 31, 1809, by Rev. Tim[oth]y P. Gillett	3	425
Benedick, s. Joel & Sarah, b. Feb. 25, 1787	3	267
Benjamin, s. John, Jr. & Eleanor, b. July 15, 1728	3	64
Benjamin, m. Lydia **GOODSELL**, b. of Branford, Apr. 27, 1780 by Warham Williams	3	269
Benjamin, s. Capt. Sam[ue]ll, 2d, & Leucy, b. Sept. 23, 1780	3	288
Benjamin, s. Capt. Benj[ami]n & Lydia, b. Feb 7, 1781	3	269
Benjamin, d. Apr. 15, 1823, in the 44th y. of his age	3	337
Ben[j]ammi, d. Apr. 22, 1823, ae 22 y.	3	337
Betsey, d. Zac[c]heus & Hannah, b. Feb. 8, 1795	3	265
Bets[e]y, wid. of Noah, d. Mar. 20, 1838	TM3	304
Betsey, d. John R. & Harriet, b. [ ], 1848	TM3	240
Betsey, d. David Beach & Sylvia, b. Oct. 13, 1851	TM3	246
Caleb, s. Sam[ue]ll & Lydia, b. Feb. 27, 1723/4	3	54
Charles, [s. David & Nancy], b. Oct. 9, 1803	3	281
Charles, [s. W[illia]m & Charlotte], b. Oct. 14, 1841	TM3	246
Clarendah, d. Capt. Sam[ue]ll, 2d, & Leucy, b. Dec. 1, 1765	3	288
Cynthia, of North Branford, m. Sylvester **JONES**, of New Haven, Sept. 12, 1824, by Charles Atwater	3	334
Daniel, s. George & Deborah, b. July 1, 1705	2	346
Daniel, s. George & Deborah, b. July 1, 1705	3	32
Daniel, s. Daniel & Thankfull, b. Oct. 18, 1731	3	85
Daniel, m. Wid. Sarah **HARRISON**, b. of Branford, May 27, 1754, by Rev. Jonathan Merrick	3	137
Daniel, Jr., m. Th[e]adosia **BARKER**, b. of Branford, Dec. 25, 1755, by Rev. Jonathan Merrick	3	140
Daniel, s. Daniel & Theodocia, b. July 12, 1766	3	191
Daniel, d. Jan. 28, 1765, ae 60	3	185
David, s. Sam[ue]ll & Lydia, b. Jan. 25, 1716/7	3	39
David, s. Daniel & Theodosia, b. Aug. 12, 1772	3	207
David, m. Nancy **BALDWIN**, Mar. 3, 1808	3	281
David, s. John R. & Hannah, b. July 23, 1851	TM3	245
Deborah, d. George & Deborah, b. Dec. 27, 1699	2	343
Deborah, m. Edward **JOHNSON**, Jr., b. of Branford, Feb. 21, 1722/3, by Nath[anie]ll Har[r]ison, J. P.	3	54
Deborah, d. Israel & Dinah, b. Oct. 19, 1731	3	100
Deborah, m. Timothy **FRISBIE**, Sept. 19, 1754, by Jonathan		

	Vol.	Page
BALDWIN, (cont.)		
Merrick	3	138
Debora[h], wid. of Dea. [George], d. Dec. 14, 1754	3	148
Debory, d. Capt. Sam[ue]ll, 2d, & Leucy, b. July 29, 1763	3	288
Desire, m. Jared **PALMER**, b. of Branford, June 17, 1790, by Jason Atwater	3	262
Dinah, d. Israel & Dinah, b. Nov. 15, 1726	3	70
Dinah, m. Dan[ie]ll **PAGE**, Jr., b. of Branford, Feb. 13, 1749, by Jon[a]th[an] Mer[r]ick	3	169
Dorothy, d. John, Jr. & Eleonor, b. Apr. 5, 1742	3	100
Ebenezer, s. Sam[ue]ll & Lydia, b. Nov. 5, 1726	3	59
Ebenezer, s. John, Jr. & Eleanor, b. Mar. 28, 1737	3	87
Eben[eze]r, s. Noah & Rebecca, b. Sept. 28, 1741	3	97
Ebenezer, s. Sam[ue]ll & Hannah, b. June 18, 1758; d. June 25, 1758	3	166
Ebenezer, s. Sam[ue]ll & Hannah, b. Feb. 18, 1760	3	166
Ebenezer, s. Lydia **FOOT**, b. Mar. 21, 1769	3	197
Ebenezer, m. Lydia **FOOT**, b. of Branford, Jan. 27, 1771, by Samuel Eells	3	205
Ebenezer, s. Noah, d. Feb. 3, 1777, ae 36 y.	3	290
Ebenezer Noah, s. Lydia **ROSE**, b. Aug. 29, 1770	3	257
Ebenezer Noah, s. Lydia **ROSE**, d. July 15, 1780	3	291
Edward, s. Rich[ar]d & Eunice, b. Nov. 25, 1749	3	120
Edward, s. Noah, Jr. & Abigail, b. May 30, 1763	3	181
Edward, s. John, 3rd, & Allethea, b. Oct. 18, 1776	3	299
Ele, s. Moses & Mary, b. Jan. 22, 1783	3	287
Eleonor, d. John, Jr. & Eleonor, b. Mar. 29, 1735	3	82
Eliada, s. Israel & Elisabeth, b. July 1, 1783	3	286
Elihu, s. John & Margery, b. Jan. 21, 1745	3	156
Elihu, m. Abigail **ROGERS**, b. of Branford, Nov. 18, 1773, by Warham Williams	3	255
Eliza Jane, [d. W[illia]m & Charlotte], b. Mar. 13, 1835	TM3	246
Elisabeth, d. George & Deborah, b. Sept. 20, 1697	2	343
Elisabeth, m. Jonathan **BUTLER**, Jr., b. of Branford, Nov. 20, 1717	3	43
Elisabeth, d. Sam[ue]ll & Lydia, b. Feb. 13, 1721/2	3	48
Elizabeth, d. John & Margery, b. May 13, 1743	3	156
Elisabeth, d. Dan[ie]ll & Thankful, b. Apr. 18, 1746	3	107
Elizabeth, d. James & Desire, b. Sept. 24, 1758	3	154
Elisabeth, of Branford, m. Elihu **ROGERS**, of New Haven, Nov. 23, 1768, by Jon[a]th[an] Merrick	3	198
Elisabeth, twin with Abigail, d. George & Hannah, b. Nov. 4, 1774	3	258
Elisabeth, [d. Israel & Elisabeth], b. Oct. 28, 1785	3	274
Elizabeth, d. Israel & Elizabeth, d. Nov. 8, 1785	3	275
Elisabeth, [d. Israel & Elisabeth], b. Oct. 6, 1788	3	274
Elizabeth, d. George & Lucretia, b. Nov. 4, 1827	3	347
Elizabeth H., m. Chester **SMITH**, Aug. 10, 1820, by Rev.		

	Vol.	Page
BALDWIN, (cont.)		
Matthew Moyes	3	414
Elizur, [s. W[illia]m & Charlotte], b. July 28, 1837	TM3	246
Emila, [d. Samuel & Flora], b. Feb. 13, 1807	3	387
Ephraim, s. Israel & Dinah, b. Oct. 7, 1743	3	100
Ephraim, m. Kaziah **WHEDON**, b. of Branford, Mar. 10, 1774	3	290
Ephraim Rogers, s. Timothy & Jerusha, b. June 21, 1822	3	421
Ephraim Rogers, s. Timothy & Jerusha, d. Aug. 12, 1828,		
ae 6 y. 1 m. 21 d.	3	351
Eunice, d. Daniel & Theodocia, b. May 20, 1769	3	198
Eunice, d. Ephraim & Keziah, b. Feb. 10, 1778	3	290
Eunice, [d. Elihu & Abigail], b. Feb. 28, 1778	3	255
Eunice, d. Ammi & Mercy, b. May 23, 1811	3	426
Eunice Parmela, [d. David & Nancy], b. Dec. 15, 1801	3	281
Gamaliel, s. James & Desire, b. Jan. 31, 1760	3	161
Gamaliel, d. Jan. 6, 1825	3	340
Georg[e], Dea., d. Oct. 26, 1728	3	148
George, s. Dan[ie]ll & Thankfull, b. Sept. 9, 1733	3	85
George, m. Hannah **FRISBIE**, b. of Branford, July 2, 1766,		
by Warham Williams	3	189
George, [s. Josiah], b. Aug. 22, 1803, in Russell, Mass.	3	409
George, s. Moses & Lucretia, b. July 1, 1819	3	366
George, of North Branford, m. Lucretia **GORDON**, of		
Branford, Dec. 12, 1826, by Rev. Timothy P. Gillett	3	343
George, [s. W[illia]m & Charlotte], b. Feb. 20, 1832	TM3	246
George, m. Marian **MONROE**, b. of Branford, Feb. 17, 1850,		
by Rev. Timothy P. Gillett	TM3	165
George, ae 19 y., m. Mary A. **MONRO[E]**, ae 16 y., Feb 17,		
1850, by Rev. T. P. Gillett	TM3	166
George A., m. Mary **HARRISON**, b. of Branford, May 14,		
1840, by Rev. T. P. Gillett	3	379
George B., of Prospect, m. Jennette C. **GOODRICH**, of		
Branford, Aug. 19, 1849, by Rev. Tim[oth]y P. Gillett	TM3	164
George B., of Prospect, m. Cornelia J. **GOODRICH**, of		
Branford, ae 17, Aug. 19, 1849, by Rev. Timothy P.		
Gillett	TM3	167
Gideon, s. John, Jr. & Eleanor, b. Aug. 3, 1730	3	69
Giles, m. Emeline **BUSH**, b. of Branford, July 2, 1829, by		
Rev. Judson A. Root	3	349
Hannah, d. John & Hannah, b. Nov. 7, 1714	3	42
Hannah, m. Edward **BARKER**, b. of Branford, Mar. 9, 1732,		
by Jonathan Mer[r]ick	3	128
Hannah, d. John, 2d & Eleanor, b. June 8, 1739	3	91
Hannah, d. Sam[ue]ll & Hannah, b. Sept. 20, 1748	3	166
Hannah, m. Bartholomew **GOODRICH**, b. of Branford, Sept.		
22, 1773, by Philemon Robbins	3	273
Hannah, w. of Zac[c]heus, d. Aug. [ ], 1820	3	428
Hannah, m. Heman **ROGERS**, b. of Branford, July 23, 1826,		

	Vol.	Page
BALDWIN, (cont.)		
by Rev. Timothy P. Gillett	3	342
Harvey Taylor, s. Henry C. & Eliza, b. [ ], 1848	TM3	240
Henry Carter, [s. Josiah], b. Aug, 18, 1805, in Russell, Mass.	3	409
Henry Carter, m. Eliza **ROSE**, b. of Branford, Nov. 25,		
1829, by Timothy P. Gillett	3	351
Hezekiah, s. George & Hannah, b. May 4, 1768	3	194
Irene, d. John, 3rd, & Allethea, b. Mar. 3, 1779	3	299
Irene, d. John & Alethea, m. Samuel **FRISBIE**, Jr., s. Samuel		
& Elizabeth, Mar. 26, 1797	3	388
Israel, s. George & Deborah, b. Dec. 13, 1694	2	343
Israel, m. Dinah **BUTLER**, b. of Branford, Dec. 10, 1718	3	43
Israel, s. Israel & Dinah, b. Dec. 21, 1721	3	47
Israel, Jr., m. Lydia **FRISBIE**, b. of Branford, Dec. 27,		
1744, by Rev. Jonath[a]n Mer[r]ick	3	109
Israel, d. Aug. 2, 1767, in the 46th y. of his age	3	194
Israel, m. Elisabeth **HATCH**, Jan. 26, 1775, by David Brunson	3	286
Israel Augustus, s. Israel & Elisabeth, b. June 26, 1780	3	286
Jacob, s. Dan[ie]ll & Thankfull, b. Jan. 7, 1735/6	3	85
Jacob, s. Israel, Jr. & Lydia, b. Oct. 2, 1746	3	109
James, m. Desier **PALMERLY**, b. of Branford, May 23, 1753,		
by Rev. Philemon Robbins	3	142
James, s. Nicod[emu]s & Martha, b. Apr. 23, 1782	3	307
James, [s. W[illia]m & Charlotte], b. July 3, 1823	TM3	246
James Calvin, s. Ammi & Mercy, b. June 29, 1823	3	426
Jane, of Branford, m. William M. **HALL**, of Wallingford,		
Dec. 16, 1829, by J. A. Root	3	351
Jane Lucy, [d. Augustus & Sally (**MONROE**)], b. Mar. 2, 1810	3	418
Jemmy, s. Ephraim & Keziah, b. Mar. 13, 1776	3	290
Jeremiah, s. John, 3rd & Allithea, b. Mar. 4, 1774	3	299
Jeremiah, [s. John & Alithea], d. Oct. 17, 1796; was lost		
at sea having sailed from Branford on Oct. 17, 1796	3	273
Jerusha, d. Aaron & Sarah, b. July 22, 1771	3	204
Jerusha, m. Eber **LINSLEY**, [1830], by J. A. Root.		
Recorded Nov. 5, 1830	3	356
Jesse, s. Ephraim & Keziah, b. Sept. 16, 1780	3	290
Joanna, m. Samuel **ROSE**, Apr. 18, 1705, by Rev. Sam[ue]ll		
Russel[l]	3	32
Joel, s. Dan[ie]ll, Jr. & Theodocia, b. July 16, 1759	3	158
Joel, of Branford, m. Sarah **GORHAM**, Apr. 25, 1783, by		
Sam[ue]ll Eells	3	312
Joel, of Branford, m. Sarah **GORHAM**, of New Haven, Apr.		
28, 1783, by Sam[ue]ll Eells	3	272
Joel, Jr., b. Sept. 5, 1811	3	396
John, s. George & Deborah, b. Jan. 13, 1690	2	343
John, m. Hannah **TYLER**, Oct. 26, 1713, by Rev. Sam[ue]ll		
Russel[l]	3	38
John, Jr., m. Joanna **GOODWRICH**, Oct. 31, 1716, by Rev.		

	Vol.	Page
BALDWIN, (cont.)		
Mr. Russel[l]	3	40
John, s. John & Hannah, b. May 9, 1717	3	40
John, s. John & Joanna, b. Dec. 29, 1717	3	41
John, 3rd, m. Abigail **WARDELL**, b. of Branford, Apr. 20, 1740	3	130
John, 4th, m. Margery **TYLER**, Mar. 18, 1741, by Jonathan Merrick	3	156
John, s. John, 3rd, & Abigail, b. Sept. 13, 1750	3	130
John, 4th, m. Lucy **TYLER**, Nov. 28, 1764, by Josiah Rogers, J. P.	3	188
John, 3rd, m. Allithea **HOBART**, b. of Branford, Oct. 20, 1772	3	299
John, [s. John & Alithea], b. Jan. 18, 1792	3	273
John, d. Jan. 3, 1817, ae 66 y., in Deerfield, Mass.	3	273
John, s. George & Betsey, b. May 8, 1851	TM3	245
Jonathan, s. Aaron & Sarah, b. Dec. 9, 1760	3	194
Jonathan, m. Kaziah **ROSE**, b. of Branford, Nov. 24, 1793, by Samuel Eells	3	264
Joseph, s. Aaron & Sarah, b. Dec. 26, 1758	3	158
Joseph, m. Rosanna **MALOYE**, b. of Branford, June 11, 1781, by Sam[ue]ll Eells	3	309
Joseph, [s. Samuel & Flora], b. May 30, 1805	3	387
Joseph, 2d, s. Timothy & Jerusha, b. Oct. 9, 1820	3	413
Josiah, s. Israel & Elisabeth, b. Jan. 21, 1778	3	286
Julia, [d. John & Alithea], b. Oct. 2, 1794	3	273
Labinius, [child of Samuel & Flora], b. Feb. 17, 1809	3	387
Lament, d. Aaron & Sarah, b. Feb. 13, 1774	3	257
Levi, s. John, 3rd, & Abigail, b. Sept. 22, 1747; d. June 20, 1750	3	130
Levi, s. John, 3rd, & Abigail, b. June 30, 1753	3	143
Levi, s. Levi & Sarah, b. Dec. 12, 1775	3	265
Levina, d. Abigail, b. Sept. 24, 1777	3	257
Linus, s. Daniel, Jr. & Theodosia, b. Apr. 8, 1763	3	180
Lois, d. Moses & Lois, b. Feb. 14, 1772	3	205
Lois, w. of Moses, d. Feb. 16, 1772	3	205
Lois, m. Peter **APPLE**, b. of Branford, May 21, 1793, by Sam[ue]l Eells	3	263
Louisa, [d. John & Alithea], b. May 31, 1798	3	273
Lucinda, d. Zaccheus & Sarah, b. July 22, 1779	3	301
Lucinda, d. Zac[c]heus & Sarah, d. Sept. 20, 1807, ae 28 y.	3	428
Lucinda, d. Ammi & Mercy, b. Oct. 18, 1812	3	426
Lucinda, of Branford, m. David C. **BISHOP**, of North Guilford, Oct. 8, 1837, by Timothy P. Gillett	3	374
Luce, d. Noah & Rebecca, b. Feb. 19, 1743/ 4	3	102
Lucy, d. Capt. Sam[ue]ll, 2d, & Leucy, b. Apr. 13, 1772	3	288
Lydia, d. John & Margery, b. Feb. 16, 1747	3	156
Lydia, m. Jonathan **FOOT**, b. of Branford, Nov. 19, 1761, by Philemon Robbins	3	174

	Vol.	Page
BALDWIN, (cont.)		
Lidia, wid. of Israel, d. Nov. 25, 1767, in the 48th y. of her age	3	194
Lydia, m. Simeon **ROSE**, b. of Branford, Feb. 6, 1774, by		
Samuel Eells	3	257
Lydia, d. Israel & Elisabeth, b. July 21, 1775	3	286
Lydia, [d. Elihu & Abigail], b. Sept. 11, 1782	3	255
Lydia, m. Samuel **FOOT**, Dec. 2, 1795	3	407
Mabel, d. Daniel, Jr. & Theodosa, b. Jan. 16, 1757	3	147
Margery, d. John & Margery, b. Feb. 9, 1742	3	156
Margery, w. of John, 4th, d. Dec. 27, 1751	3	156
Maria, [d. John & Alithea], b. Aug. 1, 1789	3	273
Marian, m. Edward **LINSLEY**, b. of North Branford, Oct. 16,		
1836, by Rev. Timothy P. Gillett	3	373
Martha, d. [George & Deborah], b. Jan. 13, 1702	3	32
Martha, d. George & Deborah, b. Jan. 13, 1702/3	2	344
Martha, m. Isaiah **BUTLER**, b. of Branford, Dec. 29, 1725,		
by Rev. Sam[ue]ll Russell	3	58
Martha, d. Israel & Dinah, b. Aug. 5, 1736	3	100
Martha, m. Nathan **HARRISON**, b. of Branford, Mar. 27,		
1758, by Jon[a]th[an] Merrick	3	165
Martha, d. Ephraim & Keziah, b. Dec. 23, 1782	3	290
Mary, d. Israel & Dinah, b. Sept. 6, 1719	3	43
Mary, w. of Phinehas, d. May 30, 1760	3	167
Mary, d. Samuel & Hannah, b. May 14, 1762	3	183
Mary, d. Aaron & Sarah, b. Jan. 18, 1766	3	194
Mary, [d. Elihu & Abigail, b. Oct. 18, 1774	3	255
Mary, m. Archelaus **BARKER**, b. of Branford, Nov. 9, 1783,		
by Sam[ue]l Eells	3	270
Mary Almira, d. Timothy & Jerusha, b. May 21, 1828	3	351
Mary Ann, [d. Josiah], b. Mar. 5, 1814	3	409
Mercy, d. Nichod[emu]s & Martha, b. Jan. 17, 1779	3	307
Micah, [s. Israel & Elisabeth], b. Nov. 2, 1790	3	274
Milla, w. Edward **LINSLY**, July 1, 1807, by Rev. Matthew		
Noyes	3	402
Miner, [s. Israel & Elisabeth], b. Apr. 1, 1793	3	274
Miner, s. Israel & Elizabeth, d. May 18, 1796	3	275
Miner, [s. Israel & Elisabeth], b. Nov. 24, 1801	3	274
Moses, [twin with Aaron], s. Aaron & Sarah, b. Dec. 17, 1749	3	134
Moses, m. Lois **WHEDON**, b. of Branford, Jan. 13, 1772, by		
Samuel Eells	3	205
Moses, Jr., s. Moses & Mary, b. Aug. 15, 1787	3	277
Moses, m. Mary **POTTER**, b. of Branford, June 20, 1782, by		
Sam[ue]ll Eells	3	287
Nancy, d. Ephraim & Kaziah, b. Sept. 17, 1774	3	290
Nancy, [d. John & Alithea], b. Nov. 28, 1786	3	273
Nancy, m. David **BALDWIN**, Mar. 3, 1808	3	281
Nancy, [d. W[illia]m & Charlotte], b. Sept. 2, 1824	TM3	246
Nicademus, s. James & Desire, b. Aug. 4, 1755	3	142

	Vol.	Page

BALDWIN, (cont.)

	Vol.	Page
Nicodemus, m. Martha **HARRISON**, b. of Branford, June 9, 1778	3	307
Noah, s. George & Deborah, b. Mar. 20, 1710	3	32
Noah, m. Rebecca **FRISBIE**, Mar. 21, 1732/3 by Rev. Philemon Robbins	3	76
Noah, s. Noah & Rebecca, b. Nov. 18, 1738	3	93
Noah, Jr., m. Abigail **FRISBIE**, b. of Branford, Jan. 12, 1763, by Philemon Robbins	3	179
Noah, Jr., d. Sept. 2, 1776, in the Army at New York	3	262
Noah, d. Nov. 23, 1799	3	256
Noah, d. Nov. 28, 1835	TM3	304
Peter, s. John, 3rd, & Abigail, b. Nov. 8, 1741	3	130
Peter, [s. David & Nancy], b. Dec. 14, 1805	3	281
Phebe, d. George & Deborah, b. Nov. 7, 1692	2	343
Phebe, m. Benjamin **BARTHOLOMEW**, Oct. 28, 1713, by Rev. Sam[ue]ll Russel[l]	3	38
Phebe, d. Daniel & Thankfull, b. Dec. 7, 1740	3	94
Phebe, d. Dan[ie]ll & Thankful, b. Dec. 7, 1740	3	107
Phebe, m. Joel **ROSE**, b. of Branford, Jan. 7, 1773, by Samuel Eells	3	208
Philemon Tyler, s. Timothy & Jerusha, b. Feb. 25, 1824	3	428
Phineas, s. John, Jr. & Eleanor, b. Feb. 23, 1732/3	3	76
Phinehas, m. Mary **HARRISON**, b. of Branford, Sept. 6, 1759, by Warham Williams	3	167
Phinehas, of Branford, m. Martha **PECK**, of Wallingford, Jan. 1, 1761, by Warham Williams	3	172
Polly, d. Joel & Sarah, b. Aug. 11, 1784	3	267
Rachel, d. Apr. 25, 1825	3	340
Rebec[c]ah, d. George & Deborah, b. Oct. 28, 1707	3	32
Rebec[c]ah, d. Sam[ue]ll & Lydia, b. Dec. 16, 1729	3	67
Rebecca, m. Mat[t]hew **LINSL[E]Y**, b. of Branford, Jan. 9, 1733/4 by Rev. Philemon Robbins	3	79
Rebecca, d. Noah & Rebecca, b. May 20, 1734	3	81
Rebecca, m. John **BLAKISTON**, Jr., b. of Branford, May 19, 1757, by Philemon Robbins	3	161
Rhoda, d. George & Hannah, b. Feb. 28, 1772	3	206
Rhoda Ellen, [d. Josiah], b. Apr. 6, 1812, in Southington	3	409
Richard, s. Jno., Jr. & Eleaner, b. Oct. 17, 1721	3	49
Richard, of Branford, m. Eunice **BASSET[T]**, of Milford, May 30, 1745, by Rev. Sam[ue]ll W[h]ittlesey, at Milford	3	120
Richard, d. Jan. 20, 1783	3	278
Rine, d. Capt. Sam[ue]ll, 2d, & Leucy, b. Dec. 5, 1776	3	288
Sabra, d. Samuel & Hannah, b. Aug. 3, 1765	3	190
Sally, m. Dan **LINSL[E]Y**, b. of Branford, Sept. 23, 1792, by Mathew Noyes	3	268
Sally, of Branford, m. Philo **HARRISON**, of North Branford, Sept. 23, 1827, by Rev. Timothy P. Gillett	3	345

	Vol.	Page

BALDWIN, (cont.)

Samuel, m. Elisabeth **FRISBEE,** b. of Branford, Mar. 14,
    1710/11, by Rev. Sam[ue]ll Russel[l] — 3, 34

Samuel, m. Lydia **SPERRY,** Jan. 8, 1713/14*, by Rev.
    Sam[uel]l Russe[ll] (*Changed to 1712/3 — 3, 38

Sam[ue]ll, s. Sam[ue]ll & Lydia, b. Jan. 4, 1713/14 — 3, 37

Sam[ue]ll, s. Israel & Dinah, b. Aug. 14, 1739 — 3, 100

Sam[ue]ll, m. Hannah **HOADL[E]Y,** b. of Branford, Apr.
    15, 1746, by Philemon Robbins — 3, 166

Sam[ue]ll, s. Sam[ue]ll & Hannah, b. Nov. 20, 1746 — 3, 166

Sam[ue]ll, s. Sam[ue]ll & Hannah, d. Sept. 20, 1752 — 3, 166

Sam[ue]ll, s. Sam[ue]ll & Hannah, b. Aug. 4, 1756 — 3, 166

Sam[ue]ll, Jr., m. Lucy **HOADL[E]Y,** b. of Branford, July 10,
    1760, by Jonathan Mer[r]ick — 3, 171

Sam[ue]ll, s. Capt. Sam[ue]ll, 2d, b. Mar. 7, 1768 — 3, 288

Samuel, s. Zaccheus & Sarah, b. Aug. 28, 1777 — 3, 301

Samuel, of Branford, m. Flora **WOODRUFF,** of Worthington,
    Nov. 28, 1799 — 3, 396

Sarah, d. John, Sr. & Hannah, b. Sept. 3, 1728 — 3, 66

Sarah, m. Jonathan **HARRISON,** Jr., b. of Branford, Aug.
    20, 1747 — 3, 280

Sarah, d. Sam[ue]ll & Hannah, b. Feb. 1, 1750 — 3, 166

Sarah, d. Aaron & Sarah, b. Apr. 17, 1751 — 3, 134

Sarah, d. James & Desier, b. Feb. 5, 1757 — 3, 152

Sarah, m. Benjamin **TYLER,** b. of Branford, Oct. 31, 1776,
    by Philemen Robbins — 3, 270

Sarah, wid. of Levi, d. May 19, 1778, in the 22nd y. of her age — 3, 265

Sarah, m. Jacob **PAGE,** b. of Branford, Nov. [ ], 1783,
    by Sam[ue]ll Eells — 3, 315

Sarah, w. of Zaccheus, d. May 29, 1784, in the 29th y. of her
    age — 3, 309

Sarah, d. Joel & Sarah, b. Oct. 7, 1794 — 3, 268

Sarah, [d. Samuel & Flora], b. Apr. 20, 1802 — 3, 387

Sarah, [d. W[illia]m & Charlotte], b. Feb. 19, 1828 — TM3, 246

Sereney, [d. Samuel & Flora], b. Aug. 12, 1803 — 3, 387

Sereney, [d. Samuel & Flora], d. Sept. 2, 1806 — 3, 387

Serene, ae 18 y., of Branford, m. James **HARRISON,** ae 23,
    of North Branford, Oct. 15, 1849, by Rev. G. P. Wood — TM3, 166

Simeon, s. John, 3rd, & Abigail, b. Nov. 24, 1744 — 3, 130

Simeon, [s. Israel & Elisabeth], b. Oct. 11, 1795 — 3, 274

Statira, d. John, 2d, & Allethea, b. Jan. 21, 1782 — 3, 299

Statira, m. Asher S. **BEACH,** b. of Branford, July 20, 1800 — 3, 389

Stephen, s. George & Hannah, b. Apr. 30, 1770 — 3, 200

Susanna, [d. Elihu & Abigail], b. Mar. 9, 1776 — 3, 255

Sylvia, m. David **BEACH,** Jan. 8, 1846, by Rev. W[illia]m
    B. Sprague, in Albany, N. Y. — TM3, 171

Talitha Oumi, d. James & Desire, b. [1763?] — 3, 179

Thankfull, d. Daniel & Thankfull, b. June 29, 1738 — 3, 94

	Vol.	Page
BALDWIN, (cont.)		
Thankful[l], d. Dan[ie]ll & Thankful[l], b. June 29, 1738	3	107
Thankfull, w. of Daniel, d. Jan. 23, 1754	3	137
Thankfull, m. Solomon **ROSE**, b. of Branford, Nov. 30,		
1763, by Jon[a]th[an] Mer[r]ick	3	180
Thankful, d. Joel & Sarah, b. Oct. 11, 1792	3	268
Timothy, m. Jerusha **TYLER**, Oct. 21, 1819, by Rev.		
Timothy P. Gillett	3	413
Timothy Gerham, s. Joel & Sarah, b. Dec. 14, 1788	3	268
Tryphena, d. Israel & Dinah, b. Aug. 12, 1729	3	70
Tryphena, d. Israel, d. Aug. 24, 1751	3	136
Tryphena, d. Aaron & Sarah, b. June 25, 1752	3	134
Tryphena, m. Reuben **LINSL[E]Y**, b. of Branford, Feb. 3,		
1779, by Samuel Eells	3	266
Tryphene, d. Nicod[emu]s & Martha, b. Jan. 29, 1781	3	307
Triphosa, d. Sam[ue]ll, Jr. & Lucy, b. Oct. 28, 1760	3	171
Vina, m. John **BEACH**, b. of Branford, Oct. 27, 1803	3	369
Wealthy, [d. Israel & Elisabeth], b. Nov. 19, 1799	3	274
William, s. Sam[ue]ll & Hannah, b. Aug. 2, 1754	3	166
William, s. Richard & Margerit, b. Oct. 4, 1761	3	282
William, [s. W[illia]m & Charlotte], b. Aug. 26, 1826	TM3	246
William Augustus, [s. Augustus & Sally], b. Sept. 1, 1812	3	418
Wyllys, s. Jos[ep]h & Rosanna, b. Mar. 10, 1783	3	309
Zac[c]heus, s. James & Desire, b. Jan. 9, 1753/4	3	142
Zaccheus, m. Sarah **BRADFIELD**, b. of Branford, Oct. 17,		
1776	3	301
Zaccheus, m. Hannah **SHELDON**, Feb. 10, 1785, by Jason		
Atwater	3	255
Zac[c]heus, m. Mrs. Welthian **JONES**, Nov. 12, 1821, by		
Charles Atwater	3	414
Zillah, m. Nath[anie]ll **PAGE**, Jr., b. of Branford, Feb.		
16, 1736/7	3	88
----, s. George & Betsey, b. June 1, 1848	TM3	239
----, d. Giles T. & Emeline, b. Jan. 8, 1849	TM3	241
BALL, Mehitabel, of New Haven, m. Lewis **BUNNELL**, of		
Branford, [Nov.] 9, [1823], by Rev. Charles Atwater	3	423
BARKER, BARKOR, Aaron, [s. Benjamin], b. June 12, 1797	3	340
Abigail, [d. William & Elisabeth, b. Apr. [ ], 1697	3	47
Abigail, d. Jon[a]th[an] & Mary, b. Jan. 26, 1716/7	3	52
Abigail, m. Jonathan **ROSE**, Jr., b. of Branford, Nov. 23,		
1724, by Rev. Sam[ue]ll Russell	3	71
Abigail, d. William, Jr. & Abigail, b. Dec. 30, 1727	3	69
Abigail, d. William, Jr. & Abigail, d. Aug. 25, 1732	3	74
Abigail, d. Dan[ie]ll, Jr. & Abigail, b. Mar. 15, 1737/8	3	89
Abigail, d. William & Abigail, b. Aug. 6, 1742	3	104
Abigail, d. James & Abigail, b. Jan. 7, 1743/4	3	109
Abigail, m. Gideon **GOODRICH**, b. of Branford, June 19,		
1746, by Rev. Philemon Robbins	3	127

	Vol.	Page
BARKER, BARKOR, (cont.)		
Abigail, d. James & Abigail, d. Aug. [ ], 1751	3	128
Adela[i]de Amelia, d. Ebeneser & Amelia, b. Aug. 8, 1840	TM3	238
Adelaide Amelia, d. Ebeneser & Amelia, d. Dec. 16, 1842	TM3	238
Amanda, d. Sam[ue]ll & Esther, b. Mar. 15, 1759; d. Sept. 21, 1761	3	154
Amanda, d. Sam[ue]ll & Esther, d. Sept. 21, 1761, ae 2 y. 6 m. 6 d.	3	173
Amanda, d. Samuel & Esther, b. Oct. 8, 1764	3	183
Amelia P., m. Julius **WILLIAMS**, Sept. 26, 1847, by Rev. F. Miller	TM3	161
Ammi Beach, [s. Chandler & Lucy], b. Feb. 22, 1811	3	411
Ann, m. Lyman **FRISBIE**, b. of Branford, Dec. 31, 1818, by Rev. Timothy P. Gillett	3	416
Anna, [d. William & Elisabeth], b. Sept. [ ], 1706	3	47
Anna, m. John **FRISBIE**, Jr., b. of Branford, Feb. 8, 1730/1, by Jno. Russell, J. P.	3	122
Anna, d. Joseph & Elisabeth, b. May 12, 1762	3	176
Anna, d. Joseph & Elisabeth, d. Aug. 20, 1762, ae 3 m. 8 d.	3	177
Anna, [d. Jonathan & Bethiah], b. June 9, 1796	3	385
Anna, wid., d. May 15, 1832, ae 71 y.	3	362
Anne, d. Jonathan & Mary, b. Mar. 13, 1700/1	2	344
Anne had s. Jabez, b. July 30, 1723	3	63
Anne, m. Ebenezer **JOHNSON**, b. of Branford, Jan. 1, 1728/9, by Rev. Sam[ue]ll Russell	3	66
Anne, d. William & Mary, b. Oct. 14, 1773	3	259
Anne, d. William & Mary, b. Oct. [ ], 1773	3	269
Archelaus, m. Mary **BALDWIN**, b. of Branford, Nov. 9, 1783, by Sam[ue]l Eells	3	270
Asa, s. John & Mary, b. May 6, 1780	3	285
Augustus, s. Sam[ue]ll & Esther, b. Jan. 23, 1749/50; d. Jan. 12, 1751, in the 1st y. of his age	3	119
Augustus, s. Sam[ue]ll & Esther, d. Jan. 12, 1750/1, in the 1st y. of his age	3	121
Augustus, s. Edward & Sarah, b. Feb. 1, 1783	3	284
Benjamin, s. Edw[ar]d & Hannah, b. Nov. 12, 1752	3	129
Benj[ami]n, m. Sarah **BEERS**, b. of Branford, Oct. 8, 1781, by Sam[ue]ll Eells	3	299
Benjamin, d. Oct. 18, 1802	3	411
Benjamin, m. Susan **HOWD**, b. of Branford, Jan. 1, 1825, by Timothy P. Gillett	3	336
Bethiah, [w. of Jonathan], d. Aug. 10, 1809	3	385
Betsey, [d. Archelaus & Mary], b. Apr. 26, 1793	3	270
Betsey A., m. Samuel B. **MILLER**, b. of Branford, Jan. 1, 1851, by Rev. Timothy P. Gillett	TM3	168
Bets[e]y A., ae 20, m. Samuel B. **MILLER**, ae 23, Jan. 1, 1851, by T. P. Gillett	TM3	170
Carolina, d. Edward & Sarah, b. Jan. 7, 1770	3	256

	Vol.	Page
BARKER, BARKOR, (cont.)		
Cate, [d. Timothy & Irene], b. May 25, 1786	3	272
Catharine Griswold, [d. Timothy & Martha], b. Apr. 28, 1834	3	378
Chandler, s. Benj[ami]n & Sarah, b. Jan. 26, 1782	3	299
Chandler, s. Benjamin & Sarah, m. Lucy **BEACH**, d. Ebenezer		
& Abigail, Oct. 18, 1810	3	411
C[h]loe, d. Joseph & Elizabeth, b. Aug. 19, 1756	3	147
Clarinda, d. William & Mary, b. May 14, 1778, at Guilford	3	269
Daniel, of Branford, m. Kez[iah] **MO[U]LT[H]ROP**, of New		
Haven, Aug. 24, 1701, by William Maltbie, J. P.	3	29
Daniel, s. Dan[ie]ll & Kezia, b. June 7, 1705	3	31
Daniel, Jr., m. Abigail **PALMER**, b. of Branford, July 8,		
1729, by Rev. Jonathan Merrick	3	69
Daniel, s. Dan[ie]ll, Jr. & Abigail, b. Aug. 14, 1735	3	89
Daniel, Lieut., d. Jan. 25, 1752, in the 75th y. of his age	3	153
Dan[ie]ll, Jr., m. Huldah **FOOT**, b. of Branford, Nov. 4, 1762,		
by Jonathan Merrick	3	178
Daniel, [s. Joel & Lois], b. Nov. 14, 1793	3	412
Daniel, m. Lucy **HARRISON**, b. of North Branford, Mar. 3,		
1825, by Timothy P. Gillett	3	339
David, s. Timothy & Hannah, b. June 14, 1759	3	156
David, [s. Timothy & Irene], b. Nov. 9, 1780	3	272
David, m. Parna **ROGERS**, Mar. 9, 1808, by [ ]	3	339
David B., [s. Benjamin], b. Sept. 21, 1800	3	340
Dolle, d. Sam[ue]ll, Jr. & Lucy, b. May 26, 1762	3	176
Dolle, m. Jacob **ROGERS**, b. of Branford, June 1, 178[ ],		
by Sam[ue]ll Eells	3	301
Dorothy, d. Daniel, Jr. & Abigail, b. Apr. 13, 1730	3	69
Dorothy, d. Will[ia]m & Abigail, b. Aug. 4, 1744	3	104
Dorithy, d. W[il]l[ia]m & Abigail, d. Sept. [ ], 1749	3	146
Dorothy, m. Reuben **WHEDON**, b. of Branford, Nov. 3, 1757,		
by Jonathan Merrick	3	166
Dorithy, d. Jacob & Lydia, b. Mar. 10, 1768	3	197
Eaton, [s. Joel & Lois], b. Dec. 20, 1799	3	412
Ebenez[e]r, s. Edward & Mary, b. Jan. 10, 1704/5	3	29
Ebenezer, s. Joseph & Hannah, b. May 23, 1736	3	84
Ebenez[e]r, s. Edw[ar]d & Hannah, b. Jan. 31, 1737	3	128
Ebenezer, m. Esther **RUSSELL**, b. of Branford, Sept. 24,		
1758, by Philemon Robbins	3	264
Ebenezer, s. Ebenezer & Esther, b. Apr. 27, 1768	3	264
Ebenezer, [s. Jonathan & Bethiah], b. Nov. 1, 1803	3	385
Ebenezer, [s. Chandler & Lucy], b. Nov. 26, 1823	3	411
Ebeneser, d. July 3, 1843, ae 39 y. 7 m. 27 d.	TM3	238
Edward, m. Hannah **BALDWIN**, b. of Branford, Mar. 9, 1732,		
by Jonathan Mer[r]ick	3	128
Edward, s. Edw[ar]d & Hannah, b. Sept. 8, 1739	3	128
Edward, Dea., d. Jan. 17, 1763, in the 55th y. of his age	3	178
Edward, m. Sarah **BROWN**, b. of Branford, Mar. 24, 1763,		

	Vol.	Page
BARKER, BARKOR, (cont.)		
by Philemon Robbins	3	179
Edward, s. Edward & Sarah, b. Oct. 24, 1766	3	256
Edward, b. May 22, 1809	3	404
Eliasaph, s. Uzal & Martha, b. June 17, 1746	3	108
Elihu, s. Uzal & Martha, b. Mar. 18, 1744	3	108
Elihu, s. Sam[ue]ll & Esther, b. June 5, 1762	3	176
Eliphelet, s. Benj[ami]n & Sarah, b. Nov. 19, 1783	3	299
Eliphalet, [s. Chandler & Lucy], b. June 6, 1817	3	411
Eliza, m. Henry **BARKER**, Aug. 9, 1837, by Rev. David		
Baldwin	3	375
Elisabeth, [d. William & Elisabeth], b. Dec. [ ], 1691	3	47
Elisabeth, w. of Edward, d. Apr. 16, 170[ ]	3	29
Elisabeth, m. Sam[ue]ll **MALTBIE**, Dec. 8, 1715, by		
Nath[anie]ll Har[r]ison, J. P.	3	46
Elisabeth, w. of Will[ia]m, d. Jan. 22, 1740/1	3	94
Elisabeth, d. Timothy & Hannah, b. Mar. 7, 1745/6	3	114
Elisabeth, d. Joseph & Elisabeth, b. Jan. 18, 1754	3	136
Elisabeth, m. Abraham **LINSLEY**, b. of Branford, Nov. 18,		
1766, by Philemon Robbins	3	192
Esther, d. Sam[ue]ll & Esther, b. Jan. 28, 1744/5; d.		
Feb. 21, 1748, in the 4th y. of her age	3	106
Esther, d. Sam[ue]ll & Esther, d. Feb. 21, 1747/8	3	114
Esther, d. Sam[ue]ll & Esther, b. Mar. 17, 1754	3	142
Esther, d. Ebenezer & Esther, b. May 27, 1771	3	264
Esther, m. Caleb **FRISBIE**, b. of Branford, Jan. 15, 1777,		
by Samuel Barker, J. P.	3	262
Esther, [d. Joel & Lois], b. Nov. 12, 1795	3	412
Estus, s. Samuel, Jr. & Lucy, b. May 23, 1766	3	189
Eunice, d. Edward & Mary, b. June 2, 1703	3	29
Eunice, m. Jonathan **RUSSELL**, b. of Branford, Dec. 12,		
1722, by Rev. Samuell Russel[l]	3	50
Eunice, d. Joseph & Hannah, b. Feb. 27, 1728/9	3	66
Eunice, d. Joseph & Elisabeth, b. Dec. 30, 1745	3	136
Eunice, d. Joseph, d. Aug. 4, 1746, in the 18th y. of her age	3	153
Eunice, d. Dan[ie]ll, Jr. & Patience, b. Aug. 28, 1747	3	117
Eunice, d. Daniel & Patience, d. Nov. 30, 1777, in the		
31st y. of her age	3	265
Eunice, m. Edmund **ROGERS**, b. of Branford, Sept. 19, 1782	3	302
Foster, [s. Archelaus & Mary], b. Jan. 7, 1789	3	270
Frank, s. Harry & Eliza, b. Nov. 20, 1850	TM3	244
Frederick, s. Edw[ard] & Sarah, b. Apr. 9, 1778	3	283
George Rogers, [s. David & Parna], b. Aug. 16, 1815	3	339
Giles, s. Edward & Sarah, b. Sept. 14, 1772	3	256
Giles, m. Hannah B. **MULFORD**, Oct. 5, 1805	3	286
Giles, d. May 17, 1843, ae 71 y.	TM3	305
Grace, [d. Archelaus & Mary[, b. Dec. 29, 1790; d. July		
10, 1796	3	270

	Vol.	Page
BARKER, BARKOR, (cont.)		
Grace, [d. Archelaus & Mary], b. Jan. 20, 1796	3	270
Grace, m. William **ROGERS**, b. of Branford, Jan. 20, 1820	3	335
Hannah, d. [Dan[ie]ll & Kezia], b. Nov. 15, 1707	3	31
Hannah, m. David **ROSE**, b. of Branford, Nov. 23, 1726,		
by Rev. Sam[ue]ll Russell	3	68
Hannah, d. Joseph & Hannah, b. May 21, 1727	3	62
Hannah, d. Jonathan & Hannah, b. Nov. 17, 1735	3	82
Hannah, d. Edw[ar]d & Hannah b. Apr. 24, 1742	3	128
Hannah, wid. of Joseph, d. Jan. 10, 1747/8	3	173
Hannah, d. Thimothy & Hannah, b. Apr. 12, 1748	3	114
Hannah, m. Dan[ie]ll **HARRISON**, Jr., b. of Branford, Apr.		
28, 1748, by Rev. Jonath[an] Mer[r]ick	3	113
Hannah, m. Eli **ROGERS**, b. of Branford, Aug. 21, 1761, by		
Philemon Robbins	3	310
Hannah, m. Obadiah **TYLER**, b. of Branford, Jan. 31, 1762,		
by Philemon Robbins	3	179
Hannah, m. John **GARRETT**, b. of Branford, Oct. 8, 1767,		
by Philemon Robbins	3	191
Hannah, [d. Archelaus & Mary], b. Apr. 11, 1801	3	397
Hannah, of Branford, m. Frederick W. **SCRANTON**, of		
Guilford, Dec. 23, 1823, by Rev. Timothy P. Gillett	3	424
Harriet Jennet, [d. Chandler & Lucy], b. June 10, 1815	3	411
Harriet Jennet, [d. Chandler & Lucy], d. Oct. 10, 1824	3	411
Harry, [s. Timothy & Irene], b. July 27, 1783	3	272
Harvey, [s. Archelaus & Mary], b. Nov. 19, 1784	3	270
Harvey R., of Branford, m. Sarah A. **HUBBARD**, of Durham,		
Feb. 5, 1850, by C. H. Topliff	TM3	165
Harvey R., ae 21 y., m. Sarah A. **HUBBARD**, ae 21 y. of		
Durham, Feb. 5, 1850, by Rev. C. H. Topliff	TM3	167
Harvey Russell, s. James & Martha, b. Dec. 2, 1828	3	360
Henry, [twin with Joseph, s. David & Parna], b. Sept. 27, 1813	3	339
Henry, m. Eliza **BARKER**, Aug. 9, 1837, by Rev. David		
Baldwin	3	375
Henry Joseph, s. Benjamin & Susan, b. July 19, 1827	3	371
Huldah, [d. William & Elisabeth], b. Oct. [ ], 1709	3	47
Iana, [d. Timothy & Irene], b. Dec. 8, 1794	3	272
Irene, d. Edward & Hannah, b. Feb. 17, 1756	3	129
Irene, [d. Timothy & Irene], b. Aug. 12, 1789	3	272
Irene, [d, Benjamin], b. June 1, 1795	3	340
Irene, [d. Benjamin], d. July 19, 1796	3	340
Irene, [d. Chandler & Lucy], b. June 4, 1819	3	411
Irene, m. Wyllys **BEACH**, b. of Branford, Dec. 27, 1846,		
by Rev. T. P. Gillett	TM3	159
Jabez, s. Anne, b. July 30, 1723	3	63
Jacob, s. Dan[ie]ll, Jr. & Abigail, b. Sept. 14, 1732	3	75
Jacob, m. Lydia **BYINTUN**, Jan. 25, 1759, by Jonathan		
Merrick	3	158

	Vol.	Page
BARKER, BARKOR, (cont.)		
James, s. Jonath[a]n & Mary, b. Jan. 11, 1709	3	31
James, m. Abigail **RUSSELL**, Oct. [ ], 1737, by Jno. Russell,		
J. P.	3	109
James, s. James & Abigail, b. Mar. 7, 1737/8; d. May 5, 1739	3	109
James, s. James & Abigail, b. May 30, 1753	3	133
James, s. William & Mary, b. Feb. 25, 1770	3	206
James, Capt., m. Lydia **MONRO[E]**, b. of Branford, Nov. 22,		
1780	3	301
James, [s. Archelaus & Mary], b. Jan. 2, 1803	3	397
James, d. Oct. 16, 1822, in the 70th y. of his age	3	423
James, m. Martha **BEACH**, b. of Branford, Nov. 12, 1826,		
by Rev. Timothy P. Gillett	3	343
James Gould, s. David & Sally, b. Oct. 9, 1829	3	378
Jane A., d. Harry & Eliza J., b. Dec. 20, 1838	TM3	240
Jane Augusta, d. Harry & Eliza J., b. Dec. 20, 1838	3	333
Jane S., m. William S. **KIRKUM**, b. of Branford, Jan. 2,		
1851, by Rev. W[illia]m Henry Rees, in Trinity Church,		
New York City	TM3	168
Jared, s. Will[ia]m, Jr. & Abigail, b. Nov. 10, 1736	3	87
Jeremiah, s. Ebenezer & Esther, b. May 28, 1774	3	264
Jeremiah, s. Ebenez[e]r & Esther, d. Sept. 2, 1783; was		
drowned	3	276
Jerusha, d. Jonath[an] & Hannah, b. Feb. 24, 1747/8	3	113
Joel, s. Jacob & Lydia, b. Mar. 9, 1764	3	188
Joel, m. Lois **PAGE**, Jan. 12, 1791	3	412
John, s. Edw[ar]d & Hannah, b. Jan. 1, 1744	3	129
John, m. Mary **ALLEN**, b. of Branford, Mar. 17, 1765, by		
Philemon Robbins	3	284
John, s. John & Mary, b. Mar. 15, 1767	3	284
John, s. Benjamin & Sarah, b. May 26, 1787	3	314
John, [s. Jonathan & Bethiah], b. Feb. 9, 1809	3	385
John, [s. Jonathan & Bethiah], d. Apr. [ ], 1809	3	386
John, m. Irene Almira **WILLIAMS**, b. of Branford, Mar. 31,		
1833, by Rev. Timothy P. Gillett	3	359
Jonathan, s. Edward, b. Jan. 28, 1674	1	174
Jonathan, m. Mary **WARDELL**, June 13, 1700, by Rev. Jno.		
Sparhauk, of Bristoll	2	344
Jonathan, s. Jonathan & Mary, b. Feb. 2, 1702/3	2	344
Jonathan, d. Mar. 22, 1727/8	3	66
Jonathan, of Branford, m. Hannah **BENTON**, of Werthersfield,		
May 21, 1734, by Rev. Stephen Mix	3	80
Jonathan, s. Timothy & Hannah, b. June 26, 1757	3	145
Jonathan, s. Joseph & Elisabeth, b. Dec. 3, 1763	3	181
Jonathan, d. Nov. 14, 1776, ae 73 y. 9 m. 1 d.	3	262
Jonathan, m. Bethiah **NORTON**, May 12, 1788	3	385
Joseph, s. Daniel & Keziah, b. Nov. 30, 1702	2	344
Joseph, s. Jon[a]th[an] & Mary, b. Aug. 13, 1719	3	52

	Vol.	Page
BARKER, BARKOR, (cont.)		
Joseph, m. Hannah **BARTHOLOMEW**, b. of Branford, Nov.		
19, 1724, by Rev. Sam[ue]ll Russell	3	56
Joseph, s. Joseph & Hannah, b. Sept. 26, 1725	3	58
Joseph, s. Joseph & Hannah, d. Feb. 6, 1726/7	3	61
Joseph, Jr., of Branford, m. Elisabeth **FOOT,** of Colchester,		
Nov. 20, 1744, by Rev. Ephraim Litter, at Colchester	3	136
Joseph, s. Dan[ei]ll & Keziah, d. May 11, 1746, in the		
44th y. of his age	3	153
Joseph, s. Joseph & Elisabeth, b. Oct. 19, 1751	3	136
Joseph, [s. Jonathan & Bethiah], b. Sept. 28, 1791	3	385
Joseph, [s. Timothy & Irene], b. Oct. 25, 1797	3	272
Joseph, [twin with Henry, s. David & Parna], b. Sept. 27, 1813	3	339
Joseph, [s. Timothy & Martha], b. Jan. 3, 1836	3	378
Joseph*, s. [Daniel?], [ ] (*Jonthn" written in the margin)	3	29
Joseph, s. Timothy & Hannah, [ ]	3	132
Jotham, s. Jacob & Lydia, b. Jan. 4, 1766	3	190
Julia G., d. Harry & Eliza J., b. Aug. 19, 1845	TM3	240
Jurdon, s. Will[ia]m, Jr. & Abigail, b. Oct. 22, 1733	3	78
Justin, [s. Jonathan & Bethiah], b. July 14, 1801	3	385
Justin Leonard, s. Timothy & Martha, b. Aug. 13, 1832	3	362
Justus, s. Jacob & Lydia, b. May 23, 1762	3	177
Kezia, d. Dan[ei]ll & Kezia, b. Apr. 3, 1710	3	31
Keziah, m. Dow **SMITH**, b. of Branford, Mar. 13, 1733, by		
Jacob Hemingway	3	188
Kezia, d. Dan[ie]ll, Jr. & Patience, b. June 3, 1744	3	117
Keziah, wid. of Lieut., d. night preceding the 1st of		
Jan. 1758, in the 77th y. of her age	3	153
Lois, [d. Joel & Lois], b. Jan. 30, 1792	3	412
Luallen Melill, s. Eliphalet & Martha, b. Aug. 6, 1850	TM3	244
Lucrecia, d. James & Abigail, b. Mar. 18, 1746/7	3	109
Lucretia, d. Russell & Elisabeth, b. July 13, 1783	3	301
Luce, d. Jonathan & Hannah, b. Oct. 18, 1738	3	90
Lucy, m. Ephraim **FOOT**, b. of Branford, July 31, 1760,		
by Philemon Robbins	3	271
Leucy, d. Capt. Sam[ue]ll & Leucy, b. Jan. 22, 1769	3	275
Lydia, d. Dan[ie]ll & Kezia, b. Dec. 22, 1712	3	41
Lydia, m. Stephen **PALMER**, b. of Branford, Dec. 27, 1732,		
by Rev. Jonathan Mer[r]ick	3	83
Lydia, d. Joseph & Hannah, b. Feb. 2, 1733/4	3	78
Lydia, d. Joseph & Hannah, b. Feb. 2, 1733/4	3	84
Lydia, m. Jonathan **RUSSELL**, Jr., b. of Branford, Oct.		
[ ], 1753, by Jonathan Russell, J. P.	3	269
Lydia, d. Ebenezer & Esther, b. Sept. 6, 1765	3	264
Lydia, d. Samuel & Esther, b. Dec. 19, 1766	3	190
Lydia, d. Jacob & Lydia, b. Apr. 14, 1770	3	257
Lydia, w. of Jacob, d. Nov. 14, 1781	3	270
Margeret, d. Joseph & Elisabeth, b. Jan. 24, 1749	3	136

	Vol.	Page
BARKER, BARKOR, (cont.)		
Marina, [d. Joel & Lois], b. Sept. 5, 1802	3	412
Martha, d. Uzal & Martha, b. Sept. 23, 1734	3	99
Martha Leonard, [d. Timothy & Martha], b. Dec. 13, 1839	3	378
Mary, d. Edward, b. Aug. 15, 1671	1	174
Mary, [d. William & Elisabeth], b. Nov. [ ], 1694	3	47
Mary, d. Jonathan & Mary, b. Oct. [ ], 170[ ]	3	29
Mary, m. Daniel **FOOT**, of Branford, Sept. 27, 1721, by		
Rev. Sam[ue]ll Russell	3	57
Mary, d. of Edward, m. John **RUSSELL**, Jr., Oct. 11, 1732,		
by Jno. Russell, J. P.	3	111
Mary, d. Edw[ar]d & Hannah, b. Oct. 26, 1734	3	128
Mary, d. Dan[ie]ll, Jr. & Patience, b. Dec. 23, 1739	3	117
Mary, d. Jonathan & Hannah, b. Aug. 31, 1740	3	97
Mary, d. Uzal & Martha, b. Apr. 6, 1748	3	119
Mary, d. Dec. 24, 1757	3	147
Mary, m. Jonathan **BAKER**, b. of Branford, Sept. 27, 1758,		
by Sam[ue]ll Barker, J. P.	3	153
Mary, d. Joseph & Elisabeth, b. Dec. 7, 1758	3	159
Mary, m. Dan[ie]ll **HOADL[E]Y**, b. of Branford, Apr. 26,		
1759, by Jon[a]th[an] Merrick	3	159
Mary, m. Timothy **FRISBIE**, b. of Branford, Mar. 29, 1764,		
by Philemon Robbins	3	182
Mary, d. William & Mary, b. Sept. 7, 1765	3	206
Mary, d. John & Mary, b. Mar. 22, 1774	3	285
Mary, m. Samuel **BEACH**, Jr., b. of Branford, Sept. 17,		
1826, by Rev. Timothy P. Gillett	3	342
Mary Ann, of Branford, m. William **FRISBIE**, of New Haven,		
June 6, 1831, [by Rev. Timothy P. Gillett]	3	357
Mary E., [d. Jonathan & Bethiah], b. Dec. 9, 1805	3	385
Mary E., m. Timothy **COOK**, b. of Branford, Jan. 1, 1844,		
by Rev. Davis T. Shailer	TM3	157
Mercy, d. Joseph & Hannah, b. Sept. 18, 1743	3	101
Mercy, d. Sam[ue]ll & Esther, b. May 23, 1752	3	126
Mercy, m. Nathaneal **PAGE**, Jr., b. of Branford, June 23,		
1763, by Jonathan Mer[r]ick	3	181
Mercy, m. Joseph **WILLFORD**, b. of Branford, Dec. 30, 1778,		
by Philemon Robbins	3	266
Mercy, [d. Archelaus & Mary], b. Mar. 5, 1808	3	397
Oliver, s. Samuel & Esther, b. July 19, 1769	3	197
Papillon, s. Edw[ar]d & Hannah, b. Aug. 12, 1732	3	128
Peter, s. Uzal & Martha, b. Apr. 13, 1740	3	99
Peter, s. Edward & Hannah, b. Feb. 19, 1750	3	129
Peter, s. John & Mary, b. June 9, 1772	3	285
Peter, [s. Benjamin], b. Apr. 14, 1790	3	340
Philemon, s. Timothy & Hannah, b. Feb. 16, 1754	3	135
Philemon, s. Timothy & Hannah, d. Aug. 14, 1761, ae		
7 y. 29 d.	3	172

	Vol.	Page
BARKER, BARKOR, (cont.)		
Pitmon, s. Capt. Sam[ue]ll & Leucy, b. July 5, 1772	3	275
Polle, d. Ebenez[e]r & Esther, b. Dec. 24, 1780	3	276
Polly, [d. Jonathan & Bethiah], b. Dec. 15, 1789	3	385
Polly, m. John **STAPLES**, b. of Branford, Sept. 16, 1827,		
by Rev. Timothy P. Gillett	3	345
Rachel, d. Edward & Sarah, b. July 25, 1764	3	256
Rachel, m. Reuel **RUSSELL**, b. of Branford, Mar. 26, 1786,		
by Sam[ue]l Eells	3	259
Ralph, s. Ebenezer & Esther, b. Feb. 27, 1778	3	276
Rebeccah, d. Jonathan & Mary, b. Apr. 3, 1712	3	52
Rebeckah, m. Nathan **PALMER**, Jan. 10, 1734, by Rev.		
Philemon Robbins	3	148
Rebecca, d. Uzal & Martha, b. Apr. 24, 1742	3	99
Rhoda, d. Timothy & Hannah, b. Nov. 20, 1763	3	180
Ruhamah, d. Jonathan & Hannah, b. June 15, 1742	3	101
Russell, s. James & Abigail, b. Mar. 30, 1757	3	145
Russell, m. Elisabeth **WILLFORD**, b. of Branford, Sept. 8,		
1779	3	301
Rutherford, s. Russell & Elisabeth, b. Dec. 17, 1779	3	301
Sabrina, d. Sam[ue]ll, Jr. & Lucy, b. Apr. 12, 1764	3	182
Sabrina, m. Nathan **MULFORD**, b. of Branford, Mar. 26,		
1782, by Sam[ue]ll Eells	3	273
Salle, d. Edw[ard] & Sarah, b. Sept. 3, 1775	3	283
Sally, [d. Archelaus & Mary], b. Sept. 21, 1786	3	270
Sally, m. Benjamin **BARTHOLOMEW**, Sept. 3, 1801	3	386
Sam[ue]ll, s. Dan[ie]ll & Kezia, b. Feb. 9, 1715/6	3	41
Samuel, s. William, Jr. & Abigail, b. Aug. 6, 1739	3	90
Sam[ue]ll, m. Esther **BAKER**, b. of Branford, Apr. 12,		
1744, by Rev. Jonathan Mer[r]ick	3	102
Sam[ue]ll, s. Samuell & Esther, b. Aug. 17, 1747; d.		
Jan. 13, 1751, in the 4th y. of his age	3	110
Sam[ue]ll, s. Sam[ue]ll & Esther, d. Jan. 13, 1750/1 in		
the 4th y. of his age	3	121
Sam[ue]ll, s. Edward & Hannah, b. June 8, 1758	3	129
Sam[ue]ll, Jr., of Branford, m. Lucy **LEETE**, of Guilford,		
Nov. 27, 1760, by [James] Sprout	3	167
Samuel A., [s. Joel & Lois], b. Nov. 22, 1797	3	412
Samuel Still Augustus, s. Samuel & Esther, b. Oct. 19, 1756	3	142
Sarah, d. Jon[a]th[an] & Mary, b. Dec. 27, 1714	3	52
Sarah, m. Joseph **TAINTOR**, b. of Branford, Apr. 10, 1743,		
by John Russell, J. P.	3	154
Sarah, d. Edw[ar]d & Hannah, b. July 28, 1747	3	129
Sarah, d. James & Abigail, b. Dec. 7, 1750	3	121
Sarah, m. John Rogers, Jr., b. of Branford, July 12, 1765	3	304
Sarah, d. William & Mary, b. Sept. 25, 1767	3	206
Silas, s. John & Mary, b. Dec. 2, 1778	3	285
Silence, d. Joseph & Hannah, b. Jan. 14, 1737/8	3	88

	Vol.	Page
BARKER, BARKOR, (cont.)_		
Silence, d. Joseph & Hannah, d. Dec. 9, 1752	3	173
Simeon, [s. Benjamin], b. Sept. 30, 1792	3	340
Solomon, s. Uzal & Martha, b. Nov. 10, 1737	3	99
Susan Lydia, d. Jonathan & Lydia, b. Sept. 1, 1814	3	344
Sibil, d. James & Abigail, b. Nov. 25, 1740 (Sybil)	3	109
Sibil, m. Ebenezer **LINSL[E]Y**, Jr., b. of Branford, Dec. 17, 1760, by Philemon Robbins (Sybil)	3	167
Thaddeus, s. Edw[ard] & Sarah, b. Oct. 19, 1780	3	283
Thankfull, d. Dan[ie]ll & Kezia, b. Apr. 19, 1719	3	43
Thankful, m. Nathan **ROSE**, b. of Branford, May 30, 1739, by Jon[a]th[an] Merrick	3	174
Thankfull, d. Joseph & Hannah, b. Jan. 1, 1740/1	3	94
Thankfull, d. Joseph & Hannah, d. May 6, 1748	3	115
Thankfull, d. Jacob & Lydia, b. May 2, 1760	3	161
Theodosia, d. Joseph & Hannah, b. Apr. 12, 1731	3	71
Th[e]adosia, m. Daniel **BALDWIN**, Jr. b. of Branford, Dec. 25, 1755, by Rev. Jonathan Merrick	3	140
Thomas, s. Ebenezer & Esther, b. Feb. 25, 1759	3	264
Thomas, [s. Jonathan & Bethiah], b. Nov. 19, 1793	3	385
Thomas, [s. Jonathan & Bethiah], d. Sept. 23, 1795	3	386
Thomas, [s. Jonathan & Bethiah], b. Sept. 15, 1798	3	385
Timothy, s. Daniel & Kezia, b. May 23, 1723	3	52
Timothy, m. Hannah **BAKER**, b. of Branford, Aug. 9, 1744, by Rev. Jon[a]th[an] Mer[r]ick	3	105
Timothy, s. Timothy & Hannah, b. Apr. 5, 1750	3	121
Timothy, [s. Timothy & Irene], b. Mar. 4, 1792	3	272
Timothy Leonard, s. Timothy & Martha, b. Mar. 13, 1828	3	362
Triphene, d. John & Mary, b. May 30, 1765	3	284
Uzal, s. Jonath[a]n & Mary, b. Feb. 8, 1707	3	31
Uzal, m. Martha **MUNSON**, b. of Branford, Jan. 6, 1731/2, by Jno, Russell, J. P.	3	75
Uzal, s. Uzal & Martha, b. Nov. 19, 1732	3	75
William, [s. William & Elisabeth], b. Feb. [ ], 1701	3	47
William, Jr., m. Abigail **FRISBE**, b. of Branford, Dec. 5, 1725, by Nath[anie]ll Har[r]ison, J. P.	3	60
William, s. William, Jr. & Abigail, b. Nov. 7, 1726	3	60
William, s. William & Abigail, d. Mar. 17, 1726/7	3	63
William, s. William, Jr. & Abigail, b. Nov. 2, 1731	3	73
William, d. Jan. 31, 1740/1	3	94
William, d. Dec. 6, 1744	3	103
William, of Branford, m. Mary **GILBERT**, of Wallingford, Dec. [ ], 1764, by Theo[philu]s Hall	3	206
William, s. William & Mary, b. Jan. 19, 1772	3	206
William Cornelius, s. Ebeneser & Amelia, b. Apr. 26, 1832	TM3	238
----, d. Oct. 16, 1707	3	30
BARNES, BARNS, BRANS, Abigail, d. Nath[anie]ll & Elisabeth, b. Sept. 1, 1735	3	82

	Vol.	Page
BARNES, BARNS, BRANS, (cont.)		
Abigail, d. Enos & Abigail, b. May 14, 1748	3	138
Ame, d. Enos & Abigail, b. May 14, 1752	3	138
Amos, s. Dan[ie]ll & Ann, b. Mar. 19, 1734/5	3	81
Asa, s. Stephen, Jr. & Martha, b. Aug. 24, 1745	3	106
Benjamin, s. Steven & Mary, b. Dec. 13, 1702	2	344
Benj[ami]n, s. John & Dorothy, b. Apr. 10, 1708	3	30
Benjamin, 2d, m. Hannah **ABBOT[T]**, b. of Branford, Dec. 7, 1727, by Rev. Sam[ue]ll Russell	3	65
Benjamin, Dea., d. July 23, 1740, in the 69th y. of his age	3	95
Daniel, of Branford, m. Ann **BROCKET**, of New Haven, Mar. 21, 1727/8, by Rev. Isaac Stiles	3	73
Daniel, s. Dan[ie]ll & Ann, b. May 11, 1729	3	73
Daniel Beach, [s. Huffman & Sally], b. Feb. 20, 1823	3	335
David, s. Ebenezer & Abigail, b. Apr. 14, 1747	3	111
Deborah, d. Benj[ami]n & Hannah, b. Nov. 10, 1734	3	113
Desire, d. Jno. & Dorothy, b. Apr. 22, 1706	3	29
Desire, m. Timothy **PARMERLE**, b. of Branford, May 3, 1727, by Rev. Sam[ue]ll Russell	3	79
Desier, of New Haven, m. Ebenezer **BUTLER**, of Branford, Mar. 30, 1757, by Josiah Rogers, J. P.	3	146
Ebenezer, s. Eben[eze]r & Abigail, b. Sept. 30, 1743	3	101
Elisabeth, d. Benj[ami]n, 3rd, & Elisabeth, b. Aug. 31, 1732	3	76
Elizabeth, of East Hampton, L. I., m. Edward **JOHNSON**, of Branford, Nov. 9, 1732, by Rev. Jonathan Merrick	3	116
Elisabeth, d. Nath[anie]ll & Elisabeth, b. Oct. 28, 1738	3	93
Enos, s. Enos & Abigail, b. Apr. 10, 1750	3	138
Enos, s. Enos & Abigail, d. Apr. 18, 1751	3	138
Eunice, d. Timothy & Phebe, b. Jan. 21, 1736/7	3	88
Eunice, d. Benj[ami]n & Hannah, b. Nov. 8, 1737	3	113
Experience, d. Stephen & Mary, b. Dec. 4, 1710 (Spelled "Exeperience")	3	35
Hannah, m. Samuel **HARRINGTON**, July 27, 1693, by William Maltbie, J. P.	2	343
Harriet, [d. Huffman & Sally], b. Jan. 24, 1808	3	335
Isaac, s. Nath[anie]ll & Elisabeth, b. Apr. 26, 1740	3	93
Johanna, of East Hampton, L. I., m. Deliverance **BUNNEL[L]**, of Branford, Dec. 25, 1730, by Rev. Jonathan Mer[r]ick	3	115
John, m. Dorothy **STENT**, Aug. 28, 1700, by Rev. Mr. Russell	2	343
John, s. John & Dorothy, b. Feb. 17, 1703/4	2	345
John Harvey, [s. Huffman & Sally], b. Jan. 12, 1812	3	335
Jonathan, s. Stephen, Jr. & Martha, b. Feb. 21, 1730/1	3	70
Laura, [d. Huffman & Sally], b. Sept. 29,. 1821	3	336
Lois, d. Timothy & Phebe, b. May 28, 1739	3	90
Luce, d. Nath[anie]ll & Elisabeth, b. Sept. 16, 1742	3	101
Lydia, d. Benj[ami]n, 2d, & Hannah, b. Oct. 22, 1728	3	65
Martha, of East Hampton, L. I., m. Isaac **BARTHOLOMEW**, of Branford, May 26, 1732, by Rev. Jonathan Mer[r]ick	3	87

	Vol.	Page
BARNES, BARNS, BRANS, (cont.)		
Martha, d. Stephen, Jr. & Martha, b. Aug. 22, 1734	3	81
Mary, d. Stephen, Jr. & Martha, b. Oct. 22, 1726	3	62
Mary, d. Benjamin & Hannah, b. June 17, 1730	3	112
Mary, m. Artemas **JOHNSON**, b. of Branford, Dec. 8, 1765,		
by Josiah Rogers, J. P.	3	263
Mehetabel, d. John & Dorothy, b. Aug. 29, 1702	2	343
Melinda had s., b. Jan. [ ], 1850	TM3	243
Melinda, of Branford, m. Horace P. **TOOKER**, of Lyme, Feb.		
16, 1851, by Rev. Timothy P. Gillett	TM3	168
Melinda, ae 19, m. Horace **TUCKER**, ae 21, Feb. 16, 1851	TM3	170
Moses, s. Dan[ie]ll & Ann, b. Aug. 8, 1732	3	78
Nathan, s. Stephen, Jr. & Martha, b. Aug. 25, 1742	3	104
Nathaniel, m. Elisabeth **BARTHOLOMEW**, b. of Branford,		
Nov. 16, 1732, by Rev. Jonathan Merrick	3	75
Nathaniel, s. Nath[anie]ll & Elisabeth, b. Oct. 1, 1733	3	82
Patience, d. John & Dorothy, b. Feb. 13, 1709	3	34
Phebe, of New Haven, m. Timothy **BARN[E]S**, of Branford,		
Dec. 6, 1733, by Rev. Jonathan Merrick	3	80
Phebe, d. Timothy & Phebe, b. May 2, 1742	3	99
Phebe, d. Timothy & Phebe, d. Oct. 9, 1743	3	102
Phebe, d. Timothy & Phebe, b. Jan. 15, 1744/5	3	108
Rachel, m. John **AUGER**, b. of Branford, Jan. 5, 1743/4,		
by Rev. Jonath[an] Mer[r]ick	3	113
Rebec[c]a, of North Haven, m. Sam[ue]ll **TOWNER**, of		
Branford, Jan. 25, 1716	3	42
Sally Eliza, [d. Huffman & Sally], b. June 10, 1814	3	335
Sarah, d. Stephen & Mary, b. May 17, 1708	3	35
Sarah, m. Ezekiel **ROGERS**, b. of Branford, Nov. 23, 1731,		
by Jno. Russell, J. P.	3	72
Sarah, d. Benja[mi]n & Hannah, b. Sept. 27, 1732	3	113
Stephen, Jr., m. Martha **WHEDON**, b. of Branford, Jan. 5,		
1725/6, by Rev. Sam[ue]ll Russell	3	62
Stephen, s. Stephen, Jr. & Martha, b. Dec. 3, 1728	3	65
Steven, s. Steven & Mary, b. Jan. 2, 1704/5	2	346
Susan E., of East Haven, m. Samuel **McQUEEN**, of Branford,		
Apr. 29, 1844, by Rev. Timothy P. Gillett	TM3	157
Timothy, of Branford, m. Phebe **BARNS**, of New Haven, Dec.		
6, 1733, by Rev. Jonathan Merrick	3	80
Timothy, s. Timothy & Phebe, b. Sept. 16, 1734	3	80
Timothy, s. Timothy & Phebe, d. Feb. 1, 1736/7	3	88
Timothy, s. Timothy & Phebe, b. Apr. 8, 1749	3	119
William, s. Stephen, Jr. & Martha, b. Nov. 10, 1738	3	95
William J., of North Haven, m. Emily **PAGE**, of Branford,		
Nov. 27, 1851, by Rev. T. P. Gillett	TM3	170
Zeruiah, of East Hampton, L. I., m. Uzziel **COOK**, of		
Branford, May 20, 1745, by Jonathan Merrick	3	187
----, s. Melinda, b. Jan. [ ], 1850	TM3	243

	Vol.	Page
BARTHOLOMEW, Abigail, d. Will[ia]m, Jr. & Abigail, b. Jan. 23,		
1724/5	3	56
Abigail, m. William **ROGERS**, Jr., b. of Branford, Nov.		
14, 1729, by Rev. Jonathan Merrick	3	68
Abner, s. Benjamin & Phebe, b. Feb. 1, 1720/1	3	53
[A]braham, s. Isaac & Rebec[c]ah, b. June 28, 1708	3	30
Abraham, m. Hannah **PAGE**, b. of Branford, June 18, 1730,		
by Rev. Jonathan Merrick	3	68
Abraham, s. Abraham & Hannah, b. Jan. 28, [1732/3]	3	95
Andrew, s. Andrew & Hannah, b. Nov. 7, 1714	3	37
Andrew, s. Benjamin & Elisabeth, b. Oct. 26, 1768	3	195
Andrew, s. Benj[ami]n & Elisabeth, d. Sept. 14, 1774,		
ae 7 y. 10 m. 19 d.	3	258
Antoinette, [d. Jacob & Hannah], b. May 9, 1809	3	399
Antionette, m. Edwin White **PARSONS**, b. of Branford, Feb.		
18, 1840, by Rev. Timothy P. Gillett	3	378
Benjamin, m. Phebe **BALDWIN**, Oct. 28, 1713, by Rev.		
Sam[ue]ll Russel[l]	3	38
Benjamin, s. Benj[ami]n & Phebe, b. Feb. 1, 1728	3	72
Benjamin, m. Elizabeth **[W]RIGHT**, b. of Branford, Feb. 2,		
1749, by Rev. Philemon Robbins	3	148
Benjamin, s. Benj[ami]n & Elisabeth, b. Oct. 13, 1752	3	127
Benjamen, s. Benjamen & Elizabeth, b. Oct. 13, 1752	3	148
Benjamin, Jr., d. Apr. 26, 1778	3	270
Benjamin, s. Gideon & Wealthean, b. Dec. 2, 1778	3	268
Benjamin, m. Sally **BARKER**, Sept. 3, 1801	3	386
Bets[e]y, d. Gideon & We[a]lthy, b. Oct. 13, 1785	3	312
Betty, d. Benjamin & Elisabeth, b. May 13, 1762	3	176
Betty, d. Benjamin & Elisabeth, d. Sept. 25, 1774, ae		
12 y. 4 m. 12 d.	3	258
Clifford, s. Rodolphus & Elizabeth, b. Apr. 1, 1849	TM3	241
Dan, s. Gersham & Elizabeth, b. Oct. 10, 1755	3	140
Dan[ie]ll, s. Andrew & Hannah, b. Oct. 16, 1708	3	30
Dan[ie]ll, s. Isaac & Martha, b. June 16, 1746	3	107
Darling, of Northford, m. Sarah H. **FOWLER**, of Guilford,		
June 11, 1827, by Rev. Timo[thy] P. Gillett	3	344
Eleaz[a]r, s. Isaac & Rebec[c]ah, b. June 10, [ ];		
[bp. July [ ], 1706]	3	29
Eli, s. Gershom & Elisabeth, b. July 13, 1761	3	176
Elizabeth, d. Isaac & Rebeccah, b. Apr. 12, 1704	2	345
Elisabeth, d. John & Marcy, b. Oct. 13, 1715	3	39
Elisabeth, m. Nathaniel **BARN[E]S**, b. of Branford, Nov.		
16, 1732, by Rev. Jonathan Merrick	3	75
Elton S., s. John J. & Charlott[e], b. Oct. 28, 1849	TM3	242
Eunice, d. Isaac & Martha, b. Dec. 25, 1742	3	102
Eunice, d. Sarah, b. Sept. 23, 1762	3	178
Ezekiel, s. Benjamin & Elisabeth, b. May 10, 1765	3	186
Ezekiel, s. Benjamin & Elisabeth, d. Oct. 9, 1774, ae 9 y.	3	258

	Vol.	Page
BARTHELOMEW, (cont.)		
4 m. 29 d.	3	258
Francis Coot, [child of Timothy, Jr. & Mariett], b. Nov. 21, 1820	3	337
Gershom, s. William, Jr. & Abigail, b. Dec. 1, 1722	3	50
Gershom, m. Elisabeth **FRISBIE**, b. of Branford, Nov. 5, 1749, by Nathan[ie]ll Harrison, J. P.	3	123
Gideon, s. Benj[ami]n & Phebe, b. Sept. 25, 1716	3	42
Gideon, s. Benjamen & Elizabeth, b. Sept. 8, 1757	3	148
Gideon, m. Wealthean **SHELDON**, b. of Branford, Feb. 5, 1778, by Philemon Robbins	3	268
Gid[eo]n, d. July 10, 1790	3	257
Hannah, d. Andrew & Hannah, b. Aug. 17, 1704	2	345
Hannah, m. Joseph **BARKER**, b. of Branford, Nov. 19, 1724, by Rev. Sam[ue]ll Russell	3	56
Hannah, d. Abraham & Hannah, b. May 9, 1731	3	72
Hannah, wid., m. Isaac **INGRAHAM**, b. of Branford, Apr. 15, 1736, by Jonathan Mer[r]ick	3	156
Hannah, m. Jacob **HARRISON**, Oct. 24, 1805	3	399
Isaac, of Branford, m. Martha **BARN[E]S**, of East Hampton, L. I., May 26, 1732, by Rev. Jonathan Mer[r]ick	3	87
Isaac, s. Isaac & Martha, b. Mar. 28, 1734	3	87
Isaac, s. Benj[ami]n & Elisabeth, b. Oct. 24, 1750	3	122
Isaac, s. Beniamen & Elizabeth, b. Oct. 24, 1750	3	148
Isaac Newton, [s. Timothy, Jr. & Mariett], b. June 4, 1824	3	337
Jacob, s. Abraham & Hannah, b. Jan. 9, 1736/7	3	95
Jerusha, d. Isaac, Sr. & Rebeccah, b. Jan. 13, 1722/3	3	52
Jesse, s. Josiah & Phebe, b. Mar. 15, 1762	3	176
John, m. wid. Marcy **FRISBEE**, Jan. 4, 1714/5, by Nathan[ie]ll Harrison, J. P.	3	39
John, s. John & Mercy, b. June 4, 1717	3	42
John, s. Andrew & Hannah, b. Feb. 8, 1723/4	3	54
John, s. Abraham & Hannah, b. Apr. 15, 1744	3	118
John J., m. Charlotte A. **SQUIRE**, b. of Branford, Aug. 24, 1837, by Rev. Leonard Bacon, of New Haven	3	374
Jonathan, s. Gershom & Elisabeth, b. Nov. 5, 1750	3	123
Joseph, s. Andrew & Hannah, b. May 6, 172[ ]	3	45
Joseph, s. Benj[ami]n & Phebe, b. June 26, 1731	3	72
Joseph, d. June 4, 1821, ae 90 y., lacking 21 d.	3	413
Josiah, s. Isaac & Rebec[c]ah, b. Jan. 18, 1710/11	3	33
Josiah, m. Lydia **HARRINGTON**, b. of Branford, June 10, 1740, by Rev. Philemon Robbins	3	96
Josiah, s. Josiah & Lydia, b. Apr. 7, 1751	3	124
Josiah, of Branford, m. wid. Phebe **MUNSON**, of Wallingford, Apr. 9, 1752, by Rev. Warham Williams	3	125
Langdon, [s. Jacob & Hannah], b. Aug. 21, 1811	3	399
Laura A., of Branford, m. James R. **WAY**, of Meriden, Aug. 22, 1849, by Rev. Timothy P. Gillett	TM3	164

	Vol.	Page
BARTHOLOMEW, (cont.)		
Laury Ann, ae 19 y., m. James R. **WAY**, ae 22 y., [ ],		
by Rev. Timothy P. Gillett	TM3	166
Levi, s. William & Hannah, b. Jan. 11, 1731/2	3	73
Luzern, s. Sam[ue]ll, Jr. & Irene, b. July 31, 1781	3	270
Lydia, d. Benjamin & Phebe, b. Sept. 8, 1725	3	72
Lydia, d. Abraham & Hannah, b. Feb. 18, 1738/9	3	95
Lydia, d. Josiah & Lydia, b. Aug. 18, 1748	3	124
Lydia, w. of Josiah, d. Oct. 6, 1751	3	124
Lydia, m. Daniel **ROGERS**, b. of Branford, June 18, 1752,		
by Rev. Philemon Robbins	3	140
Lydia, d. Sam[ue]l, Jr. & Irene, b. Jan. 25, 1777	3	267
Major, [s. Benjamin & Sally], b. Dec. 13, 1808	3	387
Marietta, [d. Benjamin & Sally], b. Jan. 17, 1810	3	387
Martha, d. Isaac & Martha, b. July 20, 1738	3	90
Mary, d. Benjamin & Phebe, b. Sept. 17, 1714	3	42
Mary, of Branford, m. Abijah **HOBART**, formerly of New		
London, Feb. 9, 1731/2, by Jno. Russell, J. P.	3	75
Mary, d. Abrahm & Hannah, b. July 19, 1741	3	118
Mercy, w. of Jno, & wid. of Ebenezer **FRISBIE**, d. Dec. 11,		
1732	3	74
Milton, [s. Benjamin & Sally], b. July 12, 1802	3	386
Minerva, [d. Benjamin & Sally], b. June 9, 1804	3	386
Moses, s. Josiah & Phebe, b. Sept. 3, 1755	3	140
Oliver, s. Josiah & Phebe, b. Oct. 20, 1757	3	159
Patience, d. Abraham & Hannah, b. May 19, 1748	3	118
Phebe, d. Benjamin & Phebe, b. Oct. 15, 1718	3	42
Phebe, m. Micah **PALMER**, Jr., b. of Branford, Mar. 5, 1741,		
by Rev. Philemon Robbins	3	103
Phebe, d. Josiah & Phebe, b. Jan. 31, 1760	3	159
Phebe, wid. Benj[ami]n, d. Feb. 26, 1760	3	160
Polle, d. Gid[eo]n & We[a]lthy, b. Aug. 29, 1787	3	254
Polle, d. Gid[eo]n & Wealthean, b. Aug. 29, 1787	3	257
Rachel, d. Benj[amin] & Phebe, b. Aug. 31, 1723	3	53
Rachel, m. Sam[ue]ll **FRISBIE**, Jr., b. of Branford, Aug.		
4, 1742, by Jno. Russell, J. P.	3	108
Rachill, d. Benjamen & Elizabeth, b. Sept. 25, 1754	3	148
Rachel, m. Samuel **TYLER**, Jr., b. of Branford, Jan. 11,		
1776, by Philemon Robbins	3	261
Rebec[c]ah, d. Andrew & Hannah, b. Mar. 28, 1712	3	35
Rebecca, d. Isaac & Martha, b. Aug. 1, 1736	3	87
Rhodolphus, m. Elisabeth S. **GRIFFING**, b. of Branford,		
June 15, 1848, by Rev. Timothy P. Gillett	TM3	162
Robert Dwight, s. Rodolphus & Elizabeth, b. Mar. 24, 1851	TM3	244
Sally, d. Gideon & We[a]lthy, b. Feb. 21, 1783	3	290
Sam[ue]ll, s. Andrew & Hannah, b. Sept. 12, 170[ ];		
[bp. Oct. [ ], 1706]	3	29
Sam[ue]ll, s. Josiah & Lydia, b. Mary 12, 1745	3	107

	Vol.	Page
BARTHOLOMEW, (cont.)		
Samuel, Jr., of Branford, m. Irene **MUNSON**, of Wallingford,		
May 14, 1776, by Warham Williams	3	267
Samuel, d. July 21, 1795, in the 89th y. of his age	3	268
Sarah, d. Isaac & Martha, b. Dec. 28, 1740	3	97
Sarah, d. Josiah & Lydia, b. Apr. 4, 1742	3	101
Sarah, m. David **TYLER**, b. of Branford, June 28, 1761,		
by Warham Williams	3	173
Sarah had d. Eunice, b. Sept. 23, 1762	3	178
Seth, s. William, Jr. & Hannah, b. Mar. 6, 1729/30	3	69
Susanna, d. Andrew & Hannah, b. Feb. 4, 1701/2	2	344
Susanna, d. William, Jr. & Hannah, b. Apr. 11, 1734	3	80
Susanna, m. Stephen **HARRISON**, b. of Branford, Mar. 16,		
1755, by Warham Williams	3	155
Thankful, d. Abraham & Hannah, b. Mar. 24, 1745/6	3	118
Timothy, s. Andrew & Hannah, b. Feb. [ ], 1716/7	3	39
Timothy, Jr., of Branford, m. Mariette **COOKE**, of		
Wallingford, Feb. 6, 1820, by Rev. Matthew Noyes	3	414
Venetia, [d. Jacob & Hannah], b. Feb. 13, 1807	3	399
We[a]lthy, d. Gideon & We[a]lthy, b. Mar. 14, 1781	3	270
William, s. Andrew & Hannah, b. Dec. 2, 1699 * (*First		
written "Feb. 4, 1701/2")	2	344
William, Jr., of Branford, m. Abigail **BROWN**, of New Haven,		
Jan. 25, 1721/2, by Rev. Jacob Heminway	3	50
William, Jr., of Branford, m. wid. Hannah **WILLIAMS**, of		
Wallingford, Dec. 7, 1726, by Theophilus Yale, J. P.	3	63
William, Jr., d. Sept. 7, 1734	3	80
BARTLETT, Henry B., of Waymait, Penn., m. Hannah C. **HALL**,		
of Branford, Aug. 28, 1836, by Rev. T. P. Gillett	3	372
Melzar F., m. Marietta **FOWLER**, b. of Guilford, Apr. 8,		
1832, by Rev. Timothy P. Gillett	3	357
William, of Westbrook, m. Parmela **STANNARD**, of Branford,		
Jan. 29, 1854, by Rev. Tim[oth]y P. Gillett	TM3	173
BASSETT, BASSET, Eunice, of Milford, m. Richard **BALDWIN**,		
of Branford, May 30, 1745, by Rev. Sam[ue]ll		
W[h]ittlesey, at Milford	3	120
Lydia, of Hamden, m. George H. **ANDREWS**, of Branford,		
May 2, 1853, by (Episcopal Minister) in New York	TM3	172
BAYLEY, [see under **BAILEY**]		
BEACH, BEECH, Abigail, [d. Elnathan & Abigail], b. June 1, 1806	3	285
Abigail, of Branford, m. Nathan **ROSE**, of North Branford,		
Apr. 21, 1827, by Rev. Timothy P. Gillett	3	344
Abigail, d. Mar. 3, 1847, ae 78	TM3	307
Ammi, [child of Eben[eze]r & Abigail], b. Dec. 25, 1790	3	282
Andrew, s. Ephraim & Sarah, b. Aug. 19, 1768	3	288
Andrew, m. Elizabeth **BRADL[E]Y**, June 14, 1792	3	389
Andrew, m. Rhoda **WAY**, b. of Branford, Apr. 20, 1824, by		
Charles Atwater	3	426

	Vol.	Page
BEACH, BEECH,(cont.)		
Andrew, d. Dec. 18, 1849, ae 80 y.	TM3	309
Angelina, [d. Asher S. & Statira], b. Oct. 9, 1807	3	389
Ann Charlotte, [d. Asa & Nancy], b. Nov. 28, 1812	3	413
Anna, w. of Samuel, d. Feb. 23, 1825	3	355
Anna, d. Samuel & Mary, b. July 27, 1827	3	355
Anna Aritta, m. Lorin D. **HOSLEY**, Sept. 30, 1822, by Rev.		
Matthew Noyes	3	421
Anne Ritte, [d. Samuel & Anne], b. Jan. 17, 1802	3	387
Asa, s. Ebenezer & Abigail, b. Aug. 30, 1776	3	289
Asa, m. Nancy **GOODRICH**, b. of Branford, Jan. 2, 1812	3	413
Asher, s. Ephraim & Sarah, b. Aug. 24, 1779	3	288
Asher S., m. Statira **BALDWIN**, b. of Branford, July 20, 1800	3	389
Asher S., d. May 3, 1811, ae 32 y., if he had lived until Aug.	3	380
Betsey, [d. Eben[eze[r & Abigail], b. Aug. 6, 1784	3	282
Betsey, d. Eb[eneze]r, d. Nov. 29, 1822	3	431
Betsey Ann, [d. Timothy & Esther], b. Sept. 21, 1838	3	377
Bette, d. Elnathan & Lydia, b. June 20, 1760	3	168
Bette, [d. Elnathan & Abigail], b. Aug. 19, 1799	3	285
Betty, m. Levi **FRISBIE**, b. of Branford, May 14, 1819	3	413
David, s. Dea. Elnathan & Lydia, b. May 30, 1767	3	191
David, [s. Elnathan & Abigail], b. July 12, 1792	3	285
David, [s. Elnathan & Abigail], d. Apr. 25, 1793	3	285
David, [s. John & Sally], b. Oct. 25, 1817	3	370
David, m. Sylvia **BALDWIN**, Jan. 8, 1846, by Rev. W[illia]m		
B. Sprague, in Albany, N. Y.	TM3	171
David Harrison, [s. John & Sally], b. Mar. 20, 1814	3	370
David Harrison, [s. John & Sally], d. Nov. 12, 1815	3	370
Delia, m. Elias **PLANT**, Jr., b. of Branford, Dec. 14, 1848,		
by Rev. T. P. Gillett	TM3	163
Eben, [s. Andrew & Elizabeth], b. Jan. 27, 1798	3	389
Ebenezor, s. Andru & Lucy, b. Mar. 16, 1750	3	152
Ebenezer, m. Abigail **LINSLEY**, b. of Branford, Dec. 6,		
1775, by Philemon Robbins	3	288
Ebenezer, [s. Eben[eze]r & Abigail], b. Sept. 26, 1788	3	282
Eber, s. Ephraim & Sarah, b. Apr. 12, 1774	3	288
Eber, m. Mary **TYLER**, Oct. 8, 1821, by Timothy P. Gillett	3	414
Edmund, [s. Elnathan & Abigail], b. Aug. 26, 1789	3	285
Edmund, [s. Elnathan & Abigail], d. Sept. 26, 1795	3	285
Edmund, [s. Elnathan & Abigail], b. Dec. 29, 1798	3	285
Edmund, m. Mary Eliza **FRISBIE**, b. of Branford, May 25,		
1819	3	417
Elizebeth, d. Phinehas & Elizebeth, b. Jan. 2, 1759	3	157
Elizabeth, [d. Andrew & Elizabeth], b. Sept. 4, 1810	3	389
Elizabeth, w. of Andrew, d. Dec. 9, 1822	3	389
Elizabeth, m. Jonathan **PALMER**, b. of Branford, Aug. 31,		
1833, by Rev. T. P. Gillett	3	361
Elnathan, s. Dea. Elnathan & Lydia, b. Dec. 10, 1764	3	184

	Vol.	Page
BEACH, BEECH, (cont.)		
Elnathan, m. Abigail **EVERTON**, May 25, 1789	3	285
Ephraim, s. Andrew & Lucy, b. June 13, 1742	3	151
Ephraim, of Branford, m. Sarah **STONE**, of Guilford, Dec.		
1, 1767, by Rev. Benj[ami]n Ruggals	3	288
Ephrain, d. July 4, 1827	3	347
Eunice, d. Elnathan & Lydia, b. Nov. 2, 1753	3	142
Hannah, d. Elnathan & Lydia, b. Nov. 15, 1751	3	125
Hannah, [d. John & Sally], b. Jan. 5, 1811	3	369
Hannah, of Branford, m. Joel **HALL**, of Wallingford, May		
4, 1830, by Timothy P. Gillett	3	353
Harvey, [s. Timothy & Esther], b. May 1, 1834	3	377
Hobart Stone, [s. Asher S. & Statira], b. Aug. 23, 1805	3	389
Hobart Stone, of Branford, m. Maria **BOOTH**, of Wallingford,		
Dec. 17, 1828, by Rev. Timothy P. Gillett	3	348
Isabelle Lee, d. Samuel, 2d & Harriette A., b. Mar. 1, 1852	TM3	245
John, m. Vina **BALDWIN**, b. of Branford, Oct. 27, 1803	3	369
John, m. Sally **TYLER**, b. of Branford, May 21, 1807	3	369
John, [s. Timothy & Esther], b. Apr. 18, 1830	3	377
John Har[r]ington, s. Elnathan & Lydia, b. Jan. 5, 1756	3	142
John [H]arrington, m. Phebe **FRISBIE**, b. of Branford,		
Oct. 2, 1776, by Sam[ue]ll Eells	3	274
John Harrington, s. of John, d. July 16, 1834	3	370
Louisa, [d. Asa & Nancy], b. Jan. 24, 1817	3	413
Louisa M., m. Timothy **PALMER**, b. of Branford, Nov. 30,		
1837, by Rev. Timothy P. Gillett	3	374
Lucy, d. Andrew & Lucy, b. Aug. 11, 1746	3	151
Lucy, m. Ebenezer **ROGERS**, b. of Branford, Sept. 10, 1772,		
by Philemon Robbins	3	258
Lucy, [d. Eben[eze]r & Abigail], b. Jan. 13, 1787	3	282
Lucy, d. Ebenezer & Abigail, m. Chandler **BARKER**, s.		
Benjamin & Sarah, Oct. 18, 1810	3	411
Lydia, d. Elnathan & Lydia, b. Apr. 18, 1758	3	154
Lydia, m. Isaac **LINSL[E]Y**, b. of Branford, Dec. 23, 1761,		
by Philemon Robbins	3	179
Lydia, m. Obed **LINSLEY**, b. of Branford, Dec. 23, 1778,		
by Philemon Robbins	3	277
Lydia, d. Ebenez[e]r & Abigail, b. Mar. 22, 1781	3	289
Lydia, [d. Elnathan & Abigail], b. Feb. 23, 1796	3	285
Lydia, m. Levi **BRADL[E]Y**, b. of Brandford, Nov. 28, 1798	3	391
Lydia Minerva, d. Edmund & Mary Eliza, b. May 14, 1820	3	417
Martha, [d. Andrew & Elizabeth], b. Dec. 8, 1805	3	389
Martha, m. James **BARKER**, b. of Branford, Nov. 12, 1826,		
by Rev. Timothy P. Gillett	3	343
Martha, M., of Branford, m. Horace B. **MEIGS**, of Berlin,		
Oct. 27, 1852, by Rev. T. P. Gillett	TM3	171
Martha Maria, [d. Timothy & Esther], b. Feb. 27, 1832	3	377
Mary, [d. John & Sally], b. Oct. 20, 1812	3	370

	Vol.	Page
BEACH, BEECH, (cont.)		
Mary, [d. John & Sally], d. Nov. 6, 1815	3	370
Mary, [d. John & Sally], b. Feb. 7, 1816	3	370
Mary, m. Hezekiah **PALMER**, b. of Branford, May 19, 1842,		
by Rev. Timothy P. Gillett	TM3	154
Mary E., d. Wyllys & Irene, b. Nov. 18, 1848	TM3	240
Mary Jane, [d. Timothy & Esther], b. May 21, 1836	3	377
Nabbe, d. John H. & Phebe, b. May 2, 1777	3	274
Nancy, [d. Elnathan, & Abigail], b. Apr. 24, 1804	3	285
Phebe, d. John & Vina, b. May 25, 1804	3	369
Phebe, m. Benjamin L. **CARTER**, b. of Branford, May 24,		
1824, by Rev. Timothy P. Gillett	3	425
Phinehas, of Wallingford, m. wid. Elizabeth **FARNUM**, of		
Branford, Mar. 27, 1758, by Ichabod Camp	3	137
Polly, [d. Samuel & Anne], b. Mar. 24, 1794	3	387
Polly, [d. Samuel & Anne], d. Oct. 11, 1795	3	387
Polly, [d. Asher S. & Statira], b. July 4, 1803	3	389
Polly, 1st, [d. Asher S. & Statira], d. Sept 26, 1804	3	389
Polly, [d. Asher S. & Statira], b. May 25, 1810	3	389
Polly, m. William **PLANT**, b. of Branford, June 30, 1831,		
by Rev. Timothy P. Gillett	3	357
Sally Eliza, [d. Timothy & Esther], b. June 16, 1828	3	377
Sally L., of Branford, m. William [S.] **HALL**, of Wallingford,		
Sept. 23, 1829, by Rev. Timothy P. Gillett	3	350
Sally Lovina, [d. John & Sally], b. Aug. 31, 1809	3	369
Samuel, s. Elnathan & Lydia, b. May 3, 1769	3	200
Samuel, m. Anne **SHELDON**, May 11, 1793	3	387
Samuel, [s. Samuel & Anne], b. Apr. 3, 1797	3	387
Samuel, 1st, [s. Samuel & Anne], d. Apr. 13, 1798	3	387
Samuel, [s. Samuel & Anne], b. Nov. 17, 1805	3	387
Samuel, Jr., m. Mary **BARKER**, b. of Branford, Sept. 17,		
1826, by Rev. Timothy P. Gillett	3	342
Samuel, s. Samuel, Jr. & Mary, b. July 27, 1827	3	355
Samuel, Jr., s. Samuel, d. July 17, 1828, was drowned	3	365
Samuel, 2d, of Branford, m. Harriet A. **COOK**, of Mendon,		
Ill., Mar. 30, 1851, by Rev. Timo[thy] P. Gillett	TM3	168
Samuel, 2d, ae 23, m. Harriett A. **COOKE**, ae 18, Mar. 30,		
1851, by Rev. T. P. Gillett	TM3	170
Sarah, d. Andru & Lucy, b. May 16, 1754	3	152
Sarah, [d. Andrew & Elizabeth], b. Jan. 23, 1793	3	389
Sarah, m. James **BLACKSTONE**, b. of Branford, Dec. 1,		
1814, by Rev. Timothy P. Gillett	3	354
Sarah, of Guilford, m. Jeremy **LINSLEY**, of Branford, Dec.		
25, 1841, by Rev. Timothy P. Gillett	TM3	153
Sarah Elizabeth, d. Eber & Mary, b. May 2, 1826	3	343
Sarah I. m. Samuel **TYLER**, b. of Branford, Jan. 21, 1849,		
by Rev. Daniel D. Lyon	TM3	163
Stephen, ae 29, m. Mary Ann **COVERT**, ae 20, July 11, 1851,		

	Vol.	Page
BEACH, BEECH, (cont.)		
by Lucius Attwater	TM3	169
Stephen A., m. Mary A. **COVERT**, b. of Branford, July 11,		
1851, by Rev. Lucius Attwater	TM3	169
Thaddeus, [s. Elnathan & Abigail], b. Dec. 11, 1790	3	285
Thaddeus, [s. Elnathan & Abigail], d. Oct. 1, 1795	3	285
Thaddeus, [s. Elnathan & Abigail], b. Aug. 12, 1801	3	285
Timothy, [s. Andrew & Elizabeth], b. Jan. 22, 1796	3	389
Vina, w. of John, d. May 4, 1806	3	369
William, [s. Andrew & Elizabeth], b. Oct. 9, 1800	3	389
William, [s. Andrew & Elizabeth], d. July 1, 1803	3	389
William Henry, [s. Timothy & Esther], b. Aug. 18, 1826	3	377
Wyllys, [s. Asher S. & Statira], b, Apr. 14, 1801	3	389
Wyllys, m. Mary **FOOT**, b. of Branford, Oct. 29, 1835, by		
Rev. Tim[othy] P. Gillett	3	371
Wyllys, m. Irene **BARKER**, b. of Branford, Dec. 27, 1846,		
by Rev. T. P. Gillett	TM3	159
Wyllys, d. Dec. 23, 1850, ae 50 y.	TM3	310
BEARDSLEY, Comfort, of Stratford, m. Jonathan **BYINTUN**, Jr.,		
of Branford, Dec. 25, 1765, by James Dana	3	200
Daniel H., m. Mary M. **LINSLEY**, Dec. [ ], 1847	TM3	162
BEAUMONT, John, of Wallingford, m. Anna **TYLER**, of Branford,		
June 3, 1827, by Rev. Timothy P. Gillett	3	344
BECKLY, Lyman, of Meriden, m. Mary Esther **PAGE**, of Branford,		
Oct. 27, 1851, by Rev. T. P. Gillett	TM3	169
BECKWITH, Lorana, of Lyme, m. Benj[ami]n **PLANT**, of		
Branford, Apr. 5, 1758, by Philemon Robbins	3	180
BEERS, Almond, s. [James & Mary], b. Sept. 4, 1806	3	388
Almon m. Betsey **HOBART**, b. of Branford, Dec. 25, 1827,		
by Rev. Timothy P. Gillett	3	346
Calvin, s. James & Mary, b. Jan. 22, 1813; d. Oct. 17, 1815	3	338
Calvin, s. James & Mary, b. Oct. 4, 1819	3	338
Eber, s. Wheeler & Lydia, b. Apr. 29, 1755	3	169
Emaline, d. [James & Mary], b. Oct. 15, 1810	3	388
Hannah, d. Sam[ue]ll & Sarah, b. Jan. 13, 1725/6	3	58
Hervey, s. Almon & Betsey, b. Aug. 17, 1828; d. Sept.		
22, 1828	3	365
James, m. Mary **HOPSON**, Sept. 2, 1805	3	388
James, s. James & Mary, b. Feb. 15, 1815	3	406
Jonathan, s. Sam[ue]ll & Sarah, b. Feb. 12, 1723/4	3	58
Lester, s. [James & Mary], b. June 22, 1808	3	388
Lester, m. Mary **STEDMAN**, b. of Branford, Apr. 18, 1830,		
by Timothy P. Gillett	3	352
Lester, d. Apr. 29, 1851, ae 43	TM3	309
Lutian, s. James & Mary, b. Feb. 23, 1821	3	338
Lydia, d. Wheeler & Lydia, b. May 17, 1757	3	169
Mary, d. Sam[ue]ll & Sarah, b. Nov. 18, 1721	3	58
Mary, m. John **POTTER**, b. of Branford, Nov. 14, 1746,		

	Vol.	Page
BEERS, (cont.)		
by Rev. Jonathan Mer[r]ick	3	112
Mary, d. James & Mary, b. Apr. 12, 1817	3	406
Mary, m. John **GORDON**, b. of Branford, Aug. 20, 1833, by		
Rev. T. P. Gillett	3	361
Mary, Mrs., m. James **LINSLEY**, b. of Branford, May 22,		
1853, by Rev. Amos W. Watrous	TM3	172
Pitman, s. Wheeler & Lydia, b. Oct. 22, 1763	3	186
Rebec[c]ah, d. Sam[ue]ll & Sarah, b. Sept. 26, 1717	3	45
Samuel, m. Sarah **WHEELER**, Apr. 8, 1712, by Nathan[ie]ll		
Harrison, J. P.	3	37
Samuel, s. Sam[ue]ll & Sarah, b. June 18, 1714	3	37
Sam[ue]ll, s. Wheeler & Lydia,˚ b. June 10, 1752	3	169
Samuel, Lieut., d. Sept. 25, 1772, ae 85 y. 7 m. 20 d.	3	207
Sarah, d. Sam[ue]ll & Sarah, b. Mar. 6, 1718/19	3	45
Sarah, w. of Lieut. Sam[ue]ll, d. June 18, 1770 in the		
86th y. of her age	3	199
Sarah, d. Wheeler & Lydia, b. May 6, 1771	3	207
Sarah, m. Benj[ami]n **BARKER**, b. of Branford, Oct. 8, 1781,		
by Sam[ue]ll Eells	3	299
Sarah, ae 18 y., m. Luther C. **ELY**, ae 23 y., June 5,		
1849, by Rev. T. P. Gillett	TM3	166
Sarah L., of Branford, m. Luther C. **ELY**, of New Haven,		
June 5, 1850, by C. H. Topliff	TM3	165
Sarah Louisa, d. Lester & Mary, b. June 2, 1832	3	359
Wheeler, s. Sam[ue]ll & Sarah, b. Feb. 4, 1715/16	3	37
Wheeler, m. Lydia **TRUSDELL**, b. of Branford, Jan. 16, 1752,		
by Jonathan Mer[r]ick	3	169
William Hervey, s. Almon & Betsey, b. Oct. 9, 1831	3	365
BEETS, [see also **BETTS**], Hannah, d. Sam[ue]ll & Hannah, b.		
Sept. 21, 1713	3	37
Martha, d. Sam[ue]ll & Hannah, b. June 12, 1715	3	37
Mary, d. Sam[ue]ll & Hannah, b. Feb. 28, 17[ ]; [bp.		
Mar. [ ], 1719]	3	43
Mary, Mrs., m. Solomon **PALMER**, b. of Branford, Feb. 9,		
1737/8, by Rev. Philemon Robbins	3	123
Sam[ue]ll, Sr., d. Feb. last, 1713/4	3	45
BELLAMY, Mary, d. John & Martha, b. Oct. 18, 1735	3	83
BENEDICT, Lois, d. Joel S. & Concurrence, b. Jan. 29, 1803	3	275
[Narcissa], d. Joel Tyler & Currance, b. Dec. 4, 1799	3	256
BENHAM, Sally, m. Jacob **MONRO[E]**, Mar. 12, 1793	3	401
BENTON, Abigail, of Weathersfield, m. Jonathan **HOADL[E]Y**, of		
Branford, Dec. 5, 1738, by David Goodrich, J. P.	3	172
Caroline, m. John **RUSSEL[L]**, Nov. 23, 1825	3	333
Hannah, of Werthersfield, m. Jonathan **BARKER**, of Branford,		
May 21, 1734, by Rev. Stephen Mix	3	80
BETTS, BETT, [see also **BEETS**], Hannah, m. Isaac **TYLER**, b. of		
Branford, Feb. 24, 1736/7, by Rev. Philemon Robbins	3	86

	Vol.	Page

BETTS, BEET, (cont.)

Jonathan, m. Mar[c]ie **WARD**, Nov. 4, [16]62	1	173
Mary, d. Roger, b. Feb. 29, 1654* (*Changed to 1653)	1	171
Petter, s. Roger, d. Oct. 3, 1653	1	170
Rogger, s. Rogger, b. Feb. 20, 1651	1	171
Roger, d. Aug. 31, 1658	1	170

BIRD, Dorcas, d. John & Abigail, b. Feb. 10, 1727/8   3   66

John, mariner, formerly of Philadelphia, now of Branford, m.
Abigail **FOOT**, of Branford, Aug. 29, 1725, by
Nath[anie]ll Har[r]ison, J. P.   3   57

Mary, d. John & Abigail, b. June 4, 1725   3   61
Robert, s. John & Abigail, b. June 4, 1730   3   70

BISHOP, BISHOPE, Amy, of Bethlehem, m. Elias **GOODRICH**,
of Branford, Dec. 3, 1803   3   283

Betsey, m. David **TOWNER**, Nov. 6, 1791, by Rev. Azel
Backus, of Bethlehem   3   283

Betsey S., of Guilford, m. Benjamin **ROGERS**, of Branford,
Mar. 1, 1828, by Rev. Jno. M. Garfield, at New Haven   3   347

David C., of North Guilford, m. Lucinda **BALDWIN**, of
Branford, Oct. 8, 1837, by Timothy P. Gillett   3   374

Mehitabell, m. John **WHITED**, Aug. 9, 1704   2   346

Sarah, of G[u]ilford, m. Joseph **FRISBIE**, of Branford,
Aug. 25, 1742, by Rev. Jonathan Todd   3   149

----, s. John & Thankful, b. Oct. 8, 1848   TM3   241
----, d. David C. & Lucinda, b. [ ], 1849   TM3   240

BLACHLY, BLATSLY, [see also **BLAKESLEE**], Mirriam, d.
Thomas, [b. Mar. 1, 1652]   1   171

Merriam, m. Samuell **POND**, Jan. 5, 1669   1   174

**BLACKSTONE, BLACISTON, BLACKISTON, BLACKSTON,
BLAKISTON**, Abigail, d. John & Elisabeth, b. Apr. 20, 1728   3   65

Abigail, m. Abraham **HOADL[E]Y**, b. of Branford, Dec. 27,
1750, by Rev. Philemon Robbins   3   122

Anne, d. John, Jr. & Rebecca, b. Oct. 15, 1758   3   161

Anne, m. John **WILLFORD**, b. of Branford, Dec. 16, 1781,
by Samuel Eells   3   276

Augustus, [s. John, Jr. & Rebeccah], b. July 25, 1802   3   387

Augustus, of Branford, m. Esther **LINSL[E]Y**, of Northford,
Nov. 28, 1822, by Rev. Oliver Wilson, of North Haven   3   421

Betsey, [d. Ralph & Sally], b. Mar. 26, 1800. (Town Clerk
adds "error")   3   429

Betsey, m. Samuel **AVERILL**, b. of Branford, Dec. 9, 1832,
by Rev. T. P. Gillett   3   359

Ebenezer, s. John & Rebecca, b. May 4, 1775   3   261
Ebenez[e]r, s. John & Rebecca, b. [ ]   3   175
Edward, s. John, Jr. & Rebecca, b. July 15, 1770   3   204

Eliza, [d. Ralph & Sally], b. Oct. 15, 1794 (Town Clerk
adds "error")   3   429

Eliza, m. William **AVERILL**, b. of Branford, Jan. 2, 1842,

	Vol.	Page

BLACKSTONE, BLACISTON, BLACKISTON, BLACKSTON,
BLAKISTON, (cont.)

by Rev. Timothy P. Gillett	TM3	154
Elisabeth, d. John & Elisabeth, b. Dec. 18, 1731	3	76
Elisabeth, w. of John, d. May 14, 1733	3	77
Elisabeth, m. Isaac **HOADL[E]Y**, b. of Branford, Mar. 31,		
1757, by Philemon Robbins	3	172
Ellen, [d. James & Sarah], b. Feb. 21, 1821	3	354
Ellen, of Branford, m. Henry B. **PLANT**, of New Haven, Sept.		
26, 1843, by Rev. Timothy P. Gillett	TM3	156
Eunice, m. Charles **HARRISON**, Oct. 10, 1821, by Timothy		
P. Gillett	3	414
Fanny, [d. Ralph & Sally], b. Apr. 10, 1797 (Town Clerk		
has marked "error")	3	429
Fanny, m. John **FOOT**, b. of Branford, Feb. 28, 1838, by		
Rev. Timothy P. Gillett	3	375
George William, [s. James & Sarah], b. Nov. 12, 1815	3	354
Grace, of Branford, m. Andrews **HOPSON**, of Wallingford,		
Nov. 27, 1823, by Rev. Timothy P. Gillett	3	424
Henry, [s. Ralph & Sally], b. Jan. 16, 1791 (Town Clerk	3	429
has marked "error")		
James, m. Sarah **BEACH**, b. of Branford, Dec. 1, 1814, by		
Rev. Timothy P. Gillett	3	354
James Linsley, s. Augustus & Esther, b. Aug. 24, 1832	3	373
Jerome, [s. Ralph & Sally], b. Dec. 18, 1715 *(Town Clerk		
has marked "error")	3	429
Jerome, m. Phebe **YALE**, b. of Branford, May 11, 1845, by		
Rev. A. C. Wheat	TM3	158
John, m. Elisabeth **FOOT**, b. of Branford, Apr. 2, 1727,		
by Nath[anie]ll Har[r]ison, J. P.	3	64
John, s. John & Elisabeth, b. May 7, 1733	3	77
John, m. Rebeckah **HARRISON**, b. of Branford, Nov. 25,		
1736, by Rev. Philemon Robbins	3	152
John, Jr., m. Rebecca **BALDWIN**, b. of Branford, May 19,		
1757, by Philemon Robbins	3	161
John, s. John, Jr. & Rebecca, b. Mar. 17, 1763	3	180
[John], Capt., had negro child of Jin, b. Sept. 26, 1784	3	313
John, Capt., d. Jan. 3, 1785, ae 85 y. 11 m. 16 d.	3	313
John, Jr., m. Rebeccah **FOOT**, b. of Branford, Nov. 13, 1789	3	387
John Adams, [s. James & Sarah], b. July 4, 1823	3	354
John Adams, m. Lucy A. **BOOTH**, b. of Branford, Dec. 31,		
1848, by Rev. T. P. Gillett	TM3	163
John Augustus, s. Augustus & Esther, b. June 28, 1829	3	373
Lorenzo, [s. James & Sarah], b. June 21, 1819	3	354
Lorenzo, of Brooklyn, N. Y., m. Emily **NORTON**, of Branford,		
Oct. 17, 1842, by Rev. Timothy P. Gillett	TM3	155
Lucy, [d. John, Jr. & Rebeccah], b. July 23, 1792	3	387

	Vol.	Page
BLACKSTONE, BLACISTON, BLACKISTON, BLACKSTON, **BLAKISTON,** (cont.)		
Lucy, m. John **TYLER**, Nov. 26, 1815, by Rev. Timothy P. Gillett	3	404
Mary A., m. Samuel O. **PLANT**, b. of Branford, Feb. 26, 1839, by Rev. Timothy P. Gillett	3	376
Mary Ann, [d. James & Sarah], b. Oct. 18, 1817	3	354
Miles, m. Lois **ROBINSON**, b. of Branford, Sept. 25, 1831, by Edw[ar]d J. Ives	3	361
Nabbe, d. John, Jr. & Rebecca, b. Apr. 15, 1768	3	195
Ralph, m. Sally **POND**, b. of Branford, [ ], 1802	3	429
Ralph, [s. Ralph & Sally], b. Mar. 22, 1823 (Town Clerk has marked "error")	3	429
Ransom, [s. John, Jr. & Rebeccah], b. Apr. 17, 1790	3	387
Rebecca, d. John & Rebecca, b. Sept. 8, 1737; d. Sept. 10, 1737	3	175
Sally, [d. Ralph & Sally], b. Sept. 13, 1821 (Town Clerk has marked "error")	3	429
Stephen, s. John & Elisabeth, b. Feb. 15, 1729/30	3	70
Stephen, m. Hannah **HARRISON**, b. of Branford, May 13, 1752, by Jon[a]th[an] Merrick	3	165
Stephen Foot, s. John, Jr. & Rebecca, b. Oct. 26, 1772	3	208
Timothy, s. John, Jr. & Rebecca, b. Sept. 27, 1765	3	189
Timothy, [s. James & Sarah], b. June 22, 1825; d. Aug. 5, [1825], ae 6 w. 3 d.	3	354
Timothy, m. Sally **GOODRICH**, b. of Branford, Jan. 12, 1826, by Rev. Timothy P. Gillett	3	341
Timothy Beach, [s. James & Sarah], b. Mar. 28, 1829	3	354
William, [s. Ralph & Sally], b. Feb. 14, 1788 (Town Clerk has marked "error")	3	429
BLAKE, Lois, m. Ebenezer **FRISBIE**, Jr., b. of Branford, June 26, 1770, by Sam[ue]ll Eells	3	304
BLAKEMAN, Emma, d. Oct. 13, 1849, ae 13 y.	TM3	309
BLAKESLEE, BLAKSLEE, [see also **BLACHLY**], Chlorane, m. Peter **AUGER**, Feb. 19, 1784	3	266
Patty, m. Stephen **BUNNELL**, May 2, 1796	3	276
Ruth, of North Haven, m. Capt. Ebenezer **ROGERS**, of Branford, Jan. 21, 1788, by Benj[ami]n Trumbull	3	258
BLATSLY, [see under **BLACHLY**]		
BLOND, Jeremiah, m. Abby Mc**CANELLY**, b. of Branford, Nov. 5, 1854, by Rev. Tim[oth]y P. Gillett	TM3	173
BOOTH, Lucy A., m. John Adams **BLACKSTONE**, b. of Branford, Dec. 31, 1848, by Rev. T. P. Gillett	TM3	163
Maria, of Wallingford, m. Hobart Stone **BEACH**, of Branford, Dec. 17, 1828, by Rev. Timothy P. Gillett	3	348
BOWERS, Ruth, m. John **FFRISSBE**, Dec. 2, [16]74	1	174
BOYINGTON, [see under **BYINGTON**]		
BOYLES, BOILES, James, s. James & Deborah, b. Dec. 21, 1735	3	84

	Vol.	Page
BOYLES, BOILES, (cont.)		
John, s. James & Deborah, b. Dec. 7, 1736	3	85
Rebec[c]ah, m. Joseph **AUGER**, b. of Branford, Feb. 20, 1775	3	267
BRACKET, [see also **BROCKETT**], Silence, of North Haven, m.		
Eben[eze]r **FRISBIE**, Jr., of Branford, Dec. 24, 1731, by		
Rev. Jonathan Mer[r]ick	3	82
BRADDOCK, Lucretia had d. Polly **STEWART**, b. Aug. 31, 177[6]	3	255
Lucretia had d. Pamela **STEWART**, b. Apr. 18, 1781	3	255
BRADFIELD, BRADFEELD, BRADFEILD, Abigail, m. Joseph		
HOADL[E]Y, b. of Branford, Feb. 15, 1738/9	3	131
Dorcas, wid. of Samuel, d. Nov. 26, 1803	3	275
John, d. Feb. 28, 1780	3	301
Lisly, d. July 26, 1655	1	170
Martha, m. John **WHITEHEAD**, Mar. 9, [16]61	1	173
Mary, d. Lisly, d. July 29, [16]55	1	170
Nathaneel, twin with Samuel, s. Samuel, b. Apr. 2, 1679	1	211
Samuel, m Sarah **GRAUES**, June 27, 1677	1	210
Samuel, twin with Nathaneel, s. Samuel, b. Apr. 2, 1679	1	211
Sarah, m. Zaccheus **BALDWIN**, b. of Branford, Oct. 17, 1776	3	301
----, wid., m. George **ADAME**, Sept.5, 1657	1	173
----, w. [John], d. Jan. 29, 1782	3	301
BRADLEY, BRADLY, Andrew Jackson, [s. Major & Rosella], b.		
Dec. 29, 1837	TM3	228
Benjamin P., s. Warren & Adelia, b. Mar. 29, 1851	TM3	243
Bets[e]y, d. Levi & Lydia, b. Aug. 28, 1799	3	391
Betsey, m. Anderson **PLANT**, b. of Branford, Dec. 23, 1818,		
by Rev. Timothy P. Gillett	3	422
Betsey Jane, [d. Timothy, Jr. & Grace Ann], b. Dec. 26, 1835	TM3	228
Cornelia, d. July 18, 1848, ae 1 y.	TM3	308
Ebeneser Y., [s. Gurdon & Ann Maria], b. Apr. 23, 1843	TM3	237
Eliza Ann, [d. John & Deborah], b. May 17, 1822	3	430
Elisabeth, d. Timothy & Sarah, b. Sept. 24, 1768, in New		
Haven	3	281
Elizabeth, m. Andrew **BEACH**, June 14, 1792	3	389
Emily Sophia, [d. Timothy, Jr. & Grace Ann], b. Jan. 6, 1838	TM3	228
Esther M., [d. Gurdon & Ann Maria], b. May 18, 1845	TM3	237
George B., ae 18, m. Louis E. **ROWLAND**, ae 17, May 25,		
1851, by Lucius Atwater	TM3	169
George G., [s. Major & Rosella], b. May 3, 1833	TM3	228
George G., m. Louis E. **ROWLAND**, b. of Branford, May 25,		
1851, by Rev. Lucius Atwater	TM3	169
George G., ae 18, m. Louis E. **ROWLAND**, May 25, 1851, by		
Lucius Atwater	TM3	170
Grace A., d. June 19, 1851, ae 43	TM3	309
Gurdon, s. Timothy & Irene, b. Sept. 27, 1819	3	425
Gurdon, m. Ann Maria **SPINK**, b. of Branford, Jan. 29,		
1843, by Rev. Pascal P. Kidder	TM3	155
Gurdon, s. Gurdon & Anna M., b. Oct. 20, 1848	TM3	241

	Vol.	Page

BRADLEY, BRADLY, (cont.)

	Vol.	Page
Irene, [d. Timothy, Jr. & Irene], b. May 25, 1799	3	391
Irene, m. William **BRIEN**, Mar. 17, 1820, by Rev. Gardiner Spring, in New York	3	424
James, [s. Timothy, Jr. & Irene], b. Sept. 25, 1798	3	391
James, [s. Timothy, Jr. & Irene], d. Nov. 27, 1802	3	391
James A., s. Timothy, Jr. & Grace Ann, b. Oct. 23, 1832	3	360
Jared, of East Haven, m. Mary **BRADLEY**, of Branford, Oct. 5, 1841, by Rev. Timothy P. Gillett	TM3	153
Jennett Johnson, d. Timothy, Jr. & Grace Ann, b. June 25, 1830	3	360
John, m. Deborah **FRISBIE**, b. of Branford, Mar. 30, 1812	3	430
John, [s. John & Deborah], b. July 4, 1817	3	430
John S., of New Haven, m. Susan C. **WHITING**, of Branford, Sept. 25, 1842, by Rev. Timothy P. Gillett	TM3	154
Julia Ann, [d. Major & Rosella], b. Sept. 25, 1834	TM3	228
Leonard, [s. Major & Rosella], b. Feb. 7, 1840	TM3	228
Levi, s. Timothy & Sarah, b. Jan. 14, 1772	3	281
Levi, m. Lydia **BEACH**, b. of Branford, Nov. 28, 1798	3	391
Lorany, d. Timothy & Sarah, b. [Apr. 19, 1780]	3	281
Lothrop, s. Timothy & Sarah, b. Dec. 14, 1764, in New Haven	3	281
Lucinday, d. Timothy & Sarah, b. Mar. 6, 1763	3	281
Lucinda, m. Abel **HOADL[E]Y**, b. of Branford, Nov. 8, 1787	3	273
Lydia, [d. Timothy, Jr. & Irene], b. Sept. 6, 1809	3	391
Lydia, of Branford, m. Aulden **PARDEE**, of East Haven, Apr. 1, 1829, by Judson A. Root	3	350
Lydia L., m. Sylvester M. **GRANNISS**, b. of Branford, Sept. 25, 1853, by Rev. L. Atwater	TM3	172
Maria, [d. Timothy, Jr. & Irene], b. Dec. 2, 1803	3	391
Mary, m. Elias **LINSL[E]Y**, Nov. 24, 1828, by J. A. Root	3	350
Mary, of Branford, m. Jared **BRADLEY**, of East Haven, Oct. 5, 1841, by Rev. Timothy P. Gillett	TM3	153
Mary J., d. Mar. 27, 1850, ae 29 y.	TM3	309
Mary Jane, [d. Timothy, Jr. & Grace Ann], b. Aug. 31, 1840	TM3	228
Mary Josephine, d. Seth & Mary Manerva, b. Oct. 28, 1840	TM3	229
Mary M., w. of Warren S., d. Feb. 7, 1845	TM3	307
Nancy, [d. Timothy, Jr. & Irene], b. July 12, 1802	3	391
Nancy, m. Sylvester **HARRISON**, b. of Branford, Aug. 1, 1821, by Rev. Timothy P. Gillett	3	413
Olive, of East Haven, m. Reuel **CHIDSEY**, of Branford, Jan. 3, 1805	3	429
Polly, [d. John & Deborah], b. May 8, 1813	3	430
Poliy, d. William & Mary Jane, b. June 10, 1848	TM3	239
Polly, d. Timothy & Sarah, b. [ ]	3	281
Rosella, of Branford, m. Alanson **PERKINS**, of Prospect, Apr. 9, 1848, by Rev. A. C. Wheat	TM3	161
Sally, d. Timothy & Sarah, b. Mar. 23, 1766, in New Haven	3	281
Sally Maria, m. James **WARDELL**, b. of Branford, Nov. 18, 1821, by Calvin Frisbie, J. P.	3	415

	Vol.	Page
BRADLEY BRADLY, (cont.)		
Seth Thomas, s. Seth & Mary M., b. Dec. 28, 1844	TM3	236
Susan C., d. Sept. 5, 1847, ae 38	TM3	307
Timothy, of East Haven, m. Sarah **GOODSELL**, of Branford,		
Sept. 12, 1762	3	280
Timothy, s. Timothy & Sarah, b. Sept. 14, 1770, in New Haven	3	281
Timothy, Jr., m. Irene **GORDON**, b. of Branford, Dec. 10,		
1797	3	391
Timothy, [d. Timothy, Jr. & Irene], b. Oct. 5, 1807	3	391
Timothy, d. May 7, 1810	3	396
Timothy Segemond, [s. Timothy, Jr. & Grace Ann], b. Oct.		
17, 1842	TM3	228
William, [s. John & Deborah], b. Sept. 17, 1818	3	430
W[illia]m, m. Ellen P. **LINSLEY**, ae 22, Oct. 27, 1850,		
by W[illia]m Henry Rees	TM3	169
----, s. Gurdon & Ann M., b. June 30, 1850	TM3	242
, d. Warren & Adilia, b. Apr [ ], 1851	TM3	243
BRAINARD, Concurrence, of Haddam, m. Roswell **SHELDON**, of		
Branford, Dec. 28, 1793	3	401
BRAY, Asa, s. John & Lydia, b. June 22, 1741	3	126
John, m. Lydia **HOADL[E]Y**, (alias) **MON[T]GOMERY**, Apr.		
28, 1737, by Rev. Philemon Robbins	3	126
Thomas, s. John & Lydia, b. Sept. 22, 1738	3	126
BRIEN, [see also **BRYAN**], Alden Parde[e], [s. William & Irene],		
b. Sept. 17, 1833	TM3	228
Bradley, [s. William & Irene], b. July 25, 1831	TM3	228
Harriet, [d. William & Irene], b. June 13, 1829	TM3	228
James, [s. William & Irene], b. Mar. 11, 1823	TM3	228
James, m. Lydia Minerva **BUSH**, b. of Branford, Aug. 4,		
1845, by Rev. Timothy P. Gillett	TM3	158
James William, [s. William & Irene], b. Mar. 11, 1823	3	424
Nancy, d. William, Jr. & Lydia A., b. Mar. 16, 1851	TM3	244
Nancy Eliza, [d. William & Irene], b. Nov. 12, 1820	TM3	228
Nancy Eliza, [d. William & Irene], b. Nov. 12, 1820	3	424
William, b. Dec. 25, 1797	TM3	228
William, m. Irene **BRADLEY**, Mar. 17, 1820, by Rev.		
Gardiner Spring, in New York	3	424
William, [s. William & Irene], b. July 16, 1826	TM3	228
William, Jr., m. Lydia A. **PALMER**, June 22, 1848	TM3	162
BRIG[G]S, George W., m. Ellen A. **JOHNSON**, b. of Branford,		
Oct. 18, 1853, by Rev.L. Atwater	TM3	172
BRISTOL, Lois, of Guilford, m. John **PAGE**, of Branford, Nov.		
26, 1766, by Nicholaus Street	3	191
BROCKETT, BROCKET, [see also **BRACKET**], Ann, of New		
Haven, m. Daniel **BARN[E]S**, of Branford, Mar. 21,		
1727/8, by Rev. Isaac Stiles	3	73
Lucius, of North Haven, m. Betsey **LINSLEY**, of Branford,		
Mar. 28, 1841, by Rev. Pascal P. Kidder	TM3	153

	Vol.	Page

BROCKETT, BROCKET, (cont.)

Obedience S., m. Stephen **SIBBEY**, of Ward, Mass., Oct. 6,
    1829, by Rev. J. A. Root — 3 — 350

BROCKWAY, Aaron, s. Edward & Abigail, b. Aug. 1, 1769 — 3 — 202

Abigail, d. Edward & Abigail, b. May 17, 1765 — 3 — 185

Abigail, w. of Edward, d. Aug. 11, 1769, ae 35 — 3 — 202

Betsey, d. Timothy & Hannah, b. Aug. 9, 1817 — 3 — 428

Betsey, of Branford, m. Richard **DIBBLE**, of Westbrook,
    Apr. 6, 1841, by Rev. Timothy P. Gillett — TM3 — 153

Edward, m. Abigail **PALMER**, b. of Branford, Feb. 5, 1760,
    by Jon[a]th[an] Merrick — 3 — 164

Edward, Jr., s. Edward & Abigail, b. Oct. 13, 1760 — 3 — 164

Edward, m. Martha **HOADL[E]Y**, b. of Branford, Mar. 13,
    1770, by Samuel Eells — 3 — 202

Eliza, of Branford, m. William P. **AUSTIN**, of Wallingford,
    Oct. 22, 1834, by Rev. Timothy P. Gillett — 3 — 367

Harriet, d. Timothy & Hannah, b. June 4, 1822 — 3 — 428

Harriet, of Branford, m. George K. **HALL**, of Wallingford,
    Oct. 3, 1844, by Rev. Timothy P. Gillett — TM3 — 157

Lorana, d. Edward & Martha, b. Dec. 29, 1772 — 3 — 258

Lydia, d. Edward & Abigail, b. June 23, 1763 — 3 — 181

Moses, s. Edward & Abigail, b. Feb. 16, 1762 — 3 — 176

Sarah, d. Edward & Abigail, b. June 13, 17[6]7 — 3 — 193

Timothy, s. Edward & Martha, b. Dec. 1, 1770 — 3 — 202

Titus, s. Edward & Martha, b. Apr. 11, 1775 — 3 — 263

BROOKER, Abraham, of Killingworth, m. Tamer **MURRAY**, of
    Guilford, Oct. 12, 1758, by Elnathan Stevens, J. P. — 3 — 171

John, s. Abraham & Tamer, b. Mar. 29, 1759 — 3 — 171

Mary, d. Abraham & Tamer, b. Dec. 18, 1760 — 3 — 171

BROOKS, Heman P., d. Jan. 17, 1822 — 3 — 417

Stephen H., m. Lavinia **FOWLER**, of Northford, [Jan.] 10,
    [1821], by Origen P. Holcomb — 3 — 413

BROW, Bity, d. Hannah, b. July 9, 1783 [Betsey?] — 3 — 283

Bets[e]y, m. Alexander **GORDON**, Jr., July 1, 1802 — 3 — 390

Hannah had d. Bity, b. July 9, 1783 — 3 — 283

BROWN, Abigail, of New Haven, m. William **BARTHOLOMEW**,
    Jr., of Branford, Jan. 25, 1721/2, by Rev. Jacob
    Heminway — 3 — 50

Abigail, m. Moses **STORK**, Sept. 4, 1755, by Rev. Philemon
    Robbins — 3 — 142

Abigail, d. Amos & Abigail, b. Nov. 3, 1758 — 3 — 167

Amos, m. Abigail **TYLER**, b. of Branford, Nov. 14, 1754,
    by Philemon Robbins — 3 — 167

Azubah, d. John & Elisabeth, b. Mar. 6, 1734/5 — 3 — 95

Charles, of New Haven, m. Lucretia **RUSSELL**, of Branford,
    Nov. 21, 1825, by Flavel S. Gaylord — 3 — 341

Dan[ie]ll, s. Joseph & Abigail, b. Jan. [24], 1751/2 — 3 — 127

Hannah had d. Milly, b. Feb. 22, 1787 — 3 — 269

	Vol.	Page
BROWN, (cont.)		
Hannah had d. Sophia, b. Mar. 20, 1791	3	269
Ichabod, s. Joseph & Abigail, b. Mar. 23, 1753	3	134
Johanna, d. John & Elisabeth, b. May 19, 1733	3	76
John, m. Elisabeth **KIRKUM**, Nov. 9, 1730, by Jno.		
Russell, J. P.	3	72
Jonathan, s. Jos[eph] & Rachell, b. Dec. 13, 1717	3	41
Joseph, m. Rachel **SWAIN**, Sept. 11, 1711, by		
Nathan[ie]ll Harrison, J. P.	3	34
Joseph, [twin with Rachel], s. Jos[eph] & Rachel,		
b. Aug. 11, 1712	3	36
Joseph, s. Joseph & Rachell, b. Oct. 4, 1714	3	36
Joceph, m. Abigail **ROGERS**, b. of Branford, Feb.		
1, 1749/50, by Nathan[ie]ll Harrison, J. P.	3	127
Ioseph, s. Joseph & Abigail, b. Jan. 11, 1750/1	3	127
Joseph, 2d, d. Dec. 24, 1752	3	127
Mary, d. Jno. & Elisabeth, b. Apr. 22, 1731	3	73
Milly, d. Hannah, b. Feb. 22, 1787	3	269
Rachel, [twin with Joseph], d. Jos[eph] & Rachel,		
b. Aug. 11, 1712	3	36
Sam[ue]ll, s. John & Elisabeth, b. Dec. 19, 1736	3	95
Sam[ue]ll, s. Amos & Abigail, b. Sept. 11, 1756	3	167
Sarah, m. Edward **BARKER**, b. of Branford, Mar 24,		
1763, by Philemon Robbins	3	179
Sophia, d. Hannah, b. Mar. 20, 1791	3	269
William, s. John & Elisabeth, b. June 30, 1740	3	95
BROWNSON, Elizur, b. Dec. [ ], 1802	3	396
BRYAN, [see also **BRIEN**], William, s. William & Emeline,		
b. May 9, 1849	TM3	241
BUCKLEY, BUCKLIE, Elesebeth, m. Mica **PAMER**, Dec.		
2, [16]62	1	173
William, m. Lydia **LUDDENTON**, Oct. 28, 1761, by		
Nicholas Street	3	173
BUEL, BEWEL, Abigail, alias **FOWLER**, had d. Betsey, b.		
Mar. 26, 1776	3	307
Abigail, alias **FOWLER**, had d. Clarissa, b. Mar. 23,		
1778	3	307
Abigail, alias **FOWLER**, had s. Hennerity, b. May 5,		
1782	3	307
Betsey, alias **FOWLER**, d. Abigail, b. Mar. 26, 1776	3	307
Clarissa, alias **FOWLER**, d. Abigail, b. Mar. 23, 1778	3	307
Hannah, d. Sam[ue]ll & Lydia, b. Feb. 4, 1746	3	117
Hannah, m. Eli **ROGERS**, b. of Branford, June 7,		
1764, by Jonathan Merrick	3	184
Hennerity, alias **FOWLER**, d. Abigail, b. May 5, 1782	3	307
Jemima, m. Jacob **HOADL[E]Y**, b. of Branford, July		
1, 1752, by Rev. Jonath[a]n Mer[r]ick	3	129
Samuel, s. Sam[ue]ll & Lydia, b. Sept. 30, 1742	3	116

	Vol.	Page
BUNNELL, BUNNEL, BONNELL, Anna, [d. John &		
Pua[r], b. Sept. 28, 1777	3	276
Augustus, [s. John & Pua[r], b. May 16, 1795	3	276
Betsey, [d. John & Pua[r], b. Oct. 24, 1792	3	276
Deliverance, of Branford, m. Johanna **BARNS**, of		
East Hampton, L. I., Dec. 25, 1730, by Rev.		
Jonathan Mer[r]ick	3	115
Elizur, [s. John & Pua[r], b. May 4, 1798	3	276
George, m. Fanny A. **ROSE**, Sept. 16, [1829], by J.		
A. Root	3	350
Hannah, d. Jacob & Mary, b. Feb. 25, 1764	3	182
Hezekiah, m. Abigail **HARRISON**, July 29, 1829, by		
Rev. J. A. Root	3	350
Jacob, s. Deliverance & Johannah, b. Apr. 3, 1734	3	115
Jacob, m. Mary **KIMBERLY**, b. of Branford, May 17,		
1756, by Jon[a]th[an] Merrick	3	171
Jacob, s. Jacob & Mary, b. Dec. 12, 1761	3	178
Jairus, d. Nov. 2, 1822, ae 78 y.	3	335
Jesse, [s. John & Pua[r], b. June 12, 1784	3	276
John, [s. John & Pua[r], b. Dec. 29, 1779	3	276
Joseph, s. Deliverance & Johannah, b. Aug. 24, 1736	3	115
Joseph, s. Jacob & Mary, b. July 23, 1757	3	171
Lewis, of Branford, m. Mehitabel **BALL**, of New		
Haven, [Nov] 9, [1823], by Rev. Charles Atwater	3	423
Lois, [d. Stephen & Patty], b. May 29, 1802	3	276
Lucy, [d. John & Pua[r], b. Nov. 22, 1789	3	276
Luther, [s. John & Pua[r], b. Mar. 20, 1782	3	276
Lydia, d. Feb. 5, 1823, ae 77 y.	3	335
Martha, d. Deliverance & Johannah, b. Mar. 9, 1732	3	115
Mary, d. Jacob & Mary, b. Apr. 26, 1759	3	171
Nathaniel, [s. John & Pua[r], b. Feb. 6, 1787	3	276
Oliver Blak[e]slee, [s. Stephen & Patty], b. Dec.		
22, 1797	3	276
Sarah A., of Middletown, m. Asher **SHELDON**, of		
Branford, Oct. 26, 1845, by Rev. T. P. Gillett	TM3	159
Sherman, s. Jacob & Mary, b. Apr. 3, 1766	3	190
Sina, m. Lemuel **COOK**, b. of Branford, July 10,		
1825, by Rev. James Keeler, of Northford	3	339
Stephen, m. Patty **BLAK[E]SLEE**, May 2, 1796	3	276
----, s. [Stephen & Patty], b. Mar. 24, 1797; d.		
same day	3	276
----, d. [Stephen & Patty], b. Mar. 17, 1800; d.		
18th of the same month	3	276
----, d. [Stephen & Patty], b. Apr. 23, 1801; d.		
25th of the same month	3	276
----, [child of Stephen & Patty], b. July 25, 1804	3	276
BURGESS, BURGES, BURGIS, Benjamin, s. Jno. & Mary,		
b. Dec. 27, 1721	3	48

	Vol.	Page

BURGESS, BURGES, BURGIS, (cont.)

Comfort, s. John & Mary, b. Jan. 7, 1709 — 3 — 48

Cumfort, m. Eunice **WHEDON**, b. of Branford, Jan. 7, 1734/5, by Rev. Jacob Heminway — 3 — 84

Comfort, d. Jan. 15, 1761, in the 52nd y. of his age — 3 — 176

Eben[ez]r, s. Comfort & Eunice, b. June 17, 1749 — 3 — 119

Ezra, s. James & Sarah, b. Apr. 3, 1747 — 3 — 113

James, s. Jno. & Mary, b. Feb. 9, 171[6] — 3 — 48

James, m. Sarah **DUNK**, b. of Branford, June 21, 1744, by Rev. Philemon Robbins — 3 — 105

James, s. James & Sarah, b. May 11, 1745 — 3 — 105

John, m. Mary **TYLER**, Nov. 28, 1709 — 3 — 32

John, s. John & Mary, b. Aug. 27, 1713 — 3 — 48

Mary, d. John & Mary, b. Dec. 30, 1724 — 3 — 56

Rebecca, d. Comfort & Eunice, b. Mar. 9, 1737/8 — 3 — 119

Rebecca, m. Amos **PAGE**, b. of Branford, Mar. 25, 1757, by Philemon Robbins — 3 — 174

Sam[ue]ll, s. Cumfort & Eunice, b. Oct. 22, 1735 — 3 — 84

Sam[ue]ll, s. Comfort & Eunice, b. Nov. 28, 1742 — 3 — 119

Sarah, d. Comfort & Eunice, b. [ ] 27, 1739/40 — 3 — 119

Thankfull, d. Jno & Mary, b. June 16, 1718 — 3 — 48

BURKE, Edward, m. Elisabeth **COOK**, Aug. 29, 1775, by Rev. Chauncey Whittelsey, of New Haven — 3 — 262

Edward, s. Edward & Elisabeth, b. Feb. 26, 1776 — 3 — 262

BURRELL, Jared, m. Mary **PALMER**, b. of Branford, Mar. [ ], 1831, by J. A. Root — 3 — 356

BUSH, Charlotte F., d. Sept. 16, 1849, ae 7 y. — TM3 — 308

Emeline, m. Giles **BALDWIN**, b. of Branford, July 2, 1829, by Rev. Judson A. Root — 3 — 349

Emily C., d. Gilbert & Hermione C., b. Dec. 19, 1850 — TM3 — 245

Lydia Minerva, m. James **BRIEN**, b. of Branford, Aug. 4, 1845, by Rev. Timothy P. Gillett — TM3 — 158

BUSHNELL, Phinehas, of Guilford, m. Mrs. Hannah **PARMELE[E]**, of Branford, Oct. 16, 1816 — 3 — 419

BUTLER, BUTLAR, Abel, m. Elizabeth **JOHNSON**, Mar. 1, 1753, by Jonathan Merrik — 3 — 138

Abel, s. Abel & Elizabeth, b. Apr. 21, 1754 — 3 — 138

Abigail, d. Silvanus & Mary, b. Mar. 7, 1742 — 3 — 100

Ann Maria, [d. Wyllys & Rebecca], b. Oct. 5, 1803 — 3 — 395

Annah, d. Jonathan & Lidia, b. May 24, 1710 — 3 — 35

Anna, m. Abraham **PALMER**, b. of Branford, Jan. 16, 1733/4, by Rev. Jon[a]th[an] Mer[r]ick — 3 — 98

Anne, d. Charles & Hannah, b. Jan. 7, 1772, in New Haven; d. Aug. 23, 1773, in New Haven — 3 — 292

Anne, d. Charles & Hannah, b. Oct. 3, 1775, in New Haven — 3 — 292

Asa, s. Abel & Elisabeth, b. May 8, 1765 — 3 — 186

Asenath, d. Nathan & Rebeccah, b. Oct. 6, 1758 — 3 — 157

	Vol.	Page
BUTLER, BUTLAR, (cont.)		
Benedick Arnold, s. Charles & Hannah, b. Jan. 7,		
1778, in Wallingford	3	292
Benjamin, s. Isaiah & Martha, b. June 24, 1749	3	118
Benjamin, s. James & Desire, b. Oct. 27, 1756	3	153
Charles, m. Hannah **ATWATER**, of New Haven, Nov.		
6, 1771, by Jon[a]th[an] Edwards	3	292
Charles, m. Caroline **PALMER**, June 7, 1847, by Rev.		
Frederick Miller	TM3	161
Charles Merit, s. Timothy & Betsey, b. Apr. 1, 1818	3	365
Charles Wyllys, [s. Wyllys & Rebecca], b. Feb. 25,		
1800	3	395
Dan[ie]ll, m. wid. Elisabeth **PELL**, May 7, 1751,		
by Rev. Jonathan Mer[r]ick	3	145
Dan[ie]ll, s. Dan[ie]ll & Elisabeth, b. Dec. 18, 1755	3	145
David, s. Isaiah & Martha, b. June 30, 1744	3	110
David, s. Matthew & Hannah, b. Oct. 3, 1772	3	289
David, m. Henrietta **ISAACS**, b. of Branford, May		
26, 1807	3	391
Desiar, d. Ebenezor & Desiar, b. Apr. 5, 1758	3	152
Dinah, d. Jonathan & Lydia, b. Apr. 4, 1699	2	344
Dinah, m. Israel **BALDWIN**, b. of Branford, Dec.		
10, 1718	3	43
Ebenezer, s. Isaiah & Martha, b. Dec. 1, 1734	3	83
Ebenezer, of Branford, m. Desier **BARNS**, of New		
Haven, Mar. 30, 1757, by Josiah Roger, J. P.	3	146
Eliza Ann, d. Timothy & Betsey, b. Mar. 6, 1814	3	365
Elisabeth, d. Jonathan, Jr. & Elisabeth, b. Apr. 20, 1721	3	52
Elisabeth, d. of Jonathan, Jr., m. Josiah **HARRISON**,		
Jr., Feb. 16, 1745/6, by Rev. Jonath[a]n Mer[r]ick	3	107
Elisabeth, d. Dan[ie]ll & Elisabeth, b. June 9, 1754	3	145
Elisabeth, w. of Jonathan, Jr., d. July 1, 1754	3	137
Elisabeth, d. Abel & Elisabeth, b. Sept. 30, 1767	3	197
Elisabeth, d. John, 2d & Elisabeth, b. Apr. 10, 1769	3	206
Elisabeth, of Branford, m. Alexander **COVENTRY**, of		
Hudson, N. Y., Mar. 11, 1787, by Jason Atwater	3	315
Elizabeth, of Hudson, N. Y., m. James W. **FRISBIE**,		
of Branford, Nov. 6, 1822, by Rev. Benjamin F.		
Staunton, of Hudson, N. Y.	3	334
Else, d. Nathan & Rebecca, b. Mar. 16, 1763	3	181
Emeline, [d. William & Rebecca], b. Apr. 19, 1807	3	394
Emeline, ae 22 y., m. John Price **COVERT**, ae 21 y.,		
Dec. 5, 1849, by Rev. C. H. Topliff	TM3	167
Emeline R., m. John P. **COVERT**, b. of Branford,		
Dec. 5, 1849, by C. H. Topliff	TM3	164
Ephraim, s. Sam[ue]ll & Luce, b. Dec. 26, 1752	3	128
George, d. Apr. 13, 1847, ae 31	TM3	307
George Augustus, s. Timothy & Betsey, b. Aug. 1,1816	3	365

	Vol.	Page

BUTLER, BUTLAR, (cont.)

Giles, s. John, 2d, & Elisabeth, b. Aug. 18, 1771   3   206

Giles, s. John & Elisabeth, b. Aug. 18, 1771   3   292

Hannah, d. John & Hannah, b. Oct. 14, 1685   1   211

Hannah, d. Silas & Hannah, b. Apr. 9, 1716   3   39

Hannah, Mrs., of Middletown, m. Rev. Sam[ue]ll
    EELLS, of Branford, Nov. 7, 1770, by Edw[ard]
    Eells   3   306

Henrietta, [d. David & Henrietta], b. May 10, 1810   3   391

Isaiah, s. Jonathan & Lydia, b. June 17, 1705   2   346

Isaiah, m. Martha **BALDWIN,** b. of Branford, Dec. 29,
    1725, by Rev. Sam[ue]ll Russell   3   58

Isaiah, s. Isaiah & Martha, b. Sept. 12, 1726   3   61

Isaiah, Jr., m. Rebecca **FOOT,** b. of Branford, Jan.
    3, 1749/50, by Rev. Jonathan Mer[r]ick   3   120

Isaiah, s. Is[a]iah, Jr. & Rebecca, b. Oct. 23, 1750   3   123

Jairus, s. Matthew & Hannah, b. Jan. 17, 1775   3   289

James, s. Nath[anie]ll & Esther, b. Mar. 15,
    1728/9, at Weathersfield   3   87

James, m. Desire **HARRISON,** b. of Branford, Jan.
    22, 1756, by Philemon Robbins   3   153

James, s. James & Desire, b. May 16, 1762   3   176

Jared, s. Nathan[ie]ll, Jr. & Rebecca, b. Feb. 18, 1745/6   3   121

Jeremiah, s. Silas & Hannah, b. Apr. 6, 1714   3   39

Jeremiah, s. Silvanus & Mary, b. Aug. 23, 1744   3   105

Jerusha, d. Joseph & Jane, b. Feb. 7, 1765   3   191

Joel, s. Samuel & Lucy, b, Mar. 11, 1763   3   186

John, m. Hannah **POTTER,** Nov. 17, 1684   1   211

John, s. John & Hannah, b. Dec. 7, 1687   1   211

John, s. Jonathan & Lidia, b. Mar. 19, 1714   3   36

John, of Branford, m. Margery **TALMAGE,** of
    Easthampton, L. I., Aug. 11, 1742, by Rev.
    Jonathan Mer[r]ick   3   101

John, s. John & Margery, b. Dec. 4, 1744   3   105

John, s. John, Jr. & Elisabeth, b. Aug. 13, 1774   3   258

John, s. John, 2d, & Elisabeth, b. Aug. 13, 1774;
    d. Aug. 19, 1775   3   292

John, 2d, m. Elisabeth **LINSL[E]Y,** b. of Branford,
    July 10, 1776, by Jon[a]th[an] Merrick   3   205

John, s. John, 2d, & Elisabeth, b. Mar. 2, 1781   3   292

Jonah, s. Jonathan & Lydia, b. July 3, 1701   2   344

Jonah, d. Feb. 28, 1710   3   34

Jonah, m. Mary **JOHNSON,** b. of Branford, Feb. 9,
    1720/1, by Nath[anie]ll Harrison, J. P.   3   51

Jonah, s. Jonah & Mary, b. May 13, 1721   3   51

Jonah, m. Anne **WILFORD,** b. of Branford, Aug. 5,
    1725, by Rev. Sam[ue]ll Russell   3   58

Jonah, s. Nathan[ie]ll, Jr. & Rebecca, b. Sept. 29, 1750   3   121

	Vol.	Page
BUTLER, BUTLAR, (cont.)		
Jonah, s. Joseph & Jane, b. Aug. 29, 1763	3	191
Jonathan, s. Jonathan & Lydia, b. July 12, 1696	2	344
Jonathan, Jr., m. Elisabeth **BALDWIN**, b. of Branford, Nov. 20, 1717	3	43
Jonathan, s. Jonath[a]n, Jr. & Elisabeth, b. June 10, 1729	3	68
Jonathan, s. Jonathan, Jr. & Elisabeth, d. Dec. 2, 1731	3	73
Jonathan, s. Isaiah & Martha, b. Aug. 13, 1739	3	110
Jonathan, d. Feb. 19, 1757	3	144
Jonathan, s. Abel & Elisabeth, b. Sept. 18, 1761	3	181
Jonathan, d. Feb. 17, 1770, in the 74th y. of his age	3	198
Joseph, m. Jane **BYINTUN**, b. of Branford, Oct. 7, 1762, by Jon[a]th[an] Mer[r]ick	3	191
Justus, s. Samuel & Lucy, b. Apr. 3, 1765	3	186
Levine, d. John, 2d, & Elisabeth, b. Aug. 2, 1776	3	292
Lois, d. Dan[ie]ll & Elisabeth, b. Oct. 31, 1752	3	145
Lorain, d. Nathan & Rebecca, b. Oct. 23, 1765	3	189
Lydia, d. Jonathan & Lydia, b. Sept. 27, 1694	2	344
Lydia, m. Sam[ue]ll **ROSE**, June 6, 1716, by Rev. Sam[ue]ll Russel[l]	3	38
Lydia, d. Jonathan, Jr. & Elisabeth, b. Dec. 22, 1726	3	63
Lydia, m. Timothy **HARRISON**, b. of Branford, June 12, 1751, by Rev. Jonath[a]n Mer[r]ick	3	136
Lydia, d. John & Margery, b. Apr. 18, 1755	3	141
Lydia, d. Mar. 13, 1847, ae 92	TM3	307
Margery, d. John & Margery, b. June 21, 1753	3	141
Mergery, d. Matthew & Hannah, b. Jan. 2, 1780	3	289
Margary, m. Chauncey **MOULTHROP**, b. of Branford, May 14, 1810	3	432
Martha, d. Isaiah & Martha, b. Nov. 19, 1741	3	110
Martha, d. Nathaniel & Esther, b. June 4, 1743	3	100
Mary, w. of Jonah, d. Jan. 15, 1723/4	3	54
Mary, d. Nath[anie]ll & Esther, b. Oct. 9, 1727, at Weathersfield	3	87
Mary, d. Salvanus & Mary, b. Oct. 6, 1746	3	113
Mary, d. Nathan[ie]ll, Jr. & Rebecca, b. Aug. 7, 1748	3	121
Mary, m. William Sidney **FOOT**, b. of [North] Branford, Aug. 27, 1827, by Rev. Timothy P. Gillett	3	345
Matthew, s. John & Margaree, b. July 21, 1748	3	116
Matthew, m. Hannah **PALMER**, b. of Branford, Apr. 20, 1772, by Philemon Robbins	3	206
Nathan, s. Iasiah & Martha, b. June 1, 1732	3	74
Nathan, m. Rebeckah **ROGERS**, b. of Branford, Dec. 8, 1755, by Warham Williams	3	140
Nathaniel, s. Jonah & Mary, b. Aug. 29, 1723	3	54
Nathaniel, s. Nath[anie]ll & Esther, b. June 24, 1731, at Weathersfield	3	87

BUTLER, BUTLAR, (cont.)	Vol.	Page
Nath[anie]ll, m. Rebecca **PALMER**, b. of Branford		
Nov. 28, 1744, by Rev. Jon[a]th[an] Mer[r]ick	3	120
Nathan[ie]ll, d. Oct. 2, 1751	3	125
Nathan[ie]ll, s. Sam[ue]ll & Rebecca, b. Jan. 14, 1753	3	128
Olive, s. Joseph & Jane, b. June 10, 1768	3	196
Olive, m. Abraham **FRISBIE**, Feb. 14, 1787	3	274
Pamelia, d. Nathan & Rebecca, b. Feb. 27, 1768	3	193
Peter, s. Sam[ue]ll & Lucy, b. Aug. 17, 1759	3	176
Polle, d. John, 2d & Elisabeth, b. Sept. 18, 1783	3	292
Polly, d. Benjamin & Lydia, b. Apr. 16, 1795	3	408
Polly, m. Lauren **PALMER**, b. of Branford, Mar. 30,		
1813	3	408
Rayner, s. Silvanus & Mary, b. June 6, 1740	3	100
Rebecca, d. Isaiah, Jr. & Rebecca, b. Mar. 1, 1752	3	125
Rebecca, d. John, 2d, & Elisabeth, b. Jan. 26, 1767	3	206
Rebecca, m. Wyllys **BUTLER**, b. of Branford, Sept.		
29, 1799	3	395
Reuben, s. Joseph & Jane, b. Sept. 12, 1766	3	191
Richard, d. Apr. 13, 1713	3	36
Rufus, s. John & Margery, b. June 1, 1750	3	141
Rufus, m. Mary **RUSSELL**, b. of North Branford, July		
25, 1824, by Timothy P. Gillett	3	334
Ruth, d. Jonathan & Lydia, b. Nov. 17, 1707	3	31
Ruth, m. Moses **FOOT**, b. of Branford, Nov. 5, 1740,		
by Rev. Jon[a]th[an] Mer[r]ick	3	98
Sally, d. John, 2d, & Elisabeth, b. Jan. 7, 1779	3	292
Salmon, s. Nathan & Rebecca, b. Mar. 5, 1761	3	171
Samuel, of Branford, m. Anne **ROBERDS**, of East		
Haven, Mar. 21, 1714, by Rev. Jacob Heminway	3	37
Samuel, s. Isaiah & Martha, b. Aug. 26, 1728	3	71
Sam[ue]ll, s. Nathan[ie]ll & Esther, b. Apr. 15, 1739	3	90
Sam[ue]ll, m. Lucy **PALMER**, b. of Branford, Nov. 5,		
1750, by Rev. Jonath[a]n Mer[r]ick	3	124
Samuel, s. Samuel & Lusee, b. Sept. 29, 1754	3	139
Sarah, d. Jonathan & Lydia, b. Oct. 6, 1718	3	44
Sarah, m. Daniel **BYINTUN**, b. of Branford, Aug. 7,		
1734, by Rev. Jonathan Mer[r]ick	3	84
Sarah, d. Nath[anie]ll & Esther, b. Sept. 1, 1734	3	87
Sarah, wid., d. Mar. 18, 1749/50	3	123
Silvanus, s. Rich[a]rd & Elisabeth, d. Apr. 5, 1713	3	36
Silvanus, s. Samuel & Anne, b. May 21, 1713	3	36
Silvanus, m. Mary **RAYNER**, b. of Branford, Oct. 30,		
1739, by Jonathan Mer[r]ick	3	93
Stephen, s. Isaiah & Martha, b. Nov. 22, 1736	3	86
Timothy, s. Nath[anie]ll & Esther, b. Feb. 9, 1736/7	3	87
Timothy, s. Silvanus & Mary, b. Mar. 15, 1749/50	3	120
Timothy, s. Benjamin & Lydia, b. Dec. 4, 1784	3	279
Titus, s. Sam[ue]ll & Lucey, b. June 27, 1757	3	145

	Vol.	Page
BUTLER, BUTLAR, (cont.)		
Tryphene, d. Jonathan & Lydia, b. Sept. 4, 1712; d. Apr. 27, 1713	3	36
Tryphena, d. John & Margery, b. Aug. 4, 1743	3	101
Triphena, m. Noah **PAGE**, b. of Branford, Dec. 26, 1772, by Samuel Eells	3	207
William, d. Mar. 2, 1807	3	394
William Harris, [s. David & Henrietta], b. July 29, 1808	3	391
Wyllys, s. Charles & Hannah, b. Jan. 7, 1781	3	292
Wyllys, m. Rebecca **BUTLER**, b. of Branford, Sept. 29, 1799	3	395
BYINGTON, BOYINGTON, BYINTON, BYINTUN,		
Anne, d. Eben[eze]r & Eunice, b. Aug. 18, 1780	3	306
Benjamin, m. Phebe **HARRISON**, b. of Branford, Sept. 24, 1770, by Sam[ue]ll Eells	3	200
Charity, d. John, Jr. & Sarah, b. Oct. 24, 1736	3	92
Chittendon, s. Benj[ami]n & Phebe, b. Mar. 1, 1775	3	295
Daniel, s. John & Jane, b. Sept. 18, 1711	3	35
Daniel, m. Sarah **BUTLER**, b. of Branford, Aug. 7, 1734, by Rev. Jonathan Mer[r]ick	3	84
Daniel, s. Daniel & Sarah, b. June 4, 1738	3	99
David, [twin with Jonathan], s. John & Jane, b. Nov. 30, 1702	3	35
David, s. David & Mercy, b. Feb. 17, 1734	3	110
Ebenezer, m. Eunice **HUFFMAN**, b. of Branford, Nov. 4, 1778, by Sam[ue]ll Eells	3	306
Elisabeth Augusta, d. Henry P. & Sally Maria, b. Dec. 3, 1837	TM3	231
Elisabeth Augusta, d. Henry P. & Sally Maria, b. Dec. 3, 1837	TM3	306
Eunice, d. David & Mercy, b. Apr. 29, 1731	3	110
Eunice, m. David **ROGERS**, b. of Branford, July 3, 1748, by Jonathan Mer[r]ick	3	184
Hannah, d. John & Jane, b. Nov. 7, 1699	3	35
Hannah, d. Jonathan & Hannah, b. Oct. 7, 1736	3	91
Hannah, d. Jon[a]th[an], Jr. & Comfort, b. Nov. 19, 1772	3	208
Henry P., of North Branford, m. Sally M. **PAGE**, of Branford, June 25, 1835, by T. P. Gillett	3	369
Henry P., m. Mary E. **McQUEEN**, b. of Branford, Apr. 26, 1843, by Rev. Timothy P. Gillett	TM3	156
Henry P., d. June 21, 1848, ae 34 y.	TM3	308
Irena, d. Benj[ami]n & Phebe, b. Mar. 20, 1771	3	295
Irene, m. Elihu **LINSL[E]Y**, Feb. 26, 1795	3	279
Isaac, [twin with Jacob], s. David & Mercy, b. May 25, 1743	3	110
Jacob, [twin with Isaac], s. David & Marcy, b. May 25, 1743	3	110

	Vol.	Page
BYINGTON, BOYINGTON, BYINTON,BYINTUN,(cont.)		
Jane, d. John & Jane, b. Jan. 16, 1707/8	3	35
Jane, d. Jon[a]th[an] & Hannah, b. Oct. 19, 1743	3	102
Jane, m. Joseph **BUTLER**, b. of Branford, Oct. 7,		
1762, by Jon[a]th[an] Mer[r]ick	3	191
Jerusha, d. David & Mercy, b. Mar. 3, 1739	3	110
John, s. John & Jane, b. Sept. 11, 1713	3	35
John, Jr., of Branford, m. Sarah **CHITTENDEN**, of		
North Guilford, Nov. 6, 1735, by Rev. Sam[ue]ll		
Russell, of North Guilford	3	92
John, s. John & Sarah, Jr., b. Sept. 1, 1740	3	95
Jonah, s. Dan[ie]ll & Sarah, b. Mar. 20, 1748	3	117
Jonathan, [twin with David], s. John & Jane, b.		
Nov. 30, 1702	3	35
Jonathan, m. Hannah **MALLERY**, b. of Branford, Dec.		
5, 1733, by Rev. Philemon Robbins	3	91
Jonathan, s. Jonathan & Hannah, b. Dec. 12, 1740	3	102
Jonathan, of Branford, m. Phebe **ALLING**, of New		
Haven, Jan. 10, 1753, by Jacob Hemingway	3	168
Jonathan, Jr., of Branford, m. Comfort **BEARDSLEY**,		
of Stratford, Dec. 25, 1765, by James Dana	3	200
Joseph, s. David & Mercy, b. Sept. 23, 1736	3	110
Lorane, d. Jonathan, Jr. & Comfort, b. July 26, 1769	3	199
Lucretia, d. Jonathan, Jr. & Comfort, b. Oct. 12,		
1766; d. July 21, 1768	3	199
Lydia, d. Dan[ie]ll & Sarah, b. Nov. 4, 1726 (The		
date "Feb. 22, 1735/6" has been added in pencil)	3	84
Lydia, m. Jacob **BARKER**, Jan. 25, 1759, by Jonathan		
Merrick	3	158
Mary, d. John & Jane, b. Jan. 8, 1709/10	3	35
Mary, m. Moses **FOOT**, b. of Branford, June 22, 1726,		
by Rev. Sam[ue]ll Russell	3	65
Mary, d. Jonathan & Hannah, b. June 3, 1739	3	91
Mary, d. Jonathan & Hannah, d. Feb. 20, 1739/40	3	102
Mintey, d. Benj[ami]n & Phebe, b. May 24, 1780	3	295
Nathan[ie]ll, s. John & Jane, b. May 20, 1706	3	35
Phebe, d. Benj[ami]n & Phebe, b. Aug. 11, 1782	3	295
Polle, d. Benj[ami]n & Phebe, b. Aug. 25, 1777	3	295
Robert, s. John & Jane, b. Oct. 5, 1704	3	35
Robert, s. John & Jane, d. May 21, 1714	3	35
Robert, s. John & Jane, b. Jan. 14, 1714/15	3	35
Sally, d. Benj[ami]n & Phebe, b. Dec. 14, 1772	3	295
Sally Maria, w. of Henry P., d. Nov. 11, 1842, ae 25 y.	TM3	306
Sarah, d. John, Jr. & Sarah, b. Oct. 3, 1738	3	92
Sarah, d. Daniel & Sarah, b. Dec. 12, 1742	3	99
Timothy, s. Jonathan & Phebe, b. Apr. 15, 1759	3	168
Timothy Augustus, s. Henry P. & Sally Maria, b.		
Mar. 31, 1836	TM3	231

	Vol.	Page
BYINGTON, BOYINGTON, BYINTON,BYINTUN,(cont.)		
Timothy Augustus, s. Henry, P. & Sally Maria, b.		
Mar. 31, 1836	TM3	306
Zeruiah, d. Jonathan & Hannah, b. Oct. 19, 1734	3	91
CARTER, CARTTAR, Abel, s. Jacob & Dorcas, b. June 4,		
1718	3	67
Abel, m. Mary **COACH,** b. of Branford, Apr. 17, 1739,		
by Rev. Jonathan Mer[r]ick	3	112
Abel, s. Abel & Mary, b. Mar. 21, 1747	3	112
Ann, of Branford, m. John **DOUGLASS,** of Northford,		
Apr. 17, 1825, by Timothy P. Gillett	3	339
Anne, d. Thomas Poledius & Sally, b. Mar. 28, 1801	3	280
Benjamin L., m. Phebe **BEACH,** b. of Branford, Mar.		
24, 1824, by Rev. Timothy P. Gillett	3	425
Benjamin L., ae 47 y., m. Flora A. **HART,** ae 38 y.		
of Cornwall, July 2, 1850, by Joshua L. Maynard	TM3	166
Benjamin Linsl[e]y, s. Thomas P. & Sally, b. June		
25, 1803	3	280
Dan[ie]ll, s. Abel & Mary, b. May 29, 1744	3	112
Dorcas, w. of Jacob, d. Jan. 10, 1735/6	3	83
Dorcas, d. Abel & Mary, b. June 28, 1739	3	112
Edwin Hopkins, s. Benjamin L. & Phebe, b. Dec. 5,		
1843	TM3	238
Henry E., s. Benjamin L. & Phebe, b. Apr. 29, 1834;		
d. Aug. 16, 1835	3	372
Jacob, m. Dorcas **TYLER,** Dec. 4, 1712, by Rev.		
Sam[ue]ll Russel[l]	3	35
Jacob, s. Jacob & Dorcas, b. Nov. 26, 1716	3	40
John, s. Abel & Mary, b. Nov. 20, 1741	3	112
John Beach, s. Benjamin L. & Phebe, b. May 11, 1825	3	341
Marie, m. Samuell **WARD,** Jan. 1, 1658	1	173
Nancy Jane, m. Isaac Hobart **PALMER,** b. of Branford,		
Jan. 3, 1839, by L. H. Corson	3	376
Phebe, d. Sept. 14, 1847, ae 43	TM3	308
Samuel B., s. Benjamin L. & Phebe, b. May 23, 1828	3	372
Sarah, d. Jacob & Dorcas, b. Feb. 4, 1714; d. Dec.		
4, 1715	3	40
CHAMBERLAIN, Abigail, d. John & Thankfull, b. Mar. 14,		
1725/6	3	58
Mary, d. John & Thankfull, b. Aug. 14, 1724	3	55
CHAPEL, Sarah E., d. Benj[ami]n F. & Nancy, b. Sept. 30,		
1849	TM3	242
CHARLES, Hannah, d. John, b. Apr. 13, 1677	1	174
Hannah, m. Christopher **PARKES,** Nov. 4, 1706, by		
W[illia]m Maltbie, J. P.	3	32
CHIDSEY, Bartholomew, s. Joseph & Sarah, b. June 17,		
1771	3	208
Betsey, [d. Reuel & Olive], b. May 13, 1810	3	429

	Vol.	Page
CHIDSEY, (cont.)		
Betsey, of Branford, m. Samuel C. **PECK**, of		
Wallingford, Sept. 29, 1831, by Edw[ar]d J. Ives	3	361
Bradley, [s. Reuel & Olive], b. July 9, 1812	3	429
Bradley, m. Mary R. **HARRISON**, b. of Branford, Jan.		
1, 1845, by Rev. Frederick Miller	TM3	157
Bradley, m. Mary R. **HARRISON**, b. of Branford, Jan.		
1, 1845, by Rev. Fred[eric]k Miller	TM3	173
Ephraim Sturdevant, of East Haven, m. Esther Ann		
WEAVER, of New Haven, Oct. 17, 1837, by		
Rev. Timothy P. Gillett	3	374
Harriet, [d. Reuel & Olive], b. Oct. 1, 1807; d.		
Oct. 12, 1811	3	429
Harriet, of Branford, m. Stephen F. **STEDMAN**, of		
New Haven, Sept. 24, 1831, by Rev. Timothy P.		
Gillett	3	357
Henry Roswell, [s. Reuel & Olive], b. Sept. 11, 1818	3	429
Jane, [d. Reuel & Olive], b. Sept. 23, 1805	3	429
Jared G., m. Harriet R. **WHEADON**, b. of Branford,		
[1830?], by J. A. Root. Recorded Nov. 5, 1830	3	356
John Street, of East Haven, m. Chloe **STENT**, of		
Branford, Feb. 14, 1842, by Rev. Timothy P.		
Gillett	TM3	154
Joseph, m. Sarah **GOODRICH**, b. of Branford, May		
17, 1769, by Nicholas Street	3	208
Laura A., m. Charles I. **HARRISON**, b. of Branford,		
Dec. 21, 1842, by Rev. Pascal P. Kidder	TM3	155
Laura Ann, [d. Reuel & Olive], b. May 12, 1823	3	429
Luther, m. Eliza **PALMER**, [Jan.] 27, [1830], by		
Judson A. Root	3	352
Mary, of East Haven, d. May 13, 1824	3	428
Polle, d. Roswell & Hannah, b. Feb. 22, 1781; d.		
Nov. 24, 1782	3	287
Polle, d. Roswell & Hannah, b. July 11, 1783	3	287
Ralph, s. Roswell & Hannah, b. Feb. 2, 1779	3	287
Ralph W[illia]m, [s. Reuel & Olive], b. Nov. 19, 1815	3	429
Reuel, s. Roswell & Hannah, b. Sept. 5, 1776	3	286
Reuel, of Branford, m. Olive **BRADLEY**, of East		
Haven, Jan. 3, 1805	3	429
Reuel, s. Bradley & Mary, b. June 15, 1848	TM3	239
Reuel, s. Bradley & Mary R., b. June 15, 1848	TM3	246
Roswell, m. Hannah **LAMFIER**, b. of Branford, Feb.		
1, 1776, by Philemon Robbins	3	286
Roswell, s. Roswell & Hannah, b. Mar. 24, 1786	3	253
Timothy, s. Joseph & Sarah, b. Feb. 26, 1770	3	208
CHITTENDEN, Sarah, of North Guilford, m. John		
BYINTUN, Jr., of Branford, Nov. 6, 1735, by		
Rev. Sam[ue]ll Russell, of North Guilford	3	92

	Vol.	Page

CHITTENDEN, (cont.)

Susan Emeline, of Branford, m. John Henry
  TILESTON, of New Haven, Dec. 20, 1854, by
  Rev. T. P. Gillett — TM3 — 173

CHURCH, Sophia T., m. James H. **FOWLER**, Apr. 10,
  1843, by Rev. Davis T. Shailer — TM3 — 156

CLANNING, Mary S., m. Lynde W. **SHEPARD**, July 18,
  1848 — TM3 — 162

CLARK, CLARKE, Fanny, d. Jonah & Hannah, b. Mar. 14,
  1777 — 3 — 267

Gerard, s. Jonah & Hannah, b. Dec. 25, 1778 — 3 — 267

Jonah, m. Hannah **TYLER**, b. of Branford, Jan. 1,
  1775, by Oliver Stanley, J. P. — 3 — 267

Nathan, of Orange, m. Caroline **FOWLER**, of Guilford,
  Mar. 7, 1824, by Rev. Timothy P. Gillett — 3 — 425

Oliver P., d. July 20, 1850, ae 19 y. — TM3 — 309

Sally, of North Haven, m. Alfred **ROSE**, of Branford,
  Jan. 1, 1812 — 3 — 400

COACH, Elisabeth, d. John & Elisabeth, b. Apr. 5, 1720 — 3 — 44

Elisabeth, m. John **ROSE**, Jr., b. of Branford, Sept
  10, 1745, by John Russell, J. P. — 3 — 164

James, s. John & Elisabeth, b. Dec. [   ] — 3 — 41

John, m. Elisabeth **PLANT**, July 23, 1712, by
  Nathan[ie]ll Harrison, J. P. — 3 — 35

John, s. John & Elisabeth, b. Aug. 6, 1725 — 3 — 57

Mary, d. Jno. & Elisabeth, b. Jan. 18, 1722/3 — 3 — 50

Mary, m. Abel **CARTER**, b. of Branford, Apr. 17,
  1739, by Rev. Jonathan Mer[r]ick — 3 — 112

Sarah, d. John & Elisabeth, b. May 2, 1715 — 3 — 36

Sarah, m. Eleazar **STENT**, Jr., b. of Branford, Sept.
  20, 1738, by Rev. Philemon Robbins — 3 — 89

COE, Rosanna, of Wallingford, m. Samuel **MALTBIE**, Jr.,
  of Branford, Feb. 11, 1768, by Caleb Merriman, J.
  P. — 3 — 193

Sarah, m. James **MALTBIE**, Mar. 8, 1786, by Oliver
  Stanley, J. P. — 3 — 315

COLLINS, Betsey, d. July 22, 1847, ae 46 — TM3 — 307

Hannah E., of Guilford, m. Luther **CRAMPTON**, of
  Madison, Mar. 12, 1843, by Rev. Pascal P. Kidder — TM3 — 155

John, m. Mrs. Dorcas **TAINTOR**, Mar. 6, 1699/1700,
  by Rev. Mr. Russell — 2 — 343

Jonathan, of Guilford, m. Betsey **JOHNSON**, of
  Branford, June 10, 1827 — 3 — 354

Sarah A., ae 21, m. William **WEDMORE**, ae 30, of
  Fair Haven, [   ], 1850, by Rev. Mr. Vibberts — TM3 — 167

Sarah Ann, d. Jonathan & Betsey, b. July 7, 1829 — 3 — 354

COMSTOCK, Zenas, m. Betsey Ann **PAGE**, b. of Branford,
  Oct. 26, 1837, by Rev. Timothy P. Gillett — 3 — 374

	Vol.	Page
CONKLIN, Jeremiah, formerly of Greenwich, Great Brittain,		
m. Hannah **ELWELL**, of Branford, Mar. 1,		
1725/6, by Nathaniel Har[r]ison, J. P.	3	61
Sarah, d. Jeremiah & Hannah, b. Oct. 19, 1726	3	61
CONNER, Sarah A., of Cheshire, m. Levins G. **FORBES**,		
of Branford, Oct. 18, 1845, by Rev. A. C. Wheat	TM3	158
CONVERSE, Elihu Williams, Dr., m. Catharine		
MONRO[E], June 8, 1823, by Charles Atwater, at		
North Branford	3	423
COOK, COOCK, COOKE, Abraham, s. Uzziel & Jeruiah,		
b. June 1, 1754	3	187
Alice Eveline, d. Samuel S. & Caroline, b. Jan. 3, 1851	TM3	244
Almira, of Guilford, m. Apollos **APPLE**, of North		
Branford, Apr. 8, 1827, by Rev. Timothy P. Gillett	3	343
Alvah Seymour, [s. Samuel & Peggy], b. Oct. 9, 1820	3	362
Ann Maria, [d. Samuel & Peggy], b. Feb. 16, 1824	3	363
Anna, m. Jonathan **WHEDON**, b. of Branford, Dec. 3,		
1749, by Rev. Philemon Robbins	3	122
Aretius Ossion, [child of Malachi & Sarah], b. Nov.		
19, 1810	3	392
Benjamin, s. Waitstill & Elisabeth, b. Apr. 6, 1771	3	204
Charles, s. Moses & Sarah, b. June 13, 1741	3	97
Cornelia, of Wallingford, m. William **EVARTS**, of		
Branford, Feb. 6, 1820, by Rev. Matthew Noyes	3	414
Demetrius, m. Elisabeth **ROGERS**, b. of Branford,		
Apr. 26, 1739, by Rev. Philemon Robbins	3	123
Demetrius, s. Demetrius & Elisabeth, b. Jan. 6, 1739/40	3	123
Desire, d. Uzziel & Zeruiah, b. Dec. 29, 1745	3	187
Ebenezer Hubbard, s. Waitstill & Elisabeth, b.		
Sept. 6, 1759	3	176
Edward Aug[us]t, s. George & Mary, b. Feb. 28, 1784	3	315
Elihu, s. Demetrius & Elizabeth, b. Oct. 11, 1755	3	142
Elihu, m. Esther **ROGERS**, b. of Branford, Mar. 8,		
1789, by Rev. Jason Atwater	3	272
Elihu, [s. Elihu & Esther], b. Dec. 5, 1792	3	272
Elihu, Jr., m. Nancy **TYLER**, b. of Branford, Dec.		
2, 1815	3	415
Elihu, [s. Elihu & Nancy], b. Dec. 5, 1824	3	374
Eliza J., of Branford, m. Erastus A. **NORTH**, of		
Berlin, May 23, 1853, by Rev. T. P. Gillett	TM3	172
Elisabeth, d. Demetrius & Elisabeth, b. Apr. 23, 1753	3	132
Elizabeth, d. Demetrius & Elizabeth, b. Apr. 23, 1753	3	142
Elisabeth, d. Waitstill & Elisabeth, b. June 13, 1764	3	204
Elisabeth, m. Edward **BURKE**, Aug. 29, 1775, by Rev.		
Chauncey Whittelsey, of New Haven	3	262
Elizur Vandee, [s. Samuel & Peggy], b. July 27, 1828	3	362
Ella Amelia, [d. Virgil N. & Mary], b. Jan. 19, 1838	TM3	229
Emeline, of Branford, m. Morris **TYLER**, of New		

	Vol.	Page

COOK, COOCK, COOKE, (cont.)

	Vol.	Page
Haven, June 27, 1831, [by Rev. Timothy P. Gillett]	3	357
Emily Cecelia, [d. Malachi & Sarah], b. Apr. 21, 1803	3	392
Esther, [d. Elihu & Esther], b. Sept. 13, 1795	3	272
Hannah, d. Waitstill & Elisabeth, b. Mar. 17, 1753	3	144
Harriet, of Wallingford, m. William Rogers **FRISBIE**, of Branford, Nov. 25, 1841, by Rev. Pascal P. Kidder, at the house of Samuel Cooke	TM3	154
Harriet, m. Bennett **ATWOOD**, b. of Wallingford, Mar. 18, 1849, by Rev. T. P. Gillett	TM3	163
Harriet, m. Henry **LINSLEY**, 2d, b. of Branford, Aug. 16, 1852, by Rev. Timothy P. Gillett	TM3	171
Harriet A., of Mendon, Ill., m. Samuel **BEACH**, 2d, of Branford, Mar. 30, 1851, by Rev. Timo[thy] P. Gillett	TM3	168
Harriett A., ae 18, m. Samuel **BEACH**, 2d, ae 23, Mar. 30, 1851, by Rev. T. P. Gillett	TM3	170
Helen Eliza, [d. Virgil N. & Mary], b. June 14, 1835	TM3	229
Henry, of Wallingford, m. wid. Mary **WHEADON**, of Branford, Feb. 13, 1710, by Nathan[ie]ll Harrison, J. P.	3	34
Henry Hobart, s. Samuel & Peggy, b. Mar. 6, 1831	3	366
Homer Stephen Malachi, [s. Malachi & Sarah], b. Apr. 3, 1805	3	392
Huldah, [twin with John], d. Waitstill & Elisabeth, b. May 14, 1768	3	204
Ichabod, s. Mary, b. June 10, 1759	3	188
Increase W., of North Guilford, m. Harriet D. **GRIFFING**, of Branford, May 13, 1832, by Tim[othy] P. Gillett	3	357
Isaac, Jr., of Branford, m. Mary **HUBBARD**, of Guilford, Nov. 14, 1739, by Rev. Thomas Ruggles	3	111
Isaac, s. Isaac, Jr. & Mary, b. Oct. 1, 1740; d. June 1, 1744	3	111
Isaac, s. Issac, Jr. & Mary, b. Mar. 14, 1746/7; d. Nov. 24, 1748	3	111
Isaac, s. Uzziel & Zeruiah, b. Oct. 9, 1757	3	187
Isaac, Jr., d. Mar. 22, 1760	3	197
Isaac, s. George & Mary, b. Dec. 10, 1781	3	315
Jacob, s. Waitstill & Elisabeth, b. July 15, 1755	3	144
Jane, d. Waitstill & Elisabeth, b. Apr. 10, 1751	3	144
Jerusha, d. Demetrius & Elisabeth, b. Jan. 19, 1760	3	187
John, [twin with Huldah], s. Waitstill & Elisabeth, b. May 14, 1768	3	204
Jonathan, s. Henry & Mary, b. Jan. 7, 1712	3	36
Joseph Whedon, [s. Elihu & Esther], b. May 20, 1790	3	272
Josiah, s. Demetrius & Elisabeth, b. Jan. 9, 1763	3	187

	Vol.	Page
COOK, COOCK, COOKE, (cont)		
Lemuel, m. Sina **BUNNELL**, b. of Branford, July 10,		
1825, by Rev. James Keeler, of Northford	3	339
Lorenzo Blackstone, s. Timothy & Mary, b. Mar. 24,		
1845	TM3	238
Lydia, d. Uzziel & Zeruiah, b. Mar. 6, 1750	3	187
Malachi, m. Sarah **TAINTER**, Dec. 25, 1802	3	392
Mariette, of Wallingford, m. Timothy		
BARTHOLOMEW, Jr., of Branford, Feb. 6,		
1820, by Rev. Matthew Noyes	3	414
Martha, [d. Elihu, Jr. & Nancy], b. July 16, 1816	3	415
Martha, m. George **PAGE**, b. of Branford, June 21,		
1835, by T. P. Gillett	3	369
Mary, d. Demetrius & Elisabeth, b. June 3, 1741	3	123
Mary had s. Ichabod **COOK**, b. June 10, 1759	3	188
Mary E., d. Dec. 22, 1847, ae 24	TM3	308
Mary Helen, d. Samuel & Peggy, b. Dec. 1, 1834	3	374
Moses, s. Moses & Sarah, b. May 19, 1744	3	104
Parnel, d. George & Mary, b. Feb. 26, 1786	3	315
Patience, d. Uzziel & Zeruiah, b. May 13, 1764	3	187
Rachel, d. Isaac, Jr. & Mary, b. Nov. 12, 1751	3	128
Ruth Hannah, d. Demetrius & Elizabeth, b. Jan. 19,		
175[ ]	3	153
Samuel, [s. Elihu & Esther], b. May 9, 1798	3	272
Samuel, [s. Elihu, Jr. & Nancy], b. Sept. 9, 1818	3	416
Samuel, m. Peggy **HOBART**, Feb. 20, 1820	3	362
Samuel, ae 24, y., m. Caroline **PAGE**, ae 20 y., Oct.		
10, 1849, by Rev. T. P. Gillett	TM3	166
Samuel S., m. Caroline C. **PAGE**, b. of Branford,		
Oct. 10, 1849, by Rev. Timothy P. Gillett	TM3	164
Samuel Scott, [s. Samuel & Peggy], b. Nov. 17, 1825	3	362
Sarah, d. Moses & Sarah, b. June 14, 1747	3	112
Silus, s. George & Mary, b. Mar. 27, 1780	3	315
Susan, m. Samuel **WILFORD**, b. of Branford, Oct. 27,		
1839	TM3	159
Timothy, [s. Elihu & Nancy], b. Mar. 27, 1822	3	374
Timothy, m. Mary E. **BARKER**, b. of Branford, Jan.		
1, 1844, by Rev. Davis T. Shailer	TM3	157
Timothy, m. Harriett **AVERILL**, b. of Branford, Oct.		
11, 1849, by Rev. Timothy P. Gillett	TM3	164
Timothy, ae 30, m. Harriett **AVERILL**, ae 32, Oct.		
11, 1849, by Rev. T. P. Gillett	TM3	167
Timothy, d. Dec. 15, 1850, ae 29	TM3	310
Uzziel, of Branford, m. Zeruiah **BARN[E]S**, of East		
Hampton, May 20, 1745, by Jonathan Merrick	3	187
Uzziel, s. Uzziel & Zeruiah, b. July 21, 1761	3	187
Virgil U., m. Mary Martha **LINSLEY**, Nov. 24, 1833,		
by W[illia]m P. Curtiss, in Trinity Church	3	362

	Vol.	Page
COOK, COOCK, COOKE, (cont.)		
Virgil Ulysses, [s. Malachi & Sarah], b. June 22, 1808	3	392
William, s. Waitstill & Elisabeth, b. May 9, 1762	3	177
----, s. Virgil U. & Mary M., b. Apr. 9, 1848	TM3	239
----, d. Jasper & Abigail, b. Feb. 21, 1849	TM3	241
COONS, Armenia F., ae 20, m. Newton A. **HALL,** ae 23,		
May 4, 1851, by Rev. Dr. Olden	TM3	170
COOPER, Charles, s. Levi **COOPER,** & Hannah **SMITH,**		
b. Jan. 13, 1808	3	432
COPES, Kalep, m. Mariet **ASHER,** June 26, 1823, by		
Charles Atwater	3	423
COREY, Jobe, s. John & Rebecca, b. Apr. 3, 1776	3	273
John, s. John & Rebecca, b. Aug. 10, 1778	3	273
Major, s. John & Rebecca, b. May 17, 1782	3	273
Sally, d. John & Rebecca, b. Oct. 27, 1780	3	273
CORNWALL, Susanna, m. Joseph **JONES,** b. of Branford,		
Sept. 20, 1764, by Philemon Robbins	3	187
COULS, [see under **COWLES**]		
COVENTRY, Alexander, of Hudson, N. Y., m. Elisabeth		
BUTLER, of Branford, Mar. 11, 1787, by Jason		
Atwater	3	315
COVERT, John P., m. Emeline R. **BUTLER,** b. of		
Branford, Dec. 5, 1849, by C. H. Topliff	TM3	164
John Price, ae 21 y., m. Emeline **BUTLER,** ae 22 y.,		
Dec. 5, 1849, by Rev. C. H. Topliff	TM3	167
Mary A., m. Stephen A. **BEACH,** b. of Branford,		
July 11, 1851, by Rev. Lucius Attwater	TM3	169
Mary Ann, ae 20, m. Stephen **BEACH,** ae 29, July 11,		
1851, by Lucius Attwater	TM3	169
William J., m. Charlotte **HOADLEY,** b. of Branford,		
Nov. 30, 1823, by Stephen W. Stebbings	3	424
----. s. John P. & Emeline, b. May 1, 1850	TM3	242
[COWLES], COWLS, COULS, Hannah, of Wallingford, m.		
Nathaniel **PENFIELD,** of Branford, May 4, 1731,		
by Rev. Theophilus Hall	3	84
Lois, of Wallingford, m. Sam[ue]ll **FRISBEE,** of		
Branford, Oct. 10, 1722, by Jno. Hall	3	50
CRAMPTON, Luther, of Madison, m. Hannah E.		
COLLINS, of Guilford, Mar. 12, 1843, by Rev.		
Pascal P. Kidder	TM3	155
CROWFOOT, Mary, of Weathersfield, m. John		
WHEADON, of Branford, Jan. 10, 1716/7, at		
Weathersfield	3	40
CUBBY, Phillis, b. Mar. 3, 1734, in Harrison's Purchase	3	419
CULLPEP[P]ER, Susan[n]a, m. Frances **LINSL[E]Y,** June		
24, , [16]55	1	170
CULVER, Ann, of Wallingford, m. Reuben **FRISBIE,** of		
Branford, Mar. 28, 1784	3	391

	Vol.	Page

CULVER, (cont.)

Charles, of Waterbury, m. Frances **DEW[E]Y**, of
  Branford, Nov. 25, 1841, by Rev. Davis T. Shailer — TM3 — 153

Ruth, of Wallingford, m. John **FOOT**, 2d, of Branford,
  Nov. 7, 1771, by Rev. Sam[ue]ll Andrus — 3 — 256

CURTIS, CURTICE, CURTISS, Abigail, Mrs., m. Solomon
  PALMER, b. of Branford, Sept. 11, 1739, by
  Rev. Philemon Robbins — 3 — 123

Fitch H., of Salem, Penn., m. Lydia **ROGERS**, of
  Branford, [Oct.] 29, 1820, by Origen P. Holcomb — 3 — 412

George Whitefield, s. Jacob & Catharina, b. July
  1, 1806 — 3 — 280

Jacob, s. Jacob & Abigail, b. Oct. 1, 1738 — 3 — 89

Lois, [d. Russell & Dorcas], b. Sept. 15, 1819,
  in East Haven — 3 — 428

Mary Thankful, [d. Russell & Dorcas], b. Mar. 12, 1822 — 3 — 428

Russell, of East Haven, m. Dorcas **ROSE**, of Branford,
  June 15, 1818 — 3 — 428

DARE, DEAR, David, s. George & Abigail, b. Aug. 23,
  1770 — 3 — 257

Georg[e], m. Abigail **WHEATON**, b. of Branford, Feb.
  4, 1755, by Rev. Philemon Robbins — 3 — 147

George, s. Georg[e] & Abigail, b. Mar. 9, 1755 — 3 — 147

Hannah, d. George & Abigail, b. Apr. 3, 1760 — 3 — 164

John, s. Georg[e] & Abigail, b. June 3, 1757 — 3 — 147

Jonathan, s. George & Abigail, b. Mar. 4, 1766 — 3 — 189

Sarah, d. George & Abigail, b. May 16, 1762 — 3 — 181

DARRIN, DARIN, [see also **DARWIN**], Adah, d. Joseph &
  Elisabeth, d. Nov. 21, 1767 — 3 — 196

Anne, d. Dan[ie]ll & Susanna, b. Sept. 21, 1759 — 3 — 159

Daniel, d. Nov. 30, 1756, in the 66-2nd y. of his age — 3 — 157

Dan[ie]ll, s. Dan[ie]ll & Susanna, b. Dec. 8, 1756 — 3 — 159

Henry, s. Dan[ie]ll & Susanna, b. Feb. 13, 1750 — 3 — 159

Hulda[h], d. Dan[ie]ll & Susanna, b. Aug. 12, 1765 — 3 — 185

Josiah, s. Dan[ie]ll & Susanna, b. Apr. 26, 1755;
  d. Jan. 14, 1756 — 3 — 159

Michael, s. Dan[ie]ll & Susanna, b. July 5, 1760 — 3 — 173

Oliver, s. Dan[ie]ll & Susanna, b. Feb. 9, 1748 — 3 — 159

Saba, d. Dan[ie]ll & Susanna, b. Sept. 30, 1752 — 3 — 159

Simeon, s. Daniel & Susanna, b. July 23, 1763 — 3 — 180

Stephen, s. Stephen & Lucy, b. Aug. 4, 1759 — 3 — 157

DARROW, Abigail, d. Rich[ar]d & Hannah, b. Apr. 7, 1745;
  d. Oct. 7, 1749 — 3 — 175

Abigail, d. Rich[ar]d & Hannah, b. Apr. 17, 1750 — 3 — 175

Amaziah, s. Rich[ar]d & Hannah, b. Dec. 26, 1747;
  d. Oct. 14, 1749 — 3 — 175

Amaziah, s. Rich[ar]d & Hannah, b. July 28, 1757 — 3 — 175

Elisabeth, d. Richard & Hannah, b. Mar. 21, 1737; d.

	Vol.	Page
DARROW, (cont.)		
Jan. 1, 1755	3	175
Hannah, d. Rich[ar]d & Hannah, b. Jan. 15, 1753	3	175
Jedediah, s. Richard & Hannah, b. Sept. 26, 1742	3	175
Mary, m. Jonathan **TOWNER**, Nov. 10, 1743, by		
Philema Robbins	3	138
Mary, d. Rich[ar]d & Hannah, b. Oct. 25, 1755; d.		
Dec. 27, 1755	3	175
Richard, m. Hannah **PARISH**, b. of Branford, Mar. 29,		
1736, by Phil[emo]n Robbins	3	175
Sarah, d. Rich[ar]d & Hannah, b. July 27, 1739	3	175
Sarah, m. Richard **LUCAS**, b. of Branford, Dec. 26,		
1758, by Philemon Robbins	3	176
Zaccheus, s. Richard & Hannah, b. Aug. 27, 1760	3	175
DARWIN, [see also **DARRIN**], Adah, [twin with Ethan], d.		
Joseph & Elisabeth, b. Sept. 5, 1746	3	110
Asenah, d. Joseph & Elisabeth, b. May 10, 1744	3	110
Clarice, d. Joseph & Elisabeth, b. Dec. 18, 1748	3	119
Ethan, [twin with Adah], s. Joseph & Elisabeth, b.		
Sept. 5, 1746	3	110
Ira, s. Joseph & Elisabeth, b. Sept. 22, 1751	3	132
Lucina, [twin with Sabrina], d. Joseph & Elisabeth,		
b. Aug. 9, 1754	3	137
Sabrina, [twin with Lucina], d. Joseph & Elisabeth,		
b. Aug. 9, 1754	3	137
[DAVENPORT], **DAUENPORT**, John, m. Abiga[i]ll		
PEIRSON, Nov. 27, [16]62	1	173
DAVIS, Charles S. A., of New Haven, m. Mary J. **DOWNS**,		
of Branford, Dec. 11, 1836, by Rev. Tim[othy] P.		
Gillett	3	373
Martha, m. Samuel **FORD**, b. of Branford, July 21,		
1762, by Jonathan Merrick	3	207
Samuel P., s. George R. & Sylvia, b. Apr. 4, 1850	TM3	243
DEAR, [see under **DARE**]		
DeBERARD, Charles Joseph, m. Polly **JOHNSON**, Aug. 10,		
1785, by Rev. Jason Atwater	3	272
Charles Joseph Jay, [s. Charles Joseph & Polly],		
b. Aug. 20, 1787	3	272
Grace, [d. Charles Joseph & Polly], b. May 3, 1794	3	272
Polly, [d. Charles Joseph & Polly], b. Oct. 21, 1791	3	272
Sally, [d. Charles Joseph & Polly], b. Nov. 24, 1797	3	272
DEE, Daniel, of Saybrook, m. Lucy **PLANT**, of Branford,		
Dec. 27, 1764, by Philemon Robbins	3	183
DENISON, Elisabeth, of South end, East Haven, m. Samuel		
HARRISON, July 3, 1707, by W[illia]m Maltbie,		
J. P.	3	32
DEW[E]Y, Frances, of Branford, m. Charles **CULVER**, of		
Waterbury, Nov. 25, 1841, by Rev. Davis T.		

	Vol.	Page
DEW[E]Y, (cont.)		
Shailer	TM3	153
DIBBLE, Caroline, d. Richard & Betsey, b. Jan. 19, 1844	TM3	230
Dency, of North Guilford, m. Roderick **HARRISON**, of		
Branford, Mar. 7, 1824, by Rev. Charles Atwater	3	425
Elizur Brockway, s. Richard & Betsey, b. June 13,		
1842	TM3	230
Phebe, m. Josiah **TALMAGE**, b. of East Hampton, Oct.		
14, 1735, by Nath[anie]ll Hunting	3	160
Richard, of Westbrook, m. Betsey **BROCKWAY**, of		
Branford, Apr. 6, 1841, by Rev. Timothy P. Gillett	TM3	153
----, s. Richard & Betsey, b. [ ], 184[8]	TM3	240
----,d. Richard & Betsey, b. May 15, 1851	TM3	245
DICKER, Thomas Frederick, of Sussex, Eng., m. Margaret		
HAMLIN, of Wallingford, Aug. 2, 1840, by Rev.		
Pascal P. Kidder	TM3	152
DICKERMAN, Charles, of Milwaukee, Wis., m. Jane E.		
FOOTE, of Branford, Feb. 22, 1848, by Rev.		
Timo[thy] P. Gillett	TM3	161
Jason, m. Lucretia **TALMAGE**, May 8, 1822, by Rev.		
Matthew Noyes	3	419
DOD[D], Ebenezer, s. Dani[e]ll, b. Dec. 11, [1651]	1	171
Mary, w. of Dani[e]ll, d. May 26, [16]57	1	170
Samuell, s. Dani[e]ll, b. May 2, [16]57	1	172
Steuen, s. Dani[e]ll, b. Feb. 16, 1654	1	172
----, d. Dani[e]ll, b. Mar. 29, 1654	1	171
DONA, [see under **DONEY**],		
DONEY, DONA, [see also **DUN**], James, m. Sarah		
FRISBIE, b. of Branford, Dec. 6, 1789	3	393
James, Capt., d. May 22, 1823, ae 80 y.	3	423
Sarah, d. Aug. 15, 1843, ae 86	TM3	305
DOUGLASS, John, s. Col. William & Hannah, b. Mar. 24,		
1775	3	266
John, of Northford, m. Ann **CARTER**, of Branford,		
Apr. 17, 1825, by Timothy P. Gillett	3	339
DOWNS, DOWN, DOWNES, Calvin, of Millford, m.		
Lucretia J. **WILLIAMS**, of Branford, June 24,		
1827, by Rev. Timothy P. Gillett	3	345
Lucy N., of Branford, m. William **PARDEE**, of		
Orange, Apr. 24, 1833, by Rev. Timothy P. Gillett	3	359
Mary, of New Haven, m. Daniel **LINSL[E]Y**, of		
Branford, Dec. 24, 1744, by Rev. Nathan Birdsey,		
of New Haven	3	104
Mary J., of Branford, m. Charles S. A. **DAVIS**, of		
New Haven, Dec. 11, 1836, by Rev. Tim[oth]y P.		
Gillett	3	373
DUDLEY, Alfred L., of Medina, O., m. Mary A.		
HARRISON, of Branford, Aug. 18, 1836, by		

	Vol.	Page
DUDLEY, (cont.)		
Rev. Timothy P. Gillett	3	372
Ann, of Guilford, m. Jacob **ROSE**, of Branford, Dec. 27, 1733, by Rev. Thomas Ruggles	3	86
Elizabeth, m. Titus **FARNON***, b. of Branford, Apr. 11, 1754, by Rev. Isaac Stiles (*First written "FARNOM")	3	140
Eunice, of Guilford, m. Jon[a]th[an] **RUSSELL**, Jr., of Branford, Dec. 5, 1787, by Thom[a]s W. Bray	3	258
Mabel, of G[u]ilford, m. Ebenezor **RUSSELL**, Apr. 30, 1754, by John Richards	3	140
Mabel, m. Elisha Davis **FORD**, Nov. 26, 1794	3	269
Mary R., m. Edmund M. **FIELD**, Aug. 9, 1835, by Rev. David Baldwin	3	371
Sarah, m. Edward **HARRISON**, b. of Branford, [Dec. 12, 1771]	3	265
DUN, [see also **DONEY**], Salley, d. of a transient woman, b. Dec. 11, 1781, at the house of John Roger, Jr.	3	304
DUNK, Sarah, m. James **BURGES**, b. of Branford, June 21, 1744, by Rev. Philemon Robbins	3	105
DURHAM, Mary, of Guilford, m. Caleb **PALMER**, of Branford, Jan. 11, 1737/8, by Rev. Thomas Ruggles, of Guilford	3	97
EARL, George W., ae 23 y., of New Haven, m. Frances M. **LAY**, ae 20 y., of Branford, Aug. 14, 1845, by Rev. Milton Bradley, at the house of Samuel Woodruff, of Richland Kalamazoo, Mich., Witnesses: Mrs. Elisabeth and Mrs. Celestia Parker	TM3	158
EBER, Magdalene, of Branford, m. John **EVERTON**, of New Haven, Jan. 10, 1767, by Samuel Barker, J. P.	3	190
Margaret, m. John **WHITE**, b. of Branford, Jan. 17, 1765, by Samuel Barker, J. P.	3	184
EELLS, Sam[ue]ll, Rev., of Branford, m. Mrs. Hannah **BUTLER**, of Middletown, Nov. 7, 1770, by Edw[ard] Eells	3	306
EG[G]LESTON, Joseph, s. Nathan[ie]ll & Hannah, b. Aug. 3, 1707	3	31
ELWELL, ELWEL, Catherine, d. Ebenezer & Catherine, b. Sept. 25, 1724	3	56
Ebenezer, s. Samuel & Sarah, b. Oct. 28, 1690	2	343
Eben[eze]r, m. Katherine **FANCHER**, Aug. 14, 1717, by Rev. Mr. Russel[l]	3	40
Ebenezer, s. Ebenezer & Catherine, b. June 9, 1721	3	48
Hannah, of Branford, m. Jeremiah **CONKLIN**, formerly of Greenwich, Great Brittain, Mar. 1, 1725/6, by Nathaniel Har[r]ison, J. P.	3	61

	Vol.	Page
ELWELL, ELWEL, (cont.)		
John, s. Joseph & Rebecca, b. Nov. 3, 1735	3	82
Jonathan, s. Ebenezer & Catherine, b. Jan. 1, 1730/1	3	70
Joseph, s. Sam[ue]ll & Sarah, b. Mar. 24, 1702/3	2	344
Joseph, m. Lydia **FINCH**, b. of Branford, Jan. 2, 1728/9, by Rev. Sam[ue]ll Russell	3	65
Joseph, s. Joseph & Lydia, b. Nov. 18, 1734	3	80
Judith, d. Ebenezer & Catherine, b. Sept. 20, 1726	3	62
Lydia, d. Eben[eze]r & Catherine, b. Aug. 9, 1728	3	66
Lydia, d. Jos[eph] & Rebecca, b. Oct. 31, 1737	3	89
Mary, m. Robert **OWENS**, b. of Branford, Feb. 23, 1725/6, by Nath[anie]ll Har[r]ison, J. P.	3	70
Mary, d. Joseph & Rebecca, b. June 5, 1740	3	94
Samuel, s. Sam[ue]ll & Sarah, b. Jan. 10, 1696/7	2	343
Sam[ue]ll, Jr., of Branford, m. Mary **JONES**, of New Haven, Oct. 12, 1720, by Sam[ue]ll Biship, J. P., at New Haven	3	45
Sarah, d. Samuel & Sarah, b. Feb. 11, 1693/4	2	343
Sarah, d. Ebenezer & Catherine, b. Jan. 4, 1722/3	3	54
Thankfull, d. Joseph & Lydia, b. July 20, 1732	3	75
---ary, d. Sam[ue]ll & Sarah, b. Mar. 8, 1707 (Mary?)	3	30
ELY, Frances Anna, d. C. Luther & Sarah L., b. Feb. 24, 1851	TM3	244
Luther C., ae 23 y., m. Sarah **BEERS**, ae 18 y., June 5, 1849, by T. P. Gillett	TM3	166
Luther C., of New Haven, m. Sarah L. **BEERS**, of Branford, June 5, 1850, by C. H. Topliff	TM3	165
EVARTS, Emely Cook, [d. William & Cornelia], b. Aug. 16, 1824	3	337
H., d. Aug. 27, 1849, ae 51 y.	TM3	309
William, of Branford, m. Cornelia **COOK**, of Wallingford, Feb. 6, 1820, by Rev. Matthew Noyes	3	414
William Augustus, [s. William & Cornelia], b. Apr. 7, 1821	3	337
EVERTON, Abigail, m. Elnathan **BEACH**, May 25, 1789	3	285
John, of New Haven, m. Magdalene **EBER**, of Branford, Jan. 10, 1767, by Samuel Barker, J. P.	3	190
FACTOR, Deborah, wid. of Jno., d. July 12, 1766, in the 64th y. of her age	3	259
John, d. Dec. 14, 1758	3	259
FALKNER, Sally, of Guilford, m. Obed **TYLER**, of Branford, June 24, 1835, by Timothy P. Gillett	3	369
FANCHER, Deborah, d. William & Thankfull, [b.] Jan. 27, 1728/9	3	66
Deborah, d. William & Thankfull, d. Dec. 5, 1739	3	66
John, s. William & Thankfull, b. June 1, 1731	3	72
Katherine, m. Eben[eze]r **ELWEL[L]**, Aug. 14, 1717, by Rev. Mr. Russel[l]	3	40
Samuel, s. William & Thankfull, b. Sept. 2, 1724	3	60
William, m. Thankfull **THOMSON**, b. of Branford, Nov. 20, 1723, by Rev. Sam[ue]ll Russell	3	54
William, s. William & Thankkfull, b. Oct. 20, 1726	3	60
FANNING, Sarah, Mrs., of New London, m. Will[ia]m **GOULD**,		

	Vol.	Page
FANNING, (cont.)		
of Branford, July 1, 1744, by Eliphalet Adams	3	102
Sarah, m. William **GOULD**, July 1, 1744	3	279
Thomas, s. Jonath[a]n & Elisabeth, b. July 10, 1720	3	45
FARLEY, John, s. Patrick & Mary, b. May 26, 1851	TM3	245
FARNUM, FARNOM, FARNO, Benjamin, of Andover, Mass., m,.		
Thankfull **FRISBEE**, wid., of Branford, Dec. 18, 1723,		
by Nath[anie]ll Har[r]ison, J. P.	3	54
Benjamin, m. Elisabeth **TYLER**, b. of Branford, June 3,		
1725, by Rev. Sam[ue]ll Russell	3	56
Benjamin, s. Benjamin & Elisabeth, b. Apr. 9, 1726	3	59
Beniamen, m. Mary **HOWD**, b. of Branford, in Northford,		
Mar. 7, 1750/1, by Rev. Warham Williams	3	149
Benjamen, s. Benjamen & Mary, b. Mar. 21, 1754	3	149
Elizabeth, d. Benjamen & Mary, b. Jan. 9, 1752	3	149
Elizebeth, wid., of Branford, m. Phinehas **BEACH**, of		
Wallingford, Mar. 27, 1758, by Ichabod Camp	3	157
Elissabeth, m. Abraham **NORTON**, Dec. 16, 1784, by Warham		
Williams	3	257
Mary, d. Benjamen & Mary, b. Sept. 22, 1756	3	149
Peter, s. Benjamin & Elisabeth, b. June 24, 1732	3	75
Peter, s. Benjamin & Elisabeth, d. Dec. 31, 1736	3	85
Peter, s. Titus & Elizabeth, b. Jan. 5, 1755	3	140
Thankfull, w. of Benj[ami]n, d. Aug. 23, 1724	3	55
Titus, m. Elizabeth **DUDLEY**, b. of Branford, Apr. 11,		
1754, by Rev. Isaac Stiles	3	140
Titus, d. Sept. 8, 1755, "in the army near Lake George"	3	140
FARRINGTON, FFARRINGTON, FARRINGTUN, Abigail, m.		
Sam[ue]ll **HOADL[E]Y**, Mar. 6, 1689	2	343
Abigail, m. William **GOULD**, June 11, 1718; d. May 25,		
1725, ae 49 y.	3	278
Desire, m. Jonathan **HAR[R]ISON**, b. of Branford, July 27,		
1726, by Rev. Sam[ue]ll Russell	3	62
Desire, d. Benjamin & Abigail, b. Mar. 30, [ ]	3	29
Jemima, of Dedham, m. Micah **PALMER**, Jr., of Branford,		
Dec. 23, 1725, by Rev. Sam[ue]ll Russell	3	61
Mary, of Dedham, Mass., m. Judah **PALMER**, of Branford,		
May 8, 1728, by Rev. Jonathan Mer[r]ick	3	78
FENN, Benjamin, of Milford, m. Mary **RUSSELL**, of Branford,		
Apr. 5, 1727, by Rev. Sam[ue]ll Russell	3	61
Benjamin, s. Benjamin & Mary, b. June 16, 1731	3	73
Benjamin, d. Jan. 3, 1731/2	3	73
Edwin, s. Clark & Sarah An[n], b. Nov. 29, 1847	TM3	239
Hubbard, of Wallingford, m. Jennett E. **WHITING**, of		
Branford, Nov. 24, 1839, by Rev. Davis T. Shailer	3	377
Mary, d. Benjamin & Mary, b. Jan. 3, 1727/8	3	73
FIELD, Chancellor Wilbur, [s. Danforth], b. Aug. 25, 1837	TM3	235
Clark Randall, [s. Danforth], b. July 12, 1844	TM3	235

	Vol.	Page
FIELD, (cont.)		
David Deforest, [s. Danforth], b. Feb. 24, 1841	TM3	235
Edmund Groving, [s. Danforth], b. Jan. 9, 1840	TM3	235
Edmund M., m. Mary R. **DUDLEY**, Aug. 9, 1835, by Rev.		
David Baldwin	3	371
Henrietta, d. May 14, 1849, ae 1 1/2 y.	TM3	308
Seneretta V., d. Danforth & Lucretia, b. Dec. 23, 1847		
(Henrietta?)	TM3	240
Stillman Kendal Wightman, [s. Danforth], b. Oct. 17, 1842	TM3	235
FINCH, FFINCE, Caleb, s. Ebenezer & Ruth, b. Feb. 5, 1774	3	259
David, of New Haven, m. Grace **TAINTER**, of Branford, Sept.		
26, 1822, by Rev. Samuel Luckey	3	420
Ebenezer, m. Ruth **FOOT**, b. of Branford, Nov. 29, 1773,		
by Samuel Andrus	3	259
Elam, s. Joseph & Chloe, b. July 25, 1756	3	156
Eunice, d. Ebenez[e]r & Ruth, b. June 11, 1792	3	261
Ichabod, s. Joseph & Chloe, b. May 9, 1768	3	263
Jesse Foot, s. Ebenezer & Ruth, b. May 27, 1777	3	269
John, s. Nath[anie]ll & Mary, [b.] 10br 20, 1699	2	346
Jonathan, s. Joseph & Chloe, b. Jan. 22, 1761	3	263
Joseph, m. wid. Chloe **TALMAGE**, b. of Branford, Sept. 16,		
1755, by Warham William	3	156
Joseph, s. Joseph & Chloe, b. Feb. 26, 1766	3	263
Joseph, d. May 17, 1768, ae 41	3	263
Lydia, d. Nath[anie]ll & Mary, b. Apr. 10, 1705	2	346
Lydia, m. Joseph **ELWELL**, b. of Branford, Jan. 2, 1728/9,		
by Rev. Sam[ue]ll Russell	3	65
Lydia had d. Bethyah **TYLER**, b. Dec. 27, 1757	3	156
Lydia had d. Bethyah **TYLER**, d. Feb. 5, 176[0]	3	159
Milton, s. Jonathan & Elizabeth, b. Sept. 13, 1789	3	264
Molle, d. Joseph & Chloe, b. Apr. 18, 1763	3	263
Nath[anie]ll, s. Nath[anie]ll & Mary, b. 8br 25, 1701	2	346
Orson, s. Jonathan & Elizabeth, b. May 15, 1795	3	264
Rumah, d. Jonathan & Elizabeth, b. July 1, 1792	3	264
Ruth, d. Ebenez[e]r & Ruth, b. Oct. 22, 1789	3	261
Sam[ue]ll, s. Ebenezer & Ruth, b. Nov. 10, 1784	3	261
Sarah, d. Joseph & Chloe, b. Aug. 27, 1758	3	156
Solomon, s. Ebenezer & Ruth, b. Sept. 19, 1781	3	261
FISK, Dorcas, of Haddam, m. Solomon **TYLER**, of Branford, Nov.		
9, 1772	3	298
Dorcas, of Haddam, m. Solomon **TYLER**, of Branford, Nov.		
10, 1772, by Eleazer May	3	208
FOOT, FOOTE, Aaron, s. Moses & Mary, b. July 5, 1738	3	98
Abiathar, [s. Rufus & Elizabeth], b. Apr. 16, 1804	3	409
Abigail, m. Jonathan **ROSE**, Aug. 15, 1697	2	345
Abigail, d. Joseph, Jr. & Anne, b. May 29, 1720	3	52
Abigail, of Branford, m. John **BIRD**, mariner, formerly		
of Philadelphia, now of Branford, Aug. 29, 1725,		

	Vol.	Page
FOOT, FOOTE, (cont.)		
by Nath[anie]ll Har[r]ison, J. P.	3	57
Abigail, d. Robert & Mary, b. June 15, 1737	3	87
Abigail, d. Robert & Mary, d. Dec. 17, 1738	3	91
Abigail, d. Robert & Mary, b. Dec. 22, 1739	3	91
Abigail, d. Ichabod & Hannah, b. Dec. 6, 1743	3	118
Abigail, d. Capt. Robert & Mary, d. Aug. 12, 1751	3	124
Abigail, d. Abraham & Abigail, b. July 25, 1752	3	170
Abigail, m. John **PLUYMERT**, b. of Branford, Sept. 10, 1782, by Warham Williams	3	265
Abigail, [d. Samuel & Lydia], b. Feb. 17, 1800	3	407
Abigail, m. W[illia]m **REYNOLDS**, Mar. 11, 1822, by Charles Atwater	3	418
Abraham, s. Joseph & Abigail, b. Dec. 28, 1704	2	345
Abraham, s. Robert & Mary, b. June 16, 1725	3	61
Abraham, of Branford, m. Abigail **ROGERS**, of Huntin[g]ton, I. I., Apr. 15, 1745, by Eben[eze]r Prime	3	170
Abraham, m. Mrs. Mary **PONSONBY**, July 20, 1784, by Bele Hubbard, Miss., New Haven	3	313
Active, d. Abraham & Abigail, b. Aug. 6, 1764	3	188
Ann, d. Joseph, Jr. & Ann, b. Sept. 15, 1729	3	67
Ann, d. Joseph, Jr. & Ann, d. Oct. 31, 1730	3	72
Ann, d. Joseph, Jr. & Ann, b. Oct. 24, 1731	3	72
Ann, m. Sam[ue]ll **ALLEN**, b. of Branford, May 8, 1754, by Rev. Philemon Robbins	3	136
Asa, s. Dan[ie]ll, Jr. & Sarah, b. July 5, 1737	3	116
Augustus, [s. Samuel & Lydia], b. Jan. 16, 1802; d. June 7, 1802	3	407
Augustus, [s. Samuel & Lydia], b. Sept. 13, 1804	3	407
Bela, [s. Rufus & Elizabeth], b. Jan. 31, 1800	3	409
Bela, [s. Rufus & Elizabeth], d. July 16, 1805	3	409
Bela Harrison, [s. Rufus & Elizabeth], b. June 28, 1816	3	409
Benjamin, s. Dan[ie]l & Mary, b. Aug. 1, 1778	3	277
Benjamin, of Branford, m. Sally P. **HALL**, of Wallingford, Apr. 24, 1803	3	277
Benjamin P., m. Sally Elisabeth **PAGE**, b. of Branford, Dec. 20, 1852, by Rev. T. P. Gillett	TM3	172
Benjamin Palmer, s. [Merit & Betsey], b. July 4, 1821	3	336
Betsey, [d. Ephraim & Mary], b. Feb. 27, 1816	3	408
Betsey, m. Harry **STEDMAN**, b. of Branford, Sept. 26, 1839, by Rev. Timothy P. Gillett	3	377
Betsey Blackstone, d. John & Fanny, b. Apr. 3, 1842	TM3	238
Celia, [d. Rufus & Elizabeth], b. May 14, 1809	3	409
Charles, [s. Walter R. & Sally A.], b. Aug. 29, 1822	3	336
Charles, [s. Walter R. & Sally A.], d. Jan. 30, 1824	3	336
Clarissa, d. Ephraim & L[e]ucy, b. Feb. 10, 1769; d. Aug. 17, 1775	3	271
Clarissa, of Branford, m. Isaac P. **LEET**, of Guilford,		

	Vol.	Page
FOOT, FOOTE, (cont.)		
Mar. 16, 1843, by Rev. Davis T. Shailer	TM3	155
Clarissa Lydia, d. Jonathan & Martha, b. June 12, 1821	3	419
Cynthia, d. Abraham & Abigail, b. Sept. 25, 1759	3	170
Daniel, s. Joseph & Abigail, b. May 19, 1695; d. about		
Nov. 19, 1695	2	345
Dan[ie]ll, s. Joseph & Abigail, b. Aug. 16, 1701	2	345
Daniel, m. Mary **BARKER**, b. of Branford, Sept. 27, 1721,		
by Rev. Sam[ue]ll Russell	3	57
Dan[ie]ll, s. Daniel, Jr. & Sarah, b. June 5, 1734	3	116
Dan[ie]ll, Jr., m. Mary **INGRAHAM**, b. of Branford, Feb.		
13, 1755, by Warham Williams	3	170
Dan[ie]ll, s. Dan[ie]ll, Jr. & Mary, b. Mar. 23, 1756;		
d. Aug. 7, 1756	3	170
Dan[ie]ll, s. Dan[ie]ll, Jr. & Mary, b. Dec. 7, 1760	3	170
David, s. Jos[e]h], Jr. & Ann, b. May 5, 1727	3	61
David, s. Moses & Mary, b. Nov. 11, 1730	3	69
David, s. Stephen, Jr. & Sybil, b. Nov. 1, 1750	3	127
David E., of Branford, m. Jane A. **ROWE**, of Fair Haven,		
Sept. 3, 1854, by Rev. T. P. Gillett	TM3	173
Delias, d. Elihu & Lucy, b. June 23, 1792	3	267
Dorcas, m. William **GOODRICH**, b. of Branford, Nov. 30,		
1720, by Rev. Sam[ue]ll Russel[l]	3	50
Dorothy, d. Moses & Mary, b. Mar. 26, 1729	3	69
Ebenezer, s. Robert & Mary, b. Jan. 7, 1733/4	3	79
Ebenezer, s. Moses & Mary, b. May 21, 1740	3	98
Ebenezer, m. Phebe **PALMER**, b. of Branford, July 8, 1755,		
by Jonathan Mer[r]ick	3	172
Edwin, s. Dan[ie]ll, Jr. & Mary, b. Aug. 20, 1759	3	170
Edwin, s. Elihu & Lucy, b. Dec. 2, 1790	3	267
Edwin Jonah, [s. David & Mary], b. Oct. 11, 1844	TM3	235
Elihu, s. Dan[ie]ll, Jr. & Mary, b. Aug. 19, 1757	3	170
Elihu, m. Lucy **WILLIAMS**, b. of Branford, Nov. 11, 1789	3	267
Elisa Charlotte, [d. David & Mary], b. Apr. 28, 1836	TM3	235
Eliza Pamelia, [d. Rufus & Elizabeth], b. June 7, 1806	3	409
[E]lisabeth, d. Stephen & Elisabeth, b. Nov. 10, 1709	3	30
Elisabeth, m. Joseph **TAINTOR**, Mar. 29, 1710, by Rev.		
Sam[ue]ll Russel[l]	3	32
Elisabeth, m. John **BLAKISTON**, b. of Branford, Apr. 2,		
1727, by Nath[anie]ll Har[r]ison, J. P.	3	64
Elisabeth, w. of John, d. Feb. 3, 1736/7	3	86
Elisabeth, of Colchester, m. Joseph **BARKER**, Jr., of Branford,		
Nov. 20, 1744, by Rev. Ephraim Litter, at Colchester	3	136
Elisabeth, d. Jonathan & Lydia, b. Sept. 5, 1767	3	198
Elizabeth, d. Jonathan & Martha, b. Mar. 6, 1816	3	419
Elizabeth, d. Jonathan & Martha, d. July 29, 1824, ae		
8 y. 4 m. 23 d.	3	355
Ellen A., ae 27, m. Miles T. **MERWIN**, ae 28, May 9, 1851 by		

	Vol.	Page
FOOT, FOOTE, (cont.)		
T. P. Gillett	TM3	170
Ellen Agnes, d. [Merit & Betsey], b. Dec. 14, 1823	3	336
Ellen Agnes, of Branford, m. Miles T. **MERWIN**, of Durham,		
May 8, 1851, by Rev. T. P. Gillett	TM3	169
Else, d. Abraham & Abigail, b. Oct. 19, 1756	3	170
Ephraim, m. Lucy **BARKER**, b. of Branford, July 31, 1760,		
by Philemon Robbins	3	271
Ephraim, s. Ephraim & Lucy, b. Sept. 1, 1775	3	271
Ephraim, d. Mar. 24, 1791, in the 64th y. of his age	3	259
Ephraim, m. Mary **HOBART**, b. of Branford, Sept. 15, 1802	3	408
Ephraim, d. Jan. 15, 1846, ae [ ]	TM3	306
Eunice, d. Jonathan & Lydia, b. July 26, 1731	3	73
Fanny, m. Jacob **PALMER**, b. of Branford, Apr. 23, 1800	3	284
Foster, d. [ ], 1823	3	424
Gideon, s. Robert & Mary, b. Feb. 19, 1729/30; d. Apr. 1. 1730	3	68
Hannah, d. Isaac & Rebec[c]ah, b. Feb. 28, 1711/12	3	33
Hannah, d. Dan[ie]ll, Jr. & Sarah, b. Apr. 22, 1730	3	77
Hannah, Mrs., m. Rev. Philemon **ROBBINS**, b. of Branford,		
Dec. 24, 1735, by Rev. Jonathan Mer[r]ick	3	83
Hannah, d. Ichabod & Hannah, b. Jan. 30, 1741/2	3	98
Hannah, m. Nathan **POTTER**, b. of Branford, Apr. 29, 1760,		
by Josiah Rogers, J. P.	3	168
Hannah, [d. Ephraim & Mary], b. Feb. 7, 1821	3	408
Harriet, d. [Merit & Betsey], b. Apr. 19, 1819	3	336
Harriet, m. Frederic **LINSLEY**, b. of Branford, Mar. 18,		
1845, by Rev. Timothy P. Gillett	TM3	157
Harrison, [s. Ephraim & Mary], b. May 27, 1803	3	408
Harrison, m. Marcia **MILLER**, b. of Branford,		
Jan. 27, 1839, by Rev. T. P. Gillett	3	376
Harrison, d. Aug. 6, 1848, ae 1 1/2 y.	TM3	308
Hulda[h], d. Dan[ie]ll, Sr. & Mary, b. Mar. 3, 1728/9	3	72
Huldah, m. Dan[ie]ll **BARKER**, Jr., b. of Branford, Nov.		
4, 1762, by Jonathan Merrick	3	178
Ichabod, m. Hannah **HARRISON**, b. of Branford, Mar. 4,		
1733/4, by Rev. Philemon Robbins	3	95
Ichabod, s. Ichabod & Hannah, b. Feb. 24, 1746/7	3	118
Ichabod, d. Sept. 11, 1773	3	256
Isaac, s. Robert, b. Dec. 14, 1672	1	174
Isaac, s. James & Rebeccah, b. July 16, 1717	3	41
Isaac, d. Feb. 11, 1758	3	150
Jacob, s. Isaac & Rebec[c]ah, b. Feb. 19, 1709/10	3	33
Jacob, s. Dan[ie]ll, Jr. & Sarah, b. Mar. 20, 1731/2	3	77
Jane E., of Branford, m. Charles **DICKERMAN**, of		
Milwaukee, Wis., Feb. 22, 1848, by Rev. Timo[thy] P.		
Gillett	TM3	161
Jared, s. Ichabod & Hannah, b. July 17, 1735	3	95
Jared, s. Nathaniel, Jr. & Mary, b. Mar. 12, 1762	3	204

	Vol.	Page
FOOT, FOOTE, (cont.)		
Jared, d. Aug. 30, 1833, ae 71	3	362
Jerusha, d. Jonathan & Lydia, b. Oct. 1, 1728	3	73
Jerusha, d. Abraham & Abigail, b. Oct. 22, 1746	3	170
John, s. Robert, b. July 24, 1670	1	174
John, m. Elisabeth **FRISBIE**, b. of Branford, Dec. 25,		
1733, by Rev. Jonathan Merrick	3	80
John, s. Ichabod & Hannah, b. Feb. 18, 1740	3	95
John, s. John & Abigail, b. Apr. 2, 1742	3	139
John, 2d, of Branford, m. Ruth **CULVER**, of Wallingford,		
Nov. 7, 1771, by Rev. Sam[ue]ll Andrus	3	256
John, s. John, 2d, & Ruth, b. July 25, 1772	3	256
John, s. Jon[a]th[an] & Lydia, b. Jan. 26, 1777	3	300
John, [s. Ephraim & Mary], b. Dec. 23, 1805	3	408
John, m. Silvia **ROSE**, b. of Branford, Jan. 6, 1831, by		
Rev. Zolva Whitman, of North Guilford	3	356
John, m. Fanny **BLACKSTONE**, b. of Branford, Feb. 28,		
1838, by Rev. Timothy P. Gillett	3	375
Jonathan, m. Lydia **SUTLIFF**, b. of Branford, June 14,		
1727, by Rev. Isaac Stiles	3	73
Jonathan, s. John & Elisabeth, b. Jan. 28, 1736/7	3	86
Jonathan, m. Lydia **BALDWIN**, b. of Branford, Nov. 19,		
1761, by Philemon Robbins	3	174
Jonathan, s. Jonathan & Lydia, b. May 3, 1765	3	198
Jonathan, s. Ephraim & Lucy, b. Mar. 13, 1772	3	271
Jonathan, m. Martha **FRISBIE**, b. of Branford, Dec. 8, 1808	3	388
Jonathan, s. Jonathan & Martha, b. Jan. 28, 1814	3	419
Jonathan, [s. Samuel & Lydia], b. Feb. 16, 1815	3	407
Joseph, s. Joseph & Abigail, b. June 20, 1691	2	345
Joseph, Jr., of Branford, m. Anne **JOHNSON**, of New Haven,		
Nov. 19, 1717, at New Haven	3	43
Joseph, s. Joseph, Jr. & Anne, b. Apr. 2, 1722	3	52
Joseph, s. Ichabod & Hannah, b. Mar. 3, 1737	3	95
Joseph, s. Joseph, Jr. & Ann, d. Aug. 4, 1727	3	63
Keturah, d. Stephen, Jr. & Sybil, b. Nov. 19, 1748	3	127
Lodemia, [d. Samuel & Lydia], b. May 10, 1810	3	407
Lodema, m. Lester **PALMER**, Nov. 4, 1829, by Rev. J. A.		
Root	3	350
Lois, d. Isaac, Jr. & Mary, b. Oct. 30, 1740	3	107
Luce, d. Dan[ie]ll, Sr. & Mary, b. Oct. 7, 1727	3	72
Lucy, d. Ephraim & Lucy, b. May 28, 1766; d. July 24, 1773	3	271
Lucy, m. Ephraim **PARRISH**, Apr. 9, 1801	3	398
Lucy, [d. Jonathan & Martha], b. Dec. 3, 1810	3	388
Lucy, d. Feb. 20, 1848, ae 37 y.	TM3	308
Lucy Clarissa, d. Ephraim & Leucy, b. Feb. 24, 1778	3	272
Lucy Clarissa, d. May 28, 1797	3	274
Lurinda, d. Abraham & Abigail, b. June 30, 1754	3	170
Lidia, d. Stephen & Elisabeth, b. Sept. 1, 1712	3	35

	Vol.	Page
FOOT, FOOTE, (cont.)		
Lydia, d. Robert & Mary, b. Mar. 23, 1727/8	3	66
Lydia, d. Robert & Mary, d. Jan. 2, 1739/40	3	91
Lydia, d. Robert & Mary, b. Apr. 12, 1743	3	100
Lydia, d. Moses & Ruth, b. Nov. 30, 1743	3	101
Lydia, d. Moses & Ruth, b. Nov. 30, 1743	3	106
Lydia had s. Ebenezer **BALDWIN**, Mar. 21, 1769	3	197
Lydia, d. Jonathan & Lydia, b. June 11, 1770	3	258
Lydia, d. Jon[a]th[an] & Lydia, b. June 11, 1770	3	300
Lydia, m. Ebenezer **BALDWIN**, b. of Branford, Jan. 27, 1771, by Samuel Eells	3	205
Lydia, [twin with Samuel], d. [Samuel & Lydia], b. Sept. 21, 1796	3	407
Lydia, [d. Foster & Mary], b. Feb. 4, 1823	3	342
Lydia, wid. of Jonathan, d. May 9, 1825	3	339
Margaret, [d. Rufus & Elizabeth], b. [ ] 10, 1813	3	409
Martha, d. Jonathan & Martha, b. Apr. 21, 1818	3	419
Mary, d. Stephen & Elisabeth, b. Sept. 27, 1715	3	39
Mary, d. Robert & Mary, b. Apr. 9, 1722	3	55
Mary, d. Dan[ie]ll & Mary, b. Dec. 8, 1724	3	57
Mary, m. Orchard **GUY**, b. of Branford, Dec. 5, 1733, by Rev. Philemon Robbins	3	80
Mary, d. Moses & Mary, b. Oct. 9, 1736	3	98
Mary, m. Jonathan **ROGERS**, b. of Branford, Dec. 6, 1738, by Jonathan Mer[r]ick	3	93
Mary, d. Abraham & Abigail, b. Oct. 15, 1748	3	170
Mary, [d. Ephraim & Mary], b. Mar. 31, 1808	3	408
Mary, [d. Foster & Mary], b. May 10, 1816	3	342
Mary, m. Wyllys **BEACH**, b. of Branford, Oct. 29, 1835, by Rev. Tim[othy] P. Gillett	3	371
Mary, d. John & Fanny, b. Feb. 26, 1848	TM3	239
Merit, b. June 19, 1795	3	339
Merit, m. Betsey **PALMER**, b. of Branford, June 18, 1818	3	336
Moses, of Branford, m. Mary **BYINTUN**, of Branford, June 22, 1726, by Rev. Sam[ue]ll Russell	3	65
Moses, s. Moses & Mary, b. Oct. 3, 1734	3	81
Moses, m. Ruth **BUTLER**, b. of Branford, Nov. 5, 1740, by Rev. Jon[a]th[an] Mer[r]ick	3	98
Nath[anie]ll, m. Hannah **FRISBEE**, Mar. 2, 1719/20, by Nath[anie]ll Harrison, J. P.	3	47
Nathaniel, s. Nath[anie]ll & Hannah, b. Oct. 15, 1723	3	53
Nath[anie]l, Jr., of Branford, m. Mary **JONES**, of Guilford, Jan. 26, 1758, by James Sproutt	3	204
Noah, s. Walter R. & Sally A., b. Jan. 17, 1825	3	339
Noah Baldwin, d. Jon[a]th[an] & Lydia, b. Mar. [ ], 1777	3	300
Obed, s. Moses & Ruth, b. Nov. 25, 1741	3	98
Pamelia, [d. Rufus & Elizabeth], b. Jan. 9, 1802	3	409
Parmelia, [d. Rufus & Elizabeth], d. July 25, 1805	3	409

	Vol.	Page
FOOT, FOOTE, (cont.)		
Phinehas, s. Ephraim & Lucy, b. Oct. 26, 1763	3	271
Polly, m. Timothy **JOHNSON**, Sept. 27, 1800	3	277
Polly Ann, [d. Rufus & Elizabeth], b. Aug. 16, 1811	3	409
Rebec[c]ah, d. Stephen & Elisabeth, b. Oct. 20, 1723	3	53
Rebeccah, d. Moses & Mary, b. Apr. 10, 1727	3	65
Rebecca, d. Isaac, Jr. & Mary, b. Apr. 25, 1739	3	107
Rebecca, m. Isaiah **BUTLAR**, Jr., b. of Branford, Jan. 3, 1749/50, by Rev. Jonathan Mer[r]ick	3	120
Rebecca, m. Sam[ue]ll **MALTBIE**, Jr., b. of Branford, Jan. 22, 1745/6, by Rev. Philemon Robbins	3	108
Rebeckah, w. of Isaac, d. Oct. 13, 1757	3	150
Rebecca, d. Ephraim & Lucy, b. May 6, 1761	3	271
Rebeccah, m. John **BLACKSTONE**, Jr., b. of Branford, Nov. 13, 1789	3	387
Robert, s. Joseph & Abigail, b. May 31, 1699	2	345
Robert, m. Mary **LINSL[E]Y**, b. of Branford, Jan. 25, 1720/1, by Rev. Sam[ue]ll Russell	3	45
Robart, Capt., d. June 14, 1761, ae 63 y.	3	290
Robert, s. Samuel & Sarah E., b. Feb. 19, 1851	TM3	244
Robert Abraham Ebenezer, s. Abraham & Abigail, b. Sept. 16, 1766	3	190
Rufus, b. Mar. 24, 1771; m. Elizabeth **HARRISON**, Mar. 12, 1799	3	409
Ruth, d. Moses & Mary, b. Aug. 1, 1732	3	80
Ruth, m. Ebenezer **FINCH**, b. of Branford, Nov. 29, 1773, by Samuel Andrus	3	259
Sally, [d. Ephraim & Mary], b. May 14, 1810; d. Apr. 20, 1817	3	408
Sally, [d. Ephraim & Mary], b. Oct. 23, 1818	3	408
Sally, m. Elizur **ROGERS**, b. of Branford, Apr. 20, 1843, by Rev. Timothy P. Gillett	TM3	156
Sally H., d. Benjamin & Sally P., b. Feb. 11, 1804; d. May 13, 1804	3	277
Sally P., w. Benjamin, d. July 25, 1804	3	277
Sam[ue]ll, s. Joseph & Abigail, b. Dec. 25, 1696	2	345
Sam[ue]ll, s. Jos[eph] & Anne, b. Jan. 8, 1718	3	43
Samuel, s. Joseph, Jr. & Ann, d. Feb. 28, 1732/3	3	76
Samuel, s. Dan[ie]ll, Jr. & Sarah, b. May 12, 1740	3	116
Samuel, s. Nath[anie]l, Jr. & Mary, b. Feb. 19, 1759	3	204
Samuel, m. Anne **HARRISON**, b. of Branford, Dec. 27, 1765, by Warham Williams	3	186
Samuel, s. Jonathan & Lydia, b. May 21, 1773	3	258
Samuel, s. Jon[a]th[an] & Lydia, b. May [ ], 1773	3	300
Sam[ue]ll, s. Ephraim & Leucy, b. May 16, 1780	3	272
Samuel, m. Lydia **BALDWIN**, Dec. 2, 1795	3	407
Samuel, [twin with Lydia], s. [Samuel & Lydia], b. Sept. 21, 1796	3	407
Samuel, [s. Ephraim & Mary], b. Sept. 18, 1812	3	408

	Vol.	Page
FOOT, FOOTE, (cont.)		
Samuel Albert, [s. David & Mary], b. May 9, 1842	TM3	235
Sarah, d. Nath[anie]ll & Hannah, b. Mar. 6, 1720/1	3	48
Sarah, d. Dan[ie]ll, Jr. & Sarah, b. Dec. 1, 1727	3	77
Sarah, m. Joseph HAR[R]ISON, b. of Branford, Apr. 10,		
1729, by Rev. Sam[ue]ll Russell	3	66
Sarah, wid., m. John TAINTOR, b. of Branford, May 9,		
1745, by Rev. Jonathan Mer[r]ick	3	116
Sarah, m. Michael TAINTOR, b. of Branford, Feb. 25,		
1747, by Jonathan Merrick	3	165
Sarah, m. Timothy GOODRIDG[E], b. of Branford, Mar. 24,		
1748, by Philemon Robbins	3	151
Sarah, d. Nathaniel, Jr. & Mary, b. Feb. 13, 1767	3	204
Sarah, [d. Walter R. & Sally A.], b. Apr. 6, 1818	3	336
Sarah Almira, d. of Stephen, m. Orin D. SQUIRE, May 23,		
1842, by Rev. Mr. Forbes, in St. Thomas Church, New		
York City	TM3	160
Silence, d. Joseph, Jr. & Ann, b. Apr. 2, 1737	3	86
Silence, d. Stephen, Jr. & Sibil, b. Apr. 28, 1753	3	135
Stephen, s. Joseph, Jr. & Anne, b. Aug. 20, 1724	3	56
Stephen, Jr., of Branford, m. Sybil FOSTER, of South		
Hampton, L. I., Nov. 5, 1747, by Rev. Jonath[a]n		
Mer[r]ick	3	127
Stephen, d. Oct. 23, 1762, in the 89th y. of his age	3	182
Stephen, [s. Foster & Mary], b. Oct. 23, 1812	3	342
Sybil, d. Nathaniel, Jr. & Mary, b. Jan. 24, 1765	3	204
Thankful, d. Sam[ue]ll & Abigail, b. Nov. 3, 1694	2	345
Thankful, m. Jonathan FRISBEE, Aug. 10, 1713, by		
Nathan[ie]ll Harrison, J. P.	3	38
Thankfull, d. Robert & Mary, b. Feb. 6, 1730/1	3	71
Thankfull, d. Jos[eph], Jr. & Ann, b. Feb. 15, 1733/4	3	86
Thankful, m. Jacob BAKER, b. of Branford, Dec. 7, 1749,		
by Rev. Jonath[a]n Mer[r]ick	3	124
Thankfull, d. Stephen, Jr. & Sibbel, b. Oct. 12, 1755	3	141
Thankful, d. Ebenezer & Phebe, b. Sept. 24, 1759	3	172
Thankfull, m. Isaac SMITH, b. of Branford, Apr. 1, 1779,		
by Sam[ue]ll Eells	3	285
Walter R., m. Sally A. HARRISON, b. of Branford, Nov. 20,		
1817, by Charles Atwater	3	336
William, s. Walter R. & Sally A., b. Jan. 27, 1827	3	351
W[illia]m Russell, s. Sam[ue]ll & Sarah, b. June 3, 1848	TM3	239
William Sidney, m. Mary BUTLER, b. of [North] Branford,		
Aug. 27, 1827, by Rev. Timothy P. Gillett	3	345
----, s. Jonathan & Lydia, b. June 24, 1762; d. day following	3	198
FORBES, FORBS, Elijah, m. [Ollive] PAGE, Dec. 23, 1780	3	283
Levi, d. Apr. 30, 1850, ae 65 y.	TM3	309
Levins G., of Branford, m. Sarah A. CONNER, of Cheshire,		
Oct. 18, 1845, by Rev. A. C. Wheat	TM3	158

	Vol.	Page
FORBES, FORBS, (cont.)		
Sam[ue]ll, s. Elijah & Ollive, b. Jan. 15, 1783	3	283
----, s. Levens & Eliza, b. Apr. [ ], 1851	TM3	243
FORD, Belinda, d. Elisha D. & Mabel, b. Jan. 6, 1796	3	269
Chloe, d. Sam[ue]ll & Hannah, b. Sept. 2, 1753	3	135
Dan[ie]ll, s. Sam[ue]ll & Hannah, b. Apr. 2, 1751	3	126
Elisha Davis, s. Samuel & Martha, b. Sept. 9, 1767	3	207
Elisha Davis, s. Sam[ue]ll & Marhta, b. Sept 9, 1767	3	299
Elisha Davis, m. Mabel **DUDLEY**, Nov. 26, 1794	3	269
Gamaliel, s. John & Hannah, b. Dec. 15, 1745	3	110
Gamalee1, s. John & Hannah, b. Feb. 6, 1749/50	3	120
Hannah, d. Sam[ue]ll & Hannah, b. July 13, 1738	3	90
Hannah, d. John & Hannah, b. July 14, 1752	3	130
Jerusha, d. Sam[ue]ll & Martha, b. Dec. 24, 1780	3	299
John, m. Hannah **HOWD**, b. of Branford, May 24, 1745, by		
Jno. Russell, J. P.	3	110
John, s. John & Hannah, b. Nov. 11, 1748	3	120
Lois, d. Sam[ue]ll & Hannah, b. Nov. 8, 1746	3	110
Lois, d. Sam[ue]ll & Martha, b. Oct. 13, 1774	3	299
Lois, m. Othniel **STENT**, b. of Branford, Feb. 13, 1782,		
by Sam[ue]ll Eells	3	288
Lois, m. Benjamin **PAGE**, b. of Branford, May 16, 1798,		
by Rev. Samuel Eells	3	271
Martin, s. Samuel & Martha, b. May 21, 1764	3	207
Martin, s. Samuel & Martha, d. Nov. 14, 1766	3	207
Rhoda, d. Sam[ue]ll & Hannah, b. Dec. 27, 1748	3	118
Rhoda, m. Eleazer **STENT**, Jr., b. of Branford, June 21,		
1769, by Philemon Robbins	3	201
Ruth, d. John & Hannah, b. Jan. 17, 1746/7	3	110
Sally, d. Sam[ue]ll & Martha, b. Mar. 16, 1783	3	299
Samuel, s. Samuel & Hannah, b. Aug. 21, 1740	3	93
Samuel, d. June 27, 1757	3	152
Samuel, m. Martha **DAVIS**, b. of Branford, July 21, 1762,		
by Jonathan Merrick	3	207
Samuel, s. Samuel & Martha, b. Nov. 5, 1769	3	207
Samuel, s. Samuel & Martha, b. Nov. 5, 1769	3	299
Sam[ue][ll, s. Sam[ue]ll & Martha, d. Oct. 6, 1775	3	299
Sam[ue]ll, s. Sam[ue]ll & Martha, b. July 18, 1778	3	299
Sarah, d. Sam[ue]ll & Hannah, b. Apr. 7, 1744	3	103
Sarah, d. Samuel & Martha, b. July 12, 1766	3	207
Sarah, d. Samuel & Martha, d. Nov. 17, 1766	3	207
Sarah, d. Sam[ue]ll & Martha, b. July 11, 1776	3	299
Sarah, d. Sam[ue]ll & Martha, d. July 21, 1777	3	299
William, s. Samuel & Martha, b. Mar. 9, 1772	3	207
William, s. Sam[ue]ll & Martha, b. Mar. 9, 1772	3	299
William, s. Sam[ue]ll & Martha, d. Sept. 13, 1774	3	299
William, s. Elisha D. & Mabel, b. June 12, 1799	3	273
William, m. Sarah **ROSE**, b. of Branford, [1830?],		

	Vol.	Page
FORD, (cont.)		
by J. A. Root. Recorded July 4, 1830	3	353
FOSDICK, Clorenda, of Weathersfield, m. Timothy **HARRISON**,		
Jr. of Branford, Mar. 14, 1776, by John March, Clerk	3	272
FOSTER, Chloe, of Long Island, m. Timothy **MORRIS**, of		
Branford, Sept. 6, 1762, on Long Island	3	294
Sybil, of South Hampton, L. I., m. Stephen **FOOT**, Jr.,		
of Branford, Nov. 5, 1747, by Rev. Jonath[a]n Mer[r]ick	3	127
William, of Meriden, m. Julia **ROGERS**, of Branford, Apr.		
25, 1826, by Rev. Timothy P. Gillett	3	341
FOWLER, Abigail, alias **BEWEL**, had d. Betsey, b. Mar. 26, 1776	3	307
Abigail, alias **BEWEL**, had d. Clarissa, b. Mar. 23, 1778	3	307
Abigail, alias **BEWEL**, had s. Hennerity, b. May 5, 1782	3	307
Abigail, of Branford, m. James **HOOPPER**, of Bristol, Feb.		
4, 1784, by Sam[ue]ll Eells	3	303
Betsey, alias **BEWEL**, d. Abigail, b. Mar. 26, 1776	3	307
Betsey, d. Eli & Mary, b. June 21, 1800	3	284
Betsey, of Branford, m. Henry E. **HODGES**, of Torrington,		
Sept. 13, 1821, by Rev. Timothy P. Gillett	3	413
Caroline, of Guilford, m. Nathan **CLARK**, of Orange, Mar.		
7, 1824, by Rev. Timothy P. Gillett	3	425
Charles Augustus, s. Ozias & Est[h]er, b. Oct. 27, 1828	3	350
Clarissa, alias **BEWEL**, d. Abigail, b. Mar. 23, 1778	3	307
Ebenezer **HOADL[E]Y**, s. Josiah, Jr. & Lydia, b. Dec. 30,		
1782	3	313
Eli, d. Sept. 30, 1850, ae 85 y.	TM3	310
Elihu, s. Josiah & Ruth, b. Aug. 4, 1754	3	137
Elihu, s. Elihu **FOWLER** & Rhoda **WAY**, b. July 27, 1810	3	346
Elihu, d. May 4, 1821, ae 67 y.	3	417
Elisabeth, of Durham, m. Benj[ami]n **MALTBIE**, of Branford,		
Oct. 26, 1752, by Nath[anie]ll Chauncey	3	171
Esther Pamela, d. Ozias & Esther Prudence, b. Mar. 16, 1825	3	341
Eunis, of G[u]ilford, m. Phinias **GOODRIDG[E]**, of Branford,		
Jan. 15, 1756, by John Richards, North G[u]ilford	3	149
Eunice, d. Eli & Mary, b. Feb. 9, 1793	3	264
Fanny, d. Eli & Mary, b. Apr. 24, 1788	3	264
Fanny, m. Abraham **ROGERS**, Jr., Nov. 16, 1809	3	404
Frederick W., of Guilford, m. Nancy **GRANT**, of Branford,		
Oct. 19, 1830, by Timothy P. Gillett	3	356
Hennerity, alias **BEWEL**, s. Abigail, b. May 5, 1782	3	307
Hervey H., of Washington, m. Betsey Ann **FRISBIE**, of		
Branford, Aug. 9, 1830, by Rev. C. A. Boardman, of New		
Haven	3	353
Isaac, s. Josiah & Ruth, b. Dec. 14, 1758	3	158
James H., m. Sophia T. **CHURCH**, Apr. 10, 1843, by Rev.		
Davis T. Shailer	TM3	156
Joseph Seth, twin with William Sereno, s. Ozias & Esther		
Prudence, b. Mar. 12, 1827	3	347

	Vol.	Page

FOWLER, (cont.)

Josiah, of Branford, m. Ruth **HALL**, of Wallingford, Feb.
13, 1752, by Rev. Sam[ue]ll Hall — 3 — 133

Josiah, s. Josiah & Ruth, b. Jan. 30, 1753 — 3 — 134

Josiah, Jr., m. Lydia **HOADL[E]Y**, b. of Branford, Feb. 17,
1779, by Warham Williams — 3 — 312

Josiah, s. Josiah, Jr. & Lydia, b. June 20, 1780 — 3 — 313

Lavinia, of Northford, m. Stephen H. **BROOKS**, [Jan.] 10,
[1821], by Origen P. Holcomb — 3 — 413

Leveret, s. Josiah, Jr. & Lydia, b. Apr. 2, 1787 — 3 — 315

Louisa Huntington, d. James H. & Sophia T., b. May 7, 1844 — TM3 — 237

Lydia, d. Josiah, Jr. & Lydia, b. Oct. 16, 1784 — 3 — 313

Marietta, m. Melzar F. **BARTLETT**, b. of Guilford, Apr. 8,
1832, by Rev. Timothy P. Gillett — 3 — 357

Mary, of Guilford, m. Sam[ue]ll **MALTBIE**, of Branford,
May 1, 1755, by Ichabod Camp — 3 — 169

Ozias, of Branford, m. Lucy **JONES**, of Wallingford, Nov.
13, 1839, by Rev. Timothy P. Gillett — 3 — 377

Polly, d. Eli & Mary, b. June 30, 1795 — 3 — 265

Polly, m. James F. **LINSLEY**, b. of Branford, Sept. 11, 1817 — 3 — 407

Rachel, of Guilford, m. Josiah **LINSL[E]Y**, of Branford,
Feb. 6, 1767, by Amos Fowler — 3 — 191

Rebecca, d. of Daniel, of Guilford, m. David **HUDSON**, of
Branford, Aug. 23, 1755, by Rev. John Richards, at
Guilford — 3 — 143

Samuel Ozias, s. Ozias & Esther Prudence, b. Aug. 31, 1822 — 3 — 432

Sarah H., of Guilford, m. Darling **BARTHOLOMEW**, of
Northford, June 11, 1827, by Rev. Timo[thy] P. Gillett — 3 — 344

Stephen, s. Josiah & Ruth, b. Mar. 8, 1756 — 3 — 145

Will[ia]m Henry, s. James & Sophia, b. Mar. [ ], 1850 — TM3 — 242

William Sereno, twin with Joseph Seth, s. Ozias & Esther
Prudence, b. Mar. 12, 1827 — 3 — 347

FOX, Sylva, of Barnards Town, Mass., m. Darius **NICHOLS**, of
Gill, Mass., May 16, 1814 — TM3 — 159

FRANKLIN, Phebe, of Sag Harbor, L. I., m. Richard Alsop
HOWD, of Branford, Dec. 14, 1801 — 3 — 427

Sally, of Sag Harbor, L. I., m. Isaac **ROGERS**, Jr., of
Branford, Nov. 30, 1813, by Rev. Timothy P. Gillett — 3 — 363

FRIEND, George, of Norwalk, m. Mary **LAMFIER**, of Branford,
June 10, 1778, by Phile[mo]n Robbins — 3 — 296

George, d. Apr. 23, 1786, in the 40th y. of his age — 3 — 257

Polle, d. George & Mary, b. May 20, 1784 — 3 — 309

Sally, d. George & Mary, b. July 4, 1782 — 3 — 296

**FRISBIE, FRISBY, FFRISSBE, FRISBE, FRISBEE, FRISBY,
FFRISBIE**, [see also **FRISSELL**], Abel, s. Caleb & Mary, b. Mar,
8, 1742/3 — 3 — 114

Abel, of Branford, m. Rebecca **HAYS**, of New Haven, June
3, 1771, by Philemon Robbins — 3 — 203

	Vol.	Page
FRISBIE, FRISBY, FFRISSBE, FRISBE, FRISBEE, FRISBY,		
FFRISBIE, (cont.)		
Abiel, s. Jonathan & Mary, b. May 26, 1695	2	343
Abiel, m. Elisabeth **ROGERS**, July 25, 1722, by Rev.		
Sam[ue]ll Russel[l]	3	49
Abiel, s. Ezekiel & Elisabeth, b. July 16, 1759	3	165
Abigail, d. Benjamin & Elisabeth, b. June 23, 1709	3	34
Abigail, d. Joseph & Abigail, b. Dec. 14, 1715	3	47
Abigail, m. William **BARKER**, Jr., b. of Branford, Dec. 5,		
1725, by Nath[anie]ll Har[r]ison, J. P.	3	60
Abigail, d. Sam[ue]ll, Jr. & Rachel, b. Dec . 6, 1742	3	108
Abigail, d. Jacob & Ruth, b. July 19, 1752	3	163
Abigail, d. Nath[anie]ll & Abigail, b. Nov. 3, 1755	3	152
Abigail, m. Noah **BALDWIN**, Jr., b. of Branford, Jan. 12,		
1763, by Philemon Robbins	3	179
Abigail, w. of Joseph, d. June 14, 1763, ae 73	3	182
Abigail, d. Timothy & Mary, b. Mar. 9, 1765	3	187
Abigail, of Woodbury, m. Rufus **LINSLEY**, of Branford, May		
29, 1777	3	291
Abigail, m. Ira **HOTCHKISS**, b. of Branford, Mar. 30, 1782,		
by Sam[ue]ll Eells	3	279
Abigail, w. of Nath[anie]l, d. Apr. 17, 1782	3	279
Abigail, d. Abraham & Olive, b. Nov. 12, 1803	3	281
Abraham, s. Caleb & Hannah, b. July 4, 1705	2	346
Abraham, s. Nath[anie]ll & Abigail, b. Aug. 23, 1762	3	185
Abraham, m. Olive **BUTLER**, Feb. 14, 1787	3	274
Adah, d. John, Jr. & Freelove, b. Dec. 10, 1769	3	202
Alfred, [s. Thomas, Jr. & Mary], b. Dec. 2, 1796	3	273
Alonso P., m. Henrietta **LINSLEY**, b. of Branford, Dec.		
25, 1844, by Rev. Frederick Miller	TM3	157
Amos, s. Eben[eze]r & Joanna, b. Feb. 17, 1728/9	3	68
Anna, d. Eben[eze]r, Jr. & Silence, b. May 7, 1734	3	82
Anne, d. John, Jr. & Freelove, b. Apr. 12, 1761	3	173
Anne, d. Lydia **GOODSELL**, b. Jan. 23, 1771	3	258
Anne, d. Ebenez[e]r, Jr. & Lois, b. Jan. 18, 1778	3	304
Annice, twin with Eunice, d. Joseph & Sarah, b. Dec. 13, 1784	3	314
Annice, m. Orin D. **SQUIRE**, June 4, 1806	3	386
Apellina, d. Edward & Martha, b. July 20, 1721; d. Sept.		
14, 1721	3	46
Asahel, s. Ezekiel & Elisabeth, b. July 2, 1756	3	165
Augustus, s. Caleb & Esther, b. Sept. 4, 1778	3	266
Augustus, s. Calib & Esther, b. Sept. 4, 1778	3	267
Augustus, s. Josiah & Sarah, b. Apr. 9, 1785	3	314
Benjamin, s. Benoni, b. Jan. 24, 1679	1	211
Benjamin, m. Elisabeth **HENLERY***, Dec. 8, 1703, by Rev.		
Sam[ue]ll Russell (***HENBRY**)	3	64
Benj[ami]n, s. Benj[ami]n & Elisabeth, b. July 16, 1705	3	64
Benj[ami]n, d. Sept. 10, 1724	3	64

	Vol.	Page
FRISBIE, FRISBY, FFRISSBE, FRISBE, FRISBEE, FRISBY,		
FFRISBIE, (cont.)		
Benjamin, s. Ebenezer, Jr. & Silence, b. Apr. 28, 1736	3	85
Benjamen, s. Joseph, 2d, & Sarah, b. Dec. 17, 1752	3	149
Betsey, d. Thomas & Deborah, b. Dec. 20, 1780	3	314
Betsey, d. Josiah & Sarah, b. May 27, 1788	3	253
Bets[e]y Ann, [d. Calvin & Polly], b. June 5, 1806	3	390
Betsey Ann, [d. Levi & Betty], b. June 6, 1824	3	413
Betsey Ann, of Branford, m. Hervey H. **FOWLER**, of		
Washington, Aug. 9, 1830, by Rev. C. A. Boardman, of		
New Haven	3	353
Betsey Ann, d. Joseph & Emeline, b. June 22, 1845	TM3	238
Caleb, s. Caleb & Hannah, b. Mar. 12, 1702/3	2	344
Caleb, m. Mary **WILFORD**, b. of Branford, Apr. 7, 1737,		
by Rev. Jonathan Mer[r]ick	3	114
Caleb, s. Caleb & Mary, b. Sept. 7, 1750	3	121
Caleb, d. Aug. 4, 1772, in the 70th y. of his age	3	206
Caleb, m. Esther **BARKER**, b. of Branford, Jan. 15, 1777,		
by Samuel Barker, J. P.	3	262
Calvin, s. Elisha & Rachel, b. Aug. 12, 1758	3	153
Calvin, s. Joseph & Sarah, b. Jan. 30, 1780	3	279
Calvin, m. Polly **HARRISON**, June 12, 1805	3	390
Calvin, [s. Lyman & Ann], b. Apr. 22, 1834	3	373
Calvin, [s. Lyman & Ann], d. May 7, 1837	3	373
Calvin, d. Jan. 7, 1846, ae 66 y.	TM3	306
Caroline, [d. Lyman & Ann], b. [ ]	3	373
Caroline B., [d. Lyman & Ann], b. Apr. 19, 1821	3	416
Charles, [s. Abraham & Olive], b. Jan. 31, 1793	3	274
Charles, s. Abraham & Olive, d. Oct. 10, 1813; "drowned		
in Long Island Sound"	3	400
Chester, [s. Abraham & Olive], b. Oct. 29, 1812	3	400
Chloe, d. Israel & Elisabeth, b. Jan. 1, 1736/7	3	86
C[h]loe, d. Israel & Elisabeth, b. May last, 1750	3	121
Chloe, d. Jan. 29, 1847, ae 87	TM3	207
Culpepper, s. Sam[ue]ll & Lydia, b. Aug. 20, 1733	3	77
Daniel, s. Caleb & Hannah, b. Feb. 17, 1709	3	31
Daniel, s. Dan[ie]ll & Ruth, b. Feb. 3, 1740/1	3	104
David, of Branford, m. Mary **WADE**, of Lyme, June 13,		
1750, by Rev. Stephen Johnson, at Lyme	3	132
David, [twin with Jonathan], s. Elisha & Rachel, b.		
Dec. 15, 1750	3	134
David, s. David & Mary, b. Apr. 18, 1751	3	132
David, d. Aug. 11, 1758	3	154
Deborah, d. Eben[eze]r & Hannah, b. Apr. 15, 1712	3	36
Deborah, d. Eben[eze]r, Jr. & Silence, b. June 8, 1732	3	82
Deborah, d. Timothy & Deborah, b. Mar. 21, 1756	3	143
Deborah, w. of Timothy, d. Apr. 12, 1756	3	143
Deborah, m. Ralph **HOADLEY**, b. of Branford, Oct. 17, 1780	3	292

	Vol.	Page

FRISBIE, FRISBY, FFRISSBE, FRISBE, FRISBEE, FRISBY, FFRISBIE, (cont.)

	Vol.	Page
Deborah, d. Ebenezer & Lois, b. Jan. 9, 1787	3	273
Deborah, m. John **BRADLEY**, b. of Branford, Mar. 30, 1812	3	430
Deborah, w. of Thomas, Sr., d. Feb. 5, 1822, in the 18th y. of her age	3	420
Dennis B., of Branford, m. Abigail F. **GOLDSMITH**, of Guilford, July 7, 1839, by L. H. Corson, in Trinity Church	3	377
Densy Ann, d. Pharez & Caroline, b. June 2, 1811	3	396
Dorcas, d. Ebenezer & Mary, b. Sept. 21, 1758	3	187
Drusilla Gertrude, d. James W. & Elizabeth, b. Aug. 7, 1726	3	350
Ebenezer, twin with Silence, s. Edward, b. Sept. 5, 1672	1	174
Ebenezer, m. Hannah **PAGE**, Apr. 21, 1703, by Eleazer Stent, J. P.	2	344
Ebinez[e]r, s. Ebenez[e]r & Hannah, b. Apr. 14, 1704	2	346
Eben[eze]r, s. Caleb & Hannah, b. Oct. 7, 1714	3	37
Ebenezer, m. Joanna **ROSE**, wid., Sept. 13, 1715, by Rev. Sam[ue]ll Russel[l]	3	49
Ebenezer, s. Sam[ue]ll & Lois, b. Feb. 26, 1724/5	3	56
Eben[eze]r, Jr., of Branford, m. Silence **BRACKET[T]**, of North Haven, Dec. 24, 1731, by Rev. Jonathan Mer[r]ick	3	82
Eben[eze]r, Jr., m. Mary **GOODRICH**, d. of Will[ia]m, b. of Branford, June 12, 1746, by Rev. Jonath[a]n Mer[r]ick	3	121
Eben[eze]r, s. Eben[eze]r, Jr. & Mary, b. Feb. 4, 1748/9	3	121
Ebenezor, m. Hannah **ABBOT**, June 29, 1758, by Sam[ue]ll Barker, J. P.	3	152
Ebenezer, d. Dec. 13, 1764, in the 85th y. of his age	3	190
Ebenezer, Jr., m. Lois **BLAKE**, b. of Branford, June 26, 1770, by Sam[ue]ll Eells	3	304
Ebenezer, d. Mar. 20, 1790	3	257
Edward, s. Edward, b. June 11, [1652]	1	171
Edward, s. John, b. Jan. 24, 1677	1	211
Edward, m. Martha **PARDEE**, Dec. 30, 1702, by Rev. Mr. Russell	2	344
Edward, s. Edward & Martha, b. Jan. 28, 1705	3	29
Edward, s. Ebenezer & Mary, b. Jan. 22, 1754	3	187
Edward, m. Jerusha **HOWD**, b. of Branford, Aug. 27, 1781, by Sam[ue]ll Eells	3	282
Elijah, s. Eben[e]z[e]r & Hannah, b. Mar. 4, 1710/11	3	34
Elijah, s. John & Susanna, b. Nov. 1, 1717	3	41
Elisha, s. Eben[eze]r & Joanna, b. Aug. 20, 1716	3	49
Elisha, m. Rachel **LEVI**, b. of Branford, July 5, 1739, by Rev. Philemon Robbins	3	104
Elisha, s. Elisha & Rachel, b. May 2[2], 1740 (First written "May 23")	3	104
Elisha, Jr., m. Martha **HARRISON**, b. of Branford, Apr. 14, 1761, by Philemon Robbins	3	171

	Vol.	Page
FRISBIE, FRISBY, FFRISSBE, FRISBE, FRISBEE, FRISBY,		
FFRISBIE, (cont.)		
Elizabeth, d. Jonathan & Mary, b. Aug. 17, 1689	2	343
Elisabeth, m. Samuel **BALDWIN**, b. of Branford, Mar. 14,		
1710/11, by Rev. Sam[ue]ll Russel[l]	3	34
Elisabeth, d. Jonathan & Thankful, b. May 3, 1715	3	36
Elisabeth, d. Abiel & Elisabeth, b. Sept. 30, 1724	3	55
Elisabeth, m. John **FOOT**, b. of Branford, Dec. 25, 1733,		
by Rev. Jonathan Merrick	3	80
Elisabeth, wid., m. Joseph **PALMER**, b. of Branford, May		
18, 1738, by Jonathan Mer[r]ick	3	96
Elisabeth, d. John & Anna, b. May 3, 1744	3	122
Elisabeth, d. Caleb & Mary, b. Aug. 29, 1745	3	114
Elisabeth, m. Gershom **BARTHOLOMEW**, b. of Branford,		
Nov. 5, 1749, by Nathan[ie]ll Harrison, J. P.	3	123
Flisabeth, d. Caleb & Mary, d. Mar. 2, 1751, ae 7	3	167
Elisabeth, d. Ezekiel & Elisabeth, b. Dec. 26, 1754	3	165
Elizabeth, d. Jedediah & Elizebeth, b. June 6, 1757	3	155
Elisabeth, w. of Israel, d. Nov. 9, 1760	3	165
Elisabeth, m. Jonathan **HOWD**, b. of Branford, Oct. 14,		
1767, by Philemon Robbins	3	201
Elisabeth, d. Ebenez[e]r, Jr. & Lois, b. Mar. 6, 1773	3	304
Elizabeth, [d. Samuel, Jr. & Irene], b. June 10, 1810	3	388
Elizabeth, d. James & Elizabeth, b. Nov. 22, 1833, in Hudson	3	350
Elizabeth, wid. Sam[ue]ll, d. Sept. 23, 1836, ae 92 y.	3	373
Elizabeth, d. Nov. 9, 1850, ae 17 y.	TM3	310
Elizabeth A., m. Eli F. **ROGERS**, b. of Branford, June 10,		
1834, by Rev. Timothy P. Gillett	3	367
Elizabeth Cornelia, twin with Henry Leonard, d. Hervey		
& Betsey, b. Sept. 1, 1835; d. Dec. 28, 1835	3	372
Elizabeth P., [d. Lyman & Ann], b. Dec. 25, 1831	3	373
Elnathan Beach, [s. Levi & Betty]. b. Aug. 22, 1820	3	413
Emeline, [d. Calvin & Polly], b. May 29, 1808	3	390
Emeline, of Branford, m. Henry **NORTON**, of Norwich,		
[June] 21, 1831, by Judson A. Root	3	356
Emeline, [d. Lyman & Ann], b. [ ]	3	373
Emily Maria, d. Judah & Sarah, b. Feb. 5, 1825	3	349
Emily Maria, d. Judah & Sarah, b. Feb. 5, 1825	3	355
Enoch, s. Thomas & Deborah, b. Feb. 7, 1766	3	194
Enoch, s. Thomas & Deborah, d. June 11, 1783, in the 18th		
y. of his age	3	272
Enoch Willford, [s. Thomas, Jr. & Mary], b. Oct. 4, 1794	3	273
Enos, s. John, Jr. & Freelove, b. Mar. 9, 1766	3	202
Eunice, d. Eben[eze]r & Joanna, b. Aug. 6, 1718	3	49
Eunice, d. Nathan & Elisabeth, b. Jan. 1, 1739/40	3	130
Eunice, d. Elisha & Rachel, b. July 28, 1744	3	104
Eunice, twin with Annice, d. Joseph & Sarah, b. Dec. 13, 1784	3	314
Ezekiel, s. Abiel & Elisabeth, b. July 12, 1723	3	53

	Vol.	Page
FRISBIE, FRISBY, FFRISSBE, FRISBE, FRISBEE, FRISBY,		
FFRISBIE, (cont.)		
Ezekiel, of Branford, m. Elisabeth **PARDEE**, of New Haven,		
Feb. 18, 1752, by Warham Williams	3	165
Fanny, d. Thomas & Deborah, b. Feb. 2, 1777	3	264
Frederic, [s. Thomas, Jr. & Mary], b. Jan. 21, 1811	3	337
George, s. Edw[ard] & Jerusha, b. Jan. 29, 1782	3	282
George, of Branford, m. Polly **ROSE**, of North Branford,		
May 3, 1835, by Rev. Tim[oth]y P. Gillett	3	368
George, s. George & Polly, b. Oct. 6, 1837	3	376
George Wrentville, s. Judah & Sarah, b. Apr. 17, 1823;		
d. Aug. 13, 1823, ae 3 m. 27 d.	3	349
George Wrentville, s. Judah & Sarah, b. Apr. 17, 1823;		
d. Aug. 13, 1823, ae 3 m. 27 d.	3	428
Gideon, s. Edward & Martha, b. June 16, 1713	3	36
Gideon, of Branford, m. Desire **GRANNIS**, of New Haven,		
Jan. 17, 1733/4, by Rev. Isaac Stiles	3	81
Gideon, s. Gideon & Desire, b. [ ], 1734	3	81
Hannah, d. John & Ruth, b. Jan. 18, 1681	1	211
Hannah, d. Jonathan & Mary, b. Aug. 14, 1693	2	343
Hannah, d. Ebinez[e]r & Hannah, b. Jan. 5, 1703	2	346
Hannah, d. Caleb & Hannah, b. Oct. 28, 1707	3	31
Hannah, m. Nath[anie]ll **FOOT**, Mar. 2, 1719/20, by		
Nath[anie]ll Harrison, J. P.	3	47
Hannah, d. John & Susanna, b. June 24, 1720	3	44
Hannah, d. Caleb & Hannah, d. Jan. 27, 1723/4	3	54
Hannah, m. Stephen **ABBOT**, b. of Branford, Jan. 6, 1724/5,		
by Rev. Sam[ue]ll Russell	3	59
Hannah, d. Abiel & Elisabeth, b. May 15, 1731	3	71
Hannah, d. Nathan & Elisabeth, b. June 20, 1744	3	130
Hannah, d. Caleb & Mary, b. Feb. 20, 1747/8	3	114
Hannah, d. Ebenezer & Mary, b. Dec. 14, 1765	3	201
Hannah, m. George **BALDWIN**, b. of Branford, July 2, 1766,		
by Warham Williams	3	189
Hannah H., m. Orin **HOADLEY**, [b.] of Branford, Nov. 15,		
1818, by Erastus Barker, J. P., Tinmouth	3	412
Hannah Hoadl[e]y, d. Will[ia]m & Rebecca, b. Aug. 17, 1788	3	257
Harvey, [s. Noah & Bets[e]y, b. Mar. 8, 1813	3	402
Harvey Jay, s. Joseph & Emeline, b. Apr. 6, 1842	TM3	238
Henry Edward, [s. Joseph & Emeline], b. July 5, 1831	3	333
Henry Leonard, twin with Elizabeth Cornelia, s. Hervey		
& Betsey, b. Sept. 1, 1835	3	372
Hervey, of Branford, m. Betsey **SHELDON**, of New Haven,		
Sept. 15, 1834, by Rev. Timothy P. Gillett	3	367
Hezekiah, s. Ebenezer, 2d, & Silence, b. July 11, 1738	3	90
Hezekiah, s. Ebenez[e]r, Jr. & Lois, b. Sept. 16, 1775	3	304
Hiram, [s. Abraham & Olive], b. Sept. 16, 1798	3	274
Huldah, d. John & Susanna, b. Nov. 16, 1715	3	39

	Vol.	Page
FRISBIE, FRISBY, FFRISSBE, FRISBE, FRISBEE, FRISBY,		
FFRISBIE, (cont.)		
Hulda[h], d. John & Susanna, b. Nov. 15, 1715	3	44
Ichabod Culpepper, s. Sam[ue]ll & Rachel, b. Aug. 1, 1760	3	164
Irene, w. of Dea. Samuel, d. Mar. 28, 1846, ae 67 y.	TM3	307
Isaac, s. Sam[ue]ll & Rachel, b. June 23, 1754	3	144
Isaac, s. John, Jr. & Freelove, b. May 2, 1764	3	183
Isaac, s. John, Jr. & Freelove, b. May 2, 1764	3	202
Israel, s. John & Susanna, b. June 22, 1709	3	33
Israel, of Branford, m. Elisabeth **GRANNIS**, of New Haven,		
July 1, 1731, by Rev. Isaac Stiles	3	81
Israel, s. Israel & Elisabeth, b. June 22, 1754	3	137
Israel, m. Hannah **JOHNSON**, b. of Branford, Dec. 15, 1762,		
by Philemon Robbins	3	181
Jacob, s. Eben[eze]r & Joanna, b. June 16, 1726	3	68
Jacob, s. John & Anna, b. Apr 4, 1740	3	122
Jacob, of Branford, m. Ruth **PORTER**, of Bethlem, Nov. 18,		
1747, by Rev. Joseph Bellamy, at Bethlem	3	120
Jacob, s. Jacob & Ruth, b. Aug. 11, 1750	3	120
James, s. Eben[eze]r & Joanna, b. July 18, 1722	3	49
James, s. Israel & Elisabeth, b. Apr. 22, 1732	3	81
James, of Branford, m. Joanna **PORTER**, of Woodbury, June		
16, 1743, by Philemon Robbins	3	165
James, s. [Samuel, 2d, & Sally], b. June 18, 1824;		
d. June 25, [1824], ae 1 wk.	3	347
James, m. Henrietta **ROSE**, Sept. 9, 1824, by Timothy P.		
Gillett	3	335
James Augustus, s. [Pharez & Caroline], b. Dec. 1, 1809	3	396
James W., [s. Samuel, Jr. & Irene], b. Mar. 29, 1798	3	388
James W., of Branford, m. Elizabeth **BUTLER**, of Hudson,		
N. Y., Nov. 6, 1822, by Rev. Benjamin F. Staunton, of		
Hudson, N. Y.	3	334
James Wrentville, s. James W. & Elizabeth, b. Aug. 31,		
1828, in Stuyvesant, N. Y.	3	350
Jane, d. Abraham & Olive, b. Nov. 23, 1806	3	281
Jarus, s. Lieut. Timothy & Mary, b. June 2, 1775	3	261
Jason, [s. Noah & Bets[e]y], b. July 28, 1814	3	402
Jedidiah, s. John & Susanna, b. Oct. 2, 1705	3	29
Jedediah, of Branford, m. Elizabeth **MUNSON**, of Wallingford,		
May 10, 1743, by Rev. Sam[ue]ll Whittelsey	3	155
Jeremiah, s. Ebenez[e]r & Mary, b. Jan. 1, 1774	3	282
Jeremiah, [s. Samuel, Jr. & Irene], b. Apr. 16, 1802	3	388
Jeremiah, s. Samuel & Irene, d. Apr. 17, 1834, ae 32 y.		
"on his passage off the coast of Virginia from Mobile"	3	363
Jerusha, d. Benj[ami]n & Elisabeth, b. Mar. 1, 1712	3	36
Joel, s. John & Anna, b. Jan. 7, 1746/7	3	122
John, s. Edward, b. July 17, [1650]	1	171
John, m. Ruth **BOWERS**, Dec. 2, [16]74	1	174

	Vol.	Page
FRISBIE, FRISBY, FFRISSBE, FRISBE, FRISBEE, FRISBY,		
FFRISBIE, (cont.)		
John, s. John, b. May 23, 1676	1	211
John, m. Susanna **HENBERRY**, Apr. 7, 1703, by Mr. Russell	2	344
John, s. John & Susanna, b. Mar. 11, 1703/4	2	345
John, Jr., m. Anna **BARKER**, b. of Branford, Feb. 8, 1730/1,		
by Jno. Russell, J. P.	3	122
John, s. John, Jr. & Anna, b. Dec. 1, 1731	3	122
John, Jr., of Branford, m. Freelove **ROGERS**, of New Haven,		
July 31, 1760, by Josiah Rogers, J. P.	3	172
John, s. John, Jr. & Freelove, b. Aug. 11, 1762	3	183
John, s. John, Jr. & Freelove, b. Aug. 11, 1762	3	202
Jonah, s. John & Susannah, b. Nov. 22, 1724	3	56
Jonah, s. Israel & Elisabeth, b. Dec. 14, 1734	3	81
Johnathan, s. Edward, b. Oct. 28, [16]59	1	172
Jonathan, s. Jonathan & Mary, b. Aug. 15, 1691	2	343
Jonathan, d. Apr. 7, 1695	2	343
Jonathan, m. Thankful **FOOT**, Aug. 10, 1713, by Nathan[ie]ll		
Harrison, J. P.	3	38
Jonathan, s. Jonathan & Thankfull, b. Oct. 4, 1717	3	42
Jonathan, d. July 13, 1722	3	51
Jonathan, s. Abiel & Elisabeth, b. Mar. 9, 1726/7	3	61
Jonathan, s. John, Jr. & Anna, b. May 23, 1734	3	122
Jonathan, [twin with David], s. Elisha & Rachel, b.		
Dec. 15, 1750	3	134
Jonathan, s. Timothy & Mary, b. Dec. 17, 1767	3	192
Joseph, s. John & Ruth, b. Aug. 15, 1688	2	343
Joseph, m. Abigail **HOADL[E]Y**, Dec. 5, 1711, by Rev. Mr.		
Sam[ue]ll Russel[l]	3	34
Joseph, s. Joseph & Abigail, b. Oct. 4, 1717	3	47
Joseph, of Branford, m. Sarah **BISHOP**, of G[u]ilford,		
Aug. 25, 1742, by Rev. Jonathan Todd	3	149
Joseph, 3d. s. Joseph, 2d, & Sarah, b. Aug. 17, 1745	3	149
Joseph, d. Apr. 26, 1758	3	152
Joseph, d. Nov. 4, 1760, ae 44	3	187
Joseph, m. Sarah **ROGERS**, b. of Branford, June 24, 1773,		
by Sam[ue]ll Eells	3	280
Joseph, s. Joseph & Sarah, b. Jan. 26, 1777	3	280
Joseph, m. Emeline **POND**, b. of Branford, July 20, 1828,		
by Timothy P. Gillett	3	347
Joseph B., [s. Lyman & Ann], b. Oct. 19, 1819	3	416
Joseph B., of Mendon, Ill., m. Sarah Ann **LAY**, d. of Dr.		
W. L., of Branford, May 6, 1845, by Rev. W. L. Wilson,		
of New Port, N. Y., at the house of Samuel Sperry in		
New York City.	TM3	158
Josiah, s. Edward, b. Jan. 19, [16]61	1	173
Josiah, s. Caleb & Hannah, b. Dec. 22, 1700	2	344
Josiah, d. Mar. 3, 1711/12	3	35

	Vol.	Page
FRISBIE, FRISBY, FFRISSBE, FRISBE, FRISBEE, FRISBY,		
FFRISBIE, (cont.)		
Josiah, s. Abiel & Elisabeth, b. Nov. 16, 1733	3	77
Josiah, s. Dan[ie]ll & Elisabeth, b. Feb. 12, 1752	3	126
Josiah, m. Sarah **ROGERS**, b. of Branford, Apr. 12, 1781,		
by Philemon Robbins	3	272
Josiah, s. Josiah & Sarah, b. Mar. 27, 1791	3	259
Josiah, m. Sarah **PALMER**, b. of Branford, Nov. 6, 1827,		
by Rev. Timothy P. Gillett	3	346
Judah, s. Sam[ue]ll & Lydia, b. Dec. 27, 1737	3	90
Judah, s. Sam[ue]ll & Rachel, b. Feb. 29, 1752	3	144
Judah, s. Sam[ue]ll, Jr. & Rachel, b. Feb. 29, 1752	3	127
Judah, s. Samuel & Elisabeth, b. Sept. 22, 1775	3	267
Judah, s. Samuel & Elizabeth, d. Sept. 2, 1795, in the		
Island of Hispaniola	3	387
Judah, [s. Samuel, Jr. & Irene], b. May 20, 1800	3	388
Judah, m. Sally **PLANT**, May 30, 1822, by Rev. Gardiner		
Spring, of New York	3	420
Judah, s. Joseph & Emeline, b. Jan. 23, 1849	TM3	241
Julia Ann had s. Thomas Julier **FRISBIE**, b. Aug. 5, 1826	3	349
Julia Ann, of Branford, m. Jeremiah **HARRISON**, of North		
Branford, Apr. 17, 1842, by Rev. Pascal P. Kidder	TM3	155
Julian, [s. Thomas, Jr. & Mary], b. Mar. 14, 1807	3	337
Keziah, d. Jedediah & Elizabeth, b. Mar. 28, 1748	3	155
Laura, [d. Thomas, Jr. & Mary], b. Feb. 19, 1793	3	273
Laura, d. Mar. 15, 1848, ae 20 y.	TM3	308
Laura S., d. Thomas & Laura, b. Feb. 20, 1848	TM3	239
Lemuel, s. Nathan & Elisabeth, b. Aug. 7, 1750	3	130
Leuy, s. Benj[ami]n & Elisabeth, b. Dec. 3, 1719	3	64
Levi, s. Elisha & Rachel, b. Mar. 31, 1747[8]	3	117
Levi, s. Josiah & Sarah, b. Apr. 12, 1794	3	267
Levi, m. Betty **BEACH**, b. of Branford, May 14, 1819	3	413
Levi, d. Nov. 4, 1846	TM3	307
Levine, d. Josiah & Sarah, b. May 5, 1786	3	315
Lewis, s. Samuel, 2d, & Sally, b. July 1, 1834	3	368
Lois, d. Sam[ue]ll & Lois, b. Feb. 24, 1725/6	3	58
Lois, w. of Sam[ue]ll, d. Mar. 28, 1728	3	90
Lois, m. Joseph **WARDELL**, May 30, 1745, by Rev. Philemon		
Robbins	3	106
Lucinda, d. Thom[a]s & Deborah, b. Jan. 20, 1783	3	305
Lucinda, d. Thomas & Deborah, b. Feb. 17, 1783	3	314
Lucinda, [d. Thomas, Jr. & Mary], b. Jan. 4, 1809	3	337
Lucinda, m. Ebenezer **LINSLEY**, Oct. 12, 1834, by Rev.		
David Baldwin	3	368
Lucretia, d. Philemon & Rhoda, b. Feb. 13, 1791	3	261
Luce, d. Nathan & Elisabeth, b. July 2, 1748	3	130
Lucy, d. Ezekiel & Elisabeth, b. Mar. 4, 1753	3	165
Luther, s. Elisha & Rachel, b. July 21, 1760	3	163

	Vol.	Page
FRISBIE, FRISBY, FFRISSBE, FRISBE, FRISBEE, FRISBY,		
FFRISBIE, (cont.)		
Lydia, d. Caleb & Hannah, b. June 1, 1698	2	344
Lydia, m. John **ROGERS**, June 17, 1713, by Nathan[ie]ll		
Harrison, J. P.	3	38
Lydia, d. Joseph & Abigail, b. May 7, 1720	3	47
Lydia, d. Sam[ue]ll & Lydia, b. June 14, 1735	3	82
Lydia, w. of Sam[ue]ll, d. Feb. 11, 1738/9	3	90
Lydia, m. Israel **BALDWIN**, Jr., b. of Branford, Dec. 27,		
1744, by Rev. Jonathan Mer[r]ick	3	109
Lydia, m. Edmund **ROGERS**, b. of Branford, Nov. 21, 1760	3	302
Lydia, d. Ebenezer & Mary, b. Dec. 3, 1761	3	187
Lydia, d. Lieut. Timothy & Mary, b. Jan. 16, 1773	3	261
Lyman, s. Joseph & Sarah, b. Feb. 23, 1794	3	270
Lyman, m. Ann **BARKER**, b. of Branford, Dec. 31, 1818, by		
Rev. Timothy P. Gillett	3	416
Lynde, s. Noah & Bets[e]y, b. Aug. 8, 1816	3	405
Lynde, m. Sarah **SPENCER**, b. of Branford, Aug. 22, 1841,		
by Rev. David T. Shailer	TM3	153
Marcy, wid., m. John **BARTHOLOMEW**, Jan. 4, 1714/5, by		
Nathan[ie]ll Harrison, J. P.	3	39
Margaret, d. Sam[ue]ll & Rebecca, b. Nov. 26, 1743	3	102
Maria, m. Chauncey **ROGERS**, b. of Branford, Oct. 25,		
1815, by Rev. Timo[thy] P. Gillett	3	364
Martha, d. Edward & Martha, b. June 10, [ ];		
[bp. July [ ], 1710	3	31
Martha, m. Josiah **ROGERS**, Jr., b. of Branford, Apr. 24,		
1728, by Rev. Jonathan Merrick	3	73
Martha, w. of Edward, d. Sept. 15, 1749	3	168
Martha, d. Samuel & Elisabeth, b. Dec. 28, 1779	3	267
Martha, m. Jonathan **FOOT**, b. of Branford, Dec. 8, 1808	3	388
Martha B., d. May 6, 1849, ae 18 y.	TM3	309
Martha Butler, d. James & Elizabeth, b. Mar. 16, 1831,		
in Stuyvesant, N. Y.	3	350
Mary, d. Jonathan & Mary, b. Jan. 1, 1685	1	210
Mary, d. Benj[ami]n & Elisabeth, b. Oct. 10, 1714	3	64
Mary, d. Caleb & Hannah, b. July 27, 1716	3	39
Mary, d. Jonathan & Thankfull, b. May 7, 1720	3	44
Mary, d. Sam[ue]ll & Lydia, b. Mar. 5, 1730/1	3	70
Mary, d. of Caleb, m. Eliphalet **HOWD**, b. of Branford,		
Oct. 11, 1738	3	130
Mary, m. Paul **TYLER**, b. of Branford, Nov. 8, 1739, by		
Rev. Jonathan Mer[r]ick	3	94
Mary, d. Caleb & Mary, b. June 27, 1740	3	114
Mary, d. Caleb & Mary, d. Mar. 8, 1751, ae 12	3	167
Mary, d. David & Mary, b. Nov. 8, 1753	3	135
Mary, d. Ebenezer & Mary, b. Apr. 26, 1756	3	187
Mary, m. Joseph **GOODRICH**, b. of Branford, June 17, 1756,		

	Vol.	Page
FRISBIE, FRISBY, FFRISSBE, FRISBE, FRISBEE, FRISBY,		
FFRISBIE, (cont.)		
by Philemon Robbins	3	199
Mary, w. of Caleb, d. June 1, 1767, in the 61st y. of her age	3	194
Mary, d. Thomas & Deborah, b. Dec. 29, 1769	3	202
Mary, [twin with Timothy], d. Timothy & Mary, b. May 17,		
1770	3	200
Mary, d. Ebenezer & Mary, d. Aug. 24, 1777	3	285
Mary, m. Hugh **MONRO**, b. of Branford, Sept. 18, 1797, by		
Rev. Bela Hubbard	3	271
Mary, of Branford, m. Alfred **HOUGH**, of Martinsburg,		
N. Y., Aug. 22, 1833, by Rev. Tim[othy] P. Gillett	3	361
Mary Adelia, d. Calvin & Polly, b. Nov. 20, 1822	3	343
Mary Ann, [d. Lyman & Ann], b. Aug. 22, 1826	3	373
Mary Eliza, [d. Thomas, Jr. & Mary], b. July 20, 1800	3	273
Mary Eliza, m. Edmund **BEACH**, b. of Branford, May 25,		
1819	3	417
Mary Eliza, d. Samuel, 2d & Sally, b. Aug. 19, 1830	3	357
Mary Elizabeth, [d. Joseph & Emeline], b. June 1, 1834	3	333
Mary Elizabeth, d. Calvin, d. Jan. 2, [1843], ae 20; bd.		
Jan. 4, 1843	TM3	304
Mary Elizabeth, d. William R. & Harriet C., b. Dec. 13,		
1842	TM3	229
Mercy, m. John **LINSL[E]Y**, Jr., b. of Branford, Jan. 13,		
1725/6, by Nath[anie]ll Har[r]ison, J. P.	3	62
Mercy, d. Sam[ue]ll, Jr. & Rachel, b. Sept. 9, 1744	3	108
Mercy, see Mercy **BARTHOLOMEW**	3	74
Miles, [s. Thomas, Jr. & Mary], b. May 4, 1805	3	336
Mirriam, d. Jedediah & Elizebeth, b. Apr. 2, 1746	3	155
Morris E., [s. Lyman & Ann], b. Jan. 30, 1830	3	373
Moses, s. Jedediah & Elizabeth, b. Sept. 30, 1754	3	155
Moses, s. Ebenezer & Mary, b. Dec. 16, 1763	3	187
Moses, m. Chloe **HOADL[E]Y**, b. of Branford, Jan. 11, 1804,		
by Sam[ue]l Eells	3	275
Myrta M., m. John **MONROE**, July 13, 1846, by Rev.		
Frederick Miller	TM3	160
Nancy, [d. Abraham & Olive], b. Oct. 17, 1789	3	274
Nancy, m. James **PALMER**, Feb. 11, 1807	3	282
Nancy, of Branford, m. Thaddeus **AVERY**, of Wallingford,		
Sept. 15, 1809	3	393
Nancy Celeste, [d. Joseph & Emeline], b. Dec. 26, 1836	3	333
Nancy M., of Branford, m. Lucius **HOPKINS**, of Harwinton,		
June 14, 1832, by Rev. Timothy P. Gillett	3	358
Nancy Maria, [d. Samuel, Jr. & Irene], b. Jan. 3, 1807	3	388
Nathan, s. Caleb & Hannah, b. Apr. 3, 1712	3	35
Nathan, of Branford, m. Elisabeth **WADE**, of Lyme, Dec.		
12, 1738, by Rev. Jonathan Parsons, at Lyme	3	130
Nathan, s. Nathan & Elisabeth, b. Oct. 10, 1746	3	130

	Vol.	Page
FRISBIE, FRISBY, FFRISSBE, FRISBE, FRISBEE, FRISBY,		
FFRISBIE, (cont.)		
Nathan[ie]ll, s. John & Susanna, b. Sept. 3, 1711	3	34
Nathaniel, s. Caleb & Hannah, b. Feb. 21, 1720/1	3	49
Nath[anie]ll, m. Abigail **HARRISON**, Oct. 25, 1745, by Rev.		
Philemon Robbins	3	152
Nathan[ie]ll, s. Elisha & Rachel, b. Apr. 15, 1753	3	134
Nathaniel, s. Nath[anie]ll & Abigail, b. Aug. 30, 1757	3	152
Nathaniel, [s. Reuben & Ann], b. Apr. 30, 1796	3	391
Nathaniel, m. Minta **OLDS**, b. of Branford, Jan. 10, 1818,		
by Orchard Gould, J. P.	3	405
Noah, s. Abiel & Elisabeth, b. Feb. 27, 1728/9	3	66
Noah, s. Will[ia]m & Rebecca, b. Mar. 7, 1782	3	285
Noah, m. Bets[e]y **WHITNEY**, Feb. 14, 1811	3	393
Obed Tyler, s. Samuel, 2d, & Sally, b. Aug. 11, 1819	3	410
Obed Tyler, m. Frances Elisa **PAGE**, b. of Branford, May		
13, 1847, by Rev. Timothy P. Gillett	TM3	160
Patience, m. Sam[ue]ll **ROSE**, 2d, b. of Branford, Oct.		
24, 1751, by Jon[a]th[an] Mer[r]ick	3	197
Peter, s. Ebenezer & Mary, b. Oct. 6, 1751	3	187
Peter, s. Eben[eze]r, Jr. & Mary, b. Oct. 6, 1751	3	131
Phares, s. Ebenezer, Jr. & Lois, b. June 20, 1784	3	277
Pharez, of Branford, m. Caroline **BAYLEY**, of Greenfield,		
N. Y, Apr. 14, 1805, at Greenfield	3	396
Phebe, m. John [H]arrington **BEACH**, b. of Branford, Oct.		
2, 1776, by Sam[ue]ll Eells	3	274
Philemon, s. Dan[ie]ll & Elisabeth, b. Nov. [9], 1759	3	161
Philemon, [s. Abraham & Olive], b. Feb. 26, 1801	3	274
Polle, d. Josiah & Sarah, b. Sept. 19, 1789	3	258
Polly, m. Chandler **PARKER**, Jan. 17, 1809	3	390
Polly, w. of Calvin, d. Jan. 3, [1843], ae 58; bd. Jan. 4, 1843	TM3	304
Rachel, d. Eben[ez]r & Joanna, b. July 24, 1720	3	49
Rachel, d. Elisha & Rachel, b. July 29, 1742	3	104
Rachel, d. Sam[ue]ll & Rachel, b. Sept. 19, 1756	3	144
Rachel, d. [ ]	3	420
Randolph, s. Samuel, 2d, & Sally, b. Apr. 6, 1821	3	347
Randolph, m. Emeline **TYLER**, b. of Branford, July 19,		
1847, by Rev. T. P. Gillett	TM3	160
Rebecca, d. Jno., b. Nov. 14, 1679	1	211
Rebec[c]ah, d. Joseph & Abigail, b. Sept. 14, 1712	3	47
Rebecca, m. Noah **BALDWIN**, Mar. 21, 1732/3, by Rev.		
Philemon Robbins	3	76
Rebecca, d. Sam[ue]ll, Jr. & Rachel, b. May 30, 1749	3	119
Rebecca, m. Isaac **PALMER**, b. of Branford, Apr. 25, 1765,		
by Philemon Robbins	3	282
Rebeccah, m. Isaac **PALMER**, Apr. 25, 1765	3	394
Rebecca, d. Samuel & Elisabeth, b. June 5, 1770	3	204
Rebecca, d. William & Rebecca, b. May 1, 1777	3	263

	Vol.	Page
FRISBIE, FRISBY, FFRISSBE, FRISBE, FRISBEE, FRISBY,		
FFRISBIE, (cont.)		
R[e]ubin, s. Nath[anie]ll & Abigail, b. Apr. 22, 1751	3	152
Reuben, of Branford, m. Ann **CULVER**, of Wallingford, Mar.		
28, 1784	3	391
Rosanna, d. [Pharez & Caroline], d. May 14, 1809	3	396
Rocksana, d. Joseph, 2d, & Sarah, b. June 14, 1757	3	149
Roxana, d. Joseph & Sarah, b. Jan. 30, 1780	3	280
Roxana, d. Samuel, 2d, & Sally, b. Nov. 21, 1822	3	347
Rufus, [s. Abraham & Olive], b. Mar. 21, 1791	3	274
Rufus, s. Abraham & Olive, b. May 21, 1807	3	396
Russel[l], [s. Thomas, Jr. & Mary], b. Nov. 2, 1812	3	337
Russell, [s. Levi & Detty], b. Jan 8, 1822	3	413
Russell Linsley, s. Alonso P. & Henrietta Linsley, b.		
Sept. 14, 1845	TM3	236
Ruth, d. John & Ruth, b. Sept. 6, 1685	1	211
Ruthe, d. John & Ruth, d. May 26, 1688	2	343
Ruth, d. Edward & Martha, b. Feb. 10, 1716	3	40
Ruth, d. Dan[ie]ll & Ruth, b. Apr. 20, 1742	3	104
Ruth, d. Jacob & Ruth, b. July 12, 1749	3	163
Ruth, [d. Jacob & Ruth], d. Sept. 1, 1749, in the 1st		
y. of her age	3	163
Ruth, d. Daniel & Elizabeth, b. Jan. 22, 1756	3	152
Ruth, of Branford, m. Dan[ie]ll **JONES**, of Long Island,		
Jan. 2, 1782, by Warham Williams	3	314
Ruth, [d. Reuben & Ann], b. July 11, 1792	3	391
Sally, d. Josiah & Sarah, b. Sept. 16, 1783	3	272
Sally, [d. Thomas, Jr. & Mary], b. Feb. 10, 1804	3	336
Samuell, s. Edward, b. Oct. [18], [1654]	1	171
Samuel, d. John & Ruth, b. Feb. 10, 1683	1	211
Sam[ue]ll, of Branford, m. Lois **COWLS**, of Wallingford,		
Oct. 10, 1722, by Jno. Hall	3	50
Samuel, s. Samuel & Lois, b. July 27, 1723	3	53
Sam[ue]ll, m. Lydia **PALMER**, b. of Branford, Dec. 5,		
1728, by Rev. Jonathan Mer[r]ick	3	66
Sam[ue]ll, Jr., m. Rachel **BARTHOLOMEW**, b. of Branford,		
Aug. 4, 1742, by Jno Russell, J. P.	3	108
Sam[ue]ll, s. Sam[ue]ll, Jr. & Rachel, b. Dec. 27, 1746	3	108
Sam[ue]ll, d. Apr. 24, 1760, in the 37th y. of his age.		
"Died a prisoner in Mar Vineca [Martineco?]"	3	164
Samuel, m. Elisabeth **TYLER**, b. of Branford, Mar. 23,		
1768, by Philemon Robbins	3	195
Samuel, s. Samuel & Elisabeth, b. June 14, 1774	3	258
Samuel, s. Josiah & Sarah, b. Sept. 12, 1792	3	267
Samuel, Jr., s. Samuel & Elizabeth, m. Irene **BALDWIN**,		
d. John & Alethea, Mar. 26, 1797	3	388
Samuel, s. Samuel & Irene, b. Mar. 6, 1813; d. Aug. 11,		
1813, ae 5 m. 5 d.	3	406

	Vol.	Page
FRISBIE, FRISBY, FFRISSBE, FRISBE, FRISBEE, FRISBY,		
FFRISBIE, (cont.)		
Samuel, Sr., d. Feb. 20, 1814, ae 67 y. 24 d.	3	407
Samuel, s. Samuel & Irene, b. Apr. 7, 1817	3	407
Samuel, 2d, s. Josiah, m. Sally **TYLER**, d. Obed, b. of		
Branford, May 17, 1818	3	410
Samuel, Jr., s. Samuel & Irene, d. Jan. 22, 1842, in the		
25th y. of his age, in Darlington, S. C.	TM3	306
Samuel Elizure, [s. Joseph & Emeline], b. Aug. 26, 1839	3	333
Samuel Judah, s. [James W. & Elizabeth], b. Mar. 18, 1824	3	334
Sarah, d. Eben[eze]r & Hannah, b. Jan. 27, 1707	3	30
Sarah, d. Joseph & Abigail, b. Nov. 12, 1729	3	66
Sarah, m. Aaron **BALDWIN**, b. of Branford, Nov. 30, 1748,		
by Rev. Jonathan Mer[r]ick	3	117
Sarah, d. Joseph, 2d, & Sarah, b. Feb. 15, 1749	3	149
Sarah, d. David & Mary, b. Mar. 13, 1756	3	142
Sarah, d. Ezekiel & Elisabeth, b. Mar. 31, 1761	3	176
Sarah, w. of Joseph, d. Sept. 5, 1773	3	280
Sarah, d. Joseph & Sarah, b. May 15, 1774	3	280
Sarah, d. Thomas & Deborah, b. Sept. 18, 1774	3	262
Sarah, m. James **DONEY**, b. of Branford, Dec. 6, 1789	3	393
Sarah, m. Samuel **PLANT**, Feb. 11, 1795	3	392
Sarah, m. Samuel **PLANT**, b. of Branford, Feb. 11, 1795	3	393
Sarah Elizabeth, d. Judah & Sarah, b. Nov. 20, 1829	3	355
Sarah Elizabeth, d. Samuel, 2d, & Sally, b. Jan. 10, 1838	3	375
Silence, twin with Ebenezer, child of Edward, b. Sept. 5, 1672	1	174
Sil[e]nce, d. Joseph, Jr. & Sarah, b. Sept. 18, 1743	3	149
Simeon, s. Jedediah & Eliz[abe]th, b. Mar. 24, 1744	3	155
Simeon, m. Hannah **MALTBIE**, b. of Branford, Feb. 11, 1768,		
by Caleb Merriman, J. P.	3	193
Simeon, s. Ebenez[e]r, Jr. & Lois, b. Sept. 5, 1782	3	305
Solomon, s. Jacob & Ruth, b. June 5, 1754	3	163
Solomon, [s. Abraham & Olive], b. Oct. 16, 1795	3	274
Statira, d. Joseph & Sarah, b. Apr. 27, 1789	3	257
Stephen, s. Ebenezer, Jr. & Lois, b. Oct. 16, 1770	3	304
Susanna, d. John & Susanna, b. May 15, 1713	3	39
Susanna, d. Jedediah & Eliz[ebe]th, b. Dec. 21, 1750	3	155
Tamar, d. Israel & Elisabeth, b. Aug. 22, 1739	3	91
Tamar, m. Abraham **PLANT**, b. of Branford, May 5, 1763,		
by Philemon Robbins	3	183
Thaddeus Watrous, s. Levi & Betty, b. Dec. 20, 1825	3	342
Thankfull, d. Edward & Martha, b. Oct. 28, 1704	2	345
[Tha]nkfull, d. Edward & Martha, b. Apr. 9, 1708	3	30
Thankfull, wid., of Branford, m. Benjamin **FARNUM**, of		
Andover, Mass., Dec. 18, 1723, by Nath[anie]ll		
Har[r]ison, J. P.	3	54
Thankfull, m. Philip **POND**, b. of Branford, Apr. 13,		
1726, by Nath[anie]ll Harrison, J. P.	3	84

	Vol.	Page
FRISBIE, FRISBY, FFRISSBE, FRISBE, FRISBEE, FRISBY, **FFRISBIE,** (cont.)		
Thankfull, d. Elisha & Rachel, b. Jan. 23, 1756	3	153
Theodore, s. Benj[ami]n & Elisabeth, b. Mar. 27, 1723	3	64
Thomas, s. Caleb & Mary, b. Feb. 21, 1737/8	3	114
Thomas, m. Deborah **GOODSELL**, b. of Branford, Feb. 28, 1765, by Josiah Rogers, J. P.	3	194
Thomas, s. Thomas & Deborah, b. Dec. 31, 1767	3	194
Thomas, Jr., m. Mary **HOADL[E]Y**, Feb. 6, 1793	3	273
Thomas, d. Jan. 30, 1829, in the 91 y. of his age	3	349
Thomas Julier, s. Julia Ann, b. Aug. 5, 1826	3	349
Timothy, m. Deborah **BALDWIN**, Sept. 19, 1754, by Jonathan Merrick	3	138
Timothy, m. Mary **BARKER**, b. of Branford, Mar. 29, 1764, by Philemon Robbins	3	182
Timothy, [twin with Mary], s. Timothy & Mary, b. May 17, 1770	3	200
Timothy, Lieut., d. May 7, 1776	3	261
Titus, s. Dan[ie]ll & Elisabeth, b. Oct. 14, 1750	3	126
Tryphena, d. John, Jr. & Freelove, b. Jan. 13, 1768	3	202
Wealthean, [d. Reuben & Ann], b. Mar. 7, 1788	3	391
Whitfield, s. Elisha & Rachel, b. July 14, 1763	3	190
Will[ia]m, s. John, Jr. & Anna, b. Feb. 14, 1736/7	3	122
Will[ia]m, s. Eben[eze]r, Jr. & Mary, b. Apr. 11, 1747	3	121
William, m. Rebec[c]a **HO[A]DLEY**, b. of Branford, July 11, 1776, by Philemon Robbins	3	261
William, s. Will[ia]m & Rebecca, b. July 24, 1779	3	285
William, f. of Rebe[c]kah, William, Noah, & Hannah **HOADLY**, by Rebe[c]kah, d. Aug. 7, 1813	3	402
William, [s. Thomas, Jr. & Mary], b. May 15, 1816	3	337
William, of New Haven, m. Mary Ann **BARKER**, of Branford, June 6, 1831, [by Rev. Timothy P. Gillett]	3	357
William Henry, s. Samuel, 2d, & Sally, b. May 11, 1826	3	347
William Rogers, s. Calvin & Polly, b. May 21, 1819	3	343
William Rogers, of Branford, m. Harriet **COOKE**, of Wallingford, Nov. 25, 1841, by Rev. Pascal P. Kidder, at the house of Samuel Cooke	TM3	154
Zebulun, s. Benj[ami]n & Elisabeth, b. May 21, 1717	3	64
-----, s. John & Susanna, b. June 22, 1709	3	30
FRISSELL, [see also **FRISBIE**], Joseph, m. Lydia **ROSE**, b. of Branford, Sept. 13, 1726, by Rev. Sam[ue]ll Russell	3	60
Joseph, s. Joseph & Lydia, b. Oct. 10, 1727	3	63
Lydia, wid., m. Abiel **PAGE**, b. of Branford, June 22, 1744, by Rev. Philemon Robbins	3	102
Sarah, d. Joseph & Lydia, b. Nov. 21, 1730	3	72
FROST, Rebe[c]cah, d. Sam[ue]ll & Sarah, b. Apr. 2, 170[ ]	3	31
Sam[ue]ll, m. Sarah **TOWNER**, Aug. 8, 1706, by W[illia]m Maltbie, J. P.	3	32

	Vol.	Page
FULLER, Jared, s. Joshua & Jemima, b. Apr. 8, 1724	3	55
Jemima, m. William **ALLEN**, b. of Branford, Dec. 17, 1739, by Jona[than] Arnold, Missionary	3	92
John, s. Joshua & Jemima, b. Apr. 2, 1728	3	68
Jonathan, s. Joshua & Jemima, b. Feb. 6, 1721/2	3	47
Joshua, of Dedham, m. Jemima **HOADL[E]Y**, of Branford, June 3, 171[ ]	3	43
Joshua, s. Joshua & Jemima, b. Mar. 10, 1719/20	3	44
Joshua, s. Joshua & Jemima, d. Aug. 22, 1735	3	83
[FYLER], **FILER**, Naomi, of Guilford, m. Judah **HOWD**, of Branford, Sept. 4, 1761, by John Richards	3	173
GARRETT, **GARRET**, Cheney, s. John & Hannah, b. Aug. 20, 1768	3	195
Hannah, d. John & Hannah, b. Sept. 6, 1776	3	262
John, m. Hannah **BARKER**, b. of Branford, Oct. 8, 1767, by Philemon Robbins	3	191
Peter, s. John & Hannah, b. Oct. 31, 1770	3	204
Samuel, s. John & Hannah, b. Apr. 16, 1773	3	208
GATES, Andrew, m. Lucinda **AUGUR**, b. of Branford, Apr. 13, 1823, by Rev. Oliver Willson, of North Haven	3	422
Andrew Monro[e], s. John & Lucinda, b. Oct. 15, 1794	3	263
John, m. Lucinda **LINSLEY**, b. of Branford, Jan. 1, 1794	3	263
John, d. Nov. 10, 1826, ae 81 y.	3	343
John M., m. Sylvia **PALMER**, Nov. 21, 1821, by Charles Atwater	3	415
John Martin, s. John & Lucinda, b. May 2, 1796	3	255
Lucinda, d. John & Lucinda, b. Mar. 29, 1802	3	275
Lucinda, m. Hanan **PALMER**, [1826?], by Rev. Matthew Noyes, of Northford	3	342
GAYLOR, Stewart, m. Thankfull **ROGERS**, Dec. [ ], 1780	3	301
GILBERT, Mary, of Wallingford, m. William **BARKER**, of Branford, Dec. [ ], 1764, by Theo[philu]s Hall	3	206
GILDERSLE[E]VE, Rebecca, of Huntington, L. I., m. Thomas **ROGERS**, of Branford, Feb. 2, 1747/8, by Jonathan Mer[r]ick	3	195
GILLETT, Timothy P., Rev., of Branford, m. Sally **HODGES**, of Torrington, Nov. 29, 1808	3	390
GLADDING, Russel S., of Saybrook, m. Eunice A. **AVERILL**, of Branford, Sept. 13, 1847, by Rev. A. C. Wheat	TM3	160
GOLDSMITH, Abigail F., of Guilford, m. Dennis B. **FRISBIE**, of Branford, July 7, 1839, by L. H. Corson, in Trinity Church	3	377
GOODNOUGH, Lucretia G., b. [ ], 1817, in New York State	TM3	236
Lucretia G., m. John **WILFORD**, Sept. 25, 1838	TM3	159
GOODRICH, **GOODRIDG**, **GOODRIDGE**, **GOODRITCH**, Abigail, m. Sam[ue]ll **POND**, June 8, 1704	2	345
Abigail, m. Samuel **POND**, b. of Branford, June 8, 1704, by W[illia]m Maltbie, J. P.	3	39

	Vol.	Page
GOODRICH, GOODRIDG, GOODRIDGE, GOODRITCH,(cont.)		
Abigail, d. Gideon & Abigail, b. June 23, 1747	3	127
Abigail, d. Gideon, d. Mar. 2, 1752	3	127
Abigail, d. Gidion & Abigail, b. Aug. 6, 1753	3	151
Amy, w. of Elias, d. Sept. 17, 1826, ae 50 y.	3	346
Anna Ritte, [d. Elias & Amy], b. June 29, 1810	3	283
Anna Retta, d. [Elias & Amy], d. [ ], 1813	3	411
Anne, d. Phinehas & Eunice, b. Mar. 18, 1759	3	160
Anne, Mrs., m. Josiah **TYLER**, Jan. 12, 1786, by Jason		
Atwater	3	255
Bartholomew, s. Timothy & Sarah, b. May 25, 1751	3	166
Bartholomew, m. Hannah **BALDWIN**, b. of Branford, Sept.		
22, 1773, by Philemon Robbins	3	273
Benjamin Eli, s. Eli & Elisabeth F., b. June 16, 1841	TM3	230
Bets[ey], d. James & Hannah, b. Mar. 3, 1785	3	390
Betsey, of Branford, m. Augustus **BALDWIN**, of Deerfield,		
Mass., June 31, (sic), 1809, by Rev. Tim[oth]y P. Gillett	3	425
Charles Parker, s. Eli & Elisabeth F., b. Feb. 29, 1840	TM3	230
Christina Maria, d. Eli & Elisabeth F., b. July 17, 1842	TM3	230
Cornelia J., ae 17, of Branford, m. George B. **BALDWIN**,		
ae 23, of Prospect, Aug. 19, 1849, by Rev. Timothy P.		
Gillett	TM3	167
Damaris, d. Phinehas & Eunice, b. Apr. 15, 1767	3	191
David, m. Lydia **RUSSELL**, b. of Branford, July 13, 1758,		
by Sam[ue]ll Hall	3	158
Desier, d. Nath[anie]ll & Mary, b. Apr. [7], 1751	3	150
Dorcus, d. Nath[anie]ll & Mary, b. Nov. 14, 1755	3	150
Ebenezer, s. Nath[anie]ll & Mary, b. Nov. 18, 1748;		
d. Jan. 22, 1751	3	150
Ebenezer, s. David & Lydia, b. Oct. 7, 1767	3	192
Ebenez[e]r, s. Bartho[lome]w & Hannah, b. Jan. 15, 1782	3	274
Edmund, s. Bartholomew & Hannah, b. Dec. 23, 1780	3	279
Edmund, s. Bartholomew, d. Aug. [ ], 1816	3	430
Edmund, [s. Will[ia]m & Mary Ann], b. Aug. 4, 1828	3	367
Eli, s. Elias & Amy, b. June 2, 1817	3	411
Eli, of Branford, m. Elisabeth Fry **PARKER**, of New Haven,		
Dec. 23, 1837, by Rev. M. Knap, in New York City	TM3	156
Elias, s. Phinehas & Eunice, b. June 27, 1773	3	256
Elias, of Branford, m. Amy **BISHOP**, of Bethlehem, Dec. 3,		
1803	3	283
Elizabeth, d. Dec. 4, 1704	2	345
Elisabeth, d. Phinehas & Eunice, b. May 25, 1761	3	173
Elisabeth Helena, d. Eli & Elisabeth F., b. Nov. 24, 1838	TM3	230
Elisur Beach, s. Joseph & Elisa, b. Apr. 24, 1830	TM3	234
Elisur Beach, s. Joseph & E[liza] A., b. Apr. 24, 1830	3	362
Ellen Eliza, d. Capt. Joseph & Eliza Adeline, b. Feb. 9, 1835	3	377
Eunice, d. Phinehas & Eunice, b. May 26, 1763	3	180
Eunice, wid., of Phinehas, d. Nov. 12, 1827, ae 95 y.	3	346

	Vol.	Page
GOODRICH, GOODRIDG, GOODRIDGE, GOODRITCH,(cont.)		
Fanney, d. James & Hannah, b. May 27, 1779	3	297
Gideon, m. Abigail **BARKER**, b. of Branford, June 19, 1746, by Rev. Philemon Robbins	3	127
Gideon, s. Gideon & Abigail b. Mar. 31, 1756	3	151
Gideon, 1st, d. Aug. 18, 1779, a prisoner in New York	3	305
Gideon, m. Jerusha **TYLER**, b. of Branford, Mar. 20, 1780	3	305
Grace, d. Bartho[lome]w & Hannah, b. Dec. 24, 1783	3	274
Grace Hannah, d. William & Mary Ann, b. Jan. 21, 1835	3	368
Hannah, m. Jonathan **STOKES**, b. of Branford, Sept. 27, 1758, by Sam[ue]ll Barker, J. P.	3	153
Hannah, [w. of James], d. July 17, 1790 in her 33rd y.	3	390
Irene, [d. Elias & Amy], b. Sept. 5, 1806	3	283
Irene, m. Woodward **PAGE**, b. of Branford, Apr. 23, 1833, by Rev. Timothy P. Gillett	3	359
James, s. Joseph & Mary, b. Apr. 21, 1758	3	199
James, m. Hannah **JOHNSON,** b. of Branford, Jan. 24, 1779, by Sam[ue]ll Eells	3	297
Jennett, [d. Will[ia]m & Mary Ann], b. July 28, 1832	3	367
Jennette C., of Branford, m. George B. **BALDWIN**, of Prospect, Aug. 19, 1849, by Rev. Tim[oth]y P. Gillett	TM3	164
Joanna, m. John **BALDWIN**, Jr., Oct. 31, 1716, by Rev. Mr. Russel[l]	3	40
John, s. Bartholomew & Hannah, b. Feb. 1, 1776	3	274
John, s. Bartholomew, d. Oct. 30, 1790	3	430
John, [s. Bartholomew & Hannah], b. Oct. 30, 1799	3	388
John Bishop, s. Elias & Amy, b. Sept. 8, 1814	3	411
John Bishop, s. Elias, d. Nov. 17, 1826, ae 12 y.	3	346
John William, [s. Will[ia]m & Mary Ann], b. Jan. 14, 1826	3	367
Joseph, m. Mary **FRISBIE**, b. of Branford, June 17, 1756, by Philemon Robbins	3	199
Joseph, s. Joseph & Mary, b. Apr. 20, 1760	3	199
Joseph, d. June 4, 1779	3	297
Joseph, d. May 23, 1790, in his 30th y.	3	390
Joseph, s. Joseph & Laida*, b. Oct. 4, 1790 (*Zada?)	3	285
Joseph, s. Joseph & Zada, b. Oct. 4, 1790	3	362
Joseph, m. Eliza A. **WILLIAMS**, b. of Branford, Aug. 2, 1826, by Rev. Timothy P. Gillett	3	342
Louisa Beach, d. Joseph & Elisa, b. Mar. 9, 1843	TM3	234
Lucy Ann, d. Capt. Joseph & Eliza Adeline, b. Jan. 11, 1837	3	377
Lydia, d. David & Lydia, b. Dec. 9, 1764	3	188
Margaret, d. Joseph & Mary, b. July 19, 1762	3	199
Mary, m. Sam[ue]ll **KIRKUM**, May 28, 1707, by Rev. Sam[ue]ll Russel[l]	3	32
Mary, d. of Will[ia]m, m. Eben[eze]r **FRISBIE**, Jr., b. of Branford, June 12, 1746, by Rev. Jonath[a]n Mer[r]ick	3	121
Mary, d. Gideon & Abigail, b. Mar. 31, 1750	3	127
Mary, m. Roger **TYLER**, b. of Branford, July 2, 1767, by		

	Vol.	Page
GOODRICH, GOODRIDG, GOODRIDGE, GOODRITCH,(cont.)		
Philemon Robbins	3	191
Morris, s. Joseph & Eliza A., b. Apr. 24, 1828	3	362
Moses, d. Dec. 18, 1748	3	158
Moses, s. Phinehas & Eunice, b. June 2, 1771	3	204
Nancy, d. James & Hannah, b. Mar. 25, 1782	3	297
Nancy, m. Asa **BEACH**, b. of Branford, Jan. 2, 1812	3	413
Nathaniel, s. William & Dorcas, b. Jan. 30, 1721/2	3	50
Nath[anie]ll, m. Mary **POND**, b. of Branford, Jan. 15,		
1746, by Rev. Philemon Robbins	3	150
Phinias, of Branford, m. Eunis **FOWLER**, of G[u]ilford,		
Jan. 15, 1756, by John Richards, North G[u]ilford	3	149
Pirmille*, d. Bertho[lome]w & Hannah, b. Aug. 25, 1774		
(^Pamelia?)	3	273
Polley, d. Gideon & Jerusha, b. Sept. 10, 1782	3	305
Rachel, d. Nath[anie]ll & Mary, b. Apr. 18, 1760	3	172
Sally, m. Timothy **BLACKSTON**, b. of Branford, Jan. 12,		
1826, by Rev. Timothy P. Gillett	3	341
Samuel, s. Nath[anie]ll & Mary, b. Dec. 15, 1757	3	150
Sam[ue]ll, s. Nath[anie]ll, d. June 14, 1760	3	172
Samuel, s. Phinehas & Eunice, b. July 24, 1765	3	186
Sarah, d. Timothy & Sarah, b. Feb. 19, 1749	3	166
Sarah, m. Joseph **CHIDSEY**, b. of Branford, May 17, 1769,		
by Nicholas Street	3	208
Sarah, d. Phinehas & Eunice, b. July 5, 1769	3	201
Sarah, d. Bartholomew & Hannah, b. Feb. 17, 1777	3	274
Sarah, d. Phinehas, d. May 1, 1822, ae 53 y.	3	426
Sarah Ann, [d. Will[ia]m & Mary Ann], b. June 11, 1830	3	367
Sarah Ann, of Branford, m. Nicholas S. **HALLENBACH**, of		
Albany, N. Y., Aug. 22, 1852, by Rev. Timothy P. Gillett	TM3	171
Solomon, s. David & Lydia, b. Dec. 28, 1761	3	176
Submit, d. Nath[anie]ll & Mary, b. June 18, 1747; d. same day	3	150
Timothy, m. Sarah **FOOT**, b. of Branford, Mar. 24, 1748,		
by Philemon Robbins	3	151
Timothy, m. Hannah **ROSE**, b. of Branford, Jan. 6, 1779,		
by Rev. Philemon Robbins	3	284
Timothy, s. Bartholomew & Hannah, b. Dec. 11, 1779	3	274
Timothy, Sr., f. of Bartholomew, d. Oct. 1, 1801	3	430
Timothy, f. of Bartholomew, d. July 23, 1802	3	388
William, m. Dorcas **FOOT**, b. of Branford, Nov. 30, 1720,		
by Rev. Sam[ue]ll Russel[l]	3	50
William, s. Nath[anie]ll & Mary, b. Sept. 30, 1746; d.		
Oct. 30, 1746	3	150
William, s. Nath[anie]ll & Mary, b. June 8, 1753	3	150
William, [s. Bartholomew & Hannah], b. Dec. 2, 1788	3	388
William, s. Bartholomew & Hannah, b. Dec. 2, 1788	3	430
William, of Branford, m. Marian **WHITING**, of North		
Branford, Feb. 27, 1826, by Rev. Timothy P. Gillett	3	341

	Vol.	Page
GOODRICH, GOODRIDG, GOODRIDGE, GOODRITCH,(cont.)		
William, d. Jan. 26, 1843, ae 54	TM3	305
Zada, d. Joseph & Eliza A., b. Oct. 16, 1826	3	362
----, s. [Phinias & Eunis], b. Aug. 7, 1757; d. in about 24 hr.	3	149
GOODSELL, GOODSEL, Deborah, d. Sam[ue]ll & Mary, b. Aug. 23, 1742	3	99
Deborah, m. Thomas FRISBIE, b. of Branford, Feb. 28, 1765, by Josiah Rogers, J. P.	3	194
Hannah, d. Jon[a]th[an] & Hannah, b. Aug. 24, 1768	3	202
Jonathan, Jr., m. Hannah TYLER, b. of Branford, Jan. 13, 1762, by Philemon Robbins	3	176
Jonathan, s. Jonathan & Hannah, b. Feb. 21, 1764	3	202
Josiah, s. Jonathan & Hannah, b. Aug. 12, 1775	3	263
Levi, s. Sam[ue]ll & Mary, b. June 17, 1745	3	106
Levi, d. July 7, 1768, in the 24th y. of his age	3	194
Lydia had d. Anne FRISBIE, b. Jan. 23, 1771	3	258
Lydia, m. Benjamin BALDWIN, b. of Branford, Apr. 27, 1780, by Warham Williams	3	269
Martha, wid., of New Haven, m. Sam[ue]ll BAKER, of Branford, Jan. 24, 1749/50, by Deodate Davenport, J. P.	3	125
Mary, d. Sam[ue]ll & Mary, b. Feb. 13, 1739/40	3	99
Mary, d. Jonathan & Hannah, b. Aug. 22, 1762	3	202
Sally, m. Samuel TYLER, Jr., May 12, 1803	3	286
Samuel, s. Sam[ue]ll & Mary, b. [Jan.] 21, 1737/8	3	89
Sarah, of Branford, m. Jeremiah WOOLCOT, of New Haven, Apr. 13, 1758, by Jonathan Merrick	3	163
Sarah, m. Jeremiah WOLCOTT, Apr. 13, 1758, by Jon[a]th[an] Mer[r]ick	3	193
Sarah, of Branford, m. Timothy BRADLEY, of East Haven, Sept. 12, 1762	3	280
Sarah, d. Jonathan & Hannah, b. Mar. 17, 1778	3	266
Simeon, s. Jonathan & Hannah, b. June 30, 1766	3	202
GORDON, Alexander, m. Lydia LINSL[E]Y, Nov. 5, 1764, by Philemon Robbins	3	199
Alexander, s. Alexander & Lydia, b. May 21, 1780	3	279
Alexander, Jr., m. Betsey [BROW], July 1, 1802	3	390
Alexander, s. Alexander & Mary b. July 1, 1835	3	376
Betsey, d. John & Lydia, b. Dec. 10, 1769	3	293
Betsey, d. Apr. 15, 1848, ae 65 y.	TM3	308
Betsey Ann, d. Alexander, Jr. & Betsey, b. July 9, 1817	3	430
Betsey Ann, [d. John & Mary], b. July 10, 1837	TM3	236
Charlotte Elen, [d. John & Mary], b. Aug. 12, 1835	TM3	236
George, s. John & Lydia, b. Dec. 7, 1779	3	293
Harriet Brow, d. Alexander, Jr. & Betsey, b. Feb. 21, 1814	3	430
Harriet Lydia, [d, John & Mary], b. Oct. 27, 1839	TM3	236
Heneretta, d. John & Lydia, b. July 30, 1774	3	293
Irene, d. Alexander & Lydia, b. July 13, 1776	3	262
Irene, m. Timothy BRADL[E]Y, Jr., b. of Branford, Dec. 10,		

	Vol.	Page
GORDON, (cont.)		
1797	3	391
Jane Alice, [d. John & Mary], b. Mar. 28, 1845	TM3	236
John, m. Lydia **JOHNSON**, b. of Branford, Oct. 30, 1765,		
by Phi[lemo]n Robbins	3	293
John, s. John & Lydia, b. Nov. 12, 1776	3	293
John, [s. Alexander, Jr. & Bets[e]y], b. Aug. 16, 1804	3	390
John, m. Harriet **HOADLEY**, b. of Branford, Oct. 25, 1827,		
by Rev. Timothy P. Gillett	3	345
John, m. Mary **BEERS**, b. of Branford, Aug. 20, 1833, by		
Rev. T. P. Gillett	3	361
Lucretia, [d. Alexander, Jr. & Bets[e]y, b. Apr. 6, 1806	3	390
Lucretia, of Branford, m. George **BALDWIN**, of North		
Branford, Dec. 12, 1826, by Rev. Timothy P. Gillett	3	343
Lydia, d. John & Lydia, b. Mar. 13, 1772	3	293
Nancy, [d. Alexander, Jr. & Bets[e]y], b. Mar. 26, 1808	3	390
Nancy, m. Edmund **PAGE**, b. of Branford, Oct. 22, 1827,		
by Rev. Timothy P. Gillett	3	345
Silvia, d. John & Lydia, b. Oct. 20, 1767	3	293
Washington, s. John & Lydia, b. Dec. 24, 1783	3	293
William, s. Alexander & Lydia, b. Dec. 22, 1787	3	277
William, s. Alexander & Lydia, b. Dec. 23, 1787	3	256
GORHAM, Judson, of Stratford, m. Nancy **STAPLES**, of Branford,		
Oct. 12, 1835, by Rev. T. P. Gillett	3	371
Parnal, m. Chauncey **LINSL[E]Y**, b. of Branford, Dec. 8,		
1803	3	282
Sarah, of New Haven, m. Joel **BALDWIN**, of Branford, Apr.		
28, 1783, by Sam[ue]ll Eells	3	272
Sarah, m. Joel **BALDWIN**, Apr. 25, 1783, by Sam[ue]ll Eells	3	312
GOULD, GOULDE, Abigail, [w. of William], d. May 25, 1725, ae		
49, y.	3	278
Abigail, d. Thomas & Lydia, b. Oct. 1, 1753	3	134
Abigail, m. Benjamin **PALMER**, Jr., b. of Branford, Mar.		
3, 1774	3	291
Abigail, m. Benjamin **PALMER**, Jr. b. of Branford, Mar.		
3, 1774	3	304
Abigail, [d. William & Mary], b. July 29, [ ]	3	278
Angeline, [d. John & Rebecca], b. Jan. 25, 1807	3	281
Ann Charlotte, d. Orchard & Polly, b. July 27, 1796	3	256
Ann Charlotte, d. Orchard & Polly, b. July 27, 1796	3	284
Anne, [d. William & Mary], b. May 1, 1738; d. June 16, 1738	3	278
Ann, [d. William & Mary], b. Jan. 9, 1739/40	3	279
Anne, m. Sam[ue]ll Holden **TORREY**, b. of Branford, Apr.		
3, 1760, by Philemon Robbins	3	163
Anne, d. Col. Will[ia]m & Mary, b. Mar. 9, 1777	3	304
Charlotte, d. John & Rebe[c]kah, b. Feb. 25, 1816	3	403
Elias, of Branford, m. Amanda **KIMBERLY**, of Guilford,		
Mar. 23, 1812	3	428

	Vol.	Page
GOULD, GOULDE, (cont.)		
Elias, [s. Elias & Amanda], b. Oct. 5, 1817	3	428
Elisabeth, d. Dr. William & Mary, b. Mar. 1, 1774	3	261
Guy, s. Samuel & Sally, b. Mar. 26, 1800	3	388
James, s. Dr. W[illia]m & Mary, b. Dec. 5, 1770	3	260
James, s. Sam[ue]l & Sally, b. Dec. 11, 1793	3	271
John, [s. William & Mary], b. Oct. 2, 1726; d. Apr. 6, [ ]	3	278
John, d. Apr. 6, 1754, in the 28th y. of his age, at sea	3	279
John, s. Thomas, d. Jan. 30, 1774, a 7 y. 1 m. 18 d.	3	292
John, s. Thomas, b. Apr. 24, 1776	3	292
John, m. Rebecca **ROGERS**, Nov. 1, 1800	3	281
John, d. Mar. 28, 1851, ae 75 y.	TM3	310
John W., s. Sam[ue]l & Sally, b. Sept. 4, 1784	3	271
John Whitehead, [s. John], b. Mar. 2, 1754	3	279
Julia, d. John & Rebeccah, b. Dec. 11, 1812	3	399
Lydia, d. Thomas & Lydia, b. Dec. 25, 1759	3	161
Lydia, m. Jonathan **PALMER**, b. of Branford, Nov. 14, 1779, by Sam[ue]ll Eells	3	282
Lydia Ann, [d. Elias & Amanda], b. May 15, 1812	3	428
Mabel, d. Thomas & Lydia, b. May 22, 1762	3	183
Mable, m. Ichabod **PAGE**, b. of Branford, July 26, 1780	3	307
Mary, [d. William & Mary], b. June 27, 1732	3	278
Mary, w. of William, d. Nov. 18, 1743, in her 39th y.	3	279
Mary, d. Wil[l]iam, Jr. & Mary, b. May [15], 1750	3	139
Mary, [w.] William, Jr., d. July 8, 1750	3	154
Mary, w. of William, d. Feb. 11, 1763, in the 37th y. of her age	3	178
Mary, d. Dr. W[illia]m & Mary, b. Dec. 20, 1765	3	260
Mary, d. Orchard & Polly, b. Dec. 1, 1791	3	268
Mary, of Branford, d. of Orchard & Mary, m. James **WASSON**, of Fairfield, Oct. 8, 1815, by Rev. Timothy P. Gillett	3	402
Mary, wid. of William & maiden name **GUY**, d. Sept. 15, 1816, in the 80th y. of her age	3	278
Mary, wid. of William, d. Sept. 15, 1816, in the 80th y. of her age, in Litchfield	3	403
Mary, see Mary **KELLOGG** & Mary **HUGGINS**	3	403
Mary Amanda, [d. Elias & Amanda], b. Mar. 23, 1821	3	428
Mahitabel, [d. William & Mary], b. Aug. 6, 1741; d. Aug. 13, 1741	3	279
Mahitabel, [d. William & Mary], b. Jan. 10, 1742/3; d. May 2, 1743	3	279
Orchard, s. Dr. William & Mary, b. Mar. 1, 1764	3	260
Orchard, m. Polly **ROGERS**, Nov. 28, 1790	3	268
Parnel, d. John & Rebe[c]kah, b. Jan. 3, 1819	3	334
Richard, formerly of North Lawton in the Parish of Oakhampton, County of Devonshire, England, d. Apr. 28, 1746, in the 84th y. of his age	3	278
Richard, [s. John & Rebecca], b. Jan. 30, 1806	3	281

	Vol.	Page
GOULD, GOULDE, (cont.)		
Sally, d. Sam[ue]l & Sally, b. May 16, 1791	3	271
Sally, w. of Samuel, d. Sept. 20, 1836, ae 71 y. 2 m. 8 d.	3	372
Samuel, s. William & Mary, b. Apr. 23, 1761	3	175
Samuel, s. Dr. William & Mary, d. [May] 10, 1765	3	260
Samuel, s. Dr. W[illia]m & Mary, b. Sept. 8, 1767	3	260
Samuel, Jr., s. Sam[ue]l & Sally, b. Sept. 2, 1788;		
d. Apr.6, 1789	3	271
Sarah, d. Thomas & Lydia, b. July 26, 1757	3	161
Thomas, [s. William & Mary], b. Apr. 14, 1730	3	278
Thomas, m. Lydia **HOADL[E]Y**, d. of Sam[ue]ll, b. of		
Branford, June 25, 1753	3	144
Thomas, s. Thomas & Lydia, b. Apr. 3, 1755	3	144
Thomas, Jr., s. Thom[a]s, d. Oct. 18, 1776, ae 21 y. 6 m.		
16 d., "by a wound received at Harlem Heights"	3	292
Thomas, d. Apr. 19, 1805, in the 76th y. of his age	3	278
Thomas, [s. Elias & Amanda], b. Jan. 2, 1816	3	428
Whitehead, [s. William & Mary], b. Feb. 18, [ ]	3	278
William, s. Richard, b. Feb. 11, 1692/3, at Parish of		
Oakhampton, England, d. Jan. 29, 1757	3	278
William, m. Abigail **FARRINGTON**, June 11, 1718	3	278
William, m. Mary **WHITEHEAD**, b. of Branford, Dec. 9,		
1725, by Rev. Sam[ue]ll Russell	3	58
William, m. Mary **WHITEHEAD**, Dec. 9, 1725	3	278
William, [s. William & Mary], b. Nov. 17, 1727	3	278
Will[ia]m, of Branford, m. Mrs. Sarah **FANNING**, of New		
London, July 1, 1744, by Eliphalet Adams	3	102
William, m. Sarah **[FANNING]**, July 1, 1744	3	279
William, Jr., of Branford, m. Mary **LORD**, of Saybrook,		
June 22, 1749, by William Hart	3	154
William, Jr., m. Mary **MALTBIE**, b. of Branford, Dec. 11,		
1751, by Philemon Robbins	3	154
William, s. W[illia]m, Jr. & Mary, b. Apr. 1, 1752	3	139
William, d. Jan. 29, 1757, in the 64th y. of his age	3	154
William, Dr., m. Mary **JOHNSON**, b. of Branford, May 5,		
1763, by Philemon Robbins	3	181
William, s. Mercy **LINSLEY**, b. Dec. 22, 1773	3	264
William, d. July 29, 1805, in the 78th y. of his age	3	278
William had negro Simeon, d. Oct. 22, 1805, in the 59th		
y. of his age	3	278
William, s. William & Mary (**MALTBY**), d. Aug. 4, 1809, in		
the 58th y. of his age, at Manchester, Vt.	3	403
GRANNIS GRANNISS, Charles H., twin s. John & Sally, b. May		
18, 1851	TM3	245
Desire, of New Haven, m. Gideon **FRISBIE**, of Branford,		
Jan. 17, 1733/4, by Rev. Isaac Stiles	3	81
Edwin, ae 23, m. Delia A **LINSLEY**, ae 21, Oct. 24, 1850,		
by T. P. Gillett	TM3	170

	Vol.	Page

GRANNIS, GRANNISS, (cont.)

Edwin H., of East Haven, m. Delia Ann **LINSLEY**, of
Branford, Oct. 24, 1850, by Rev. T. P. Gillett ... TM3 ... 168

Elisabeth, of New Haven, m. Israel **FRISBIE**, of Branford,
July 1, 1731, by Rev. Isaac Stiles ... 3 ... 81

John, m. Sally E. **GRIFFING**, b. of Branford, Dec. 24,
1838, by Rev. Timothy P. Gillett ... 3 ... 376

Sylvester M., m. Lydia L. **BRADLEY**, b. of Branford, Sept.
25, 1853, by Rev. L. Atwater ... TM3 ... 172

----, d. John & Sally, b. Jan. 3, 1848 ... TM3 ... 239

----, s. John d. May 13, 1851, ae 1 d. ... TM3 ... 310

GRANT, Catharine, d. Peter & Ellanah, b. Dec. 30, 1775 ... 3 ... 275

Daniel, s. Peter & Ellanah, b. Mar. 4, 1778 ... 3 ... 275

James, s. Peter & Ellanah, b. May, 12, 1780 ... 3 ... 275

Nancy, of Branford, m. Frederick W. **FOWLER**, of Guilford,
Oct. 19 1830, by Timothy P. Gillett ... 3 ... 356

Polly, of Branford, m. Roswell C. **HART**, of Harwinton,
Mar. 11, 1827, by Rev. Timothy P. Gillett ... 3 ... 343

[GRAVES], GRAUES, Sarah, m. Samuel **BRADFEILD**, June 27,
1677 ... 1 ... 210

Thankfull, of Guilford, m. Moses **PAGE**, of Branford,
Oct. 20, 1731, by Rev. Thomas Ruggles ... 3 ... 74

GRIFFING, GRIFFIN, Aaron, m. Elizabeth **GRIFFING**, Aug. 5,
1784 ... 3 ... 388

Bets[e]y, [d. Aaron & Elizabeth], b. Dec. 20, 1793 ... 3 ... 388

Elizabeth, m. Aaron **GRIFFING**, Aug. 5, 1784 ... 3 ... 388

Elisabeth S., m. Rhodolphus **BARTHOLOMEW**, b. of
Branford, June 15, 1848, by Rev. Timothy P. Gillett ... TM3 ... 162

Harriet D., of Branford, m. Increase W. **COOK**, of North
Guilford, May 13, 1832, by Tim[othy] P. Gillett ... 3 ... 357

Henry, [s. Aaron & Elizabeth], b. May 8, 1797 ... 3 ... 388

Henry Augustus, s. [John & Jenny, colored], b. Mar. 7, 1800 ... 3 ... 399

Jared, [s. Aaron & Elizabeth], b. Jan. 19, 1788 ... 3 ... 388

Jared, s. [Aaron & Elizabeth], d. Sept. 26, 1806 ... 3 ... 388

Jenny, [colored], d. Mar. 20, 1847, ae 86 ... TM3 ... 307

Lucy Leura, [d. John & Jenny, colored], b. Dec. 25, 1801 ... 3 ... 399

Mindwell, d. Timothy & Thankfull, b. Nov. 30, 1784 ... 3 ... 279

Nancy, [d. Aaron & Elizabeth], b. Apr. 30, 1785 ... 3 ... 388

Nancy, m. Joel **IVES**, Jr., b. of Branford, Nov. 8, 1821,
by Timothy P. Gillett ... 3 ... 415

Nancy, m. John **SPENCER**, b. of Branford, May 12, 1849,
by Rev. T. P. Gillett ... TM3 ... 163

Sally E., m. John **GRANNISS**, b. of Branford, Dec. 24,
1838, by Rev. Timothy P. Gillett ... 3 ... 376

Samuel, [s. Aaron & Elizabeth], b. July 5, 1790 ... 3 ... 388

Teresa Eleonora, [d. John & Jenny, colored], b. Dec. 24, 1812 ... 3 ... 399

----, d. William & Elizabeth, b. Sept. 14, 1848 ... TM3 ... 240

GRISWOLD, Betsey, of Branford, m. Nathan N. **TUCKER**, of

	Vol.	Page
GRISWOLD, (cont.)		
North Madison, Nov. 29, 1832, by Levi Bradley, J. P.	3	358
GUDSILL , [see under **GUTSILL**]		
GUN[N], Joseph, s. Nathani[e]ll, b. Apr. 19, [16]63	1	173
Nathaniell, s. Nathani[e]ll, b. Apr. 23, [16]61	1	172
GUTSILL, GUDSELL, GUDSILL, John, s. Jonathan & Elizabeth,		
b. Aug. 15, 1747	3	146
Jonathan, s. J[o]nathan & Elizabeth, b. Feb. 27, 1740/1	3	146
Josiah, s. Jonathan & Elizabeth, b. Mar. 27, 1742;		
d. [Sept. 19, 1743]	3	146
Josiah, s. Jonathan & Elizabeth, b. Dec. 2, 1743;		
d Oct. 15, 1744	3	146
Josiah, s. Jonathan & Elizabeth, b. Jan. 22, 1750	3	146
Lydia, d. Thomas & Sarah, b. May 3, 1692 (First		
written "May 2")	2	343
Mary, d. Thomas & Sarah, b. Dec. 22, 1686	1	210
Samuel, s. Thomas & Sarah, b. Feb. 28, 1684	1	210
Samuel, s. Jonathan & Elizabeth, b. Mar. 10, 1756	3	146
Sarah, d. Thomas & Sarah, b. Sept. 14, [1689]	2	343
Sarah, d. Jonathan & Elizabeth, b. Oct. 24, 1745	3	146
Thomas, m. Sarah **HEMINWAY**, June 4, 1684	1	210
GUY, Anna, d. Orchard & Mary, b. July 17, 1740	3	95
Anna, d. Mar. 28, 1814, in the 74th y. of her age	3	400
Anne, d. Orch[ar]d, Jr. & Abigail, b. Jan. 18, 1768	3	195
Elisabeth, d. Orchard & Mary, b. Dec. 5, 1738	3	90
Elisabeth, m. Sam[ue]ll **HUGGINS**, b. of Branford, July 3,		
1760, by Philemon Robbins	3	162
John, s. Orchard & Mary, b. May 26, 1742	3	98
Lydia, d. Dec. 21, 1821	3	420
Mary, d. Orchard & Mary, b. May 13, 1737	3	87
Mary, of Branford, m. Timothy **JOHNSON**, of Guilford, Feb.		
10, 1757, by Rev. Philemon Robbins	3	145
Mary, see Mary **GOULD**	3	403
Orchard, m. Mary **FOOT**, b. of Branford, Dec. 5, 1733, by		
Rev. Philemon Robbins	3	80
Orchard, s. Orchard & Mary, b. July 27, 1744	3	102
Orchard, Jr. m. Abigail **BALDWIN**, b. of Branford, Aug.		
20, 1767, by Philemon Robbins	3	195
Orchard, s. Orchard & Abigail b. July 25, 1770	3	260
Rebe[c]kah, d. Orchard & Abigail, b. July 5, 1773	3	260
Sarah, d. Orchard & Mary, b. Nov. 27, 1734	3	80
Will[ia]m, s. Orchard & Mary, b. [Apr. 20, 1754]	3	136
HALL, Alanson, of Litchfield, m. Rebe[c]kah **WALKER**, of		
Branford, Dec. 10, 1829, by Rev. Timothy P. Gillett	3	351
Andrews, [s. Alanson & Rebecca], b. Apr. 14, 1832	3	379
Ann, Mrs., of Wallingford, m. Warham **WILLIAMS**, of		
Branford, Nov. 30, 1752, by Rev. Sam[ue]ll Hall	3	133
George K., of Wallingford, m. Harriet **BROCKWAY**, of		

	Vol.	Page

HALL, (cont.)

	Vol.	Page
Branford, Oct. 3, 1844, by Rev. Timothy P. Gillett	TM3	157
Hannah, of Wallingford, m. Berijah **TYLER**, of Branford, Apr. 7, 1751, by Rev. Warham Williams	3	125
Hannah, of Guilford, m. John **PAMELE**, of Branford, July 2, 1808	3	392
Hannah C., of Branford, m. Henry B. **BARTLETT**, of Waymait, Penn., Aug. 28, 1836, by Rev. T. P. Gillett	3	372
Henry, [s. Alanson & Rebecca], b. Feb. 4, 1839	3	379
Joel, of Wallingford, m. Hannah **BEACH**, of Branford, May 4, 1830, by Timothy P. Gillett	3	353
Newton A., ae 23, m. Armenia F. **COONS**, ae 20, May 4, 1851, by Rev. Dr. Olden	TM3	170
Rebecka, d. Oct. 31, 1848, ae 38 y.	TM3	309
Roger, [s. Alanson & Rebecca], b. Feb. 20, 1831	3	379
Ruhama Trowbridge, d. Elias & Ruhama, m. Elias **PLANT**, s. Benjamin & Lorana, Mar. 30, 1799	3	392
Ruth, of Wallingford, m. Josiah **FOWLER**, of Branford, Feb. 13, 1752, by Rev. Sam[ue]ll Hall	3	133
Sally P., of Wallingford, m. Benjamin **FOOT**, of Branford, Apr. 24, 1803	3	277
Sarah, [d. Alanson & Rebecca], b. Apr. 23, 1834	3	379
William M., of Wallingford, m. Jane **BALDWIN**, of Branford, Dec. 16, 1829, by J. A. Root	3	351
William [S], of Wallingford, m. Sally L. **BEACH**, of Branford, Sept. 23, 1829, by Rev. Timothy P. Gillett	3	350
----, d. Eli & Thankful, b. Dec. 17, 1850	TM3	245
----, d. Eli, d. Dec. 17, 1850, ae 1 d.	TM3	310
HALLENBACH, Nicholas S., of Albany, N. Y., m. Sarah Ann **GOODRICH**, of Branford, Aug. 22, 1852, by Rev. Timothy P. Gillett	TM3	171
HALLOCK, HALLIOCK, Dennis, s. Nath[a]n & Lucretia, b. Sept. 21, 1782	3	279
Leucrecy, w. of Nathan & d. of Benj[ami]n, Jr. & Lydia **HOADLEY**, b. Mar. 22, 1762	3	291
Nathan, b. Nov. 22, 1760, on Long Island	3	291
Nathan, m. Lucretia [**HOADLEY**], June 13, 1782, by Sam[ue]ll Eells	3	279
HAMLIN, Margaret, of Wallingford, m. Thomas Frederick **DICKER**, of Sussex, Eng., Aug. 2, 1840, by Rev. Pascal P. Kidder	TM3	152
HAND, Esther, of East Guilford, m. John **HUGGINS**, of Branford, Apr. 14, 1756, by Rev. Jon[a]th[an] Todd	3	158
HARDING, Michael, s. Francis & Ellen, b. Apr. 15, 1850	TM3	242
HARLOW, Ransom Byrom, Dr., m. Sarah **WOLCUT**, Nov. 18, 1775, by Josiah Rogers, J. P.	3	261
HARRINGTON, HARRINTON, HERRINGTON, Hannah, d. Sam[ue]ll & Hannah, b. Mar. 25, 170[ ]	3	31

	Vol.	Page
HARRINGTON, HARRINTON, HERRINGTON, (cont.)		
Hannah, m. Joseph **TALMAGE**, b. of Branford, June 22, 1739,		
by Rev. Jonathan Merrick	3	91
John, s. Samuel & Hannah, b. Aug. 27, 1712	3	35
John, m. Lydia **ROGERS**, b. of Branford, Mar. 20, 1732,		
by Rev. Jacob Heminway	3	96
Lydia, d. Sam[ue]ll & Hannah, b. Nov. 22, 1714	3	36
Lydia, m. Josiah **BARTHOLOMEW**, b. of Branford, June 10,		
1740, by Rev. Philemon Robbins	3	96
Mehetabell, d. Sam[ue]ll, b. Oct. 3, 1681	1	211
Naomi, m. Sam[ue]ll **ROSE**, 3rd, b. of Branford, Apr. 15,		
1752, by Rev. Philemon Robbins	3	125
Samuel, m. Hannah **BARNES**, July 27, 1693, by William		
Maltbie, J. P.	2	343
Sam[ue]ll, m. Hannah **ROSE**, Jan 5, 1703/4, by W[illia]m		
Maltbie, J. P.	2	345
Sam[ue]ll, Sr., d. July 25, 1719	3	43
Sam[ue]ll, Jr., d. Aug. 25, 1729	3	67
Sam[ue]ll, Dea., d. Dec. 2, 1760, in the 82nd y. of his age	3	176
Sarah, d. Sam[ue]ll & Hannah, b. Apr. 29, 1709	3	33
HARRISON, HARISON, Aaron, s. Thom[as] & Marg[are]t, b. Mar.		
4, 1704	3	29
Aaron, s. Thom[as] & Margeret, d. Nov. 30, 1708	3	30
Aaron, s. Benjamin & Mary, b. Apr. 20, 1726	3	65
Abel, s. Thomas & Hannah, b. Feb. 2, 1731/2	3	78
Abel, s. Thomas & Hannah, b. Feb. 2, 1731/2	3	84
Abigail, d. Thom[as] & Margeret, b. Nov. 17, 169[ ]	3	29
Abigail, d. Nath[anie]ll & Thankfull, b. Mar. 6, 1721/2	3	51
Abigail, d. Benj[ami]n & Mary, b. Dec. 14, 1735	3	83
Abigail, d. Jon[a]th[an] & Desire, b. July 11, 1736	3	93
Abigail, m. Josiah **POND**, b. of Branford, Dec. 9, 1736,		
by Rev. Philemon Robbins	3	90
Abigail, m. Nath[anie]ll **FRISBIE**, Oct. 25, 1745, by Rev.		
Philemon Robbins	3	152
Abigail, m. Phinehas **TYLER**, b. of Branford, Mar. 16,		
1760, by Philemon Robbins	3	170
Abigail, d. Jairus & Mary, b. Oct. 27, 1777	3	309
Abigail, m. Hezekiah **BONNELL**, July 29, 1829, by Rev. J.		
A. Root	3	350
Abraham, s. Nath[anie]ll & Hannah, b. Feb. 28, 1700	3	33
Abraham, s. Nathan[ie]ll & Hannah, d. Aug. 27, 1714	3	33
Abraham, s. Dan[ie]ll & Hannah, b. Nov. 20, 1728	3	173
Abraham, m. Hannah **JOHNSON**, b. of Branford, Jan. 26,		
1764, by Jon[a]th[an] Mer[r]ick	3	185
Abraham, s. Abraham & Hannah, b. Aug. 19, 1767	3	192
Alexander, [s. Butler & Mercy], b. Mar. 23, 1795	3	340
Ammi, Jr., s. Ammi & Elizabeth, b. July 28, 1790	3	271
Ammi, d. Mar. 14, 1850, ae 86 y.	TM3	309

	Vol.	Page
HARRISON, HARISON, (cont.)		
Amos, s. Nathan[ie]ll & Hannah, b. Mar. 11, 1707	3	33
Amos, m. Esther **MALTBIE**, b. of Branford, Mar. 11, 1729/30,		
by Jno. Russell, J. P.	3	75
Amy, w. of Ithiel, d. Oct. 27, 1817	3	370
An[n], d. Richard, b. Nov. 2, [16]57	1	172
Ann, d. Richard, [d.] Nov. 8, [16]57	1	170
Anna, m. Titus **MUNSON**, Dec. 6, 1821, by Rev. Matthew		
Noyes	3	415
Anne, m. Samuel **FOOT**, b. of Branford, Dec. 27, 1765, by		
Warham Williams	3	186
Anne, d. Nathan & Martha, b. Aug. 30, 1769	3	204
Anne Maria, m. Willoughby L. **LAY**, Aug. 16, 1818, by Rev.		
Timothy P. Gillett	3	415
Apollos, [s. Butler & Mercy], b. Dec. 15, 1791	3	340
Asahel, Capt., m. Elisabeth **HARRISON**, b. of Branford,		
Mar. 11, 1779	3	306
Beniamin, s. Richard, b. July 30, 1655	1	172
Benjamin, s. Thom[as] & Margeret, b. Aug. 7, 1698	3	29
Benjamin, m. Mary **SUTLIEF**, b. of Branford, Oct. 19,		
1720, by Rev. Sam[ue]ll Russell	3	50
Benjamin, s. Benjamin & Mary, b. Nov. 14, 1721	3	51
Benjamin, s. Jonathan & Desire, b. Dec. 21, 1730	3	71
Benjamin, s. Edward & Sarah, b. Jan. 12, 1776; d.		
Sept. 3, 1795	3	312
Betey, d. Farrington & Hannah, b. Mar. 18, 1777	3	276
Betsey, d. Sam[ue]ll & Rebecca, b. Aug. 19, 1779	3	289
Betsey, d. Ammi & Elizabeth, b. May 28, 1786	3	270
Betsey, m. Augustus **PALMER**, Dec. 23, 1804	3	282
Betsey E., [d. Israel M. & Nancy], b. Apr. 30, 1822	3	370
Butler, s. Timothy & Lydia, b. Feb. 16, 1757	3	160
Butler, m. Mercy **LINSLEY**, b. of Branford, Feb. 14, 1782,		
by Nicholas Street	3	272
Caroline, [d. Increase & Lucy], b. Aug. 19, 1825	3	340
Charles, [s. Butler & Mercy], b. May 9, 1790	3	340
Charles, m. Eunice **BLACKSTONE**, Oct. 10, 1821, by		
Timothy P. Gillett	3	414
Charles I., m. Laura A. **CHIDSEY**, b. of Branford, Dec.		
21, 1842, by Rev. Pascal P. Kidder	TM3	155
Chloe, d. Timothy, Jr. & Clor[i]nda, b. Aug. 4, 1784	3	311
Cornelia, d. [John & Betsey], b. Aug. 15, 1826	TM3	233
Cornelia, d. John & Betsey, d. Feb. 28, 1828, ae		
1 y. 6 m. 13 d.	TM3	306
Dan[ie]ll, s. Nathan[ie]ll & Hannah, b. Sept. 12, 1694	3	33
Dan[ie]ll, m. Hannah **HOADL[E]Y**, b. of Branford, June 30,		
1720, by Rev. Sam[ue]ll Russell	3	53
Daniel, s. Daniel & Hannah, b. Aug. 5, 1722	3	53
Dan[ie]ll, Jr., m. Hannah **BARKER**, b. of Branford, Apr. 28,		

	Vol.	Page
HARRISON, HARISON, (cont.)		
1748, by Rev. Jonath[an] Mer[r]ick	3	113
Dan[ie]ll, s. Dan[ie]ll & Hannah, b. Feb. 2, 1751	3	133
Dan[ie]ll, d. Oct. 10, 1752	3	173
Daniel, Jr., m. Hannah **PAGE**, b. of Branford, Dec. 10,		
1772, by Samuel Eells	3	207
Danniel Foot, m. Zada **MONRO[E]**, b. of Branford, Mar. 7,		
1780	3	283
David, s. Thom[as] & Ma[r]g[are]t, b. Feb. 7, 1702	3	29
David, of Branford, m. Mary **WOOSTER**, of Stratford, Jan.		
1, 1728/9, by Rev. Jedidiah Mills	3	65
David, s. Nathan & Martha, b. Sept. 22, 1772	3	257
David, s. Farrington & Hannah, b. Aug. 20, 1781	3	276
David, s. [John & Betsey], b. Feb. 10, 1819	TM3	233
Deborah, d. Abraham & Hannah, b. Apr. 24, 1765	3	185
Desire, d. Jonathan & Desire, b. Apr. 16, 1733	3	93
Desire, m. James **BUTLER**, b. of Branford, Jan. 22, 1756,		
by Philemon Robbins	3	153
Desire, d. Jon[a]th[an], Jr. & Sarah, b. Jan. 29, 1757	3	280
Doratha, d. Nath[anie]ll & Hannah, b. Mar. 1, 1702	3	33
Dorothy, d. Timothy & Lydia, b. Dec. 26, 1762	3	179
Edward m. Sarah **DUDLEY**, b. of Branford, [Dec. 12, 1771]	3	265
Elihu, s. Thomas & Hannah, b. Feb. 25, 1739/40	3	92
Elizabeth, d. John & Rebeccah, b. Oct. 20, 1703	2	346
Elisabeth, d. Isaac & Patience, b. [ ]; [bp. Feb. 9, 1719]	3	32
Elisabeth, d. of Jno., m. John **WILLFORD**, b. of Branford,		
Feb. 6, 1752, by Rev. Philemon Robbins	3	125
Elisabeth, m. John **PALMER**, b. of Branford, Apr. 10, 1754,		
by Jon[a]th[an] Merrick	3	286
Elisabeth, d. Timothy & Lydia, b. Oct. 2, 1755	3	160
Elisabeth, m. Capt. Asahel **HARRISON**, b. of Branford,		
Mar. 11, 1779	3	306
Elizabeth, b. July 22, 1779; m. Rufus **FOOT**, Mar. 12, 1799	3	409
Elizur, [s. Butler & Mercy], b. Apr. 3, 1797	3	340
Elizur, [s. Increase & Lucy], b. June 13, 1823	3	340
Elizur, [s. Butler & Mercy], b. Aug. 9, 1823	3	340
Ephraim, s. Thomas & Hannah, b. Dec. 28, 1726	3	78
Esther, d. Amos & Esther, b. May 17, 1731	3	75
Esther, d. Daniel & Hannah, b. Oct. 15, 1767; d. Nov. 23, 1767	3	192
Esther, d. Timothy & Lydia, b. May 13, 1770	3	199
Esther, d. Edward & Sarah, b. Oct. 1, 1772; d. Aug. 1, 1773	3	265
Eunice, m. Ithiel **RUSSELL**, Jr. b. of Branford, Nov. 20,		
1771, by Samuel Eells	3	205
Eunice, m. Eliada **ROSE**, b. of Branford, Oct. 19, 1796	3	270
Eunice, d. Sam[ue]ll, Jr. & Rebecca, b. May 16, [ ]	3	289
Farringtun, s. Jon[a]th[an] & Desire, b. July [ ], 1735;		
d. Aug. following	3	93
Farringtun, s. Jon[a]th[an] & Desire, b. Oct. 1, 1738	3	93

	Vol.	Page
HARRISON, HARISON, (cont.)		
Farrington, m. Hannah **WILLFORD**, b. of Branford, Sept.		
29, 1772, by Philemon Robbins	3	276
Fosdick, s. Timothy, Jr. & Clorenda, b. Aug. 10, 1782	3	272
George, s. Richard, b. Dec. 31, [16]58	1	172
Gideon, s. Thomas, Jr. & Hannah, b. Aug. 5, 1724	3	55
Hannah, d. Nathan[ie]ll & Hannah, b. July 28, 1690	3	33
Hannah, d. Isaac & Patience, b. Oct. 3, 1711	3	32
Hannah, w. of Capt. Nathaniel, d. Sept. 27, 1723	3	53
Hannah, d. Nath[anie]ll & Thankfull, b. Nov. 8, 1725	3	57
Hannah, d. Dan[ie]ll & Hannah, b. May 9, 1726	3	173
Hannah, m. Ichabod **FOOT**, b. of Branford, Mar. 4, 1733/4,		
by Rev. Philemon Robbins	3	95
Hannah, w. of Dan[ie]ll, d. Jan. 15, 1747/8	3	173
Hannah, d. Jon[a]th[an], Jr. & Sarah, b. Apr. 23, 1749	3	280
Hannah, m. Sam[ue]ll **ROGERS**, b. of Branford, Dec. 5,		
1751, by Nathan[ie]ll Harrison, J. P.	3	131
Hannah, m. Stephen **BLAKISTON**, b. of Branford, May 13,		
1752, by Jon[a]th[an] Merrick	3	165
[Hannah], w. of Isaac, d. Oct. 4, 1753	3	134
Hannah, d. Isaac & Rebec[c]ah, b. Nov. 20, 1757	3	150
Hannah, d. Stephen & Susanna, b. July 24, 1758	3	156
Hannah, d. Stephen & Susanna, d. Jan. 29, 1770	3	201
Hannah, m. Mason **HOBART**, b. of Branford, Nov. 28, 1776,		
by Philemon Robbins	3	287
Hannah, wid. of Capt. Farrington, d. Dec. 1, 1843, ae 90 y.	TM3	305
Hannah Venelia, b. June 12, 1819	3	399
Harvey, m. Lydia **LEWIS**, b. of North Branford, May 1,		
1853, by Rev. Lucius Atwater	TM3	172
Henry, s. Justus & Sarah, b. Dec. 28, 1783	3	296
Henry G., s. [John & Betsey], b. Apr. 5, 1831	TM3	233
Hervey, [s. Israel M. & Nancy], b. Jan. 31, 1830	3	370
Horace, s. Jared & Mary, b. Apr. 15, 1788	3	269
Increase, [s. Butler & Mercy], b. June 2, 1799	3	340
Isaac, m. Patience **TYLER**, Dec. 12, 1706, by Rev. Sam[ue]ll		
Russel[l]	3	32
Isaac, s. Isaac & Patience, b. May 22, 1722	3	49
Isaac, m. Hannah **JOHNSON**, b. of Branford, May 21, 1752,		
by Rev. Philemon Robbins	3	134
Isaac, m. Rebecca **ROGERS**, d. of Noah, b. of Branford,		
Aug. 26, 1756, by Rev. P. Robbins	3	143
Isaac, d. Sept. 11, 1770, ae 48, 2 m. 20 d.	3	200
Israel, s. Capt. Josiah & Lydia, b. Feb. 15, 1757	3	297
Israel M., m. Nancy **PAGE**, b. of Branford, July 22, 1819	3	370
Ithiel, s. Capt. Josiah & Lydia, b. July 27, 1759	3	297
Ithiel, d. Jan. 1, 1818	3	370
Jacob, s. Thomas & Margeret, b. Oct. 23, 1708	3	30
Jacob, s. Thomas & Hannah, b. Oct. 7, 1734	3	84

	Vol.	Page
HARRISON, HARISON, (cont.)		
Jacob, s. Jon[a]th[an], Jr. & Sarah, b. Apr. 19, 1765	3	280
Jacob, s. Nathan & Martha, b. July 16, 1765	3	204
Jacob, m. Lois **RUSSELL**, Dec. 13, 1781, by Sa[mue]ll Eells	3	309
Jacob, m. Hannah **BARTHOLOMEW**, Oct. 24, 1805	3	399
Jairus, m. Mary **HARRISON**, b. of Branford, Apr. 8, 1777,		
by Sam[ue]ll Eells	3	308
James, s. Sam[ue]ll & Elisabeth, b. Mar. 23, 1720/1	3	54
James, ae 23 y., of North Branford, m. Serene **BALDWIN**,		
ae 18 y., of Branford, Oct. 15, 1849, by Rev. G. P. Wood	TM3	166
Jared, s. Sam[ue]ll & Elisabeth, b. May 31, 1716	3	41
Jared, of Branford, m. Mary **McCLEAVE**, of New Haven, July		
25, 1776, by Cha[u]ncey Whittlccey	3	284
Jemima, d. Thomas & Marg[ar]et, b. Mar. 12, 1691/2	2	343
Jeremiah, m. Harriet **LINSLEY**, b. of Branford, Oct. 13,		
1824, by Charles Atwater	3	336
Jeremiah, of North Branford, m. Julia Ann **FRISBIE**, of		
Branford, Apr. 17, 1842, by Rev. Pascal P. Kidder	TM3	155
Jerome, s. Thaddeus & Elizabeth, b. Oct. 26, 1806	3	340
Jerusha, m. Ithiel **RUSSELL**, b. of Branford, Jan. 3, 1727/8,		
by Rev. Sam[ue]ll Russell	3	67
Jiles, s. Sam[ue]ll, Jr. & Rebecca, b. Oct. 4, 1765	3	289
Joel, s. Dan[ie]ll & Hannah, b. Mar. 21, 1753	3	133
John, s. Thomas, b. Mar. 1, 1670/1	1	210
John, m. Rebeccah **TRUESDELL**, Dec. 24, 1702, by Rev. Mr.		
Russell	2	344
John, s. John & Rebec[c]ah, b. July 27, 1712	3	35
John, s. John & Lydia, b. Sept. 12, 1742	3	113
John, s. Jon[a]th[an], Jr. & Sarah, b. Nov. 29, 1761	3	280
John, s. [John & Betsey], b. Aug. 6, 1821	TM3	233
John, s. John & Betsey, d. Aug. 6, 1821, ae 6 y. 5 m. 6 d.	TM3	306
John, [s. Israel M. & Nancy], b. Sept. 21, 1824	3	370
Jonathan, s. Nath[anie]ll & Hannah, b. July 8, 1704	3	33
Jonathan, m. Desire **FARRINTON**, b. of Branford, July 27,		
1726, by Rev. Sam[ue]ll Russell	3	62
Jonathan, s. Jon[a]th[an] & Desire, b. May 22, 1727	3	62
Jonathan, Jr., m. Sarah **BALDWIN**, b. of Branford, Aug.		
20, 1747	3	280
Joseph, s. Thom[as] & Margeret, b. May 25, 1700	3	29
Joseph, m. Sarah **FOOT**, b. of Branford, Apr. 10, 1729,		
by Rev. Sam[ue]ll Russell	3	66
Joseph, s. Joseph & Sarah, b. June 4, 1731	3	98
Joseph, d. July 23, 1748, in the 49th y. of his age	3	156
Joseph, s. Joseph, d. June 29, 1750, in the 19th y. of his age	3	156
Joseph, s. Daniel & Hannah, b. Feb. 23, 1758	3	152
Josiah, s. Nath[anie]ll & Hannah, b. Feb. 1, 1698	3	33
Josiah, m. Lydia **HO[A]DLY**, b. of Branford, June 12,		
1723, by Rev. Sam[ue]ll Russell	3	70

	Vol.	Page
HARRISON, HARISON, (cont.)		
Josiah, s. Josiah & Lydia, b. July 19, 1724	3	70
Josiah, Jr., m. Elisabeth **BUTLER**, d. of Jonathan, Jr., Feb. 16, 1745/6, by Rev. Jonath[a]n Mer[r]ick	3	107
Josiah, s. Josiah, Jr. & Elisabeth, b. Jan. 6, 1746/7	3	112
Josiah, m. wid. Lydia **HARRISON**, Oct. 24, 1754, by Jon[a]th[an] Merrick	3	297
Josiah, d. Dec. 13, 1773, in the 76th y. of his age	3	257
Josiah, Jr., d. Feb. 12, 1774	3	296
Juliette, d. [John & Betsey], b. Mar. 11, 1817	TM3	233
Juliette, d. John & Betsey, d. Dec. 7, 1817, ae 8 m. 11 d.	TM3	306
Justus, s. Capt. Josiah & Lydia, b. Oct. 3, 1755	3	297
Justus, m. Sarah **RUSSELL**, d. of Dea. Ebenez[e]r, b. of Branford, Nov. 7, 1779, by Sam[ue]ll Eells	3	296
Justus, s. Ammi & Elizabeth, b. Apr. 16, 1784	3	270
Justus, d. Aug. 13, 1826	3	376
Laveret, s. Daniel F. & Zada, b. Sept. 17, 1781	3	283
Leah, d. Joseph & Sarah, b. Apr. 14, 1736	3	98
Leah, d. Joseph, d. Aug. 11, 1751, in the 16th y. of her age	3	156
Lemuel, s. Thomas & Hannah, b. Mar. 23, 1737/8	3	88
Lemuel, s. Edward & Sarah, b. Oct. 6, 1781; d. Oct. 29, 1781	3	265
Leviney, d. Jared & Mary, b. July 8, 1783	3	284
Lois, d. Stephen & Susanna, b. Sept. 23, 1769	3	201
Lucretia, d. Sept. 5, 1849, ae 83 y.	TM3	309
Lucy, m. Benjamin **HOADLEY**, b. of Branford, Nov. 1, 1738	3	278
Lucy, m. Daniel **BARKER**, b. of North Branford, Mar. 3, 1825, by Timothy P. Gillett	3	339
Luther, s. Daniel & Hannah, b. July 4, 1769	3	197
Lydia, d. Thomas & Marg[ar]et, b. Aug. 24, 1690	2	343
Lydia, m. Joseph **MORRIS**, Mar. 4, 1712/3, by Rev. Sam[ue]ll Russel[l]	3	37
Lydia, d. Timothy & Lydia, b. Jan. 12, 1754	3	136
Lydia, wid., m. Josiah **HARRISON**, Oct. 24, 1754, by Jon[a]th[an] Merrick	3	297
Lydia, m. Joseph **SMITH**, b. of Branford, Feb. 24, 1762, by Philemon Robbins	3	176
Lydia, d. Capt. Josiah & Lydia, b. Jul.y 19, 1762	3	297
Lydia, m. Abijah **ROGERS**, b. of Branford, Aug. 9, 1775, by Warham Williams	3	259
Lydia, d. Butler & Mercy, b. May 4, 1782	3	272
Lydia, d. Jared & Mary, b. June 13, 1785	3	269
Lydia, d. Dec. 20, 1849, ae 65 y.	TM3	309
Lyman, of North Branford, m. Emily **ROGERS**, of Branford, Apr. 15, 1840, by Rev. T. P. Gillett	3	379
Marcus, [s. Butler & Mercy], b. May 18, 1793	3	340
Marie, m. Thomas **PEIRSON**, Nov. 27, [16]62	1	173
Martha, d. Nathanael & Mary, b. June 21, 1760	3	165
Martha, m. Elisha **FRISBIE**, Jr., b. of Branford, Apr. 14, 1761,		

	Vol.	Page
HARRISON, HARISON, (cont.)		
by Philemon Robbins	3	171
Martha, m. Nicodemus **BALDWIN**, b. of Branford, June 9, 1778	3	307
Mary, d. Thomas, b. Feb. 10, 1668	1	210
Mary, d. Nath[anie]ll & Hannah, b. Apr. 24, 1696	3	33
Mary, m. John **LINSL[E]Y**, June 6, 1699, by Rev. Sam[ue]ll Russel[l]	3	32
Mary, d. John & Rebec[c]ah, b. July 25, 1710	3	35
Mary, m. William **HOADL[E]Y**, Jr., b. of Branford, Jan. 7, 1718, by Rev. Sam[ue]ll Russell	3	44
Mary, d. Nathan[ie]ll & Thankfull, b. Apr. 19, 1718	3	41
Mary, m. Timothy **HOADL[E]Y**, b. of Branford, Feb. 20, 1732/3, by Rev. Jonathan Mer[r]ick	3	85
Mary, m. Daniel **MALTBIE**, Sept. [16], 1736	3	142
Mary, w. of James, d. June 12, 1749	3	125
Mary, m. Phinehas **BALDWIN**, b. of Branford, Sept. 6, 1759, by Warham Williams	3	167
Mary, m. Jairus **HARRISON**, b. of Branford, Apr. 8, 1777, by Sam[ue]ll Eells	3	308
Mary, m. George A. **BALDWIN**, b. of Branford, May 14, 1840, by Rev. T. P. Gillett	3	379
Mary A., of Branford, m. Alfred L. **DUDLEY**, of Medina, O., Aug. 18, 1836, by Rev. Timothy P. Gillett	3	372
Mary Ann, [d. Israel M. & Nancy], b. May 28, 1820	3	370
Mary Eliza, d. Charles J. & Laura, b. Mar. 20, 1844	TM3	246
Mary R., m. Bradley **CHIDSEY**, b. of Branford, Jan. 1, 1845, by Rev. Frederic Miller	TM3	157
Mary R., m. Bradley **CHIDSEY**, b. of Branford, Jan. 1, 1845, by Rev. Fred[eric]k Miller	TM3	173
Molle, d. Moses & Elisabeth, b. Oct. 4, 1759	3	182
Molle, d. Jared & Mary, b. Sept 6, 1780	3	284
Moses, s. Timothy & Lydia, b. Dec. 10, 1764	3	185
Nabbe [W]right, d. Timothy, Jr. & Clorenda, b. June 25, 1778	3	272
Nabby Wright, of Branford, m. Erastus **STRONG**, of Chesterfield, N. Y., Nov. 14, 1802, by Samuel Eells	3	353
Nancy, d. Ammi & Elizabeth, b. May 2, 1793	3	271
Nancy, m. Henry **LINSLEY**, b. of Branford, May 6, 1838, by Rev. Timothy P. Gillett	3	375
Nathan, s. Josiah & Lydia, b. Mar. 18, 1730/1	3	71
Nathan, m. Martha **BALDWIN**,, b. of Branford, Mar. 27, 1758, by Jon[a]th[an] Merrick	3	165
Nathan, s. Nathan & Martha, b. Mar. 25, 1762	3	179
Nathan, d. Aug. 17, 1773, in the 43rd y. of his age	3	257
Nathan[ie]ll, s. Nathan[ie]ll & Hannah, b. Jan. 26, 1692	3	33
Nathan[ie]ll, Jr., [of Branford], m. Thankfull **WILKINSON**, of Milford, Apr. 18, 1717 by Sam[ue]ll Eells	3	41
Nathaniel, d. Jan. 1, 1727/8	3	63

	Vol.	Page
HARRISON, HARISON, (cont.)		
Nathaniel, s. Josiah & Lydia, b. Sept. 16, 1734	3	80
Nathaniel, [twin with Sarah], s. Nath[anie]ll & Thankful,		
b. Aug. 3, 1735	3	83
Nath[anie]ll, Jr., m. Mary **TYLER**, b. of Branford, Dec.		
19, 1758, by Nath[anie]ll Harrison, J. P.	3	154
Nathan[ie]ll, d. Feb. 3, 1760	3	159
Nathanael, s. Timothy & Lydia, b. July 30, 1767	3	195
Noah, s. Dan[ie]ll & Hannah, b. Mar. 19, 1737	3	173
Offana, d. Jacob & Lois, b. Dec. 9, 1783	3	309
Patience, [twin with Silence], d. Nathan[ie]ll & Hannah,		
b. July 30, 1710; d. July [ ], 1711	3	33
Patience, d. Isaac & Patience, b. Aug. 16, 1724	3	55
Patiance, m. Binjamin **PALMER**, b. of Branford, Feb. 6,		
1746, by Phi[lemo]n Robbins	3	290
Patiance, wid., d. Jan. 15, 1762	3	175
Patiance, m. Samuel **ROSE**, 3rd, b. of Branford, Sept. 19,		
1782, by Sam[ue]ll Eells	3	308
Peter, s. Dan[ie]ll & Hannah, b. Nov. 11, 1739	3	173
Phebee, d. Josiah, Jr. & Elizabeth, b. Oct. 10, 1748	3	117
Phebe, m. Benjamin **BYINTUN**, b. of Branford, Sept. 24,		
1770, by Sam[ue]ll Eells	3	200
Philo, of North Branford, m. Sally **BALDWIN**, of Branford,		
Sept. 23, 1827, by Rev. Timothy P. Gillett	3	345
Polle, d. Edward & Sarah, b. Apr. 6, 1783	3	312
Polle, d. Farrington & Hannah, b. Jan. 13, 1784	3	276
Polly, m. Calvin **FRISBIE**, June 12, 1805	3	390
Rachel, d. Joseph & Sarah, b. Jan. 13, 1739	3	98
Rachel, m. Stephen **PALMER**, Jr., b. of Branford, Feb. 8,		
1759, by Jon[a]th[an] Merrick	3	154
Rachel, d. Timothy & Lydia, b. Mar. 13, 1760	3	160
Rachel, d. Edward & Sarah, b. Jan. 30, 1778	3	265
Rachel, d. Edward & Sarah, b. Jan. 30, 1778	3	312
Rebeccah, d. John & Rebeccah, b. June 17, 1705	2	346
Rebeccah, d. Nathaniel & Thankfull, b. May 23, 1731	3	71
Rebeckah, m. John **BLA[C]KISTON**, b. of Branford, Nov. 25,		
1736, by Rev. Philemon Robbins	3	152
Rebeckah, d. John & Lydia, b. Nov. 16, 1745	3	113
Rebecca, m. John **JOHNSON**, b. of Branford, Feb. 22, 1759,		
by Nath[anie]ll Harrison, J. P.	3	155
Rebecca, m. Samuel **HARRISON**, Jr., b. of Branford, June		
19, 1765, by Jon[a]th[an] Merrick	3	289
Rebecca, d. Sam[ue]ll, Jr. & Rebecca, b. Feb. 26, 1767	3	289
Reuben, s. Stephen & Susanna, b. Apr. 28, 1762	3	178
Reuben, s. Daniel, Jr. & Hannah, b. July 3, 1774	3	258
Richard, Sr., d. Oct. 25, [1653]	1	170
Roderick, of Branford, m. Dency **DIBBLE**, of North Guilford,		
Mar. 7, 1824, by Rev. Charles Atwater	3	425

	Vol.	Page
HARRISON, HARISON, (cont.)		
Roger, s. Sam[ue]ll, Jr. & Rebecca, b. Feb. 2, 1769	3	289
Rosanna, d. Stephen & Susanna, b. Nov. 3, 1767	3	192
Rufus, s. Nathan & Martha, b. Apr. 16, 1759	3	165
Russell, s. Justus & Sarah, b. July 19, 1781	3	296
Ruth, d. David & Mary, b. Jan. 5, 1729/30	3	69
Salle, d. Edward & Sarah, b. Mar. 19, 1774; d. Mar. 25, 1784	3	312
Salle, d. Timothy, Jr. & Clorenda, b. Dec. 12, 1776;		
d. May 19, 1777	3	272
Salle, d. Farrington & Hannah, b. Mar. 28, 1779	3	276
Sally, d. Ammi & Elizabeth, b. Nov. 22, 1787	3	270
Sally, m. Rufus **PALMER**, b. of Branford, Feb. 2, 1809	3	281
Sally A., m. Walter R. **FOOT**, b. of Branford, Nov. 20,		
1817, by Charles Atwater	3	336
Samuell, s. Thomas, b. Aug. 11, 1673	1	174
Samuel, m. Elisabeth **DENISON**, of Southend, East Haven,		
July 3, 1707, by W[illia]m Malthie, J. P.	3	32
Samuel, s. Sam[ue]ll & Elisabeth, b. Dec. 15, 1712	3	36
Samuel, Jr., m. Rebecca **HARRISON**, b. of Branford, June		
19, 1765, by Jon[a]th[an] Merrick	3	289
Sam[ue]ll, Capt., d. July 28, 1772	3	289
Samuel, s. Farrington & Hannah, b. Dec. 25, 1774	3	276
Samuel, s. [John & Betsey], b. Nov. 11, 1814	TM3	233
Sarah, d. Joseph & Sarah, b. Feb. 8, 1729/30	3	71
Sarah, [twin with Nathaniel], d. Nath[anie]ll & Thankfull,		
b. Aug. 3, 1735	3	83
Sarah, d. Jon[a]th[an], Jr. & Sarah, b. Mar. 28, 1753	3	280
Sarah, wid., m. Daniel **BALDWIN**, b. of Branford, May 27,		
1754, by Rev. Jonathan Merrick	3	137
Sarah, d. Stephen & Susanna, b. Feb. 24, 1756	3	155
Sarah Hall, d. Jared & Mary, b. July 19, 1778	3	284
Silence, [twin with Patience], d. Nathan[ie]ll & Hannah,		
b. July 30, 1710; d. Apr. 6, 1713	3	33
Simeon, d. Oct. 13, 1760, "in the Army"	3	165
Stephen, s. Joseph & Sarah, b. Nov. 14, 1733	3	98
Stephen, m. Susanna **BARTHOLOMEW**, b. of Branford, Mar.		
16, 1755, by Warham Williams	3	155
Stephen, s. Stephen & Susanna, b. Feb. 24, 1772	3	207
Sybil, d. Stephen & Susanna, b. Jan. 13, 1765	3	185
Sylvester, m. Nancy **BRADLEY**, b. of Branford, Aug. 1,		
1821, by Rev. Timothy P. Gillett	3	413
Thankfull, d. Nathan[ie]ll & Thankfull, b. Apr. 29, 1720	3	41
Thankful, m. John **ROGERS**, Jr., b. of Branford, Dec. 29,		
1743, by Rev. Philemon Robbins	3	119
Thankful, w. of Nath[anie]ll, d. July 19, 1761	3	173
Thankful, d. Dan[ie]ll & Hannah, b. July 13, 1764	3	183
Thomas, s. Thomas & Margeret, b. Oct. 12, 1694	3	29
Thomas, Jr., m. Hannah **SUTLI[E]F**, b. of Branford, Apr.		

	Vol.	Page
HARRISON, HARISON, (cont.)		
12, 1721, by Rev. Sam[ue[ll] Russel[l]	3	46
Thomas, s. Thomas, Jr. & Hannah, b. Dec. 14, 1722	3	55
Timothy, s. Josiah & Lydiah, b. Aug. 31, 1729	3	70
Timothy, m. Lydia **BUTLAR**, b. of Branford, June 12, 1751,		
by Rev. Jonath[a]n Mer[r]ick	3	136
Timothy, s. Timothy & Lydia, b. July 8, 1752	3	136
Timothy, Jr., of Branford, m. Clorenda **FOSDICK**, of		
Weathe[r]sfiel d, Mar. 14, 1776, by John March	3	272
Timothy Ithiel, s. Sylvester & Nancy, b. Feb. 21, 1835	3	373
Titus, s. Thomas & Hannah, b. Nov. 30, 1728	3	78
Westouer, [twin with Wostor], s. David & Mary, b. Feb. 21,		
1736/7	3	138
Willard, s. Sylvester & Nancy, b. May 19, 1823	3	366
William, s. Jonathan & Desire, b. Jan. 13, 1728/9	3	65
William, s. Sylvester & Nancy, b. Jan. 7, 1826	3	366
Wostor, [twin with Westouer], s. David & Mary, b. Feb.		
21, 1736/7	3	138
----, d. Sam[ue]ll & Elisabeth, b. Nov. 26, 1709	3	30
----, child of Dan[ie]ll & Hannah, st. b. Nov. 3, 1762	3	178
----, child of Daniel, Jr. & Hannah, b. July 8, 1773;		
d. July 10, 1773	3	208
HARROS, Will[ia]m, s. Lydia **HOADLEY**, b. Dec. 19, 1781	3	295
HART, Dennis, of Long Island, m. Rebecca **PALMER**, of Branford,		
May 18, 1783, by Sam[ue]ll Eells	3	306
Dennis, s. Dennis & Rebecca, b. Nov. 6, 1783	3	306
Flora A., ae 38 y., of Cornwall, m. Benjamin L. **CARTER**,		
ae 47 y., July 2, 1850, by Joshua L. Maynard	TM3	166
Roswell C., of Harwinton, m. Polly **GRANT**, of Branford,		
Mar. 11, 1827, by Rev. Timothy P. Gillett	3	343
HASSAN, Sybel, m. John **HUG[G]INS**, b. of Branford, Mar. 26,		
1783, by Sam[ue]ll Eells	3	282
HATCH, Elisabeth, m. Israel **BALDWIN**, Jan. 26, 1775, by David		
Brunson	3	286
HAWKINS, Moses, s. Joseph & Mahitable, b. Sept. 3, 1756	3	151
Samuel, s. Joseph & Mahitable, b. Dec. 3, 1763	3	311
HAYDEN, Hannah, d. Kate **LANFAIR**, b. Apr. [ ], 1799	3	386
Hannah had s. Lewis Benajah **PENFIELD**, b. Nov. 26, 1818	3	426
HAYES, HAYS, Abigail, d. Ezekiel & Rebecca, b. Jan. 15, 1764	3	182
Abigail, d. Ezekiel & Rebecca, d. Aug. 4, 1767	3	191
Elisabeth, d. [Capt.] Ezekiel & Abigail, b. Aug. 22, 1780	3	280
Ezekiel, m. Rebecca **RUSSELL**, b. of Branford, Dec. 26,		
1749, by Jno. Russell, J. P.	3	119
Ezekiel, s. Ezekiel & Rebecca, b. Feb. 19, 1753	3	133
Ezekiel, s. Ezekiel & Rebecca. b. Feb. 19, 1753	3	144
Martha, d. Ezekiel & Abigail, b. May 27, 1783	3	280
Mary, d. Ezekiel & Rebecca. b. May 13, 1761	3	172
Rebecca, d. Ezekiel & Rebecca, b. Oct. 13, 1750	3	121

	Vol.	Page
HAYES, HAYS, (cont.)		
Rebecca, d. Ezekiel & Rebecca, b. Oct. 13, 1750	3	144
Rebecca, of New Haven, m. Abel **FRISBIE**, of Branford,		
June 3, 1771, by Philemon Robbins	3	203
Rutherford, s. Ezekiel & Rebecca, b. July 29, 1756	3	144
HEACOX, Rachel, of Durham, m. Isaac **INGRAHAM**, Jr., of		
Branford, Feb. 25, 1767, by Elihu Chauncey, J. P.	3	266
HEATON, Sarah, of New Haven, m. John **HUGGINS**, of Branford,		
Sept. 25, 1729, by Rev. Joseph Noyes, of New Haven	3	89
HEMIN[G]WAY, Sarah, m. Thomas **GUTSILL**, June 4, 1684	1	210
HENBERRY, Susanna, m. John **FFRISSBE**, Apr. 7, 1703, by Mr.		
Russell	2	344
HENBRY, Elisabeth, see Elisabeth **HENLERY**	3	64
HENDRICK, Mary L., of New Haven, m. Roswell b. **SHELDON**,		
of Branford, Sept. 8, 1839, by Rev. Stephen Dodd, of East		
Haven	3	376
HENLERY*, Elisabeth, m Benjamin **FRISB[I]E**, Dec. 8, 1703, by		
Rev. Sam[ue]ll Russell (***HENBRY**?)	3	64
HICKSCOCK, [see under **HITCHCOCK**]		
HILL, Anna, d. Luke & Hannah, b. Dec. 30, 1692, at Simsbury	2	346
Asa, s. Eben[eze]r & Martha, b. Nov. 22, 1719	3	44
Ebenezer, s. Luke & Hannah, b. Nov. 23, 1687 at G[u]ilford	2	346
Eleanor, of Springfield, Mass., m. Prince B. **WARNER**, of		
Branford, May 27, 1835, by Rev. Timo[thy] P. Gillett	3	369
Harriet, m. Horace **LANDON**, b. of Guilford, June 14, 1829,		
by Timothy P. Gillett	3	349
Isaac, s. Luke & Hannah, b. May 27, 1703, at Branford	2	346
Keziah, d. Luke & Hannah, b. Feb. 24, 1695, at Wethersfield	2	346
Luke, s. Luke & Hannah, b. Sept. 16, 1698, at Simsbury	2	346
Lydia, d. Luke & Hannah, b. Feb. 25, 1700, at Simsbury	2	346
Marie A., ae 22 m. Leveret F. **LINSLEY**, ae 21, Mar. 18,		
1851, by Theodore A. Lovejoy	TM3	169
HINMAN, Phebe, of Durham, m. Edmund **TYLER**, of Branford,		
Feb. 14, 1802	3	409
[HITCHCOCK], HICKSCOCK, Edward m. Frances **INGLAND**,		
May 20, [16]56	1	170
HITT, Abraham, s. John & Hannah, b. Apr. 30, 1721	3	77
Hannah, d. John & Hannah, b. June 10, 1719	3	77
Lydia, d. Jno. & Hannah, b. Aug. 26, 1726	3	77
Nathan, s. Jno. & Hannah, b. May 1, 1724	3	77
Sam[ue]ll, s. Jno. & Hannah, b. Oct. 26, 1731	3	77
Sarah, d. John & Hannah, b. July 12, 1715	3	77
HOADLEY, HOADLY, HODLE, Abell, s. Abram & Elisabeth, b.		
Dec. 24, 1705	3	29
Abel, s. Dan[ie]ll & Elisabeth, b. Dec. 1, 1740	3	105
Abel, s. Daniel & Mary, b. June 19, 1760	3	180
Abel, m. Lucinda **BRADLEY**, b. of Branford, Nov. 8, 1787	3	273
Abel, d. Mar. 29, 1845, ae 80 y.	TM3	306

	Vol.	Page

HOADLEY, HOADLY, HODLE, (cont.)

Abel, of Branford, m. Amelia **ALLEN**, of New Haven,

[1839?], by Rev. Timothy P. Gillett	3	376
Abigail, d. Samuel & Abigail, b. Jan. 5, 1690	2	343

Abigail, m. Joseph **FRISBEE**, Dec. 5, 1711, by Rev. Sam[ue]ll

Russel[l]	3	34
Abigail, d. John & Mercy, b. Sept. 12, 1714	3	60
Abigail, d. Sam[ue]ll & Lydia, b. Aug. 24, 1722	3	132
Abigail, d. Abel & Martha, b. May 14, 1731	3	82
Abigail, d. Benj[ami]n & Lucy, b. May 20, 1746	3	278

Abigail, m. Stephen **WADE**, Feb. 16, 1747/8, by Rev. P.

Robbins	3	135
Abigail, d. Jonathan & Abigail, b. Sept. 16, 1752	3	134
Abigail, d. Benj[ami]n, d. Nov. 20, 1752	3	279
Abigaill, d. Jonathan, d. May 21, 1754	3	147
Abigail, d. W[illia]m & Abigail, b. July 28, 175[7]	3	150
Abigail, d. Abraham & Abigail, b. May 1, 1758	3	267
Abiga[i]l, d. Capt. William & Abiga[i]l, d. Mar. 7, 1760	3	260
Abigail, d. Isaac & Elisabeth, b. May 9, 1777	3	295

Abigail, m. Timothy **PAGE**, b. of Branford, Sept. 21, 1779,

by Sam[ue]ll Eells	3	306
Abigail, [d. Jonathan & Rachel], d. Dec. 21, 1806	3	384
Abigail B., [d. Abraham & Olive], b. July 27, 1800	3	285

Abraham, m. Elizabeth **MALTBIE**, Mar. 14, 1697/8, by

W[illia]m Maltbie, J. P.	2	346
Abraham, s. Abram & Elisabeth, b. July 16, 1708	3	30
Abraham, s. Jonathan & Abigail, b. Feb. 16, 1747/8	3	118
Abraham, d. July 14, 1748	3	147

Abraham, m. Abigail **BLACKISTON**, b. of Branford, Dec. 27,

1750, by Rev. Philemon Robbins	3	122
Abraham, s. Jonathan, d. Mar. 20, 1752	3	147
Abraham, s. Isaac & Elisabeth, b. Nov. 11, 1768	3	195
Abraham, m. Olive **PRICE**, Oct. 10, 179[2]	3	285
Alonzo, s. Orin & Hannah H., b. Feb. 24, 1821	3	343
Alvan, s. Jonathan, Jr. & Rachel, b. Dec. 31, 1779	3	270
Amanday, d. Jonathan, Jr. & Rachel, b. Aug. 19, 1778	3	270
Ambrus, s. James & Lydia, b. Aug. 15, 1771	3	279

Ammi, m. Mary **SPENCER**, b. of Branford, Feb. 5, 1837, by

Rev. Timothy P. Gillett	3	373
Andrew, s. Nathan[ie]ll & Anne, b. Nov. 1, 1747	3	131
Ann, [d. Orin & Julia M.], b. Feb. 6, 1833	TM3	320
Anna Tyler, [d. Isaac & Laura], b. June 8, 1815	3	408
Anne, d. Jonathan & Abigail, b. May 15, 1742	3	106
Anne, d. Nathan[ie]ll & Anne, b. June 15, 1749	3	131
Anne, twin with Mary, d. Rufus & Ruth, b. Aug. 4, 1785	3	312
Anne, [d. Jonathan & Rachel], d. July 4, 1809	3	384
Asa, s. Daniel & Mary, b. July 23, 1776	3	264
Benjamin, s. Samuel & Abigail, b. July 24, 1704	2	345

	Vol.	Page
HOADLEY, HOADLY, HODLE, (cont.)		
Benjamin, m. Lucy **HARRISON**, b. of Branford, Nov. 1, 1738	3	278
Benjamin, [twin with Lucy], s. Benj[ami]n & Lucy, b.		
June 22, 1739	3	278
Benjamin, s. Benj[ami]n, Jr. & Lydia, b. July 9, 1764	3	279
Benj[ami]n, d. Apr. 26, 1768	3	279
Benj[ami]n, Jr., d. June 1, 1768	3	279
Betsey, [d. Abraham & Olive], b. July 29, 1802	3	285
Betsey, m. Dan E. **LINSLEY**, Aug. 6, 1820, by Timothy P.		
Gillett	3	411
Charles, m. Nancy **ANDREWS**, July 2, 1843, by Rev. Davis		
T. Shailer	TM3	156
Charles Edwin, s. Orin & Julia M., b. Jan. 20, 1844	TM3	230
Charles Edwin, s. Orin & Julia M., d. Feb. 23, 1844, ae 5 wk.	TM3	305
Charles Elizur, [s. Isaac & Laura], b. June 10, 1818	3	408
Charlotte, m. William J. **COVERT**, b. of Branford, Nov.		
30, 1823, by Stephen W. Stebbins	3	424
Chloe, d. Sam[ue]ll & Sybil, b. Feb. 5, 1760	3	168
Chloe had s. Augustus **AMES**, b. Apr. 8, 1785	3	280
Chloe had s. Augustus **AMES**, b. Apr. 8, 1785	3	390
Chloe, m. Moses **FRISBIE**, b. of Branford, Jan. 11, 1804,		
by Sam[ue]l Eells	3	275
Clarenda, d. Benj[ami]n & Lucy, b. Nov. 6, 1741	3	278
Clarissa, d. Samuel, Jr. & Desire, b. Nov. 4, 1778	3	269
Clarissa had s. Chandler **PARKER**, b. Nov. 6, 1788	3	390
Daniel, s. Sam[ue]ll & Abigail, b. Dec. 9, 1706	3	30
Daniel, m. Elizabeth **HOWD**, b. of Branford, Nov. 24, 1735,		
by Rev. Jonathan Mer[r]ick	3	105
Daniel, s. Daniel & Elisabeth, b. Oct. 21, 1736	3	105
Dan[ie]ll, d. Apr. 7, 1744	3	105
Dan[ie]ll, m. Mary **BARKER**, b. of Branford, Apr. 26, 1759,		
by Jon[a]th[an] Merrick	3	159
Daniel, s. Daniel & Mary, b. Nov. 13, 1763	3	181
Demon, [s. Silas & Rachel], b. Mar. 28, 1785	3	286
Demon, [s. Silas & Rachel], d. Mar. 12, 1808	3	286
Dennis, s. Sam[ue]ll & Hannah, b. Oct. 7, 1781	3	281
Dinah, d. John & Mercy, b. Sept. 11, 1716	3	60
Dorothy, d. Jonathan & Abigail, b. Mar. 20, 1749/50	3	121
Eben[eze]r, s. Sam[ue]ll & Lydia, b. Nov. 9, 1729	3	132
Eben[eze]r, s. Timothy & Mary, b. Mar. 7, 1746/7	3	135
Eben[eze]r, m. Martha **HOADL[E]Y**, b. of Branford, Sept.		
27, 1756, by Rev. Philemon Robbins	3	143
Ebenezer, s. Eben[eze]r & Martha, b. June 26, 1757	3	168
Eli, [s. Silas & Rachel], b. May 23, 1795	3	286
Eli, [s. Silas & Rachel], d. May 2, 1796	3	286
Eliphalet, s. Dan[ie]ll & Elisabeth, b. Sept. 26, 1738	3	105
Elis, [d. Silas & Rachel], b. Feb. 7, 1796	3	286
Eliza, [d. Silas & Rachel], b. Mar. 4, 1804	3	286

	Vol.	Page
HOADLEY, HOADLY, HODLE, (cont.)		
Elizabeth, d. William, b. June 15, 1668	1	210
Elisabeth*, m. John **KINKEAD**, b. of Branford, Nov. 28, 1725, by Nath[anie]ll Har[r]ison, J. P. (*Written Uisabeth")	3	63
Elisabeth, d. Dan[ie]ll & Elisabeth, b. Mar. 11, 1742/3	3	105
Elisabeth, d. Sam[ue]ll & Leucy, b. Mar. 24, 1744	3	278
Elisabeth, d. Jonathan & Abigail, b. Sept. 24, 1744	3	106
Elizabeth, w. of Abraham, d. Dec. 14, 1747	3	147
Elisabeth, d. Sam[ue]ll & Sybil, b. May 24, 1758	3	168
Elisabeth, d. Daniel & Mary, b. Sept. 23, 1771	3	206
Elisabeth, d. Isaac & Elisabeth, b. Mar. 12, 1773	3	295
Elisabeth, m. Benjamin **HOWD**, b. of Branford, Oct. 11, 1775, by Sam[ue]ll Eells	3	281
Elisabeth, d. Jon[a]th[an], d. Apr. 8, 1792	3	260
Elizabeth, [d. Jonathan & Rachel], d. Apr. 8, 1792	3	384
Elisabeth, [d. Orin & Julia M.], b. Sept. 24, 1839	TM3	230
Erastus, s. Ralph & Deborah, b. Aug. 10, 1781	3	292
Eunice, [d. Silas & Rachel], b. Mar. 18, 1806	3	286
Eunice, [d. Silas & Rachel], d. Dec. 27, 1809	3	286
[Evander], s. Jonathan, Jr. & Rachel, b. Sept. 25, 1783	3	283
Evander, [s. Jonathan & Rachel], d. Oct. 15, 1798	3	384
Phane, d. Lydia, b. Feb. 8, 1779	3	279
Fanny, [d. Peleg & Phebe], b. Aug. 3, 1800	3	391
George, s. Capt. Timothy & Rebecca, b. Dec. 15, 1781	3	271
George, [s. Isaac & Laura], b. Feb. 14, 1814	3	408
Gideon, s. Samuel & Abigail, b. Apr. 17, 1699	2	343
Gideon, s. Sam[ue]ll & Lydia, b. Nov. 24, 1724	3	132
Hannah, d. William, b. Nov. 8, 1670* (*First written 1640)	1	210
Hannah, d. William & Abigail, b. Apr. 27, 1693	2	343
Hannah, d. Samuel & Abigail, b. Dec. 10. 1694	2	343
Hannah, d. John & Marcy, b. Apr. 18, 1708	3	34
Hannah, m. Dan[ie]ll **HAR[R]ISON**, b. of Branford, June 30, 1720, by Rev. Sam[ue]ll Russell	3	53
Hannah, d. John & Lydia, b. May 8, 1733	3	79
Hannah, m. Sam[ue]ll **BALDWIN**, b. of Branford, Apr. 15, 1746, by Philemon Robbins	3	166
Hannah, d. W[illia]m & Abigail, b. Mar. 10, 1748	3	150
Hannah, d. Benj[ami]n & Lucy, b. Oct. 6, 1748	3	278
Hannah, m. Abraham **PLANT**, b. of Branford, May 9, 1751, by Philemon Robbins	3	183
Hannah, d. Nath[anie]ll & Anne, b. June 12, 1752	3	131
Hannah, d. Jacob & Jemima, b. July 1, 1767	3	195
Hannah, d. Capt. Will[ia]m & Abigail, d. Nov. 12, 1769, ae 21	3	199
Hannah, m. Asahel **PALMER**, b. of Branford, Nov. 23, 1773	3	300
Hannah, d. Sam[ue]ll & Hannah, b. [Feb. 7, 1775]* (*First written March 26th, 1777)	3	281
Hannah had d. Betsey **PALMER**, b. Apr. 18, 1804	3	390

	Vol.	Page
HOADLEY, hOADLY, HODLE, (cont.)		
Hannah H., w. of Orin, d. Sept. 24, 1825	3	343
Harriet, m. John **GORDON**, b. of Branford, Oct. 25, 1827,		
by Rev. Timothy P. Gillett	3	345
Harvey, [s. Jonathan & Rachel], d. Dec. 9, 1803	3	384
Harvey, s. Harvey & Eliza, b. Nov. 25, 1849	TM3	242
Heli, s. Rufus & Ruth, b. Aug. 29, 1776	3	267
Hervey, s. Jonathan, Jr. & Rachel, b. Aug. 22, 1781	3	270
Hervey, m. Sally **HOBART**, b. of Branford, Nov. 27, 1828,		
by Rev. Timothy P. Gillett	3	348
Hulda[h], d. Joseph & Abigail, b. June 29, 1747	3	131
Ira, s. Daniel & Mary, b. Sept. 20, 1765	3	192
Ira, s. Rufus & Ruth, b. Jan. 16, 1772	3	205
Ira, [s. Rufus, Jr. & Hannah], b. Apr. 19, 1803	3	404
Irena, d. Abraham & Abigail, b. Nov. 3, 1765	3	267
Isaac, s. Abel & Martha, b. Dec. 31, 1728	3	82
Isaac, m. Elisabeth **BLAKISTON**, b. of Branford, Mar. 31,		
1757, by Philemon Robbins	3	172
Isaac, s. Isaac & Elisabeth, d. Jan. 14, 1777	3	295
Isaac, [s. Abel & Lucinda], b. Feb. 21, 1790	3	273
Isaac, s. Abel & Lucinda, m. Laura **TYLER**, d. Solomon &		
Dorcas, b. of Branford, Nov. 3, 1813	3	408
Jacob, s. Sam[ue]ll & Lydia, b. Mar. 8, 1731	3	132
Jacob, m. Jemima **BEWEL**, b. of Branford, July 1, 1752,		
by Rev. Jonath[a]n Mer[r]ick	3	129
Jacob, s. Jacob & Jemima, b. Aug. 19, 1759	3	169
Jairus, s. Rufus, & Ruth, b. Nov. 21, 1769	3	98
James, s. Sam[ue]ll & Lydia, b. Feb. 25, 1738	3	132
James, m. Lydia **HOADL[E]Y**, b. of Branford, Mar. 31, 1768,		
by Philemon Robbins	3	201
James, s. James & Lydia, b. Dec. 9, 1768	3	201
Jane, d. Orin & Julia M., d. Oct. 2, 1833, ae 13 d.	TM3	305
Jane, [d. Orin & Julia M.], b. June 17, 1835	TM3	230
Jared, s. Jacob & Jemima, b. Mar. 18, 1753	3	132
Jared, s. Daniel & Mary, b. Jan. 1, 1774	3	257
Jared, s. Daniel & Mary, d. May 2, 1777, in the 4th y.		
of his age	3	264
Jehiel, s. Timothy & Mary, b. Feb. 14, 1743/4	3	103
Jemima, d. William & Abigail, b. Mar. 24, 1695/6	2	343
Jemima, of Branford, m. Joshua **FULLER**, of Dedham,		
June 3, 171[ ]	3	43
Jemima, d. Jacob & Jemima, b. Jan. 30, 1762	3	177
Jarame, s. James & Lydia, b. July 27, 1776	3	279
Jerusha, d. Sam[ue]ll & Lydia, b. Feb. 20, 1736	3	132
Jerusha, m. Stephen **ROGERS**, b. of Branford, Oct. 16,		
1760, by Philemon Robbins	3	181
John, s. John & Marcy, b. Mar. 5, 1709/10	3	34
John, m. Lydia **ROGERS**, b. of Branford, Feb. 17, 1730,		

	Vol.	Page
HOADLEY, HOADLY, HODLE, (cont.)		
by Jno. Russell, J. P.	3	117
John, s. John & Lydia, b. July 1, 1758	3	157
John, s. Rufus & Ruth, b. Mar. 2, 1768	3	198
John, d. Mar. 23, 1776, in the 67th y. of his age	3	261
John, d. Oct. 7, 1833	3	364
John P., [s. Abraham & Olive], b. Dec. 23, 1794	3	285
Jonathan, s. Abraham & Elisabeth, b. Jan. 16, 1713	3	37
Jonathan, of Branford, m. Abigail **BENTON**, of Weathersfield, Dec. 5, 1738, by David Goodrich, J. P.	3	172
Jonathan, s. Jonathan & Abigail, b. May [5, 1755]	3	140
Jonathan, Jr., of Branford, m. Rachel **LEETE**, of Guilford, Feb. 19, 1777	3	290
Jonathan, [s. Jonathan & Rachel], d. Nov. 5, 1793	3	384
Jonathan, d. Oct. 31, 1822	3	343
Jonathan, d. Oct. 31, 1842, ae 67 y.	TM3	305
Joseph, s. John & Mercy, b. Apr. 17, 1712	3	60
Joseph, m. Abigail **BRADFIELD**, b. of Branford, Feb. 15, 1738/9	3	131
Julia, d. Aug. 20, 1848, ae 40 y.	TM3	308
Levi, [twin with Simeon], s. Rufus & Ruth, b. July 4, 1780	3	269
Liment, d. Mary **ROSE**, b. Jan. 16, 1775	3	261
Lorenzo, s. Orin & Hannah H., b. Oct. 5, 1822	3	343
Lorenzo, d. July [ ], 1848, ae 26 y.	TM3	308
Louisa, [d. Abraham & Olive], b. Dec. 5, 1809	3	285
Leucrecy, d. Benj[ami]n, Jr. & Lydia, b. Mar. 22, 1762; m. Nathan **HALLOCK**	3	291
Lucretia, m. Nathan **HALLIOCK**, June 13, 1782, by Sam[ue]ll Eells	3	279
Lucretia, [d. Abraham & Olive], b. Feb. 24, 1793	3	285
Luce, d. Timothy & Mary, b. May 7, 1737	3	87
Lucy, [twin with Benjamin], d. Benj[ami]n & Lucy, b. June 22, 1739	3	278
Lucy, d. Jacob & Jemima, b. May 21, 1757	3	169
Lucy, m. Sam[ue]ll **BALDWIN**, Jr., b. of Branford, July 10, 1760, by Jonathan Mer[r]ick	3	171
Luther, s. Sam[ue]ll & Hannah, b. Mar. 26, 1777	3	281
Luther, s. Sam[ue]l & Hannah, d. Feb. 2, 1794	3	390
Luther, [s. Silas & Rachel], b. Feb. 9, 1798	3	286
Lydia, d. Sam[ue]ll & Abigail, b. Dec. 23, 1701	2	344
Lydia, m. Josiah **HAR[R]ISON**, b. of Branford, June 12, 1723, by Rev. Sam[ue]ll Russell	3	70
Lydia, d. Sam[ue]ll & Lydia, b. Jan. 1, 1734	3	132
Lydia, (alias) **MON[T]GOMERY**, m. John **BRAY**, Apr. 28, 1737, by Rev. Philemon Robbins	3	126
Lydia, d. Timothy & Mary, b. May 24, 1740	3	135
Lydia, d. John & Lydia, b. Sept. 14, 1747	3	115
Lydia, d. Benj[ami]n & Lucy, b. Feb. 22, 1751	3	279

	Vol.	Page
HOADLEY, HOADLY, HODLE, (cont.)		
Lydia, d. of Sam[ue]ll, m. Thomas **GOULD**, b. of Branford,		
June 25, 1753	3	144
Lydia, d. Isaac & Elisabeth, b. Dec. 25, 1757	3	172
Lydia, wid. of Sam[ue]ll, d. Feb. 6, 1759, ae 59	3	167
Lydia, d. Jacob & Jemima, b. Nov. 20, 1764	3	195
Lydia, m. James **HOADLEY**, b. of Branford, Mar. 31, 1768,		
by Philemon Robbins	3	201
Lydia, d. James & Lydia, b. Dec. 17, 1773	3	279
Lydia, d. James & Lydia, d. Oct. 21, 1776	3	279
Lydia had d. Phane, b. Feb. 8, 1779	3	279
Lydia, m. Josiah **FOWLER**, Jr., b. of Branford, Feb. 17,		
1779, by Warham Williams	3	312
Lydia had s. Will[ia]m **HARROS**, b. Dec. 19, 1781	3	295
Lydia, [d.] June 4, 1840	TM3	304
Lydia, d. June 4, 1840, ae 91 y.	TM3	305
Lydia Charlotte, [d. Abraham & Olive], b. June 25, 1805	3	285
Martha, d. Abel & Martha, b. Feb. 18, 1732/3	3	82
Martha, m. John **HOWD**, b. of Branford, Jan. 9, 1735, by		
Philemon Robbins	3	197
Martha, d. Isaac & Elisabeth, b. Feb. 10, 1762	3	181
Martha, m. Eben[eze]r **HOADL[E]Y**, b. of Branford, Sept.		
27, 1756, by Rev. Philemon Robbins	3	143
Martha, m. Edward **BROCKWAY**, b. of Branford, Mar. 13,		
1770, by Samuel Eells	3	202
Martha, d. Isaac & Elisabeth, d. Sept. 28, 1783	3	295
Martha, [d. Abel & Lucinda], b. Dec. 5, 1788	3	273
Martha, m. Wyllys **ROGERS**, May 30, 1811	3	408
Martin, m. Parna **PAGE**, b. of Branford, Dec. 2, 1810	3	389
Martin, s. Sam[ue]ll & Hannah, b. [ ]	3	281
Mary, d. William & Abigail, b. May 22, 1691	2	343
Mary, w. of W[illia]m, d. May 12, 1703	2	344
Mary, d. John & Marcy, b. Apr. 18, 1706	3	34
Mary, m. Adam **RAYNER**, Oct. 7, 1713, by Nathan[ie]ll		
Harrison, J. P.	3	38
Mary, d. Timothy & Mary, b. Nov. 18, 1734	3	90
Mary, d. Jonathan & Abigail b. Nov.7, 1739	3	106
Mary, d. William & Abigail, b. Feb. 5, 1740	3	150
Mary, m. Samuel **ROSE**, 2d, b. of Branford, Feb. 19, 1742,		
by Will[ia]m Gould, J. P.	3	196
Mary, m. William **MONRO[E]**, b. of Branford, July 11, 1760,		
by William Hoadley, J. P.	3	259
Mary, d. Jacob & Jamima, b. Feb. 1, 1770	3	199
Mary, d. Isaac & Elisabeth, b. Mar. 24, 1775	3	295
Mary, twin with Anne, d. Rufus & Ruth, b. Aug. 4, 1785	3	312
Mary, m. Thomas **FRISBIE**, Jr., Feb. 6, 1793	3	273
Mary, d. Orin & Hannah H., b. Aug. 4, 1824; d. Oct. 13, [ ]	3	343
Mary, [d. Orin & Julia M.], b. Sept. 8, 1831	TM3	230

	Vol.	Page
HOADLEY, HOADLY, HODLE, (cont.)		
Mary Ann, [d. Silas & Rachel], b. Aug. 14, 1808	3	286
Mary E., d. Ammi & Polly, b. July 3, 1848	TM3	239
Mary E., m. Albert **PALMER**, May 6, 1851, by Rev. Camp	TM3	170
Matilda, d. Isaac & Elisabeth, b. Feb. 21, 1760	3	172
Matilda had s. Edmund **PALMER**, b. Apr. 10, 1784	3	278
Mercy, [d. Silas & Rachel], b. June 23, 1793	3	286
Mercy, m. Ammi **BALDWIN**, Dec. 24, 1810	3	386
Merwin, [s. Rufus, Jr. & Hannah], b. Dec. 3, 1809	3	404
Miles, [s. Abraham & Olive], b. Sept. 8, 1796	3	285
Miles Albert, [s. Orin & Julia M.], b. Sept 29, 1840	TM3	230
Nancy, [d. Silas & Rachel], b. May 3, 1790	3	286
Nathaniel, s. John & Mercy, b. Apr. 11, 1720	3	60
Nathan[ie]ll, m. Anne **SCARIT**, b. of Branford, Dec. 12,		
1745, by Rev. Philemon Robbins	3	131
Noah, s. Daniel & Mary, b. June 22, 1767	3	192
Olive, d. Daniel & Mary, b. Aug. 16, 1769	3	198
Oliver, [s. Silas & Rachel], b. Nov. 1, 1787	3	286
Orrin, s. Jon[a]th[an], Jr. & Rachel, b. June 11, 1788	3	257
Orin, m. Hannah H. **FRISBIE**, [b.] of Branford, Nov. 15,		
1818, by Erastus Barker, J. P., Tinmouth	3	412
Orin Harvey, [s. Orin & Julia M.], b. July 29, 1827	TM3	230
Parna, [d. Peleg & Phebe], b. Apr. 26, 1802	3	391
Pascal Kidder, s. Orin & Julia M., b. June 9, 1845	TM3	232
Peleg, m. Phebe **TOWNER**, b. of Branford, Sept. 12, 1796	3	271
Philemon, s. Jacob & Jemmiah, b. June 11, 1755	3	141
Philemon, of Martinsburg, N. Y., m. Betsey **PLANT**, of		
Branford, May 8, 1827, by Rev. Timothy P. Gillett	3	344
Polle, d. Sam[ue]ll, Jr., alias **PARRISH**, & Desire, b.		
Oct. 12, 1781	3	270
Polly, [d. Abraham & Olive], b. June 17, 1798	3	285
Polly, [d. Peleg & Phebe], b. Jan. 7, 1808	3	391
Rachel, m. Noah **TUTTLE**, b. of Branford, Dec. 1, 1720,		
by Rev. Sam[ue]ll Russel[l]	3	52
Rachel, d. Samuel & Sybil, b. Jan. 23, 1764	3	185
Rachel, m. Silas **HOADL[E]Y**, Jan. 6, 1785	3	286
Rachel, wid. of Jonathan, d. May 7, 1843, ae 89 y.	TM3	305
Rachel, d. Abram & Elizabeth, b. Aug. 31, [ ]	3	29
Ralph, s. Abraham & Abigail, b. Sept. 28, 1751	3	267
Ralph, m. Deborah **FRISBIE**, b. of Branford, Oct. 17, 1780	3	292
Ralph, [s. Abel & Lucinda], b. Dec. 11, 1795	3	273
Ralph, d. May 29, 1849, ae 52 y.	TM3	308
Rebecca, d. Joseph & Abigail, b. July 20, 1741	3	131
Rebecca, d. John & Lydia, b. Feb. 13, 1743/4	3	103
Rebecca, d. Abraham & Abigail, b. Sept. 20, 1754	3	267
Rebec[c]a, m. William **FRISBIE**, b. of Branford, July 11,		
1776, by Philemon Robbins	3	261
Rebe[c]kah, [w. of Capt. Timothy], d. Apr. 18 1819, ae 72	3	420

	Vol.	Page
HOADLEY, HOADLY, HODLE, (cont.)		
Reuel, s. James & Lydia, b. Nov. 11, 1783	3	279
Reuel, of Scott, N. Y. m. Nancy **AVERY**, of Branford, Mar.		
19, 1823, by Rev. Timothy P. Gillett	3	422
Rufus, s. Timothy & Mary, b. Feb. 26, 1740/1	3	97
Rufus, of Branford, m. Ruth **PECK**, of Wallingford, May		
28, 1767, by Warham Williams	3	192
Rufus, s. Rufus & Ruth, b. May 8, 1774	3	259
Rufus, Jr., m. Hannah **PAGE**, Nov. 15, 1801	3	404
Ruth, d. Rufus & Ruth, b. Nov. 2, 1782	3	312
Sally, d. Peleg & Phebe, b. May 19, 1797	3	271
Sally Sophronia, [d. Abel & Lucinda], b. Feb. 24, 1798	3	273
Sam[ue]ll, m. Abigail **FFARRINGTON**, Mar. 6, 1689	2	343
Samuel, s. Samuel & Abigail, b. Feb. 20, 1696	2	343
Sam[ue]ll, s. Sam[ue]ll & Lydia, b. June 24, 1727	3	132
Sam[ue]ll, of Branford, m. Sybil **JONES**, of Guilford,		
Sept. 16, 1756, by James Sproutt	3	168
Sam[ue]ll, d. Feb. 22, 1756, in the 59th y. of his age	3	168
Samuel, s. Samuel & Sybil, b. Aug. 1, 1762, in Guilford	3	185
Samuel, m. Hannah **PALMER**, wid. of Dan[ie]l, b. of		
Branford, Feb. 16, 1774	3	281
Samuel, Jr., m. Desire **WHEDON**, b. of Branford, June 13,		
1778, by Philemon Robbins	3	269
Samuel, [s. Abel & Lucinda], b. Nov. 29, 1793	3	273
Samuel, d. June 6, 1804	3	391
Sarah, d. John & Lydia, b. July 9, 1742	3	98
Sarah, d. of Will[ia]m, 3rd, m. John **MONRO[E]**, b. of		
Branford, Feb. 14, 1748/9, by Rev. Philemon Robbins	3	135
Sarah, d. W[illia]m & Abigail, b. Apr. 7, 1753	3	150
Sarah, d. Capt. W[illia]m & Abigail, d. Feb. 11, 1760	3	260
Sarah, d. Daniel & Mary, b. Jan. 7, 1762	3	180
Silas, m. Rachel **HOADLL[E]Y**, Jan. 6, 1785	3	286
Simeon, [twin with Levi], s. Rufus & Ruth, b. July 4, 1780	3	269
Sophia, [d. Jonathan & Rachel], b. Dec. 10, 1797	3	384
Sylvia, d. Jonathan & Rachel, d. Jan. 22, 1843, ae 46 y.	TM3	305
Tamse, d. John & Mary*, b. Nov. 30, 1702 (*Marcy)	3	34
Thirza, m. Joseph K. **PALMER**, b. of Branford, Aug. 21, 1833	TM3	159
Thirsa Elisabeth, [d. Orin & Julia M.], b. May 13, 1829	TM3	230
Thirsa Elizabeth, d. Orin & Julia M., d. Oct. 15, 1837,		
ae 8 y. 5 m.	TM3	305
Thirza R., of Tinmouth, Vt., m. Joseph K. **PALMER**, Aug.		
21, 1833, by Rev. T. P. Gillett	3	361
[Ti]mothy, s. Samuel & Abigail, b. July 14, 1709	3	30
Timothy, m. Mary **HARRISON**, b. of Branford, Feb. 20,		
1732/3, by Rev. Jonathan Mer[r]ick	3	85
Timothy, s. Timothy & Mary, b. Oct. 2, 1738	3	97
Timothy, d. July 19, 1772, ae 62 y. 11 m. 24 d.	3	206
Timothy, Capt., m. Rebecca **TAINTOR**, b. of Branford, Jan.		

	Vol.	Page
HOADLEY, HOADLY, HODLE, (cont.)		
28, 1781, by Warham Williams	3	271
Timothy, s. Capt. Timothy & Rebecca, b. Apr. 13, 1784	3	311
Timothy, Jr., d. May 6, 1814, ae 30	3	420
Timothy, Capt., d. Nov. 23, 1816, ae 77	3	420
William, s. Samuel & Abigail, b. Dec. 10, 1692	2	343
W[illia]m, s. W[illia]m & Elisabeth, b. Feb. 13, 1707	3	31
William, Jr., m. Mary **HARRISON**, b. of Branford, Jan. 7, 1718, by Rev. Sam[ue]ll Russell	3	44
William, Capt., m. Abigail **BALDWIN**, b. of Branford, Dec. 19, 1739, by Rev. Philemon Robbins	3	150
W[illia]m, s. W[illia]m & Abigail, b. May 27, 1742; d. Sept. 1, 1744	3	150
William, 2d, s. W[illia]m & Abigail, b. May 13, 1746; d. June 6, 1753	3	150
William, s. Abraham & Abigail, b. Mar. 27, 1760	3	267
William, Capt., d. Oct. 28, 1769, ae [ ]3	3	199
HOBART, [see also **HUBBARD**], Abijah, formerly of New London, m. Mary **BARTHOLOMEW**, of Branford, Feb. 9, 1731/2, by Jno. Russell, J. P.	3	75
Aletheia, d. Abijah & Mary, b. May 22, 1744	3	102
Alithea, d. Abijah & Mary, d. Nov. 9, 1747	3	110
Aleathea, d. Abijah & Mary, b. Dec. 7, 1755	3	147
Allithea, m. John **BALDWIN**, 3rd, b. of Branford, Oct. 20, 1772	3	299
Betsey, d. Mason & Hannah, b. Mar. 28, 1790	3	344
Betsey, m. Edmund **PALMER**, 2d, Dec. 15, 1808	3	344
Betsey, [d. Samuel & Esther], b. Nov. 14, 1810	3	367
Betsey, m. Almon **BEERS**, b. of Branford, Dec. 25, 1827, by Rev. Timothy P. Gillett	3	346
Isaac, ? s. Mason & Hannah, b. Jan. 18, 1779	3	287
Jerusha, of Guilford, M. Sam[ue]ll **ROGERS**, Jr., of Branford, Jan. 7, 1789, by Thom[a]s Wells Bray	3	253
John, s. Abijah & Mary, b. June 22, 1747	3	110
John, m. Mary **TYLER**, b. of Branford, Oct. 25, 1770, by P. Robbins	3	297
John, Lieut., d. Apr. 3, 1813, ae 66	3	367
John, [s. Samuel & Esther], b. Jan. 5, 1815	3	367
Lauretta, d. John & Lydia A., b. Dec. 23, 1842	TM3	237
Margeret, d. Abijah & Mary, d. Sept. 9, 1751	3	126
Margaret, d. Mason & Hannah, b. Dec. 12, 1781	3	287
Margaret, d. Feb. 2, 18[ ], ae 85	3	367
Mary, d. John & Mary, b. July 7, 1775	3	297
Mary, w. of John, d. July 13, 1775	3	297
Mary, d. John & Mary, d. Nov. 20, 1775	3	297
Mary, [d. Samuel & Esther], b. Apr. 6, 1801	3	367
Mary, m. Ephraim **FOOT**, b. of Branford, Sept. 15, 1802	3	408
Mary, m. Andrew S. **PAGE**, b. of Branford, May 27, 1820,		

	Vol.	Page
HOBART, (cont.)		
by Rev. Timo[thy] P. Gillett	3	419
Mason, s. Abijah & Mary, b. Nov. 1, 1752	3	126
Mason, m. Hannah **HARRISON**, b. of Branford, Nov. 28,		
1776, by Philemon Robbins	3	287
Peggy, [d. Samuel & Esther], b. Aug. 22, 1803	3	367
Peggy, m. Samuel **COOK**, Feb. 20, 1820	3	362
Rebecca, d. Abijah & Mary, b. Feb. 28, 1731/2 [1732/3]	3	75
Rebecca, m. Thomas **ROGERS**, b. of Branford, Oct. 12, 1752,		
by Philemon Robbins	3	196
Rebecca, d. Mason & Hannah, b. Sept. 26, 1777	3	287
Rebecca, m. Linus **ROBINSON**, b. of Branford, Apr. 26,		
1797, by Lynde Huntington	3	270
Sally, [d. Samuel & Esther], b. Aug. 17, 1806	3	367
Sally, m. Hervey **HOADLEY**, b. of Branford, Nov. 27, 1828,		
by Rev. Timothy P. Gillett	3	348
Samuel, s. John & Mary, b. Aug. 19, 1771	3	297
Samuel, m. Esther **IVES**, b. of Branford, Apr. 6, 1800	3	367
Saritea, [d. Samuel & Esther], b. Aug. 4, 1813	3	367
Sariett, of Branford, m. Philo **WALDEN**, of Wallingford,		
Sept. 11, 1831, by Rev. Timo[thy] P. Gillett	3	357
HODGES, Henry E., of Torrington, m. Betsey **FOWLER**, of		
Branford, Sept. 13, 1821, by Rev. Timothy P. Gillett	3	413
Sally, of Torrington, m. Rev. Timothy P. Gillett, of		
Branford, Nov. 29, 1808	3	390
HOFFMAN, [see under **HUFFMAN**]		
HOLCOMB, Fanny Frisbie, d. Frederick Alonzo & Mary Ann, b.		
Mar. 9, 1833	3	364
Frances C., d. Origen P., b. Nov. 27, 1822	3	422
Frederick, m. Mary Ann **ROGERS**, Sept. 20, 1827, by Rev.		
David Baldwin	3	346
Jairus Rogers, s. Frederick Alonzo & Mary Ann, b. Feb.		
4, 1829	3	364
John Henry, s. Frederick Alonzo & Mary Ann, b. Feb. 11, 1831	3	364
----, s. Frederick A. & Mary, b. May 10, 1849	TM3	241
HOLLAND, Sam[ue]ll, formerly of London, now of Branford, d.		
Dec. 17, 1729	3	67
HOOPPER, James, of Bristol, m. Abigail **FOWLER**, of Branford,		
Feb. 4, 1784, by Sam[ue]ll Eells	3	303
HOPEWELL, Thomas, m. ---- [O'CINNE], May 22, [16]56	1	170
HOPKINS, Ellen Maria, d. Lucius & Nancy Maria, b. Mar. 12, 1833	3	361
Lucius, of Harwinton, m. Nancy M. **FRISBIE**, of Branford,		
June 14, 1832, by Rev. Timothy P. Gillett	3	358
HOPSON, Andrew E., d. Sept. 18, 1848, ae 1 y.	TM3	308
Andrew P., s. Charles R. & Caroline, b. Aug. 30, 1847	TM3	240
Andrews, of Wallingford, m. Grace **BLACKSTONE**, of		
Branford, Nov. 27, 1823, by Rev. Timothy P. Gillett	3	424
Jerusha, m. Nicholas **ANDREWS**, Sept. 24, 1807	3	387

	Vol.	Page
HOOPSON, (cont.)		
Mary, m. James **BEERS**, Sept. 2, 1805	3	388
----, s. Charles R. & Caroline M., b. Apr. 6, 1851	TM3	244
HOSLEY, Abigail, [s. Loring D. & Anna Aritta], b. June 14, 1841	TM3	232
Benjamin Adolphus, [s. Loring D. & Anna Aritta], b. June 1, 1824	TM3	232
Charlotte, [d. Loring D. & Anna Aritta], b. Dec. 28, 1832	TM3	232
David Beach, [s. Loring D. & Anna Aritta], b. Apr. 29, 1834	TM3	232
George, [s. Loring D. & Anna Aritta], b. Sept. 27, 1839	TM3	232
Lorin D., m. Anna Aritta **BEACH**, Sept. 30, 1822, by Rev. Matthew Noyes	3	421
Loring D., d. Feb. [ ], 1851, ae 54	TM3	309
Loring Davis, Jr., [s. Loring D. & Anna Aritta], b. Sept. 3, 1827	TM3	232
Malintha, [d. Loring D. & Anna Aritta], b. Nov. 2, 1835	TM3	232
Mary Ann, [d. Loring D. & Anna Aritta], b. Feb. 24, 1831	TM3	232
Samuel, [s. Loring D. & Anna Aritta], b. July 14, 1829	TM3	232
Thaddeus, [s. Loring D. & Anna Aritta], b. Apr. 23, 1843	TM3	232
William Beach, [s. Loring D. & Anna Aritta], b. Feb. 14, 1845, ("1823" written under 1845)	TM3	232
HOTCHKISS, Abigail, m. William **MONRO[E]**, Apr. 19, 1848	TM3	162
Elizabeth, d. John & Georgeanna, b. Oct. 14, 1847	TM3	239
Ira, m. Abigail **FRISBIE**, b. of Branford, Mar. 30, 1782, by Sam[ue]ll Eells	3	279
John, m. Georgeanna **TUCKER**, b. of Branford, Aug. 2, 1846, by Rev. A. C. Wheat	TM3	159
Lancelot, d. Ira & Abigail, b. Oct. 19, 1783	3	279
Lancelot, d. Feb. 9, 1834, ae 50 y.	3	368
Sophronia, of East Haven, m. Lambert **MOULTHROP**, of New Haven, Oct. 18, 1829, by Rev. Timo[thy] P. Gillett	3	351
HOUGH, Alfred, of Martinsburg, N. Y., m. Mary **FRISBIE**, of Branford, Aug. 22, 1833, by Rev. Tim[othy] P. Gillett	3	361
Joel, of Hamden, m. Ruth **MUNSON**, of Branford, Dec. 20, 1820, by Rev. Matthew Noyes	3	414
HOW, [see also **HOWD**], Elizabeth, m. Joseph **WILFORD**, b. of Branford, Dec. 19, 1751, by Nath[anie]ll Harrison, J. P.	3	141
Philip, s. Philip & Elisabeth, b. Nov. 30, 1748	3	120
Phillip, 2d, d. Sept. 3, 175[7], at Jonathan Towners	3	150
Samuel, m. Sarah **ROSE**, b. of Branford, Jan. 11, 1770, by Samuel Eells	3	204
Samuel, s. Samuel & Sarah, b. May 30, 1770	3	204
Thankfull, of Wallingford, m. John **PALMER**, Jr., of Branford, Jan. 24, 1722/3, by John Hall	3	51
HOWD, [see also **HOW**], Aaron, [twin with Moses], s. Dan[ie]ll & Martha, b. Sept. 9, 1745; d. Sept. 14, 1746	3	107
Abigail, d. Sam[ue]ll & Ame, b. July 2, 1757	3	149
Abigail, d. Pennock & Katharine, b. Feb. 17, 1775	3	308
Abraham, s. Pennock & Katharine, b. Oct. 21, 1781	3	308

	Vol.	Page
HOWD, (cont.)		
Abraham, m. Eunice **WHITNEY**, b. of Branford, May 6, 1811	3	427
Adella, [d. Watrous & Charlotte], b. Aug. 11, 1837	3	378
Adellah, d. June [ ], 1850, ae 12 y.	TM3	309
Alithea, d. Samuel & Amy, , b. Feb. 6, 1763	3	180
Amos, s. Josiah & Hannah, b. Mar. 19, 1770	3	264
Amy, d. Samuel & Amy, b. Dec. 2, 1754	3	139
[Ame], m. John **WHITNEY**, Jr., b. of Branford, Dec. 18,		
1776, by P. Robbins	3	293
Anna, d. Joel & Abigail, b. Sept. 13, 1773	3	300
An[n]ah, d. Josiah & Hannah, b. Aug. 19, 1774	3	264
Anthony, s. Anthony, b. Nov. 11, 1674	1	174
Anthony, s. Samuel & Amy, b. July 6, 1768	3	201
Bani. s. Benj[ami]n & Elisabeth, b. May 15, 1776	3	281
Benjamin, m. Elizabeth **WHITEHEAD**, Oct. 1, 1705, by		
Eleazar Stent, J. P.	2	346
Benjamin, s. Benjamin & Elisabeth, b. Aug. 20, 1707	3	31
Benjamen, s. Eliphalet & Mary, b. Aug. 22, 1756	3	149
Benjamin, s. Joel & Abigail, b. Dec. 5, 1770	3	300
Benjamin, m. Elisabeth **HOADLEY**, b. of Branford, Oct. 11,		
1775, by Sam[ue]ll Eells	3	281
Benoni, s. Anthony, b. Sept. 10, 1676	1	211
Charlotte, [d. Richard Alsop & Phebe], b. Sept. 23, 1811	3	427
Charlotte, m. Watrous **HOWD**, b. of Branford, Feb. 14,		
1831, by Rev. Timothy P. Gillett	3	356
Clarinda, d. Dan[ie]ll & Martha, b. [ ], 1742; d. Oct. 10, 1742	3	106
Clorinda, d. Dan[ie]ll & Martha, b. Apr. 5, 1749	3	128
Cornelia, d. May 19, 1848, ae 19 y.	TM3	308
Daniel, s. John & Hannah, b. May 23, 1715	3	37
Daniel, m. Martha **MALTBIE**, b. of Branford, May 9, 1739,		
by Rev. Philemon Robbins	3	106
Daniel, d. Jan. 1, 1756	3	149
Daniel, s. Wilkinson & Thankful, b. Aug. 12, 1764	3	183
Edmund, s. Josiah & Hannah, b. Aug. 4, 1776	3	264
Edward, s. John & Hannah, b. Nov. 14, 1720	3	45
Edward, [twin with John], s. John & Martha, b. Nov. 11, 1735	3	197
Eliphalet, s. Benj[ami]n & Elisabeth, b. Jan. 24, 1709/10	3	36
Eliphalet, m. Mary **FRISBIE**, d. of Caleb, b. of Branford,		
Oct. 11, 1738	3	130
Eliza Evelina, [d. Abraham & Eunice], b. Apr. 5, 1820	3	427
Elisabeth, m. John **NASH**, Aug. 22, 1677	1	210
Elisabeth, d. Benj[ami]n & Elisabeth, b. Dec. 18, 1711	3	36
Elisabeth, m. Daniel **HOADL[E]Y**, b. of Branford, Nov. 24,		
1735, by Rev. Jonathan Mer[r]ick	3	105
Elisabeth, w. of Jonathan, d. Apr. 18, 1768	3	201
Elisabeth, d. Pennock & Katherine, b. Oct. 19, 1779;		
d. Aug. 20, 1781	3	308
Emily Frances, d. [Watrous & Charlotte], b. May 10, 1834;		

	Vol.	Page
HOWD, (cont.)		
d. June 18, 1836	3	378
George William, [s. Abraham & Eunice], b. Apr. 9, 1814	3	427
Hannah, d. John & Hannah, b. Nov. 24, 1717	3	40
Hannah, d. Eliphalet & Mary, b. Apr. 29, 1739	3	99
Hannah, m. John **FORD**, b. of Branford, May 24, 1745, by Jno. Russell, J. P.	3	110
Hannah, m. Dan[ei]ll **PALMER**, b. of Branford, Mar. 19, 1761, by Philemon Robbins	3	174
Hannah, m. Micah **PALMER**, Jr., b. of Branford, Dec. 30, 1762, by Philemon Robbins	3	179
Hannah, d. Samuel & Ame, b. Oct. 24, 1764	3	183
Hannah, d. Pennock & Katherine, b. Feb. 7, 1765	3	307
Jerusha, d. Pennock & Katherine, b. Sept. 12, 1763	3	307
Jerusha, m. Edward **FRISBIE**, b. of Branford, Aug. 27, 1781, by Sam[ue]ll Eells	3	282
Jime, s. Benj[ami]n & Elisabeth, b. Sept. 30, 1778	3	281
Joel, m. Abigail **POND**, b. of Branford, Feb. 5, 1769	3	300
Joel, s. Joel & Abigail, b. Oct. 7, 1777	3	300
John, s. Anthony, b. Sept. 27, 1673	1	174
John, of Branford, m. Hannah **WILKINSON**, of Milford, sometime in the year 1705, or 1706, by Sam[ue]ll Eells, J. P.	3	197
John, m. Martha **HOADL[E]Y**, b. of Branford, Jan. 9, 1735, by Philemon Robbins	3	197
John, [twin with Edward], s. John & Martha, b. Nov. 11, 1735	3	197
John Jackson, s. Richard Alsoph & Ruth, b. Aug. 1, 1835	3	373
Jonathan, s. Eliphalet & Mary, b. Jan. 7, 1744/5	3	130
Jonathan, m. Elisabeth **FRISBIE**, b. of Branford, Oct. 14, 1767, by Philemon Robbins	3	201
Jonathan, s. Jonathan & Elisabeth, b. Mar. 8, 1768	3	201
Jonathan Peck, s. Wilkinson & Thankful, b. Apr. 12, 1766	3	191
Joseph, s. John & Hannah, b. Sept. 1, 1709	3	34
Joseph, s. Pennock & Katharine, b. Dec. 5, 1769	3	307
Josiah, s. Eliphalet & Mary, b. Apr. 10, 1741	3	99
Josiah, of Branford, m. Hannah **LEETE**, of Guilford, June [ ], 1767, by Philemon Robbins	3	264
Judah, of Branford, m. Noami **FILER**, of Guilford, Sept. 4, 1761, by John Richards	3	173
Lavina, d. Benj[ami]n & Elisabeth, d. Feb. 4, 1784	3	282
Levine, d. Benj[ami]n & Elisabeth, b. Nov. 8, 1780	3	281
Lois, d. Josiah & Hannah, b. Dec. 23, 1767	3	264
Mariet, [d. Richard Alsop & Phebe], b. Nov. 15, 1802	3	427
Maretta, m. Malachi **LINSLEY**, Jr. b. of Branford, Dec. 24, 1823, by Rev. Timothy P. Gillett	3	424
Martha, d. Eliphalet & Mary, b. Oct. 12, 1752	3	130
Martha, d. Wilkinson & Thankful, b. Nov. 23, 1762	3	181
Martha, m. Elias **POND**, b. of Branford, Jan. 11, 1774,		

	Vol.	Page
HOWD, (cont.)		
by Sam[ue]ll Eells	3	305
Martha, d. Benjamin & Elisabeth, b. May 12, 17[ ];		
[bp. May 27, 1716]	3	43
Mary, d. Eliphalet & Mary, b. Nov. 11, 1749	3	130
Mary, m. Jonathan **PALMER**, May 6, 1750, by Rev. Philemon		
Robbins	3	123
Mary, m. Beniamen **FARNOM**, b. of Branford, in Northford,		
Mar. 7, 1750/1, by Rev. Warham Williams	3	149
Mary, d. Pennock & Katherine, b. Jan. 15, 1767	3	307
Mary, m. Isaac **ROGERS**, b. of Branford, Apr. 8, 1773, by		
Sam[ue]ll Eells	3	302
Mary Jane, d. Richard Alsop & Ruth, b. June 20, 1837	TM3	230
Mary Parmelia, [d. Abraham & Eunice], b. Feb. 22, 1822	3	427
Moses, [twin with Aaron], s. Dan[ie]ll & Martha, b. Sept.		
9, 1745	3	107
Nelson, m. Cornelia **ROGERS**, b. of Branford, Jan. 12,		
1841, by Rev. A. B. Goldsmith, of Guilford	TM3	152
Nelson, d. Sept. 9, 1847, ae 39	TM3	307
Pennock, of Branford, m. Katherine **KIMBERLY**, of Guilford,		
Feb. 11, 1761, by Rev. John Richards, in North Guilford	3	282
Pennock, m. Katharine **KIMBE[R]LY**, of Guilford, Feb. 11,		
1761	3	307
Richard, A., m. Ruth **HULL**, b. of Branford, June 11, 1829,		
by Chandler Barker, J. P.	3	349
Richard Alsop, s. Pennock & Katharine, b. Feb. 29, 1777	3	308
Richard Alsop, of Branford, m. Phebe **FRANKLIN**, of Sag		
Harbor, L. I., Dec. 14, 1801	3	427
Richard Alsoph, s. Richard Alsoph & Ruth, b. Sept. 18, 1832	3	373
Sabrina, d. Josiah & Hannah, b. June 6, 1772	3	264
Sally, d. Joel & Abigail, b. July 24, 1783	3	300
Samuel, s. John & Hannah, b. Dec. 1, 1712	3	36
Samuel, m. Amy **BALDWIN**, Feb. 14, 1754, by Philemon		
Robbins	3	139
Sam[ue]ll, s. Sam[ue]ll & Amy, b. Apr. 26, 1758	3	163
Samuel, s. Joel & Abigail, b. Dec. 10, 1779	3	300
Sarah, d. Dan[ie]ll & Martha, b. Sept. 15, 1743	3	107
Sarah, m. Joseph **PERMELE**, b. of Branford, Dec. 1, 1763,		
by Philemon Robbins	3	296
Sarah, m. Joseph **PARMELE**, b. of Branford, Dec. 2, 1763,		
by Philemon Robbins	3	181
Sarah, d. Pennock & Katharine, b. Oct. 13, 1772	3	308
Susan, m. Benjamin **BARKER**, b. of Branford, Jan. 1, 1825,		
by Timothy P. Gillett	3	336
Susan J., of Branford, m. Levi H. **NORTON**, of New Haven,		
Apr. 25, 1833, by Rev. Timothy P. Gillett	3	359
Susan Jennet, [d. Abraham & Eunice], b. Apr. 25, 1812	3	427
Watrous, m. Charlotte **HOWD**, b. of Branford, Feb. 14,		

	Vol.	Page
HOWD, (cont.)		
1831, by Rev. Timothy P. Gillett	3	356
Wilkinson, s. Dan[ie]ll & Martha, b. June 5, 1740	3	106
Wilkinson, of Branford, m. Thankful **PECK**, of Parish of		
Northford, Dec. 17, 1761, by Warham Williams	3	174
----, s. Benj[ami]n & Elisabeth, b. Jan. 13, 1784;		
d. 14th of the month	3	281
HUBBARD, [see also **HOBART**, Daniel, Jr., m. Susan **RUSSELL**,		
May 28, 1828, by Rev. David Baldwin	3	360
George, m. Rebecca **KNOWL[E]S**, b. of Branford, Jan. 10,		
1753, by Jonathan Mer[r]ick	3	178
George, d. Nov. 2, 1762	3	178
Mary, of Guilford, m. Isaac **COOK**, Jr., of Branford, Nov.		
14, 1739, by Rev. Thomas Ruggles	3	111
Sarah A., of Durham, m. Harvey R. **BARKER**, of Branford,		
Feb. 5, 1850, by C. H. Topliff	TM3	165
Sarah A., ae 21 y., of Durham, m. Harvey R. **BARKER**, ae		
21 y., Feb. 5, 1850, by Rev. C. H. Topliff	TM3	167
Susan L., m. Edward **SPENCER**, Dec. 28, 1851, by Rev.		
Lucius T. Atwater	TM3	171
HUDSON, David, s. David & Keziah, d. Jan. 14, 1755	3	176
David, of Branford, m. Rebecca **FOWLER**, of Guilford,		
d. of Daniel, Aug. 23, 1755, by Rev. John Richards, at		
Guilford	3	143
David, s. David & Rebecca, b. Feb. 16, 1761	3	171
John, s. David & Rebecca, b. Nov. 6, 1762	3	178
Kezia, d. David & Rebecca, b. Sept. 30, 1756	3	143
Timothy, s. David & Rebeccah, b. Nov. 12, 1758	3	156
HUFFMAN, Eunice, d. Henry & Eunice, b. Oct. 10, 1758	3	180
Eunice, m. Ebenezer **BYINTON**, b. of Branford, Nov. 4,		
1778, by Sam[ue]ll Eells	3	306
Henry, m. Eunice **PALMER**, b. of Branford, Sept. 2, 1755,		
by Jonathan Mer[r]ick	3	180
Lucy, d. Henry & Eunice, b. Mar. 5, 1769	3	196
Nancy, d. Henry & Eunice, b. Apr. 10, 1764	3	182
Nancy, m. Josiah **ROGERS**, b. of Branford, July 25, [17--],		
by Sam[ue]l Eells	3	261
Samuel, s. Henry & Eunice, b. Apr. 21, 1766	3	194
Thankful, d. Henry & Eunice, b. May 10, 1756	3	180
Timothy, s. Henry & Eunice, b. Aug. 15, 1761	3	180
HUGGINS, HUGINS, Eben[eze]r, s. John & Sarah, b. Dec. 17,		
1748	3	122
Ebenez[e]r, s. John & Sarah, b. Dec. 17, 1748	3	129
James, s. John & Sarah, b. May 19, 1752	3	129
John, of Branford, m. Sarah **HEATON**, of New Haven, Sept.		
25, 1729, by Rev. Joseph Noyes, of New Haven	3	89
John, s. John & Sarah, b. Feb. 12, 1733/4	3	89
John, of Branford, m. Esther **HAND**, of East Guilford,		

	Vol.	Page
HUGGINS, HUGINS, (cont.)		
Apr. 14, 1756, by Rev. Jon[a]th[an] Todd	3	158
John, d. Sept. 16, 1757	3	147
John, s. John & Esther, b. Dec. 29, 1758	3	158
John, d. May 22, 1773	3	258
John, m. Sybel **HASSAN,** b. of Branford, Mar. 26, 1783,		
by Sam[ue]ll Eells	3	282
John Kasson, s. John & Cybil, b. Aug. 6, 1785	3	278
Mary, s. Mary Kellogg	3	403
Mellescent, d. Samuel & Elisabeth, b. Sept. 24, 1763	3	183
Rebecca, d. Samuel & Elisabeth, b. Mar. 1, 1761	3	183
Sam[ue]ll, s. John & Sarah, b. Sept. 30, 1738	3	89
Sam[ue]ll, m. Elisabeth **GUY,** b. of Branford, July 3,		
1760, by Philemon Robbins	3	102
Samuel, s. Sam[ue]ll & Elisabeth, b. Nov. 19, 1765	3	188
Sarah, d. John & Sarah, b. Feb. 29, 1743/4	3	129
William, s. John & Esther, b. Aug. 20, 1765	3	187
William Charl[e]s, s. John & Sarah, b. Nov. 27, 1756;		
d. Oct. 14, 1757	3	147
HULL, Lorenda, of Branford, m. William B. **NORTON,** of		
Guilford, Nov. 26, 1829, by Chandler Barker, J. P.	3	351
Marietta, of Branford, m. William K. **PORTER,** of New		
Haven, Apr. 10, 1842, by Rev. Pascal P. Kidder	TM3	154
Ruth, m. Richard A. **HOWD,** b. of Branford, June 11, 1829,		
by Chandler Barker, J. P.	3	349
HUMISTON, Polly, of West Springfield, m. Daniel **PALMER,** Oct.		
4, 1808	3	363
HUNTINGTON, Louisa Almira, [d. Rev. Lynde & Anna], b. Jan.		
26, 1802	3	401
Lynde, Rev., m. Anne **ATWATER,** wid. of Rev. Jason, June		
15, 1796	3	401
Lynde, Rev., d. Sept. 19, 1804, in the 38th y. of his		
age and 9th y. of his ministry	3	401
Lynde Atwater, [s. Rev. Lynde & Anne], b. Jan. 12, 1804	3	401
Sophia, [d. Rev. Lynde & Anne], b. Apr. 1, 1797	3	401
----, s. [Rev. Lynde & Anne], b. Oct. 2, 1798; d. Oct. 16, 1798	3	401
HURD, Betsey, of Huntington, m. Wyllys **LINDSLEY,** of North		
Branford, June 20, 1819, by Rev. Menzies Rayner, of		
Huntington. Witnesses: B. L. Rayner, M. P. Rayner,		
Maria Shelton, Levinia Todd, Charles J. Todd	3	415
Mary, of Roxbury, m. Benjamin **PAGE,** of Branford, Dec.		
25, 1814, by Rev. Fosdic Harrison, at Roxbury	3	338
IGO, John, of Winsted, m. Mary A. **LINSLEY,** of Branford, Mar.		
21, 1852, by Rev. T. P. Gillett	TM3	170
INGLAND, Frances, m. Edward **HICKSCOCK,** May 20, [16]56	1	170
John, d. Nov. 30, [1655]	1	170
INGRAHAM, Bede, d. Isaac, Jr. & Rachel, b. Aug. 7, 1772	3	266
Elisabeth, [d. Isaac & Hannah], b. June 17, 1745	3	157

	Vol.	Page
INGRAHAM, (cont.)		
Hannah, d. Isaac, Jr. & Rachel, b. Sept. 4, 1777	3	266
Irena, d. Isaac, Jr. & Rachel, b. July 18, 1775; d. June 3, 1777	3	266
Isaac, m. wid. Hannah **BARTHOLOMEW**, b. of Branford,		
Apr. 15, 1736, by Jonathan Mer[r]ick	3	156
Isaac, [s. Isaac & Hannah], b. Sept. 4, 1742	3	157
Isaac, Jr., of Branford, m. Rachel **HEACOX**, of Durham,		
Feb. 25, 1767, by Elihu Chauncey, J. P.	3	266
Mary, [d. Isaac & Hannah], b. Oct. 8, 1736	3	157
Mary, m. Dan[ie]ll **FOOT**, Jr., b. of Branford, Feb. 13,		
1755, by Warham Williams	3	170
Rachel, d. Isaac, Jr. & Rachel, b. Oct. 31, 1767	3	266
Sybil, [d. Isaac & Hannah], b. Feb. 5, 1739	3	157
Sybil, m. David **TYLER**, b. of Branford, Jan. 26, 1758,		
by Warham Williams	3	154
Sibyl, d. Isaac, Jr. & Rachel, b. Aug. 17, 1770	3	266
ISAACS, Billy, s. Ralph & Mary, b. Aug. 7, 1780	3	275
Henrietta, d. Mercy **LINSL[E]Y**, b. May 10, 1786	3	273
Henrietta, m. David **BUTLER**, b. of Branford, May 26, 1807	3	391
Salle, d. Ralph & Mary, b. Jan. 12, 1778	3	275
Sophia, d. Ralph & Mary, b. Nov. 6, 1782	3	275
ISBELL, Edward E., s. Elisha & Mindwell, b. Oct. 27, 1849	TM3	242
Elisha S., of Meriden, m. Mindwell **SPENCER**, of Branford,		
Nov. 30, 1848, by Rev. T. P. Gillett	TM3	163
IVES, IUES, Elizabeth, m. John **MALTBIE**, b. of Branford, Oct.		
5, 1791, by Matthew Noyes	3	264
Esther, m. Samuel **HOBART**, b. of Branford, Aug. 6, 1800	3	367
Joel, Jr., m. Nancy **GRIFFING**, Nov. 8, 1821, by Timothy		
P. Gillett	3	415
Joel, d. Aug. 14, 1825, in the 78th y. of his age	3	341
Jonah, s. Lazarus & Mehetabel, b. June 16, 1752	3	128
Martha, of New Haven, m. Eleazer **STENT**, of Branford,		
Jan. 6, 1713/14, by Abram Bradl[e]y, J. P., at New Haven	3	38
Olive, m. Richard **LINSL[E]Y**, June 30, 1801	3	280
Sarah, m. Eleazur **STENT**, Jr., Mar.7, 1810	3	404
JACOBS, Abigail, d. Isaac & Judith, b. Apr. 19, 1721	3	45
JEROME, Emely W., of New Hartford, Conn., m. Charles M.		
OWEN, of Stockbridge, Mass., July 10, 1845, by Rev.		
Timothy P. Gillett	TM3	158
Sarah E., of Bloomfield, m. Norman B. **MERRILL**, of New		
Hartford, Oct. 10, 1850, by Rev. T. P. Gillett	TM3	168
Sarah E., m. Norman B. **MERRILL**, Oct. 10, 1850, by T. P.		
Gillett	TM3	170
JOHNSON, Abigail, m. Bezaliel **TYLER**, Jan. 23, 1711/12, by Rev.		
Sam[ue]ll Russel[l]	3	34
Alpheus, s. Timothy & Hannah, b. Feb. 1, 1749/50	3	120
Amanda, d. Stephen & Submit, b. Oct. 13, 1763	3	203
Amos, s. Edward & Esther, b. Jan. 30, 1692/3	2	344

	Vol.	Page
JOHNSON, (cont.)		
Amos, s. Edward & [Elizabeth], b. July 18, 1739	3	116
Amos, d. July 19, 1760, in the 68th y. of his age	3	163
Anaritter, d. Joseph W[illia]m & Statira, b. Jan. 10, 1814	3	370
Anaritta had d. Ellen Augusta **JOHNSON**, b. Mar. 16, 1834	3	370
Annah, d. Edward & Elizabeth, b. Oct. 17, 1743	3	116
Anne, of New Haven, m. Joseph **FOOT**, Jr., of Branford,		
Nov. 19, 1717, at New Haven	3	43
Anne, d. Ebenezer & Anne, b. May 1, 1734	3	85
Anne, d. Ebene[ze]r & Anne, b. May 1, 1734	3	81
Artemas, m. Mary **BARNS**, b. of Branford, Dec. 8, 1765,		
by Josiah Rogers, J. P.	3	263
Asahel, s. Artemas & Mary, b. Feb. 28, 1768, at Woodbury	3	263
Beda J., m. Roswell **TYLER**, b. of Branford, Mar. 13, 1844,		
by Rev. Davis T. Shailer	TM3	157
Betsey, [d. Jeremiah & Lydia], b. June 14, 1801	3	429
Betsey, of Branford, m. Jonathan **COLLINS**, of Guilford,		
June 10, 1827	3	354
Charles, [s. Jeremiah & Lydia], b. Oct. 7, 1806	3	429
Charles, m. Henrietta **TYLER**, b. of Branford, Jan. 28,		
1830, by Rev. Timothy P. Gillett	3	352
Charlotte, [d. Nath[anie]l & Sarah], b. Apr. 30, 1787	3	262
Charlotte Maria, d. Timothy & Polly, b. July 6, 1801	3	277
Cornelius, s. Edward & Esther, b. Aug. 18, 1705	3	29
Daniel, s. Edward, Jr. & Deborah, b. Mar. 14, 1727/8	3	69
Dan[ie]ll, m. Bathsheba **POND**, b. of Branford, Oct. 17,		
1753, by Rev. Jonath[a]n Mer[r]ick	3	133
Deborah, d. Edward, Jr. & Deborah, b. Nov. 14, 1730	3	69
Deborah, w. of Edward, Jr., d. Nov. 24, 1730	3	69
Deborah, d. Dan[ie]ll & Bathsheba, b. May 5, 1757	3	145
Ebenezer, s. Edward & Esther, b. Mar. 8, 1702/3	2	344
Ebenezer, m. Anne **BARKER**, b. of Branford, Jan. 1, 1728/9,		
by Rev. Sam[ue]ll Russell	3	66
Ebenezer, s. Eben[eze]r & Anne, b. Dec. 3, 1735	3	85
Edward, s. Edward & Esther, b. June 12, 1697	2	344
Edward, Jr., m. Deborah **BALDWIN**, b. of Branford, Feb.		
21, 1722/3, by Nath[anie]ll Har[r]ison, J. P.	3	54
Edward, of Branford, m. Elizabeth **BARNS**, of East Hampton,		
L. I., Nov. 9, 1732, by Rev. Jonathan Merrick	3	116
Edward, s. Edward & Elizabeth, b. Mar. 30, 1735	3	116
Edward, s. Charles & Henrietta, b. Aug. 27, 1832	3	372
Elizabeth, d. Edward & Esther, b. Dec. 6, 1690	2	344
Elisabeth, d. Nath[anie]ll & Elisabeth, b. Dec. 2, 1729	3	69
Elisabeth, d. Edward & Elizabeth, b. July 28, 1733	3	116
Elisabeth, d. Nath[anie]ll & Elisabeth, d. Sept. 2, 1738	3	167
Elizabeth, m. Abel **BUTLER**, Mar. 1, 1753, by Jonathan		
Merrik	3	138
Elisabeth, w. of Lieut. Nathaniel, d. Sept. 14, 1775	3	261

	Vol.	Page
JOHNSON, (cont.)		
Ellen A., m. George W. **BRIG[G]S**, b. of Branford, Oct.		
18, 1853, by Rev. L. Atwater	TM3	172
Ellen Augusta, d. Anaritta **JOHNSON**, b. Mar. 16, 1834	3	370
Esther, d. Edward & Esther, b. June 12, 1700	2	344
Esther, d. Edward & Elizabeth, b. Aug. 21, 1737	3	116
Esther, d. July 19, 175[7]	3	147
Eunice, d. Stephen & Submit, b. Nov. 14, 1769	3	203
Experience, d. Edward & Esther, b. May 20, 1695	2	344
Experience, m. Robert **SLOOPER**, Jan. 9, 1717/8, by Rev.		
Sam[ue]ll Russell	3	54
Exsperance, d. Edward & Elizabeth, b. Nov. 25, 1745	3	116
Frederick W., of Wallingford, m. Nancy **LINDLEY**, of North		
Branford, Apr. 6, 1824, by Charles Atwater	3	426
George Guy, s. Timothy & Polly, b. Dec. 21, 1802	3	277
George Timothy, s. George W[illia]m, b. June 1, 1835	3	370
George W[illia]m, s. Joseph W[illia]m & Statira, b. Apr.		
25, 1810	3	370
Hannah, m. Daniel **PAGE**, Jan. 3, 1710, by Rev. Sam[ue]ll		
Russel[l]	3	33
Hannah, d. Edward, Jr. & Deborah, b. Dec. 22, 1725	3	69
Hannah, w. of Nath[anie]ll, d. Jan. 15, 1725/6	3	58
Hannah, d. Nath[anie]ll & Elisabeth, b. Sept. 21, 1735	3	83
Hannah, d. Timothy & Hannah, b. Jan. 26, 1744/5	3	110
Hannah, d. Timothy & Hannah, b. Jan. 26, 1744/5	3	120
Hannah, m. Isaac **HARRISON**, b. of Branford, May 21, 1752,		
by Rev. Philemon Robbins	3	134
Hannah, m. Israel **FRISBIE**, b. of Branford, Dec. 15,		
1762, by Philemon Robbins	3	181
Hannah, m. Abraham **HARRISON**, b. of Branford, Jan. 26,		
1764, by Jon[a]th[an] Mer[r]ick	3	185
Hannah, m. James **GOODRICH**, b. of Branford, Jan. 24, 1779,		
by Sam[ue]ll Eells	3	297
Hannah, [d. Nath[anie]l & Sarah], b. Apr. 2, 1794	3	262
Harriet Louisa, of Branford, m. William **TALMADGE**,, of		
North Branford, May 12, 1852, by Rev. T. P. Gillett	TM3	171
Henry, s. Stephen & Submit, b. Nov. 1, 1758	3	203
Henry, m. Huldah **PAGE**, b. of Branford, Mar. 24, 1784,		
by Sam[ue]ll Eells	3	309
Henry, s. Charles & Henrietta, b. Apr. 15, 1835	3	372
Isaac, s. Nathaniel & Elisabeth, b. Feb. 28, 1740/1	3	97
Isaac, s. Nath[anie]ll & Elisabeth, d. Feb. 14, 1756	3	167
Isaac, s. John & Rebecca, b. Apr. 7, 1773; d. Apr. 10, [1773]	3	256
Jeremiah, s. Willford & Sarah, b. Aug. 12, 1770	3	257
Jeremiah, m. Lydia **SPINK**, b. of Branford, Mar. 4, 1796	3	429
Jeremiah, d. May 1, 1825	3	339
Jerusha, d. Daniel & Bathsheb[a], b. Oct. 26, 1754	3	139
John, s. Nathan[ie]ll & Hannah, b. Sept. 5, 1706	3	29

	Vol.	Page
JOHNSON, (cont.)		
John, s. Nathan[ie]ll & Elisabeth, b. Oct. 21, 1732	3	76
John, m. Rebecca **HARRISON**, b. of Branford, Feb. 22, 1759,		
by Nath[anie]ll Harrison, J. P.	3	155
John, s. John & Rebecca, b. Aug. 18, 1764	3	185
John, s. Nath[anie]ll & Hannah, d. Dec. [ ]	3	29
Jonathan, s. Ebenezer & Ann, b. Apr. 15, 1739	3	92
Joseph, s. Ebenezer & Anne, b. July 31, 174[2]	3	105
Joseph W[illia]m, d. Sept. 1, 1826	3	370
Keturah, m. Thomas **KASSAN**, b. of Branford, Aug. 11, 1760,		
by Deod[a]t[e] Davenport, J. P., New Haven	3	161
Lydia, d. Timothy & Hannah, b. May 24, 1741	3	100
Lydia, m. John **GORDON**, b. of Branford, Oct. 30, 1765, by		
Phi[lemo]n Robbins	3	293
Mary, d. Nathan[ie]ll & Hannah, b. July 18, 1703	2	345
Mary, m. Jonah **BUTLER**, b. of Branford, Feb. 9, 1720/1,		
by Nath[anie]ll Harrison, J. P,	3	51
Mary, d. Ebenezer & Ann, b. Aug. 25, 1731	3	73
Mary, m. Dr. William **GOULD**, b. of Branford, May 5, 1763,		
by Philemon Robbins	3	181
Mary, d. Stephen & Submit, b. June 10, 1766	3	203
Mary, d. Artemas & Mary, b. Sept. 18, 1777	3	263
Mehetabel, of New Haven, m. Timothy **ROSE**, of Branford,		
Sept. 22, 1730, by Jno, Russel[l], J. P.	3	103
Mercy, d. Stephen & Submit, b. Mar. 28, 1756; d. May 5, 1759	3	203
Nancy, [d. Jeremiah & Lydia], b. May 27, 1799	3	429
Nathaniel, Jr., m. Elisabeth **WILFORD**, b. of Branford,		
June 17, 1725, by Rev. Sam[ue]ll Russell	3	57
Nath[anie]ll, d. Sept. 8, 1726	3	59
Nathaniel, s. Nathaniel & Elisabeth, b. Jan. 14, 1726/7	3	64
Nath[anie]ll, s. John & Rebecca, b. Mar. 16, 1767	3	192
Nathaniel, Lieut., d. June 17, 1773, ae 74 y. 4m. 17 d.	3	256
Nath[anie]l, m. Sarah **TYLER**, Apr. 13, 1786	3	262
Orret C., of North Guilford, m. John **WHEADON**, of North		
Branford, Jan. 8, 1824, by Rev. Charles Atwater	3	425
Phebe, d. Edward & Elizabeth, b. July 29, 1748	3	116
Pilanah, d. Henry & Huldah, b. Nov. 15, 1784	3	331
Polle, d. Willford & Sarah, b. Dec. 29, 1760	3	257
Polly, m. Charles Joseph **DeBERARD**, Aug. 10, 1785, by Rev.		
Jason Atwater	3	272
Polly, d. Timothy & Polly, b. Mar. 24, 1790	3	260
Polly, w. of Timothy, d. Dec. 29, 1796, in the 33rd y.of her age	3	270
Rebecca, [d. Nath[anie]l & Sarah], b. Mar. 3, 1792	3	262
Rebecca Anne, d. Stephen & Submit, b. Mar. 2, 1761	3	203
Reuben, s. Timothy & Hannah, b. Apr. 21, 1743	3	100
Sally, [d. Nath[anie]l & Sarah], b. Jan. 15, 1789	3	262
Sally, [d. Jeremiah & Lydia], b. Sept. 24, 1804;		
d. Oct. 24, 1804	3	429

	Vol.	Page
JOHNSON, (cont.)		
Sally Eliza, d. Timothy & Polle, b. Jan. 7, 1794	3	262
Sally Maria, d. Charles & Henrietta, b. Nov. 6, 1830;		
d. Nov. 24, 1832	3	371
Sam[ue]ll, s. Nathan[ie]ll & Hannah, b. Jan. 13, 1707/8;		
d. [Jan.] 29, [1707/8]	3	31
Samuel, s. Nathan[ie]ll & Elisabeth, b. Mar. 2, 1737/8	3	89
Sam[ue]ll, s. Nath[anie]ll & Elisabeth, d. May 26, 1754	3	167
Statira, m. John Augustus WILFORD, b. of Branford, Dec.		
9, 1841, by Rev. Timothy P. Gillett	TM3	153
Stephen, m. Submit LUD[D]INGTON, b. of Branford, June 28,		
1754, by Jon[a]th[an] Russell, J. P.	3	136
Timothy, s. Edward & Esther, b. July 17, 1709	3	41
Timothy, m. Hannah WHEDON, b. of Branford, Nov. 30,		
1738, by Rev. Philemon Robbins	3	89
Timothy, s. Timothy & Hannah, b. Nov. 15, 1739	3	91
Timothy, of Guilford, m. Mary GUY, of Branford, Feb. 10,		
1757, by Rev. Philemon Robbins	3	145
Timothy, s. Tim[oth]y & Mary, b. Aug. 1, 1757	3	304
Timothy, d. Aug. 22, 1758, in the 26th y. of his age	3	304
Timothy, d. Mar. 11, 1760	3	165
Timothy, m. Polly FOOT, Sept. 27, 1800	3	277
Timothy F., s. Joseph W[illia]m & Statira, b. Jan. 21, 1812	3	370
Trueman, s. Artemas & Mary, b. Oct. 9, 1775	3	263
Wilford, s. Nathan[ie]ll & Elisabeth, b. Oct. 13, 1744	3	109
Willford, m. Sarah LANFERE, b. of Branford, Aug. 8, 1768,		
by Elihu Hall, J. P.	3	256
Willford, d. Aug. 13, 1783, in the 39th y. of his age	3	287
Willford, [s. Jeremiah & Lydia], b. Dec. 11, 1797	3	429
William, s. Artemas & Mary, b. Apr. 14, 1772, at Woodbury	3	263
William R., s. Timothy & Polly, b. Dec. 17, 1787	3	260
W[illia]m R., d. Oct. 17, 1849, ae 61 y.	TM3	309
William Russell, s. Timothy & Polly, b. Dec. 17, 1787	3	426
Zacharias, s. Edward & Elizabeth, b. Sept. 12, 1741	3	116
Zadok, s. Edward, Jr. & Deborah, b. Mar. 31, 1724	3	55
JONES, Anna, d. Daniel & Dorothy, b. June 8, 1803	3	276
Anna, d. Daniel, d. Nov. 25, 1823	3	425
Dan[ie]l, of Long Island, m. Ruth FRISBIE, of Branford,		
Jan. 2, 1782, by Warham Williams	3	314
Daniel, Jr., s. Daniel, b. Feb. 3, 1800	3	273
Huldah, d. Asa & Leucy, b. Mar. 16, 1783	3	272
Joseph, m. Susanna CORNWALL, b. of Branford, Sept. 20,		
1764, by Philemon Robbins	3	187
Lucy, of Wallingford, m. Ozias FOWLER, of Branford, Nov.		
13, 1839, by Rev. Timothy P. Gillett	3	377
Mary, of New Haven, m. Sam[ue]ll ELWELL, Jr., of		
Branford, Oct. 12, 1720, by Sam[ue]ll Bishop, J. P., at		
New Haven	3	45

	Vol.	Page
JONES, (cont.)		
Mary, of Guilford, m. Nath[anie]l **FOOT**, Jr., of Branford,		
Jan. 26, 1758, by James Sproutt	3	204
Nancy, d. Dan[ie]l & Ruth, b. Mar. 30, 1785; d. Apr. 29, 1786	3	314
[Patty], d. Dan[ie]l & Ruth, b. May 11, 1783	3	314
Polly, m. Daniel **LINSL[E]Y**, Dec. 22, 1790	3	275
Rachel, d. Joseph & Susanna, b. Jan. 30, 1767	3	257
Sybil, of Guilford, m. Sam[ue]ll **HOADL[E]Y**, of Branford,		
Sept. 16, 1756, by James Sproutt	3	168
Sylvester, of New Haven, m. Cynthia **BALDWIN**, of North		
Branford, Sept. 12, 1824, by Charles Atwater	3	334
Welthian, Mrs., m. Zacheus **BALDWIN**, Nov. 12, 1821, by		
Charles Atwater	3	414
Willl[ia]m, s. Joseph & Susanna, b. June 21, 1765	3	187
JOSLIN, Amaziah, s. Nathan[ie]ll & Anne, b. Sept. 1, 1744	3	128
Nathan[ie]ll, of East Haven, m. Anne **WADE**, of Lyme, Dec.		
1, 1743, by Rev. Jonath[a]n Mer[r]ick	3	128
Simeon, s. Nathan[ie]ll & Anne, b. Oct. 22, 1746	3	128
KASSAN, Thomas, m. Keturah **JOHNSON**, b. of Branford, Aug.		
11, 1760, by Deod[a]te Davenport, J. P., New Haven	3	161
[KEITH], **KIETH**, Lydia, of Milford, m. Stephen Moitson **SMITH**,		
of North Haven, Nov. 14, 1824, by Jacob Frisbie, J. P.	3	336
KELLOGG, Mary, w. Frederic W., & wid. of John **HUGGINS**, of		
New Haven, & d. of William & Mary **GOULD**, d. Nov.		
15, 1812, in the 47th y. of her age, at Whitestown,		
Newhartford settlement, N. Y..	3	403
KIMBERLY, **KIMBELY**, Abigail, of Guilford, m. Ammi		
PALMER, of Branford, Mar. 14, 1810	3	390
Amanda, of Guilford, m. Elias **GOULD**, of Branford, Mar.		
23, 1812	3	428
Clarissa, m. David **STAPLES**, b. of Branford, Oct. 17, 1790	3	264
Katharine, of Guilford, m. Pennock **HOWD**, Feb. 11, 1761	3	307
Katherine, of Guilford, m. Pennock **HOWD**, of Branford,		
Feb. 11, 1761, by John Richards, minister, in North		
Guilford	3	282
Mary, m. Jacob **BUNNEL**, b. of Branford, May 17, 1756, by		
Jon[a]th[an] Merrick	3	171
KINKEAD, Andrew, s. John & Elisabeth, b. Aug. 9, 1744	3	102
Crownidge, s. John & Elisabeth, b. Dec. 19, 1727	3	63
Elisabeth, d. John & Elisabeth, b. May 23, 1739	3	90
John, m. Uisabeth* **HOADL[E]Y**, b. of Branford, Nov. 28,		
1725, by Nath[anie]ll Har[r]ison, J. P. (*Elisabeth)	3	63
John, s. John & Elisabeth, b. Sept. 13, 1730	3	69
Mary, d. John & Elisabeth, b. Oct. 24, 1741	3	96
Robert, s. John & Elisabeth, b. Feb. 26, 1735/6	3	83
Thomas, s. John & Elisabeth, b. July 23, 1733	3	76
KIRKUM, **KERKUM**, Elisabeth, d. Sam[ue]ll & Mary, b. June 16,		
1708	3	30

	Vol.	Page

KIRKUM, KERKUM, (cont.)

Elisabeth, m. John **BROWN**, Nov. 9, 1730, by Jno. Russell, J. P. — 3 — 72

Joanna, d. Sam[ue]ll & Mary, b. Mar. [   ] * (*Overwritten to read "Feb. 23,") — 3 — 39

John, s. Sam[ue]ll & Mary, b. Sept. 11, 1722 — 3 — 49

Lydia, d. Sam[ue]ll & Mary, b. July 10, 1720 — 3 — 45

Mercy, d. Sam[ue]ll & Mary, b. June 29, 1725 — 3 — 65

Patience, d. Sam[ue]ll & Mary, b. Jan. 31, 171[ ] — 3 — 39

Rebec[c]ah, d. Sam[ue]ll & Mary, b. Mar. [   ] — 3 — 39

Sam[ue]ll, m. Mary **GOODRITCH**, May 28, 1707, by Rev. Sam[ue]ll Russel[l] — 3 — 32

Sam[ue]ll, s. Sam[ue]ll & Mary, b. Feb. 1, 17[ ] — 3 — 41

Sarah, d. Sam[ue]ll & Mary, b. Jan. 27, 1730/1 — 3 — 90

William S., m. Jane S. **BARKER**, b. of Branford, Jan. 2, 1851, by Rev. W[illia]m Henry Rees, in Trinity Church, New York City — TM3 — 168

KNERINGER, Julia, d. Mathias & Hannah, b. Jan. 29, 1848 — TM3 — 240

Julia, d. Nov. 15, 1849, ae 2 y. — TM3 — 309

KNOWL[E]S, Mary, of Branford, m. William **LUDDINTON**, of East Haven, Nov. 5, 1730, by Jacob Heminway — 3 — 70

Rebecca, m. George **HUBBARD**, b. of Branford, Jan. 10, 1753, by Jonathan Mer[r]ick — 3 — 178

LAKE, Henry D., m. Mrs. Jane **STENT**, May 4, 1845, by Rev. Frederic Miller — TM3 — 158

LAMPHERE, LAMFIER, LANFAIR, LAMPHIER, LANFARE, LANFERE, Aaron Stephen, [s. Oliver], b. Sept. 27, 1824 — 3 — 338

Betsey, [d. Oliver], b. Apr. 27, 1816 — 3 — 338

Betsey, [d. Oliver], d. Dec. 23, 1822 — 3 — 338

Betsey, of Branford, m. Edward **PECK**, of N. Haven, Jan. 2, 1850, by Rev. Timothy P. Gillett — TM3 — 165

Betsey, ae 24, m. Edwin **PECK**, ae 32, of New Haven, Jan. 2, 1850, by Rev. T. P. Gillett — TM3 — 167

Cate, d. Oliver, Jr. & Phebe, b. Mar. 2, 1778 — 3 — 266

Hannah, d. Oliver & Temperance, b. Sept. 6, 1754 — 3 — 177

Hannah, m. Roswell **CHIDSEY**, b. of Branford, Feb. 1, 1776, by Philemon Robbins — 3 — 286

Henry, s. Oliver & Temperance, b. Apr. 4, 1752 — 3 — 177

Henry, [s. Oliver], b. July 10, 1822 — 3 — 338

Horace, of Branford, m. Julia M. **SHELTON**, of Huntington, Apr. 5, 1829, by Rev. Timothy P. Gillett — 3 — 349

James S., d. Nov. 1, 1847, ae 16 — TM3 — 308

Kate had d. Hannah **HAYDEN**, b. Apr. [ ], 1799 — 3 — 386

Katy, m. Jeremiah **SHELDON**, June 29, 1801 — 3 — 386

Louisa, [d. Oliver], b. Mar. 28, 1818 — 3 — 338

Martha, d. [Oliver, Jr. & Lois], b. June 5, 1810 — 3 — 396

Martha, of Branford, m. Almon **ROCKWELL**, of Granby, Nov. 11, 1832, by Rev. Timothy P. Gillett — 3 — 358

	Vol.	Page

LAMPHERE, LAMFIER, LANFAIR, LAMPHIER, LANFARE,
LANFERE, (cont.)

	Vol.	Page
Mary, of Branford, m. George **FRIEND**, of Norwalk, June 10, 1778, by Phile[mo]n Robbins	3	296
Oliver, Jr., m. Phebe **ROGERS**, b. of Branford, June 28, 1777, by Philemon Robbins	3	266
Oliver, s. Oliver, Jr. & Phebe, b. Dec. 20, 1779; d. Nov. 20, 1780	3	269
Oliver, 3rd, s. Oliver, Jr. & Phebe, b. Feb. 4, 1783	3	271
Oliver, Jr., of Branford, m. Lois **WILLARD**, of East Guilford, June 5, 1808	3	396
Oliver, d. May 7, 1812, ae 62	3	398
Oliver, Sr., d. May 7, 1812	3	426
Oliver, of Branford, m. Chloe **STEELE**, of New Hartford, Mar. 14, 1826, by Rev. Timothy P. Gillett	3	341
Phebe, d. Dec. 14, 1847, ae 94	TM3	308
Sarah, m. Willford **JOHNSON**, b. of Branford, Aug. 8, 1768, by Elihu Hall, J. P.	3	256
Temperance, d. Oliver & Temperance, b. Jan. 27, 1757	3	177
Temperance, m. John **WATTERS**, b. of Branford, Jan. 15, 1777, by Philemon Robbins	3	287
William, [s. Oliver], b. Apr. 1, 1820	3	338
William Swan, [s. Oliver], b. June 13, 1814	3	338
William Swan, [s. Oliver], d. Oct. 5, 1816; "was drowned"	3	338
LANDON, Horace, m. Harriet **HILL**, b. of Guilford, June 14, 1829, by Timothy P. Gillett	3	349
LANE, ----, d. Ezra & Martha, b. Apr. 30, 1848	TM3	239
LANFARE, LANFAIR, LANFERE, [see under **LAMPHERE,**]		
LATIMER, Eliza Jane, d. [John & Louisa], b. Mar. 29, 1831	TM3	234
Eliza Jane, d. John & Louisa, b. Mar. 29, 1831	TM3	307
George, s. [John & Louisa], b. Dec. 25, 1833	TM3	234
George, s. [John & Louisa], b. Dec. 25, 1833	TM3	307
George, s. John & Louisa, d. Feb. 25, 1834	TM3	307
John Edmund, s. [John & Louisa], b. Aug. 15, 1832	TM3	234
John Edmund, s. John & Louisa, b. Aug. 15, 1832	TM3	307
Louisa Ann, d. [John & Louisa], b. Apr. 7, 1835	TM3	234
Louisa Ann, d. [John & Louisa], b. Apr. 7, 1835	TM3	307
LAWRANCE, LARANCE, Eldad, s. Richard, b. July 14, [1654]	1	171
Eldad, s. Richard, d. Nov. 12, [16]55	1	170
Eleazer, s. Richard, b. Jan. 17, 1651	1	171
Sary, d. Richard, b. Mar. 25, [16]57	1	172
LAY, Cornelia Loisa, d. [Willoughby L. & Ann Maria], b. Aug. 22, 1826	3	352
Emeline Frisbie, [d. Willoughby L. & Ann Maria], b. Aug. 3, 1831	3	352
Frances M., ae 20 y., of Branford, m. George W. **EARL**, ae 23 y., of New Haven, Aug. 14, 1845, by Rev. Milton Bradley, at the house of Samuel Woodruff, of Richmond		

	Vol.	Page

LAY, (cont.)

Kalamasoo, Mich. Witnesses: Mrs. Elisabeth &
Mrs. Celestia Parker — TM3 — 158

Frances Maria, d. [Willoughby L. & Ann Maria], b. Sept.
9, 1824 — 3 — 352

James, s. [Willoughby L. & Anne Maria], b. Feb. 14, 1820 — 3 — 415

James, s. Willoughby L. & Ann Maria, d. Sept. 1, 1823,
ae 3 y. 6 m. 4 d. — 3 — 352

James Willoughby, s. [Willoughby L. & Ann Maria], b. Nov.
16, 1829 — 3 — 352

Sarah Ann, d. [Willoughby L. & Anne Maria], b. Aug. 16,
1821 — 3 — 415

Sarah Ann, 2d, d. Willoughby L. & Ann Maria, b. Jan. 29,
1823 — 3 — 352

Sarah Ann, d. Willoughby L. & Ann Maria, d. Sept. 9, 1823,
ae 2 y. 5 d. — 3 — 352

Sarah Ann, d. of Dr. W. L., of Branford, m. Joseph B.
FRISBIE, of Mendon, Ill., May 6, 1845, by Rev. W. L.
Wilson, of New Port, N. Y., at the house of Samuel
Sperry, in New York City — TM3 — 158

Willoughby L., m. Anne Maria **HARRISON**, Aug. 16, 1818,
by Rev. Timothy P. Gillett — 3 — 415

LEAVITT, LEAVETT, LEAVIT, LUVIT, David, s. David &
Rebeckah, b. Sept. 17, 1756 — 3 — 143

Rebecca, d. [David, Jr.] & Rebecca, b. Nov. 4, 1750 — 3 — 122

Sarah d. David & Rebeccah, b. Mar. 21, 1759 — 3 — 156

Silence, d. David, Jr. & Rebecca, b. July 19, 1753 — 3 — 132

LEETE, LEET, Addam Raynor, s. Asa & Hannah, b. Mar. 3, 1757 — 3 — 146

Benjamin, s. Asa & Hannah, b. Jan. 17, 1753 — 3 — 134

Elisabeth, d. Asa & Hannah, b. Nov. 4, 1750 — 3 — 134

Hannah, of Guilford, m. Josiah **HOWD**, of Branford, June
[ ], 1767, by Philemon Robbins — 3 — 264

Isaac P., of Guilford, m. Clarissa **FOOT**, of Branford,
Mar. 16, 1843, by Rev. Davis T. Shailer — TM3 — 155

James T., of Guilford, m. Julia A. **PLANT**, of Branford,
Aug. 6, 1839, by Rev. Timo[thy] P. Gillett — 3 — 376

Lucy, of Guilford, m. Sam[ue]ll Barker, Jr., of Branford,
Nov. 27, 1760, by [James] Sprout — 3 — 167

Rachel, of Guilford, m. Jonathan **HOADLEY**, Jr., of Branford,
Feb. 19, 1777 — 3 — 290

Sarah, d. Asa & Hannah, b. Dec. 29, 1754 — 3 — 139

LEVI, Rachel, m. Elisha **FRISBIE**, b. of Branford, July 5, 1739,
by Rev. Philemon Robbins — 3 — 104

LEWIS, Lydia, m. Harvey **HARRISON**, b. of North Branford, May
1, 1853, by Rev. Lucius Atwater — TM3 — 172

Sam[ue]ll, of Colchester, m. Mary **TAINTOR**, of Branford,
Feb. 24, 1729/30, by Rev. Sam[ue]ll Russell — 3 — 68

LINDSLEY, LINDLEY, LINLY, LINSLEY, LINSLY, Abiel, s.

	Vol.	Page
LINDSLEY, LINDLEY, LINLY, LINSLEY, LINSLY, (cont.)		
Benjamin & Mary, b. Mar. 22, 1700	2	346
Abigail, d. Joseph & Lydia, b. Aug. 8, 1742	3	101
Abigail, d. Sam[ue]ll & Lydia, b. Nov. 27, 1750	3	121
Abigail, d. Ebenezer, Jr. & Sybil, b. June 2, 1767	3	203
Abigail, m. Ebenezer **BEACH**, b. of Branford, Dec. 6, 1775,		
by Philemon Robbins	3	288
Abigail, d. Rufus & Abigail, b. Oct. 3, 1782	3	291
Abigail, d. John & Jerusha, b. Oct. 16, 1789	3	259
Abigail, [d. Daniel & Polly], b. July 22, 1795	3	275
Abigail Ann, d. Richard & Olive, b. Apr. 16, 1813	3	404
Abraham, m. Elisabeth **BARKER**, b. of Branford, Nov. 18,		
1766, by Philemon Robbins	3	192
Abram, s. Israel & Priscilla, b. Feb. 17, 1744/5	3	104
Alfred, [s. Elihu & Irene], b. Apr. 30, 1796	3	279
Almira, [d. Ebenezer, Jr. & Bets[e]y], b. Mar. 29, 1796	3	406
Almira Jerusha, d. Rich[ar]d & Olive, d. Oct. 1, 1824, ae 22 y.	3	342
Ammi, s. Rufus & Abigail, b. Mar. 12, 1789	3	256
Ann Catharine, [d. Dan & Sally], b. July 9, 1809	3	399
Anna, m. Medad **TAINTER**, b. of Branford, Apr. 20, 1780	3	266
Anne, d. Israel & Priscilla, b. Nov. 18, 1742	3	104
Anne, m. Dow **SMITH**, Jr., b. of Branford, May 24, 1767,		
by Jon[a]th[an] Merrick	3	305
Anne, d. Mercy, b. Oct. 23, 1780	3	298
Apollino, d. John, Jr. & Elizabeth, b. Apr. 6, 1757;		
d. Nov. 26, 1758	3	154
Asenah, d. Ebenezor & Sarah, b. May 15, 1757	3	152
Asenath, m. John **POTTER**, Jr., b. of Branford, Nov. 27,		
1781, by Nicholas Street	3	262
Asenath, m. John **POTTER**, Jr., b. of Branford, Nov. 27,		
1781, by Nicholas Street	3	298
Beniamin, s. John, b. July 10, [16]56	1	172
Beniamin, s. John, d. Mar. 29, [16]60	1	170
Benjamin Douglass, [s. Daniel & Polly], b. July 7, 1793	3	275
Bethia, d. Franses, b. Mar. 4, 1660	1	172
Bethiah, d. Benj[ami]n & Mary, b. Mar. 21, [ ];		
[bp. Apr. [ ], 1706	3	29
Bethiah, m. David **TYLER**, Dec. 8, 1726, by Nath[anie]ll		
Har[r]ison, J. P.	3	62
Bets[e]y, [d. Ebenezer, Jr. & Bets[e]y], b. Dec. 5, 1791	3	406
Bets[e]y, [d. Daniel & Polly], b. Feb. 14, 1792	3	275
Bets[e]y, m. Charles Jacob **PAGE**, Sept. 19, 1796	3	384
Betsey, of Branford, m. Lucius **BROCKETT**, of North Haven,		
Mar. 28, 1841, by Rev. Pascal P. Kidder	TM3	153
Caroline Elizabeth, d. [Ralph & Lydia], b. Dec. 14, 1820;		
d. Apr. 1, 1821, ae 3 m. 17 d.	3	420
Charlotte, [d. Joseph & Lorany], b. Apr. 23, 1799	3	398
Charlotte, [d. Joseph & Lorany], b. Apr. 23, 1799	3	431

	Vol.	Page
LINDSLEY, LINDLEY, LINLY, LINSLEY, LINSLY, (cont.)		
Chaunc[e]y, s. Dr. Reubin & Tryphene, b. Mar. 27, 1781	3	294
Chauncey, m. Parnal **GORHAM**, b. of Branford, Dec. 8, 1803	3	282
Clarissa, w. of Obed, d. Oct. 18, 1826	3	359
Damaris, w. of Jonathan, d. July 16, 1754	3	137
Dan, s. Joseph & Lydia, b. Oct. 27, 1734	3	80
Dan, m. Sally **BALDWIN**, b. of Branford, Sept. 23, 1792,		
by Mathew Noyes	3	268
Dan E., m. Betsey **HOADLEY**, Aug. 6, 1820, by Timothy P.		
Gillett	3	411
Daniel, of Branford, m. Mary **DOWN**, of New Haven, Dec.		
24, 1744, by Rev. Nathan Birdsey, of New Haven	3	104
Daniel, m. Polly **JONES**, Dec. 22, 1790	3	275
Daniel, d. Nov. 23, 1799, in the 84th y. of his age	3	256
David, s. Sam[ue]ll & Lydia, b. May 21, 1745	3	105
David, m. Lois **PALMER**, b. of Branford, Aug. 31, 1768, by		
Philemon Robbins	3	195
David, s. Dr. Reubin & Tryphene, b. Apr. 6, 1780;		
d. Apr. 14, 1780	3	294
David, [s. Joseph & Lorany], b. July 16, 1805	3	398
David, [s. Joseph & Lorany], b. July 16, 1805	3	431
Debbora[h], d. Franses, b. Apr. 22, [16]56	1	172
Delia A., ae 21 m. Edwin **GRANNISS**, ae 23, Oct. 24, 1850,		
by T. P. Gillett	TM3	170
Delia Ann, [d. Elijah & Delia], b. Oct. 28, 1829	TM3	230
Delia Ann, of Branford, m. Edwin H. **GRANNIS**, of East		
Haven, Oct. 24, 1850, by Rev. T. P. Gillett	TM3	168
Dorcas, m. Eli **ROGERS**, b. of Branford, Jan. 21, 1768,		
by Josiah Rogers, J. P.	3	194
Drusilla, [d. Malachi & Rebe[c]kah], b. Dec. 2, 1790	3	411
Ebene[e]r, s. John & Mary, b. Nov. 7, 1711	3	34
Ebenezer, m. Sarah **WILFORD**, b. of Branford, Dec. 10,		
1734, by Rev. Philemon Robbins	3	81
Ebenezer, s. Eben[eze]r & Sarah, b. July 18, 1736	3	86
Ebenezer, Jr., m. Sibil **BARKER**, b. of Branford, Dec. 17,		
1760, by Philemon Robbins	3	167
Ebenezer, s. Ebenezer, Jr. & Sybil, b. Oct. 15, 1764	3	185
Ebenezer, Jr., m. Bets[e]y **RUSSELL**, Oct. 18, 1789	3	406
Ebenezer, m. Lucinda **FRISBIE**, Oct. 12, 1834, by Rev.		
David Baldwin	3	368
Ebenezer, d. Feb. 10, 1851, ae 87	TM3	309
Eber, m. Jerusha **BALDWIN**, [1830], by J. A. Root.		
Recorded Nov. 5, 1830	3	356
Edmund, s. John, Jr. & Elisabeth, b. Nov. 22, 1770	3	272
Edward, s. Obed & Lydia, b. Sept. 23, 1779	3	277
Edward, [s. Isaac, Jr. & Lucinda], b. May 11, 1804	3	410
Edward, m. Milla **BALDWIN**, July 1, 1807, by Rev. Matthew		
Noyes	3	402

	Vol.	Page

LINDSLEY, LINDLEY, LINLY, LINSLEY, LINSLY, (cont.)

	Vol.	Page
Edward, m. Marian **BALDWIN**, b. of North Branford, Oct. 16, 1836, by Rev. Timothy P. Gillett	3	373
Edward, d. Mar. 5, 1851, ae 72	TM3	309
Elam, s. Stephen & Elisabeth, b. June 12, 1783	3	307
Elias, [s. Daniel & Polly], b. Aug. 28, 1803	3	275
Elias, m. Mary **BRADLEY**, Nov. 24, 1828, by J. A. Root	3	350
Elihu, s. Samuel, Jr. & Hannah, b. June 26, 1769	3	205
Elihu, m. Irene **BYINGTON**, Feb. 26, 1795	3	279
Elihu, [s. Elihu & Irene], b. July 18, 1797	3	279
Elihu, Jr., m. Nancy **PARDY**, b. of Branford, Nov. 7, 1824, by Charles Atwater	3	336
Elijah, s. Solomon & Thankfull, b. June 29, 1784	3	312
Elijah Plumb, s. Wyllys & Betsey, b. Sept. 13, 1822	3	427
Eleseheth, [said to be illeg. d. John], [b.] June 18, [16]58	1	172
Elesebeth, d. John, d. July 11, [16]59	1	170
Elesebet[h], d. Gaberill, b. Feb. 24, [16]61	1	173
Elisabeth, d. John & Mary, b. Jan. 20, 1705	3	31
Elisabeth, d. John & Mary, d. Sept. 16, 1712	3	35
Elisabeth, d. Joseph & Lydia, b. Mar. 11, 1744/5	3	118
Elisabeth, d. Eben[eze]r & Sarah, b. July 9, 1745	3	118
Elisabeth, m. Sam[ue]ll **RUSSELL**, Dec. 22, 1748, by Jno. Russell, J. P.	3	117
Elisabeth, d. Sam[ue]ll & Lydia, b. Oct. 6, 1760	3	164
Elisabeth, m. Jonathan **TYLER**, b. of Branford, Dec. 28, 1769, by Warham Williams	3	202
Elisabeth, d. John, Jr. & Elisabeth, b. May 1, 1776	3	273
Elisabeth, m. John **BUTLER**, 2d. b. of Branford, July 10, 1776, by Jon[a]th[an] Merrick	3	205
Elizabeth, [d. Malachi & Rebe[c]kah], b. Aug. 24, 1797	3	411
Ellen P., ae 22, m. W[illia]m **BRADLEY**, Oct. 27, 1850, by W[illia]m Henry Rees	TM3	169
Ellen Phebe, d. Malachi, Jr. & Mariette, b. Dec. 20, 1828	3	355
Emeline, [d. Ebenezer, Jr. & Bets[e]y, b. Oct. 25, 1805	3	406
Emerett, m. Leveritt **THOMPSON**, Dec. 24, 1846, by Rev. Frederick Miller	TM3	160
Erastus, s. Josiah & Rachel, b. July 9, 1770	3	200
Esther, of Northford, m. Augustus **BLACKSTON**, of Branford, Nov. 28, 1822, by Rev. Oliver Wilson, of North Haven	3	421
Frances, m. Susan[n]a **CULLPEPER**, June 24, [16]55	1	170
Franklin Bartholomew, s. Malachi, Jr. & Mariette, b. June 11, 1827	3	355
Frederic, [s. Elihu & Irene], b. Nov. 19, 1801	3	279
Frederic, m. Harriet **FOOT**, b. of Branford, Mar. 18, 1845, by Rev. Timothy P. Gillett	TM3	157
Frederic A., s. Benjamin C. & Lydia, b. Mar. 6, 1842	TM3	237
George, s. Dan & Sally, b. Apr. 2, 1803; d. Oct. 2, 1803	3	277
George, [s. Dan & Sally], d. Oct. 2, 1803, ae 6 m.	3	399

	Vol.	Page
LINDSLEY, LINDLEY, LINLY, LINSLEY, LINSLY, (cont.)		
George, [s. Elias & Mary], b. May 29, 1829	TM3	228
George Washington, [s. Elijah & Delia], b. May 11, 1815	TM3	230
Giles, s. John, Jr. & Elisabeth, b. Oct. 4, 1767	3	192
Grace Ann, [d. Malachi & Rebe[c]kah, b. Sept. 19, 1817	3	411
Hannah, wid., d. Feb. 16, 1736/7	3	90
Hannah, d. Ebenezer & Sarah, b. Jan. 27, 1763	3	179
Hannah, d. Stephen & Elisabeth, b. May 26, 1782	3	307
Harriot, [d. Ebenezer, Jr. & Bets[e]y], b. June 15, 1790	3	406
Harriot, [d. Elihu & Irene], b. Jan. 1, 1804	3	279
Harriot, [d. Dan & Sally], b. Feb. 2, 1805	3	399
Harriot, d. Elihu & Irene, b. Jan. 1, 1806	3	282
Harriott, d. Ebenezer, Jr. & Bets[e]y, m. Anson **TYLER,**		
s. of Philemon & Lucy, July 10, 1811	3	398
Harriet, m. Jeremiah **HARRISON**, b. of Branford, Oct. 13,		
1824, by Charles Atwater	3	336
Harriet M., d. Benjamin C. & Lydia, b. June 12, 1840	TM3	237
Harvey Jones, [s. Daniel & Polly], b. Aug. 24, 1797	3	275
Henrietta, m. Alonso P. **FRISBIE**, b. of Branford, Dec.		
25, 1844, by Rev. Frederic Miller	TM3	157
Henry, s. Elihu & Irene, b. Dec. 2, 1807	3	282
Henry, [s. Elijah & Delia], b. Mar. 20, 1825	TM3	230
Henry, m. Nancy **HARRISON**, b. of Branford, May 6, 1838,		
by Rev. Timothy P. Gillett	3	375
Henry, 2d, m. Harriet **COOKE**, b. of Branford, Aug. 16,		
1852, by Rev. Timothy P. Gillett	TM3	171
Henry Bradley, s. Henry & Nancy, b. May 31, 1842	TM3	234
Henry Davis, [s. Elias & Mary], b. Feb. 12, 1843	TM3	228
Henry Davis, s. Elias & Mary, b. Feb. 12, 1843	TM3	237
Herman, [s. Elihu & Irene], b. Sept. 17, 1798	3	279
Irene, d. Rufus & Abigail, b. Oct. 24, 1780	3	291
Isaac, m. Lydia **BEACH**, b. of Branford, Dec. 23, 1761, by		
Philemon Robbins	3	179
Isaac, of Branford, m. Esther **MONSON**, of Wallingford,		
June 30, 1768, by Warham Williams	3	275
Isaac, s. Isaac & Esther, b. Oct. 4, 1771	3	275
Isaac, Jr., m. Lucinda **ROSE**, Jan. 3, 1798	3	410
Isaac, Sr., d. July 12, 1818, ae 79 y.	3	410
Israel, s. Jonathan & Dorcas, b. Mar. 8, 1712	3	36
Israel, m. Priscilla **WHEDON**, b. of Branford, [ ] 6, 1739,		
by Rev. Jon[a]th[an] Merrick	3	104
Israel, s. Israel & Priscilla, b. Aug. 27, 1740	3	104
Israel, Jr., of Branford, m. Hannah **MO[U]LTRUP**, of New		
Haven, Sept. 22, 1763, by Nicolaus Street	3	186
Israel, d. Oct. 19, 1803	3	275
Jacob, s. Rufus & Abigail, b. Aug. 25, 1791	3	256
James, [twin with John], s. Joseph & Lydia, b. Feb. [6],		
1749/50	3	124

	Vol.	Page
LINDSLEY, LINDLEY, LINLY, LINSLEY, LINSLY, (cont.)		
James, s. Joseph & Lydia, d. June 2, 1757, in the 8th y. of his age	3	170
James, s. Ebenezer, Jr. & Sybil, b. Oct. 12, 1762; d. Apr. 11, 1763	3	179
James, s. Ebenezer, Jr. & Sybil, b. July 27, 1772	3	259
James, m. Sarah **MALTBIE**, b. of Branford, Sept. 28, 1786, by Warham Williams	3	253
James, s. Rufus & Abigail, b. Oct. 3, 1793	3	256
James, [s. Joseph & Lorany], b. Apr. 26, 1809	3	398
James, [s. Joseph & Lorany], b. Apr. 26, 1809	3	431
James, m. Mrs. Mary **BEERS**, b. of Branford, May 22, 1853, by Rev. Amos W. Watrous	TM3	172
James F., m. Polly **FOWLER**, b. of Branford, Sept. 11, 1817	3	407
James Francis, [s. Ebenezer, Jr. & Bets[e]y], b. Sept. 26, 1802	3	406
James Henry, s. [James & Sarah], b. May 5, 1787	3	253
Jane Eliza, [d. Elias & Mary], b. May 24, 1836	TM3	228
Jane Eliza, d. Elias & Mary, d. July 7, 1841, ae 5 y. 1 m. 13 d.	TM3	305
Jared Taintor, s. Josiah & Rachel, b. Dec. 15, 1779	3	255
Jared Tainter, s. Josiah & Rachel, b. Dec. 15, 1780	3	268
Jason, [s. Isaac, Jr. & Lucinda], b. Oct. 22, 1799	3	410
Jason, m. Betsey **RUSSELL**, b. of Branford, Jan. 1, 1824, by Rev. Timothy P. Gillett	3	424
Jeremiah, s. David & Lois, b. July 31, 1769	3	198
Jeremiah, s. John, Jr. & Elisabeth, b. Jan. 24, 1774	3	273
Jeremy, [s. Daniel & Polly], b. May 21, 1799	3	275
Jeremy, of Branford, m. Sarah **BEACH**, of Guilford, Dec. 25, 1841, by Rev. Timothy P. Gillett	TM3	153
Jerusha, d. Dan[ie]ll & Mary, b. Aug. 25, 1756	3	158
Jerusha, m. John **LINSLEY**, 3rd, b. of Branford, Mar. 11, 1778, by Rev. Sam[ue]ll Eells	3	269
Jesse, s. Reuben & Tryfene, b. Apr. 27, 1787	3	255
Jesse, Capt., m. Abigail **BALDWIN**, b. of Branford, Apr. 27, 1817, by Rev. Elijah Plumb	3	335
Joel, s. Abraham & Elisabeth, b. Oct. 5, 1768	3	203
John, m. Sarah **POND**, July 6, [16]55	1	170
John, m. Mary **HARRISON**, June 6, 1699, by Rev. Sam[ue]ll Russel[l]	3	32
John, s. John & Mary, b. Feb. 20, 1703	3	31
John, Jr., m. Mercy **FRISBE**, b. of Branford, Jan. 13, 1725/6, by Nath[anie]ll Har[r]ison, J. P.	3	62
John, s. John, Jr. & Mercy, b. May 20, 1727	3	62
John, [twin with James], s. Joseph & Lydia, b. Feb. [6], 1749/50	3	124
John, Jr., m. Elisabeth **BAKER**, b. of Branford, June 8, 1754, by Rev. Jon[a]th[an] Mer[r]ick	3	137
John, s. John, Jr. & Elisabeth, b. Nov. 1, 1759	3	159
John, 3rd, m. Jerusha **LINSLEY**, b. of Branford, Mar. 11,		

	Vol.	Page

LINDSLEY, LINDLEY, LINLY, LINSLEY, LINSLY, (cont.)

	Vol.	Page
1778, by Rev. Sam[ue]ll Eells	3	269
John, [s. Isaac, Jr. & Lucinda], b. June 8, 1808	3	410
John, s. Richard & Olive, b. Apr. 4, 1811	3	396
John Allword*, [s. Elias & Mary], b. Mar. 4, 1845 (*Atwood?)	TM3	228
John Atwood, s. Elias & Mary, b. Mar. 3, 1845	TM3	237
John B., m. Lucinda **MONRO[E]**, b. of Branford, Aug. 16,		
1835, by Rev. Tim[othy] P. Gillett	3	369
John Bradl[e]y, [s. Joseph & Lorany], b. Apr. 12, 1807	3	398
John Bradley, [s. Joseph & Lorany], b. Apr. 12, 1807	3	431
John Hancock, [s. Elijah & Delia], b. Sept. 13, 1827	TM3	230
John M., s. W[illia]m & Harriet, b. Dec. 2, 1850	TM3	245
Jonathan, m. Dorcas **PHIPPEN**, Sept. 24, 1706, by Jonathan		
Law, J. P., at Milford	3	32
Jonathan, s. Jonathan & Dorcas, b. June 13, 1707	3	31
Jonathan, d. May 3, 1725	3	57
Jonathan, Jr., m. Eunice **ROGERS**, b. of Branford, Dec. 8,		
1767, by Josiah Rogers, J. P.	3	192
Joseph, s. John & Mary, b. Nov. 28, 1707	3	31
Joseph, s. Joseph & Lydia, b. Apr. 30, 1732	3	76
Joseph, m. Lydia **WILFORD**, b. of Branford, May 27, 1733,		
by Rev. Jonath[a]n Mer[r]ick	3	76
Joseph, b. Sept. 13, 1772; m. Lorany **LINSL[E]Y**, Sept.		
10, 1797	3	398
Joseph, Sr., d. Jan. 2, 1786	3	255
Joseph, s. John, Jr. & Jerusha, b. Mar. 6, 1786; d. May		
29, 1790	3	259
Joseph, d. Apr. 16, 1803	3	397
Joseph Bartholomew, [s. Malachi & Rebe[c]kah], b. May		
21, 1807	3	411
Joseph N., m. Harriet M. **WHITING**, b. of Branford, Jan.		
29, 1843, by Rev. Davis T. Shailer	TM3	155
Joseph Nelson, [s. Joseph & Lorany], b. July 20, 1817	3	431
Josiah, s. Joseph & Lydia, b. July 12, 1737	3	86
Josiah, of Branford, m. Rachel **FOWLER**, of Guilford, Feb.		
6, 1767, by Amos Fowler	3	191
Josiah James, s. Josiah & Rachel, b. Feb. 4, 1767	3	191
Justus B., m. Nancy **MONROE**, June 14, 1846, by Rev.		
Frederick Miller	TM3	160
Leveret F., ae 21, m. Marie A. **HILL**, ae 22, Mar. 18,		
1851, by Theodore A. Lovejoy	TM3	169
Levi, s. Rufus & Abigail, b. Sept. 13, 1796	3	256
Lois, d. Daniel & Mary, b. Sept. 14, 1751	3	158
Lois, m. Nathan **ROSE**, Jr., b. of Branford, Dec. 29, 1779,		
by Samuel Eells	3	267
Lorany, b. Apr. 19, 1780; m. Joseph **LINSL[E]Y**, Sept. 10,		
1797	3	398
Lorany, [d. Joseph & Lorany], b. Feb. 12, 1815	3	431

	Vol.	Page
LINDSLEY, LINDLEY, LINLY, LINSLEY, LINSLY, (cont.)		
Lucinda, m. John GATES, b. of Branford, Jan. 1, 1794	3	263
Lucy, d. Isaac & Lydia, b. Apr. 13, 1764	3	182
Lucy, m. Philemon TYLER, b. of Branford, Apr. 27, 1785,		
by Jason Atwater	3	254
Lucy, m. Jesse ROBINSON, June 29, 1845, by Rev. Frederick		
Miller	TM3	160
Lucy Hoadl[e]y, [d. Edward & Milla], b. June 29, 1808	3	402
Liddia, d. Benjamin & Marry, b. Sept. 15, 1703	2	346
Lydia, m. Richard TRUESDELL, b. of Branford, Feb. 20,		
1723/4, by Rev. Sam[ue]ll Russell	3	56
Lydia, d. Joseph & Lydia, b. Jan. 30, 1739/40	3	96
Lydia, d. Sam[ue]ll & Lydia, b. Mar. 8, 1746/7	3	108
Lydia, m. Alexander GORDON, Nov. 5, 1764, by Philemon		
Robbins	3	199
Lydia, d. Isaac & Esther, b. Jan. 28, 1779	3	275
Lydia, d. Obed & Lydia, b. Nov. 1, 1781	3	277
Lydia, [d. Malachi & Rebe[c]kah], b. Dec. 4, 1792	3	411
Lydia, [d. John & Anna], d. Feb. 7, 1810	3	385
Lydia, m. Frederick RUSSELL, b. of Branford, Apr. 25, 1816	3	422
Lydia, m. Elias PLANT, b. of Branford, Nov. 10, 1842, by		
Rev. Timothy P. Gillett	TM3	155
Malachi, s. Eben[eze]r, Jr. & Sybil, b. Aug. 20, 1769	3	203
Malachi, [s. Malachi & Rebekah], b. Mar. 20, 1800	3	411
Malachi, Jr., m. Maretta HOWD, b. of Branford, Dec. 24,		
1823, by Rev. Timothy P. Gillett	3	424
Malachi, m. Nancy E. MORTON, Apr. 25, 1849, by Rev.		
David Baldwin	TM3	164
Marcy, d. Benj[ami]n & Mary, b. Oct. 22, 1710	3	33
Margeret, d. Gaberill, b. Feb. 8, 1659	1	172
Marietta, [d. Ebenezer, Jr. & Bets[e]y], b. Sept. 28, 1808	3	406
Martha, d. Eben[eze]r & Sarah, b. Mar. 12, 1749/50	3	122
Martha, m. Robert OLDS, b. of Branford, Nov. 6, 1769, by		
Philemon Robbins	3	259
Martha, d. Capt. Ebenez[e]r & Sibble, b. Jan. 13, 1778	3	275
Martha, w. of Isaac, Sr., d. Oct. 16, 1819, in the 79th		
y. of her age	3	410
Martin, s. John, Jr. & Elisabeth, b. Mar. 12, 1762	3	176
Mary, d. John & Mary, b. June 1, 1701	3	31
Mary, m. Robert FOOT, b. of Branford, Jan. 25, 1720/1,		
by Rev. Sam[ue]ll Russell	3	45
Mary, d. Eben[eze]r & Sarah, b. Sept. 5, 1738	3	89
Mary, w. of John, d. Jan. 27, 1738/9	3	90
Mary, d. Dan[ie]ll & Mary, b. Mar. 3, 1745/6	3	108
Mary, w. of Daniel, d. Aug. 22, 1759	3	158
Mary, m. John RUSSELL, b. of Branford, Aug. 4, 1762, by		
Jon[a]th[an] Russell, J. P.	3	182
Mary, d. Daniel, d. June 18, 1773, in the 27th y. of her age	3	257

	Vol.	Page
LINDSLEY, LINDLEY, LINLY, LINSLEY, LINSLY, (cont.)		
Mary, d. John, 3rd & Jerusha, b. Apr. 16, 1781	3	270
Mary, d. Richard & Olive, b. Jan. 28, 1808	3	282
Mary, d. Chauncey & Parnal, b. Aug. 29, 1809	3	282
Mary A., of Branford, m. John **IGO**, of Winsted, Mar. 21, 1852, by Rev. T. P. Gillett	TM3	170
Mary L., d. Joseph N. & Harriet, b. Mar. 4, 1851	TM3	243
Mary M., m. Daniel H. **BEARDSLEY**, Dec. [ ], 1847	TM3	162
Mary Martha, [d. Malachi & Rebe[c]k ah], b. Oct. 16, 1812	3	411
Mary Martha, m. Virgil N. **COOK**, Nov. 24, 1833, by W[illia]m P. Curtiss, in Trinity Church	3	362
Mary Thankful, [d. Elijah & Delia], b. Dec. 20, 1817	TM3	230
[M]at[t]hew, s. Benjamin & Mary, b. May 3, 1708	3	30
Mat[t]hew, m. Rebecca **BALDWIN**, b. of Branford, Jan. 9, 1733/4, by Rev. Philemon Robbins	3	79
Mercy, d. Eben[eze]r & Sarah, b. Mar. 11, 1753	3	134
Mercy, d. John, Jr. & Elizabeth, b. Sept. 14, 1754	3	139
Mercy had s. William **GOULD**, b. Dec. 22, 1773	3	264
Mercy had d. Anne, b. Oct. 23, 1780	3	298
Mercy, m. Butler **HARRISON**, b. of Branford, Feb. 14, 1782, by Nicholas Street	3	272
Mercy had d. Henrietta **ISAACS**, b. May 10, 1786	3	273
Meriam, d. Dan[ie]ll & Mary, b. May 31, 1749	3	119
Merrick, s. John, Jr. & Jerusha, b. Sept. 1, 1783	3	259
Mille Sophronia, [d. Edward & Milla], b. Oct. 26, 1814	3	402
Molle, d. David & Lois, b. Nov. 8, 1771	3	205
Munson, s. Isaac & Esther, b. Apr. 20, 1769	3	275
Nancy, twin with Statira, d. John, Jr. & Elisabeth, b. Nov. 13, 1778	3	273
Nancy, [d. Joseph & Lorany], b. July 25, 1801	3	398
Nancy, [d. Joseph & Lorany], b. July 25, 1801	3	431
Nancy, [d. Elihu & Irene], b. Dec. 21, 1802	3	279
Nancy, of North Branford, m. Frederick W. **JOHNSON**, of Wallingford, Apr. 6, 1824, by Charles Atwater	3	426
Nancy, wid. of Russell, d. Apr. 23, 1847, ae 47	TM3	307
Noah, s. Josiah & Rachel, b. Jan. 26, 1774	3	263
Obed, s. Eben[eze]r & Sarah, b. Aug. 13, 1747	3	118
Obed, m. Lydia **BEACH**, b. of Branford, Dec. 23, 1778, by Philemon Robbins	3	277
Obed, m. Clarissa **RUSSELL**, b. of Branford, June 17, 1806	3	359
Olive, [d. James & Sarah], b. Sept. 21, 1789	3	253
Olive, w. of Richard, d. Oct. 23, 1827, ae 55 y.	3	352
Olive Maria, d. Rich[ar]d & Olive, d. Oct. 11, 1827, in the 22nd y. of her age	3	352
Petor, s. Samuel & Lidia, b. Jan. 27, 1756	3	141
Peter, s. Sam[ue]ll & Lydia, d. Dec. 24, 1756	3	144
Philemon, s. Abraham & Elisabeth, b. Apr. 16, 1767	3	192
Philo, [s. Elihu & Irene], b. Sept. 2, 1800	3	279

	Vol.	Page
LINDSLEY, LINDLEY, LINLY, LINSLEY, LINSLY, (cont.)		
Polley, d. Dr. Reuben & Tryfene, b. June 21, 1785	3	313
Polly Hall, d. Dan & Sally, b. July 25, 1795	3	268
Rachel, d. Josiah & Rachel, b. Sept. 20, 1768	3	196
Rachel, w. of Josiah, d. Feb. 4, 1785	3	255
Rachel, d. Josiah & Rachel, d. Mar. 3, 1787, in the 19th		
y. of her age	3	255
Ralp[h], s. Solomon & Thankfull, b. Oct. 13, 1779	3	271
Ralph, m. Lydia **TYLER**, b. of Branford, June 16, 1818,		
by Rev. Matthew Noyes	3	420
Rebecca, d. Joseph & Lydia, b. Aug. 24, 1747	3	118
Rebecca, m. Jared **TAINTER**, b. of Branford, Dec. [ ],		
1772, by Warham Williams	3	257
Rebe[c]kah, w. of Malachi, d. Jan. 16, 1837, ae 66 y.		
7 m. 11 d.	3	373
Rebe[c]kah Amelia, [d. Malachi & Rebe[c]kah], b. May 21,		
1803	3	411
Reuben, s. Daniel & Mary, b. Nov. 1, 1753, N. S.	3	158
Reuben, m. Tryphena **BALDWIN**, b. of Branford, Feb. 3,		
1779, by Samuel Eells	3	266
Reuben Walcott, s. Wyllys & Betsey, b. Oct. 24, 1820	3	415
Richard, s. John, 3rd, & Jerusha, b. June 31 (sic), 1778	3	269
Richard, m. Olive **IVES**, June 30, 1801	3	280
Rufus, of Branford, m. Abigail **FRISBIE**, of Woodbury,		
May 29, 1777	3	291
Rufus, s. Rufus & Abigail, b. Apr. 8, 1779	3	291
Russell, [s. Ebenezer, Jr. & Bets[e]y], b. Nov. 7, 1793	3	406
Ruth, d. Franses, b. Feb. 4, [1658]	1	172
Sally, d. Rufus & Abigail, b. Feb. 12, 1787	3	255
Sally, [d. Ebenezer, Jr. & Bets[e]y], b. May 29, 1798	3	406
Sally, d. Dan & Sally, b. Aug. 20, 1798	3	255
Sally, [d. Joseph & Lorany], b. June 4, 1812	3	398
Sally, d. [Capt. Jesse & Abigail], b. June 7, 1822	3	335
Sally, of Branford, m. Sidney **UMBERFIELD**, of Bethany,		
Nov. 26, 1835, by Rev. T. P. Gillett	3	371
Sam[ue]ll, s. Jonathan & Dorcas, b. Oct. 22, 1709	3	36
Sam[ue]ll, m. Lydia **MORRIS**, b. of Branford, Nov. 27, 1740,		
by Rev. Jonathan Mer[r]ick	3	93
Samuel, s. Samuel & Lydia, b. Sept. 15, 1741;		
d. Jan. 22, 1741/2	3	97
Samuel, s. Sam[ue]ll & Lydia, b. July 23, 1743	3	100
Samuel, Jr., m. Hannah **ROSE**, b. of Branford, Sept. 7,		
1767, by Jonathan Mer[r]ick	3	205
Samuel Baker, s. John, Jr. & Elisabeth, b. Mar. 11, 1765	3	185
Samuel David, [s. Joseph & Lorany], b. Nov. 30, 1822	3	431
Sam[ue]l Edward, [s. Edward & Milla], b. Oct. 29, 1812	3	402
Samuel Still William, s. Simeon & Sarah, b. May 25, 1775	3	260
Sarah, d. Eben[eze]r & Sarah, b. Dec. 23, 1742	3	118

	Vol.	Page

LINDSLEY, LINDLEY, LINLY, LINSLEY, LINSLY, (cont.)

	Vol.	Page
Sarah, m. Dan[ie]ll **OLDS**, b. of Branford, Oct. 28, 1748, by Rev. Jon[a]th[an] Mer[r]ick	3	131
Sarah, m. Stephen **POTTER**, b. of Branford, July 3, 1766, by Philemon Robbins	3	194
Sarah, d. Ebenez[e]r & Sibbil, b. Aug. 27, 1775	3	275
Sarah, w. of Timothy, b. Aug. 27, 1775	3	397
Sarah, d. Dr. Reubin & Tryphene, b. Aug. 12, 1782	3	294
Sarah, d. of Ebenezer & Sybil, m. Timothy **RUSSELL**, Sept. 11, 1799	3	397
Silence, d. Abraham & Elisabeth, b. Jan. 24, 1771	3	203
Simeon, s. Sam[ue]ll & Lydia, b. Feb. 20, 1748/9	3	118
Solomon, s. Joseph & Lydia, b. Oct. 30, 1752	3	128
Solomon, s. Rufus & Abigail, b. Nov. 13, 1784	3	255
Solomon, [s. Elijah & Delia], b. June 22, 1819	TM3	230
Sophronia, d. Dan & Sally, b. June 30, 1793	3	268
Statira, twin with Nancy, d. John, Jr. & Elisabeth, b. Nov. 13, 1778	3	273
Stephen, m. Elisabeth **TYLER**, b. of Branford, Apr. 16, 1781, by Sam[ue]ll Eells	3	307
Sukey Elizabeth, d. Martin & Lucinda, b. May 18, 1789	3	263
Susan, m. Uri **ANDREWS**, July 27, 1845, by Rev. Frederick Miller	TM3	160
Susan Adelia, [d. Malachi & Rebe[c]kah], b. Apr. 24, 1810	3	411
Susannah, d. Benjamin & Marry, b. Feb. 18, 1698	2	346
Susanna, m. John **PAGE**, b. of Branford, Jan. 22, 1734/5, by Rev. Jon[a]th[an] Mer[r]ick	3	87
Sibble, d. Capt. Ebenez[e]r & Sibble, b. Sept. 19, 1782	3	275
Sylvia, [d. Daniel & Polly], b. June 10, 1801	3	275
Thankful, m. David **AVERY**, Feb. 4, 1838, by Rev. David Baldwin	3	375
Thomas Russell, s. Obed & Clarissa, b. Sept. 10, 1809	3	359
Vina Eliza, [d. Edward & Milla], b. Aug. 12, 1810	3	402
Walter F., s. Frederick & Harriet, b. May 13, 1848	TM3	239
Walter F., d. Oct. 2, 1848, ae 1 1/2 y.	TM3	308
William, [s. Malachi & Rebe[c]kah], b. Jan. 20, 1795	3	411
William, [s. Elijah & Delia], b. Feb. 3, 1823	TM3	230
William Augustus, s. Josiah & Rachel, b. Mar. 4, 1776	3	263
William F., d. Oct. 2, 1847, ae 2	TM3	308
William Joseph, s. Malachi, Jr. & Marriette, b. Dec. 25, 1825	3	355
William S., m. Emeline **TYLER**, b. of Branford, Nov. 28, 1849, by Rev. Timothy P. Gillett	TM3	164
Winfield Scott, s. John B. & Lucinda, b. Oct. 16, 1847	TM3	239
Winfield Scott, d. Jan. 27, 1849, ae 1 y.	TM3	309
Wyllys, of North Branford, m. Betsey **HURD**, of Huntington, June 20, 1819, by Rev. Menzier Rayner, of Huntington. Witnesses: B. L. Rayner, M. P. Rayner, Maria Shelton, Levinia Todd, Charles J. Todd	3	415

	Vol.	Page
LINDSLEY, LINDLEY, LINLY, LINSLEY, LINSLY, (cont.)		
----, s. Isaac & Lydia, b. Feb. 22, 1763; d. Feb. 23, 1763	3	179
----, s. Obed & Lydia, b. Sept. 22, 1780; d. Dec. 1, following	3	277
----, s. Charles & Jane Ann, b. [ ], 1850	TM3	243
LINSE*, Margeret, d. Gaberill, b. Feb. 8, 1659 (***LINDSLEY?**)	1	172
LITTLE, Emeline, of Branford, m. Edmund H. **MEIGS**, of		
Madison, May 6, 1850, by Rev. Tim[oth]y P. Gillett	TM3	165
Emeline, ae 21 y., m. Edmund **MEIGS**, ae 27, y., July 28,		
1850, by Rev. T. P. Gillett	TM3	167
LOOMIS, J. O., Dr., m. Jennett A. **SQUIRE**, Jan. 1, 1836, by		
Rev. H. B. Camp	3	371
LORD, Mary, of Saybrook, m. William **GOULD**, Jr., of Branford,		
June 22, 1749, by William Hart	3	154
LOUNSBURY, David, m. Ann **SPENCER**, b. of Branford, Dec. 23,		
1840, by Rev. Davis T. Shailer	TM3	152
John Hobart, b. June 18, 1843	TM3	229
William, s. David & Ann, b. Nov. 11, 1845	TM3	232
LUCAS, Asahel, s. Richard & Sarah, b. Sept. 22, 1762	3	178
Edmund, s. Richard & Sarah, b. Oct. 31, 1759	3	176
Richard, m. Sarah **DARROW**, b. of Branford, Dec. 26, 1758,		
by Philemon Robbins	3	176
LUDDINGTON, LUDDENTON, LUDDINTON, LUDINGTON,		
Abigail Kimberly [d. Caleb L. & Mary], b. July 18, 1843	TM3	235
Ammi Palmer, [s. Caleb L. & Mary], b. Aug. 10, 1840, in		
East Haven	TM3	235
Anna, of East Haven, m. Dan[ie]ll **OLDS**, of Branford,		
Feb. 28, 1754, by Philemon Robbins	3	172
Anne, d. Will[ia]m & Mary, b. June 20, 1750	3	133
Anne, [d. Will[ia]m, d. May 20, 1754, ae 4 y.	3	136
Caleb L., of East Haven, m. Mary **PALMER**, of Branford,		
Nov. 17, 1840, by John D. Baldwin	TM3	152
Caleb L., of East Haven, m. Mary **PALMER**, of Branford,		
Nov. 17, 1840	TM3	159
Henry, s. Will[ia]m & Mary, b. May 25, 1739	3	109
Lydia, d. Will[ia]m & Mary, b. July 25, 1741	3	109
Lydia, m. William **BUCKLEY**, Oct. 28, 1761, by Nicholas		
Street	3	173
Mary, d. Will[ia]m & Mary, b. May 20, 1736	3	109
Mary, w. of Will[ia]m, d. Apr. 16, 1759	3	160
Mary, [d. Caleb L. & Mary], b. Oct. 28, 1845	TM3	235
Rebeckah, d. William & Mary, b. May 10, 1747	3	112
Rebecca, [d. Will[ia]m], d. May 20, 1754, ae 7 y.	3	136
Sam[ue]ll, s. Will[ia]m & Mary, b. Apr. 30, 1744	3	109
Stephen, s. Will[ia]m & Mary, b. Oct. 18, 1753	3	136
Submit, d. William & Mary, b. Feb. 10, 1732/3	3	78
Submit, m. Stephen **JOHNSON**, b. of Branford, June 28, 1754,		
by Jon[a]th[an] Russell, J. P.	3	136
William, of East Haven, m. Mary **KNOWL[E]S**, of Branford,		

	Vol.	Page

LUDDINGTON, LUDDENTON, LUDDINTON, LUDINGTON, (cont.)

Nov. 5, 1730, by Rev. Jacob Heminway	3	70
William, m. Mary **WILKENSON**, b. of Branford, Apr. 17, 1760, by Jonathan Merrick	3	160
----, d. Caleb & Mary, b. June [ ], 1850	TM3	243
[LYMAN], LIMAN, Elesebeth, d. John, b. Nov. 6, [16]55	1	172
John, of Harfoord, m. Dorcas **PLUM**, d. John, Jan. 12, [16]64	1	170
MABBATT, Samuel Robinson, m. Caroline **SQUIRE**, Aug. 12, 1840, by Rev. Pascal P. Kidder, at the house of O. D. Squire	TM3	152
MALLERY, Hannah, m. Jonathan **BYINTUN**, b. of Branford, Dec. 5, 1733, by Rev. Philemon Robbins	3	91
MALOYE, [see under **MELOY**]		
MALTBIE, MALTBY, MALTBYE, Abigail, [w. of William], d. Oct. 24, 1710	3	31
Abigail, d. Dan[ie]ll & Esther, b. Mar. 6, 1713	3	37
Abigail, d. Sam[ue]ll & Elisabeth, b. Oct. 29,. 1716	3	46
Abigail, d. Sam[ue]ll, Jr. & Abigail, b. Apr. 22, 1744	3	106
Abigail, m. Ephraim **PARISH**, b. of Branford, July 19, 1744, by Jno. Russell, J. P	3	102
Abigail, m. Bille **TYLER**, b. of Branford, Mar. 10, 1765, by Rev. Bela Hubbard	3	185
Adonijah Morris, s. Sam[ue]ll, Jr. & Rosanna, b. Sept. 11, 1772	3	310
Ama, d. Sam[ue]ll & Rosanna, b. Mar. 30, 1775	3	310
Ama, d. Sam[ue]ll, Jr. & Rosanna, d. Feb. 23, 1777, in the 2nd y. of her age	3	310
Anne, d. James & Sarah, b. Aug. 31, 1793	3	261
Augustus W[illia]m, s. Stephen & Abigail, b. Oct. 22, 1789	3	268
Belizur, s. Stephen & Abigail, b. Mar. 9, 1789	3	268
Benjamin, s. Dan[ie]ll & Esther, b. June 20, 1717	3	40
Beniamen, s. Daniel & Mary, b. May 13, 1751	3	143
Benj[ami]n, of Branford, m. Elisabeth **FOWLER**, of Durham, Oct. 26, 1752, by Nath[anie]ll Chauncey	3	171
Benj[ami]n, s. Benj[ami]n & Elisabeth, b. Jan. 20, 1755	3	171
Benjamin, Jr., m. Rebecca **TAINTOR**, b. of Branford, Jan. 23, 1778	3	300
Benjamin, s. Benj[ami]n, Jr. & Rebecca, b. Nov. 15, 1780	3	301
Bille, s. James & Sarah, b. Oct. 31, 1796	3	271
Dan[ie]ll, s. William, b. May 19, 1679	1	211
Daniel, m. Esther **MOSS**, Oct. 27, 1702	2	344
Dan[ie]ll, s. Dan[ie]ll & Esther, b. June 16, 1708	3	30
Dan[ie]ll, s. Dan[ie]ll & Esther, b. Oct. 29, 1715	3	37
Dan[ie]ll, d. Dec. 26, 1731	3	72
Daniel, m. Mary **HARRISON**, Sept. [16], 1736	3	142
Daniel, s. Daniel & Mary, b. Jan. 7, 1742	3	142
Daniel, Jr., m. Margaret **MUNSON**, b. of Northford, Branford,		

	Vol.	Page
MALTBIE, MALTBY, MALTBYE, (cont.)		
Dec. 22, 1763, by Warham Williams	3	184
Degrass, s. Benj[ami]n, Jr. & Rebecca, b. Sept. 11, 1782	3	301
Elizabeth, d. William, b. Apr. 30, 1676	1	211
Elizabeth, m. Abraham **HODLE**, Mar. 14, 1697/8, by		
W[illia]m Maltbie, J. P.	2	346
Elisabeth, d. Sam[ue]ll & Elisabeth, b. July 8, 1723	3	53
Elisabeth, [w. Capt. Sam[ue]ll], d. Dec. 7, 1752	3	123
Elizabeth, wid. of Capt. [Samuell], d. Dec. 7, 1752, in		
the 61st y. of her age	3	151
Elisabeth, d. Benjamin & Elisabeth, b. May 16, 1761	3	174
Esther, m. Amos **HAR[R]ISON**, b. of Branford, Mar. 11,		
1729/30, by Jno. Russell, J. P.	3	75
Esther, d. Daniel & Mary, b. Aug. 30, 1739	3	142
Eunice, d. James & Sarah, b. Apr. 18, 1788	3	253
Hannah, d. Daniel & Mary, b. Sept. 25, 1746	3	143
Hannah, m. Simeon **FRISBIE**, b. of Branford, Feb. 11, 1768,		
by Caleb Merriman, J. P.	3	193
James, s. Sam[ue]ll & Elis[abet]h, b. June 2, 1721; d.		
May 24, 1722	3	46
James, s. Sam[ue]ll & Rebecca, b. May 30, 1749	3	118
James, m. Sarah **COE**, Mar. 8, 1786, by Oliver Stanely, J. P.	3	315
James, s. James & Sarah, b. July 18, 1789	3	253
James, of Branford, m. Lydia **WILLIAMS**, of Wallingford,		
Mar. 21, 1819	3	419
John, s. Dan[ie]ll & Esther, b. Apr. 25, 1722	3	48
John, s. Samuel, Jr. & Rosanna, b. Dec. 8, 1768	3	196
John, m. Elizabeth **IVES**, b. of Branford, Oct. 5, 1791,		
by Matthew Noyes	3	264
John, Jr., s. John & Elizabeth, b. May 8, 1795	3	255
Jonath[a]n, s. W[illia]m & Abigail, b. July 26, 1698	2	346
Jonathan, s. Sam[ue]ll, Jr. & Rebecca, b. Oct. 21, 1751	3	123
Jonathan, s. Benj[ami]n & Elisabeth, b. Apr. 21, 1759	3	171
Joseph, s. Dan[ie]ll & Esther, [b.] May 31, 1712	3	37
Juliana, d. John & Elizabeth, b. May 17, 1797	3	255
Lucresia, d. Daniel & Mary, b. May 22, 1749	3	143
Lydia, d. Dan[ie]ll & Mary, b. Oct. 12, 1760	3	169
Martha, d. Dan[ie]ll & Esther, b. Sept. 10, 1720	3	44
Martha, m. Daniel **HOWD**, b. of Branford, May 9, 1739, by		
Rev. Philemon Robbins	3	106
Mary, d. Daniel & Est[h]er, b. Dec. 7, 1703	2	346
Mary, d. Sam[ue]ll & Elisabeth, b. Feb. 28, 1725/6	3	58
Mary, d. Daniel & Mary, b. June 5, 1744	3	143
Mary, m. William **GOULD**, Jr., b. of Branford, Dec. 11,		
1751, by Philemon Robbins	3	154
Polly, m. Calvin **MANSFIELD**, Apr. 12, 1797, by John		
Russell	3	417
Razana, m. John **PAGE**, b. of Branford, Nov. 30, 1787	3	265

	Vol.	Page

MALTBIE, MALTBY MALTBYE, (cont.)

	Vol.	Page
Rebecca, d. Sam[ue]ll & Elisabeth, b. July 28, 1732;		
d. Apr. 19, 1734	3	74
Rebecca, d. Sam[ue]ll & Rebecca, b. Mar. 25, 1754	3	137
Rebeckah, w. of Sam[ue]ll, Jr., d. Feb. 9, 1755, in the		
32nd y. of her age	3	151
Rebeckah, d. Sam[ue]ll, d. May 16, 1755, ae 1 y. 2 m.	3	151
Sabra, d. Daniel & Mary, b. May 10, 1756	3	143
Salina, d. John & Elizabeth, b. Mar. 4, 1794	3	264
Sally, d. James & Sarah, b. May 15, 1787	3	315
Sally, m. Augustus **TYLER**, Dec. 28, 1814, by Rev. James		
Noyes, of Wallingford	3	416
Sam[ue]ll, s. W[illia]m & Abigail, b. Aug. 7, 1693	2	346
Sam[uell], m. Elisabeth **BARKER**, Dec. 8, 1715, by		
Nath[anie]ll Har[r]ison, J. P.	3	46
Samuel, s. Sam[ue]ll & Elis[abet]h, b. Oct. 21, 1718	3	46
Sam[ue]ll, Jr., m. Abigail **WILLFORD**, b. of Branford,		
Oct. 13, 1743, by Rev. Philemon Robbins	3	101
Sam[ue]ll, Jr., m. Rebecca **FOOT**, b. of Branford, Jan.		
22, 1745/6, by Rev. Philemon Robbins	3	108
Sam[ue]ll, s. Sam[ue]ll, Jr. & Rebecca, b. Nov. 15, 1746	3	108
Sam[ue]ll, Capt., d. Dec. 2, 1751	3	123
Sam[ue]ll, Capt., d. Dec. 2, 1751, in the 59th y. of his age	3	151
Sam[ue]ll, of Branford, m. Mary **FOWLER**, of Guilford,		
May 1, 1755, by Ichabod Camp	3	169
Samuel, Jr., of Branford, m. Rosanna **COE**, of Wallingford,		
Feb. 11, 1768, by Caleb Merriman, J. P.	3	193
Samuel, d. Dec. 1, 1770, in the 53rd y. of his age	3	201
Sam[ue]ll, Jr., d. Aug. 18, 1774, in the 28th y. of his age	3	310
Samuel Chauncey, s. John & Elizabeth, b. July 17, 1792	3	264
Sarah, d. Sam[ue]ll & Elisabeth, b. Nov. 10, 1729	3	67
Sarah, d. of Capt. Sam[ue]ll, m. Edward **RUSSELL**, b. of		
[Branford], May 30, 1753, by Rev. Philemon Robbins	3	135
Sarah, d. of Capt. Sam[ue]ll, m. Edward **RUSSELL**, b. of		
Branford, May last, 1753, by Rev. Philemon Robbins	3	145
Sarah, d. Benj[ami]n & Elisabeth, b. May 5, 1763	3	183
Sarah, d. Capt. Daniel & Mary, b. June 23, 1765	3	185
Sarah, m. James **LINSLEY**, b. of Branford, Sept. 28, 1786,		
by Warham Williams	3	253
Sarah Elizabeth, d. James & Lydia, b. Jan. 30, 1820	3	419
Stephen, m. Abigail **WILLIAMS**, b. of Branford, Sept. 27,		
1788	3	268
Thaddeus, s. Benj[ami]n & Elisabeth, b. Dec. 19, 1756	3	171
Thaddeus, s. Benj[ami]n, Jr. & Rebecca, b. Jan. 15, 1779	3	300
Thankfull, d. Daniel & Mary, b. Feb. 5, 1758	3	151
Timothy, s. Samuel, Jr. & Rosanna, b. Apr. 9, 1770	3	201
William, s. William, b. Jan. 9, [16]73	1	174
William, s. Dan[ie]ll & Esther, b. Feb. 17, 1705	3	29

	Vol.	Page
MALTBIE, MALTBY, MALTBYE, (cont.)		
William, d. Sept. [ ], 1710	3	31
Zacc[h]eus, s. Daniel & Mary, b. June [ ], 1754	3	143
MANN, Lewis, of [Wahara], Wis., m. Ellen M. **RUSSELL,** of		
Branford, May 13, 1848, by Rev. Frederick Miller, in		
Trinity Church	TM3	162.
MANSFIELD, , Calvin, m. Polly **MALTBY,** Apr. 12, 1797, by		
John Russell	3	417
Celina, [d. Calvin & Polly], b. Nov. 15, 1799	3	417
Celina, [d. Calvin & Polly], d. Sept. 11, 1805	3	417
Emily Celina, [d. Calvin & Polly], b. Oct. 27, 1814	3	417
Hiram, [s. Calvin & Polly], b. Mar. 15, 1811	3	417
Jared, [s. Calvin & Polly], b. Oct. 9, 1820	3	417
John Calvin, [s. Calvin & Polly], b. May 15, 1816	3	417
Liverius, m. Jane **OSBORNE,** June 27, 1833, by Rev. David		
Daldwin	3	360
Mary Achsah, [d. Calvin & Polly], b. May 5, 1804	3	417
Nathan, [s. Calvin & Polly], b. Nov. 28, 1798,		
d. Dec. 1, 1798, ae 3 d.	3	417
Nathan, 2d, [s. Calvin & Polly], b. Dec. 3, 1801	3	417
Sherlock, [s. Calvin & Polly], b. Oct. 9, 1806	3	417
W[illia]m Henry, [s. Calvin & Polly], b. Nov. 19, 1808	3	417
MARKS, Hannah, m. Joseph **ABBOT[T],** b. of Branford, Apr. 14,		
1730, by Jno. Russell, J. P.	3	70
MARSHALL, Lydia, m. Stephen **PALMER,** Jr., b. of Branford,		
Feb. 28, 1790	3	387
MASON, Eunice, m. Moses **STORK,** Apr. 10, 1763, by [ ] Boyle,		
New London	3	311
Peter, [colored], d. Apr. 2, 1848, ae 70 y.	TM3	308
McCABE, Susanna, d. James & Catharine, b. July 20, 1851	TM3	245
McCANELLY, Abby, m. Jeremiah **BLOND,** b. of Branford, Nov. 5,		
1854, by Rev. Tim[oth]ly P. Gillett	TM3	173
McCLEAVE, Mary, of New Haven, m. Jared **HARRISON,** of		
Branford, July 25, 1776, by Cha[u]ncey Whittlecey	3	284
McDERMOTT, Mary Ann, d. Sept. 22, 1850, ae 2 y.	TM3	310
McMILLAN, Hugh, of New Haven, m. Jane A. **O[L]MSTEAD,** of		
Branford, Nov. 7, 1841, by Rev. Davis T. Shailer	TM3	153
McNEIL, Archibald, s. Archibald & Mary, b. Sept. 20, 1736	3	106
John, s. Archibald, & Mary, b. Aug. 2, 1745	3	106
McQUEEN, James, [s. William & Triphena], b. Aug. 12, 1785	3	395
James, m. Lydia **TYLER,** Mar. 12, 1807	3	392
Jillen, [child of William & Triphena], b. Feb. 14, 1780	3	395
Jillen, [child of William & Triphena], d. Aug. 26, 1784	3	395
John, s. William & Triphena, d. Sept. 1, 1807	3	395
John Still William, s. William & Tryphena, b. May 29, 1775	3	277
John Still William, [s. James & Lydia], b. Dec. 30, 1807	3	392
Lucy Ann, [d. James & Lydia], b. Aug. 11, 1809	3	392
Mary E., m. Henry P. **BOYINGTON,** b. of Branford, Apr. 26,		

	Vol.	Page
McQUEEN, (cont.)		
1843, by Rev. Timothy P. Gillett	TM3	156
Polly, [d, William & Triphena], b. Sept. 14, 1778	3	395
Sally, [d. William & Triphena], b. May 18, 1782	3	395
Sally, [d. William & Triphena], d. Feb. 14, 1794	3	395
Samuel, of Branford, m. Susan E. **BARNES**, of East Haven, Apr. 29, 1844, by Rev. Timothy P. Gillett	TM3	157
Triphena, m. Isaac **PALMER**, Feb. 6, 1794	3	394
William, m. Triphena **ROSE**, Jan. 12, 1775	3	394
William, [s. William & Triphena], b. May 8, 1788	3	395
MEIGS, Edmund, ae 27 y., m. Emeline **LITTLE**, ae 21 y., July 28, 1850, by Rev. T. P. Gillett	TM3	167
Edmund H., of Madison, m. Emeline **LITTLE**, of Branford, May 6, 1850, by Rev. Tim[oth]y P. Gillett	TM3	165
Horace B., of Berlin, m. Martha M. **BEACH**, of Branford, Oct. 27, 1852, by Rev. T. P. Gillett	TM3	171
Lucretia, of Guilford, m. Reuben **ROSE**, of Branford, Jan. 1, 1772, by Jon[a]th[an] Todd	3	205
MELOY, MALOYE, Henry Stark, s. Edward & Mary, b. Mar. 25, 1778	3	265
Rosanna, m. Joseph **BALDWIN**, b. of Branford, June 11, 1781, by Sam[ue]ll Eells	3	309
MERRIAM, Eliza C., of Meriden, m. Benjamin **ROGERS**, of Branford, May 28, 1848, by Rev. Frederick Miller, in Trinity Church	TM3	162
MERRICK, MERICK, C[h]loe, d. Rev. Jonathan & Jerusha, b. Apr. 3, 1738	3	88
Chloe, m. Timothy **RUSSELL**, b. of Branford, Nov. 24, 1764, by Jon[a]th[an] Mer[r]ick	3	198
Jerusha, d. Rev. Jonathan & Jerusha, b. Mar. 3, 1732/3	3	76
Jerusha, wid. of Rev. Jon[a]th[an], d. July 23, 1777	3	287
Jonathan, Rev., of Branford, m. Mrs. Jerusha **MINOR**, of Stonington, Mar. 28, 1732, by Dan[ie]ll Palmer, J. P.	3	76
Jonathan, Rev., of North Branford, d. June 27, 1772	3	287
Lucretia, d. Rev. Jonathan & Jerusha, b. Jan. 5, 1742/3	3	99
Mary, d. Rev. Jonathan & Jerusha, b. Mar. 20, 1740	3	99
Mary, d. Rev. Jonathan & Jerusha, d. Dec. 2, 1761, in the 22nd y. of her age	3	176
Minor, s. Rev. Jonathan & Jerusha, b. June 23, 1735	3	82
Minor, m. Abigail **RUSSELL**, b. of Branford, June 28, 1764, by Jonathan Mer[r]ick	3	185
Sarah, d. Rev. Jonath[an] & Jerusha, b. Nov. 9, 1746	3	112
Sarah, m. Frederick **MONROE**, b. of Branford, Mar. 17, 1824, by Charles Atwater	3	425
MERRILL, Norman B., of New Hartford, m. Sarah E. **JEROME**, of Bloomfield, Oct. 10, 1850, by Rev. T. P. Gillett	TM3	168
Norman B., m. Sarah E. **JEROME**, Oct. 10, 1850, by T. P. Gillett	TM3	170

	Vol.	Page
MERWIN, Miles T., of Durham, m. Ellen Agnes **FOOT**, of		
Branford, May 8, 1851, by Rev. T. P. Gillett	TM3	169
Miles T., ae 28, m. Ellen A. **FOOT**, ae 27, May 9, 1851,		
by T. P. Gillett	TM3	170
MILLER, Caroline Anna, d. Frederick & Susan C., b. Jan. 3, 1848	TM3	239
David, s. Henry & Deliverance, b. June 5, 1734	3	88
Elisabeth, d. Henry & Deliverance, b. Nov. 16, 1724	3	88
F., Rev., d. Oct. 3, 1849, ae 38 y.	TM3	309
Frederick, s. Fred[eric]k H. & Susan, b. Sept. [ ], 1849	TM3	242
Harriet Frances, d. Rev. Frederic & Susan C., b. July 21, 1844	TM3	231
Henry, of Lime, m. Deliverance **PAGE**, of Branford, Sept.		
23, 1723, by Rev. Eliphalet Adams	3	88
Herbert Clarkson, s. Rev. Frederick & Susan, b. June 2, 1846	TM3	238
Jonathan, s. Henry & Deliverance, b. Sept. 30, 1726	3	88
Louesa Abigail, d. Rev. Frederic & Susan C., b. Oct. 27,		
1842, at Cheshire	TM3	231
Lydia, d. Henry & Deliverance, b. Jan. 2, 1732	3	88
Marcia, m. Harrison **FOOT**, b. of Branford, Jan. 27, 1839,		
by Rev. T. P. Gillett	3	376
Mary, d. Henry & Deliverance, b. Dec. 30, 1728	3	88
Samuel, s. Henry & Deliverance, b. May 16, 1737	3	89
Samuel B., m. Betsey A. **BARKER**, b. of Branford, Jan. 1,		
1851, by Rev. Timothy P. Gillett	TM3	168
Samuel B., ae 23, m. Bets[e]y A. **BARKER**, ae 20, Jan. 1,		
1851, by T. P. Gillett	TM3	170
MINOR, Jerusha, Mrs., of Stonington, m. Rev. Jonathan		
MER[R]ICK of Branford, Mar. 28, 1732, by Dan[ie]ll		
Palmer, J. P.	3	76
William P., of Roxbury, m. Clorinda F. **STRONG**, of Branford,		
June 2, 1829, by Rev. Fosdic Harrison, of Roxbury	3	349
MONROE, MONRO, MUNRO, Alvin, twin with Josiah, s. Samuel		
& Damaris, b. May 4 & 5, 1829, (Probably born May 5		
as Alvin is mentioned last in the entry)	3	364
Andrew, m. Deborah **TYLER**, b. of Branford, Oct. 26, 1721,		
by Rev. Sam[ue]ll Russell	3	52
Andrew, s. Andrew & Deborah, b. Sept. 28, 1724	3	96
Andrew, m. Deborah **PALMER**, b. of Branford, Jan. 4, 1750,		
by Isaac Stiles	3	189
Andrew, s. Andrew & Deborah, b. Sept. 5, 1754	3	189
Andrew, [s. Jacob & Sally], b. Sept. 26, 1800	3	401
Ann, [d. Jacob & Sally], b. Apr. 8, 1794	3	401
Anna, of Branford, m. William **REDFIELD**, of East Haven,		
Apr. 29, 1814	3	430
Baverly, s. Will[ia]m & Mary, b. June 22, 1772	3	260
Beverly, [s. Jacob & Sally], b. July 28, 1812	3	401
Catharine, m. Dr. Elihu Williams **CONVERSE**, June 8, 1823,		
by Charles Atwater, at North Branford	3	423
Charlotte, [d. Jacob & Sally], b. May 31, 1798	3	401
Cynthia, d. William & Mary, b. May 3, 1762	3	260

	Vol.	Page

MONROE, MONRO, MUNRO, (cont.)

Cynthya, d. William & Mary, d. Oct. 20, 1778	3	288
Daniel, s. Andrew & Deborah, b. May 4, 1750	3	189
Elisabeth, d. Andrew & Deborah, b. Sept. 11, 1726	3	96
Elisabeth, m. Aaron **MORRIS**, Nov. 29, 1744, by W[illia]m Gould, J. P.	3	103
Elisabeth, d. Andrew & Deborah, b. Feb. 15, 1752	3	189
Eunice, m. David **RUSSELL**, b. of Branford, July 19, 1793	3	263
Frederick, s. William & Mary, b. Feb. 8, 1767	3	260
Frederick, m. Sarah **MERRICK**, b. of Branford, Mar. 17, 1824, by Charles Atwater	3	425
Hannah, [d. Jacob & Sally], b. June 1, 1796	3	401
Harriett F., d. William & Abagail, b. Aug. 1, 1849	TM3	243
Hugh, s. Andrew & Deborah, b. July 5, 1763	3	189
Hugh, m. Mary **FRISBIE**, b. of Branford, Sept. 18, 1797, by Rev. Bela Hubbard	3	271
Jacob, m. Sally **BENHAM**, Mar. 12, 1793	3	401
Jeremiah, s. William & Mary, b. Dec. 1, 1775	3	260
John, s. Andrew & Deborah, b. Aug. 22, 1722	3	52
John, m. Sarah **HOADL[E]Y**, d. of Will[ia]m, 3rd, b. of Branford, Feb. 14, 1748/9, by Rev. Philemon Robbins	3	135
John, [s. Jacob & Sally], b. Oct. 31, 1795	3	401
John, m. Myrta M. **FRISBIE**, July 13, 1846, by Rev. Frederick Miller	TM3	160
John Factor, s. Andrew & Deborah, b. July 17, 1757	3	189
Josiah, twin with Alvin, s. Samuel & Damaris, b. May 4, & 5, 1829 (Probably born May 4 as Josiah is mentioned first in the entry)	3	364
Josiah T., m. Mary J. **PAGE**, Apr. 9, 1852, by Rev. Lucius T. Atwater	TM3	171
Lavinia, d. W[illia]m & Mary, b. Apr. 22, 1769	3	260
Lavinia, m. Eliada **ROSE**, b. of Branford, Dec. 19, 1792	3	270
Lucinda, d. Andrew & Deborah, b. Sept. 11, 1760	3	189
Lucinda, m. John B. **LINSLEY**, b. of Branford, Aug. 16, 1835, by Rev. Tim[othy] P. Gillett	3	369
Lydia, [twin with Sarah], d. John & Sarah, b. Feb. 3, 1753	3	135
Ladye, d. W[illia]m & Mary, b. Oct. 24, 1760	3	260
Lydia, m. Capt. James **BARKER**, b. of Branford, Nov. 22, 1780	3	301
Marian, m. George **BALDWIN**, b. of Branford, Feb. 17, 1850, by Rev. Timothy P. Gillett	TM3	165
Mary, d. Andrew & Deborah, b. Oct. 9, 1731	3	96
Mary, d. John & Sarah, b. Feb. 18, 1749/50	3	135
Mary, d. Will[ia]m & Mary, b. Oct. 22, 1779	3	288
Mary, [d. Jacob & Sally], b. May 5, 1804	3	401
Mary, of Branford, m. Nathaniel **PAGE**, of North Branford, May 13, 1840, by Rev. David T. Shailer	3	379
Mary A., ae 16 y., m. George **BALDWIN**, ae 19 y., Feb. 17,		

	Vol.	Page
MONROE, MONRO, MUNRO, (cont.)		
1850, by Rev. T. P. Gillett	TM3	166
Nancy, m. Justus B. **LINSLEY,** June 14, 1846, by Rev.		
Frederick Miller	TM3	160
Sally, [d. Jacob & Sally], b. Jan. 23, 1802	3	401
Sally, m. Augustus **BALDWIN,** May 4, 1808, by Rev. Aaron		
Dutton, of Guilford	3	418
Samuel, m. Damaris **TYLER,** b. of Branford, Jan. 29, 1826,		
by Rev. Timothy P. Gillett	3	341
Sarah, [twin with Lydia], d. John & Sarah, b. Feb. 3, 1753	3	135
Sarah, m. Samuel **RUSSELL,** Jr., b. of Branford, June 12, 1774	3	278
Sarah, d. Will[ia]m & Mary, b. Oct. 17, 1782	3	288
William, s. Andrew & Deborah, b. Sept. 9, 1733	3	96
William, m. Mary **HOADL[E]Y,** b. of Branford, July 11, 1760,		
by William Hoadley, J. P.	3	259
William, s. William & Mary, b. July 15, 1765	3	260
William, m. Abigail **HOTCHKISS,** Apr. 19, 1848	TM3	162
Zada, m. Danniel Foot **HARRISON,** b. of Branford, Mar. 7,		
1780	3	283
----, d. William & Abagial, b. May 5, 1849	TM3	241
[MONTGOMERY], MONGOMERY, Lydia (alias) **HOADL[E]Y,**		
m. John **BRAY,** Apr. 28, 1737, by Rev. Philemon		
Robbins	3	126
MORRIS, MORRISS, Aaron, m. Elisabeth **MONROE,** Nov. 29,		
1744, by W[illia]m Gould, J. P.	3	103
Aaron, s. Aaron & Elisabeth, b. July 17, 1768	3	203
Aaron, d. Jan. 5, 1784	3	294
Aaron, s. Andrew & Lucretia, b. Mar. 3, 1812	3	398
Andrew, s. Aaron & Elisabeth, b. Oct. 31, 1749	3	202
Andrew, m. Lucretia **RUSSELL,** b. of Branford, June 25, 1795	3	393
Andrew, [s. Andrew & Lucretia], b. Jan. 8, 1803	3	393
Betsey, d. Daniel & Betsey, b. Oct. 14, 1801	3	280
Daniel, s. Timothy & Chloe, b. Oct. 4, 1770	3	294
Edmund, s. Aaron & Elisabeth, b. Dec. 14, 1758	3	203
Edmund, [s. Capt. Edmund & Hannah], b. Apr. 21, 1795	3	366
Edmund, d. Feb. 17, 1851, ae 92	TM3	309
Elisabeth, d. Timothy & Chloe, b. Aug. 9, 1780	3	294
Elisabeth, w. of Aaron, d. Dec. 12, 1781	3	294
Elisabeth, d. William S. & Sally, b. Nov. 14, 1841	TM3	232
Ellen, ae 25, m. Abraham **AUGUR,** ae 40, of Georgia, July		
28, 1850, by Rev. Lucius Atwater	TM3	167
Ellen, of Branford, m. Abraham **AUGUR,** of Georgia, July		
29, 1850, by Rev. Lucius Atwater	TM3	165
Elvira, [d. Capt. Edmund & Hannah], b. Mar. 11, 1805	3	366
Emeline, d. Dan[ie]l & Betsey, b. Nov. 21, 1803	3	280
Emeline Stewart, d. James F. & Harriet, b. May 20, 1842	TM3	232
Esther Hannah, [d. Capt. Edmund & Hannah], b. Dec. 5, 1802	3	366
Eunice Ann, [d. Capt. Edmund & Hannah], b. Oct. 24, 1806;		

	Vol.	Page
MORRIS, MORRISS, (cont.)		
d. Aug. [ ], 1828, ae 22 y.	3	366
Foster, s. Timothy & Chloe, b. June 25, 1766	3	294
Grace, [d. Capt. Edmund & Hannah], b. June 17, 1793	3	366
Grace, [d. Capt. Edmund & Hannah], d. Oct. 13, 1833, ae 40 y.	3	366
Harriet, d. James F. & Harri[e]tt, b. Mar. 8, 1849	TM3	241
Harriett R., d. Jan. 28, 1850, ae 11 m.	TM3	309
James, s. Timothy & Chloe, b. Aug. 29, 1772	3	294
James F., m. Harriet **PLANT**, b. of Branford, Feb. 28, 1839,		
by Rev. T. P. Gillett	3	376
James Foster, s. Dan[ie]l & Betsey, b. Dec. 29, 1805	3	280
Jane, [d. Capt. Edmund & Hannah], b. Aug. 9, 1808	3	366
John Russell, [s. Andrew & Lucretia], b. Mar. 1, 1806	3	393
Joseph, m. Lydia **HARRISON**, Mar. 4, 1712/3, by Rev.		
Sam[ue]ll Russel[l]	3	37
Joseph, s. Joseph & Lydia, b. Jan. 1, 1713/14	3	37
Joseph, s. Timothy & Chloe, b. Mar. 8, 1764	3	294
Keturah, d. Timothy & Chloe, b. Oct. 26, 1775	3	294
Keturah, d. Apr. 25, 1850, ae 76 y.	TM3	309
Lewis Foster, s. James F. & Harriet, b. Apr. 12, 1840	TM3	232
Louisa, d. Aaron & Elisabeth, b. Mar. 11, 1755	3	203
Louisa, [d. Capt. Edmund & Hannah], b. Mar. 25, 1801	3	366
Louesa, d. William S. & Sally, b. Feb. 28, 1839	TM3	232
Lucretia, [d. Andrew & Lucretia], b. Feb. 14, 1799	3	393
Lydia, d. Jos[eph] & Lydia, b. Oct. 15, 1715	3	37
Lydia, m. Sam[ue]l **LINSL[E]Y**, b. of Branford, Nov. 27,		
1740, by Rev. Jonathan Mer[r]ick	3	93
Lydia Ann, [d. Andrew & Lucretia], b. Mar. 1, 1801	3	393
Margaret, d. Aaron & Elisabeth, b. June 16, 1745	3	202
Mary, m. Nath[anie]ll **WHEDON**, Jr., b. of Branford, Nov.		
20, 1755, by Philemon Robbins	3	162
Mary Elizabeth, [d. Andrew & Lucretia], b. Feb. 13, 1797	3	393
Polly, [d. Capt. Edmund & Hannah], b. May 28, 1789	3	366
Robert Hamilton, s. William S. & Sally, b, Jan. 21, 1844	TM3	232
Sally, [d. Andrew & Lucretia], b. July 12, 1809	3	393
Sarah, d. Aaron & Elisabeth, b. Apr. 11, 1747	3	118
Sybil, d. Timothy & Chloe, b. June 11, 1768; d. Dec. 4, 1769	3	294
Timothy, of Branford, m. Chloe **FOSTER**, of Long Island,		
Sept. 6, 1762, on Long Island	3	294
Tim[o]thy, s. Timothy & Chloe, b. Dec. 1, 1777	3	294
Walter Leet, s. James F. & Harriet, b. Jan. 4, 1844	TM3	232
William S., m. Sally E. **STEDMAN**, b. of Branford, Oct.		
1, 1837, by Timothy P. Gillett	3	374
Zayda, d. Aaron & Elisabeth, b. Aug. 13, 1764	3	203
----, s. W[illia]m s. & Sally, b. July 21, 1850	TM3	242
MORSE, MOSS, Esther, m. Daniel **MALTBIE**, Oct. 27, 1702	2	344
John, s. Seth & Hannah, b. Aug. 17, 1711	3	34
Martha, m. Sam[ue]ll **STENT**, Nov. 27, 1706, by Rev.		

	Vol.	Page
MORSE, MOSS, (cont.)		
Sam[ue]ll Street, of Wallingford	3	32
Seth, s. Seth & Desire, b. Dec. 12, 1776	3	265
MORTON, John, d. Nov. 22, 1847, ae 40	TM3	308
Nancey E., m. Malachi **LINSLEY,** Apr. 25, 1849, by Rev.		
David Baldwin	TM3	164
MOSS, [see under **MORSE**]		
MOULTHROP, MOLTHROP, MOLTROP, MOLTRUP,		
MULTRUP, Amy, b. Oct. 8, 1777, in East Haven; m. Samuel N.		
WILLIAMS, June 7, 1799	3	418
Chauncey, b. Jan. 5, 1788	3	432
Chauncey, m. Margary **BUTLER,** b. of Branford, May 14,		
1810	3	432
Delia Eliza, [d. Chauncey & Margary], b. Apr. 19, 1811	3	432
Dorothy, m. Samuel **POTTER,** June 1, 1738, by Rev. Jacob		
Heminway	3	100
Hannah, of New Haven, m. Israel **LINSL[E]Y,** Jr., of Branford,		
Sept. 22, 1763, by Nicolaus Street	3	186
Hannah Maria, [d. Chauncey & Margary], b. Oct. 10, 1815	3	432
Joseph Chauncey, [s. Chauncey & Margary], b. Apr. 17, 1822	3	432
Kez[iah], of New Haven, m. Daniel **BARKER,** of Branford,		
Aug. 24, 1701, by William Maltbie, J. P.	3	29
Lambert, of New Haven, m. Sophronia **HOTCHKISS,** of East		
Haven, Oct. 18, 1829, by Rev. Timo[thy] P. Gillett	3	351
Laura Ann, [d. Chauncey & Margary], b. Apr. 25, 1819	3	432
Lois, d. of Israel & Lydia, b. Mar. 26, 1745, at New Haven;		
m. Charles **PAGE**	3	198
Lois, of New Haven, m. Charles **PAGE,** of Branford, Oct.		
31, 1765, by Nicolaus Street	3	188
Lucretia Bradley, [d. Chauncey & Margary], b. Dec. 21, 1812	3	432
MOWRY, Bedford, of Pittsburg, Penn., m. Lucretia **WOLCOTT,** of		
Branford, [Feb] 18, [1822], by Rev. Origen P. Holcomb	3	418
MULFORD, Augustus, s. Nath[a]n & Sabrina, b. Sept. 1, 1782	3	273
Barnabas, m. Hannah **PETTY,** b. of Branford, Apr. 30, 1740,		
by Rev. Jonath[an] Mer[r]ick	3	113
Barnabas, s. Barnabas & Hannah, b. Feb. 13, 1744/5	3	113
David, s. Barnabas & Hannah, b. June 13, 1744	3	113
Edward, s. Barnabas & Hannah, b. Feb. 1, 1741/2	3	98
Hannah, d. Barnabas & Hannah, b. May 21, 1749	3	119
Hannah B., m. Giles **BARKER,** Oct. 5, 1805	3	286
Joel, s. Barnabas & Hannah, b. Dec. 17, 1754	3	135
Lucresha, d. Barnibas & Hannah, b. Aug. 15, 1756	3	146
Lucretia, d. Dea. Barnabas & Hannah, d. Sept. 6, 1775	3	261
Mary, d. Barnabas & Hannah, b. Sept. 27, 1761	3	173
Molly, m. Thomas **ROGERS,** Jr., b. of Branford, Aug. 5,		
1784, by Sam[ue]l Eells	3	260
Nathan, s. Barnabas & Hannah, b. July 25, 1759	3	156
Nathan, m. Sabrina **BARKER,** b. of Branford, Mar. 26, 1782,		

	Vol.	Page
MULFORD, (cont.)		
by Sam[ue]ll Eells	3	273
MUNGER, Truman, d. Oct. 27, 1850, ae 50 y.	TM3	309
MUNROE, [see under **MONROE**]		
MUNSON, MONSON, Abigail, m. Amaziah **ROSE**, Dec. 23, 1795	3	266
Albert, s. Asahel & Ruth, b. June 2, 1792	3	256
Almira, d. Asahel & Ruth, b. July 26, 1794	3	256
Almond, s. Levi & Mary, b. Oct. 3, 1761	3	183
Elizebeth, of Wallingford, m. Jedediah **FRISBIE**, of Branford, May 10, 1743, by Rev. Sam[ue]ll Whittlesley	3	155
Elizabeth, d. Asahel & Ruth, b. Dec. 23, 1798	3	256
Esther, of Wallingford, m. Isaac **LINSLEY**, of Branford, June 30, 1768, by Warham Williams	3	275
Irene, of Wallingford, m. Samuel **BARTHOLOMEW**, Jr., of Branford, May 14, 1776, by Warham Williams	3	267
Jesse, s. Ephraim & Comfort, b. Dec. 1, 1740	3	96
Juliana, d. Asahel & Ruth, [b.] Dec. 29, 1796	3	256
Lucy, m. Amaziah **ROSE**, Apr. 17, 1782	3	266
Margaret, m. Daniel **MALTBIE**, Jr., b. of Northford, Branford, Dec. 22, 1763, by Warham Williams	3	184
Martha, m. Uzal **BARKER**, b. of Branford, Jan. 6, 1731/2, by Jno. Russell, J. P.	3	75
Mehetabel, of Wallingford, m. Dan **POND**, of Branford, Aug. 29, 1750, by Rev. Sam[ue]ll Whittlesey, at Wallingford	3	124
Phebe, wid., of Wallingford, m. Josiah **BARTHOLOMEW**, of Branford, Apr. 9, 1752, by Rev. Warham Williams	3	125
Ruth, of Branford, m. Joel **HOUGH**, of Hamden, Dec. 20, 1820, by Rev. Matthew Noyes	3	414
Ruth, d. Asahel & Ruth, [b.] [ ]	3	256
Titus, m. Anna **HARRISON**, Dec. 6, 1821, by Rev. Matthew Noyes	3	415
MURRAY, Tamer, of Guilford, m. Abraham **BROOKER**, of Killingworth, Oct. 12, 1758, by Elnathan Stevens, J. P.	3	171
NASH, Elizabeth, d. John, b. Aug. 15, 1681	1	211
John, m. Elisabeth **HOWD**, Aug. 22, 1677	1	210
Joseph, s. Jno. b. Jan. 28, 1679	1	211
Thomas, s. Jno., b. Jan. 28, 1679	1	211
NETTLETON, Hanna[h], m. Thomas **SMITH**, July 10, [16]56	1	170
Marie, w. of Samuell, d. Oct. 29, [16]58	1	170
NICHOLS, Catharine, d. [Darius & Sylva], b. June 7, 1820	TM3	233
Charlotte Maria, d. [Darius & Sylva], b. Jan. 24, 1831	TM3	233
Darius, of Gill, Mass., m. Sylva **FOX**, of Barnards Town, Mass., May 16, 1814	TM3	159
Darius, s. [Darius & Sylva], b. July 2, 1823, in New Port, N. Y.	TM3	233
Darius, s. Darius & Sylva, d. Mar. 11, 1834	TM3	306
Darius, d. Sept. 18, 1847, ae 57	TM3	308
Elisabeth, d. [Darius & Sylva], b. Jan. 23, 1819	TM3	233

	Vol.	Page
NICHOLS, (cont.)		
Henry Z., m. Eliza Ann **POND**, b. of Branford, June 13,		
1850, by Rev. W[illia]m Henry Rees	TM3	165
Henry Z., ae 22, m. Eliza A. **POND**, ae 19, June 10, 1850,		
by Rev. W. H. Reeves	TM3	167
Henry Zina, [s. Darius & Sylva], b. Aug. 18, 1827	TM3	233
Lydia Almena, d. Darius & Sylva, b. Mar. 30, 1815, in		
Colerain, Mass.	TM3	233
Mary Jane, d. [Darius & Sylva], b. July 30, 1837	TM3	233
May Jane, d. Darius, d. Jan. 12, 1843	TM3	306
Ruggles Green, s. [Darius & Sylva], b. Feb. 25, 1816,		
in Barnardston, Mass	TM3	233
Sarah Manerva, d. [Darius & Sylva], b. Feb. 17, 1833	TM3	233
Sylva, d. [Darius & Sylva], b. Dec. 7, 1825, in New Port, N. Y.	TM3	233
Sylvia, d. Jan. 1, 1850, ae 56 y.	TM3	309
William Edmund, s. [Darius & Sylva], b. Aug. 24, 1829	TM3	233
Zina Kelsey, s. [Darius & Sylva], b. Feb. 3, 1822, in		
New Port, N. Y.	TM3	233
Zina Kelsey, s. Darius & Sylva, d. Apr. 22, 1834	TM3	306
NORTH, Erastus A., of Berlin, m. Eliza J. **COOK**, of Branford,		
May 23, 1853, by Rev. T. P. Gillett	TM3	172
NORTON, Abraham, m. Elissabeth **FARNUM**, Dec. 16, 1784, by		
Warham Williams	3	257
Abraham, s. Abraham & Elisabeth, b. Dec. 25, 1789	3	257
Bethiah, m. Jonathan **BARKER**, May 12, 1788	3	385
Dorratha, d. John, b. Mar. 1, [1649]	1	171
Doratha, w. of John, d. Jan. 24, 1652	1	170
Elesebeth, w. of John, d. Nov. 6, [1657]	1	170
Elizabeth, d. [Asa & Sophia Amelia], b. Oct. 24, 1811	3	400
Elizabeth, m. Abrahan **ROGERS**, Jr. b. of Branford, Nov.		
30, 1837, by Rev. Timo[thy] P. Gillett	3	374
Elissabeth Mary, d. Abraham & Elissabeth, b. July 14, 1787	3	257
Emily, d. Asa & Sophia A., b. July 19, 1820	3	348
Emily, of Branford, m. Lorenzo **BLACKSTONE**, of Brooklyn,		
N. Y., Oct. 17, 1842, by Rev. Timothy P. Gillett	TM3	155
Harriett D., d. Aug. 28, 1849, ae 37 y.	TM3	309
Henry, of Norwich, m. Emeline **FRISBIE**, of Branford,		
[June] 21, 1831, by Judson A. Root	3	356
Henry Barker, s. Asa & Sophia Amelia, b. May 5, 1807	3	400
Jehiel Forbes, s. [Asa & Sophia Amelia], b. Apr. 5, 1809	3	400
Joel, m. Elisabeth **PALMER**, Jan. 29, 1783, by Sam[ue]ll Eells	3	279
John, s. John, b. Mar. 24, [1651]	1	171
John, s. John, b. Oct. 14, [16]57	1	172
John, s. John, d. Jan. 15, [1658?]	1	170
Laura, m. George **ROGERS**, b. of Branford, Oct. 14, 1844,		
by Rev. E. Edwin Hall	TM3	157
Levi H., of New Haven, m. Susan J. **HOWD**, of Branford,		
Apr. 25, 1833, by Rev. Timothy P. Gillett	3	359

	Vol.	Page
NORTON, (cont.)		
Marcy, d. Oct. 21, 1824, ae 87 y.	3	348
Mary, d. Asa & Sophia, b. Apr. 21, 1814	3	405
Mary, d. Asa & Sophia A., b. Apr. 21, 1814	3	406
Matte, d. Thomas & Mercy, b. Oct. 20, 1761	3	178
Stephen Potter, s. Thomas, Jr. & Sarah, b. May 17, 1792	3	260
Thomas, m. Mercy **TYLER**, b. of Branford, Apr. 29, 1761, by Philemon Robbins	3	178
Thomas, s. Thomas & Mercy, b. July 27, 1764; d. Sept. 6, 1764	3	189
Thomas, s. Thomas & Mercy, b. July 22, 1766	3	189
Thomas, Jr., m. Sarah **POTTER**, b. of Branford, Nov. 16, 1789, by Jason Atwater	3	260
Timothy, s. Thomas & Mercy, b. Dec. 18, 1762; d. next day	3	178
Timothy, s. Asa & Sophia, b. Nov. 23, 1816	3	405
Timothy Parmele, s. Asa & Sophia A., b. Nov. 23, 1816	3	406
William, s. Asa & Sophia A., b. Aug. 3, 1823; d. June 13, 1826	3	348
William B., of Guilford, m. Lorenda **HULL**, of Branford, Nov. 26, 1829, by Chandler Barker, J. P.	3	351
William Tyler, s. Asa & Sophia, b. Dec. 5, 1826	3	348
William Tyler, of Norwich, m. Mary Eliza **PLANT**, of Branford, Nov. 29, 1852, by Rev. T. P. Gillett	TM3	172
NORVILL, William, s. John & Anne, b. Mar. 6, 1763	3	189
NOYES, Almira Jerusha, [d. Matthew], b. June 11, 1802	3	280
Mary Ann, d. Rev. Matthew & Mary, b. Mar. 29, 1796	3	255
Olive Maria, [d. Rev. Matthew], b. Feb. 25, 1805	3	280
O'BRIEN, John, s. Michael & Mary, b. June 30, 1850	TM3	242
John, d. [ ], 1851, ae 4 y.	TM3	310
Thomas, ae 24, m. Bridget [ ], ae 22, July 30, 1851	TM3	169
O'CINNE, ____, m. Thomas **HOPEWELL**, May 22, [16]56	1	170
OLDS, OALDS, Anna, w. of Dan[ie]ll, d. May 27, 1758	3	172
Dan[ie]ll, m. Sarah **LINSL[E]Y**, b. of Branford, Oct. 28, 1748, by Rev. Jon[a]th[an] Mer[r]ick	3	131
Dan[ie]ll, s. Dan[ie]ll & Sarah, b. Sept. 10, 1750	3	131
Dan[ie]ll, of Branford, m. Anna **LUDDINTON**, of East Haven, Feb. 28, 1754, by Philemon Robbins	3	172
Dan[ie]ll, of Branford, m. Sarah **ROW**, of New Haven, Jan. 17, 1759, by Nicholas Street	3	172
Daniel, Jr., m. Sarah **RUSSELL**, b. of Branford, Dec. 2, 1772	3	278
Daniel, s. Daniel, Jr. & Sarah, b. Feb. 5, 1781, in Guilford	3	278
Francis, s. Daniel, Jr. & Sarah, b. Dec. 20, 1776	3	278
Jared, s. Daniel, Jr. & Sarah, b. Dec. 20, 1778	3	278
John Daniel, s. Stephen & Clorinda, b. Apr. 9, 1775	3	259
Minta, m. Nathaniel **FRISBIE**, b. of Branford, Jan. 10, 1818, by Orchard Gould, J. P.	3	405
Robert, s. Dan[ie]ll & Sarah, b. Apr. 17, 1749	3	131
Robert, m. Martha **LINSL[E]Y**, b. of Branford, Nov. 6, 1769, by Philemon Robbins	3	259

	Vol.	Page
OLDS, OALDS, (cont.)		
Robart, d. Sept. 30, 1783, in the 35th y. of his age	3	298
Samuel, s. Robert & Martha, b. Mar. 27, 1771	3	259
Sarah, d. Dan[ie]ll & Anna, b. Nov. 9, 1756	3	172
Stephen, s. Dan[ie]ll & Sarah, b. June 10, 1752	3	131
Stephen, d. Dec. 26, 1777, in the 26th y. of his age	3	265
William, s. Daniel, Jr. & Sarah, b. May 25, 1773	3	278
OMSTEAD, Jane A., of Branford, m. Hugh **McMILLAN**, of New		
Haven, Nov. 7, 1841, by Rev. Davis T. Shailer	TM3	153
OSBORNE, Jane, m. Liverius **MANSFIELD,** June 27, 1833, by		
Rev. David Baldwin	3	360
OWENS, OWEN, Charles M., of Stockbridge, Mass., m. Emely W.		
JEROME, of New Hartford, Conn., July 10, 1845, by		
Rev. Timothy P. Gillett	TM3	158
Robert, m. Mary **ELWELL**, b. of Branford, Feb. 23, 1725/6,		
by Nath[anie]ll Har[r]ison, J. P.	3	70
William, s. Robert & Mary, b. Jan. 19, 1730/1	3	70
PAGE, Abel, s. George & Mary, b. Feb. 10, 1716/7	3	42
Abel, m. Sarah **TOWNER**, b. of Branford, Jan. 15, 1756, by		
Philemon Robbins	3	159
Abel, s. Abel, b. Sept. 25, 1761	3	174
Abiel, s. George & Mary, b. July 7, 1707	3	31
Abiel, m. Lydia **FRISSELL**, wid., b. of Branford, June 22,		
1744, by Rev. Philemon Robbins	3	102
Abigail, d. Nath[anie]ll & Abigail, b. Mar. 29, 1722	3	49
Abigail, d. Abraham & Abigail b. May 6, 1742	3	105
Abigail, d. David & Elisabeth, b. Oct. 2, 1746	3	109
Abigail, m. William **WHEDON**, b. of Branford, Apr. 11,		
1770, by Samuel Eells	3	199
Abraham, s. Dan[ie]ll & Hannah, b. Sept. 4, 17[ ]; d.		
[bp. Aug. 31, 1717]	3	41
Abraham, m. Abigail **POND**, b. of Branford, Nov. 22, 1739,		
by Rev. Philemon Robbins	3	91
Abraham, s. Abraham & Abigail, b. Dec. 27, 1740	3	105
Alice, d. Sam[ue]ll, Jr. & Sarah, b. Oct. [ ], 1766,		
in New Haven	3	193
Amelia, d. John & Rosanna, b. Mar. 6, 1793	3	265
Amos, s. Sam[ue]ll & Mary, b. Feb. 12, 1737	3	164
Amos, m. Rebecca **BURGESS**, b. of Branford, Mar. 25, 1757,		
by Philemon Robbins	3	174
Andrew S., m. Mary **HOBART**, b. of Branford, May 27, 1820,		
by Rev. Timo[thy] P. Gillett	3	419
Anna, wid., d. Oct. 8, 1842	TM3	304
Anne, d. Sam[ue]ll & Sarah, b. Sept. 19, 1770	3	292
Asa, of Wallingford, m. Eunice **PAGE**, of Branford, May 7,		
1759, by Elizer Goodrich	3	190
Asa, s. Asa & Eunice, b. July 5, 1760; d. Oct. [ ], 1760	3	190
Asa, s. Asa & Eunice, b. Aug. 15, 1761	3	190

	Vol.	Page
PAGE, (cont.)		
Augustus, m. Sarah **WEBBER**, b. of Branford, Nov. 28, 1813	3	337
Augustus Newton, [s. Augustus & Sarah], b. Dec. 28, 1821	3	337
Barsheba, d. Sam[ue]ll & Mindwell, b. Jan. 25, 1715/16	3	39
Bathsheba, m. James **PLANT**, b. of Branford, Sept. 22, 1740, by Rev. Jonathan Mer[r]ick	3	101
Benjamin, m. Lois **FORD**, b. of Branford, May 16, 1798, by Rev. Samuel Eells	3	271
Benjamin, [s. Benjamin & Lois], b. Aug. 11, 1806	3	283
Benjamin, of Branford, m. Mary **HURD**, of Roxbury, Dec. 25, 1814, by Rev. Fosdic Harrison, at Roxbury	3	338
Betsey, d. Ichabod & Mable, b. July 20, 1781	3	307
Betsey Ann, m. Zenas **COMSTOCK**, b. of Branford, Oct. 26, 1837, by Rev. Timothy P. Gillett	3	374
Betsey Ann, [d. Woodward], b. Oct. 2, 1838	TM3	229
Betsey Augusta, [d. Martin & Nancy], b. July 3, 1815	TM3	236
Betsey Augusta, d. Martin & Nancy, d. Feb. 26, 1836	TM3	307
Bets[e]y Eliza, [d. Charles Jacob & Bets[e]y], b. Sept. 9, 1810	3	384
Bette, d. David & Elisabeth, b. June 23, 1749	3	120
Caroline, ae 20 y.,m. Samuel **COOK**, ae 24 y., Oct. 10, 1849, by Rev. T. P. Gillett	TM3	166
Caroline C., m. Samuel S. **COOK**, b. of Branford, Oct. 10, 1849, by Rev. Timothy P. Gillett	TM3	164
Caroline Celinda, d. Chandler & Lucy Loretta, b. Mar. 4, 1830	3	372
Caroline E., d. Charles & Carolin, b. Dec. 1, 1847	TM3	240
Caroline E., d. Dec. 1, 1847, ae 25	TM3	308
Caroline E., d. Sept. 18, 1848, ae 1 y.	TM3	308
Caroline Elisabeth, [d. Martin & Nancy], b. Apr. 29, 1822	TM3	236
Chandler, [s. Sam[ue]ll], b. July 4, 1788	3	396
Charles, s. Abiel & Lydia, b. Apr. 21, 1745	3	107
Charles, of Branford, m. Lois **MOLTHROP**, of New Haven, Oct. 31, 1765, by Nicolaus Street	3	188
Charles, d. Dec. 3, 1769, in the 25th y. of his age. He was drowned in the passage from the West Indies in the sloop Greyhound, Edmund Rogers, master	3	198
Charles, [s. Charles Jacob & Bets[e]y], b. Dec. 2, 1799	3	384
Charles, [s. Charles & Caroline], b. Mar. 12, 1841	TM3	237
Charles Jacob, s. Charles & Lois, b. July 7, 1766	3	191
Charles Jacob, m. Betsey **LINSL[E]Y**, Sept. 19, 1796	3	384
Chloe, d. Ephraim & Martha, b. Apr. 13, 1758	3	284
Daniel, s. George, b. May 2, 1683	1	211
Daniel, m. Hannah **JOHNSON**, Jan. 3, 1710, by Rev. Sam[ue]ll Russel[l]	3	33
Dan[ie]ll, s. Dan[ie]ll & Hannah, d. Nov. 30, 1710	3	41
Dan[ie]ll, s. Dan[ie]ll & Hannah, b. Aug. 4, 1715	3	37
Daniel, s. Dan[ie]ll & Hannah, b. Apr. 17, 1724	3	55
Dan[ie]ll, Jr., m. Dinah **BALDWIN**, b. of Branford, Feb. 13, 1749, by Jon[a]th[an] Mer[r]ick	3	169

	Vol.	Page
PAGE, (cont.)		
Dan[ie]ll, s. Abel & Sarah, b. Dec. 12, 1756	3	159
Dan[ie]ll, s. Dan[ie]ll, Jr. & Dinah, b. Sept. 18, 1757	3	170
Daniel, Dea., d. Apr. 7, 1766, in the 83rd y. of his age	3	189
Daniel, s. Timothy & Abigail, b. Dec. 22, 1780	3	306
Daniel, [s. Benjamin & Lois], b. Feb. 24, 1801	3	283
Daniel, d. Dec. 2, 1817, ae 16 y. 10 m. 5 d.	3	338
Daniel Everit, [s. Benjamin & Mary], b. Aug. 1, 1820	3	338
Daniel Everitt, d. Feb. 29, 1821, ae 7 m., wanting one day	3	338
Darwin, [s. Benjamin & Mary], b. Oct. 29, 1822	3	338
David, s. Nathan[ie]ll & Abigail, b. Mar. 23, 1716	3	41
David, m. Elisabeth **RAYNER**, b. of Branford, Apr. 3, 1740,		
by Rev. Jonathan Mer[r]ick	3	109
David, s. David & Elisabeth, b. Apr. 1, 1741	3	109
David, s. John & Lois, b. Oct. 2, 1780	3	309
David, m. Nancy **ROSE**, b. of Branford, [Aug.] 26, [1823],		
by Charles Atwater	3	423
Deliverance, d. Sam[ue]ll & Mindwell, b. Apr. 30, 1702	3	38
Deliverance, of Branford, m. Henry **MILLER**, of Lime, Sept.		
23, 1723, by Rev. Eliphalet Adams	3	88
Dennis, [s. Dennis S. & Almira Louisa], b. Mar. 9, 1833	3	378
Dennis Smith, s. Joel & Mabel, b. June 7, 1809	3	349
Dinah, d. Dan[ie]ll, Jr. & Dinah, b. Mar. 14, 1752	3	169
Dinah, 2d, m. John **AUGER**, Jr., b. of Branford, Nov. 20,		
1776, by Warham Williams	3	313
Dinah, d. Sept. 23, 1819, ae 92 y.	3	338
Ebenezer, s. Ephraim & Martha, b. May 15, 1764	3	284
Edgar Delos, s. Chandler & Lucy Loretta, b. Mar. 24, 1827	3	372
Edmund, s. Amos & Rebecca, b. Nov. 10, 1761	3	174
Edmund, m. Nancy **GORDON**, b. of Branford, Oct. 22, 1827,		
by Rev. Timothy P. Gillett	3	345
Edward, s. Abraham & Abigail, b. May 20, 1745	3	105
Edward, m. Elisabeth **TYLER**, b. of Branford, Nov. 14, 1771,		
by Josiah Rogers, J. P.	3	204
Edward C., s. Harvey & Harritt, b. Apr. [ ], 1850	TM3	242
Eli, s. Ephraim & Martha, b. Feb. 7, 1772	3	284
Elisabeth, d. Sam[ue]ll & Mindwell, b. July 13, 1713	3	38
Elisabeth, d. George & Mary, b. Feb. 12, 1714/15	3	38
Elisabeth, d. Sam[ue]ll & Sarah, b. Mar. 14, 1772	3	293
Ellen, d. Charles & Caroline, b. [ ], 1850	TM3	242
Emily, of Branford, m. William J. **BARNES**, of North Haven,		
Nov. 27, 1851, by Rev. T. P. Gillett	TM3	170
Emely Lovina, d. George & Martha, b. Dec. 30, 1841	TM3	237
Ephraim, s. Dan[ie]ll & Hannah, b. July 21, 1730	3	71
Ephraim, s. Amos & Rebecca, b. Jan. 10, 1760	3	174
Ephraim, s. Ephraim & Martha, b. Jan. 28, 1769	3	284
Erastus, of Branford, m. Delight **ROSE**, of Northford, Nov.		
27, 1827, by Rev. Timothy P. Gillett	3	346

	Vol.	Page
PAGE, (cont.)		
Esther, d. Dan[ie]ll, Jr. & Dinah, b. Sept. 11, 1749;		
d. Sept. 10, 1751	3	169
Esther, d. Dan[ie]ll, Jr. & Dinah, b. Oct. 10, 1754	3	169
Esther Jerusha, [d. Benjamin & Lois], b. July 1, 1799	3	283
Esther Jerusha, m. Samuel Augustus **ROGERS**, Sept. 28, 1820,		
by Charles Atwater	3	412
Eunice, d. Sam[ue]ll & Mary, b. [Jan. 8, 1742]	3	164
Eunice, of Branford, m. Asa **PAGE**, of Wallingford, May 7,		
1759, by Elizer Goodrich	3	190
Eunice, d. Asa & Eunice, [b.] Oct. 2, 1764	3	190
Eunice, [d. Sam[ue]l], b. Aug. 13, 1794	3	395
Eunice, d. Sept. 4, 1842, ae 48	TM3	304
Fanny Eliza, [d. Dennis S. & Almira Louisa], b. June 30, 1831	3	378
Frances Elisa, m. Obed Tyler **FRISBIE**, b. of Branford,		
May 13, 1847, by Rev. Timothy P. Gillett	TM3	160
Frances Maria, [d. Woodward], b. Jan. 23, 1840	TM3	229
Frank, [s. Charles & Caroline], b. Apr. 5, 1845	TM3	237
George, s. George, b. Feb. 2, 1672	1	210
George, d. Nov. 22, 1759	3	159
George, [s. Charles Jacob & Bets[e]y], b. May 13, 1807	3	384
George, m. Martha **COOK**, b. of Branford, June 21, 1835,		
by T. P. Gillett	3	369
George Henry, s. George & Martha, b. June 20, 1836	3	378
Gilbert Smith, [s. Augustus & Sarah], b. Feb. 6, 1824	3	337
Hanna[h], d. George, b. Dec. 17, 1677	1	210
Hannah, m. Ebenezer **FFRISSBE**, Apr. 21, 1703, by Eleazar		
Stent, J. P.	2	344
Hannah, d. Dan[ie]ll & Hannah, b. July 3, 1713	3	36
Hannah, m. Abraham **BARTHOLOMEW**, b. of Branford, June		
18, 1730, by Rev. Jonathan Merrick	3	68
Hannah, d. [John & Susanna], b. Feb. 15, 1736	3	87
Hannah, d. Abraham & Abigail, b. June 10, 1754	3	145
Hannah, m. Daniel **HARRISON**, Jr., b. of Branford, Dec.		
10, 1772, by Samuel Eells	3	207
Hannah, d. Ephraim & Martha, b. Mar. 24, 1775	3	284
Hannah, d. John & Lois, b. Sept. 10, 1782	3	309
Hannah, m. Rufus **HOADL[E]Y**, Jr., Nov. 15, 1801	3	404
Harriet, [d. Martin & Nancy], b. Feb. 4, 1825	TM3	236
Harriett, m. Harvey **PAGE**, b. of Branford, May 23, 1849,		
by Rev. T. P. Gillett	TM3	163
Harve[y], s. Ichabod & Mable, b. June 29, 1783	3	307
Harvey, m. Harriett **PAGE**, b. of Branford, May 23, 1849,		
by Rev. T. P. Gillett	TM3	163
Henrietta, [d. Charles Jacob & Bets[e]y], b. Apr. 9, 1802	3	384
Henrietta, m. Almon **TYLER**, b. of Branford, June 21, 1823,		
by James Noyes	3	423
Henry Brooks, [s. Woodward], b. July 6, 1842	TM3	229

	Vol.	Page
PAGE, (cont.)		
Horace Edward, [s. Augustus & Sarah], b. June 13, 1819	3	337
Huldah, d. Ephraim & Martha, b. Feb. 28, 1762	3	284
Huldah, d. Sam[ue]ll & Sarah, b. June 10, 1776	3	293
Huldah, m. Henry **JOHNSON**, b. of Branford, Mar. 24, 1784,		
by Sam[ue]ll Eells	3	309
Ichabod, m. Mable **GOULD**, b. of Branford, July 26, 1780	3	307
Isaac, s. Sam[ue]ll & Mary, b. June 29, 1748	3	164
Isaac, s. John & Rosanna, b. May 27, 1790	3	265
Jacob, s. Ephraim & Martha, b. Oct. 29, 1753	3	136
Jacob, m. Sarah **BALDWIN**, b. of Branford, Nov. [ ], 1783,		
by Sam[ue]ll Eells	3	315
Jacob, s. Jacob & Sarah, b. May 13, 1790	3	259
Joel, s. Amos & Rebecca, b. Oct. 27, 1763	3	193
John, s. Georg[e], b. Mar. 12, 1664	1	210
John, d. Apr. 10, 1712	3	39
John, s. Nathan[ie]ll & Abigail, b. May 19, 1714	3	36
John, m. Susanna **LINSL[E]Y**, b. of Branford, Jan. 22,		
1734/5, by Rev. Jon[a]th[an] Mer[r]ick	3	87
John, s. John & Susanna, b. Jan. 6, 1745	3	157
John, d. Mar. 24, 1754, in the 41st y. of his age	3	157
John, of Branford, m. Lois **BRISTOL**, of Guilford, Nov.		
26, 1766, by Nicholaus Street	3	191
John, s. John & Lois, b. Mar. 3, 1768	3	193
John, s. John & Lois, d. Feb. 2, 1770	3	207
John, s. John & Lois, b. Dec. 26, 1770	3	207
John, m. Razana **MALTBIE**, b. of Branford, Nov. 30, 1787	3	265
John, [s. Charles Jacob & Bets[e]y], b. Sept. [ ], 1804	3	384
John, [s. Charles & Caroline], b. Jan. 26, 1839, in New Haven	TM3	237
Jonathan, s. George, b. Sept. 15, 1675	1	210
Jonathan, d. Feb. 8, 1707	3	30
Jonathan, s. Nathan[ie]ll & Abigail, b. Oct. 10, 1717	3	41
Jonathan, s. Nathan[ie]ll & Zillah, b. Sept. 23, 1743	3	107
Jonathan, s. Nath[anie]ll, Jr. & Mercy, b. Jan. 18, 1768	3	196
Joseph, s. Nathan[ie]ll & Abigail, b. Apr. 9, 1720	3	45
Judson, [s. Benjamin & Mary], b. Dec. 16, 1816	3	338
Leonord, s. Jacob & Sarah, b. Dec. 14, 1785	3	315
Lois, wid., of Charles & d. of Israel & Lydia **MOLTHRUP**,		
b. Mar. 26, 1745, at New Haven	3	198
Lois, d. John & Lois, b. Sept. 13, 1775	3	309
Lois, w. of John, d. Nov. 27, 1786	3	265
Lois, m. Joel **BARKER**, Jan. 12, 1791	3	412
Lois, [d. Benjamin & Lois], b. Nov. 24, 1802	3	283
Lois, w. of Benjamin, d. June 25, 1810, ae 35 y. 8 m. 12 d.	3	283
Louisa, d[. Sam[ue]ll], b. July 8, 1802	3	395
Louisa Maria, [d. Dennis S. & Almira Louisa], b. Aug. 30,		
1838	3	378
Lucrecy, d. Amos & Rebecca, b. Feb. 14, 1774	3	274

	Vol.	Page
PAGE, (cont.)		
Lucy, d. John & Susanna, b. Nov. 10, 1740	3	157
Lucy Caroline, d. Edgar D. & Jane, b. Feb. 15, 1851	TM3	245
Luther, s. Ephraim & Martha, b. June 27, 1756	3	284
Lydia, d. Sam[ue]ll & Mindwell, b. Jan. 16, 1704/5	3	38
Lydia, d. Timothy & Abigail, b. Jan. 24, 1783	3	306
Lydia, [d. Charles Jacob & Bets[e]y], b. Oct. 14, 1797	3	384
Lydia, [d. Charles & Caroline], b. Feb. 10, 1843	TM3	237
Lydia, d. Sept. 15, 1848, ae 6 y.	TM3	308
Martha, d. Dan[ie]ll & Hannah, b. July 23, 1727	3	63
Martha, d. Ephraim & Martha, b. Aug. 15, 1766	3	284
Mary, d. George & Mary, b. Mar. 5, 1712/13	3	37
Mary, d. Dan[ie]ll & Hannah, b. Sept. 16, 1719	3	44
Mary, m. Thomas **WHEDON**, Jr., b. of Branford, Apr. 19, 1744, by Rev. Jonathan Mer[r]ick	3	114
Mary, d. Sam[ue]ll & Mary, b. Apr. 31 (sic), 1751	3	164
Mary, d. Dan[ie]ll, Jr. & Dinah, b. Nov. 5, 1760	3	170
Mary, d. Sam[ue]ll & Sarah, d. June 10, 1778	3	293
Mary, [d. Sam[ue]ll], b. Mar. 8, 1782	3	395
Mary, [d. Benjamin & Mary], b. Nov. 4, 1815	3	338
Mary Ann, [d. Martin & Nancy], b. Sept. 1, 1813	TM3	236
Mary Esther, of Branford, m. Lyman **BECKLY**, of Meriden, Oct. 27, 1851, by Rev. T. P. Gillett	TM3	169
Mary J., m. Josiah T. **MONROE**, Apr. 9, 1852, by Rev. Lucius T. Atwater	TM3	171
Mary Jane, d. Woodward & Irene, b. Feb. 14, 1834	3	367
Moses, s. George & Mary, b. Mar. 1, 1704/5	2	346
Moses, of Branford, m. Thankfull **GRAUES**, of Guilford, Oct. 20, 1731, by Rev. Thomas Ruggles	3	74
Moses, s. Moses & Thankfull, b. Sept. 1, 1732	3	74
Nancy, [d. Sam[ue]ll], b. July 15, 1800	3	395
Nancy, m. Israel M. **HARRISON**, b. of Branford, July 22, 1819	3	370
Nathan, s. Nathaniel & Abigail, b. Jan. 8, 1724/5	3	56
Nathan, s. David & Elisabeth, b. Feb. 1, 1743/4	3	109
Nathaniel, s. George, b. Jan. 18, 1679	1	210
Nathan[ie]ll, s. Nathan[ie]ll & Abigail, b. Jan. 29, 1710	3	34
Nathan[ie]ll, m. Abigail **WHEADON**, May 10, 1710, by Rev. Mr. Russel[l]	3	33
Nath[anie]ll, Jr., m. Zillah **BALDWIN**, b. of Branford, Feb. 16, 1736/7	3	88
Nath[anie]ll, s. Nath[anie]ll, Jr. & Zillah, b. Dec. 29, 1737	3	88
Nathanael, Jr., m. Mercy **BARKER**, b. of Branford, June 23, 1763, by Jonathan Mer[r]ick	3	181
Nathaniel, of North Branford, m. Mary **MONROE**, of Branford, May 13, 1840, by Rev. David T. Shailer	3	379
Noah, s. Nathan[ie]ll & Zillah, b. Mar. 1, 1739/40	3	107
Noah, s. John & Lois, b. Mar. 20, 1772	3	207

	Vol.	Page

PAGE, (cont.)

	Vol.	Page
Noah, m. Triphena **BUTLER**, b. of Branford, Dec. 26, 1772,		
by Samuel Eells	3	207
Olive, d. Amos & Rebecca, b. Feb. 5, 1758	3	174
[Ollive], m. Elijah **FORB[E]S**, Dec. 23, 1780	3	283
Parna, m. Martin **HOADL[E]Y**, b. of Branford, Dec. 2, 1810	3	389
Patience, d. Sam[ue]ll & Mindwell, b. Apr. 2, 1710	3	38
Phebe Amelia, [d. Benjamin & Lois], b. Nov. 25, 1804	3	283
Philo, s. Amos & Rebecca, b. July 6, 1771	3	274
Phinias, [twin with Sarah], s. Abraham & Abigail, b.		
July 10, 1757	3	145
Prudence, d. Dan[ie]ll & Hannah, b. Sept. 7, 1711	3	34
Prudence, m. Isaac **WHEDON**, b. of Branford, May 28, 1731,		
by Rev. Jonathan Merrick	3	71
Rayner, s. David & Ellsabeth, b. Apr. 5, 1752	3	126
Reuben, d. Nathan[ie]ll & Zillah, b. Mar. 20, 1745/6	3	107
Rebecca, d. Amos & Rebecca, b. Sept. 29, 1767	3	193
Reuben, s. Abel & Sarah, b. Feb. 15, 1758	3	159
Reuben, s. Nathanael, Jr. & Mercy, b. Nov. 28, 1764	3	190
Rosanna, d. John & Rosanna, b. Apr. 14, 1788	3	265
Sally Elisabeth, m. Benjamin P. **FOOTE**, b. of Branford,		
Dec. 20, 1852, by Rev. T. P. Gillett	TM3	172
Sally M., of Branford, m. Henry P. **BYINGTON**, of North		
Branford, June 25, 1835, by T. P. Gillett	3	369
Sally Maria, [d. Martin & Nancy], b. Aug. 31, 1817	TM3	236
Sam[ue]ll, s. Georg[e], b. Mar. 1, 1670/1	1	210
Sam[ue]ll, s. Sam[ue]ll & Mindwell, b. Sept. 21, 1707	3	38
Sam[ue]ll, m. Mary **ROSE**, b. of Branford, Jan. 27, 1736,		
by Philemon Robbins	3	164
Sam[ue]ll, Jr., s. Sam[ue]ll & Mary, b. July 7, 1740	3	164
Samuel, Jr., of Branford, m. Sarah **WOODWARD**, of New		
Haven, Apr. 3, 1766, by Jon[a]th[an] Merrick	3	193
Sam[ue]l, [s. Sam[ue]l], b. Apr. 15, 1785	3	395
Samuel, of Branford, m. Mrs. Mary **TUTTLE**, of East Haven,		
July 23, 1823, by Charles Atwater, at North Branford	3	423
Sarah, d. Georg[e], b. May 28, 1666	1	210
Sarah, d. Sam[ue]ll & Mindwell, b. Sept. 6, 1709	3	38
Sarah, d. Sam[ue]ll & Mindwell, d. Jan. [ ], 1712/13	3	39
Sarah, d. Sam[ue]ll & Mindwell, b. Feb. 16, 1722	3	88
Sarah, d. Daniel & Hannah, b. Dec. 20, 1732	3	74
Sarah, [twin with Phinias], d. Abraham & Abigail, b.		
July 10, 1757	3	145
Sarah, d. Abel & Sarah, b. Oct. 14, 1759	3	159
Sarah, w. of Sam[ue]ll, d. Mar. 31, 1780	3	293
Sarah Ann, [d. Andrew S. & Mary], b. Jan. 17, 1822;		
d. Feb. 6, following	3	419
Selina, [d. Benjamin & Lois], b. July 30, 1808; d. May		
14, 1810, ae 1 y. 9 m. 14 d.	3	283

	Vol.	Page
PAGE, (cont.)		
Solomon, s. Asa & Eunice, b. May 29, 1767	3	191
Stephen Decatur, [s. Augustus & Sarah], b. Jan. 9, 1815	3	337
Susanna, d. John & Susanna, b. Nov. 15, 1735	3	87
Susanna, wid. of John, d. Apr. 21, 1759, in the 61st y.		
of her age	3	157
Thankful, d. Abraham & Abigail, b. Apr. 19, 1752	3	127
Timothy, s. Sam[ue]ll & Mindwell, b. Sept. 7, 1700	3	38
Timothy, s. Ephraim & Martha, b. June 9, 1760	3	284
Timothy, m. Abigail **HOADLEY**, b. of Branford, Sept. 12,		
1779, by Sam[ue]ll Eells	3	306
Timothy, [s. Dennis S. & Almira Louisa], b. Oct. 26, 1836	3	378
William Lewis, [s. Augustus & Sarah], b. Apr. 11, 1817	3	337
Woodward, s. Sam[ue]ll & Sarah, b. May 29, 1774	3	293
Woodward, [s. Sam[ue]l], b. Oct. 15, 1805	3	395
Woodward, m. Irene **GOODRICH**, b. of Branford, Apr. 23,		
1833, by Rev. Timothy P. Gillett	3	359
----, s. Dennis S. & Almira, b. [ ], 1849	TM3	240
PALMER, PAMER, Abiah, d. John & Phebe, b. Sept. 23, 1706	3	30
Abigail, d. Micah & Damaris, b. Mar. 12, 1710/11	3	34
Abigail, d. Joseph & Elisabeth, b. Oct. 21, 1723	3	63
Abigail, m. Daniel **BARKER**, Jr., b. of Branford, July 8,		
1729, by Rev. Jonathan Merrick	3	69
Abigail, d. Judah & Mary, b. Feb. 2, 1733/4	3	78
Abigail, d. Judah & Mary, d. Sept. 29, 1734	3	82
Abigail, d. Micah, Jr. & Jemima, b. Nov. 20, 1734	3	81
Abigail, d. Nathan & Rebeckah, b. Oct. 31, 1743	3	148
Abigail, m. Edward **BROCKWAY**, b. of Branford, Feb. 5,		
1760, by Jon[a]th[an] Merrick	3	164
Abigail, d. John & Elisabeth, b. Oct. 21, 1762	3	286
Abigail, d. Rufus & Abigail, b. Jan. 10, 1774	3	258
Abigail had child b. Dec. 1, 1783	3	306
Abigail, w. of Isaac, d. Apr. 11, 1793	3	394
Abigail, m. Nathaniel **PALMER**, b. of Branford, Nov. 29,		
[1798], by Samuel Eells	3	255
Abigail, wid. of Ammi, d. Dec. 2, 1845	TM3	307
Abraham, m. Anna **BUTLER**, b. of Branford, Jan. 16, 1733/4,		
by Rev. Jon[a]th[an] Mer[r]ick	3	98
Achsah, d. Micah, Jr. & Hannah, b. Oct. 8, 1763	3	181
Albert, m. Mary E. **HOADLEY**, May 6, 1851, by Rev. Camp	TM3	170
Alvan Kimberly, [s. Joseph K. & Thirsa], b. Sept. 5, 1847	TM3	235
Ambrus, s. Isaac & Rebecca, b. Apr. 28, 1765	3	282
Ambrose, [s. Isaac & Rebeccah], b. May 10, 1765	3	394
Ambrus, s. Isaac & Rebecca, d. Sept. 14, 1770	3	283
Ambrose, [s. Isaac & Rebeccah], d. Sept. 14, 1770	3	394
Ambrus, s. Isaac & Abigail, b. Sept. 29, 1773	3	283
Ambrose, [s. Isaac & Abigail], b. Sept. 29, 1774	3	394
Ambrose, [s. Isaac & Abigail], d. Jan. 5, 1795	3	394

	Vol.	Page
PALMER, PAMER, (cont.)		
Amelia, [d. John], b. Jan. 25, 1811	3	348
Amme, s. Isaac & Abigail, b. May 22, 1783	3	283
Ammi, [s. Isaac & Abigail], b. May 25, 1783	3	394
Ammi, of Branford, m. Abigail **KIMBERLY**, of Guilford, Mar. 14, 1810	3	390
Ammi, d. Oct. 9, 1840, ae 57 y.	TM3	304
Ammi, d. Oct. 9, 1840	TM3	307
Ammi Barker, s. Timothy & Louisa, b. Jan. 17, 1843	TM3	234
Amee, d. Dan[ie]ll & Elisabeth, b. July 8, 1713	3	37
Angenett, d. Jonathan & Elizabeth, b. July 30, 1847	TM3	234
Anna, d. Abraham & Anna, b. Jan. 31, 1738/9	3	98
Anne, d. Judah & Mary, b. Aug. 2, 1738	3	89
Anne, d. Stephen, Jr. & Rachel, b. Jan. 4, 1761	3	170
Asahel, s. Stephen & Lydia, b. Apr. 14, 1747	3	112
Asahel, m. Hannah **HOADLEY**, b. of Branford, Nov. 23, 1773	3	300
Asenath, d. Nathan & Rebeckah, b. Mar. 22, 1747	3	148
Augustus, s. Jonathan & Lydia, b. May 31, 1784	3	278
Augustus, s. Jonathan & Lydia, b. May 31, 1786	3	267
Augustus, m. Betsey **HARRISON**, Dec. 23, 1804	3	282
Augustus, [twin with James, s. James & Nancy], b. Mar. 2, 1815	3	368
Augustus, d. July 8, 1816, in Cuba	3	282
Barnabas, s. Nathan[ie]ll & Rebecca, b. Feb. 12, 1748	3	129
Barnebas, m. Sarah **SMITH**, b. of Branford, Nov. 15, 1781, by Sam[ue]ll Eells	3	302
Barsheba, d. Dan[ie]ll & Elisabeth, b. Apr. 14, 1707	3	30
Bathsheba, m. Ephraim **PARISH**, b. of Branford, Nov. 27, 1729, by Rev. Samuell Russell	3	67
Belah, s. Jabez & Hannah, b. Sept. 4, 1761	3	173
Benjamin, s. Dan[ie]ll & Elisabeth, b. Apr. 5, 1721	3	45
Binjamin, m. Patiance **HARRISON**, b. of Branford, Feb. 6, 1746, by Phi[lemo]n Robbins	3	290
Benjamin, s. Benj[ami]n & Patience, b. Jan. 5, 1752	3	290
Benjamin, Jr., m. Abigail **GOULD**, b. of Branford, Mar. 3, 1774	3	291
Benjamin, Jr., m. Abigail **GOULD**, b. of Branford, Mar. 3, 1774	3	304
Benjamin, s. John & Elisabeth, b. Aug. 29, 1774	3	286
Benjamin, d. Apr. 26, 1808, ae 87 y.	3	395
Benj[ami]n, d. May 17, 1848, ae 54 y.	TM3	308
Benjamin Butler, [s. Lauren & Polly], b. July 24, 1820	3	408
Bets[e]y, [d. Benjamin & Abigail], b. May 6, 1794	3	395
Betsey, d. Hannah **HOADL[E]Y**, b. Apr. 18, 1804	3	390
Betsey, m. Merit **FOOT**, b. of Branford, June 18, 1818	3	336
Betsey, w. of Edmund, 2d, d. Sept. 17, 1827	3	345
Betsey Matilda, [d. Edmund, 2d, & Betsey], b. June 25, 1824	3	344
Caleb, s. Micah & Damaris, b. Apr. 6, 1696	2	345

	Vol.	Page
PALMER, PAMER, (cont.)		
Caleb, of Branford, m. Mary **DURHAM**, of Guilford, Jan.		
11, 1737/8, by Rev. Thomas Ruggles, of Guilford	3	97
Caroline, m. Charles **BUTLER**, June 7, 1847, by Rev.		
Frederick Miller	TM3	161
Cate, d. Asahel & Hannah, b. Apr. 2, 1779	3	300
Chandler, s. Asahel & Hannah, b. Apr. 8, 1776	3	300
Charles Wilman, s. Wilman & Susan Cornelia, b. Apr. 10,		
1838	3	375
Charlotte, w. of Justin, d. July 6, 1841	TM3	307
C[h]loe, d. Caleb & Mary, b. Apr. 1, 1739	3	97
Chloe, d. Judah & Mary, b. Oct. 31, 1740	3	99
Cobadia*, s. William, b. Mar. 31, 1650 (*Oobadia?)	1	171
Cornelia Augusta, d. Wilman & Susan Cornelia, b. Jan. 27,		
1833	3	365
Cornelia Augusta, d. Wilman & Susan Cornelia, d. Feb. 21,		
1837	TM3	305
Cornelia Augusta, d. Wilman & Susan C., b. Oct. 31, 1844	TM3	232
Daniel, s. Michael, b. Sept. 13, 1675	1	174
Dan[ie]ll, s. Dan[ie]ll & Elisabeth, b. Mar. 16, 1702	3	30
Daniel, s. Nathan[ie]ll & Rebecca, b. Apr. 29, 1734	3	79
Daniel, d. Dec. 20, 1757	3	290
Dan[ie]ll, m. Hannah **HOWD**, b. of Branford, Mar. 19, 1761,		
by Philemon Robbins	3	174
Daniel, d. Jan. 22, 1768, in the 34th y. of his age	3	193
Daniel, s. Dan[ie]ll & Hannah, b. Apr. 12, 1768	3	193
Daniel, s. Barnebas & Sarah, b. Feb. 22, 1782	3	302
Daniel, of Branford, m. Polly **HUMISTON**, of West		
Springfield, Oct. 4, 1808	3	363
Daniel, [s. Daniel & Polly], b. May 12, 1816	3	363
Daniel, s. Daniel, d. Sept. 17, 1820, ae 4 y. 4 m.	3	363
Daniel W[illia]m, [s. Daniel & Polly], b. Mar. 1, 1826	3	363
David, s. Micah, Jr. & Jemima, b. Mar. 7, 1727/8	3	64
David, s. Micah & Jemima, d. Jan. 28, 1748/9	3	118
David, [twin with Jonathan], s. Stephen, Jr. & Rachel,		
b. Jan. 20, 1772	3	205
Deborah, d. John & Phebe, b. Apr. 26, 1691	2	344
Deborah, d. Joseph & Elisabeth, b. Oct. 4, 1727	3	63
Deborah, m. Andrew **MONRO[E]**, b. of Branford, Jan. 4,		
1750, by Isaac Stiles	3	189
Desire, d. Judah & Mary, b. Sept. 2, 1735	3	82
Ebenezer, s. Stephen & Lydia, b. Oct. 1, 1743	3	101
Edmund, s. Nath[anie]ll & Lydia, b. Sept. 12, 1782	3	291
Edmund, s. Matilda **HOADL[E]Y**, b. Apr. 10, 1784	3	278
Edmund, 2d, b. Apr. 10, 1784	3	345
Edmund, 2d, m. Betsey **HOBART**, Dec. 15, 1808	3	344
Edmund, [s. Edmund, 2d, & Betsey], b. Dec. 17, 1820	3	344
Elijah, m. Mary **TRUSDELL**, b. of Branford, Apr. 16, 1745,		

	Vol.	Page
PALMER, PAMER, (cont.)		
by Rev. Jonath[a]n Mer[r]ick	3	125
Elijah, s. Elijah & Mary, b. Feb. 27, 1751/2	3	125
Eliza, m. Luther **CHIDSEY**, [Jan.] 27, [1830], by Judson		
A. Root	3	352
Eliza L., m. Lyman Luzerne **SQUIRE**, b. of Branford, July		
22, 1830, by Timo[thy] P. Gillett	3	353
Elizabeth, d. Michaell, b. Oct. 13, 1663	1	173
Elisabeth, d. Joshua & Marcy, b. June 2, 1701	3	34
Elisabeth, d. Dan[ie]ll & Elisabeth, b. Mar. 14, 1718	3	42
Elisabeth, d. John & Thankful, b. Dec. 22, 1736	3	117
Elisabeth, d. John & Elisabeth, b. Sept. 17, 1757	3	286
Flisabeth, d. Benj[ami]n & Patience, b. Jan. 5, 1765	3	290
Elisabeth, m. Levi **ROGERS**, Jr., b. of Branford, July 6, 1776,		
by Sam[ue]ll Eells	3	289
Elisabeth, w. of Sam[ue]ll, d. Oct. 9, 1782	3	280
Ellsabeth, m. Joel **NORTON**, Jan. 29, 1783, by Sam[ue]ll Eells	3	279
Elizabeth Beach, d. Jonathan & Elisabeth, b. Sept. 29, 1841	TM3	234
Elizabeth Lydia, d. [Augustus & Betsey], b. May 6, 1805	3	282
Ellen Miller, d. Isaac & Nancy, b. [ ], 1849	TM3	242
Enos, s. Elijah & Mary, b. May 24, 1748	3	125
Erastus, s. Barnabas & Sarah, b. Jan. 31, 1785	3	255
Esther, d. Stephen & Lydia, b. Nov. 27, 1751	3	158
Eugene Hoadley, [s. Joseph K. & Thirsa], b. May 10, 1834	TM3	235
Eugene Hoadley, [s. Joseph K. & Thirza], b. May 10, 1834	3	373
Eunice, d. John, Jr. & Thankfull, b. Jan. 12, 1732/3	3	80
Eunice, m. Henry **HUFFMAN**, b. of Branford, Sept. 2, 1755,		
by Jonathan Mer[r]ick	3	180
Ezra, s. John, Jr. & Thankfull, b. Jan. 21, 1726/7	3	61
Frederic, [s. Benjamin & Abigail], b. Dec. 2, 1784	3	395
George, [s. James & Nancy], b. May 3, 1819	3	368
George, s. Lauren & Polly, b. Dec. 3, 1828	3	364
George, d. July 4, 1850, ae 16 y.	TM3	309
Hanan, [s. John], b. Aug. 25, 1798	3	348
Hanan, m. Lucinda **GATES**, [1826?], by Rev. Matthew		
Noyes, of Northford	3	342
Hannah, d. Micah & Damaris, b. Nov. 28, 1694	2	345
Hannah, d. Dan[ie]ll & Elisabeth, b. May 10, 1716	3	37
Hannah, m. Peter **TYLER**, Jr., Jan. 31, 1733/4, by Rev.		
Jonathan Mer[r]ick	3	81
Hannah, d. Nathan[ie]ll & Rebecca, b. June 26, 1740	3	129
Hannah, d. Jabez & Hannah, b. Jan. 12, 1749/50	3	119
Hannah, d. Benj[ami]n & Patience,, b. June 27, 1750	3	290
Hannah, m. Matthew **BUTLER**, b. of Branford, Apr. 20, 1772,		
by Philemon Robbins	3	206
Hannah, m. Abraham **ROGERS**, b. of Branford, Mar. 11, 1773	3	301
Hannah, wid. of Dan[ie]ll, m. Samuel **HOADLEY**, b. of		
Branford, Feb. 16, 1774	3	281

	Vol.	Page
PALMER, PAMER, (cont.)		
Hannah, d. Asahel & Hannah, b. Apr. 28, 1775; d. June 7,		
1775	3	300
Hannah Rebecca, d. Nath[anie]l & Lydia, b. Jan. 18, 1775	3	291
Harriet, w. of Edmund, 2d, d. May 16, 1830, ae 40 y.	3	365
Harriet, [d. Justin & Mary Ann], b. Dec. 29, 1844	TM3	237
Harriet Alice, d. Wilman & Susan Cornelia, b. Oct. 18, 1842	TM3	230
Harrison, s. Rufus & Sally, b. Nov. 8, 1809	3	284
Henry, [s. Ammi & Abigail], b. Dec. 31, 1814	3	358
Henry, [s. Ammi & Abigail], b. Apr. 5, 1822	3	358
Henry, 1st, s. [Ammi & Abigail], d. June 14, 1822, ae 7 y.	3	358
Henry, m. Irene **AVERILL**, b. of Branford, Jan. 15, 1846,		
by Rev. Timothy P. Gillett	TM3	159
Henry Ammi, [s. Joseph K. & Thirsa], b. May 9, 1842, in		
Michigan	TM3	235
Henry Ammi, s. Joseph K. & Thirsa, d. May 10, 1842	TM3	307
Henry Pitman, [s. Joseph K. & Thirsa], b. July 17, 1843,		
in Michigan	TM3	235
[H]ezekiah, s. Dan[ie]ll & Elisabeth, b. Feb. 26, 1704	3	30
Hezekiah, s. Benj[ami]n & Patience, b. May 21, 1754	3	290
Hezekiah, d. Apr. 26, 1810, ae 56 y.	3	395
Hezekiah, [s. James & Nancy], b. July 30, 1811	3	368
Hezekiah, s. James & Nancy, b. July 30, 1811	3	399
Hezekiah, m. Mary **BEACH**, b. of Branford, May 19, 1842,		
by Rev. Timothy P. Gillett	TM3	154
Hulda[h], d. Nathan & Rebeckah, b. Jan. 11, 1740	3	148
Irene, d. Stephen, Jr. & Rachel, b. Jan. 7, 1769	3	196
Irene, m. Eliphalet **ROGERS**, b. of Branford, Jan. 18,		
1795, by Sam[ue]l Eells	3	271
Isaac, s. Benj[ami]n & Patiance, b. Dec. 26, 1746	3	290
Isaac, m. Rebecca **FRISBIE**, b. of Branford, Apr. 25, 1765,		
by Philemon Robbinis	3	282
Isaac, m. Rebeccah **FRISBIE**, Apr. 25, 1765	3	394
Isaac, m. Abigail **TYLER**, b. of Branford, Feb. 19, 1773,		
by Philemon Robbins	3	283
Isaac, m. Abigail **TYLER**, Feb. 19, 1773	3	394
Isaac, s. Isaac & Abigail, b. Dec. 4, 1775	3	283
Isaac, [s. Isaac & Abigail], b. Dec. 16, 1776	3	394
Isaac, m. Triphena **McQUEEN**, Feb. 6, 1794	3	394
Isaac, 2d, s. Isaac & Abigail, d. Mar. 28, 1798	3	394
Isaac, [s. Ammi & Abigail], b. ᵀov. 7, 1819; d. Mar. 12,		
1820, ae 4 m.	3	358
Isaac Hobart, [s. Edmund, 2d, & Betsey], b. Aug. 4, 1813	3	344
Isaac Hobart, m. Nancy Jane **CARTER**, b. of Branford, Jan.		
3, 1839, by L. H. Corson	3	376
Jacob, s. Nathan[ie]ll & Rebecca, b. Feb. 7, 1738	3	129
Jacob, s. Daniel & Hannah, b. Nov. 12, 1765	3	193
Jacob, s. Rufus & Abigail, b. Nov. 11, 1771	3	207

	Vol.	Page
PALMER, PAMER, (cont.)		
Jacob, m. Fanny **FOOT**, b. of Branford, Apr. 23, 1800	3	284
James, s. Jos[eph] & Elisabeth, b. Oct. 1, 1740	3	96
James, s. Jon[a]th[an] & Lydia, b. July 31, 1781	3	282
James, m. Nancy **FRISBIE**, Feb. 11, 1807	3	282
James, [s. James & Nancy], b. Feb. 18, 1810; d. Mar. 11, 1810	3	368
James, s. James & Nancy, b. Feb. 18, 1810; d. Mar. 11,		
of the same year	3	399
James, [s. James & Nancy], b. Sept. 25, 1813; d. Mar. 2, 1814	3	368
James, [twin with Augustus, s. James & Nancy], b. Mar.		
2, 1815; d. Nov. 22, 1831	3	368
James, Sr., d. Nov. 22, 1831	3	368
James Bradley, s. Jonathan & Elisabeth, b. Sept. 8, 1837	TM3	234
James Bradley, s. Jonathan & Elisabeth, b. Sept. 8, 1837	TM3	300
James Frances, [s. Daniel & Polly], b. Oct. 4, 1811	3	363
James Goodrich, s. Timothy & Louisa, b. Mar. 30, 1841	TM3	234
Jane Amanda, [d. Joseph K. & Thirsa], b. Mar. 21, 1840	TM3	235
Jane Elisabeth, d. Isaac H. & Nancy Jane, b. Sept. 29, 1839	TM3	237
Jared, s. Isaac & Rebecca, b. Aug. 8, 1767	3	282
Jared, [s. Isaac & Rebeccah], b. Aug. 8, 1767	3	394
Jared, m. Desire **BALDWIN**, b. of Branford, June 17, 1790,		
by Jason Atwater	3	262
Jared, [s. Lauren & Polly], b. Sept. 29, 1814	3	408
Jarib, s. Jabis & Hannah, b. Feb. 15, 1755	3	139
Jemima, m. Ephraim **PARISH**, b. of Branford, May 15, 1760,		
by Philemon Robbins	3	163
Jemima, d. Micah, Jr. & Jemima, b. [ ]	3	65
Jerusha, [twin with Luce], d. Judah & Mary, b. May 6, 1746	3	109
Job, s. Joshua & Marcy, b. Sept. 18, 1707	3	35
Joel, s. John & Elisabeth, b. Sept. 16, 1767	3	286
Joel, [s. John], b. June 22, 1787	3	348
John, s. Michaell, b. Dec. 22, 1666	1	173
John, s. John & Phebe, b. Jan. [ ], 1692/3	2	344
John, Jr., of Branford, m. Thankfull **HOW**, of Wallingford,		
Jan. 24, 1722/3, by John Hall	3	51
John, s. John, Jr. & Thankfull, b. May 13, 1730	3	74
John, 1st, d. Jan. 13, 1737/8	3	148
John, s. Jabez & Hannah, b. June 29, 1752	3	132
John, m. Elisabeth **HARRISON**, b. of Branford, Apr. 10,		
1754, by Jon[a]th[an] Merrick	3	286
John, s. John & Elisabeth, b. Feb. 8, 1765	3	286
John, d. May 23, 1765, in the 73rd y. of his age	3	185
John, s. Isaac & Abigail, b. June 18, 1778	3	283
John, [s. Isaac & Abigail], b. June 18, 1779	3	394
John, [s. John], b. Apr. 18, 1792	3	348
John, d. Sept. 22, 1849, ae 3 y.	TM3	309
John Albert, s. Hanan, b. July 9, 1827	3	348
John Bradley, s. Wilman & Susan Cornelia, b. Sept. 26, 1834	3	368

	Vol.	Page
PALMER, PAMER, (cont.)		
John Bradley, s. Wilman & Susan Cornelia, d. Feb. 26, 1837	TM3	305
John Hobart, [s. Edmund, 2d, & Betsey], b. Nov. 21, 1817;		
d. Jan. 15, 1818	3	344
John Hobart, [s. Edmund 2d, & Betsey], b. Nov. 10, 1818	3	344
Jonathan, s. Micah, Jr. & Jemima, b. Sept. 24, 1726	3	61
Jonathan, m. Mary **HOWD**, May 6, 1750, by Rev. Philemon		
Robbins	3	123
Jonathan, s. Benj[ami]n & Patiance, b. Nov. 9, 1758	3	290
Jonathan, [twin with David], s. Stephen, Jr. & Rachel,		
b. Jan. 20, 1772	3	205
Jonathan, m. Lydia **GOULD**, b. of Branford, Nov. 14, 1779,		
by Sam[ue]ll Eells	3	282
Jonathan, d. Jan. 13, 1805	3	282
Jonathan, [s. James & Nancy], b. Apr. 12, 1808	3	368
Jonathan, s. [James & Nancy], b. Apr. 12, 1809	3	282
Jonathan, m. Elizabeth **BEACH**, b. of Branford, Aug. 31,		
1833, by T. P. Gillett	3	361
Joseph, s. John & Phebe, b. Aug. 28, 1698	2	344
Joseph, m. Elisabeth **TRUSDELL**, b. of Branford, Mar. 29,		
1719/20, by Rev. Sam[ue]ll Russell	3	51
Joseph, s. Joseph & Elisabeth, b. Jan. 22, 1720/1	3	51
Joseph, m. wid. Elisabeth **FRISBIE**, b. of Branford, May		
18, 1738, by Jonathan Mer[r]ick	3	96
Joseph K., [s. Ammi & Abigail], b. Jan. 9, 1811	3	358
Joseph K., m. Thura **HOADLEY**, b. of Branford, Aug. 21,		
1833, by [ ]	TM3	159
Joseph K., m. Thirza R. **HOADLEY**, of Tinmouth, Vt., Aug.		
21, 1833, by Rev. T. P. Gillett	3	361
Joseph Kimberly, s. [Ammi & Abigail], b. Jan. 9, 1811	3	390
Joshua, s. Michael, b. Dec. 25, 1677	1	174
Joshua, s. Joshua & Marcy, b. Mar. 18, 1705	3	35
Judah, s. Micah & Damaris, b. Mar. 18, 1701/2	2	345
Judah, of Branford, m. Mary **FARRINGTUN**, of Dedham,		
Mass., May 8, 1728, by Rev. Jonathan Mer[r]ick	3	78
Judah, s. Judah & Mary, b. Sept. 26, 1742	3	99
Julia, [d. Nathaniel, Jr. & Abigail], b. Aug. 12, 1799	3	391
Julius Russell, [s. Daniel & Polly], b. Jan. 2, 1818	3	363
Justin, [s. Nathaniel, Jr. & Abigail], b. Oct. 23, 1812	3	391
Justus, s. John & Elisabeth, b. Apr. 1, 1769	3	286
Justus, [s. Isaac & Abigail], b. July 25, 1786	3	394
Justus, [s. John], b. June 4, 1807	3	348
Lauraen, s. Jared & Desire, b. May 23, 1791	3	262
Lauren, m. Polly **BUTLER**, b. of Branford, Mar. 30, 1813	3	408
Lazarus, s. Joshua & Marcy, b. Jan. 21, 1709	3	35
Lester, [s. Nathaniel, Jr. & Abigail], b. Sept. 20, 1803	3	391
Lester, m. Lodema **FOOT**, Nov. 4, 1829, by Rev. J. A. Root	3	350
Lois, d. Jabez & Hannah, b. Feb. 28, 1747/8	3	118

	Vol.	Page

PALMER, PAMER, (cont.)

Lois, m. David **LINSL[E]Y**, b. of Branford, Aug. 31, 1768,
    by Philemon Robbins — 3 — 195
Lois, d. John & Elisabeth, b. July 9, 1777 — 3 — 286
Lois, [d. John], b. Aug. 16, 1803 — 3 — 348
Lois, m. Chauncey **STONE**, b. of Branford, [Sept], 23, [1824],
    by Charles Atwater — 3 — 334
Luce, d. Dan[ie]ll, Jr. & Patience, b. Jan. 18, 1732/3 — 3 — 76
Luce, [twin with Jerusha], d. Judah & Mary, b. May 6, 1746 — 3 — 109
Lucy, m. Sam[ue]ll **BUTLAR**, b. of Branford, Nov. 5, 1750,
    by Rev. Jonath[a]n Mer[r]ick — 3 — 124
Lurenda, [d. Daniel & Polly], b. Feb. 4, 1822 — 3 — 363
Luzern Augustus, s. Jonathan & Elisabeth, b. June 6, 1839 — TM3 — 234
Lydia, d. Micah & Damaris, b. Feb. 17, 169'//8 — 2 — 315
Lydia, m. Sam[ue]ll **FRISBE**, b. of Branford, Dec. 5, 1728,
    by Rev. Jonathan Mer[r]ick — 3 — 66
Lydia, d. Jos[eph] & Elisabeth, b. Mar. 26, 1739 — 3 — 96
Lydia, d. John & Elisabeth, b. Sept. 3, 1760 — 3 — 286
Lydia, w. of Stephen, d. Apr. 13, 1781, ae 68 y. 3 m. 21 d. — 3 — 269
Lydia, w. of Stephen, d. Apr. 13, 1781 — 3 — 270
Lydia, m. Heman **ROGERS**, b. of Branford, Feb. 15, 1784,
    by Sam[ue]ll Eells — 3 — 275
Lydia, w. of Jonathan, d. Aug. 15, 1796 — 3 — 282
Lydia A., m. William **BRIEN**, Jr., June 22, 1848 — TM3 — 162
Malachi, s. Benj[ami]n, Jr. & Abigail, b. June 21, 1774 — 3 — 304
Marietta, [d. Nathaniel, Jr. & Abigail], b. July 7, 1802 — 3 — 391
Marietta, [d. Nathaniel, Jr. & Abigail], d. Sept. 27, 1802 — 3 — 391
Mariett[a], [d. Daniel & Polly], b. Jan. 17, 1820 — 3 — 363
Martha, d. Micah & Damaris, b. Feb. 27, 1705/6 — 3 — 39
Mary, d. Michael, b. May 25, 1673 — 1 — 174
Mary, d. Michaell, b. Oct. 24, 1669 — 1 — 173
Mary, d. Dan[ie]ll & Elisabeth, b. June 1, 1701 — 3 — 30
Mary, d. Micah & Damaris, b. June 4, 1708 — 3 — 39
Mary, of Branford, m. Jonah **RICHARDS**, of Hartford, July
    27, 1726, by Rev. Sam[ue]ll Russell — 3 — 62
Mary, d. Judah & Mary, b. June 17, 1731 — 3 — 78
Mary, d. Nathan & Rebeckah, b. Aug. [6], 1737 — 3 — 148
Mary, d. Jonath[a]n & Mary, b. Jan. 29, 1750/1 — 3 — 123
Mary, d. Elijah & Mary, b. Jan. 10, 1754 — 3 — 139
Mary, d. Nathan & Rebecca, d. May 2[9], 1776 — 3 — 262
Mary, [d. Ammi & Abigail], b. Dec. 25, 1812 — 3 — 358
Mary, m. Jared **BURRELL**, b. of Branford, Mar. [ ], 1831,
    by J. A. Root — 3 — 356
Mary, of Branford, m. Caleb L. **LUD[D]INGTON**, of East
    Haven, Nov. 17, 1840, by John D. Baldwin — TM3 — 152
Mary, of Branford, m. Caleb L. **LUD[D]INGTON**, of East
    Haven, Nov. 17, 1840 — TM3 — 159
Mary Abigail, [d. Joseph K. & Thirsa], b. July 16, 1838,

	Vol.	Page
PALMER, PAMER, (cont.)		
in Michigan	TM3	235
Mary Ann, [d. Justin & Mary Ann], b. Aug. 15, 1842	TM3	237
Mary Eugene, d. Joseph & Thirsa, d. Aug. 17, 1837	TM3	307
Mary Eugenia, [d. Joseph K. & Thirsa], b. Aug. 14, 1836	TM3	235
Mary Eugenia, [d. Joseph K. & Thirsa], b. Aug. 14, 1836	3	373
Mica, m. Elesebeth **BUCKLIE**, Dec. 2, [16]62	1	173
Micah, s. Michael, b. Aug. 19, 1671	1	174
Micah, m. Damaris **WHITEHEAD**, Feb. 14, 1693/4	2	345
Micah, s. Micah & Damaris, b. Mar. 17, 1699/1700	2	345
Micah, Jr., of Branford, m. Jemima **FARRINGTON**, of		
Dedham, Dec. 23, 1725, by Rev. Sam[ue]ll Russell	3	61
Micah, s. Micah, Jr. & Jemima, b. Oct. 27, 1732	3	75
Micah, Jr., m. Phebe **BARTHOLOMEW**, b. of Branford, Mar.		
5, 1741, by Rev. Philemon Robbins	3	103
Micah, Jr., m. Hannah **HOWD**, b. of Branford, Dec. 30, 1762,		
by Philemon Robbins	3	179
Micah, s. Micah, Jr. & Hannah, b. Feb. 14, 1770	3	199
Micah, Jr., d. Aug. 15, 1770, in the 38th y. of his age	3	200
Micah, d. Aug. 20, 1770, in the 71st y. of his age	3	200
Micah, s. Micah, Jr. & Hannah, d. Apr. 12, 1771, in the		
2d y. of his age	3	203
Michell, s. Michaell, b. Jan. 8, 1664	1	173
Nancy, w. of James, d. Sept. 19, 1835	3	370
Nancy Elizabeth, [d. James & Nancy], b. Apr. 4, 1822	3	368
Nathan, s. John & Phebe, b. Mar. 10, 1700	2	344
Nathan, m. Rebeckah **BARKOR**, Jan. 10, 1734, by Rev.		
Philemon Robbins	3	148
Nathan, s. Nathan & Rebeckah, b. July 18, 1750	3	148
Nathan, s. Nathan & Rebeckah, d. Oct. 29, 1751	3	148
Nathan, s. Jabez & Hannah, b. Sept. 20, 1757	3	146
Nathan, d. June 2, 1776	3	263
Nathan[ie]ll, s. Dan[ie]ll & Elisabeth, b. Mar. 27, 1711	3	34
Nathaniel, m. Rebecca **TYLER**, b. of Branford, Sept. 11,		
1733, by Rev. Philemon Robbins	3	76
Nathan[ie]ll, s. Nathan[ie]ll & Rebecca, b. Feb. 21, 1736	3	129
Nathan[ie]ll, d. Aug. 14, 1755, ae 45	3	167
Nathaniel, m. Lydia **ROSE**, b. of Branford, Mar. 9, 1774,		
by Samuel Eells	3	257
Nathaniel, s. Nanth[anie]l & Lydia, b. Dec. 1, 1776	3	291
Nathaniel, m. Abigail **PALMER**, b. of Branford, Nov. 29,		
[1798], by Samuel Eells	3	255
Nathaniel, d. Oct. 3, 1807, in his 72nd y.	3	391
Noah, s. Micah, Jr. & Hannah, b. Aug. 30, 1765	3	199
Obadia[h](?), s. William, b. Mar. 31, 1650	1	171
Oren, s. Asahel & Hannah, b. Dec. 10, 1781	3	300
Orphana, twin with Rufus, d. Rufus & Abigail, b. June 22,		
1776	3	262

	Vol.	Page
PALMER, PAMER, (cont.)		
Patience, d. Benj[ami]n & Patience, b. Nov. 30, 1766	3	290
Patience, w. of Benjamin, d. Oct. 18, 1793	3	265
Patty, [d. John], b. Oct. 17, 1794	3	348
Paul, s. Nathan[ie]ll & Rebecca, b. Sept. 6, 1745	3	129
Peter, [s. John], b. Oct. 18, 1789	3	348
Pharez, [s. Isaac & Abigail], b. Mar. 21, 1791	3	394
Pharez, [s. Isaac & Abigail], d. Mar. 21, 1792	3	394
Phebe, d. John & Phebe, b. Apr. 2, 1694	2	344
Phebe, d. Stephen & Lydia, b. Mar. 3, 1737/8	3	90
Phebe, w. of John, d. July 12, 1738	3	148
Phebe, m. Ebenezer **FOOT**, b. of Branford, July 8, 1755,		
by Jonathan Mer[r]ick	3	172
Phebe, wid. of Micah, d. Mar. 19 1800	3	284
Phebe Ann, [d. Daniel & Polly], b. May 31, 1814	3	363
Philemon(?), s. Dan[ie]ll & Elisabeth, b. Apr. 16, 1709	3	30
Polly, [d. Benjamin & Abigai], b. Mar. 29, 1788	3	395
Polly, m. Alfred **ROSE**, June 27, 1835, by Rev. Smith Dayton	3	369
Polly Elizabeth, [d. Daniel & Polly], b. Dec. 19, 1830	3	363
Rebecca, d. Dan[ie]ll, Jr. & Patience, b. Apr. 28, 1728	3	76
Rebeckah, d. Nathan & Rebeckah, b. Dec. 24, 1734	3	148
Rebecca, d. Caleb & Mary, b. Apr. 12, 1741	3	97
Rebecca, d. Nathan[ie]ll & Rebecca, b. Nov. 12, 1742	3	129
Rebecca, m. Nath[anie]ll **BUTLAR**, b. of Branford, Nov. 28,		
1744, by Rev. Jon[a]th[an] Mer[r]ick	3	120
Rebeckah, d. Nath[a]n & Rebeckah, d. Oct. 18, 1751	3	148
Rebeckah, 2d, d. Nathan & Rebeckah, b. Jan. 2, 1753	3	148
Rebecca, d. Nat[hanie]ll & Rebecca, d. May 6, 1760, ae 17	3	167
Rebecca, w. of Isaac, d. Sept. 10, 1770, in the 22nd y.		
of her age	3	282
Rebecca, w. of Isaac, d. Sept. 10, 1770	3	394
Rebecca, w. of Nathan, d. May 23, 1776	3	262
Rebecca, of Branford, m. Dennis **HART**, of Long Island,		
May 18, 1783, by Sam[ue]ll Eells	3	306
Rebeccah, [d, Isaac & Abigail], b. Feb. 14, 1789	3	394
Richard Lewis, s. James F., b. June 14, 1847	TM3	240
Robert, [s. Benjamin & Abigail], b. Oct. 15, 1789	3	395
Rosanna, d. Nath[anie]l & Lydia, b. July 18, 1778	3	291
Rufus, s. Micah, Jr. & Phebe, b. Nov. 9, 1744	3	103
Rufus, m. Abigail **ROSE**, b. of Branford, Dec. 26, 1770,		
by Sam[ue]ll Eells	3	207
Rufus, twin with Orphana, s. Rufus & Abigail, b. June 22,		
1776	3	262
Rufus, d. Oct. 23, 1776, in the 32nd y. of his age	3	262
Rufus, m. Sally **HARRISON**, b. of Branford, Feb. 2, 1809	3	281
Rufus, d. Dec. 27, 1845, in the 70th y. of his age	TM3	306
Ruth, d. Abraham & Anna, b. Nov. 22, 1734	3	98
Sally Elizabeth, [d. Edmund, 2d, & Betsey], b. Oct. 1, 1815	3	344

	Vol.	Page
PALMER, PAMER, (cont.)		
Samuel, s. Micah & Damaris, b. Mar. 28, 1704	2	346
Sam[ue]ll, s. Micah & Damaris, b. Mar. 28, 1704	3	39
Samuel, s. Daniel & Hannah, b. Aug. 30, 1763	3	187
Samuel, d. Mar. 12, 1779	3	280
Samuel Augustus, [s. Daniel & Polly], b. Oct. 4, 1809	3	363
Samuel Augustus, s. Daniel, d. Sept. 20, 1827, in the		
18th y. of his age	3	363
Sarah, d. Judah & Mary, b. Mar. 8, 1728/9	3	78
Sarah, d. Nath[anie]ll & Rebecca, b. Jan. 15, 1753	3	129
Sarah, d. John & Elisabeth, b. Nov. 21, 1754	3	286
Sarah, d. Benj[ami]n, Jr. & Abigail, b. May 7, 1778	3	304
Sarah, m. Josiah **FRISBIE**, b. of Branford, Nov. 6, 1827,		
by Rev. Timothy P. Gillett	3	346
Solomon, m. Mrs. Mary **BEETS**, b. of Branford, Feb. 9,		
1737/8, by Rev. Philemon Robbins	3	123
Solomon, [s. Isaac & Abigail], b. Mar. 1, 1793	3	394
Solomon, [s. Isaac & Abigail], d. Apr. 1, 1793	3	394
Solomon, m. Mrs. Abigail **CURTIS**, b. of Branford, Sept.		
11, 1739, by Rev. Philemon Robbins	3	123
Stephen, m. Lydia **BARKER**, b. of Branford, Dec. 27, 1732,		
by Rev. Jonathan Mer[r]ick	3	83
Stephen, s. Stephen & Lydiah, b. Oct. 1, 1735	3	83
Stephen, Jr., m. Rachel **HARRISON**, b. of Branford, Feb.		
8, 1759, by Jon[a]th[an] Merrick	3	154
Stephen, s. Stephen, Jr. & Rachel, b. Jan. 27, 1765	3	184
Stephen, d. Apr. 6, 1782, in the 77th y. of his age	3	270
Stephen, Jr., m. Lydia **MARSHALL**, b. of Branford, Feb.		
28, 1790	3	387
Stephen, Sr., d. July 19, 1809	3	387
Steven, s. John & Phebe, b. July 15, 1703	2	344
Susan, [d. Edmund, 2d, & Betsey], b. June 14, 1809;		
d. Nov. 27, 1810	3	344
Susan, [d. Edmund, 2d, & Betsey], b. Mar. 28, 1811	3	344
Susan, of Branford, m. Atwater **ANDREWS**, of Wallingford,		
Mar. 27, 1831, by Edw[ar]d J. Ives	3	361
Silvey, [d. John], b. Apr. 28, 1800 (Sylvia)	3	348
Sylvia, m. John M. **GATES**, Nov. 21, 1821, by Charles		
Atwater	3	415
Timothy, s. Jno, Jr. & Thankfull, b. Jan. 4, 1723/4	3	55
Timothy, s.[Augustus & Betsey], b. June 6, 1810	3	282
Timothy, m. Louisa M. **BEACH**, b. of Branford, Nov. 30,		
1837, by Rev. Timothy P. Gillett	3	374
Tryphene, d. John & Elisabeth, b. Dec. 11, 1771;		
d. Feb. 14, 1772	3	286
Ursula, [d. James & Nancy], b. Aug. 28, 1817	3	368
William, s. Nathan[ie]ll & Rebecca, b. July 17, 1750	3	129
William, [s. Isaac & Abigail], b. Jan. 25, 1781	3	394

	Vol.	Page
PALMER, PAMER, (cont.)		
William, s. Isaac & Abigail, b. Jan. 27, 1781	3	283
William, m. Eliza A. **SPENCER**, b. of Branford, July 16, 1837, by Rev. Timothy P. Gillett	3	374
William Bradley, s. Wilman & Susan Cornelia, b. Oct. 30, 1840	TM3	229
William Isaac, [s. Lauren & Polly], b. Oct. 2, 1816	3	408
Wilman, s. Jacob & Fanny, b. Apr. 2, 1802	3	284
----, d. Nathaniel & Lydia, d. Apr. 8, 1780	3	291
----, child of Abigail, b. Dec. 1, 1783	3	306
PARDEE, PARDY, Aulden, of East Haven, m. Lydia **BRADLEY**, of Branford, Apr. 1, 1829, by Judson A. Root	3	350
Elisabeth, of New Haven, m. Ezekiel **FRISBIE**, of Branford, Feb. 18, 1752, by Warham Williams	3	165
Elizabeth, of Guilford, m. Samuel **STENT**, of Branford, Dec. 17, 1806	3	427
James R., m. Betsey **STEVENS**, b. of North Madison, Mar. 3, 1828, by Rev. Timothy P. Gillett	3	346
Julia Ann, d. Alden & Lydia, b. Mar. 19, 1830	TM3	237
Martha, m. Edward **FFRISSBE**, Dec. 30, 1702, by Rev. Mr. Russell	2	344
Nancy, m. Elihu **LINDLEY**, Jr., b. of Branford, Nov. 7, 1824, by Charles Atwater	3	336
Susanna, of New Haven, m. Joseph **ROGERS**, of Branford, Aug. 23, 1748, by Rev. Isaac Stiles, of New Haven	3	157
William, of Orange, m. Lucy N. **DOWNES**, of Branford, Apr. 24, 1833, by Rev. Timothy P. Gillett	3	359
PARKER, Chandler, s. Clarissa **HOADL[E]Y**, b. Nov. 6, 1788; m. Polly **FRISBIE**, Jan. 17, 1809	3	390
David H., d. Sept. 13, 1849,ae 1 1/2 y.	TM3	309
Eliada, s. Titus & Martha, b. June 18, 1766	3	197
Elisabeth Fry, of New Haven, m. Eli **GOODRICH**, of Branford, Dec. 23, 1837, by Rev. M. Knap, in New York City	TM3	156
Henry, s. Chandler & Polly, b. June 25, 1809	3	390
Linus, s. Titus & Martha, b. May 22, 1758	3	153
Martha, of Wallingford, m. Titus **PARKER**, of Branford, July 16, 1752, by Rev. Sam[ue]ll Hall, at Wallingford	3	133
Martha, d. Titus & Martha, b. Jan. 12, 1764	3	182
Rufus, s. Titus & Martha, b. Nov. 19, 1760	3	169
Sarah, d. Titus & Martha, b. Mar. 13, 1769	3	197
Titus, of Branford, m. Martha **PARKER**, of Wallingford, July 16, 1752, by Rev. Sam[ue]ll Hall, at Wallingford	3	133
Titus, s. Titus & Martha, b. Oct. 27, 1755	3	142
William, of Wallingford, m. Louisa **WHITING**, of Branford, June 3, 1849, by Rev. T. P. Gillett	TM3	163
PARKES, Christopher, m. Hannah **CHARLES**, Nov. 4, 1706, by W[illia]m Maltbie, J. P.	3	32

	Vol.	Page
PARMELEE, PALMERLE, PALMERLY, PAMERLE,		
PARMELE, PERMELE, Abigail, d. Caleb, Jr. & Elisabeth, b.		
Apr. 16, 1721	3	55
Amelia, d. Joseph & Sarah, b. Jan. 9, 1775	3	296
Ann, d. Jonathan & Sarah, b. Sept. 16, 1737	3	89
Asaph, s. Jonathan & Sarah, b. Apr. 2, 1746	3	116
Desire, d. Timothy & Desire, b. Feb. 15, 1728/9	3	79
Desier, m. James **BALDWIN**, b. of Branford, May 23, 1753,		
by Rev. Philemon Robbins	3	142
Dorothy, d. Timothy & Desire, b. May 8, 1731	3	79
Esther, d. Joseph & Sarah, b. Oct. 16, 1769	3	296
Esther, d. Joseph & Sarah, d. Nov. 6, 1781	3	296
Hannah, d. Joseph & Sarah, b. Mar. 29, 1768	3	296
Hannah, Mrs., of Branford, m. Phinehas **BUSHNELL**, of		
Guilford, Oct. 16, 1816	3	419
Jared, s. Jonathan & Sarah, b. Aug. 1, 1748	3	116
Jemima, d. Caleb, Jr. & Jemima, b. Feb. 16, 1728/9	3	83
Jeremiah, s. Joseph & Sarah, b. Feb. 14, 1777	3	296
John, s. Joseph & Sarah, b. Jan. 10, 1772	3	296
John, s. Timothy & Matty, b. Oct. 4, 1789	3	278
John, of Branford, m. Hannah **HALL**, of Guilford, July 2, 1808	3	392
John, d. Mar. 15, 1813, ae 40 y. 2 m. 5 d.	3	392
Jonathan, s. Jonathan & Sarah, b. Oct. 7, 1743	3	115
Joseph, m. Sarah **HOWD**, b. of Branford, Dec. 1, 1763, by		
Philemon Robbins	3	296
Joseph, m. Sarah **HOWD**, b. of Branford, Dec. 2, 1763, by		
Philemon Robbins	3	181
Joseph, d. Nov. 20, 1807	3	392
Lydia, of Branford, m. John **YOUNG**, formerly of Exeter,		
Mass., Feb. 3, 1725/6, by Rev. Sam[ue]ll Russell	3	59
Margaret, d. Joseph & Sarah, b. May 1, 1770	3	296
Mary, d. Caleb, Jr. & Elisabeth, b. Dec. 25, 1722	3	55
Samuel, s. Joseph & Sarah, b. Oct. 19, 1782	3	296
Sarah, d. Caleb, Jr. & Elisabeth, b. Oct. 16, 1724	3	56
Sarah, d. Timothy & Desire, b. Mar. 22, 1732/3	3	79
Sarah, d. Jonathan & Sarah, b. Oct. 7, 1743* (*Changed		
to Nov. 1, 1739)	3	115
Sarah, m. Noah **ROGERS**, Jr., b. of Branford, Oct. 23,		
1755, by Philemon Robbins	3	141
Sarah, d. Joseph & Sarah, b. Apr. 5, 1766	3	296
Sarah, m. Jeremiah **RUSSELL**, b. of Branford, Nov. 29,		
1832, by Rev. Timothy P. Gillett	3	358
Timothy, m. Desire **BARNS**, b. of Branford, May 3, 1727,		
by Rev. Sam[ue]ll Russell	3	79
Timothy, s. Joseph & Sarah, b. Oct. 25, 1764	3	184
Timothy, s. Joseph & Sarah, b. Oct. 25, 1764	3	296
PARRISH, PARISH, David, s. Ephiram & Jemima, b. July 28,		
1764	3	259

	Vol.	Page
PARRISH, PARISH, (cont.)		
Diana, d. Ephraim & Bathsheba, b. Apr. 23, 1734	3	79
Elisabeth, d. Josiah & Elisabeth, b. Aug. 3, 1751	3	167
Ephraim, m. Bathsheba **PALMER**, b. of Branford, Nov. 27,		
1729, by Rev. Sam[ue]ll Russell	3	67
Ephraim, s. [Ephraim] & Bathsheba, b. July 15, 1732	3	78
Ephraim, m. Abigail **MALTBIE**, b. of Branford, July 19,		
1744, by Jno. Russell, J. P.	3	102
Ephraim, m. Jemima **PALMER**, b. of Branford, May 15, 1760,		
by Philemon Robbins	3	163
Ephraim, s. Ephraim & Jemima, b. Oct. 30, 1768; d. Jan.		
6, 1773	3	259
Ephraim, m. Lucy **FOOT**, Apr. 9, 1801	3	398
Ephraim, d. Mar. 15, 1810, in the 78th y. of his age	3	398
Hannah, m. Richard **DARROW**, b. of Branford, Mar. 29, 1736,		
by Phil[emo]n Robbins	3	175
Hannah, d. Josiah & Elisabeth, b. July 11, 1756	3	167
Hezekiah, s. Ephraim & Bathsheba, b. Nov. 6, 1730	3	78
Jemima, d. Ephiram & Jemimah, b. Nov. 14, 1765	3	259
Jerusha, d. Ephraim & Bathsheba, b. Apr. 3, 1737	3	90
John, d. Mar. 23, 1748	3	166
[John], s. Josiah & Elisabeth, b. May 16, 1762	3	178
Jonathan, s. Ephraim & Jemima, b. Feb. 27, 1761	3	170
Jonathan, s. Capt. Ephraim, m. Mary **RUSSELL**, d. of Edward,		
b. of Branford, Nov. 25, 1784, by Jason Atwater	3	310
Josiah, s. John & Hannah, b. Mar. 20, 1724/5	3	56
Josiah, m. Elisabeth **PLANT**, b. of Branford, Sept. 21,		
1748, by Philemon Robbins	3	166
Josiah, s. Josiah & Elisabeth, b, Apr. 6, 1749	3	167
Josiah, Jr., m. Thankfull **PLANT**, b. of Branford, Dec. 25,		
1770, by Philemon Robbins	3	201
Luce, d. John & Hannah, b. Oct. 6, 1722	3	49
Lucy, m. Timothy **PLANT**, b. of Branford, Feb. 12, 1745,		
by Rev. Philemon Robbins	3	151
Lucy, m. Timothy **PLANT**, b. of Branford, Feb. 12, 1745,		
by Philemon Robbins	3	162
Lucy, w. of Ephraim, d. Apr. 30, 1730, in the 92nd y.		
of her age	3	355
Mary, d. Ephraim & Bathsheba, b. July 22, 1739	3	92
Mary, d. Josiah & Elisabeth, b. June 7, 1759	3	167
Polle, see under Polle **HOADLEY**	3	270
Russell, s. Jon[a]th[an] & Mary, b. Oct. 27, 1789	3	263
Submit, d. Ephraim & Jemima, b. Sept. 28, 1762	3	178
Sibil, d. Josiah & Elisabeth, b. Mar. 28, 1753 (Sybil)	3	167
PARSONS, Edwin, s. Edwin & Anto[i]nett[e], b. May 4, 1849	TM3	241
Edwin White, m. Antionette **BARTHOLOMEW**, b. of		
Branford, Feb. 18, 1840, by Rev. Timothy P. Gillett	3	378
Frances Gertrude, d. Levi S. & Elvira, b. June 10, 1834, at		

	Vol.	Page

PARSONS, (cont.)

Sandisfield, Mass.	TM3	231
Homer Lee, s. Levi S. & Elvira, b. July 26, 1836	TM3	231
Levi S., of Sandersfield, Mass., m. Elvira **SQUIRE**, of		
Branford, Sept. 11, 1833, by Rev. Judson A. Root	3	361
----, s. Edwin & Antoinette, b. June 17, 1851	TM3	244

PECK, Edward, of N. Haven, m. Betsey **LANPHIER**, of Branford,

Jan. 2, 1850, by Rev. Timothy P. Gillett	TM3	165
Edwin, ae 32, of New Haven, m. Betsey **LAMPHIER**, ae 24,		
Jan. 2, 1850, by Rev. T. P. Gillett	TM3	167
Martha, of Wallingford, m. Phinehas **BALDWIN**, of Branford,		
Jan. 1, 1761, by Warham Williams	3	172
Ruth, of Wallingford, m. Rufus **HOADL[E]Y**, of Branford,		
May 28, 1767, by Warham Williams	3	192
Samuel C., of Wallingford, m. Betsey **CHIDSEY**, of Branford,		
Sept. 29, 1831, by Edw[ar]d J. Ives	3	361
Thankful, of Parish of Northford, m. Wilkinson **HOWD**, of		
Branford, Dec. 17, 1761, by Warham Williams	3	174

PELL, Elisabeth, wid., m. Dan[ie]ll **BUTLAR**, May 7, 1751, by

Rev. Jonath[a]n Mer[r]ick	3	145

PENFIELD, Abigail, d. Sam[ue]ll & Bethiah, b. Apr. 22, 1731

	3	71
Abigail, d. Sam[ue]ll & Bethiah, b. Nov. 11, 1736	3	86
Bethiah, d. Sam[ue]ll & Bethiah, b. May 31, 1744	3	103
Bethyah, m. Thomas **RUSSELL**, b. of Branford, May 9, 1765,		
by Philemon Robbins	3	265
Hannah, d. Sam[ue]ll & Bethiah, b. Sept. 8, 1728	3	64
Isaac, s. Nath[anie]ll & Hannah, b. July 4, 1733	3	85
Lewis Benajah, s. Hannah **HAYDEN**, b. Nov. 26, 1818	3	426
Lois, d. Nath[anie]ll & Hannah, b. Oct. 10, 1736	3	85
Lydia, d. Sam[ue]ll & Bethiah, b. Sept. 4, 1733	3	76
Nathaniel, of Branford, m. Hannah **COULS**, of Wallingford,		
May 4, 1731, by Rev. Theophilus Hall	3	84
Nathaniel, s. Nath[anie]ll & Hannah, b. Apr. 6, 1732	3	85
Sam[ue]ll, m. Bethiah **ROSE**, b. of Branford, Dec. 1, 1727,		
by Rev. Sam[ue]ll Russell	3	63
Samuel, s. Nath[anie]ll & Hannah, b. Mar. 7, 1734/5	3	85
Samuel, s. Sam[ue]ll & Bethiah, b. Apr. 17, 1740	3	93
Sarah, d. Nath[anie]ll & Hannah, b. Nov. 23, 1740	3	95

PERKINS, Alanson, of Prospect, m. Rosella **BRADLEY**, of

Branford, Apr. 9, 1848, by Rev. A. C. Wheat	TM3	161
Rosella, d. [ ], 1849, ae 36 y.	TM3	308

PERSON, [see under **PARSONS** and **PIERSON**]

PETTY, Edward, d. June 23, 1773, ae 82y. 3 m. 24 d.

	3	256
Elisabeth, w. of Edward, d. Mar. 27, 1772	3	205
Hannah, m. Barnabas **MULFORD**, b. of Branford, Apr. 30,		
1740, by Rev. Jonath[an] Mer[r]ick	3	113

PHIPPEN, Dorcas, m. Jonathan **LINSL[E]Y**, Sept. 24, 1706, by

Jonathan Law, J. P., at Milford	3	32

	Vol.	Page
[PIERSON], PEIRSON, PERSON, Abiga[i]ll, m. John		
DAUENPORT, Nov. 27, [16]62	1	173
Grace, d. Abraham, b. July 13, [1650]	1	171
Rebecka, d. Abraham, b. Dec. [10, 1654]	1	171
Susan[n]a, d. Abraham, b. Dec. 10, [1652]	1	171
Theophelus, s. Abraham, b. May 15, [16]59	1	172
Thomas, m. Marie HAR[R]ISON, Nov. 27, [16]62	1	173
PLANT, Abraham, s. John & Hannah, b. Sept. 20, 1727	3	62
Abraham, m. Hannah HOADL[E]Y, b. of Branford, May 9,		
1751, by Philemon Robbins	3	183
Abraham, m Tamar FRISBIE, b. of Branford, May 5, 1763,		
by Philemon Robbins	3	183
Abraham, twin with Anne, s. Abraham & Thamar, b. night		
following Aug. 3, 1778	3	265
Albert Edward, s. [William & Polly], b. Nov. 6, 1841	TM3	233
Alonzo Augustus, s. [William & Polly], b. Oct. 27, 1834	TM3	233
Alonzo Austin, [s. William & Polly], b. Oct. 27, 1834	3	333
Amos Page, s. Sarah, b. Nov. 30, 1775	3	265
Anderson, s. Benj[ami]n & Lorana, b. Nov. 18, 1765	3	189
Anderson, [s. Samuel & Sarah], b. Jan. 2, 1796	3	392
Anderson, [s. Samuel & Sarah], b. Jan. 2, 1796	3	393
Anderson, m. Betsey BRADLEY, b. of Branford, Dec. 23,		
1818, by Rev. Timothy P. Gillett	3	422
Anderson, d. June 22, 1847, ae 20	TM3	307
Ann Louisa, d. William & Polly, b. Feb. 14, 1832	3	360
Anne, twin with Abraham, d. Abraham & Thamar, b. night		
following Aug. 3, 1778	3	265
Benjamin, s. John & Hannah, b. July 22, 1732	3	74
Benj[ami]n, of Branford, m. Lorana BECKWITH, of Lyme,		
Apr. 5, 1758, by Philemon Robbins	3	180
Benj[ami]n, s. Benjamin & Lorana, b. Oct. 1, 1763	3	189
Benjamin, [s. Samuel & Sarah], d. Aug. 11, 1808, ae 76	3	392
Benjamin, d. Aug. 11, 1808, ae 76	3	393
Betsey, of Branford, m. Philemon HOADLEY, of Martinsburg,		
N. Y., May 8, 1827, by Rev. Timothy P. Gillett	3	344
Ebenez[e]r, s. James & Bathsheba, b. Oct. 26, 1741	3	126
Edw[ar]d, [s. Elias & Ruhama Trowbridge], b. Sept. 8,1806	3	392
Edwin Ezra, s. [William & Polly], b. Feb. 6, 1837	TM3	233
Edwin Ezra, [s. William & Polly], b. Feb. 6, 1837	3	333
Electa, d. Abraham & Thamar, b. Sept. 27, 1765	3	186
Eli, s. Abraham & Tamar, b. Aug. 4, 1763	3	183
Elias, s. Benjamin & Lorana, m. Ruhama Trowbridge HALL,		
d. Elias & Ruhama, Mar. 30, 1799	3	392
Elias, [s. Elias & Ruhamah], b. Mar. 16, 1817	3	432
Elias, of Branford, m. Lydia LINSLEY, of Branford, Nov.		
10, 1842, by Rev. Timothy P. Gillett	TM3	155
Elias, Jr., m. Delia BEACH, b. of Branford, Dec. 14, 1848,		
by Rev. T. P. Gillett	TM3	163

	Vol.	Page

PLANT, (cont.)

Elisabeth, m. John **COACH**, July 23, 1712, by Nathan[ie]ll
    Harrison, J. P. | 3 | 35

Elisabeth, d. John & Hannah, b. Aug. 1, 1720 | 3 | 44

Elisabeth, m. Josiah **PARISH**, b. of Branford, Sept. 21,
    1748, by Philemon Robbiins | 3 | 166

Elisabeth, d. Abraham & Thamar, b. Oct. 12, 1775 | 3 | 265

Ellen Blackstone, d. [Samuel O. & Mary Ann], b. May 28,
    1840 | TM3 | 234

Emely Maria, d. [Samuel O. & Mary Ann], b. Apr. 2, 1842 | TM3 | 234

Emely Maria, d. Samuel O. & Mary Ann, d. Jan. 10, 1843 | TM3 | 306

Hannah, d. John & Hannah, b. July 16, 1708 | 3 | 34

Hannah, m. Abraham **WHEDON**, b. of Branford, Mar. 3, 1730,
    by Jonathan Merrick | 3 | 162

Hannah, d. Timothy & Luce, b. Mar. 15, 1747 | 3 | 126

Hannah, wid. of John, d. Nov. 5, 1754, ae 69 | 3 | 165

Hannah, w. of Abraham, d. Apr. 4, 1755 | 3 | 183

Hannah, d. Benj[ami]n & Lorana, b. Jan. 26, 1759 | 3 | 180

Hannah, d. Abraham & Tamar, b. Mar. 14, 1773 | 3 | 256

Hannah, m. John **RUSSELL**, Jr., b. of Branford, June 31 (sic),
    1779, by Philemon Robbins | 3 | 277

Harriet, [d. Elias & Ruhamah], b. Dec. 5, 1812 | 3 | 432

Harriet, m. James F. **MORRIS**, b. of Branford, Feb. 28,
    1839, by Rev. T. P. Gillett | 3 | 376

Henry B., of New Haven, m. Ellen **BLACKSTONE**, of
    Branford, Sept. 26, 1843, by Rev. Timothy P. Gillett | TM3 | 156

Henry Bradley, s. Anderson & Betsey, b. Oct. 27, 1819 | 3 | 422

Ithael, s. Timothy & Lucey, b. July 8, 1755 | 3 | 149

James, s. John & Hannah, b. Nov. 18, 1716 | 3 | 39

James, m. Bathsheba **PAGE**, b. of Branford, Sept. 22, 1740,
    by Rev. Jonathan Mer[r]ick | 3 | 101

James, s. James & Bathsheba, b. Sept. 10, 1742 | 3 | 101

James, [s. Elias & Ruhamah], b. Nov. 26, 1810 | 3 | 432

Jane, [d. Elias & Ruhama Trowbridge], b. Mar. 1, 1808 | 3 | 392

Jane, d. Elias & Ruhamah, d. Nov. 6, 1815 | 3 | 432

Jane F., d. Elias, Jr. & Adelia, b. Nov. [ ], 1850 | TM3 | 243

Jane Maria, [d. Elias & Ruhamah], b. Feb. 9, 1819 | 3 | 432

Jason, s. Abraham & Tamer, b. Aug. 17, 1782 | 3 | 253

Joel, s. Timothy & Lucey, b. Mar. 25, 1753 | 3 | 149

John, s. John, b. Mar. 3, 1678/9 | 1 | 210

John, s. John & Hannah, b. Sept. 19, 1711 | 3 | 35

John, d. Feb. 10, 1752, ae 74 | 3 | 165

John, s. Benjamin & Lorana, b. Dec. 1, 1761 | 3 | 180

John, [s. Samuel & Sarah], b. May 19, 1806 | 3 | 392

John, [s. Samuel & Sarah], b. May 19, 1806 | 3 | 393

Jonathan, s. John & Hannah, b. July 29, 1714 | 3 | 37

Julia A., of Branford, m. James T. **LEET**, of Guilford,
    Aug. 6, 1839, by Rev. Timo[thy] P. Gillett | 3 | 376

	Vol.	Page
PLANT, (cont.)		
Julia Ann, [d. Elias & Ruhamah], b. May 22, 1815	3	432
Louisa Ann, d. [William & Polly], b. Feb. 14, 1832	TM3	233
Lucy, d. Timothy & Lucy, b. May 27, 1745	3	126
Lucy, of Branford, m. Daniel **DEE**, of Saybrook, Dec. 27, 1764, by Philemon Robbins	3	183
Luzern Lewis, s. [William & Polly], b. July 26, 1839	TM3	233
Lydia, d. Abraham & Tamar, b. Dec. 28, 1767	3	256
Mari, [d. Samuel & Sarah], b. Oct. 9, 1808	3	392
Mary, [d. Elias & Ruhama Trowbridge], b. Sept. 3, 1801	3	392
Mary Eliza, of Branford, m. William Tyler **NORTON**, of Norwich, Nov. 29, 1852, by Rev. T. P. Gillett	TM3	172
Mary R., [d. Samuel & Sarah], b. Oct. 9, 1808	3	393
Moses, s. James & Bathsheba, b. Mar. 17, 1760	3	161
Pegge, d. Benjamin & Lorane, b. May 29, 1769	3	206
Polly, [d. Samuel & Sarah], b. Oct. 16, 1798	3	392
Polly, [d. Samuel & Sarah], b. Oct. 16, 1798	3	393
Polly, [d. Samuel & Sarah], d. Apr. 20, 1800	3	392
Polly, [d. Samuel & Sarah], d. Apr. 20, 1800	3	393
Rebecca, d. Abraham & Tamar, b. Mar. 7, 1770	3	256
Sally, [d. Samuel & Sarah], b. Sept. 17, 1801	3	392
Sally, [d. Samuel & Sarah], b. Sept. 17, 1801	3	393
Sally, m. Judah **FRISBIE**, b. of Branford, May 30, 1822, by Rev. Gardiner Spring, of New York	3	420
Samuel, s. James & Bathsheba, b. Dec. 27, 1744	3	104
Samuel, s. Benjamin & Lorane, b. Apr. 1, 1772	3	205
Samuel, m. Sarah **FRISBIE**, Feb. 11, 1795	3	392
Samuel, m. Sarah **FRISBIE**, b. of Branford, Feb. 11, 1795	3	393
Samuel O., m. Mary A. **BLACKSTONE**, b. of Branford, Feb. 26, 1839, by Rev. Timothy P. Gillett	3	376
Samuel Orin, [s. Samuel & Sarah], b. Jan. 24, 1815	3	393
Sarah, d. James & Bathshaba, b. May 6, 1754	3	153
Sarah had s. Amos Page **PLANT**, b. Nov. 30, 1775	3	265
Sarah Frisbie, [d. Samuel O. & Mary Ann], b. Sept. 11, 1845	TM3	234
Solomon, s. James & Bathsheba, b. May 20, 1741	3	101
Stephen, s. James & Bathsheba, b. Feb. 2, 1746/7	3	110
Thankfull, m. Josiah **PARISH**, Jr., b. of Branford, Dec. 25, 1770, by Philemon Robbins	3	201
Thomas, [s. Elias & Ruhama Trowbridge], b. Apr. 14, 1804	3	392
Timothy, s. John & Hannah, b. Apr. 6, 1724	3	55
Timothy, m. Lucy **PARRISH**, b. of Branford, Feb. 12, 1745, by Rev. Philemon Robbins	3	151
Timothy, m. Lucy **PARISH**, b. of Branford, Feb. 12, 1745, by Philemon Robbins	3	162
Timothy, s. Timothy & Luce, b. July 4, 1750	3	126
Timothy, s. Timothy & Lucey, b. July 4, 1750	3	149
William, [s. Elias & Ruhama Trowbridge], b. Jan. 4, 1800	3	392
William, m. Polly **BEACH**, b. of Branford, June 30, 1831,		

	Vol.	Page

PLANT, (cont.)

by Rev. Timothy P. Gillett — 3 — 357

----, s. John & Angeline, b. Apr. 7, 1849 — TM3 — 241

PLUM, Dorcas, d. John, m. John **LIMAN,** of Har[t]foord, Jan.
12, [16]54 — 1 — 170

Doratha, d. Samuell, b. Mar. 26, [16]60 — 1 — 172

Elesebeth, d. Samuell, b. Jan. 18, [1650] — 1 — 171

Johanna, d. Samuell, b. Mar. 11, [16]65 — 1 — 173

John, s. Samuell, b. Oct. 28, 1657 — 1 — 172

Joship, s. Samuell, b. Aug. 3, [16]62 — 1 — 173

Mary, d. Samuell, b. Apr. 1, 1653 — 1 — 171

Samuell, s. Samuell, b. Mar. 22, [1654] — 1 — 172

PLUYMERT, Abigail Amelia, d. John & Abigail, b. May 14, 1793 — 3 — 265

Har[r]iot, d. John & Abigail, b. Nov. 19, 1788 — 3 — 265

John, m. Abigail **FOOT,** b. of Branford, Sept. 10, 1782,
by Warham Williams — 3 — 265

John, Jr., s. John & Abigail, b. Dec. 24, 1784 — 3 — 265

Joseph, s. John & Abigail, b. July 11, 1791 — 3 — 265

Sarah, d. John & Abigail, b. Dec. 29, 1786 — 3 — 265

William Champlin, s. John & Abigail, b. May 2, 1783 — 3 — 265

POND, Abagail, d. Sam[ue]ll, d. Oct. 19, 1679 — 1 — 211

Abigail, m. Isaac **TYLER,** Nov. 6, 1704 — 2 — 345

Abigail, d. Sam[ue]ll & Abigail, b. July 7, 1713 — 3 — 39

Abigail, m. Abraham **PAGE,** b. of Branford, Nov. 22, 1739,
by Rev. Philemon Robbins — 3 — 91

Abigail, d. Phineas & Martha, b. Mar. 6, 1746/7 — 3 — 127

Abigail, d. Roswell & Lydia, b. Dec. 18, 1767 — 3 — 208

Abigail, m. Joel **HOWD,** b. of Branford, Feb. 5, 1769 — 3 — 300

Amanda, d. Elias & Martha, b. Oct. 29, 1782 — 3 — 305

Asher, [twin with Gad], s. Moses & Mary, b. Aug. 12, 1727 — 3 — 63

Asher, s. Aaron & Martha, b. Jan. 31, 1749/50 — 3 — 121

Bartholomew, s. Sam[ue]ll & Abigail, b. Jan. 19, 1708 — 3 — 39

Bartholomew, [twin with Rebecca], s. Philip & Thankfull,
b. Apr. 13, 1736 — 3 — 84

Bathsheba, d. Moses & Mary, b. Jan. 2, 1724/5 — 3 — 58

Bathsheba, m. Dan[ie]ll **JOHNSON,** b. of Branford, Oct.
17, 1753, by Rev. Jonath[a]n Mer[r]ick — 3 — 133

Charles, s. Russell & Lydia, b. Apr. [ ], 1850 — TM3 — 241

Dan, s. Philip & Thankfull, b. Nov. 4, 1726 — 3 — 84

Dan, of Branford, m. Mehetabel **MONSON,** of Wallingford,
Aug. 29, 1750, by Rev. Sam[ue]ll Whittlesey, at
Wallingford — 3 — 124

Dan, s. Dan & Mehetabel, b. Apr. 22, 1751 — 3 — 124

Elias, s. Aaron & Martha, b. Sept. 23, 1751 — 3 — 132

Elias, m. Martha **HOWD,** b. of Branford, Jan. 11, 1774,
by Sam[ue]ll Eells — 3 — 305

Eliphelet, s. Elias & Martha, b. Aug. 20, 1775 — 3 — 305

Eliza A., ae 19, m. Henry Z. **NICHOLS,** ae 22, June 10, 1850,

	Vol.	Page
POND, (cont.)		
by Rev. W. H. Reeves	TM3	167
Eliza Ann, m. Henry Z. **NICHOLS**, b. of Branford, June 13,		
1850, by Rev. W[illia]m Henry Rees	TM3	165
Emeline, m. Joseph **FRISBIE**, b. of Branford, July 20,		
1828, by Timothy P. Gillett	3	347
Gad, [twin with Asher], s. Moses & Mary, b. Aug. 12, 1727	3	63
Jonathan, s. Phineas & Martha, b. June 24, 1740	3	127
Joseph, m. Elvira E. **AVERILL**, June 5, 1845, by Rev.		
Frederick Miller	TM3	160
Josiah, s. Sam[ue]ll & Miriam, b. Sept. 25, 1688	2	343
Josiah, s. Sam[ue]ll & Abigail, b. Mar. 19, 1710/11	3	39
Josiah, m. Abigail **HARRISON**, b. of Branford, Dec. 9, 1736		
by Rev. Philemon Robbins	3	90
Josiah, s. Roswell & Lydia, b. Sept. 27, 1765	3	188
Lois, d. Moses & Mary, b. June 20, 1730	3	69
Lois, d. Aaron & Martha, b. Mar. 22, 1756	3	161
Martha, d. Aaron & Martha, b. Apr. 17, 1758	3	161
Mary, m. Nath[anie]ll **GOODRIDG[E]**, b. of Branford, Jan.		
15, 1746, by Rev. Philemon Robbins	3	150
Mary, d. Aaron & Martha, b. Apr. 22, 1748	3	121
Mary, d. Roswell & Lydia, b. Nov. 14, 1769	3	208
Mene Mene Tekel Uphorsin, s. Sam[ue]ll & Abigail, b.		
Mar. 5, 1720/1	3	48
Mindwell d. Moses & Mary, b. July 12, 1742	3	98
Naomi, d. Aaron & Martha, b. Sept. 18, 1753	3	133
Nathaniel, s. Sam[ue]ll, b. Feb. 14, 1676	1	174
Nelson, m. Harriet **WRIGHT**, of North Branford, Apr. 23,		
1849, by Rev. Mr. Chase	TM3	164
Paul, s. Moses & Mary, b. May 12, 1736	3	85
Peter, s. Sam[ue]ll & Abigail, b. Jan. 22, 1718/9	3	40
Phillip, s. Sam[ue]ll & Abigail, b. Jan. 15, 1706	3	39
Philip, m. Thankfull **FRISBIE**, b. of Branford, Apr. 13,		
1726, by Nath[anie]ll Harrison, J. P.	3	84
Philip, s. Philip & Thankfull, b. Feb. 7, 1740/1	3	97
Phineas, s. Sam[ue]ll & Abigail, b. June 9, 1715	3	39
Phineas, s. Phineas & Martha, b. June [15], 1737	3	127
Pitman, s. Elias & Martha, b. Nov. 3, 1778	3	305
Putnam*, d. Jan. 6, 1847, ae 67 (*Pitman?)	TM3	307
Rachell, d. Moses & Mary, b. May 26, 1733	3	77
Rebecca, [twin with Bartholomew], d. Philip & Thankfull,		
b. Apr. 13, 1736	3	84
Rosewell, s. Josiah & Abigail, b. Oct. 10, 1738	3	90
Roswell, m. Lydia **ROGERS**, b. of Branford, Nov. 22, 1764,		
by Philemon Robbins	3	188
Roswell, s. Roswell & Lydia, b. July 15, 1772	3	256
Sally, m. Ralph **BLACKSTON**, b. of Branford, [ ], 1802	3	429
Samuell, m. Mirriam **BLACHLY**, Jan. 5, 1669	1	174

	Vol.	Page
POND, (cont,)		
Samuel, s. Sam[ue]ll, b. July 1, 1679	1	211
Sam[ue]ll, m. Abigail **GOODRICH**, June 8, 1704	2	345
Sam[ue]ll, m. Abigail **GOODRICH**, b. of Branford, June 8, 1704, by W[illia]m Maltbie, J. P.	3	39
Sam[ue]ll, s. Sam[ue]ll & Abigail, b. May 7, 1705	3	39
Sam[ue]ll, s. Moses & Mary, b. June 24, 1739	3	91
Samuel L., s. Eliphalet, b. Dec. 7, 1823	TM3	235
Sarah, m. John **LINSL[E]Y**, July 6, [16]55	1	170
Thankfull, d. Philip & Thankfull, b. Apr. 27, 1733	3	84
Timothy, s. Philip & Thankfull, b. Oct. 7, 1730	3	84
PONSONBY, Mary, Mrs. m. Abraham **FOOT**, July 20, 1784, by Bele Hubbard, Missionary, New Haven	3	313
PORTER, Joanna, of Woodbury, m. James **FRISBIE**, of Branford, June 16, 1743, by Philemon Robbins	3	165
John, of Middletown, m. Fanny **SCOVIL**, of Haddam, Dec. 22, 1834, by Rev. T. P. Gillett	3	368
Ruth, of Bethlem, m. Jacob **FRISBIE**, of Branford, Nov. 18, 1747, by Rev. Joseph Bellamy, at Bethlem	3	120
William K., of New Haven, m. Marietta **HULL**, of Branford, Apr. 10, 1842, by Rev. Pascal P. Kidder	TM3	154
POTTER, Achsah, d. John & Mary, b. Sept. 26, 1747	3	112
Ard, s. John & Mary, b. Dec. 26, 1748	3	119
Ard, s. John & Mary, d. May 26, 1766	3	196
Bela, s. John & Asenath, b. Mar. 18, 1785	3	262
Daniel, s. Nathan & Hannah, b. July 24, 1768	3	203
Hannah, m. John **BUTLER**, Nov. 17, 1684	1	211
Isaac, s. Nathan & Hannah, b. Aug. 23, 1762	3	177
Jacob, s. Sam[ue]ll & Dorothy, b. June 26, 1741	3	100
James, s. John, Jr. & Asenath, b. Jan. 3, 1782	3	262
James, s. John, Jr. & Asenath, b. Jan. 3, 1782	3	298
John, m. Mary **BEERS**, b. of Branford, Nov. 14, 1746, by Rev. Jonathan Mer[r]ick	3	112
John, Jr., m. Asenath **LIN[S]L[E]Y**, b. of Branford, Nov. 27, 1781, by Nicholas Street	3	262
John, Jr., m. Asenath **LINSLEY**, b. of Branford, Nov. 27, 1781, by Nicholas Street	3	298
John, s. John & Asenath, b. Apr. 29, 1789	3	262
John, d. Nov. 1, 1792	3	267
Jonathan Beers, s. John, Jr. & Asenath, b. [ ] 9, 1787	3	262
Lucinda, d. Stephen & Sarah, b. Apr. 4, 1767	3	194
Mary, w. of John, d. May 30, 1780	3	267
Mary, m. Moses **BALDWIN**, b. of Branford, June 20, 1782, by Sam[ue]ll Eells	3	287
Merit, s. John & Asenath, b. Oct. 17, 1792	3	262
Nathan, m. Hannah **FOOT**, b. of Branford, Apr. 29, 1760, by Josiah Rogers, J. P.	3	168
Nathan, s. Nathan & Hannah, b. Apr. 29, 1765	3	203

	Vol.	Page
POTTER, (cont.)		
Orin H., of Plymouth, m. Miriam **SHEPHERD**, of Branford,		
Jan. 26, 1824, by Rev. Timothy P. Gillett	3	425
Priscilla, d. John & Asenath, b. Oct. 1, 1795	3	267
Samuel, m. Dorothy **MULTRUP**, June 1, 1738, by Rev. Jacob		
Heminway	3	100
Samuel, s. Sam[ue]ll & Dorothy, b. Sept. 10, 1739	3	100
Sarah, m. Thomas **NORTON**, Jr., b. of Branford, Nov. 16,		
1789, by Jason Atwater	3	260
Stephen, m. Sarah **LINSL[E]Y**, b. of Branford, July 3,		
1766, by Philemon Robbins	3	194
PRESTON, Lydia, d. Eben[eze]r & Martha, b. Mar. 22, 1747/8	3	121
Sam[ue]ll, s. Eben[eze]r & Martha, b. Mar. 27, 1746	3	121
PRICE, Olive, m. Abraham **HOADL[E]Y**, Oct. 10, 179[2]	3	285
PRIMUS, Ham, negro, b. June 7, 1787	3	411
Peter, s. Cambridge & Moriah, negro, b. July 9, 1784	3	406
PRINDLE, Elisabeth A., of Newburyport, Mass., m. William Y.		
ROGERS, of Branford, Sept. 15, 1846, by Rev. A. C.		
Wheat	TM3	159
RAINER, [see under **RAYNER**]		
RAYMOND, Elnathan Tyler, s. Lucius T. & Hannah, b. Sept. 10,		
1820; d. Jan. 18, 1822	3	416
Lucius Tyler, m. Hannah **ROBINSON**, b. of Branford, Jan.		
2, 1820	3	416
RAYNER, RAINER, Abigail, d. Adam & Mary, b. Aug. 5, 1723	3	53
Abigail, d. Adam & Mary, d. Nov. 25, 1736, ae 14 y.	3	85
Adam, m. Mary **HOADL[E]Y**, Oct. 7, 1713, by Nathan[ie]ll		
Harrison, J. P.	3	38
Adam, s. Adam & Mary, b. Sept. 13, 1720	3	44
Adam, s. Adam & Mary, d. Nov. 9, 1722	3	60
Adam, d. Feb. 1, 1754, in the 64th y. of his age	3	134
Elisabeth, d. Adam & Mary, b. Feb. 8, 1717/8	3	42
Elisabeth, m. David **PAGE**, b. of Branford, Apr. 3, 1740,		
by Rev. Jonathan Mer[r]ick	3	109
Hannah, d. Adam & Mary, b. Oct. 10, 1726	3	59
Lydia, d. Adam & Mary, b. Feb. 22, 1732/3	3	76
Lydia, m. George **TYLER**, b. of Branford, Jan. 14, 1756,		
by Rev. Jonath[a]n Mer[r]ick	3	144
Mary, d. Adam & Mary, b. July 27, 1715	3	37
Mary, m. Silvanus **BUTLER**, b. of Branford, Oct. 30, 1739,		
by Jonathan Mer[r]ick	3	93
Rebeccah, d. Adam & Mary, b. Nov. 27, 1729	3	67
REDFIELD, Charles, [s. William & Anna], b. July 25, 1820	3	430
Harriet, [d. William & Anna], b. Jan. 16, 1815	3	430
John, [s. William & Anna], b. Feb. 18, 1817	3	430
William, of East Haven, m. Anna **MONRO[E]**, of Branford,		
Apr. 29, 1814	3	430
REYNOLDS, W[illia]m, m. Abigail **FOOT**, Mar. 11, 1822, by		

	Vol.	Page
REYNOLDS, (cont.)		
Charles Atwater	3	418
RICE, John, d. June 26, 1851, ae 61 y.	TM3	310
RICHARDS, Jonah, of Hartford, m. Mary **PALMER**, of Branford,		
July 27, 1726, by Rev. Sam[ue]ll Russell	3	62
RIGHT, [see under **WRIGHT**]		
ROBBINS, ROBINS, Ammi Ruhamah, s. Rev. Philemon & Hannah,		
b. Aug. 25, 1740	3	93
Beniamin, s. John, b. Oct. 24, 1660	1	172
Chandler, s. Rev. Philemon & Hannah, b. Aug. 13, 1738	3	88
Hannah, d. Rev. Philemon & Hannah, b. Sept. 1, 1742	3	99
Hannah, d. Philemon & Hannah, d. Nov. 11, 1747	3	124
Hannah Rebecca, d. Philemon & Hannah, b. Apr. 18, 1751	3	124
Irene, d. Philemon & Hannah, b. Nov. 16, 1746	3	107
Irene, Mrs., m. George Douglass **THOMSON**, b. of Branford,		
Nov. 5, 1772, by Philemon Robbins	3	208
James Elizur, [s. Eleazer & Else], b. Jan. 6, 1808	3	283
John, m. Marie **ABUT**, Nov. 4, 1659	1	173
John, s. John, b. July 2, [16]62	1	173
John, m. Janne **TILLISON**, June 23, 167[0]* (*First written		
1679)	1	174
Lucy Delia, [d. Eleazer & Else], b. Apr. 10, 1806	3	283
Olive Eliza, [d. Eleazer & Else], b. Mar. 9, 1810	3	283
Philemon, Rev., m. Mrs. Hannah **FOOT**, b. of Branford, Dec.		
24, 1735, by Rev. Jonathan Mer[r]ick	3	83
Philemon, s. Rev. Philemon & Hannah, b. Nov. 1, 1736	3	85
Philemon, s. Rev. Philemon & Hannah, d. Sept. 6, 1756,		
ae 19 y. "Was a student at Yale College"	3	144
Rebecca, d. Rev. Philemon & Hannah, b. July 27, 1744	3	102
Rebeccah, d. Philemon & Hannah, d. Feb. 7, 1750/1	3	124
Rebecca Hannah, d. Philemon & Hannah, b. Apr. 7, 1753	3	137
Sarah, d. Philemon & Hannah, b. Jan. 11, 1748/9	3	118
Sarah, d. Philemon & Hannah, b. Jan. 11, 1748/9	3	124
ROBERDS, Anne, of East Haven, m. Samuel **BUTLAR**, of		
Branford, Mar. 21, 1714, by Rev. Jacob Heminway	3	37
ROBINSON, Desire, m. Nathaniel **BAYLEY**, July 6, 1807	3	282
Erastus, [s. John & Lucy], b. May 8, 1803	3	276
Hannah, m. Lucius Tyler **RAYMOND**, b. of Branford, Jan.		
2, 1820	3	416
Harriet Elisabeth, [d. John Hobart & Julia Ann], b.		
Dec. 25, 1840	TM3	234
Hobart Wyllys, [s. John Hobart & Julia Ann], b. July 10, 1845	TM3	234
Jesse, m. Lucy **LINSLEY**, June 29, 1845, by Rev. Frederick		
Miller	TM3	160
John H., m. Julia Ann **TYLER**, b. of Branford, Feb. 13,		
1840, by Rev. L. H. Corson	3	377
Linus, m. Rebecca **HOBART**, b. of Branford, Apr. 26, 1797,		
by Lynde Huntington	3	270

	Vol.	Page

ROBINSON, (cont.)

Lois, m. Miles **BLACKSTONE**, b. of Branford, Sept. 25,
1831, by Edw[ar]d J. Ives ... 3 ... 261

Lydia, of New Haven, m. Roger **TYLER**, of Branford, May
7, 1760, by Jon[a]th[an] Merrick ... 3 ... 166

Rebecca, [d. John & Lucy], b. Feb. 7, 1801 ... 3 ... 276

Rebecca, of North Branford, m. John B. **SPENCER**, of Derby,
May 26, 1822, by Charles Atwater ... 3 ... 419

Rebecca Hobart, [d. John Hobart & Julia Ann], b. Feb.
22, 1843 ... TM3 ... 234

Wyllys T., s. John H. & Julia Ann, b. Sept. 28, 1848 ... TM3 ... 240

----, d. John & Julia, b. Sept. 14, 1848 ... TM3 ... 241

ROCKWELL, Almon, of Granby, m. Martha **LANFARE**, of
Branford, Nov. 11, 1832, by Rev. Timothy P. Gillett ... 3 ... 358

ROGERS, Abiather, s. David & Eunice, b. Aug. 23, 1758 ... 3 ... 184

Abigail, d. Noah & Elisabeth, b. [Oct. 8], 1723 ... 3 ... 63

Abigail, of Huntin[g]ton, L. I., m. Abraham **FOOT**, of
Branford, Apr. 15, 1745, by Eben[eze]r Prime ... 3 ... 170

Abigail, m. Joseph **BROWN**, b. of Branford, Feb. 1, 1749/50,
by Nathan[ie]ll Harrison, J. P. ... 3 ... 127

Abigail, d. Joseph & Susanna, b. Dec. 27, 1751 ... 3 ... 157

Abigail, m. Elihu **BALDWIN**, b. of Branford, Nov. 18, 1773,
by Warham Williams ... 3 ... 255

Abijah, s. Thomas & Rebecca, b. Dec. 2, 1753 ... 3 ... 196

Abijah, m. Lydia **HARRISON**, b. of Branford, Aug. 9, 1775,
by Warham Williams ... 3 ... 259

Abraham, [twin with Isaac], s. John, Jr. & Thankful, b.
Dec. 13, 1749 ... 3 ... 119

Abraham, m. Hannah **PALMER**, b. of Branford, Mar. 11, 1773 ... 3 ... 301

Abraham, s. Abr[aha]m & Hannah, b. June 25, 1783 ... 3 ... 301

Abraham, Jr., m. Fanny **FOWLER**, Nov. 16, 1809 ... 3 ... 404

Abraham, [s. Abraham, Jr. & Fanny], b. June 11, 1813 ... 3 ... 404

Abraham, Jr., m. Elizabeth **NORTON**, b. of Branford, Nov.
30, 1837, by Rev. Timo[thy] P. Gillett ... 3 ... 374

Abraham, Jr., d. Sept. 24, [ ], in the 78th y. of his age ... 3 ... 345

Albert Towner, s. Henry & Nancy, b. Apr. 15, 1833 ... 3 ... 368

Ambros[e], s. Stephen & Jerusha, b. Dec. 4, 1765 ... 3 ... 190

Ammi, s. Thomas & Rebecca, b. May 26, 1769 ... 3 ... 197

Ammi, [s. Jairus & Fanny], b. Sept. 16, 1802 ... 3 ... 360

Amos, s. Ezekiel & Sarah, b. Feb. 3, 1732/3 ... 3 ... 75

Anna, m. John **TYLER**, b. of Branford, Nov. 20, 1786, by
Jason Atwater ... 3 ... 385

Anne, d. Dan[ie]ll & Lydia, b. July 11, 1760 ... 3 ... 171

Annis, d. Thomas, Jr. & Molly, b. Aug. 11, 1788 ... 3 ... 261

Asa, s. Levi & Johanna, b. Jan. 22, 1765 ... 3 ... 184

Barnabas, s. Thomas, Jr. & Molly, b. June 23, 1793 ... 3 ... 261

Bela, [s. Hobart & B[e]ula[h], b. Feb. 3, 1802 ... 3 ... 274

Benjamin, [s. Noadiah], b. July 3, 1802 ... 3 ... 386

	Vol.	Page

ROGERS, (cont.)

Benjamin, of Branford, m. Betsey S. **BISHOP**, of Guilford,
    Mar. 1, 1828, by Rev. Jno, M. Garfield, at New Haven   3   347

Benjamin, of Branford, m. Eliza C. **MERRIAM**, of Meriden,
    May 28, 1848, by Rev. Frederick Miller, in Trinity
    Church   TM3   162

Beriah, s. Stephen & Jerusha, b. July 23, 1774   3   282

Betsey, d. Edm[un]d & Lydia, b. Dec. 8, 1770   3   302

Betsey, d. Eli & Hannah, b. May 10, 1779   3   310

Betsey, [d. Isaac, Jr. & Sally], b. Mar. 12, 1822   3   363

Betsey S., w. of Benjamin, d. May 13, 1847, ae 41   TM3   307

Caroline, [d. Wyllys & Martha], b. June 14, 1821, in
    Charleston, S. C.; d. May 18, 1822   3   408

Charles, s. Gideon & Eunice, b. Mar. 3, 1768   3   194

Charles, [s. Chauncey & Maria], b. Dec. 1, 1831   3   364

Charles Henry, s. Eli F. & Elizabeth A. F., b. Mar. 22, 1835   3   369

Charles Henry, s. Eli F. & Elizabeth A. F., b. Mar. 22, 1835   3   370

Charles William, [s. Chauncey & Maria], b. Dec. 14, 1816   3   364

Charles W[illia]m, [s. Chauncey & Maria], d. Mar. 15, 1826   3   364

Charlotte, [d. Chauncey & Maria], b. Jan. 3, 1821   3   364

Charlotte, of Branford, m. Elihu **WATROUS**, of Westbrook,
    Mar. 17, 1845, by Rev. E. Edwin Hall   TM3   157

Chauncey, s. Isaac & Mary, b. May 5, 1788   3   258

Chauncey, m. Maria **FRISBIE**, b. of Branford, Oct. 25,
    1815, by Rev. Timo[thy] P. Gillett   3   364

Clarissa Thankfull, d. Eli & Hannah, b. Aug. 13, 1784   3   310

Cornelia, [d. Isaac, Jr. & Sally], b. Mar. 20, 1819   3   363

Cornelia, m. Nelson **HOWD**, b. of Branford, Jan. 12, 1841,
    by Rev. A. B. Goldsmith, of Guilford   TM3   152

Culpepper, s. Edm[un]d & Lydia, b. May 22, 1766   3   302

Culpepper, s. Edmund & Lydia, d. Mar. 5, 1794 "on his
    passage from Dominico to St. Croix"   3   269

Daniel, s. John & Lydia, b. June 2, 1727   3   62

Daniel, m. Lydia **BARTHOLOMEW**, b. of Branford, June 18,
    1752, by Rev. Philemon Robbins   3   140

Daniel, s. Daniel & Lidiah, b. Mar. 31, 1757   3   145

Daniel, s. David & Eunice, b. Jan. 1, 1765   3   184

Daniel, s. Daniel & Lydia, d. Jan. 5, 1777, in the 20th
    y. of his age, at Fairfield, on his return home from the
    Army   3   262

Daniel, s. Ephraim & Martha, b. Mar. 18, 1785   3   314

Daniel, d. July 9, 1801   3   275

Dan[ie]l, [s. John & Anna], d. July 9, 1801   3   385

David, m. Eunice **BYINTUN**, b. of Branford, July 3, 1748,
    by Jonathan Mer[r]ick   3   184

David, s. David & Eunice, b. Dec. 24, 1763   3   184

Dunover, [child of Isaac, Jr. & Sally], b. Sept. 1, 1831   3   363

Ebenezer, s. Josaih, Jr. & Martha, b. Jan. 29, 1747/8   3   113

	Vol.	Page

ROGERS, (cont.)

	Vol.	Page
Ebenezer, m. Lucy **BEACH**, b. of Branford, Sept. 10, 1772,		
by Philemon Robbins	3	258
Ebenezer, s. Capt. Ebenezer & Lucy, b. Dec. 13, 1785	3	258
Ebenezer, Capt., of Branford, m. Ruth **BLAKESLEE**, of		
North Haven, Jan. 21, 1788, by Benj[ami]n Trumbull	3	258
Edmund, m. Lydia **FRISBIE**, b. of Branford, Nov. 21, 1760	3	302
Edmund, s. Edm[un]d & Lydia, b. May 13, 1761	3	302
Edmund, m. Eunice **BARKER**, b. of Branford, Sept. 19, 1782	3	302
Edmund, m. Esther **WHEDON**, Apr. 22, 1784, by Rev. Jason		
Atwater	3	272
Edmund sailed from Branford Jan. 6, 1785* and was lost		
at sea. (*First written 1795)	3	268
Edmund, Jr., [s. Edmund]., sailed from Branford Jan. 6,		
17[85]* and was lost at sea (*First written 1795)	3	268
Edmund, s. Edmund & Esther, b. Jan. 18, 1785	3	272
Edmund James, s. Jonathan & Orphana, b. Dec. 7, 1800	3	274
Edward, s. Noah & Elisabeth, b. Apr. 14, 1735	3	84
Edward, s. Josiah, Jr. & Martha, b. Jan. 12, 1735/6	3	85
Eli, m. Hannah **BARKER**, b. of Branford, Aug. 21, 1761,		
by Philemon Robbins	3	310
Eli, m. Hannah **BUEL**, b. of Branford, June 7, 1764, by		
Jonathan Merrick	3	184
Eli, m. Dorcas **LINSL[E]Y**, b. of Branford, Jan. 21, 1768,		
by Josiah Rogers, J. P.	3	194
Eli F., m. Elizabeth A. **FRISBIE**, b. of Branford, June		
10, 1834, by Rev. Timothy P. Gillett	3	367
Eli Fowler, [s. Abraham, Jr., & Fanny], b. July 15, 1811	3	404
Elihu, s. Josiah, Jr. & Martha, b. Jan. 28, 1745/6	3	113
Elihu, of New Haven, m. Elisabeth **BALDWIN**, of Branford,		
Nov. 23, 1768, by Jon[a]th[an] Merrick	3	198
Eliphalet, s. Thomas & Rebecca, b. June 2, 1764	3	196
Eliphalet, m. Irene **PALMER**, b. of Branford, Jan. 18, 1795,		
by Sam[ue]l Eells	3	271
Eliza, [d. Hobart & B[e]ula[h], b. July 16, 1800	3	274
Eliza, [d. Isaac, Jr. & Sally], b. Aug. 10, 1816	3	363
Elisabeth, d. John & Lydia, b. Sept. 24, 1720	3	46
Elisabeth, m. Abiel **FRISBE[E]**, July 25, 1722, by Rev.		
Sam[ue]ll Russel[l]	3	49
Elisabeth, d. Noah & Elisabeth, b. Nov. 9, 1727	3	64
Elisabeth, wid., d. Dec. 9, 1732	3	74
Elisabeth, m. Demetrius **COOK**, b. of Branford, Apr. 26,		
1739, by Rev. Philemon Robbins	3	123
Elizabeth, w. of Noah, d. Aug. 25, 1755	3	147
Elisabeth, d. Nehemiah & Rachel, b. Feb. 24, 1766	3	190
Elisabeth, d. Elihue & Elisabeth, b. Jan. 7, 1782	3	270
Elizur, s. Abraham, Sr. & Fanny, b. Nov. 2, 1816	3	405
Elizur, m. Sally **FOOT**, b. of Branford, Apr. 20, 1843,		

	Vol.	Page
ROGERS, (cont.)		
by Rev. Timothy P. Gillett	TM3	156
Elsee, d. Ebenezer & Lucy, b. Sept. 13, 1780	3	269
Els[e]y, d. Josiah & Nancy, b. May 13, 1788	3	261
Emily, [d. Isaac, Jr. & Sally], b. Aug. 20, 1820	3	363
Emily, of Branford, m. Lyman **HARRISON**, of North		
Branford, Apr. 15, 1840, by Rev. T. P. Gillett	3	379
Ephraim, s. Dan[ie]ll & Lydia, b. Oct. 23, 1752	3	127
Ephraim, s. Daniel & Lidiah, b. Oct. 23, 1752	3	151
Ephraim, [s. John & Anna], d. Jan. 15, 1804	3	385
Esther, m. Elihu **COOK**, b. of Branford, Mar. 8, 1789, by		
Rev. Jason Atwater	3	272
Esther P., d. Eliphalet & Irene, b. Feb. 25, 1798	3	271
Ethan, s. Levi & J[o]hannah, b. Oct. 21, 1759	3	169
Ethan, [s. Heman & Eunice], b. Feb. 6, 1794	3	281
Ethan, [s. Heman & Eunice], d. Nov. 3, 1803	3	281
Eunice, d. David & Eunice, b. Apr. 9, 1749	3	184
Eunice, m. Jonathan **LINSL[E]Y**, Jr., b. of Branford, Dec.		
8, 1767, by Josiah Rogers, J. P.	3	192
Eunice, d. Gideon & Eunice, b. Aug. 13, 1772	3	206
Eunice, w. of Edm[un]d, d. May 16, 1783	3	302
Eunice, [d. Heman & Eunice], b. Nov. 23, 1798	3	281
Eunice, w. of Heman, d. Nov. 24, 1808	3	281
Ezekiel, m. Sarah **BARN[E]S**, b. of Branford, Nov. 23,		
1731, by Jno, Russell, J. P.	3	72
Fanny Minerva, [d. Jairus & Fanny], b. Aug. 14, 1816	3	360
Frank, s. Elizur & Sally, b. May 6, 1848	TM3	240
Frank Abraham, s. Elizur & Sally, b. May 6, 1848	TM3	241
Frederic, [s. Samuel & Jerusha], b. Feb. 26, 1802	3	284
Frederick, [s. Isaac, Jr. & Sally], b. Jan. 28, 1827	3	363
Freelove, of New Haven, m. John **FRISBIE**, Jr., of Branford,		
July 31, 1760, by Josiah Rogers, J. P.	3	172
George, [s. Chauncey & Maria], b. Sept. 16, 1818	3	364
George, m. Laura **NORTON**, b. of Branford, Oct. 14, 1844,		
by Rev. E. Edwin Hall	TM3	157
Gideon, s. Josiah, Jr. & Martha, b. Nov. 11, 1738	3	100
Giles, s. Ebenezer & Ruth, b. Dec. 24, 1796	3	270
Grace, d. Edm[un]d & Lydia, b. Jan. 28, 1779	3	302
Hannah, d. John & Lydia, b. July 10, 1718	3	43
Hannah, d. John & Lydia, d. Nov. 20, 1721	3	46
Hannah, d. Noah & Elisabeth, b. May 8, 1737	3	87
Hannah, d. Levi & J[o]hanna, b. Aug. 9,. 1750	3	169
Hannah, d. Sam[ue]ll & Hannah, b. Oct. 15, 1752	3	131
Hannah, d. Eli & Hannah, b. Jan. 23, 1766	3	189
Hannah, w. of Eli, d. Feb. 2, 1766, in the 19th y. of her age	3	189
Hannah, m. Asher **SHELDON**, Jr., b. of Branford, Mar. 25,		
1778, by Philemon Robbins	3	268
Hannah, d. Abr[aha]m & Hannah, b. Aug. 13, 1779	3	301

	Vol.	Page
ROGERS, (cont.)		
Hannah, w. of Dea. Samuel, d. May 18, 1782	3	271
Hannah, w. of Abraham, d. Apr. 11, 1826, ae 76 y.	3	342
Harriet, [d. Isaac, Jr. & Sally], b. Nov. 16, 1833	3	363
Harriet Louisa, d. [Henry & Nancy], b. Mar. 24, 1837,		
in Wallingford	TM3	234
Heman, s. Levi & J[o]hanna, b. June 22, 1757	3	169
Heman, m. Lydia **PALMER**, b. of Branford, Feb. 15, 1784,		
by Sam[ue]ll Eells	3	275
Heman, m. Eunice **WHEDON**, Mar. 29, 1787	3	281
Heman, m. Hannah **BALDWIN**, b. of Branford, July 23, 1826,		
by Rev. Timothy P. Gillett	3	342
Henry, [s. Jairus & Fanny], b. Dec. 24, 1806	3	360
Henry, s. Abraham, Jr. & Fanny, b. July 31, 1821	3	414
Henry, m. Nancy **TOWNER**, b. of Branford, Dec. [ ], 1832,		
by Edw[ar]d J. Ives	3	361
Henry, m. Elizabeth **TOWNSEND**, May 16, 1849, by Rev.		
Franklin A. Spencer, of Westmoreland, N. Y.	TM3	246
Henry Franklin, s. Henry & Nancy, d. Apr. 17, 1837, in		
Wallingford	TM3	306
Henry Franklin, [s. Henry & Nancy], b. Apr. 18, 1835,		
in Wallingford	TM3	234
Hervey, [s. Samuel & Jerusha], b. June 21, 1809	3	284
Hiram, s. Eliphalet & Irene, b. Oct. 23, 1795	3	271
Hobart, s. Thomas & Rebecca, b. Apr. 12, 1773	3	208
Hobart, m. B[e]ula[h] **WARNER**, July 25, 1799	3	274
Homer Lewis, s. [Henry & Nancy], b. Feb. 13, 1839	TM3	234
Irene, d. Thomas & Rebecca, b. Nov. 28, 1766	3	196
Irene, d. Thomas, Jr. & Molly, b. Dec. 20, 1790	3	261
Iritte, d. Levi, Jr. & Elisabeth, b. Dec. 18, 1785	3	314
Isaac, m. Mary **HOWD**, b. of Branford, Apr. 8, 1773, by		
Sam[ue]ll Eells	3	302
Isaac, s. Isaac & Mary, b. July 13, 1782	3	303
Isaac, s. Ebenez[e]r & Ruth, b. Oct. 13, 1792	3	268
Isaac, Jr., of Branford, m. Sally **FRANKLIN**, of Sag Harbor,		
L. I., Nov. 30, 1813, by Rev. Timothy P. Gillett	3	363
Isaac, [s. Isaac, Jr. & Sally], b. Dec. 12, 1817	3	363
Jacob, s. John, Jr. & Thankfull, b. Sept. 27, 1752	3	132
Jacob, m. Dolle **BARKER**, b. of Branford, June 1, 178[ ],		
by Sam[ue]ll Eells	3	301
Jacob, s. Jacob & Dolly, b. Mar. 25, 1785	3	312
Jairus, s. Isaac & Mary, b. Feb. 17, 1777	3	303
James, s. Edm[un]d & Lydia, b. Feb. 7, 1776	3	302
James, s. Edmund & Lydia, d. Oct. 27, 1795, at Philadelphia	3	269
James, [s. Chauncey & Maria], b. Dec. 31, 1823	3	364
James, s. Benjamin & Betsey S., b. Aug. 28, 1831	3	360
James Harrison, [s. Wyllys & Martha], b. Oct. 20, 1822,		
in New Haven	3	408

	Vol.	Page
ROGERS, (cont.)		
Jane, [d. Isaac, Jr. & Sally], b Jan. 10, 1824	3	363
Jane, of Branford, m. Henry **TRION**, of Middletown, May 1,		
1843, by Rev. Timothy P. Gillett	TM3	156
Jared, s. Stephen & Jerusha, b. Dec. 10, 1777	3	282
Jason, [twin with Joel], s. Joseph & Susanna, b. Dec. 2, 1748	3	157
Jemima, d. David & Eunice, b. Dec. 31, 1761	3	184
Jeremy, s. Eli & Hannah, b. Nov. 13, 1775	3	310
Jerusha, d. Stephen & Jerusha, b. Feb. 28, 1770	3	202
Jerusha, d. Levi, Jr. & Elisabeth, b. Jan. 12, 1777	3	289
Jerusha, d. Dec. 30, 1819, in the 83rd y. of her age	3	430
Joel, [twin with Jason], s. Joseph & Susanna, b. Dec. 2, 1748	3	157
John, s. Noah, b. Nov. 8, 1677	1	210
John, m. Lydia **FRISBEE**, June 17, 1713, by Nathan[ie]ll		
Harrison, J. P.	3	38
John, s. John & Lydia, b. Oct. 14, 1722	3	50
John, Jr., m. Thankfull **HARRISON**, b. of Branford, Dec.		
29, 1743, by Rev. Philemon Robbins	3	119
John, s. John, Jr. & Thankful, b. Nov. 13, 1744	3	119
John, d. Feb. 9, 1764, in the 88th y. of his age	3	181
John, Jr., m. Sarah **BARKER**, b. of Branford, July 12, 1765	3	304
John, s. John, Jr. & Sarah, b. Dec. 22, 1768	3	304
John, d. July 21, 1809	3	285
John, [s. Jairus & Fanny], b. Sept. 17, 1822	3	360
Jonah Westover, s. David & Eunice, b. Nov. 15, 1766	3	190
Jonathan, s. Josiah & Lydia, b. Dec. 12, 1715	3	37
Jonathan, m. Mary **FOOT**, b. of Branford, Dec. 6, 1738,		
by Jonathan Mer[r]ick	3	93
Jonathan, s. John, Jr. & Sarah, b. Feb. 9, 1780	3	304
Jonathan, m. Orphana **ROGERS**, Sept. 15, 1799	3	274
Joseph, s. John & Lydia, b. Apr. 29, 1725	3	57
Joseph, of Branford, m. Susanna **PARDEE**, of New Haven,		
Aug. 23, 1748, by Rev. Isaac Stiles, of New Haven	3	157
Joseph, s. Joseph & Susanna, b. Apr. 27, 1755	3	157
Josiah, s. Noah, b. Jan. 31, 1679	1	210
Josiah, Jr., m. Martha **FRISBIE**, b. of Branford, Apr. 24,		
1728, by Rev. Jonathan Merrick	3	73
Josiah, s. Josiah, Jr. & Martha, b. Sept. 16, 1733	3	85
Josiah, Ensign, d. Dec. 29, 1757	3	168
Josiah, s. Thomas & Rebecca, b. Nov. 22, 1761	3	196
Josiah, s. Gideon & Eunice, b. Aug. 3, 1766	3	194
Josiah, d. Oct. 5, 1783, in the 76th y. of his age	3	258
Josiah, s. Ebenez[e]r & Ruth, b. Feb. 24, 1795	3	268
Jo[s]iah, m. Nancy **HUFFMAN**, b. of Branford, July 25,		
[17--], by Sam[ue]l Eells	3	261
Julia, [d. Heman & Eunice], b. July 11, 1802	3	281
Julia, of Branford, m. William **FOSTER**, of Meriden, Apr.		
25, 1826, by Rev. Timothy P. Gillett	3	341

	Vol.	Page
ROGERS, (cont.)		
Justus, s. Jacob & Dolle, b. Feb. 7, 1782	3	301
Justus, s. Samuel & Jerusha, b. Feb. 10, 1812	3	399
Levi, m. J[o]hannah **TRU[E]SDELL**, b. of Branford, Dec.		
14, 1743, by Jacob Hemingway	3	169
Levi, s. Levi & J[o]hanna, b. June 19, 1755	3	169
Levi, Jr., m. Elisabeth **PALMER**, b. of Branford, July 6,		
1776, by Sam[ue]ll Eells	3	289
Levi, s. Josiah & Lydia, b. Feb. [ ]	3	43
Lovisa, [d. Isaac, Jr. & Sally], b. Feb. 17, 1815	3	363
Lucrece, d. Levi, Jr. & Elisabeth, b. Oct. 11, 1778	3	289
Lucey, d. Ebenezer & Lucy, b. Apr. 26, 1776	3	261
Lucy, w. of Capt. Ebenezer, d. Oct. 13, 1786, in the		
42nd y. of her age	3	258
Lydia, d. Josiah & Lydia, b. Feb. 28, 1713/14	3	37
Lydia, d. John & Lydia, b. May 12, 1714	3	37
Lydia, m. John **HOADL[E]Y**, b. of Branford, Feb. 17, 1730,		
by Jno Russell, J. P.	3	117
Lydia, m. John **HARRINGTON**, b. of Branford, Mar. 20,		
1732, by Rev. Jacob Heminway	3	96
Lydia, d. Jon[a]th[an] & Mary, b. June 1, 1747	3	113
Lydia, d. David & Eunice, b. Jan. 24, 1751	3	184
Lidia, w. of John, d. June 30, 1751	3	147
Lydia, d.Edm[un]d & Lydia, b. June 4, 1763	3	302
Lydia, m. Roswell **POND**, b. of Branford, Nov. 22, 1764,		
by Philemon Robbins	3	188
Lydia, d. Daniel & Lydia, b. Nov. 29, 1765	3	195
Lydia, d. Stephen & Jerusha, b. Apr. 18, 1768	3	202
Lydia, d. Stephen & Jerusha, d. Oct. 14, 1773	3	283
Lydia, w. of Edm[un]d, d. Mar. 20, 1782	3	302
Lydia, d. Heman & Lydia, b. May 11, 1784	3	310
Lydia, w. of Heman, d. May 20, 1784	3	310
Lydia, d. Noahiah & Rebeccah, b. Oct. 21, 1797	3	274
Lydia, [d. John & Anna], d. Jan. 20, 1800	3	385
Lydia, w. of Daniel, d. Dec. 20, 1800	3	275
Lydia, of Branford, m. Fitch H. **CURTISS**, of Salem, Penn.,		
[Oct] 29, [1820], by Origen P. Holcomb	3	412
Lydia, d. Oct. 6, 1827, in the 62nd y. of her age	3	346
Lydia Beach, d. Ebeneze r & Lucy, b. June 19, 1773	3	258
Major, [s. Wyllys & Martha], b. Apr. 7, 1817	3	408
Malachi, s. Joseph & Susanna, b. Nov. 28, 1763	3	183
Maria Louisa, [d. Chauncey & Maria], b. Nov. 30, 1833	3	364
Martha, d. Ezekiel & Sarah, b. Nov. 27, 1738	3	93
Martha, d. Josiah, Jr. & Martha, b. June 6, 1741	3	100
Martha, d. Samuel & Hannah, b. Oct. 25, 1765	3	187
Martha, w. of Josiah, d. Dec. 17, 1791	3	268
Martha, d. Benj[ami]n & Eliza, b. Sept. 28, 1849	TM3	242
Martha Frisbie, d. Eben[eze]r & Lucy, b. Jan. 19, 1775	3	259

	Vol.	Page
ROGERS, (cont.)		
Mary, d. Noah, b. Apr. 14, 1675	1	210
Mary, d. John & Lydia, b. Mar. 30, 1715; d. Jan. 30, 1717/8	3	41
Mary, d. Jon[a]th[an] & Mary, b. Aug. 13, 1743	3	113
Mary, d. Josiah, Jr. & Martha, b. Oct. 13, 1743	3	113
Mary, d. Josiah, d. Dec. 8, 1749	3	168
Mary, d. Sam[ue]ll & Hannah, b. May 5, 1762	3	177
Mary, d. Gideon & Eunice, b. Sept. 23, 1770	3	206
Mary, d. Isaac & Mary, b. Nov. 4, 1773; d. Dec. 4, 1773	3	302
Mary, d. Isaac & Mary, b. June 3, 1776	3	302
Mary, d. Eli & Hannah, b. July 8, 1782	3	310
Mary, w. of John, d. Dec. 20, 1798	3	285
Mary, [d. Jairus & Fanny], b. July 26, 1812	3	360
Mary, d. Benjamin & Betsey S., b. Jan. 25, 1829	3	350
Mary, d. Benjamin & Betsey S., d. Mar. 11, 1831	3	356
Mary Ann, [d. Chauncey & Maria], b. Aug. 7, 1828	3	364
Mary Ann, m. Frederick **HOLCOMB**, Sept. 20, 1827, by Rev. David Baldwin	3	346
Mason, s. Elisur & Sally, b. Apr. 25, 1844	TM3	231
Matilda, [d. Noadiah], b. Apr. 11, 1808	3	386
Matilda, of Branford, m. [ ] **WALKER**, of Guilford, June 27, 1832, by Edw[ar]d J. Ives	3	361
Mercy, d. David & Eunice, b. Mar. 13, 1753	3	135
Mercy, d. David & Eunice, b. Mar. 13, 1753	3	184
Minor, [s. Wyllys & Martha], b. Sept. 1, 1813	3	408
Ned, s. Stephen & Jerusha, b. Apr. 14, 1772	3	282
Ned, s. Noadiah & Rebeccah, b. Nov. 29, 1800	3	274
Nehemiah, m. Rachel **AUGUR**, b. of Branford, Mar. 1, 1763, by Jon[a]th[an] Mer[r]ick	3	190
Nelson, [s. Jairus & Fanny], b. July 25, 1808	3	360
Nic[h]olas, s. Thomas, Jr. & Molly, b. July 9, 1786	3	260
Niobe, [child of Isaac, Jr. & Sally], b. July 5, 1829	3	363
Noahdiah, s. Stephen & Jerusha, b. Mar. 8, 1761	3	181
Noadiah, m. Rebecca **TYLER**, b. of Branford, Oct. 16, 1793, by Rev. David Butler	3	261
Noah, m. Elisabeth **TAINTOR**, Apr. 8, 1673	1	174
Noah, m. Elisabeth **WHEELER**, b. of Branford, Nov. 28, 1722, by Nath[anie]ll Harrison, J. P.	3	51
Noah, Sr., d. Oct. 8, 1725	3	57
Noah, s. Noah & Elisabeth, b. May 8, 1732	3	74
Noah, Jr., m. Sarah **PALMERLY**, b. of Branford, Oct. 23, 1755, by Philemon Robbins	3	141
Noah, 3rd, s. Noah, 2d, & Sarah, b. Aug. 14, 1756; d. Aug. 16, 1756	3	147
Noah, d. Apr. 28, 1760, in the 72nd y. of his age	3	165
Noah, s. Levi & Joanna, b. June 15, 1767	3	192
Noah, s. Noadiah & Rebecca, b. Sept. 27, 1794	3	263
Olive, d. Capt. Ebenezer & Ruth, b. Sept. 28, 1790	3	258

	Vol.	Page
ROGERS, (cont.)		
Orphana, d. Edm[un]d & Lydia, b. Mar. 20, 1782	3	302
Orphana, m. Jonathan **ROGERS**, Sept. 15, 1799	3	274
Parne, d. Isaac & Mary, b. Nov. 3, 1783	3	303
Parna, m. David **BARKER**, Mar. 9, 1808	3	339
Peter, s. John, Jr. & Sarah, b. Feb. 2, 1772	3	304
Peter, s. Jacob & Dolly, b. Nov. 24, 1797	3	255
Phebe, d. Daniel & Lidia, b. May 1, 1754	3	140
Phebe, m. Oliver **LANFAIR**, Jr., b. of Branford, June 28,		
1777, by Philemon Robbins	3	266
Philemon, s. David & Eunice, b. Oct. 12, 1755	3	184
Polly, d. Edm[un]d & Lydia, b. Nov. 4, 1768	3	302
Polley, d. Josiah & Nancy, b. Jan. 30, 1790	3	261
Polly, m. Orchard **GOULD**, Nov. 28, 1790	3	268
Polly, [d. Heman & Eunice], b. Sept. 6, 1791	3	281
Polly, [d. Heman & Eunice], d. Sept. 26, 1793	3	281
Polly Menta, [d. Heman & Eunice], b. Dec. 26, 1795	3	281
Rebec[c]ah, d. Noah & Elisabeth, b. Jan. 20, 1729/30	3	68
Rebeccah, d. Josiah, Jr. & Martha, b. June 10, 1731	3	73
Rebecca, w. of Thomas, d. Sept. 10, 1751	3	195
Rebeckah, m. Nathan **BUTLER**, b. of Branford, Dec. 8, 1755,		
by Warham Williams	3	140
Rebecca, d. of Noah, m. Isaac **HARRISON**, b. of Branford,		
Aug. 26, 1756, by Rev. P. Robbins	3	143
Rebecca, d. John, Jr. & Sarah, b. Oct. 21, 1765;		
d. Sept. 13, 1775	3	304
Rebecca, d. Isaac & Mary, b. Jan. 13, 1779	3	303
Rebecca, d. Noadiah & Rebecca, b. Mar. 25, 1796	3	269
Rebecca, m. John **GOULD**, Nov. 1, 1800	3	281
Rebecca, w. of Thomas, d. May 7, 1801	3	273
Reuel, s. Levi, Jr. & Elisabeth, b. Dec. 25, 1782	3	289
Rufus, s. Thomas & Rebecca, b. Aug. 3, 1756	3	196
Rufus, s. Thomas, Jr. & Molly, b. Sept. 1, 1784	3	260
Rufus, s. Josiah & Nancy, b. Sept. 4, 1794	3	264
Ruth, d. Josiah, Jr. & Martha, b. Oct. 18, 1728	3	73
Ruth, m. Amos **SEAWARD**, b. of Branford, Jan. 16, 1750/1,		
by Warham Williams	3	168
Ruth, d. Levi & J[o]hanna, b. Aug. 31, 1752	3	169
Ruth, d. Samuel & Hannah, b. Mar. 17, 1770	3	199
Ruth, d. Capt. Ebenezer & Ruth, b. Nov. 31 (sic), 1788	3	258
Salley, d. Edm[un]d & Lydia, b. June 13, 1773	3	302
Sally, [d, Heman & Eunice], b. Sept. 28, 1787	3	281
Sally, m. Jared **WHITNEY**, b. of Branford, Sept. 14, 1790	3	389
Sally, d. John & Mary, b. Feb. 14, 1794	3	386
Sam[ue]ll, s. John & Lydia, b. Oct. 5, 1729	3	67
Sam[ue]ll, m. Hannah **HARRISON**, b. of Branford, Dec. 5,		
1751, by Nathan[ie]ll Harrison, J. P.	3	131
Samuel, s. Samuel & Hannah, b. Aug. 21, 1755	3	140

	Vol.	Page
ROGERS, (cont.)		
Sam[ue]ll, s. Sam[ue]ll & Hannah, b. Mar. 3, 1760	3	161
Samuel, s. Nehemiah & Rachel, b. June 17, 1764	3	190
Sam[ue]ll, Jr., of Branford, m. Jerusha **HOBART**, of Guilford,		
Jan. 7, 1789, by Thom[a]s Wells Bray	3	253
Samuel, s. Samuel & Jerusha, b. Apr. 7, 1795	3	269
Samuel, Dea., d. Apr. 30, 1795	3	269
Samuel, [s. Samuel & Jerusha], d. June 24, 1797	3	284
Samuel, [s. Samuel & Jerusha], b. Oct. 13, 1798	3	284
Samuel Augu[s]tus, s. Josiah & Nancy, b. Mar. 1, 1792	3	261
Samuel Augustus, m. Esther Jerusha **PAGE**, Sept. 28, 1820,		
by Charles Atwater	3	412
Sarah, w. of Noah, Jr., d. Jan. 7, 1757	3	147
Sarah, d. Samuel & Hannah, b. Nov. 16, 1757	3	152
Sarah, m. Joseph **FRISBIE**, b. of Branford, June 24, 1773,		
by Sam[ue]ll Eells	3	280
Sarah, d. Abraham & Hannah, b. Apr. 26, 1776	3	301
Sarah, d. Ebenezer & Lucy, b. Mar. 28, 1778	3	265
Sarah, m. Josiah **FRISBIE**, b. of Branford, Apr. 12, 1781,		
by Philemon Robbins	3	272
Sherman, [s. Samuel & Jerusha], b. Apr. 10, 1806	3	284
Simeon, s. Levi & Johanna, b. Aug. 17, 1762	3	177
Solomon, s. Elihu & Elisabeth, b. July 11, 1778	3	265
Staty, d. Josiah & Nancy, b. May 27, 1786	3	261
Stephen, m. Jerusha **HOADL[E]Y,,** b. of Branford, Oct. 16,		
1760, by Philemon Robbins	3	181
Stephen, s. Stephen & Jerusha, b. Dec. 21, 1763	3	181
Stephen, d. Nov. 9, 1791, in the 60th y. of his age	3	260
Stephen, s. Noadiah & Rebeccah, b. Mar. 29, 1799	3	274
Stephen, [s. Noadiah], d. May 4, 1803	3	386
Stephen, [s. Noadiah], b. June 12, 1806	3	386
Silvia, d. Abraham & Hannah, b. May 25, 1773 (Sylvia)	3	301
Silvestus, s. Samuel & Jerusha, b. Nov. 19, 1792;		
d. July 2, 1793	3	269
Temperance, d. Noah, Jr. & Elisabeth, b. Sept. 9, 1725	3	57
Thankful, d. John, Jr. & Thankful, b. Sept. 23, 1760	3	166
Thankfull, d. Eli & Hannah, b. Feb. 22, 1762; d. July 3, 1783	3	310
Thankfull, m. Stewart **GAYLOR**, Dec. [ ], 1780	3	301
Thankfull, w. of John, d. Feb. 28, 1792, ae 71 y. 9 m. 29 d.	3	259
Thirza, d. Jacob & Dolle, b. Aug. 20, 1788	3	254
Thomas, of Branford, m. Rebecca **GILDERSLE[E]VE**, of		
Huntington, L. I., Feb. 2, 1747/8, by Jonathan Mer[r]ick	3	195
Thomas, m. Rebecca **HOBART**, b. of Branford, Oct. 12, 1752,		
by Philemon Robbins	3	196
Thomas, s. Thomas & Rebecca, b. Feb. 24, 1759	3	196
Thomas had negro Peg, b. Oct. 13, 1771	3	256
Thomas, Jr., m. Molly **MULFORD**, b. of Branford, Aug. 5,		
1784, by Sam[ue]l Eells	3	260

	Vol.	Page
ROGERS, (cont.)		
Thomas had negro Dick, b. Jan. 2, 1788 and negro Titis,		
b. July 10, 1792	3	256
Tryphene, d. Levi, Jr. & Elisabeth, b. Mar. 26, 1781	3	289
Violete, d. Capt. Ebenezer & Lucy, b. Nov. 17, 1782	3	258
William, Jr., m. Abigail **BARTHOLOMEW**, , b. of Branford,		
Nov. 14, 1729, by Rev. Jonathan Merrick	3	68
William, s. Noadiah & Rebecca, b. Oct. 18, 1812;		
d. Feb. 18, 1814	3	430
William, m. Grace **BARKER**, b. of Branford, Jan. 20, 1820	3	335
William, [s. Chauncey & Maria], b. Feb. 3, 1826	3	364
William, [s. Chauncey & Maria], d. May 9, 1826	3	364
William Frisbie, s. [William & Grace], b. Jan. 27, 1824	3	335
William Hubbard, [s. Wyllys & Martha], b. Dec. 29, 1811	3	408
William Y., of Branford, m. Elisabeth A. **PRINDLE**, of		
Newburyport, Mass., Sept. 15, 1846, by Rev. A. C. Wheat	TM3	159
Wyllys, s. Samuel & Jerusha, b Nov 18, 1790	3	269
Wyllys, m. Martha **HOADLEY**, May 30, 1811	3	408
----, s. Noah & Elisabeth, b. Feb. 21, 1733/4; d. Mar. 4, 1733/4	3	78
----, s. Thomas & Rebecca, b. Mar. 14, 1749;		
d. tenth day after birth	3	195
ROOT, Ellena, d. James & Serenna, b. Feb. 14, 1851	TM3	245
ROSE, Abigail, d. Jonathan & Abigail, b. July 15, 1708	3	34
Abigail, d. Timothy & Mehetabel, b. Mar. 12, 1736/7	3	103
Abigail, d. Sam[ue]ll, 2d, & Mary, b. June 9, 1744	3	196
Abigail, m. Rufus **PALMER**, b. of Branford, Dec. 26, 1770,		
by Sam[ue]ll Eells	3	207
Abigail, d. Justus & Lydia, b. Sept. 9, 1772	3	208
Abigail, d. Justus & Lydia, b. Sept. 9, 1772	3	298
Alfred, s. Nathan & Lois, b. Nov. 5, 1790	3	282
Alfred, of Branford, m. Sally **CLARKE**, of North Haven,		
Jan. 1, 1812	3	400
Alfred, m. Polly **PALMER**, June 27, 1835, by Rev. Smith		
Dayton	3	369
Amaziah, s. Sam[ue]ll, 3rd, & Naomi, b. Dec. 29, 1757	3	153
Amaziah, m. Lucy **MUNSON**, Apr. 17, 1782	3	266
Amaziah, m. Abigail **MUNSON**, Dec. 23, 1795	3	266
Amaziah, d. Oct. 3, 1820	3	415
Amie, d. Timothy & Mehetabel, b. June 25, 1731	3	103
Anne, d. Jacob & Anne, b. Sept. 20, 1735	3	92
Anne, w. of Jacob, d. Sept. 1, 1767, in the 63rd y. of her age	3	192
Belah, s. John, Jr. & Elisabeth, b. Apr. 12, 1747	3	164
Belah, s. John, Jr. & Elisabeth, d. Sept. 16, 1759	3	164
Belah, s. John, 2d, & Elisabeth, b. Jan. 31, 1765	3	199
Benjamin, s. Nathan & Thankful,, d. Feb. 9, 1758	3	175
Benj[ami]n, s. Nathan & Thankful, b. [ ]	3	174
Bethiah, d. John & Hannah, b. Oct. 2, 1705	2	346
Bethiah, m. Sam[ue]ll **PENFIELD**, b. of Branford, Dec. 1,		

	Vol.	Page
ROSE, (cont.)		
1727, by Rev. Sam[ue]ll Russell	3	63
Bets[e]y, d. Justus & Lydia, b. Apr. 5, 1776	3	298
Bille, s. Jacob & Anne, b. Jan. 13, 1739/40	3	93
Bille, m. wid. Abigail **BALDWIN**, b. of Branford, Apr. 15,		
1778, by Samuel Eells	3	264
Bille, s. Amaziah & Lucy, b. Dec. 9, 1783; d. Dec. 18, 1783	3	266
Bille, d. Jan. 15, 1786, ae 46 y. 2 d.	3	313
C[h]loe, d. Jacob & Anne, b. Nov. 14, 1736	3	92
Damas, [twin with Lucretia], d. Capt. Reubin & Lucretia,		
b. May 10, 1780	3	303
Daniel, s. John, b. Mar. 11, 1682/3	1	211
Daniel, s. Jonathan & Abigail, b. Nov. 27, 1705	3	34
Daniel, s. Sam[ue]ll & Lydia, b. Mar. 25, 1722;		
d. Feb. 14, 1723/4	3	48
Daniel, s. Sam[ue]ll & Lydia, b. Feb. 10, 1731/2	3	73
Daniel, s. David & Hannah, b. July 21, 1743	3	101
Daniel, s. Samuel, 2d, & Naomi, b. Jan. 31, 1772	3	205
David, s. Jonathan & Abigail, b. Dec. 6, 1700	2	345
David, m. Hannah **BARKER**, b. of Branford, Nov. 23, 1726,		
by Rev. Sam[ue]ll Russell	3	68
David, s. David & Hannah, b. Dec. 11, 1736	3	90
David, s. Solomon & Thankful, b. Apr. 24, 1770	3	200
Deborah, d. John, b. June 6, 1671	1	174
Delight, of Northford, m. Erastus **PAGE**, of Branford,		
Nov. 27, 1827, by Rev. Timothy P. Gillett	3	346
Dorcas, d. Robert, m. Daniell **SWAINE**, s. William,		
July 26, 1653	1	170
Dorcas, d. Nathan, Jr. & Lois, b. Feb. 13, 1782	3	270
Dorcas, of Branford, m. Russell **CURTISS**, of East Haven,		
June 15, 1818	3	428
Eliada, s. Solomon & Thankful, b. Mar. 28, 1766	3	200
Eliada, m. Lavinia **MONRO[E]**, b. of Branford, Dec. 19, 1792	3	270
Eliada, m. Eunice **HARRISON**, b. of Branford, Oct. 19, 1796	3	270
Eliza, m. Henry Carter, **BALDWIN**, b. of Branford, Nov. 25,		
1829, by Timothy P. Gillett	3	351
Elisabeth, d. John, b. Apr. 28, 1668	1	173
Elisabeth, d. Sam[ue]ll & Lydia, b. Sept. 14, 1719	3	43
Elisabeth, w. of Dea. John, d. Jan. 21, 1720 or 1719/20	3	51
Elizabeth, d. John & Elizabeth, b. Jan. 28, 1747	3	114
Elisabeth, of Branford, m. Sam[ue]ll **ALLEN**, of Stratford,		
Jan. 23, 1748/9, by Rev. P. Robbins	3	120
Elisabeth, d. John, Jr. & Elisabeth, b. Apr. 21, 1753	3	164
Elisabeth, m. Allin **SMITH**, b. of Branford, Aug. 23, 1775,		
by Philemon Robbins	3	295
Eunice, d. Jonathan, Jr. & Abigail, b. July 13, 1727	3	71
Fanne, d. Capt. Reubin & Lucretia, b. June 11, 1782	3	303
Fanny A., m. George **BONNELL**, Sept. 16, [1829], by J. A.		

ROSE, (cont.)	Vol.	Page
Root	3	350
Hannah, d. Jno., b. Mar. 15, 1676/7	1	211
Hannah, m. Sam[ue]ll **HARRINGTON**, Jan. 5, 1703/4, by		
W[illia]m Maltbie, J. P.	2	345
Hannah, d. John & Hannah, b. Mar. 25, 1705	3	31
Hannah, d. Sam[ue]ll & Lydia, b. Jan. 24, 1729/30	3	68
Hannah, d. John & Elizabeth, b. Feb. 5, 1742	3	114
Hannah, d. Nathan & Thankful, b. May 11, 1744	3	174
Hannah, d. Sam[ue]ll, 3rd, & Noami, b. Sept. 24, 1762	3	178
Hannah, m. Samuel **LINSL[E]Y**, Jr., b. of Branford, Sept.		
7, 1767, by Jonathan Mer[r]ick	3	205
Hannah, m. Timothy **GOODRICH**, b. of Branford, Jan. 6,		
1779, by Rev. Philemon Robbins	3	284
Hannah, m. Jonathan **ROSE**, Apr. 1, 1787	3	267
Henrietta, m. James **FRISBIE**, Sept. 9, 1824, by Timothy		
P. Gillett	3	335
Henrietta Noami, d. Jonathan & Hannah, b. July 24, 1793;		
d. Mar. 6, 1796	3	267
Ira, s. Amaziah & Lucy, b. May 17, 1786	3	266
Irene, d. Nathan, Jr. & Lois, b. Apr. 29, 1785	3	254
Isaac, s. Jon[a]th[a]n, Jr. & Abigail, b. Oct. 7, 1735	3	83
Jacob, s. Jonathan & Abigail, b. Mar. 20, 1702/3	2	345
Jacob, of Branford, m. Ann **DUDLEY**, of Guilford, Dec. 27,		
1733, by Rev. Thomas Ruggles	3	86
Jerusha, d. Timothy & Mehetabel, b. July 24, 1750	3	126
Jerusha, d. Sam[ue]ll, 2d, & Patience, b. Oct. 24, 1758	3	197
Joanna, wid., m. Ebenezer **FRISBEE**, Sept. 13, 1715, by		
Rev. Sam[ue]ll Russel[l]	3	49
Joanna, d. Timothy & Mehetabel, b. Jan. 31, 1739/40	3	103
Joel, s. David & Hannah, b. Dec. 13, 1739	3	93
Joel, m. Phebe **BALDWIN**, b. of Branford, Jan. 7, 1773,		
by Samuel Eells	3	208
John, s. John, b. Oct. 28, 1679	1	211
John, Jr., of Branford, m. Hannah **WILLIAMS**, of Kelinworth,		
Dec. 9, 1702	2	344
John, s. John & Hannah, b. Sept. 8, 1707	3	31
John, d. Apr. 17, 1712	3	35
John, s. Sam[ue]ll & Lydia, b. June 25, 1717	3	40
John, Dea., d. Dec. 27, 1722	3	51
John, s. John & Elizabeth, b. Jan. 22, 1740	3	114
John, Jr., m. Elisabeth **COACH**, b. of Branford, Sept. 10,		
1745, by John Russell, J. P.	3	164
John, s. John, Jr. & Elisabeth, b. Jan. 4, 1745/6	3	164
John Me[i]gs, s. Capt. Reubin & Leucretia, b. July 6, 1775	3	303
Jonathan, m. Abigail **FFOOT**, Aug. 15, 1697	2	345
Jonathan, s. Jonathan & Abigail, b. Aug. 15, 1698	2	345
Jonathan, Jr., m. Abigail **BARKER**, b. of Branford, Nov.		
23, 1724, by Rev. Sam[ue]ll Russell	3	71

	Vol.	Page
ROSE, (cont.)		
Jonathan, s. Jonathan, Jr. & Abigail, b. Apr. 4, 1730	3	72
Jonathan, s. Sam[ue]ll, 2d, & Patience, b. July 3, 1756	3	197
Jonathan, s. Justus & Lydia, b. Aug. 30, 1781	3	298
Jonathan, m. Hannah **ROSE**, Apr. 1, 1787	3	267
Jonathan, [s.] Charles, m. [ ]	1	174
Joseph, s. Nathan & Thankful, b. Mar. 18, 1741; d. Feb.		
3, 1746	3	174
Joseph, s. Nathan & Thankful, b. Aug. [ ], 1760;		
d. "When but 6 days old"	3	175
Joseph Lester, s. Alfred & Sally, b. Mar. 1, 1813	3	400
Justus, s. Jonathan, Jr. & Abigail, b. Oct. 15, 1732	3	74
Justus, m. Lydia **RUSSELL**, b. of Branford, Nov. 4, 1771,		
by Jon[a]th[an] Russell, J. P.	3	208
Kezia, d. David & Hannah, b. Feb. 25, 1729/30	3	68
Kezia, d. Solomon & Thankful, b. Sept. 18, 1764	3	200
Kaziah, m. Jonathan **BALDWIN**, b. of Branford, Nov. 24,		
1793, by Samuel Eells	3	264
Lavinia, w. of Eliada, d. Feb. 10, 1793	3	270
Levi, s. David & Hannah, b. Dec. 15, 1751	3	133
Lois, d. Justus & Lydia, b. Apr. 26, 1774	3	298
Lucina, d. John, Jr. & Elisabeth, b. Apr. 11, 1759	3	164
Luccinda, d. Solomon & Thankfull, b. July 6, 1773	3	294
Lucinda, m. Isaac **LINSLEY**, Jr., Jan. 3, 1798	3	410
Lucretia, [twin with Damas], d. Capt. Reubin & Lucretia,		
b. May 10, 1780	3	303
Luce, d. Jacob & Anne, b. Apr. 4, 1743	3	108
Lucy, d. Capt. Reubin & Lucrecy, b. Apr. 30, 1784	3	311
Lucy, w. of Amaziah, d. Sept. 29, 1795	3	266
Lieda, d. Jonathan, b. Sept. 20, 1671 (Lydia?)	1	211
Lydia, d. John & Hannah, b. Sept. 29, 1703	2	344
Lydia, d. Sam[ue]ll & Lydia, b. Sept. 21, 1725	3	58
Lydia, m. Joseph **FRISSELL**, b. of Branford, Sept. 13,		
1726, by Rev. Sam[ue]ll Russell	3	60
Lydia, d. Sam[ue]ll 2d & Mary, b. Jan. 19, 1743	3	196
Lydia, m. Sam[ue]ll **TYLER**, b. of Branford, Jan. 5, 1748/9,		
by Rev. Philemon Robbins	3	123
Lidia, d. Sam[ue]ll & Neomy, b. May 4, 1753	3	141
Lydia had s. Ebenezer Noah **BALDWIN**, b. Aug. 29, 1770	3	257
Lydia, m. Nathaniel **PALMER**, b. of Branford, Mar. 9, 1774,		
by Samuel Eells	3	257
Lydia, d. Justus & Lydia, b. Apr. 25, 1778	3	298
Lydia had s. Ebenezer Noah **BALDWIN**, d. July 15, 1780	3	291
Lydia, d. Sam[ue]ll, 3rd, & Patience, b. Feb. 12, 1783;		
d. Feb. 14, 1783	3	308
Lydia, m. Augustus **RUSSELL**, b. of Branford, Apr. 6, 1800,		
by Rev. Matthew Noyes, of Northford	3	280
Mary, d. Robert, b. Apr. 15, [1654]	1	172

	Vol.	Page
ROSE, (cont.)		
Mary, m. Sam[ue]ll **PAGE**, b. of Branford, Jan. 27, 1736, by Philemon Robbins	3	164
Mary, d. Jacob & Anne, b. Apr. 6, 1738	3	92
Mary, w. of Samuel, 2d, d. Oct. 28, 1747	3	196
Mary, d. Sam[ue]ll, 2d, & Patience, b. Nov. 27, 1754	3	197
Mary had d. Liment **HOADLEY**, b. Jan. 16, 1775	3	261
Mary E., d. Stephen & Rebecca, b. Oct. 14, 1850	TM3	245
Mary Emeline, d. Alfred & Sally, b. Mar. 22, 1825	3	345
Mary Goodsell, d. Sam[ue]ll, 3rd, & Sarah, b. Sept. 2, 1791; d. Feb. 11, 1792	3	260
Mehetabel, d. Timothy & Mehetabel, b. Mar. 12, 1734/5	3	103
Nancy, m. David **PAGE**, b. of Branford, [Aug.] 26, [1823], by Charles Atwater	3	423
Naomi, d. Sam[ue]ll, 3rd, & Naomi, b. Feb. 22, 1760	3	160
Naomi, s. of Samuel, d. Aug. 26, 1794	3	270
Noami, d. Daniel & Phebe, b. Sept. 11, 1795	3	266
Nathan, m. Thankful **BARKER**, b. of Branford, May 30, 1739, by Jon[a]th[an] Merrick	3	174
Nathan, s. Nathan & Thankful, b. June 3, 1757	3	175
Nathan, Jr., m. Lois **LINSL[E]Y**, b. of Branford, Dec. 29, 1779, by Samuel Eells	3	267
Nathan, [d.] Mar. 19, 1789	3	257
Nathan, of North Branford, m. Abigail **BEACH**, of Branford, Apr. 21, 1827, by Rev. Timothy P. Gillett	3	344
Nathan[ie]ll, s. Sam[ue]ll & Joanna, b. Feb. 12, 1709	3	31
Patience, w. of Sam[ue]l, 3d, d. Sept. 8, 1784, ae 19 y. 11 m. 20 d.	3	314
Philemon, s. Sam[ue]ll & Patience, b. Mar. 1, 1766; d. Mar. 5, 1766	3	197
Polly, of North Branford, m. George **FRISBIE**, of Branford, May 3, 1835, by Rev. Tim[oth]y P. Gillett	3	368
Rebec[c]ah, d. Jonathan & Abigail, b. Feb. 1, 1710	3	34
Rebecca, d. Jacob & Anne, b. July 5, 1745	3	108
R[e]uben, s. Jacob & Anne, b. July 16, 1741	3	108
Reuben, of Branford, m. Lucretia **MEIGS**, of Guilford, Jan. 1, 1772, by Jon[a]th[an] Todd	3	205
Robert, s. Jonathan & Hannah, b. May 7, 1788	3	267
Robert, s. Alfred & Sally, b. May 24, 1815	3	427
Robert, s. Alfred & Sally, d. Apr. 26, 1827, in the 12th y. of his age	3	345
Roderic Randal[l], s. Jonathan & Hannah, b. June 18, 1791	3	267
Samuel, s. John & Elisabeth, b. Dec. 1, 1690	3	38
Samuel, m. Joanna **BALDWIN**, Apr. 18, 1705, by Rev. Sam[ue]ll Russel[l]	3	32
Sam[ue]ll, s. Sam[ue]ll & Joanna, b. Mar. 27, 1706	3	29
Sam[ue]ll, m. Lydia **BUTLER**, June 6, 1716, by Rev. Sam[ue]ll Russel[l]	3	38

	Vol.	Page
ROSE, (cont.)		
Sam[ue]ll, s. Sam[ue]ll & Lydia, b. Aug. 12, 1728	3	68
Samuel, s. Timothy & Mehetabel, b. Mar. 17, 1732/3	3	103
Samuel, 2d, m. Mary **HOADL[E]Y**, b. of Branford, Feb. 19, 1742, by Will[ia]m Gould, J. P.	3	196
Sam[ue]ll, 2d, m. Patience **FRISBIE**, b. of Branford, Oct. 24, 1751, by Jon[a]th[an] Mer[r]ick	3	197
Sam[ue]ll, 3d, m. Naomi **HARRINGTON**, b. of Branford, Apr. 15, 1752, by Rev. Philemon Robbins	3	125
Samuel, s. Sam[ue]ll, 2d, & Patience, b. July 17, 1752	3	197
Sam[ue]ll, s. Sam[ue]ll & Neomy, b. Aug. 18, 1755	3	141
Samuel, s. Samuel, Jr. & Naomi, d. May 9, 1778	3	266
Samuel, 3d, m. Patience **HARRISON**, b. of Branford, Sept. 19, 1782, by Sam[ue]ll Eells	3	308
Samuel, s. Amaziah & Lucy, b. Sept. 17, 1789	3	266
Sarah, d. John, b. Nov. 26, 1673	1	174
Sarah, d. Sam[ue]ll & Lydia, b. July 19, 1734	3	79
Sarah, d. Dea. Sam[ue]ll & Lydia, d. Jan. 5, 1738/9	3	90
Sarah, d. Nathan & Thankful, b. Apr. 24, 1748	3	174
Sarah, d. John, Jr. & Elisabeth, b. Oct. 21, 1750	3	164
Sarah, m. Samuel **HOW**, b. of Branford, Jan. 11, 1770, by Samuel Eells	3	204
Sarah, w. of Sam[ue]l, 3d, d. June 8, 1794, in the 43d y. of her age	3	262
Sarah, m. William **FORD**, b. of Branford, [1830?], by J. A. Root. Recorded July 4, 1830	3	353
Simeon, s. David & Hannah, b. July 12, 1747	3	115
Simeon, m. Lydia **BALDWIN**, b. of Branford, Feb. 6, 1774, by Samuel Eells	3	257
Solomon, s. David & Hannah, b. Apr. 13, 1733	3	81
Solomon, m. Thankfull **BALDWIN**, b. of Branford, Nov. 30, 1763, by Jon[a]th[an] Mer[r]ick	3	180
Stephen Whedon, s. Alfred & Sally, b. Sept 19, 1821	3	427
Silvia, m. John **FOOTE**, b. of Branford, Jan. 6, 1831, by Rev. Zolva Whitman, of North Guilford (Sylvia)	3	356
Thomas, s. John & Elizabeth, b. May 24, 1744	3	114
Timothy, of Branford, m. Mehetabel **JOHNSON**, of New Haven, Sept. 22, 1730, by Jno. Russel[l], J. P.	3	103
Timothy, s. Timothy & Mehetabel, b. Feb. 7, 1746	3	126
Triphena, d. John, Jr. & Elisabeth, b. Apr. 22, 1755	3	164
Triphena, m. William **McQUEEN**, Jan. 12, 1775	3	394
Urania, d. Timothy & Mehetabel, b. Dec. 19, 1742	3	103
----, s. Eliada & Lavinia, b. Feb. 3, 1793; d. Feb. 7 following	3	270
----, child of Stephen W. & Miriam R., b. Nov. 9, 1847	TM3	239
ROSEWELL, [see also **RUSSELL**], Elizabeth, d. William, b. Oct. 1, 1679	1	211
ROWE, ROW, Jane A., of Fair Haven, m. David E. **FOOTE**, of Branford, Sept. 3, 1854, by Rev. T. P. Gillett	TM3	173

	Vol.	Page
ROWE, ROW, (cont.)		
Sarah, of New Haven, m. Dan[ie]ll **OLDS**, of Branford,		
Jan. 17, 1759, by Nicholas Street	3	172
ROWLAND, Louis E., ae 17, m. George B. **BRADLEY**, ae 18,		
May 25, 1851, by Lucius Atwater	TM3	169
Louis E., m. George G. **BRADLEY**, b. of Branford, May 25,		
1851, by Rev. Lucius Atwater	TM3	169
Louis E., m. George G. **BRADLEY**, ae 18, May 25, 1851, by		
Lucius Atwater	TM3	170
----, d. John & Mary, b. Mar. 10, 1851	TM3	244
RUSSELL, RUSSEL,[see also **ROSEWELL**], Abigail, d. Sam[ue]ll		
& Abigail, b. Aug. 16, 1690	2	345
Abigail, d. John & Sarah, b. Dec. 24, 1717	3	33
Abigail, d. Jonathan & Eunice, b. Nov. 5, 1734	3	80
Abigail, m. James **BARKER**, Oct. [ ], 1737, by Jno.		
Russell, J. P.	3	109
Abigail, m. Minor **MER[R]ICK**, b. of Branford, June 28,		
1764, by Jonathan Mer[r]ick	3	185
Abigail, d. Edward & Sarah, b. Nov. 24, 1765; d. Mar.		
21, 1768	3	277
Abigail, d. Edward & Sarah, b. July 11, 1770	3	277
Abigail, m. Joseph E. **TROWBRIDGE**, b. of Branford, June		
18, 1794, by Nicholas Street	3	263
Anne, d. Ithiel & Eunice, b. Sept. 19, 1774	3	259
Asahel, s. John, 2d, & Hannah, b. Feb. 23, 1787	3	263
Augustus, s. Jonathan & Lydia, b. Feb. 9, 1775	3	269
Augustus, m. Lydia **ROSE**, b. of Branford, Apr. 6, 1800,		
by Rev. Matthew Noyes, of Northford	3	280
Benjamin, s. John & Mary, b. Feb. 12, 1779	3	277
Benj[ami]n, [s. John, 2d, & Hannah], b. Feb. 9, 1793	3	263
Betsey, d. Capt. Sam[ue]ll & Elisabeth, b. Feb. 9, 1765	3	275
Bets[e]y, m. Ebenezer **LINSL[E]Y**, Jr., Oct. 18, 1789	3	406
Bets[e]y, d. Jon[a]th[an], Jr. & Eunice, b. Aug. 28, 1791	3	259
Betsey, m. Jason **LINSLEY**, b. of Branford, Jan. 1, 1824,		
by Rev. Timothy P. Gillett	3	424
Chaunc[e]y, s. Jon[a]th[an], Jr. & Eunice, b. Mar. 8, 1790;		
d. Mar. 27, 1790	3	259
Chauncey, [s. Augustus & Lydia], b. Sept. 30, 1801	3	280
Clarissa, d. Timothy & Chloe, b. Oct. 16, 1765	3	198
Clarissa, d. Thomas & Bethyah, b. Apr. 23, 1769	3	265
Clarissa, [d. Timothy & Sarah], b. Feb. 17, 1806	3	397
Clarissa, m. Obed **LINSLEY**, b. of Branford, June 17, 1806	3	359
Daniel, s. Sam[ue]ll & Abigail, b. June 19, 1698	2	345
David, s. Jonathan, Jr. & Lydia, b. May 31, 1762	3	178
David, m. Eunice **M[O]NRO[E]**, b. of Branford, July 19, 1793	3	263
Ebenezer, s. Sam[ue]ll & Abigail, b. May 4, 1703	2	345
Ebenezer, s. Jonathan & Eunice, b. Mar. 21, 1727/8	3	64
Ebenezer, s. Ithiel & Jerusha, b. Nov. 23, 1731	3	73

	Vol.	Page
RUSSELL, RUSSEL, (cont.)		
Eben[eze]r, s. [John, Jr. & Mary], b. Dec. 26, 1747	3	111
Ebenezor, m. Mabel **DUDLEY**, of G[u]ilford, Apr. 30, 1754,		
by John Richards	3	140
Ebenezer, s. Ebenezer & Mabel, b. Aug. 19, 1758	3	153
Ebenezer Linsl[e]y, [s. Timothy & Sarah], b. June 21, 1800	3	397
Edward, s. [John, Jr. & Mary], b. Aug. 19, 1733	3	111
Edward, m. Sarah **MALTBIE**, d. of Capt. Sam[ue]ll, b. of		
[Branford], May 30, 1753, by Rev. Philemon Robbins	3	135
Edward, m. Sarah **MALTBIE**, d. of Capt. Sam[ue]ll, b. of		
Branford, May last, 1753, by Rev. Philemon Robbins	3	145
Edward, s. John, Jr. & Hannah, b. Nov. 20, 1783	3	278
Elisabeth, d. Sam[ue]ll & Dorothy, d. Dec. 22, 1721	3	46
Ellen Juliet, [d. Timothy & Sarah], b. Mar. 26, 1808	3	397
Ellen M., of Branford, m. Lewis **MANN**, of [Wahara], Wis.,		
May 13, 1848, by Rev. Frederick Miller, in Trinity		
Church	TM3	162
Emeline, d. Lydia **RUSSELL**, b. Oct. 24, 1827	3	355
Emily, d. Jeremiah & Sarah E., b. Dec. 29, 1833	3	372
Erastus, s. Ithiel & Eunice, b. June 15, 1778	3	266
Esther, d. Thomas & Abigail, b. Apr. last Tues., 1737	3	111
Esther, m. Ebenezer **BARKER**, b. of Branford, Sept. 24,		
1758, by Philemon Robbins	3	264
Esther, d. Jon[a]th[an], Jr. & Lydia, b. Dec. 3, 1767	3	192
Eunice, d. Jonathan & Eunice, b. Nov. 6, 1725	3	58
Eunice, d. Jonathan & Lidia, b. Dec. 7, 1754	3	139
Eunice, d. Jon[a]th[an], Jr. & Lydia, d. Dec. 31, 1767	3	192
Eunice, d. John, Jr. & Hannah, b. Dec. 14, 1779	3	278
Eunice, d. Ithiel & Eunice, b. Dec. 16, 1780	3	295
Eunice, m. Benjamin Rose **SMITH**, b. of Branford, Oct. 31,		
1805	3	335
Frederick, m. Lydia **LINSLEY**, b. of Braanford, Apr. 25, 1816	3	422
George Lewis, Rev., d. July 11, 1844, ae 38 y.	TM3	305
Hannah, d. Sam[ue]ll, Jr. & Dorothy, b. Sept. 26, 1722	3	49
Irena, d. Jon[a]th[an], Jr. & Lydia, b. Jan. 22, 1760	3	161
Irene, d. John, Jr. & Hannah, b. Nov. 28, 1781	3	278
Ithiel, m. Jerusha **HAR[R]ISON**, b. of Branford, Jan. 3,		
1727/8, by Rev. Sam[ue]ll Russell	3	67
Ithiel, Jr., m. Eunice **HARRISON**, b. of Branford, Nov. 20,		
1771, by Samuel Eells	3	205
Ithiel, s. Ithiel & Eunice, b. Feb. 20, 1773	3	256
Ithiel Samuel, s. Ithiel & Eunice, b. Apr. 25, 1776	3	263
James, s. Sam[ue]ll, Jr. & Sarah, b. Dec. 18, 1774	3	278
James, [s. Timothy & Sarah], b. Jan. 7, 1804	3	397
James W[illia]m, [s. Frederick & Lydia], b. Sept. 29, 1818	3	422
Jay Edward, s. Jeremiah & Sarah E., b. Nov. 19, 1835	3	372
Jeremiah, s. John & Hannah, b. Aug. 7, 1801	3	372
Jeremiah, m. Sarah **PARMELE[E]**, b. of Branford, Nov. 29,		

	Vol.	Page
RUSSELL, RUSSEL, (cont.)		
1832, by Rev. Timothy P. Gillett	3	358
Jerusha, d. Ithiel & Jerusha, b. Aug. 23, 1729	3	67
John, s. Sam[ue]ll & Abigail, b. Jan. 24, 1686	2	345
John, of Branford, m. Sarah **TROWBRIDGE**, of New Haven,		
Dec. 17, 1707, by John Alling	3	33
John, s. John & Sarah, b. Sept. 13, 1710	3	33
John, Jr., m. Mary **BARKER**, d. of Edward, Oct. 11, 1732,		
by Jno. Russell, J. P.	3	111
John, s. [John, Jr. & Mary], b. Oct. 11, 1736	3	111
John, Jr., d. Mar. 12, 175[ ]	3	111
John, Jr., d. Mar. 12, 1750/1, ae 40 y. 6 m.	3	122
John, s. Edward & Sarah, b. Sept. 11, 1756	3	145
John, Col., d. July 7, 1757	3	147
John, m. Mary **LINSL[E]Y**, b. of Branford, Aug. 4, 1762,		
by Jon[a]th[an] Russell, J. P.	3	182
John, Jr., m. Hannah **PLANT**, b. of Branford, June 31,		
1779, by Philemon Robbins	3	277
John, m. Caroline **BENTON**, Nov. 23, 1825	3	333
John Benton, [s. John & Caroline], b. Jan. 16, 1836	3	333
John Edward, s. John & Mary, b. Jan. 18, 1777	3	277
John Maltbie, s. [John, 2d, & Hannah], b. Dec. 12, 1788	3	263
Jonathan, m. Eunice **BARKER**, b. of Branford, Dec. 12, 1722,		
by Rev. Sam[ue]ll Russel[l]	3	50
Jonathan, s. Jonathan & Eunice, b. July 25, 1731	3	71
Jonathan, Jr., m. Lydia **BARKER**, b. of Branford, Oct.		
[ ], 1753, by Jonathan Russell, J. P.	3	269
Jonathan, s. Jonathan, Jr. & Lydia, b. Dec. 15, 1764	3	185
Jonathan, s. Sam[ue]ll & Abigail, b. Aug. 21, 1700	2	345
Jon[a]th[an], Jr., of Branford, m. Eunice **DUDLEY**, of		
Guilford, Dec. 5, 1787, by Thom[a]s W. Bray	3	258
Joseph, s. [John, Jr. & Mary], b. Dec. 14, 1746	3	111
Joseph, [s. Timothy & Molly], b. Nov. 16, 1798	3	397
Julia, d. Reuel & Rachel, b. Mar. 28, 1787	3	259
Julia Ann, [d. John & Caroline], b. Dec. 21, 1826;		
d. Oct. 9, 1829	3	333
Julia Eliza, d. David & Eunice, b. Mar. 12, 1794	3	263
Lemma, s. Jonathan, Jr. & Eunice, b. Apr. 21, 1794	3	255
Lemma, s. Jonathan, Jr. & Eunice, d. Oct. 4, 1798	3	255
Lois, d. Jonathan, Jr. & Lydia, b. June 25, 1757	3	153
Lois, m. Jacob **HARRISON**, Dec. 13, 1781, by Sam[ue]ll Eells	3	309
Lois, d. Augustus & Lydia, b. May 8, 1808	3	281
Lois, m. Alonzo **APPELL**, Sept. 6, 1829, by J. A. Root	3	350
Lucretia, d. John & Mary, b. Jan. 11, 1769	3	277
Lucretia, d. Jonathan, Jr. & Lydia, b. Apr. 18, 1770	3	201
Lucretia, m. Andrew **MORRIS**, b. of Branford, June 25, 1795	3	393
Lucretia, of Branford, m. Charles **BROWN**, of New Haven,		
Nov. 21, 1825, by Flavel S. Gaylord	3	341

	Vol.	Page
RUSSELL, RUSSEL, (cont.)		
Lucy, d. Ebenezer & Mabel, b. May 24, 1760	3	163
Lydia, d. Thomas & Abigail, b. July [ ], 1735	3	111
Lydia, d. Jonathan & Eunice, b. May 18, 1741	3	97
Lydia, m. David **GOODRICH**, b. of Branford, July 13, 1758,		
by Sam[ue]ll Hall	3	158
Lydia, m. Justus **ROSE**, b. of Branford, Nov. 4, 1771, by		
Jon[a]th[an] Russell, J. P.	3	208
Lydia, d. John & Mary, b. Apr. 2, 1772	3	277
Lydia had d. Emeline, b. Oct. 24, 1827	3	355
Martha Eliza, [d. Timothy & Sarah], b. July 10, 1810	3	397
Mary, d. John & Sarah, b. Sept. 12, 1720	3	44
Mary, d. John & Sarah, b. Sept. 12, 1720	3	111
Mary, of Branford, m. Benjamin **FENN**, of Milford, Apr. 5,		
1727, by Rev. Sam[ue]ll Russell	3	61
Mary, d. [John, Jr. & Mary], b. Apr. 28, 1739	3	111
Mary, d. Jonathan & Eunice, b. July 25, 1744	3	102
Mary, d. Edward & Sarah, b. Apr. 17, 1763	3	277
Mary, d. Timothy & Chloe, b. Dec. 24, 1767	3	198
Mary, d. of Edward, m. Jonathan **PARRISH**, s. of Capt.		
Ephraim, b. of Branford, Nov. 25, 1784, by Jason Atwater	3	310
Mary, m. Rufus **BUTLER**, b. of North Branford, July 25,		
1824, by Timothy P. Gillett	3	334
Mary Ann, [d. John & Caroline], b. Aug. 3, 1831;		
d. Sept. 14, 1833	3	333
Mary Jane, [d. Frederick & Lydia], b. May 14, 1820	3	422
Molly, d. Joseph & Martha, b. Dec. 18, 1778	3	397
Molly, m. Timothy **RUSSELL**, Oct. 1, 1797	3	397
Molly, w. of Timothy, d. Nov. 25, 1798	3	397
Nancy, d. John & Mary, b. Apr. 25, 1783	3	277
Orphana, d. John, Jr. & Mary, b. Sept. 18, 1751	3	123
Philemon, s. Ebenezer & Mabel, b. Mar. 20, 1764	3	182
Polly, d. John & Mary, b. June 25, 1764	3	277
Rebecca, d. John & Sarah, b. Feb. 6, 1722/3	3	111
Rebecca, m. Ezekiel **HAYS**, b. of Branford, Dec. 26, 1749,		
by Jno. Russell, J. P.	3	119
Reuel, s. John, b. Oct. 30, 1762	3	182
Reuel, m. Rachel **BARKER**, b. of Branford, Mar. 26, 1786,		
by Sam[ue]ll Eells	3	259
Robart, s. Reuel & Rachel, b. July 25, 1789	3	259
Rutherford, s. Thomas & Bethyah, b. Sept. 17, 1771	3	265
Rutherford, Capt., m. Betsey **SMITH**, b. of Branford, June		
20, 1838, by Rev. David T. Shailer, at the house of Capt.		
Russell	3	375
Sally, d. John & Mary, b. Jan. 29, 1774	3	277
Sally, d. Sam[ue]ll, Jr. & Sarah, b. Sept. 18, 1782	3	278
Sally, m. Chester **AVERILL**, Mar. 8, 1809	3	396
Sam[ue]ll, s. Sam[ue]ll & Abigail, b. Sept. 28, 1693	2	345

	Vol.	Page
RUSSELL, RUSSEL, (cont.)		
Sam[ue]ll, s. John & Sarah, b. Sept. 23, 1726	3	111
Sam[ue]ll, m. Elisabeth **LINSL[E]Y**, Dec. 22, 1748, by		
Jno. Russell, J. P.	3	117
Sam[ue]ll, s. Sam[ue]ll & Elisabeth, b. Feb. 21, 1753	3	144
Sam[ue]ll, s. Sam[ue]ll & Elisabeth, b. Feb. 22, 1753	3	133
Samuel, Jr., m. Sarah **MUNRO[E]**, b. of Branford, June 12,		
1774	3	278
Samuel, [s. Timothy & Molly], b. Nov. 16, 1798	3	397
Samuel, s. of Timothy, d. Feb. 13, 1809	3	397
Samuel Penfield, s. Thomas & Bethyah, b. Feb. 22, 1767	3	265
Sarah, d. John & Sarah, b. Dec. 24, 1715	3	33
Sarah, d. Sam[ue]ll & Elisabeth, b. Nov. 12, 1749	3	119
Sarah, d. Ebenezer & Mabel, b. Mar. 10, 1755	3	140
Sarah, d. Edward & Sarah, b. July 29, 1759	3	158
Sarah, m. Daniel **OLDS**, Jr., b. of Branford, Dec. 2, 1772	3	278
Sarah, d. of Dea. Ebenez[e]r, m. Iustus **HARRISON**, b. of		
Branford, Nov. 7, 1779, by Sam[ue]ll Eells	3	296
Sarah, of Branford, m. Caleb **SMITH**, of New Haven, Oct.		
10, 1782, by Sam[ue]ll Eells	3	309
Sarah, d. John, 2d, & Hannah, b. June 10, 1785	3	263
Sarah Elizabeth, [d. Frederick & Lydia], b. Feb. 3, 1817	3	422
Sarah Molly, [d. Timothy & Sarah], b. Sept. 16, 1801	3	397
Submit, d. Ithiel & Jerusha, b. Apr. 15, 1735	3	90
Susan, [d. Augustus & Lydia], b. Oct. 31, 1803	3	280
Susan, m. Daniel **HUBBARD**, Jr., May 28, 1828, by Rev.		
David Baldwin	3	360
Tempe, d. Eben[eze]r & Mabel, b. Aug. 18, 1761	3	173
Thomas, s. John & Sarah, b. Sept. 15, 1712	3	33
Thomas, s. [John, Jr. & Mary], b. July 31, 1743	3	111
Thomas, m. Bethyah **PENFIELD**, b. of Branford, May 9, 1765,		
by Philemon Robbins	3	265
Thomas, s. Ithiel & Eunice, b. May 28, 1785	3	314
Timothy, s. Sam[ue]ll & Abigail, b. Nov. 18, 1695	2	345
Timothy, s. Jonathan & Eunice, b. Apr. 10, 1738	3	88
Timothy, m. Chloe **MER[R]ICK**, b. of Branford, Nov. 24,		
1764, by Jon[a]th[an] Mer[r]ick	3	198
Timothy, s. Capt. Sam[ue]ll & Elisabeth, b. Dec. 22, 1774	3	276
Timothy, s. Samuel & Elizabeth, b. Dec. 22, 1774	3	397
Timothy, d. Jonathan, Jr. & Eunice, b. Nov. 6, 1796	3	255
Timothy, m. Molly **RUSSELL**, Oct. 1, 1797	3	397
Timothy, m. Sarah **LINSL[E]Y**, d. of Ebenezer & Sybil,		
Sept. 11, 1799	3	397
William, s. Ebenezer & Mable, b. May 30, 1756	3	142
William, s. John & Mary, b. Aug. 30, 1766	3	277
Wyllys, s. [John, 2d, & Hannah], b. Mar. 3, 1791	3	263
SAGE, Anna, d. June 2, 1851, ae 76	TM3	309
SARGANT, Goodwife, d. Dec. 19, 1651	1	170

	Vol.	Page
SARGANT, (cont.)		
Johnathan, d. Dec. 19, 1652	1	170
SCARRITT, SCARRIOT, SCRAIT, SCARIT, Abigail, d.		
Rich[a]rd & Hannah, b. May 12, 172[ ]	3	45
Andrew, s. Rich[ar]d & Hannah, b. Mar. 9, 1718/9	3	43
Ann, d. Richard & Hannah, b. May 28, 1726	3	59
Anne, m. Nathan[ie]ll **HOADL[E]Y**, b. of Branford, Dec. 12,		
1745, by Rev. Philemon Robbins	3	131
James, s. Rich[a]rd & Hannah, b. Sept. 2, 1737	3	108
Jarimiah, m. Mary **WHEADON**, Apr. 22, 1756, by Mr. Merrik	3	142
Richard, s. Richard & Hannah, b. Aug. 17, 1723	3	53
Sarah E., d. Oct. 3, 1848	TM3	308
Sarah Louisa, d. Marcus C. & Sally A., b. Oct. 19, 1839	3	378
William C., m. Mary S. **WILLIAMS**, b. of Branford, Jan.		
9, 1848, by Rev. A. C. Wheat	TM3	161
----, infant of William, d. [ ], 1848, ae 16 d.	TM3	309
----, d. William C. & Mary J., b. Apr. 1, 1849	TM3	241
SCOVIL, Fanny, of Haddam, m. John **PORTER**, of Middletown,		
Dec. 22, 1834, by Rev. T. P. Gillett	3	368
SCRANTON, Frederick W., of Guilford, m. Hannah **BARKER**, of		
Branford, Dec. 23, 1823, by Rev. Timothy P. Gillett	3	424
SEWARD, SEAWARD, Amos, m. Ruth **ROGERS**, b. of Branford,		
Jan. 16, 1750/1, by Warham Williams	3	168
Chloe, of Durham, m. Joseph **TALMAGE**, of Branford, Jan.		
1, 1752, by Rev. Nathan[ie]ll Chauncey, at Durham	3	135
Dinah, m. John **WHEDON**, Sr., b. of Branford, July 9, 1728,		
by Rev. Jonathan Merrick	3	67
Nathan, s. Amos & Ruth, b. Oct. 10, 1758	3	168
Ruth, d. Amos & Ruth, b. Sept. 16, 1755	3	168
Sarah, d. Amos & Ruth, b. Dec. 9, 1751	3	168
SHELDON, Abigail, d. Asher & Wealthean, b. Nov. 28, 1771	3	268
Abigail, d. Asher & Wealthean, d. Apr. 9, 1773	3	268
Ann, d. Asher & Wealthean, b. Dec. 3, 1768	3	268
Anne, m. Samuel **BEACH**, May 11, 1793	3	387
Apollas, [s. Jeremiah & Katy], b. May 24, 1810	3	386
Apollas, s. Jeremiah & Caty, d. Mar. 20, 1825	3	339
Asher, of Branford, m. Wealthean **STEEL**, of Hartford,		
Aug. 22, 1751, by Elnathan Whitman	3	268
Asher, Jr., s. Asher & Wealthean, b. Jan. 30, 1756	3	268
Asher, Jr., m. Hannah **ROGERS**, b. of Branford, Mar. 25,		
1778, by Philemon Robbins	3	268
Asher, Jr., d. Apr. 26, 1780, ae 24 y. 2 m. 26 d.	3	268
Asher, f. of Asher, Wealthean, Daniel, Mary, Roswell,		
Ann, d. Feb. 19, 1794	3	402
Asher, [s. Jere & Katy], b. Mar. 12, 1814	3	426
Asher, of Branford, m. Sarah A. **BUNNELL**, of Middletown,		
Oct. 26, 1845, by Rev. T. P. Gillett	TM3	159
Austin, [s. Jeremiah & Katy], b. June 20, 1806	3	386

	Vol.	Page
SHELDON, (cont.)		
Betsey, [d. Jere & Katy], b. Jan. 5, 1812	3	426
Betsey, of New Haven, m. Hervey **FRISBIE**, of Branford, Sept. 15, 1834, by Rev. Timothy P. Gillett	3	367
Daniel, s. Asher & Wealthean, b. [Nov. 11, 1760]	3	268
Edwards Doolittle, [s. Truman & Almira], b. Apr. 18, 1843	TM3	238
Franklin Luther, [s. Truman & Almira], b. Mar. 13, 1847	TM3	238
George Lewis, [s. Truman & Almira], b. Apr. 7, 1845	TM3	238
Hannah, m. Zaccheus **BALDWIN**, Feb. 10, 1785, by Jason Atwater	3	255
Jephthae Brainard, [s. Roswell & Concurrence], b. Mar. 8, 1802	3	401
Jere[miah], s. Asher, Jr. & Hannah, b. Feb. 17, 1779	3	268
Jeremiah, m. Katy **LANFAIR**, June 29, 1801	3	386
Mary, d. Asher & Wealthean, b. Apr. 15, 1766	3	268
Mary Ann, [d. Roswell & Concurrence], b. Dec. 12, 1798	3	401
Nicholas, [s. Jeremiah & Katy], b. Oct. 15, 1804	3	386
Phoebe Sophia, [d. Jere & Katy], b. Nov. 25, 1820	3	426
Roswell, s. Asher & Wealthean, b. June 28, 1763	3	268
Roswell, of Branford, m. Concurrence **BRAINARD**, of Haddam, Dec. 28, 1793	3	401
Roswell B., of Branford, m. Mary L. **HENDRICK**, of New Haven, Sept. 8, 1839, by Rev. Stephen Dodd, of East Haven	3	376
Roswell Beach, [s. Jere & Katy], b. Oct. 24, 1817	3	426
Sarah Cornelia, [d. Truman & Almira], b. Aug. 2, 1841	TM3	238
Sophronia, [d. Jeremiah & Katy], b. Mar. 5, 1802	3	386
Truman, [s. Jeremiah & Katy], b. May 17, 1803	3	386
Truman, m. Almira **APPALY**, May 27, 1840	TM3	161
Wealthean, d. Asher & Wealthean, b. Sept. 5, 1753; d. Nov. 2, 1753	3	268
Wealthean, d. Asher & Wealthean, b. Mar. 17, 1758	3	268
Wealthean, w. of Asher, d. Mar. 13, 1772	3	268
Wealthean, m. Gideon **BARTHOLOMEW**, b. of Branford, Feb. 5, 1778, by Philemon Robbins	3	268
Wealthy Ann, [d. Jere & Katy], b. Mar. 13, 1816	3	426
Wilson, [d. Jeremiah & Katy], b. Apr. 9, 1808	3	386
SHELLY, Austin H., m. Philona R. **SMITH**, Apr. 9, 1852, by Rev. Lucius T. Atwater	TM3	171
Oliver A., s. Jacob A. & Elizabeth, b. Feb. 27, 1848	TM3	239
Zillah, m. David **WHEDON**, b. of Branford, Nov. 25, 1759, by Sam[ue]ll Barker, J. P.	3	161
SHELTON, Julia M., of Huntington, m. Horace **LANFARE**, of Branford, Apr. 5, 1829, by Rev. Timothy P. Gillett	3	349
SHEPHERD, SHEPARD, Baldwin, [s. Jared & Martha], b. Jan. 12, 1811	3	431
Benjamin T., m. Hannah **STENT**, b. of Branford, Feb. 7, 1833, by Rev. T. P. Gillett	3	359
Benjamin Tyler, s. Elihu & Sarah, b. May 8, 1812	3	429

	Vol.	Page
SHEPHERD, SHEPARD, (cont.)		
Betsey, [d. Jared & Martha], b. Aug. 30, 1813	3	431
Charles Benjamin, [s. Benjamin T. & Hannah], b. Sept. 4 1843	TM3	231
Elihu, d. July 25, 1848, ae 63 y.	TM3	308
Harvey, s. [Benjamin T. & Hannah], b. July 25, 1834	TM3	231
Henry, [s. Jared & Martha], b. July 3, 1822	3	431
Hiram, [s. Jared & Martha], b. Oct. 27, 1806	3	431
Hiram, s. Henry & Sarah, C., b. May 27, 1851	TM3	244
Jared, Jr., [s. Jared & Martha], b. Apr. 3, 1808	3	431
Jared, m. Mary Ann **AVERILL**, Sept. 4, 1837, by Rev.		
David Baldwin	3	375
John Ford, s. [Benjamin T. & Hannah], b. Mar. 31, 1841	TM3	231
Lind, see under Lynde		
Lydia, d. [Benjamin T. & Hannah], b. Feb. 17, 1840	TM3	231
Lyman D., s. Henry & Sarah C., b. Aug. 15, 1849	TM3	242
Lyman D., d. Jan. 4, 1850, ae 5 m.	TM3	309
Linde, [s. Jared & Martha], b. Dec. 1, 1819 (Lynde?)	3	431
Lynde W., m. Mary S. **CLANNING**, July 18, 1848	TM3	162
Major, [s. Jared & Martha], b. Aug. 25, 1816	3	431
Martha, d. Apr. 13, 1851, ae 66	TM3	309
Miriam, [d. Jared & Martha], b. Aug 5, 1803	3	431
Miriam, of Branford, m. Orin H. **POTTER**, of Plymouth,		
Jan. 26, 1824, by Rev. Timothy P. Gillett	3	425
Samuel, s. [Benjamin T. & Hannah], b. Jan. 3, 1838	TM3	231
Sarah Jane, [d. Benjamin T. & Hannah], b. Feb. 26, 1836	TM3	231
Willoughby F., s. Willoughby L. & Mary, b. Jan. 5, 1850	TM3	242
SIBBEY, Stephen, of Ward, Mass., m. Obedience S. **BROCKETT**,		
Oct. 6, 1829, by Rev. J. A. Root	3	350
SKELLINX, Mercy, d. Jacob, decd., m. Sam[ue]ll **BAKER**, s. of		
Thomas, decd., b. of Easthampton, N. Y., Oct. 18, (1721),		
by Rev. Nath[anie]ll Hunting, of Easthampton	3	94
SLINEY, Catharine, d. David & Bets[e]y, b. Jan. 20, 1851	TM3	245
SLOOPER, Daniel, s. Robert & Experience, b. Jan. 5, 1726/7	3	71
Elisabeth, d. Robert & Experience, b. Oct. 22, 1723	3	54
Jehiel, s. Robert & Experience, b. Aug. 7, 1729	3	71
John, s. Robert & Experience, b. Jan. 31, 1720/1	3	54
Robert, m. Experience **JOHNSON**, Jan. 9, 1717/8, by Rev.		
Sam[ue]ll Russell	3	54
Robert, s. Robert & Experience, b. Feb. 14, 1731/2	3	75
Thomas, s. Robert & Experience, b. Feb. 8, 1718/9	3	54
SMITH, Allin, m. Elisabeth **ROSE**, b. of Branford, Aug. 23,		
1775, by Philemon Robbins	3	295
Anne, d. Dow & Anne, b. Jan. 9, 1772	3	305
Augustus, s. Isaac & Thankfull, b. July 12, 1782	3	285
Benjamin Rose, [s. Allin & Elisabeth], b. Apr. 8, 1776	3	295
Benjamin Rose, m. Eunice **RUSSELL**, b. of Branford, Oct.		
31, 1805	3	335
Betsey, d. Isaac & Thankfull, b. Nov. 15, 1779	3	285

	Vol.	Page
SMITH, (cont.)		
Betsey, d. Stephen & Hannah, b. Jan. 14, 1783	3	309
Betsey, m. Capt. Rutherford **RUSSELL**, b. of Branford,		
June 20, 1838, by Rev. David T. Shailer, at the house of		
Capt. Russell	3	375
Caleb, of New Haven, m. Sarah **RUSSELL**, of Branford, Oct.		
10, 1782, by Sam[ue]ll Eells	3	309
Chester, m. Elizabeth H. **BALDWIN**, Aug. 10, 1820, by Rev.		
Matthew Noyes	3	414
Dan, s. Stephen, Jr. & Hannah, b. June 18, 1780, in New		
Haven	3	309
Dan, s. Stephen & Hannah, b. Mar. 16, 1786	3	276
Daniel, s. Dow & Keziah, b. Jan. 23, 1748	3	188
Deborah, m. John **WHITNE[Y]**, b. of Branford, Jan. 17,		
1750/1, by Rev. Philemon Robbins	3	130
Dow, m. Keziah **BARKER**, b. of Branford, Mar. 13, 1733,		
by Jacob Hemingway	3	188
Dow, s. Dow & Keziah, b. Mar. 21, 1745	3	188
Dow, Jr., m. Anne **LINSLEY**, b. of Branford, May 24, 1767,		
by Jon[a]th[an] Merrick	3	305
Ebenez[e]r, s. Elisha & Elisabeth, b. Feb. 11, 1750/1	3	131
Edward Russell, s. Caleb & Sarah, b. Oct. 12, 1783	3	309
Elisabeth, d. Elisha & Elisabeth, b. Dec. 7, 1747	3	131
Elisabeth, [d. Allin & Elisabeth], b. Oct. 29, 1777	3	295
Elizabeth, d. [Benjamin Rose & Eunice], b. July 22, 1819	3	335
Elizabeth, w. of Allen, d. Feb. [ ], 1823	3	432
Elisur Grant, s. Grant & Rebecca, b. Sept. 25, 1843	TM3	234
Eunice, [d. Jordon & Sarah], b. Dec. 13, 1774	3	298
Hannah, [d. Allin & Elisabeth], b. Apr. 4, 1779	3	295
Hannah, d. Dow & Anne, b. Sept. 8, 1781	3	305
Hannah had s. Charles **COOPER**, b. Jan. 13, 1808; reputed		
f. Levi **COOPER**	3	432
Hiram, s. Benjamin & Eunecia, b. Mar. 3, 1807	3	396
Isaac, s. Dow & Keziah, b. Apr. 21, 1754	3	188
Isaac, m. Thankfull **FOOT**, b. of Branford, Apr. 1, 1779,		
by Sam[ue]ll Eells	3	285
Jemima, d. Stephen & Jemima, b. Sept. 12, 1748	3	123
John, [s. Jordon & Sarah], b. Nov. 19, 1781	3	298
John, [s. Allin & Elisabeth], b. Sept. 22, 1783	3	295
Jordon, s. Dow & Keziah, b. Sept. 1, 1733	3	188
Joseph, s. Dow & Keziah, b. Apr. 12, 1739	3	188
Joseph, m. Lydia **HARRISON**, b. of Branford, Feb. 24, 1762,		
by Philemon Robbins	3	176
Justus, [s. Jordon & Sarah], b. Jan. 27, 1777	3	298
Keziah, d. Dow & Keziah, b. Aug. 28, 1751	3	188
Leonard, of Branford, m. Mrs. Harriet **YALE**, of Meriden,		
Oct. 19, 1845, by Rev. A. C. Wheat	TM3	158
Lois, [d. Jordon & Sarah], b. Oct. 20, 1770	3	298

	Vol.	Page
SMITH, (cont.)		
Lucinda, m. Doan **SNOW**, Nov. 17, 1833, by Samuel N.		
Shepard, Int. pub.	3	362
Lurena, d. Mar. 3, 1851, ae 66 y.	TM3	310
Lydia, d. Dow & Keziah, b. Jan. 1, 1743	3	188
Mabel, [d. Jordon & Sarah], b. Oct. 25, 1768	3	298
Margeret, d. Jan. 10, 1728/9, ae 93 y.	3	66
Mary C., d. Leonard & Harriett, b. Jan. 1, 1848	TM3	240
Phebe, [d. Jordon & Sarah], b. Sept. 13, 1766	3	298
Philona R., m. Austin H. **SHELLY**, Apr. 9, 1852, by Rev.		
Lucius T. Atwater	TM3	171
Polly, d. Allen & Elizabeth, b. Dec. 28, 1785	3	432
Rebecca, d. Dow & Anne, b. May 3, 1775	3	305
Samuel M., s. Thomas M. & Lorana, b. Sept. 22, 1849	TM3	242
Sarah, d. Dow & Keziah, b. Aug. 31, 1736; d. Jan. 15,		
1757, in the 21st y. of her age	3	188
Sarah, d. Dow & Anne, b. May 18, 1769	3	305
Sarah, m. Barnebas **PALMER**, b. of Branford, Nov. 15, 1781,		
by Sam[ue]ll Eells	3	302
Saymore, s. Benj[ami]n & Anna, b. Sept. 9, 1751	3	131
Seth, s. John & Kezia, b. July 16, 1752	3	130
Simeon, s. Joseph & Lydia, b. Dec. 29, 1762	3	179
Stephen Moitson, of North Haven, m. Lydia **KIETH**, of		
Milford, Nov. 14, 1824, by Jacob Frisbie, J. P.	3	336
Thomas, m. Hanna[h] **NETTLETON**, July 10, [16]56	1	170
Thomas, s. Allen & Elizabeth, b. Mar. 22, 1892*		
(*Probably 1792?)	3	432
----, d. Lorenzo & Lucy, b. Feb. 15, 1849	TM3	241
SNOW, Doan, m. Lucinda **SMITH**, Nov. 17, 1833, by Samuel N.		
Shepard, Int. Pub.	3	362
SPENCER, Ann, m. David **LOUNSBURY**, b. of Branford, Dec. 23,		
1840, by Rev. Davis T. Shailer	TM3	152
Edward, m. Susan L. **HUBBARD**, Dec. 28, 1851, by Rev.		
Lucius T. Atwater	TM3	171
Eliza A., m. William **PALMER**, b. of Branford, July 16,		
1837, by Rev. Timothy P. Gillett	3	374
John, m. Nancy **GRIFFING**, b. of Branford, May 12, 1849,		
by Rev. T. P. Gillett	TM3	163
John B., of Derby, m. Rebecca **ROBINSON**, of North		
Branford, May 26, 1822, by Charles Atwater	3	419
Mary, m. Ammi **HOADLEY**, b. of Branford, Feb. 5, 1837,		
by Rev. Timothy P. Gillett	3	373
Mindwell, of Branford, m. Elisha S. **ISBELL**, of Meriden,		
Nov. 30, 1848, by Rev. T. P. Gillett	TM3	163
Sarah, m. Lynde **FRISBIE**, b. of Branford, Aug. 22, 1841,		
by Rev. Davis T. Shailer	TM3	153
SPERRY, Arsneth, d. Feb. 9, 1850, ae 76 y.	TM3	309
Cornelia M., d. Hart & Lucinda, b. June 21, 1851	TM3	244

	Vol.	Page
SPERRY, (cont.)		
Lydia, m. Samuel **BALDWIN**, Jan. 8, 1713/14* by Rev.		
Sam[ue]ll Russel[l] (*Changed to 1712/3)	3	38
SPICER, Luce, d. Jeremiah & Hannah, b. Oct. 11, 1741	3	126
SPINK, Ann Maria, d. Samuel & Hester, b. May 22, 1825	3	344
Ann Maria, m. Gurdon **BRADLEY**, b. of Branford, Jan. 29,		
1843, by Rev. Pascal P. Kidder	TM3	155
Emily Malissa, d. Samuel & Eunice, b. Feb. 14, 1833	3	366
Esther Eliza, d. Samuel & Esther, b. June 18, 1830	3	366
George Richard, s. Samuel & Eunice, b. Oct. 12, 1834	3	372
Lydia, m. Jeremiah **JOHNSON**, b. of Branford, Mar. 4, 1796	3	429
Samuel, m. Eunice **TYLER**, b. of Branford, Nov. 6, 1831,		
by Timothy P. Gillett	3	357
Shubael Tillotson, s. Samuel & Esther, b. Sept. 9, 1828	3	366
William, s. Richard & Elizabeth, b. June 23, 1787	3	279
SOUIRE, Annice E., [child of Orin D. & Annice], b. Sept. 4, 1829	3	410
Caroline, [d. Orin D. & Annis], b. Mar. 5, 1821	3	410
Caroline, m. Samuel Robinson **MABBATT**, Aug. 12, 1840, by		
Rev. Pascal P. Kidder, at the house of O. D. Squire	TM3	152
Charlotte A., m. John J. **BARTHOLOMEW**, b. of Branford,		
Aug. 24, 1837, by Rev. Leonard Bacon, of New Haven	3	374
Charlotte Ann, [d. Orin D. & Annis], b. Aug. 14, 1819	3	410
Eliza Ann, [d. Lyman L. & Elizabeth L.], b. Mar. 12, 1831	3	333
Eliza Ann, m. Lewis B. **STAPLES**, b. of Branford, Mar. 15,		
1849, by Rev. T. P. Gillett	TM3	163
Ellen M., [d. Orin D. & Annice], b. Apr. 29, 1832	3	410
Elvira, [d. Orin D. & Annis], b. Nov. 14, 1811	3	410
Elvira, of Branford, m. Levi S. **PARSONS**, of Sandersfield,		
Mass., Sept. 11, 1833, by Rev. Judson A. Root	3	361
Emeranse, [s. Orin D. & Annice], b. Aug. 26, 1808, in Guilford	3	386
Henry Bishop, [s. Orin D. & Annis], b. Jan. 29, 1823;		
d. Mar. 14, 1826	3	410
Horatio Nelson, [s. Orin D. & Annis], b. Apr. 16, 1817	3	410
Jennette, [d. Orin D. & Annis], b. Oct. 25, 1815	3	410
Jennnett A., m. Dr. J. O. **LOOMIS**, Jan. 1, 1836, by Rev.		
H. B. Camp	3	371
Jennette Melissa, [d. Lyman L. & Elizabeth L.], b. June 9, 1834	3	333
John Newton, [s. Orin D. & Annis], b. Sept. 17, 1813	3	410
Lewis Lysander, [s. Orin D. & Annice], b. Feb. 23, 1807,		
in Guilford	3	386
Lyman Frisbie, s. Lyman L. & Elisa, b. Dec. 22, 1842	TM3	231
Lyman Luzerne, [s. Orin D. & Annice], b. Feb. 18, 1810	3	386
Lyman Luzerne, m. Eliza L. **PALMER**, b. of Branford, July		
22, 1830, by Timo[thy] P. Gillett	3	353
Orin D., m. Annice **FRISBIE**, June 4, 1806	3	386
Orin D., [s. Orin D. & Annis], b. Feb. 1, 1825	3	410
Orin D., of Branford, m. Sarah Almira **FOOTE**, d. of Stephen,		
May 23, 1842, by Rev. Mr. Forbes, in St. Thomas		

	Vol.	Page
SQUIRE, (cont.)		
Church, New York City	TM3	160
Sarah F., [d. Orin D. & Annice], b. May 31, 1827	3	410
Sarah F., m. John F. **WOODHULL**, July 26, 1847, by Rev. Frederick Miller	TM3	161
STALK, [see under **STORK**]		
STANNARD, Hulda[h], of Saybrook, m. Jacob M. **TYLER**, of Branford, May 1, [18__]	3	283
Lynde H., d. Jan. 5, 1849, ae 43 y.	TM3	308
Parmela, of Branford, m. William **BARTLETT**, of Westbrook, Jan. 29, 1854, by Rev. Tim[oth]y P. Gillett	TM3	173
STAPLES, Abigail, d. David & Clarissa, b. Sept. 14, 1795	3	268
David, s. Enoch & Abigail, b. Apr. 22, 1770	3	258
David, m. Clarissa **KIMBERLY**, b. of Branford, Oct. 17, 1790	3	264
Enoch, m. Abigail **WILLFORD**, b. of Branford, Oct. 15, 1769, by Phile[mo]n Robbins	3	197
Enoch, s. Enoch & Abigail, b. Oct. 18, 1782	3	280
Enoch, s. Enoch & Abigail, b. [ ]	3	276
Georg[e] Lewis, s. Lewis & Eliza Ann, b. Sept. [ ], 1849	TM3	242
Grace, d. Enoch & Abigail, b. Dec. 9, 1780; d. Nov. 3, 1781	3	280
Grace, d. Enoch & Abigail, b. Sept. 5, 1787	3	253
Grace, d. Enoch & Abigail, b. [ ]; d. Nov. 3, [ ]	3	276
Harriet, of Branford, m. Benjamin **STILLMAN**, of Humphreysville, Oct. 27, 1833, by Rev. T. P. Gillett	3	362
Henry Augustus, s. John & Polly, b. Sept. 3, 1828	3	366
John, s. Enoch & Abigail, b. Mar. 12, 1777	3	280
John, m. Polly **BARKER**, b. of Branford, Sept. 16, 1827, by Rev. Timothy P. Gillett	3	345
John, d. Aug. 20, 1848, ae 71 y.	TM3	308
John, s. Enoch & Abigail, b. [ ]	3	276
John Enoch, s. John & Ellis, b. Dec. 26, 1820	3	366
Joseph, s. Enoch & Abigail, b. July 25, 1772	3	258
Joseph, s. David & Clarissa, b. June 11, 1792; d. Mar. 16, 1795	3	264
Joseph, s. David & Clarissa, b. Dec. 17, 1797	3	271
Lewis B., m. Eliza Ann **SQUIRE**, b. of Branford, Mar. 15, 1849, by Rev. T. P. Gillett	TM3	163
Lewis Barker, s. John & Polly, b. Jan. 7, 1830	3	366
Nancy, of Branford, m. Judson **GORHAM**, of Stratford, Oct. 12, 1835, by Rev. T. P. Gillett	3	371
Polly, d. July 20, 1851, ae 62 y.	TM3	310
Robert, s. Enoch & Abigail, b. Dec. 1, 1774	3	258
Robert, s. David & Clarissa, b. Nov. 14, 1793	3	264
Sarah, d. David & Sarah, b. July 13, 1801	3	275
STEDMAN, Benjamin, [s. Benjamin & Mary], b. Jan. 31, 1820	3	431
Benjamin Foot, s. Stephen f. & Harriet, b. Aug. 18, 1832	3	359
Grace Rogers, [d. Henry & Betsey], b. Aug. 20, 1845	TM3	235
Hannah, [d. Henry & Betsey], b. Nov. 7, 1844	TM3	235
Harry, [s. Benjamin & Mary], b. Apr. 4, 1812	3	431

	Vol.	Page
STEDMAN, (cont.)		
Harry, m. Betsey **FOOT**, b. of Branford, Sept. 26, 1839,		
by Rev. Timothy P. Gillett	3	377
Henry Harrison, [s. Henry & Betsey], b. Apr. 24, 1840	TM3	235
Mary, [d. Benjamin & Mary], b. July 21, 1810	3	431
Mary, m. Lester **BEERS**, b. of Branford, Apr. 18, 1830,		
by Timothy P. Gillett	3	352
Mary Foot, [d. Henry & Betsey], b. Mar. 4, 1842	TM3	235
Sally, [d. Benjamin & Mary], b. Nov. 3, 1815	3	431
Sally E., m. William S. **MORRIS**, b. of Branford, Oct. 1,		
1837, by Timothy P. Gillett	3	374
Stephen F., [s. Benjamin & Mary], b. Jan. 24, 1806	3	431
Stephen F., of New Haven, m. Harriet **CHIDSEY**, of Branford,		
Sept. 24, 1831, by Rev. Timothy P. Gillett	3	357
STEELE, STEEL, Chloe, of New Hartford, m. Oliver **LANFARE**,		
of Branford, Mar. 14, 1826, by Rev. Timothy P. Gillett	3	341
Wealthean, of Hartford, m. Asher **SHELDON**, of Branford,		
Aug. 22, 1751, by Elnathan Whitman	3	268
STENT, STENTT, Asahel, [s. Samuel & Elizabeth], b. Aug. 31,		
1811	3	427
Chloe, d. Eleazer & Rhoda, b. May 10, 1786	3	254
Chloe, twin with Hannah, d. [Samuel & Elizabeth], b. Dec. 21,		
1815	3	427
Chloe, of Branford, m. John Street **CHIDSEY**, of East Haven,		
Feb. 14, 1842, by Rev. Timothy P. Gillett	TM3	154
Dorothy, d. Eleazar, b. Sept. 13, 1672	1	174
Dorothy, m. John **BARNES**, Aug. 28, 1700, by Rev. Mr.		
Russell	2	343
Eaton, [s. Eleazur, Jr. & Sarah], b. Aug. 9, 1812	3	404
Eleazar, s. Eleazar, b. Apr. 26, 1680	1	211
Eleaz[a]r, Capt., d. Feb. 8, 1705/6	3	29
Eleazer, of Branford, m. Martha **IUES**, of New Haven, Jan.		
6, 1713/14, by Abram Bradl[e]y, J. P., at New Haven	3	38
Eleazer, s. Eleaz[e]r & Martha, b. Oct. 23, 1715	3	37
Eleazar, Jr., m. Sarah **COACH**, b. of Branford, Sept. 20,		
1738, by Rev. Philemon Robbins	3	89
Eleazar, s. Eleazar & Sarah, b. Jan. 19, 1743/4	3	101
Eleazer, Capt., s. of Eleazar, d. Jan. 12, 1745/6, being		
64 years past	3	107
Eleazer, Jr., m. Rhoda **FORD**, b. of Branford, June 21,		
1769, by Philemon Robbins	3	201
Eleazer, d. June 30, 1772, ae 56 y. 8 m. 8 d.	3	206
Eleazer, s. Eleazer & Rhoda, b. Nov. 28, 1781	3	270
Eleazur, Jr., m. Sarah **IVES**, Mar. 7, 1810	3	404
Eleazer, d. Feb. 24, 1817	3	431
Elizabeth, d. Eleazar, b. Apr. 25, 1676	1	174
Elisabeth, w. of Capt. Ele[a]z[e]r, d. Aug. 12, 1712	3	36
Elisabeth, d. Eleazar & Martha, b. May 31, 1717	3	40

	Vol.	Page
STENT, STENTT, (cont.)		
Elisabeth, wid. of Samuel, d. Oct. 5, 1835, ae 53	TM3	306
Elizabeth Adela[i]de, d. John & Polly, b. May 23, 1844	TM3	234
Elnathan, s. Eleazar & Elizabeth, d. Nov. 6, 1701	2	343
Hannah, d. Eleazar & Rhoda, b. May 7, 1777	3	263
Hannah, twin with Chloe, d. [Samuel & Elizabeth], b. Dec. 21, 1815	3	427
Hannah, m. Benjamin T. **SHEPHERD,** b. of Branford, Feb. 7, 1833, by Rev. T. P. Gillett	3	359
Jane, Mrs.,m. Henry D. **LAKE,** May 4, 1845, by Rev. Frederic Miller	TM3	158
Jane Eliza, d. Asahel & Sarah Eliza b. May 30, 1845	TM3	234
John, s. Eleaz[e]r & Sarah, b. Jan. 15, 1749/50	3	122
John, d. Mar. 21, 1772	3	122
John, [s. Samuel & Elizabeth], b. Jan. 9, 1808	3	427
John Ford, s. Eleazer & Rhoda, b. Mar. 29, 1790	3	258
John Judson, s. John & Polly, b. Aug. 11, 1850	TM3	244
Joseph, s. Eleazar & Elizabeth, b. Sept. 27, 1691	2	343
Lois, [d. Eleazur, Jr. & Sarah], b. Dec. 17, 1810	3	404
Martha, s. of Capt. Eleazer, d. Jan. 17, 1727/8	3	64
Martha, d. Eleazer, Jr. & Sarah, b. June 29, 1741	3	96
Martha, m. Roger **TYLER,** Jr., b. of Branford, May 15, 1767, by Philemon Robbins	3	195
Mary, d. Eleazar, b. Nov. 28, 167(4,5,or 6)? (Was typed over)	1	174
Mary, d. Eleazar, d. Oct. 5, 1679	1	211
Mehetabell, d. Eleazar, b. Jan. 16, 1681	1	211
Mehetabell, d. Eleazar & Elizabeth, d. Sept. 14, 1699	2	343
Newton, [s. Eleazur, Jr. & Sarah], b. May 29, 1814	3	404
Othniel, s. Eleaz[e]r & Sarah, b. Apr. 15, 1752	3	126
Othniel, m. Lois **FORD,** b. of Branford, Feb. 13, 1782, by Sam[ue]ll Eells	3	288
Rhoda, d. Eleazar & Rhoda, b. Nov. 24, 1772	3	208
Rhoda, d. Eleazer & Rhoda, d. Sept. 27, 1774, ae 1 y. 10 m. 3 d.	3	257
Rhoda, d. Eleazer & Rhoda, b. Oct. 30, 1774	3	263
Rhoda, wid. of Eleaser, d. Feb. 10, 1837, ae 88	TM3	306
Sally, [d. Eleazur, Jr. & Sarah], b. Feb. 5, 1817	3	404
Samuel, s. Eleazar, b. Mar. 5, [16]77/8	1	174
Sam[ue]ll, m. Martha **MOSS,** Nov. 27, 1706, by Rev. Sam[ue]ll Street, of Wallingford	3	32
Samuel, s. Eleazar, Jr. & Sarah, b. June 24, 1739	3	90
Samuel, s. Eleazar & Sarah, d. Mar. 21, 1763, in the 24th y. of his age	3	179
Samuel, s. Eliazar & Rhoda, b. Oct. 14, 1779	3	267
Samuel, of Branford, m. Elizabeth **PARDEE,** of Guilford, Dec. 17, 1806	3	427
Samuel, d. Nov. 13, 1822, ae 43 y.	TM3	306
Samuel, f. of John, Asahel, Hannah & Chloe, d. Nov. 13, 1822,		

	Vol.	Page
STENT, STENTT, (cont.)		
ae 43 y.	3	427
Sarah, w. of Eleazar, d. Mar. 26, 1763, in the 48th y. of her age	3	179
Sarah, d. Eleazer, Jr. & Rhoda, b. Feb. 6, 1771	3	201
Thomas, s. Eleazar, b. Sept. 10, 1671; d. Sept. 20, 1671	1	174
Thomas, s. Eleazar & Sarah, d. Mar. 22, 1764, ae 17 y.		
1 m. 24 d.	3	182
Thomas, s. Ele[a]z[e]r & Sarah, b. Feb. 18, 1746/7	3	109
Thomas, s. Eleaz[e]r & Rhoda, b. Jan. 8, 1784	3	296
----, child of John & Polly A., b. July 12, 1848	TM3	240
STEVENS, Betsey, m. James R. **PARDY**, b. of North Madison,		
Mar. 3, 1828, by Rev. Timothy P. Gillett	3	346
STEWART, Betsey, d. Will & Margaret, b. June 8, 1778	3	294
Elisabeth, d. Will[ia]m & Margaret, d. Sept. 8, 1773	3	294
Pamela, d. Lucretia **BRADDOCK**, b. Apr. 18, 1781	3	255
Polly, d. Lucretia **BRADDOCK**, b. Aug. 31, 177[6]	3	255
William, d. Oct. 22, 1779, "in an engagement with a		
British ship at sea"	3	294
STILLMAN, Benjamin, of Humphreysville, m. Harriet **STAPLES**,		
of Branford, Oct. 27, 1833, by Rev. T. P. Gillett	3	362
STOCKWELL, Eleazar, s. Quintan, b. Apr. 25, 1679	1	211
STOKES, Jonathan, m. Hannah **GOODRICH**, b. of Branford, Sept.		
27, 1758, by Sam[ue]ll Barker, J. P.	3	153
Jonathan, s. Jonathan & Hannah, b. Mar. 17, 1760;		
d. Apr. 4, 1760	3	177
Jonathan, s. Jonathan & Hannah, b. Feb. 23, 1761	3	177
Miriam, d. Jonathan & Hannah, b. Jan. 7, 1759	3	177
STONE, Arch, s. Elihu, b. Feb. 20, 1770	3	306
Chauncey, m. Lois **PALMER**, b. of Branford, [Sept] 23,		
[1824], by Charles Atwater	3	334
Chloe, d. Elihu, b. Oct. 5, 1761	3	306
Edmund, s. Elihu, b. Aug. 31, 1768	3	306
John, s. Elihu & Thankful, b. Oct. 7, 1759	3	173
Mary, d. Elihu & Thankfull, b. Jan. 12, 1758	3	152
Noah, s. Elihu, b. Dec. 3, 1769	3	306
Polle, [twin with Salley], d. Elihu, b. Jan. 21, 1777	3	306
Rachel, d. Elihu, b. June 10, 1766	3	306
Ruth, d. Elihu, b. Nov. 21, 1779	3	306
Salley, [twin with Polle], d. Elihu, b. Jan. 21, 1777	3	306
Sarah, of Guilford, m. Ephraim **BEACH**, of Branford, Dec.		
1, 1767, by Rev. Benj[ami]n Ruggals	3	288
Thankfull, d. Elihu, b. Feb. 10, 1763	3	306
STORK, STALK, Abigail, d. Moses & Abigail, b. Dec. 4, 1758;		
d. Oct. 16, 1759	3	163
Abigail, w. of Moses, d. Dec. 11, 1758	3	163
Abigail, d. Moses & Eunice, b. Oct. 13, 1763, in New London	3	311
Calvin, twin with Luther, s. Moses & Eunice, b. May 16, 1780	3	311
Christopher Still Moses, s. Moses & Eunice, b. May 11, 1767	3	311

	Vol.	Page
STORK, STALK, (cont.)		
Daniel, s. Moses & Eunice, b. Jan. 7, 1772	3	311
John, s. Moses & Eunice, b. Mar. 10, 1776	3	311
Luther, twin with Calvin, s. Moses & Eunice, b. May 16, 1780	3	311
Moses, m. Abigail **BROWN**, Sept. 4, 1755, by Rev. Philemon		
Robbins	3	142
Moses, m. Eunice **MASON**, Apr. 10, 1763, by [ ] Boyle,		
New London	3	311
Moses, Jr., s. Moses & Deborah, d. [ ]	3	311
Noah, s. Moses & Abigail, b. Oct. 13, 1757	3	151
William, s. Moses & Eunice, b. Dec. 10, 1770	3	311
STREET, Horatio Gates, s. Jesse & Lois, b. Nov. 12, 1777	3	265
STRONG, Clorinda, [d. Erastus & Nabby Wright], b. May 11, 1807,		
in Chesterfield, N. Y.	3	353
Clorinda F., of Branford, m. William P. **MINOR**, of Roxbury,		
June 2, 1829, by Rev. Fosdic Harrison, of Roxbury	3	349
Erastus, of Chesterfiel d, N. Y., m. Nabby Wright **HARRISON**,		
of Branford, Nov. 14, 1802, by Samuel Eells	3	353
Erastus, of Branford, m. Sally **THOMPSON**, of East Haven,		
May 28, 1827, by Rev. Henry Lines, of New Haven	3	354
Erastus Albert, [s. Erastus & Nabby Wright], b. Aug. 19,		
1809, in Chesterfield, N. Y.	3	353
Idea Sophronia, [d. Erastus & Nabby Wright], b. Oct. 2, 1818	3	354
Martha Louisa, [d. Erastus & Nabby Wright], b. Feb. 24, 1812	3	353
Nabby W., w. of Erastus, d. Mar. 14, 1825	3	354
SUMMERS, Lydia, d. Jan. 5, 1796	3	266
SUTLIFF, SUTLIF, SUTLIEF, Hannah, m. Thomas		
HAR[R]ISON, Jr., b. of Branford, Apr. 12, 1721, by Rev.		
Sam[ue]ll Russel[l]	3	46
Lydia, m. Jonathan **FOOT**, b. of Branford, June 14, 1727,		
by Rev. Isaac Stiles	3	73
Mary, m. Benjamin **HARRISON**, b. of Branford, Oct. 19,		
1720, by Rev. Sam[ue]ll Russell	3	50
SWAIN, SWAINE, SWANE, Christean, d. Samuell, b. Apr. 25,		
[16]59	1	172
Dani[e]ll, s. William, m. Dorcas **ROSE**, d. Robert, July		
26, 1653	1	170
Dani[e]ll, s. Dani[e]ll, b. Dec. 23, [16]55	1	172
Daniel, s. Jno. & Hannah, b. Nov. 4, 1725	3	57
Debora[h], d. Dani[e]ll, b. Apr. 24, 1654	1	171
Deborah, m. Peter **TYLER**, Nov. 20, 1671	1	174
Dorcas, d. Dani[e]ll, b. [Dec.] 2, [16]57	1	172
Eunice, d. John & Jane, b. Aug. [ ], 1692	3	35
Eunice, m. Thomas **WHEADON**, May 6, 1714, by Nathan[ie]ll		
Harrison, J. P.	3	38
Hannah, d. Jno. & Hannah, b. July 10, 1722	3	50
Hannah, d. Jno . & Hannah, d. July 13, 1725	3	57
Hannah, d. Jno. & Hannah, b. Feb. 28, 1726/7	3	64

	Vol.	Page
SWAIN, SWAINE, SWANE, (cont)		
Isaac, s. John & Hannah, b. Aug. 17, 1729; d. Dec. 12, 1729	3	69
James, s. Jno. & Hannah, b. Mar. 8, 1727/8	3	64
John, s. Dani[e]ll, b. May 22, 1660	1	172
John, s. John & Jane, b. Dec. 13, 1693	3	35
John, of Branford, m. Hannah **[W]RIGHT**, of Glausenbury,		
Oct. 17, 1721, by Rev. Mr. Stephens, at Glausenbury	3	48
John, s. John & Hannah, b. Dec. 30, 1723	3	55
Johnathan, s. Dani[e]ll, b. Jan. 12, [16]62	1	173
Jonathan, s. John & Hannah, b. Feb. 20, 1730/1	3	72
Mary, d. Samuell, b. Mar. 1, [1649]	1	171
Mary, d. Samuel, d. Nov. 10, [16]55	1	170
Mary, d. Samuell, b. Jan. 12, [16]56	1	172
Mary, d. John & Hannah, b. Dec. 14, 1732	3	78
Phebe, d. Samuell, b. May 24, 1654	1	171
Rachel, m. Joseph **BROWN**, Sept. 11, 1711, by Nathan[ie]ll		
Harrison, J. P.	3	34
Sarah, d. Samuell, b. Oct. 7, [16]61	1	173
TAINTOR, TAINTER, TAINTR,[see also **TENTER**], Abigail, d.		
Michael & Sarah, b. Aug. 13, 1747	3	165
Anna, [d. Medad & Anna], b. Mar. 4, 1787	3	266
Benjamin, s. Joseph & Sarah, b. June 7, 1751	3	155
Dorcas, Mrs., m. John **COLLINS**, Mar. 6, 1699/1700, by		
Rev. Mr. Russell	2	343
Elisabeth, m. Noah **ROGERS**, Apr. 8, 1673	1	174
Elisabeth, d. Joseph & Elisabeth, b. Oct. 28, 1716	3	32
Elizebeth, d. Joseph & Sarah, b. Mar. 25, 1748	3	154
Elizebeth, d. Joseph & Sarah, d. Oct. 23, 1751	3	155
Elizabeth, d. Nath[anie]ll & Submit, b. Mar. 11, 1754	3	140
Eunice, d. Nath[anie]ll & Submit, b. Dec. 31, 1760	3	177
Eunice, m. Stephen **WILLIAMS**, b. of Branford, Jan. 23,		
1778, by Warham Williams	3	291
Eunecy, [d. Medad & Anna], b. June 29, 1790	3	266
Grace, of Branford, m. David **FINCH**, of New Haven, Sept.		
26, 1822, by Rev. Samuel Luckey	3	420
Henry, [s. Medad & Anna], b. May 19, 1793	3	266
Isaac, s. Nath[anie]ll & Submit, b. Jan. 17, 1768	3	196
Jared, s. John & Sarah, b. May 25, 1746	3	116
Jared, m. Rebecca **LINSLEY**, b. of Branford, Dec. [ ],		
1772, by Warham Williams	3	257
John, m. wid. Sarah **FOOT**, b. of Branford, May 9, 1745,		
by Rev. Jonathan Mer[r]ick	3	116
John, s. Jared & Rebecca, b. Aug. 24, 1774	3	258
Joseph, m. Elisabeth **FOOT**, Mar. 29, 1710, by Rev. Sam[ue]ll		
Russel[l]	3	32
Joseph, s. Joseph & Elisabeth, b. Nov. 29, 1714	3	32
Joseph, m. Sarah **BARKER**, b. of Branford, Apr. 10, 1743,		
by John Russell, J. P.	3	154

	Vol.	Page

TAINTOR, TAINTER, TAINTR, (cont.)

Joseph, s. Joseph & Sarah, b. Sept. 8, 1745	3	154
Joseph, d. Oct. 15, 1750	3	155
Mary, d. Joseph & Elisabeth, b. July 11, 1711	3	32
Mary, of Branford, m. Sam[ue]ll **LEWIS**, of Colchester, Feb. 24, 1729/30, by Rev. Sam[ue]ll Russell	3	68
Mary, d. Michael & Sarah, b. Sept. 2, 1755	3	166
Medad, s. Michael & Sarah, b. Nov. 13, 1757	3	166
Medad, m. Anna **LINDSLEY**, b. of Branford, Apr. 20, 1780	3	266
Michael, m. Sarah **FOOT**, b. of Branford, Feb. 25, 1747, by Jonathan Merrick	3	165
Michael, s. Michael & Sarah, b. June 22, 1752	3	165
Nathaniel, m. Submit **TYLER**, b. of Branford, Jan. 4, 1753, by Warham Williams	3	140
Nath[anie]ll, s. Nath[anie]ll & Submit, b. Mar. 3, 1756	3	141
Nath[anie]ll, s. Nath[anie]ll & Submit, d. Mar. 25, 1762, in the 7th y. of his age	3	177
Rebeccah, d. Nath[anie]ll & Submit, b. Sept. 20, 1758	3	177
Rebecca, m. Benjamin **MALTBIE**, Jr., b. of Branford, Jan. 23, 1778	3	300
Rebecca, m. Capt. Timothy **HOADL[E]Y**, b. of Branford, Jan. 28, 1781, by Warham Williams	3	271
Reuben, [s. Medad & Anna], b. Mar. 11, 1785	3	266
Salle, d. Michael & Sarah, d. Oct. 10, 1776, in the 12th y. of her age	3	262
Sarah, d. Joseph & Sarah, b. Nov. 17, 1743	3	154
Sarah, wid., m. Paul **TYLER**, b. of Branford, Oct. 26, 1761, by Josiah Rogers, J. P.	3	184
Sarah, w. of Michael, d. Oct. 27, 1776, in the 48th y. of her age	3	262
Sarah, [d. Medad & Anna], b. Jan. 15, 1783	3	266
Sarah, m. Malachi **COOK**, Dec. 25, 1802	3	392
Submit, d. Nathanael & Submit, b. Oct. 20, 1763	3	183

TALMADGE, TALMAGE, Chloe, wid., m. Joseph **FINCH**, b. of

Branford, Sept. 16, 1755, by Warham Williams	3	156
D[avis], s. Solomon & Lucretia, b. Apr. 2, 1787	3	258
Enos Todd, s. Solomon & Lucretia, b. Nov. 21, 1784	3	258
Hannah, d. Joseph & Hannah, b. Nov. 18, 1740	3	94
Hannah, [d. Josiah & Hannah], b. Jan. 17, 1751	3	160
Hannah, w. of Joseph, d. Apr. 16, 1751	3	135
Hannah, d. Joseph & Hannah, d. Nov. 20, 1751	3	135
Ichabod, [s. Josiah & Phebe], b. Jan. 18, 1747	3	160
Jacob, [s. Josiah & Hannah], b. Sept. 2, 1749	3	160
John, [s. Josiah & Hannah], b. Mar. 8, 1755	3	160
Jonathan, [s. Josiah & Phebe], b. Mar. 30, 1742	3	160
Joseph, [s. Josiah & Phebe], b. Apr. 4, 1739	3	160
Joseph, m. Hannah **HERRINTON**, b. of Branford, June 22, 1739, by Rev. Jonathan Merrick	3	91

	Vol.	Page
TALMADGE, TALMAGE, (cont.)		
Joseph, of Branford, m. Chloe **SEWARD**, of Dunham, Jan. 1,		
1752, by Rev. Nathan[ie]ll Chauncey, at Durham	3	135
Josiah, m. Phebe **DIBBLE**, b. of East Hampton, Oct. 14,		
1735, by Nath[anie]ll Hunting	3	160
Josiah, [s. Josiah & Phebe], b. Nov. 25, 1736	3	160
Josiah, m. Hannah **WILLIAMS**, b. of Branford, July [ ],		
1748, by Jon[a]th[an] Merrick	3	160
Josiah, Jr., m. Sybil **TODD**, b. of Branford, Mar. 15, 1759,		
by Warham Williams	3	160
Lois, [d. Josiah & Hannah], b. Feb. 23, 1753	3	160
Lucretia, d. Solomon & Lucretia, b. July 4, 1789	3	258
Lucretia, m. Jason **DICKERMAN**, May 8, 1822, by Rev.		
Matthew Noyes	3	419
Margery, of Easthampton, L. I., m. John **BUTLER**, of		
Branford, Aug. 11, 1742, by Rev. Jonathan Mer[r]ick	3	101
Phebe, [d. Josiah & Phebe], b. Aug. 4, 1744	3	160
Phebe, w. of Josiah, d. Jan. 28, 1747	3	160
Salla, [d. Josiah & Hannah], b. Aug. 4, 1758	3	160
Samuel, s. Josiah, Jr. & Sybil, b. Feb. 2, 1760	3	160
Solomon, s. Joseph & Chloe, b. Dec. 13, 1753	3	135
Solomon, m. Lucretia **TODD**, b. of Branford, May 2, 1782	3	258
Solomon had negro Phene, b. July 6, 1784	3	258
William, of North Branford, m. Harriet Louisa **JOHNSON**, of		
Branford, May 12, 1852, by Rev. T. P. Gillett	TM3	171
----, s. Orson C. & Clarra, b. Jan. 9, 1850	TM3	243
TANTTEPAN, Elisabeth, d. William & Sarah, b. Nov. 13, 1760	3	257
Hannah, d. William & Sarah, b. Mar. 26, 1769	3	257
TAYLOR, John, s. Charles & Hannah, b. Sept. 14, 1744	3	106
TENTER,[see also **TAINTOR**], Elesebeth, d. Micaell, b. June		
22, [16]55	1	172
Elesebeth, w. of Micaell, d. July 22, [16]59	1	170
Johan[n]a, d. Micaell, b. Apr. 29, [16]57	1	172
John, s. Mica[e]ll, b. May 26, 1650	1	171
Mica, s. Micah, b. Oct. 12, [1652]	1	171
Sarie, d. Micaell, b. Oct. 12, [16]58	1	172
THARP, Hannah, m. John **TYLER**, Jr., July 11, 1716, by Rev.		
Sam[ue]ll Russel[l]	3	38
THOMAS, Caroline, d. May 25, 1851, ae 82 y.	TM3	310
John, s. James & Anne, b. Oct. 14, 1783	3	312
THOMPSON, THOMSON, George Douglass, m. Mrs. Irene		
ROBBINS, b. of Branford, Nov. 5, 1772, by Philemon		
Robbins	3	208
Leveritt, m. Emerett **LINSLEY**, Dec. 24, 1846, by Rev.		
Frederick Miller	TM3	160
Sally, of East Haven, m. Erastus **STRONG**, of Branford,		
May 28, 1827, by Rev. Henry Lines, of New Haven	3	354
Thankfull, m. William **FANCHER**, b. of Branford, Nov. 20,		

	Vol.	Page
THOMPSON, THOMPSON, (cont)		
1723, by Rev. Sam[ue]ll Russell	3	54
TILLOTSON, TILESTON, TILLISON, Janne, m. John		
ROBINES, June 23, 167[0] (First written 1679)	1	174
John Henry, of New Haven, m. Susan Emeline		
CHITTENDEN, of Branford, Dec. 20, 1854, by Rev. T.		
P. Gillett	TM3	173
Shubael, m. Eliza **TYLER,** Sept. 1, 1825, by Stephen Dodd	3	340
Shubael, of New Haven, m. Betsey A. **AVERILL,** of Branford,		
Oct. 27, 1836, by Rev. Timothy P. Gillett	3	373
TODD, Charl[e]s, s. Josiah & Esther, b. Aug. 28, 1752	3	139
Elnathan, s. Jno. & Hannah, b. Jan. 7, 1738/9	3	92
Hannah, d. Jno. & Hannah, b. Apr. 23, 1734	3	92
John, s. John & Hannah, b. Jan. 8, 1731/2	3	92
Lole, d. Josiah & Esther, b. Sept. 16, 1754	3	139
Lucretia, m. Solomon **TALMAGE,** b. of Branford, May 2,		
1782	3	258
Mindwell, d. Jno. & Hannah, b. Feb. 9, 1736	3	92
Rebecca, of Northford, m. Harry **WILLIAMS,** of Wallingford,		
Dec. 24, [1820], by Origen P. Holcomb	3	412
Sybil, m. Josiah **TALMAGE,** Jr., b. of Branford, Mar. 15,		
1759, by Warham Williams	3	160
TOPPING, Lydia, Mrs., [formerly **WILFORD**), d. Nov. 3, 1694	2	343
TORREY, Oliver, s. Samuel H. & Anne, b. Feb. 15, 1764	3	182
Sam[ue]ll Holden, m. Anne **GOULD,** b. of Branford, Apr. 3,		
1760, by Philemon Robbins	3	163
Sam[ue]ll Holden, s. Sam[ue]ll H. & Anna, b. Jan. 21, 1761	3	171
TOWNER, Amos B., [s. David & Betsey], b. Dec. 12, 1804	3	284
Amos B., s. David & Betsey, d. Nov. 9, 1805	3	284
Anne, d. Jacob & Diana, b. May 26, 1776	3	285
Asenath, d. Jon[a]th[an], Jr. & Abigail, b. Nov. 14, 1783	3	274
Augustus, s. Jon[a]th[an], Jr. & Abigail, b. Sept. 2, 1787	3	257
David, s. Jon[a]th[an] & Mary, b. Aug. 19, 1768	3	274
David, m. Betsey **BISHOP,** Nov. 6, 1791, by Rev. Azel		
Backus, of Bethlehem	3	283
Davis, s. David & Betsey, b. Feb. 2, 1813	3	334
Eber, s. Jacob & Diana, b. Oct. 11, 1771	3	285
Eliza, [d. David & Betsey], b. Feb. 13, 1810	3	284
Eliza, d. David & Betsey, d. June 2, 1823	3	334
Elizabeth, d. Jonathan & Mary, b. Sept. 4, 1744	3	138
Elizabet[h], d. Jonathan & Mary, d. Jan. 12, 1752	3	138
Elisabeth, d. Jacob & Diana, b. Mar. 15, 1758;		
d. June 21, 1759	3	285
Elisabeth, d. Jon[a]th[an] & Mary, b. Dec. 14, 1761	3	274
Elisabeth, wid. of Richard, d. May 11, 1778, in the 86th		
y. of her age	3	265
Harriett, [d. David & Betsey], b. Jan. 28, 1800	3	283
Jacob, s. Richard, Jr. & Elisabeth, b. Mar. 29, 1726	3	59

	Vol.	Page
TOWNER, (cont.)		
Jerusha, d. Jacob & Diana, b. Oct. 17, 1765	3	285
John, [s. David & Betsey], b. Sept. 15, 1793	3	283
John, m. Martha **TYLER**, b. of Branford, Feb. 6, 1825, by		
Rev. Timothy P. Gillett	3	337
Jonath[an], s. Richard, Jr. & Elisabeth, b. Nov. 16, 1721	3	48
Jonathan, m. Mary **DARROW**, Nov. 10, 1743, by Philema		
Robbins	3	138
Jonathan, s. Jonathan & Mary, b. Aug. 28, 1758	3	274
Jon[a]th[an], Jr., m. Abigail **BALDWIN**, b. of Branford,		
Mar. 10, 1782, by Sam[ue]ll Eells	3	274
Jonathan, d. Apr. 19, 1804	3	284
Joseph, s. Jonathan & Mary b. Apr. 11, 1746; d. Apr. 19, 1746	3	138
Joseph, s. Jonathan & Mary, b. Mar. 10, 1754	3	139
Joseph, s. Jonathan & Mary, d. Mar. 29, 1757	3	150
Mary, m. Samuel **TYLER**, Oct. 22, 1713, by Rev. Sam[ue]ll		
Russel[l]	3	38
Mary, d. Richard & Elisabeth, b. Jan. 19, 1732/3	3	79
Mary, d. Jonathan & Mary, b. Nov. 1, 1751	3	138
Mary, wid. of Jonath[an], d. Feb. 15, 1806	3	284
Moses, s. Jacob & Diana, b. Aug. 6, 1760; d. Sept. 6, 1777	3	285
Nancy, [d. David & Betsey], b. Oct. 6, 1806	3	284
Nancy, m. Henry **ROGERS**, b. of Branford, Dec. [ ], 1832,		
by Edw[ar]d J. Ives	3	361
Phebe, d. Sam[ue]ll & Rebec[c]a, b. Sept. 14, 1717	3	42
Phebe, d. Jacob & Diana, b. Apr. 27, 1774	3	285
Phebe, m. Peleg **HOADLEY**, b. of Branford, Sept. 12, 1796	3	271
Rebecca, d. Jacob & Diana, b. May 14, 1764	3	285
Richard, Jr., m. Elisabeth **TYLER**, b. of Branford, Sept.		
28, 1720, by Nath[anie]ll Harrison, J. P.	3	45
Richard, Sr., d. Aug. 22, 1727	3	62
Richard, s. Richard & Elisabeth, b. Oct. 9, 1730	3	72
Richard, 2d, d. Feb. 28, 1753	3	132
Rreamy, d. Jonathan & Mary, b. Nov. 27, 1749; d. Jan. 23,		
1752	3	138
Ruhamah, d. Jon[a]th[an] & Mary, b. Apr. 11, 1764	3	274
Sam[ue]ll, of Branford, m. Rebec[c]a **BARN[E]S**, of North		
Haven, Jan. 25, 1716	3	42
Sarah, m. Sam[ue]ll **FROST**, Aug. 8, 1706, by W[illia]m		
Maltbie, J. P.	3	32
Sarah, d. Rich[ar]d, Jr. & Elisabeth, b. Nov. 29, 1723	3	53
Sarah, m. Abel **PAGE**, b. of Branford, Jan. 15, 1756, by		
Philemon Robbins	3	159
Sarah, d. Jacob & Diana, b. Feb. 23, 1768	3	285
Thankfull, d. Jonathan & Mary, b. June 11, 1747	3	138
TOWNSEND, Elizabeth, m. Henry **ROGERS**, May 16, 1849, by		
Rev. Franklin A. Spencer, of Westmoreland, N. Y.	TM3	246
TROWBRIDGE, Joseph E., m. Abigail **RUSSELL**, b. of Branford,		

	Vol.	Page
TROWBRIDGE, (cont.)		
June 18, 1794, by Nicholas Street	3	263
Sarah, of New Haven, m. John **RUSSEL[L]**, of Branford, Dec.		
17, 1707, by John Alling	3	33
TRUESDELL, TRUSDELL, TRUSDILL, TRUSDIL, Ebenezer, s.		
Richard & Lydia, b. Feb. 27, 1736/7	3	86
Elisabeth, m. Joseph **PALMER**, b. of Branford, Mar. 29,		
1719/20, by Rev. Sam[ue]ll Russell	3	51
James, s. Richard & Lydia, b. Jan. 25, 1731/2	3	75
Johanna, d. Richard & Lydia, b. Jan. 3, 1724	3	56
J[o]hanna, m. Levi **ROGERS**, b. of Branford, Dec. 14, 1743,		
by Jacob Hemingway	3	169
John, s. Will[ia]m & Martha, b. July 1, 1720	3	45
Jonathan, s. Richard & Lydia, b. Dec. 25, 1733	3	83
Jonathan, d. June 10, 1771	3	204
Justice, s. Richard & Lusee, b. Aug. 7, 1751	3	137
Lusee, d. Richard & Lusee, b. Dec. 6, 1752	3	137
Lydia, d. Richard & Lydia, b. Dec. 21, 1729	3	68
Lydia, m. Wheeler **BEERS**, b. of Branford, Jan. 16, 1752,		
by Jonathan Mer[r]ick	3	169
Lydia, b. Aug. 3, 1783	3	266
Mary, d. Richard & Lydia, b. Oct. 10, 1727	3	66
Mary, m. Elijah **PALMER**, b. of Branford, Apr. 16, 1745,		
by Rev. Jonathan Mer[r]ick	3	125
Rebeccah, m. John **HARRISON**, Dec. 24, 1702, by Rev. Mr.		
Russell	2	344
Richard, m. Lydia **LINSL[E]Y**, b. of Branford, Feb. 20,		
1723/4, by Rev. Sam[ue]ll Russell	3	56
Richard, m. Lusee **TRION**, June 8, 1750, by Jon[a]th[an]		
Mer[r]ick	3	137
Sam[ue]ll, s. Richard & Lydia, b. June 24, 1739	3	108
Thomas, s. William & Martha, b. Oct. 16, 1726	3	59
William, m. Martha **TYLER**, b. of Branford, Apr. 21, 1719,		
by Rev. Sam[ue]ll Russell	3	60
TRYON, TRION, Benjamin, of Wethersfield, m. Luce **WHEDON**,		
of Branford, Apr. 25, 1738, by Rev. Philemon Robbins	3	92
Eunice, d. Benj[ami]n & Luce, b. Aug. 6, 1739	3	92
Hannah, d. Benjamin & Luce, b. May 12, 1742	3	137
Henry, of Middletown, m. Jane **ROGERS**, of Branford, May		
1, 1843, by Rev. Timothy P. Gillett	TM3	156
Lusee, m. Richard **TRUSDILL**, June 8, 1750, by Jon[a]th[an]		
Mer[r]ick	3	137
TUCKER, Georgeanna, [d. Nathan Nelson & Betsey], b. June 19,		
1831	TM3	231
Georgeanna, m. John **HOTCHKISS**, b. of Branford, Aug. 2,		
1846, by Rev. A. C. Wheat	TM3	159
Horace, ae 21, m. Melinda **BARNES**, ae 19, Feb. 16, 1851	TM3	170
Horace P., of Lyme, m. Melinda **BARNS**, of Branford, Feb.		

	Vol.	Page
TUCKER, (cont.)		
16, 1851, by Rev. Timothy P. Gillett	TM3	168
James Telly, s. [Nathan Nelson & Betsey], b. Aug. 21, 1841	TM3	231
Lewis Montgomery, s. [Nathan Nelson & Betsey], b. Jan. 19, 1834	TM3	231
Mary Olds, d. [Nathan Nelson & Betsey],, b. Nov. 5, 1837	TM3	231
Nathan N., of North Madison, m. Betsey **GRISWOLD**, of Branford, Nov. 29, 1832, by Levi Bradley, J. P.	3	358
Stephen Olds, s. [Nathan Nelson & Betsey], b. May 27, 1843	TM3	231
----, d. Nelson & Betsey, b. June [ ], 1850	TM3	243
TUTTLE, Desire, d. Noah & Rachel, b. Sept. 17, 1730	3	72
Elisabeth, d. Noah & Rachel, b. Jan. 8, 1727/8	3	72
Joseph, s. Noah & Rachel, b. July 18, 1734	3	80
Lydia, d. Noah & Rachel, b. June 27, 1722	3	52
Mary, Mrs., of East Haven, m. Samuel **PAGE**, of Branford, July 23, 1823, by Charles Atwater, at North Branford	3	423
Noah, m. Rachel **HOADL[E]Y**, b. of Branford, Dec. 1, 1720, by Rev. Sam[ue]ll Russel[l]	3	52
Rachel, of North Haven, m. Joseph **TYLER**, Jr., of Branford, June 23, 1763, by Benjamin Trumble	3	180
Timothy, s. Noah & Rachel, b. Apr. 3, 1724	3	72
TYLER, Abel, s. Eben[eze]r & Anne, b. Oct. 25, 1722	3	49
Abiel, s. Ebenezer & Anne, b. Feb. 3, 1724/5	3	56
Abigail, d. Ffrancis, b. Apr. 6, 1681	1	211
Abigail, d. Isaac & Abigail, b. Dec. 23, 1705	2	346
Abigail, d. Isaac & Abigail, b. Dec. 22, [ ]; [bp. Dec. [ ], [1705]	3	29
Abigail, [twin with Amos], d. Bezaleel & Abigail, b. Mar. 24, 1725/6	3	60
Abigail, d. Joseph, Jr. & Hannah, b. Jan. 12, 1752	3	125
Abigail, m. Amos **BROWN**, b. of Branford, Nov. 14, 1754, by Philemon Robbins	3	167
Abigail, w. of Joseph, d. Oct. [ ], 1759	3	163
Abigail, d. Bille & Abigail, b. Apr. 18, 1768	3	194
Abigail, m. Isaac **PALMER**, b. of Branford, Feb. 19, 1773, by Philemon Robbins	3	283
Abigail, m. Isaac **PALMER**, Feb. 19, 1773	3	394
Abigail, [d. William, 2d, & Abigail], b. Oct. 31, 1828	3	365
Abraham, s. Isaac & Abigail, b. Feb. 11, 1706/7	3	30
Agnis, d. John & Hannah, b. Oct. 21, 1715	3	44
Almira, [d. Philemon & Lucy], b. Aug. 23, 1801	3	384
Almira, d. Philemon, d. July 22, 1840, ae 39 y.	TM3	304
Almond, s. Sam[ue]l & Sally, b. Mar. 10, 1804	3	286
Almon, m. Henrietta **PAGE**, b. of Branford, June 21, 1823, by James Noyes	3	423
Almon, s. Almon & Henrietta, b. Jan. 14, 1828	3	371
Amos, [twin with Abigail], s. Bezaleel & Abigail, b. Mar. 24, 1725/6	3	60

	Vol.	Page
TYLER, (cont.)		
Anna, d. Solomon & Dorcas, b. June 16, 1775	3	298
Anna, [d. John & Anna], b. July 24, 1804	3	385
Anna, of Branford, m. John **BEAUMONT**, of Wallingford,		
June 3, 1827, by Rev. Timothy P. Gillett	3	344
Anna, [d. Benjamin R. & Hannah], b. Nov. 17, 1829	3	365
Anne, d. George, b. June 20, 1682	1	211
Anne, d. Isaac & Abigail, b. Aug. 10, 1710	3	33
Anne, d. Peter, Jr. & Hannah, b. July 18, 1738	3	97
Anne, d. Peter & Hannah, b. Apr. 30, 1773	3	257
Anne, d. Solomon & Dorcas, b. July 16, 1775 (Perhaps 1778?)	3	265
Anson, [s. Philemon & Lucy], b. Dec. 6, 1788	3	384
Anson, s. Philemon & Lucy, m. Harriott **LINSL[E]Y**, d. of		
Ebenezer, Jr. & Bets[e]y, July 10, 1811	3	398
Anson, [Sr.], d. Nov. 22, 1822	3	421
Asa, s. Sam[ue]l & Rachel, b. Aug. 22, 1793	3	269
Asa, [s. Edmund & Phebe], b. Aug. 6, 1811	3	409
Asa, s. Samuel & Rebekah, d. May 28, 1816	3	403
Asahel, s. Paul & Mary, b. Dec. 9, 1744	3	186
Asahel, s. Solomon & Dorcas, b. Nov. 3, 1780	3	298
Asahel, d. July 16, 1849, ae 68 y.	TM3	309
Augustus, m. Sally **MALTBY**, Dec. 28, 1814, by Rev. James		
Noyes, of Wallingford	3	416
Augustus, d. Sept. 4, 1822	3	421
Benjamin, s. Bezaleel & Abigail, b. Sept. 10, 1721	3	49
Benj[ami]n, s. Joseph, Jr. & Hannah, b. Nov. 16, 1742	3	99
Benjamin, s. Joseph, & Hannah, d. Sept. 23, 1743	3	163
Benjamin, s. Joseph, Jr. & Jerusha, b. July 21, 1755	3	163
Benjamin, m. Sarah **BALDWIN**, b. of Branford, Oct. 31, 1776,		
by Philemon Robbins	3	270
Benjamin, [s. Obed & Eunice], b. Dec. 16, 1805	3	405
Benjamin, s. Benjamin R. & Hannah, b. Aug. 21, 1837	TM3	232
Berijah, s. David & Bethiah, b. June 18, 1728 (Probably 1729)	3	67
Berijah, s. David & Bathiah, b. June 18, 1729	3	139
Berijah, of Branford, m. Hannah **HALL**, of Wallingford,		
Apr. 7, 1751, by Rev. Warham Williams	3	125
Bethyah, d. Lydia **FINCH**, b. Dec. 27, 1757	3	156
Bethyah, d. Lydia **FINCH**, d. Feb. 5, 176[0]	3	159
Betsey, d. Sam[ue]ll, Jr. & Rachel, b. Nov. 24, 1776	3	305
Betsey, d. John, Jr. & Eunice, b. Nov. 21, 1829	3	355
Betsey, d. John, d. Aug. 13, 1842	TM3	309
Betsey, d. John & Eunice, b. [ ]	TM3	243
Bets[e]y Ann, [d. Malachi S. & Lucy], b. Feb. 29, 1816	3	417
Bezaliel, m. Abigail **JOHNSON**, Jan. 23, 1711/2, by Rev.		
Sam[ue]ll Russel[l]	3	34
Bezaleel, s. Bezaleel & Abigail, b. Nov. 6, 1715	3	37
Bille, s. Paul & Mary, b. July 9, 1742	3	186
Bille, m. Abigail **MALTBIE**, b. of Branford, Mar. 10, 1765,		

	Vol.	Page
TYLER, (cont.)		
by Rev. Bela Hubbard	3	185
Calvin, s. Obadiah & Hannah, b. May 28, 1762	3	179
Calvin, s. Obadiah & Hannah, d. May 12, 1765, ae 2 d.	3	186
Calvin, s. Obadiah & Hannah, b. Sept. 13, 1767	3	198
Caroline Christiana, [d. Malachi S. & Lucy], b. Oct. 15, 1817	3	417
Charles, s. Bezaleel & Abigail, b. Jan. 6, 1723/4	3	55
Charles, d. about Sept. 12, 1738	3	88
Dameris, [d. Obed & Eunice], b. Apr. 12, 1802	3	405
Damaris, m. Samuel **MONRO[E]**, b. of Branford, Jan. 29,		
1826, by Rev. Timothy P. Gillett	3	341
Daniel, m. Eunice **TYLER**, b. of Branford, Feb. 11, 1741/2,		
by W[illia]m Gould, J. P.	3	97
Daniel, s. Daniel & Eunice, b. Jan. 9, 1744/5	3	105
David, s. John & Hannah, b. Mar. 9, 1706/7	3	31
David, m. Bethiah **LINSL[E]Y**, of Branford, Dec. 8, 1726,		
by Nath[anie]ll Har[r]ison, J. P.	3	62
David, s. David & Bethyah, b. July 22, 1730	3	112
David, m. Sybil **INGRAHAM**, b. of Branford, Jan. 26, 1758,		
by Warham Williams	3	154
David, s. David & Sybil, b. June 4, 1760	3	160
David, m. Sarah **BARTHOLOMEW**, b. of Branford, June 28,		
1761, by Warham Williams	3	173
David, [s. John & Anna], b. Mar. 18, 1791	3	385
David Atwater, [s. Augustus & Sally], b. Nov. 10, 1818	3	416
David Morse, s. Jacob M. & Huldah, b. Apr. 24, 1818	3	407
Deborah, d. Peter, b. Mar. 15, 1676/7	1	211
Deborah, d. George & Mary, b. Nov. 24, 1700	2	343
Deborah, d. Peter & Elizabeth, b. Apr. 23, 1701	2	343
Deborah, m. Andrew **MONRO[E]**, b. of Branford, Oct. 26,		
1721, by Rev. Sam[ue]ll Russell	3	52
Dennis, [s. Edmund & Phebe], b. Apr. 14, 1803	3	409
Diana, d. Jacob M. & Hulda[h], b. Apr. 7, 1813	3	402
Dorcas, d. Peter, b. May 3, 1680	1	211
Dorcas, m. Jacob **CARTER**, Dec. 4, 1712, by Rev. Sam[ue]ll		
Russel[l]	3	35
Dorcus, d. David & Bethyah, b. Nov. 30, 1742	3	115
Ebenezer, s. George & Mary, b. Mar. 29, 1703	2	344
Ebenezer, s. Eben[eze]r & Anna, b. Jan. 3, 1716/7	3	39
Ebenezer, s. John, Jr. & Hannah, b. Apr. 20, 1723	3	52
Ebenezer, s. George & Mary, d. May 2, 1723	3	52
Ebenezer, s. Joseph & Jerusha, b. Nov. 5, 1761	3	176
Ebenezer, [s. William, 2d, & Abigail], b. Aug. 11, 1824	3	365
Eber, s. Obadiah & Hannah, b. Feb. 17, 1771	3	201
Edmund, s. Sam[ue]ll, Jr. & Rachel, b. Feb. 2, 1783	3	305
Edmund, of Branford, m. Phebe **HINMAN**, of Durham, Feb.		
14, 1802	3	409
Eliza, [d. Philemon & Lucy], b. Jan. 1, 1797	3	384

	Vol.	Page
TYLER, (cont.)		
Eliza, m. Shubael **TILLOTSON**, Sept. 1, 1825, by Stephen Dodd	3	340
Elizabeth, d. George, b. Nov. 6, 1687	1	211
Elizabeth, d. George & Mary, b. Feb. 9, 1693/4	2	343
Elizabeth, d. Peter & Elizabeth, b. Sept. 6, 1705	2	346
Elisabeth, m. Richard **TOWNER**, Jr., b. of Branford, Sept. 28, 1720, by Nathan[ie]ll Harrison, J. P.	3	45
Elisabeth, m. Benjamin **FARNUM**, b. of Branford, June 3, 1725, by Rev. Sam[ue]ll Russell	3	56
Elisabeth, d. John, Sr. & Hannah, b. Aug. 20, 1728	3	64
Elisabeth, d. Peter, Jr. & Hannah, b. Nov. 5, 1743	3	103
Elisabeth, d. Paul & Mary, b. Aug. 7, 1750	3	186
Elizabeth, d. Sam[ue]ll & Lidia, b. Dec. 5, 1757	3	151
Elisabeth, m. Samuel **FRISBIE**, b. of Branford, Mar. 23, 1768, by Philemon Robbins	3	195
Elisabeth, m. Edward **PAGE**, b. of Branford, Nov. 14, 1771, by Josiah Rogers, J. P.	3	204
Elisabeth, m. Stephen **LINSLEY**, b. of Branford, Apr. 16, 1781, by Sam[ue]ll Eells	3	307
Elnathan, s. John & Hannah, b. Jan. 26, 1704/5	2	345
Elnathan, s. John & Hannah, d. Feb. 13, 1708/9	3	30
Elnathan, s. John & Hannah, b. Apr. 9, 1711	3	34
Elnathan, s. Elnathan & Lucy, b. Mar. 30, 1755	3	155
Elnathan, d. June 1, 1763	3	180
Elsee, [d. John & Anna], b. Jan. 12, 1793	3	385
Elsee, d. Sept. 6, 1811, ae 18 y.	3	342
Emeline, d. John, Jr. & Lucy, b. Aug. 9, 1823	3	340
Emeline, [d. Benjamin R. & Hannah], b. July 19, 1826	3	365
Emeline, m. Randolph **FRISBIE**, b. of Branford, July 19, 1847, by Rev. T. P. Gillett	TM3	160
Emeline, m. William S. **LINSLEY**, b. of Branford, Nov. 28, 1849, by Rev. Timothy P. Gillett	TM3	164
Esther, [d. Philemon & Lucy], b. Jan. 13, 1795	3	384
Eunice, d. John, Jr. & Hannah, b. Oct. 8, 1717	3	40
Eunice, m. Daniel **TYLER**, b. of Branford, Feb. 11, 1741/2, by W[illia]m Gould, J. P.	3	97
Eunice, d. Jonathan & Elisabeth, b. Dec. 12, 1770	3	202
Euncey, [d. Obed & Eunice], b. Oct. 14, 1796	3	405
Eunice, m. Samuel **SPINK**, b. of Branford, Nov. 6, 1831, by Timothy P. Gillett	3	357
Esra*, s. Ebenezer & Anne, b. Oct. 3, 1718 (*Ezra)	3	42
Ezra, [s. John & Anna], b. Oct. 11, 1799	3	385
George, d. Mar. 22, 1730/1	3	71
George, s. Roger & Martha, b. Oct. 7, 1732	3	75
George, m. Lydia **RAYNER**, b. of Branford, Jan. 14, 1756, by Rev. Jonath[a]n Mer[r]ick	3	144
Gideon, s. Bezaleel & Abigail, b. Oct. 10, 1717	3	42

	Vol.	Page
TYLER, (cont.)		
Grace, d. Roger, Jr. & Martha, b. Apr. 24, 1783	3	308
Hannah, d. Peter, b. Feb. 10, 1682	1	211
Hannah, d. George & Hannah, b. Mar. 10, 1690/1	2	343
Hannah, d. Peter & Hannah, b. May 8, 1693	2	345
Hannah, d. John & Hannah, b. June 3, 1713	3	44
Hannah, m. John **BALDWIN**, Oct. 26, 1713, by Rev. Sam[ue]ll		
Russel[l]	3	38
Hannah, d. John & Hannah, b. Sept. 28, 1733	3	77
Hannah, d. Joseph, Jr. & Hannah, b. Aug. 14, 1744	3	104
Hannah, d. Elnathan & Lucy, b. Mar. 10, 1745	3	155
Hannah, w. of Joseph, Jr., d. Jan. 31, 1752	3	163
Hannah, m. Jonathan **GOODSELL**, Jr., b. of Branford, Jan.		
13, 1762, by Philemon Robbins	3	176
Hannah, d. Samuel & Lydia, b. Apr. 30, 1763	3	185
Hannah, m. Peter **TYLER**, b. of Branford, Feb. 16, 1764,		
by Warham Williams	3	198
Hannah, d. Bille & Abigail, b. Apr. 24, 1770	3	200
Hannah, m. Jonah **CLARK**, b. of Branford, Jan. 1, 1775,		
by Oliver Stanley, J. P.	3	267
Hannah, d. Benjamin & Sarah, b. Feb. 4, 1779	3	271
Hannah, m. Daniel **AVERILL**, Nov. 3, 1796	3	286
Hannah, [d. Malachi S. & Lucy], b. Jan. 8, 1822	3	417
Hannah, d. Feb. 2, 1848, ae 65 y.	TM3	308
Harriet, [d. Malachi S. & Lucy], b. May 2, 1819	3	417
Harriet, [d. Benjamin R. & Hannah], b. Sept. 18, 1831	3	365
Harriet Loisa, d. Anson & Harriet, b. Aug. 10, 1819	3	421
Harvey, [s. John & Anna], b. Aug. 18, 1801	3	385
Hervey, d. July 17, 1826, ae 25 (Harvey)	3	342
Henrietta, m. Charles **JOHNSON**, b. of Branford, Jan. 28,		
1830, by Rev. Timothy P. Gillett	3	352
Henry, [s. Malachi S. & Lucy], b. Jan. 17, 1814	3	417
Henry Butler, s. Samuel Maltby & Celestia, b. Apr. 13, 1835	3	371
Isaac, s. George, b. Feb. 25, 1679	1	211
Isaac, m. Abigail **POND**, Nov. 6, 1704	2	345
Isaac, s. Isaac & Abigail, b. Oct. 31, 1708	3	30
Isaac, m. Hannah **BETTS**, b. of Branford, Feb. 24, 1736/7,		
by Rev. Philemon Robbins	3	86
Isaac, s. Isaac & Hannah, b. Apr. 11, 1743	3	101
Isaac, d. Aug. 28, 1772	3	298
Jacob, s. Paul & Mary, b. Mar. 18, 1754	3	186
Jacob, s. Phinehas & Abigail, b. Oct. 20, 1760	3	170
Jacob M., of Branford, m. Hulda[h] **STANNARD**, of Saybrook,		
May 1, [18--]	3	283
Jacob Maltbie, s. Bille & Abigail, b. Aug. 1, 1782	3	297
James, s. Daniel & Eunice, b. Feb. 25, 1742/3	3	100
James, s. Samuel & Rachel, b. Jan. 7, 1785	3	269
James W., [s. William, 2d, & Abigail], b. Jan. 1, 1826	3	365

	Vol.	Page
TYLER, (cont.)		
Jehiel, s. John, Sr. & Hannah, b. June 24, 1725	3	60
Jemima, d. Peter & Elizabeth, b. Sept. [28], 1702	2	343
Jemima, d. John & Hannah, b. Mar. 13, 1717/18	3	44
Jemima, d. Elnathan & Lucy, b. Oct. 3, 1755	3	155
Jeremiah, s. Roger, Jr. & Martha, b. Jan. 30, 1771	3	308
Jerusha, d. John, Jr. & Hannah, b. Aug. 16, 1730	3	69
Jerusha, m. Joseph **TYLER**, Jr., b. of Branford, July		
[ ], 1752, by Philemon Robbins	3	163
Jerusha, d. Joseph, Jr. & Jerusha, b. Oct. 14, 1757	3	163
Jerusha, m. Gideon **GOODRICH**, b. of Branford, Mar. 20,		
1780	3	305
Jerusha, d. Philemon & Lucy, b. June 7, 1787	3	254
Jerusha, m. Timothy **BALDWIN**, Oct. 21, 1819, by Rev.		
Timothy P. Gillett	3	413
John, s. Peter, b. Nov. 22, 1674	1	174
John, s. George & Mary, b. Jan. 6, 1695/6	2	343
John, Jr., m. Hannah **THARP**, July 11, 1716, by Rev.		
Sam[ue]ll Russel[l]	3	38
John, s. John, Sr. & Hannah, b. Jan. 23, 1722/3	3	60
John, s. Joseph, Jr. & Jerusha, b. Aug. 26, 1759	3	163
John, m. Anna **ROGERS**, b. of Branford, Nov. 20, 1786, by		
Jason Atwater	3	385
John, Jr., [s. John & Anna], b. Sept. 15, 1789	3	385
John, m. Lucy **BLACKSTONE**, Nov. 26, 1815, by Rev.		
Timothy P. Gillett	3	404
John, Jr., m. Eunice **AVERILL**, b. of Branford, July 23,		
1828, by Rev. Timothy P. Gillett	3	347
John Rogers, s. John, Jr. & Eunice, b. Oct. 27, 1834	3	371
Jonathan, s. John & Hannah, b. Jan. 17, 1708/9	3	30
Jonathan, s. Ebenezer & Anne, b. June 7, 1732	3	74
Jonathan, s. Paul & Mary, b. Sept. 12, 1740	3	94
Jonathan, m. Elisabeth **LINSL[E]Y**, b. of Branford, Dec.		
28, 1769, by Warham Williams	3	202
Joseph, s. Peter & Hannah, b. Oct. 26, 1691	2	345
Joseph, Jr., m. Hannah **WARDELL**, b. of Branford, Dec. 28,		
1737, by Rev. Philemon Robbins	3	91
Joseph, s. Joseph, Jr. & Hannah, b. Aug. 10, 1740	3	95
Joseph, Jr., m. Jerusha **TYLER**, b. of Branford, July		
[ ], 1752, by Philemon Robbins	3	163
Joseph, d. Nov. 19, 175[9]	3	163
Joseph, Jr., of Branford, m. Rachel **TUTTLE**, of North Haven,		
June 23, 1763, by Benjamin Trumble	3	180
Josiah, s. Dan[ie]ll & Eunice, b. Nov. 1, 1749	3	122
Josiah, s. Sam[ue]ll & Lydiah, b. Feb. 1, 1755	3	151
Josiah, s. Joseph & Jerusha, b. June 6, 1770	3	206
Josiah, m. Mrs. Anne **GOODRICH**, Jan. 12, 1786, by Jason		
Atwater	3	255

	Vol.	Page
TYLER, (cont.)		
Julia Ann, m. John H. **ROBINSON**, b. of Branford, Feb. 13,		
1840, by Rev. L. H. Corson	3	377
Julia Elizabeth, d. Samuel M. & Celestia, b. Oct. 23, 1832	3	360
Julia Matilda, [d. Jacob M. & Hulda[h], b. Mar. 13, 1808	3	283
Julian, d. Anson & Harriet, b. May 29, 1815	3	421
Julius, [s. John & Anna], b. Nov. 24, 1806	3	385
Laura, d. Sollomon & Dorcas, b. Sept. 19, 1789	3	253
Laura, d. Solomon & Dorcas, m. Isaac **HOADLEY**, s. Abel &		
Lucinda, b. of Branford, Nov. 3, 1813	3	408
Lemuel, s. Elnathan & Lucy, b. Aug. 17, 1761	3	180
Lucrecia, d. Dan[ie]ll & Eunice, b. July 10, 1747	3	111
Lucy, d. Elnathan & Lucy, b. July 3, 1752	3	155
Lucy, m. John **BALDWIN**, 4th, Nov. 28, 1764, by Josiah		
Rogers, J. P.	3	188
Lucy, [d. Philemon & Lucy], b. Sept. 24, 1792	3	384
Lucy, w. of John, Jr., d. Nov. 5, 1825, ae 34 y.	3	340
Luther, s. Obadiah & Hannah, b. May 6, 1765	3	186
Lydia, d. Sam[ue]ll & Lydia, b. Dec. 13, 1749	3	123
Lydia, w. of Roger, d. Nov. 28, 1760	3	166
Lydia, d. Peter & Hannah, b. Nov. 19, 1769	3	199
Lydia, d. Bille & Abigail, b. Mar. 8, 1774	3	297
Lydia, d. Benjamin & Sarah, b. Sept. 23, 1781	3	271
Lydia, [d. John & Anna], b. Mar. 5, 1787	3	385
Lydia, m. James **McQUEEN**, Mar. 12, 1807	3	392
Lydia, d. Jan. 13, 1813, ae 26	3	342
Lydia, d. John, Jr. & Lucy, b. Dec. 5, 1816	3	406
Lydia, m. Ralph **LINSLEY**, b. of Branford, June 16, 1818,		
by Rev. Matthew Noyes	3	420
Lydia Beach, d. Philemon & Lucy, b. Nov. 20, 1785	3	254
Lydia Diana, d. Jacob M. & Huldah, b. Apr. 7, 1813	3	407
Major, [s. William, 2d, & Abigail], b. Aug. 19, 1820	3	365
Malachi, s. Peter & Hannah, b. Apr. 11, 1746	3	106
Malachi, d. Apr. 15, 1769	3	199
Malachi, s. Roger, Jr., & Martha, b. July 14, 1777	3	308
Malachi, s. Peter & Hannah, b. Dec. 2, 1781	3	262
Margery, m. John **BALDWIN**, 4th, Mar. 18, 1741, by Jonathan		
Merrick	3	156
Marietta, [d. Philemon & Lucy], b. Dec. 10, 1803	3	384
Mariette, m. Samuel **AVERILL**, b. of Branford, May 9, 1843,		
by Rev. Timothy P. Gillett	TM3	156
Martha, d. John & Hannah, b. Nov. 25, 1702	2	343
Martha, m. William **TRUESDELL**, b. of Branford, Apr. 21,		
1719, by Rev. Sam[ue]ll Russell	3	60
Martha, d. Roger & Martha, b. May 26, 1731	3	74
Martha, d. Joseph, Jr. & Jerusha, b. Apr. 15, 1753	3	163
Martha, d. Roger, Jr. & Martha, b. June 28, 1779	3	308
Martha, [d. John & Anna], b. Sept. 19, 1795	3	385

	Vol.	Page
TYLER, (cont.)		
Martha, m. John **TOWNER**, b. of Branford, Feb. 6, 1825,		
by Rev. Timothy P. Gillett	3	337
Martha Laurens, [d. Augustus & Sally], b. Sept. 25, 1815	3	416
Mary, d. George & Mary, b. Apr. 8, 1709	3	30
Mary, m. John **BURGES**, Nov. 28, 1709	3	32
Mary, d. Roger & Martha, b. Nov. 19, 1735	3	82
Mary, d. Isaac & Hannah, b. May 3, 1739	3	90
Mary, d. Joseph, Jr. & Hannah, b. Dec. 14, 1746	3	111
Mary, d. Paul & Mary, b. Feb. 7, 1747; d. [ ]	3	186
Mary, d. Paul & Mary, b. Apr. 30, 1757	3	186
Mary, m. Nath[anie]ll **HARRISON**, Jr., b. of Branford,		
Dec. 19, 1758, by Nath[anie]ll Harrison, J. P.	3	154
Mary, w. of Paul, d. Nov. 13, 1760	3	186
Mary, m. John **HOBART**, b. of Branford, Oct. 25, 1770, by		
P. Robbins	3	297
Mary, d. Bille & Abigail, b. Oct. 1, 1772	3	297
Mary, d. Solomon & Dorcas, b. Apr. 3, 1774; d. Apr. 6, 1774	3	298
Mary, d. Roger, Jr. & Martha, b. Oct. 24, 1775	3	308
Mary, m. Eber **BEACH**, Oct. 8, 1821, by Timothy P. Gillett	3	414
Mary, d. John, Jr. & Eunice, b. Sept. 26, 1833	3	367
Mary, d. Aug. 13, 1848, ae 1 y.	TM3	308
Mercy, d. Roger & Martha, b. July 20, 1737	3	88
Mercy, m. Thomas **NORTON**, b. of Branford, Apr. 29, 1761,		
by Philemon Robbins	3	178
Milly, d. Samuel & Rachel, b. Mar. 9, 1791	3	269
Molly, [d. Philemon & Lucy], b. Feb. 1, 1799	3	384
Morris, of New Haven, m. Emeline **COOK**, of Branford, June		
27, 1831, [by Rev. Timothy P. Gillett]	3	357
Nancy, d. Sam[ue]l & Rachel, b. Jan. 5, 1796	3	269
Nancy, m. Elihu **COOK**, Jr., b. of Branford, Dec. 2, 1815	3	415
Nathan, s. Francis & Sarah, b. Nov. 23, 1706	3	31
Nathan, s. Eben[eze]r & Anne, b. Oct. 28, 1720	3	49
Nathaniel, s. Bezaleel & Abigail, b. July 13, 1731	3	76
Nehemiah, s. Joseph, Jr. & Hannah, b. Sept. 27, 1738	3	91
Nehemiah, s. Joseph, Jr. & Hannah, d. Sept. 27, 1743	3	163
Nehemiah, s. Joseph & Jerusha, b. Oct. 8, 1765	3	187
Noah, s. Ebenezer & Anne, b. Aug. 12, 1727	3	74
Obed, s. Joseph & Jerusha, b. Apr. 2, 1768	3	206
Obed, of Branford, m. Sally **FALKNER**, of Guilford, June		
24, 1835, by Timothy P. Gillett	3	369
Obed, d. Mar. 29, 1840, ae 71 y.	TM3	304
Obed, s. Benjamin R. & Hannah, b. Dec. 14, 1841	TM3	232
Obediah, s. George & Mary, b. Feb. 21, 1705	3	31
Obadiah, s. Roger & Martha, b. July 22, 1739	3	92
Obadiah, m. Hannah **BARKER**, b. of Branford, Jan. 31, 1762,		
by Philemon Robbins	3	179
Oliver Tillotson, s. William, 2d, & Abigail, b. May 10, 1834	3	377

	Vol.	Page
TYLER, (cont.)		
Ozias, s. Elnathan & Lucy, b. Sept. 17, 1747	3	155
Pamela, d. Sept. 16, 1848,. ae 37 y.	TM3	308
Pamelia Amelia, d. Jacob M. & Huldah, b. Jan. 11, 1811	3	407
Pamela Amelia, d. Jacob M. & Huldah, b Jan. 25, 1811	3	398
Patience, d. Peter & Hannah, b. Sept. 25, 1689	2	345
Patience, m. Isaac **HARRISON**, Dec. 12, 1706, by Rev.		
Sam[ue]ll Russel[l]	3	32
Patience, d. John, Sr. & Hannah, b. Aug. 23, 1720	3	60
Paul, m. Mary **FRISBIE**, b. of Branford, Nov. 8, 1739, by		
Rev. Jonathan Mer[r]ick	3	94
Paul, m. wid. Sarah **TAINTOR**, b. of Branford, Oct. 26,		
1761, by Josiah Rogers, J. P.	3	184
Peter, m. Deborah **SWANE**, Nov. 20, 1671	1	174
Peter, s. Peter, b. Jan. 28, [16]72/73	1	174
Peter, Sr., m. Hannah **WHITEHEAD**, Dec. 25, 1688	2	345
Peter, Jr., m. Hannah **PALMER**, Jan. 31, 1733/4, by Rev.		
Jonathan Mer[r]ick	3	81
Peter, s. Peter, Jr. & Hannah, b. Jan. 5, 1734/5	3	81
Peter, s. Peter, Jr. & Hannah, b. Feb. 17, 1740/1	3	97
Peter, s. Sam[ue]ll & Lydia, b. Oct. 24, 1760	3	171
Peter, m. Hannah **TYLER**, b. of Branford, Feb. 16, 1764,		
by Warham Williams	3	198
Peter, s. Peter & Hannah, b. Feb. 22, 1767	3	199
Peter, of Northford, d. Dec. 5, 1807	3	281
Philemon, s. Joseph & Jerusha, b. Nov.. 3, 1763	3	184
Philemon, m. Lucy **LINSLEY**, b. of Branford, Apr. 27, 1785,		
by Jason Atwater	3	254
Phinehas, s. David & Bethyah, b. Dec. 12, 1736	3	115
Phinehas, m. Abigail **HARRISON**, b. of Branford, Mar. 16,		
1760, by Philemon Robbins	3	170
Polly, d. Samuel & Rachel, b. Feb. 16, 1788	3	269
Rachel, d. Peter & Hannah, b. July 2, 1778	3	262
Rebec[c]ah, d. Bezaleel & Abigail, b. Apr. 3, 1713	3	36
Rebecca, m. Nathaniel **PALMER**, b. of Branford, Sept. 11,		
1733, by Rev. Philemon Robbins	3	76
Rebecca, d. David & Sybil, b. Nov. 22, 1758	3	154
Rebecca, d. Bille & Abigail, b. Jan. 8, 1766	3	194
Rebecca, d. Roger, Jr. & Martha, b. Nov. 12, 1772	3	308
Rebecca, d. Sam[ue]ll, Jr. & Rachel, b. Jan. 31, 1779	3	305
Rebecca, m. Noadiah **ROGERS**, b. of Branford, Oct. 16, 1793,		
by Rev. David Butler	3	261
Roger, s. Georg[e] & Mary, b. Feb. 26, 1697	2	343
Roger, s. Roger & Martha, b. Jan. 25, 1740/1	3	101
Roger, of Branford, m. Lydia **ROBINSON**, of New Haven,		
May 7, 1760, by Jon[a]th[an] Merrick	3	166
Roger, Jr., m. Martha **STENT**, b. of Branford, May 15, 1767,		
by Philemon Robbins	3	195

	Vol.	Page
TYLER, (cont.)		
Roger, m. Mary **GOODRICH**, b. of Branford, July 2, 1767,		
by Philemon Robbins	3	191
Roger, s. Roger, Jr. & Martha, b. May 27, 1774	3	308
Roger, d. Jan. 17, 1784, ae 85 y. 10 m. 8 d.	3	300
Roswell, s. Josiah & Anne, b. Dec. 10, 1786	3	255
Roswell, m. Beda J. **JOHNSON**, b. of Branford, Mar. 13,		
1844, by Rev. Davis T. Shailer	TM3	157
Roxany, d. Josiah & Anna, b. Mar. 17, 1789	3	257
Sally, [d. Obed & Eunice], b. Dec. 31, 1793	3	405
Sally, m. John **BEACH**, b. of Branford, May 21, 1807	3	369
Sally, w. of Samuel, Jr., d. Nov. 20, 1815	3	403
Sally, d. Obed, m. Samuel **FRISBIE**, 2d, s. of Josiah, b.		
of Branford, May 17, 1818	3	410
Sally, w. of Obed, d. Dec. 28, 1839, ae 58 y.	TM3	304
Sally Loisa, d. Jacob M. & Huldah, b. Dec. 25, 1815	3	407
Samuel, s. George, b. Feb. 25, 1684	1	211
Samuel, m. Mary **TOWNER**, Oct. 22, 1713, by Rev. Sam[ue]ll		
Russel[l]	3	38
Sam[ue]ll, m. Lydia **ROSE**, b. of Branford, Jan. 5, 1748/9,		
by Rev. Philemon Robbins	3	123
Samuel, s. Samuel & Lydiah, b. Mar. 21, 1753	3	151
Samuel, Jr., m. Rachel **BARTHOLOMEW**, b. of Branford,		
Jan. 11, 1776, by Philemon Robbins	3	261
Samuel, s. Sam[ue]ll, Jr. & Rachel, b. Oct. 15, 1780	3	305
Samuel, Jr., m. Sally **GOODSELL**, May 12, 1803	3	286
Samuel, Jr., d. Nov. 29, 1815	3	403
Samuel, d. Mar. 18, 1816	3	403
Samuel, s. Almon & Henrietta, b. Jan. 24, 1824	3	371
Samuel, s. John & Eunice, b. Aug. 14, 1837	TM3	243
Samuel, m. Sarah I. **BEACH**, b. of Branford, Jan. 21, 1849,		
by Rev. Daniel D. Lyon	TM3	163
Sam[ue]ll Bet[t]s, s. Isaac & Hannah, b. Mar. 13, 1740/1	3	95
Samuel Maltby, [s. Jacob M. & Hulda[h], b. Nov. 1, 1806	3	283
Sarah, d. John & Hannah, Jr., b. Oct. 24, 1720	3	45
Sarah, d. Joseph, Jr. & Hannah, b. Aug. 11, 1749	3	120
Sarah, d. Peter & Hannah, b. Mar. 4, 1765	3	199
Sarah, d. Roger, Jr. & Martha, b. Sept. 17, 1767	3	195
Sarah, d. Benj[ami]n & Sarah, b. Apr. 25, 1785	3	312
Sarah, m. Nath[anie]l **JOHNSON**, Apr. 13, 1786	3	262
Sarah J., d. Samuel & Sarah, b. Sept. 8, 1850	TM3	243
Simeon, s. John, Jr. & Hannah, b. Apr. 6, 1729	3	66
Solomon, s. Ebenezer & Anne, b. July 12, 1729	3	74
Solomon, of Branford, m. Dorcas **FISK**, of Haddam, Nov.		
9, 1772	3	298
Solomon, of Branford, m. Dorcas **FISK**, of Haddam, Nov. 10,		
1772, by Eleazer May	3	208
Solomon, s. Solomon & Dorcas, b. Nov. 22, 1776	3	266

	Vol.	Page
TYLER, (cont.)		
Solomon, s. Solomon & Dorcas, b. Nov. 22, 1776	3	298
Solomon, d. Dec. 23, 1819	3	340
Statira, [d. Obed & Eunice], b. Aug. 4, 1787	3	405
Submit, d. Peter, Jr. & Hannah, b. Mar. 8, 1735/6	3	83
Submit, m. Nathaniel **TAINTER**, b. of Branford, Jan. 4, 1753, by Warham Williams	3	140
Susan, [d. Benjamin R. & Hannah], b. Mar. 13, 1828	3	365
Sybil, w. of David, d. Aug. 17, 1760, in the 22nd y. of her age	3	161
Thankful, d. Paul & Mary, b. Oct. 23, 1760	3	186
Thomas, s. Roger, Jr. & Martha, b. Sept. 5, 1781	3	308
Timothy, s. Bezaleel & Abigail, b. Nov. 7, 1719	3	45
Wells, [s. Edmund & Phebe], b. Aug. 15, 1805	3	409
William, s. David & Bethyah, b. Mar. 25, 1733	3	112
William, s. Roger, Jr. & Martha, b. June 30, 1769	3	308
William, [s. Obed & Eunice], b. May 10, 1799	3	405
William Augustine, s. Jacob M. & Huldah, b. Apr. 17, 1821	3	407
Will[ia]m Augustus, s. Bille & Abigail, b. Dec. 9, 1779	3	297
William Averill, s. John & Eunice, b. Apr. 13, 1839	TM3	243
Wyllys, [s. Philemon & Lucy], b. Dec. 9, 1790	3	384
Wyllys, s. Anson & Harriot, b. Jan. 10, 1812	3	398
UMBERFIELD, Sidney, of Bethany, m. Sally **LINSLEY**, of Branford, Nov. 26, 1835, by Rev. T. P. Gillett	3	371
UTTER, Mary, d. Abraham & Lydia, b. Nov. 14, 1727	3	66
WADE, Abigail, d. Stephen & Abigail, b. Aug. 18, 1757	3	256
Amasa, s. Stephen & Abigail, b. Mar. 16, 1751	3	136
Anne, of Lyme, m. Nathan[ie]ll **JOSLIN**, of East Haven, Dec. 1, 1743, by Rev. Jonath[a]n Mer[r]ick	3	128
Edward, s. Stephen & Abigail, b. May 25, 1754	3	256
Elisabeth, of Lyme, m. Nathan **FRISBIE**, of Branford, Dec. 12, 1738, by Rev. Jonathan Parsons, at Lyme	3	130
Mary, of Lyme, m. David **FRISBIE**, of Branford, June 13, 1750, by Rev. Stephen Johnson, at Lyme	3	132
Solomon, s. Stephen & Abigail, b. Nov. 23, 1748	3	135
Stephen, m. Abigail **HOADL[E]Y**, Feb. 16, 1747/8, by Rev. P. Robbins	3	135
WALDEN, Charles E., s. Philo & Sariett, b. May 13, 1831	3	364
Philo, of Wallingford, m. Sariett **HOBART**, of Branford, Sept. 11, 1831, by Rev. Timo[thy] P. Gillett (1830?)	3	357
WALKER, Elisabeth Rebecca, [d. John N. & Matilda], b. Oct. 25, 1838	TM3	236
Jane Amelia, [d. John N. & Matilda], b. Jan. 16, 1841	TM3	236
John Rogers, [s. John N. & Matilda], b. Aug. 12, 1834, in East Haven	TM3	236
Rebekah, of Branford, m. Alanson **HALL**, of Litchfield, Dec. 10, 1829, by Rev. Timothy P. Gillett	3	351
Sybil Smith, [s. John N. & Matilda], b. May 5, 1836, in East Haven	TM3	236

	Vol.	Page
WALKER, (cont.)		
----, of Guilford, m. Matilda **ROGERS**, of Branford, June		
27, 1832, by Edw[ar]d J. Ives (Probably John N. Walker)	3	361
----, s. J. Nelson & Matilda, b. June 22, 1851	TM3	245
WALSTON, WALLSTON, Esther, d. Thom[as] & Susanna, b. Jan.		
13, 1709/10	3	36
John, s. Thom[as] & Susanna, b. Mar. 23, 1719	3	43
Rebec[c]ah, d. Thom[as] & Susanna, b. Apr. 8, 1711	3	36
Ruth, d. Thom[as] & Susanna, b. Mar. 23, 1715	3	43
Thankful, d. Thom[as] & Susanna, b. Mar. 10, 1713	3	36
Thomas, s. Thomas & Susanna, b. May 9, 1730	3	87
WARD, WARDE, Abiga[i]ll, d. John, b. Apr. 20, [1]65[5]* *(First		
written 1653)	1	173
Abiga[i]ll, d. John, b. June 4, 1658	1	172
Dorkas, d. John, b. Mar. 10, [16]62	1	173
Elisebeth, d. John, b. Jan. 24, [16]60	1	173
George, d. Apr. 7, 1653	1	170
Hannah, d. John, b. Nov. 20, [16]58	1	172
John, s. John, b. Apr. 10, [1650]	1	171
John, s. John, b. Mar. 29, 1654	1	171
Josiah, s. John, b. Nov. 15, [16]61	1	173
Mar[c]ie, m. Johnathan **BETT**, Nov. 4, [16]62 (Marie)	1	173
Marie, d. John, b. June 11, [1654]	1	171
Marie, d. Samuell, b. Oct. 20, [16]62	1	173
Nathani[e]ll, s. John, b. Nov. 3, [16]56	1	172
Samuell, s. John, b. Sept. 22, [16]56	1	172
Samuell, m. Marie **CARTTAR**, Jan. 1, 1658	1	173
Sarah, d. John, b. Mar. 22, [1651]	1	171
Tabatha, d. Samuell, b. Oct. 23, [16]59	1	172
WARDELL, WARDEL, Abigail, d. Uzall & Phebe, b. Dec. 14,		
1718	3	42
Abigail, m. John **BALDWIN**, 3rd, b. of Branford, Apr. 20,		
1740	3	130
Hannah, d. Uzal & Phebe, b. Jan. 4, 1714/5	3	36
Hannah, m. Joseph **TYLER**, Jr., b. of Branford, Dec. 28,		
1737, by Rev. Philemon Robbins	3	91
James, m. Sally Maria **BRADLEY**, b. of Branford, Nov. 18,		
1821, by Calvin Frisbie, J. P.	3	415
Joseph, s. Uzal & Phebe, b. May 31, 1721	3	45
Joseph, m. Lois **FRISBIE**, May 30, 1745, by Rev. Philemon		
Robbins	3	106
Maria, d. James & Sally Maria, b. June 9, 1833	3	364
Mary, m. Jonathan **BARKER**, June 13, 1700, by Rev. Jno.		
Sparhauk, of Bristoll	2	344
Mary, d. Uzal & Phebe, b. June 8, 1708	3	30
Matildah, d. Aug. 18, 1848, ae 88 y.	TM3	308
Phebe, d. Uzal & Phebe, b. July 18, 1712	3	35
Phebe, m. Thomas **ALLEN**, b. of Branford, Apr. 10, 1740,		

	Vol.	Page
WARDELL, WARDEL, (cont.)		
by Rev. Philemon Robbins	3	96
Rebec[c]ah, d. Uzal & Phebe, b. Nov. 21, 1716	3	39
Samuel Bradley, s. James & Sal[l]y Maria, b. Nov. 25, 1824	3	339
Sarah, d. Uzal & Phebe, b. Jan. 13, 1709	3	31
Uzal, s. Uzal & Phebe, b. Oct. 20, 1723	3	53
WARNER, WARNEER, B[e]ula[h], m. Hobart **ROGERS**, July 25,		
1799	3	274
Frances A., d. Abiram A. & Hannah, b. Dec. 9, 1850	TM3	244
John, s. John, b. Oct. 18, 1657	1	172
Marie, d. John, d. Dec. 9, [16]55	1	170
Prince B., of Branford, m. Eleanor **HILL**, of Springfield,		
Mass., May 27, 1835, by Rev. Timo[thy] P. Gillett	3	369
----, s. Prince & Jane, (colored), b. July 2, 1849	TM3	241
WASSON, James, of Farifield, m. Mary **GOULD**, of Branford, d.		
of Orchard & Mary, Oct. 8, 1815, by Rev. Timothy P.		
Gillett	3	402
WATERS, WATTERS, WOOTERS, Eunice, w. of John, d. Feb. 6,		
1824, ae 39 y.	3	365
Jacob Johnson, s. John, b. Dec. 31, 1672	1	174
John, m. Temperance **LAMFIER**, b. of Branford, Jan. 15,		
1777, by Philemon Robbins	3	287
John, s. John & Tem[peranc]e, b. June 23, 1777	3	287
John, d. Jan. 20, 1783, "on board a prison ship in New York"	3	287
Samuel, s. John & Eunice, b. July 1, 1820	3	365
Silvias, s. John & Temp[eranc]e, b. Mar. 26, 1781	3	287
WATROUS, Elihu, of Westbrook, m. Charlotte **ROGERS**, of		
Branford, Mar. 17, 1845, by Rev. E. Edwin Hall	TM3	157
WAY, Abigail, d. May & Abigail, b. Sept. 8, 1729, at East Haven	3	74
Ashband, s. John & Mary, b. Sept. 11, 1721	3	45
Chloe, d. May & Abigail, b. Oct. 14, 1731	3	74
James R., of Meriden, m. Laura A. **BARTHOLOMEW**, of		
Branford, Aug. 22, 1849, by Rev. Timothy P. Gillett	TM3	164
James R., ae 22 y., m. Laury Ann **BARTHOLOMEW**, ae 19		
y., [1849?] by Rev. Timothy P. Gillett	TM3	166
John, of Branford, m. Mary **ASHBAND**, of Milford, Oct. 30,		
1718, by Rev. Jacob Hemingway, at East Haven	3	44
John, s. John & Mary, b. July 4, 1719	3	44
Joseph, s. May & Abigail, b. Nov. 19, 1742	3	193
May, s. May & Abigail, b. May 14, 1736	3	193
Philemon, s. May & Abigail, b. Nov. 11, 1733	3	77
Rhoda had s. Elihu **FOWLER**, b. July 27, 1810; reputed f.		
Elihu **FOWLER**	3	346
Rhoda, m. Andrew **BEACH**, b. of Branford, Apr. 20, 1824,		
by Charles Atwater	3	426
WEAVER, Esther Ann, of New Haven, m. Ephraim Sturdevant		
CHIDSEY, of East Haven, Oct. 17, 1837, by Rev.		
Timothy P. Gillett	3	374
WEBBER, Sarah, m. Augustus **PAGE**, b. of Branford, Nov. 28,		

	Vol.	Page
WEBBER, (cont.)		
1813	3	337
WEDMORE, William, ae 30, of Fair Haven, m. Sarah A.		
COLLINS, ae 21, [ ], 1850, by Rev. Mr. Vibberts	TM3	167
WHEATON, WHEADON, WHEDON, Abel, s. John, Jr. &		
Rebecca, b. Apr. 26, 1735	3	82
Abigail, m. Nathan[ie]ll **PAGE**, May 10, 1710, by Rev. Mr.		
Russell	3	33
Abigail, d. Nath[anie]ll & Rhoda, b. Jan. 26, 1726/7	3	79
Abigail, m. Georg[e] **DARE**, b. of Branford, Feb. 4, 1755,		
by Rev. Philemon Robbins	3	147
Abinoam, s. John, Jr. & Rebecca, b. Dec. 4, 1737	3	89
Abraham, s. John & Marry, b. 9br 20, 1705	2	346
Abraham, m. Hannah **PLANT**, b. of Branford, Mar. 3, 1730,		
by Jonathan Merrick	3	162
Abraham, s. Reuben & Dorothy, b. June 5, 1761	3	173
Abraham, d. Aug. 6, 1762, in the 57th y. of his age	3	177
Amaziah, s. Will[ia]m & Abigail, b. Sept. 6, 1779	3	273
Amaziah H., s. Amaziah & Sally, b. Oct. 27, 1805	3	335
Ann, d. John & Marry, b. Jan. 29, 1696	2	346
Anna, d. Jno., Jr. & Rebec[c]ah, b. Aug. 2, 1731	3	78
Benjamin, s. Solomon & Sarah, b. Apr. 29, 1777	3	271
Benoni, s. Thomas & Elisabeth, b. Oct. 1, 1735	3	83
Catharine, d. Edward & Eunice, b. Nov. 11, 1801	3	421
C[h]loe, d. Jonathan & Anna, b. Apr. 16, 1751	3	122
Daniel, s. Thomas & Eunice, b. May 6, 1726	3	59
Daniel, s. Reuben & Dorothy, b. Apr. 7, 1763	3	186
Daniel, [s. Reuben & Lydia], b. July 29, 1787	3	256
David, s. Nath[anie]ll & Rhoda, b. Apr. 28, 1731	3	79
David, m. Zillah **SHELLY**, b. of Branford, Nov. 25, 1759,		
by Sam[ue]ll Barker, J. P.	3	161
Debborah, d. John & Marry, b. 8br 2, 1701	2	346
Deborah, d. Abraham & Hannah, b. Jan. 27, 1744	3	162
Desiah, d. Thomas & Mary, b. May [ ], 1754	3	137
Desire, m. Samuel **HOADLEY**, Jr., b. of Branford, June 13,		
1778, by Philemon Robbins	3	269
Dorcas, d. Thomas & Eunice, b. Aug. 25, 1720	3	45
Eben[eze]r, s. Nath[anie]ll, Jr. & Mary, b. Jan. 2, 1759;		
d. Jan. 23, 1759	3	162
Edmund, s. David & Zillah, b. Aug. 22, 1760	3	172
Edward, s. Will[ia]m & Abigail, b. Mar. 29, 1776	3	273
Elisabeth, d. John & Mary, b. July 27, 1725	3	57
Ephraim, s. Thomas & Eunice, b. Sept. 22, 1730	3	70
Esther, d. Nath[anie]ll, Jr. & Mary, b. June 9, 1760	3	162
Esther, m. Edmund **ROGERS**, Apr. 22, 1784, by Rev. Jason		
Atwater	3	272
E[s]ther, d. Solomon & Sarah, b. May 22, 1787	3	257
Eunice, d. Thomas & Eunice, b. Jan. 13, 1714/15	3	39

	Vol.	Page
WHEATON, WHEADON, WHEDON, (cont.)		
Eunice, m. Cumfort **BURGIS**, b. of Branford, Jan. 7, 1734/5,		
by Rev. Jacob Heminway	3	84
Eunis, d. Thomas, Jr. & Mary, b. Jan. 13, 1744/5	3	114
Eunice, d. Reuben & Dorothy, b. Mar. 5, 1759	3	166
Eunice, d. Reuben & Dorothy, d. June 21, 1761	3	174
Eunice, d. James & Dynah, b. June 14, 1762	3	303
Eunice, m. Heman **ROGERS**, Mar. 29, 1787	3	281
Eunice, [d. Reuben & Lydia], b. Feb. 2, 1790	3	256
Hannah, d. Thomas, b. July 21, 1674	1	174
Hannah, d. Thomas & Eunice, b. Nov. 6, 1716	3	40
Hannah, d. Abraham & Hannah, b. Apr. 5, 1731	3	162
Hannah, m. Timothy **JOHNSON**, b. of Branford, Nov. 30,		
1738, by Rev. Philemon Robbins	3	89
Harriet R., m. Jared G. **CHIDSEY**, b. of Branford, [1830?],		
by J. A. Root	3	356
Irene, d. James & Dynah, b. Nov. 17, 1767	3	303
Isaac, m. Prudence **PAGE**, b. of Branford, May 28, 1731,		
by Rev. Jonathan Merrick	3	71
Isaac, s. James & Dynah, b. Aug. 17, 1770	3	303
Jacob, s. Abraham & Hannah, b. Sept. 10, 1742	3	162
Jacob, d. Nov. 20, 1755	3	162
James, s. James & Dynah, b. Jan. 6, 1774	3	303
Jane, d. Thomas & Eunice, b. Feb. 12, 1723/4	3	54
Jehiel, s. Thomas & Eunice, b. Jan. 9, 1727/8	3	63
Jehoiada, s. John, Sr. & Dinah, b. Aug. 25, 1729	3	67
John, s. Thomas, b. Dec. 22, 1671	1	211
John, s. John & Marry, b. 10br 25, 1699	2	346
John, of Branford, m. Mary **CROWFOOT**, of Weathersfield,		
Jan. 10, 1716/7, at Weathersfield	3	40
John, Jr., m. Rebec[c]ah **WHEDON**, b. of Branford, Dec. 9,		
1725, by Nath[anie]ll Har[r]ison, J. P.	3	59
John, s. John, Jr. & Rebeccah, b. Mar. 8, 1727/8	3	65
John, Sr., m. Dinah **SEWARD**, b. of Branford, July 9, 1728,		
by Rev. Jonathan Merrick	3	67
John, s. Thomas & Mary, b. Oct. 1, 1752	3	137
John, of North Branford, m. Orret C. **JOHNSON**, of North		
Guilford, Jan. 8, 1824, by Rev. Charles Atwater	3	425
Jonathan, s. John & Mary, b. July 7, 172[1]	3	55
Jonathan, s. John & Mary, b. July 15, 1721	3	45
Jonathan, [twin with Rhoda], s. Nath[anie]ll & Rhoda,		
b. Sept. 15, 1735	3	83
Jonathan, m. Anna **COOK**, b. of Branford, Dec. 3, 1749, by		
Rev. Philemon Robbins	3	122
Jonathan, s. Jonath[a]n & Ann, b. Nov. 7, 1752; d. Jan. 6, 1753	3	128
Jonathan, s. Jonathan & Anna, b. Jan. 26, 1755	3	147
Joseph, s. Nath[anie]ll, Jr. & Mary, b. July 18, 1756	3	162
Kaziah, m. Ephraim **BALDWIN**, b. of Branford, Mar. 10, 1774	3	290

	Vol.	Page
WHEATON, WHEADON, WHEDON, (cont.)		
Lemissa, d. Solomon & Sarah, b. Mar. 6, 1792	3	259
Lois, m. Moses **BALDWIN**, b. of Branford, Jan. 13, 1772,		
by Samuel Eells	3	205
Lois, d. James & Dynah, b. Oct. 17, 1776	3	303
Lucene, d. Jonathan & Anne. b. Dec. 15, 1753	3	134
Lucretia, d. Solomon & Sarah, b. July 21, 1782	3	271
Luce, d. Thomas & Eunice, b. May 1, 1718	3	42
Luce, of Branford, m. Benjamin **TRYON**, of Wethersfield,		
Apr. 25, 1738, by Rev. Philemon Robbins	3	92
Lurene, d. Nath[anie]l, Jr. & Mary, b. Dec. 8, 1762	3	206
Lydia, d. Nath[anie]ll & Rhoda, b. Apr. 10, 1733	3	79
Lydia Sophronia, [d. Reuben & Lydia], b. Dec. 24, 1795	3	256
Martha, m. Stephen **BARNS**, Jr., b. of Branford, Jan. 5,		
1725/6, by Rev. Sam[ue]ll Russell	3	62
Martha, d. Abraham & Hannah, b. Aug. 30, 1732	3	162
Marry, d. John & Marry, b. Mar. 14, 1702	2	346
Mary, wid., of Branford, m. Henry **COOK**, of Wallingford,		
Feb. 13, 1710, by Nathan[ie]ll Harrison, J. P.	3	34
Mary, d. John & Mary, b. Nov. 18, 1717	3	40
Mary, m. Jarimiah **SCARRIOT**, Apr. 22, 1756, by Mr. Merrik	3	142
Mercy, d. James & Dynah, b. Mar. 17, 1763; d. Aug. 6, 1778	3	303
Mercy, d. Solomon & Sarah, b. Aug. 9, 1779	3	271
Milicent, [d. Reuben & Lydia], b. Mar. 2, 1798	3	256
Nathan, s. Thomas & Eunice, b. May 9, 1731	3	82
Nath[anie]ll, m. Rhoda **WHEELER**, b. of Branford, Nov. 8,		
1725, by Nath[anie]ll Harrison, J. P.	3	79
Nathan[ie]ll, s. Nath[anie]ll & Rhoda, b. Jan. 17, 1728/9	3	79
Nath[anie]ll, Jr., m. Mary **MORRISS**, b. of Branford, Nov.		
20, 1755, by Philemon Robbins	3	162
Noah, s. Abraham & Hannah, b. July 18, 1748	3	162
Noah, s. Will[ia]m & Abigail, b. June 29, 1772	3	273
Olive, d. James & Dynah, b. June 20, 1765	3	303
Ozias, s. Will[ia]m & Abigail, b. Dec. 17, 1774	3	273
Pitman, s. James & Dynah, b. June 17, 1773	3	303
Polley, d. Will[ia]m & Abigail, b. Dec. 2, 1770	3	273
Priscilla, d. John & Mary, b. Aug. 24, 1719	3	43
Priscilla, m. Israel **LINSL[E]Y**, b. of Branford, [ ] 6,		
1739, by Rev. Jon[a]th[an] Merrick	3	104
Rebec[c]ah, m. John **WHEDON**, Jr., b. of Branford, Dec. 9,		
1725, by Nath[anie]ll Har[r]ison, J. P.	3	59
Rebec[c]ah, d. Jno. Jr. & Rebec[c]ah, b. Dec. 6, 1729	3	78
Reuben, s. Abraham & Hannah, b. Feb. 25, 1734	3	162
Reuben, m. Dorothy **BARKER**, b. of Branford, Nov. 3, 1757,		
by Jonathan Merrick	3	166
Rhoda, [twin with Jonathan], d. Nath[anie]ll & Rhoda, b.		
Sept. 15, 1735	3	83
Rufus, s. James & Dynah, b. Jan. 3, 1760	3	303

	Vol.	Page
WHEATON, WHEADON, WHEDON, (cont.)		
Ruth, d. Nath[anie]ll & Rhoda, b. Oct. 30, 1737	3	106
Sally, d. Solomon & Sarah, b. Nov. 24, 1774	3	271
Samuel, s. John, Jr. & Rebec[c]ah, b. Nov. 4, 1726	3	59
Sam[ue]ll, s. Jno., Jr. & Rebec[c]ah, b. Mar. 20, 1732/3	3	78
Samuel, s. Nath[anie]ll & Rhoda, b. Aug. 25, 1744	3	106
Sarah, d. Abraham & Hannah, b. Apr. 10, 1737	3	162
Stephen, s. Solomon & Sarah, b. Dec. 7, 1784	3	257
Submit, d. Abraham & Hannah, b. July 23, 1735	3	162
Thomas, m. Eunice **SWAIN**, May 6, 1714, by Nathan[ie]ll		
Harrison, J. P.	3	38
Thomas, s. Thomas & Eunice, b. July 10, 1722	3	51
Thomas, Jr., m. Mary **PAGE**, b. of Branford, Apr. 19, 1744,		
by Rev. Jonathan Mer[r]ick	3	114
Thomas, s. Thomas, Jr. & Mary, b. May 24, 1747	3	114
Timothy, s. Abraham & Hannah, b. Dec. 20, 1738	3	162
Timothy, d. June 5, 1739	3	162
Timothy, s. Abraham & Hannah, b. July 22, 1740	3	162
William, s. Abraham & Hannah, b. Sept. 21, 1746	3	162
William, m. Abigail **PAGE**, b. of Branford, Apr. 11, 1770,		
by Samuel Eells	3	199
----, s. Nath[anie]ll, Jr. & Mary, b. Dec. 23, 1757;		
d. Dec. 24, 1757	3	162
WHEDON, [see under **WHEATON**]		
WHEELER, Elisabeth, m. Noah **ROGERS**, b. of Branford, Nov.		
28, 1722, by Nath[anie]ll Harrison, J. P.	3	51
Rhoda, m. Nath[anie]ll **WHEDON**, b. of Branford, Nov. 8,		
1725, by Nath[anie]ll Harrison, J. P.	3	79
Sarah, m. Samuel **BEERS**, Apr. 8, 1712, by Nathan[ie]ll		
Harrison, J. P.	3	37
WHITE, John, m. Margaret **EBER**, b. of Branford, Jan. 17, 1765,		
by Samuel Barker, J. P.	3	184
John sailed from Branford Jan. 6, 17[85]* and was lost		
at sea (* first written "1795")	3	269
Salle, d. John & Margaret, b. July 12, 1765	3	258
WHITEHEAD, WHITHEAD, WHITED, Damaras, d. John, b.		
Jan. 20, 1669	1	210
Damaris, m. Micah **PAMER**, Feb. 14, 1693/4	2	345
Eliphalet, s. John, b. Sept. 27, 1674	1	174
Elizabeth, d. Jno., b. Oct. [ ], 1677	1	211
Elizabeth, m. Benjamin **HOWD**, Oct. 1, 1705, by Eleazar		
Stent, J. P.	2	346
Hana, d. John, b. Mar. 10, [16]64	1	173
Hannah, m. Peter **TYLER**, Sr., Dec. 25, 1688	2	345
John, m. Martha **BRADFEELD**, Mar 9, [16]61	1	173
John, s. John, b. Feb. 20, 1665	1	210
John, m. Mehitabell **BISHOPE**, Aug. 9, 1704	2	346
Martha, d. John, b. Jan. 10, 1667	1	210

	Vol.	Page
WHITEHEAD, WHITHEAD, WHITED, (cont.)		
Mary, d. John, b. May 6, [16]62	1	173
Mary, d. John & Mehetabeel, b. Nov. 3, 17[ ];		
[bp. Dec. [ ], 1705]	3	29
Mary, m. William **GOULD**, b. of Branford, Dec. 9, 1725,		
by Rev. Sam[ue]ll Russell	3	58
Mary, m. William **GOULD**, Dec. 9, 1725	3	278
Samuel, s. John, b. Nov. 24, 1672	1	210
Thomas, s. Jno., b. Feb. 27, 1680	1	211
WHITING, Abel, d. Oct. 5, 1835	3	371
Harriet M., m. Joseph N. **LINSLEY**, b. of Branford, Jan.		
29, 1843, by Rev. Davis T. Shailer	TM3	155
Jennett E., of Branford, m. Hubbard **FENN**, of Wallingford,		
Nov. 24, 1839, by Rev. Davis T. Shailer	3	377
Louisa, of Branford, m. William **PARKER**, of Wallingford,		
June 3, 1849, by Rev. T. P. Gillett	TM3	163
Marian, of North Branford, m. William **GOODRICH**, of		
Branford, Feb. 27, 1826, by Rev. Timothy P. Gillett	3	341
Susan C., of Branford, m. John S. **BRADLEY**, of New Haven,		
Sept. 25, 1842, by Rev. Timothy P. Gillett	TM3	154
William Ambrose, s. Abel & Mary, b. June 7, 1825	3	369
William Chandler, s. Abel, d. June 10, 1824	3	369
WHITNEY, WHITNE, Betsey, d. John, Jr. & Ame, b. Feb. 24,		
1781	3	293
Bets[e]y, m. Noah **FRISBIE**, Feb. 14, 1811	3	393
Catharine, [d. Jared & Sally], b. Apr. 4, 1810	3	389
Deborah, d. John & Deborah, b. June 30, 1763	3	186
Enos, s. John & Deborah, b. Aug. 10, 1761	3	186
Eunice, [d. Jared & Sally], b. Dec. 17, 1794	3	389
Eunice, m. Abraham **HOWD**, b. of Branford, May 6, 1811	3	427
Grasey, d. John, Jr. & Ame, b. Nov. 18, 1783	3	293
Hannah, d. John & Deborah, b. Dec. 7, 1751	3	130
Hannah, [d. Jared & Sally], b. Aug. 3, 1796	3	389
Harriot, [d. Jared & Sally], b. Apr. 2, 1808	3	389
Horace, [s. Jared & Sally], b. Feb. 27, 1793	3	389
Jared, s. John & Deborah, b. Sept. 13, 1765	3	187
Jared, m. Sally **ROGERS**, b. of Branford, Sept. 14, 1790	3	389
Jared, [s. Jared & Sally], b. June 2, 1798	3	389
John, m. Deborah **SMITH**, b. of Branford, Jan. 17, 1750/1,		
by Rev. Philemon Robbins	3	130
John, s. John & Deborah, b. Apr. 13, 1754	3	168
John, Jr., m. [Ame] **HOWD**, b. of Branford, Dec. 18, 1776,		
by P. Robbins	3	293
Joseph, s. John & Deborah, b. Aug. 9, 1759	3	168
Joseph, s. John, Jr. & Ame, b. July 29, 1778	3	293
Joseph, [s. Jared & Sally], b. Oct. 19, 1802	3	389
Lucy Bindy, [d. Jared & Sally], b. Dec. 16, 1805	3	389
Mary, d. John, Jr. & Ame, b. Jan. 8, 1777	3	293

	Vol.	Page
WHITNEY, WHITNE, (cont.)		
Sarah, d. John & Deborah, b. Dec. 10, 1757	3	168
William, [s. Jared & Sally], b. June 16, 1800	3	389
WHITWAY, Thomas, d. Dec. 12, 1651	1	170
WILFORD, WILLFORD, Abigail, d. Richard & Elisabeth, b. Sept. 17, 1720	3	96
Abigail, m. Sam[ue]ll **MALTBIE,** Jr., b. of Branford, Oct. 13, 1743, by Rev. Philemon Robbins	3	101
Abigail, d. Joseph & Elizabeth, b. Mar. 11, 1752	3	141
Abigail, m. Enoch **STAPLES,** b. of Branford, Oct. 15, 1769, by Phile[mo]n Robbins	3	197
Ann, d. Richard & Elizabeth, b. Sept. 13, 1702* (*First written Mar. 29, 1703)	2	344
Anne, m. Jonah **BUTLER,** b. of Branford, Aug. 5, 1725, by Rev. Sam[ue]ll Russell	3	58
Anne, d. Joseph & Elisabeth, b. Apr. 24, 1767	3	200
Charles Henry, [s. John & Lucretia G.], b. Mar. 3, 1843	TM3	236
Ebeneser, [s. John & Lucretia G.], b. Dec. 28, 1840	TM3	236
Edwin Lusern, s. [Samuel & Susan], b. Mar. 13, 1842	TM3	238
Elisabeth, d. Rich[a]rd & Elisabeth, b. Jan. 25, 1706/7	3	34
Elisabeth, m. Nathaniel **JOHNSON,** Jr., b. of Branford, June 17, 1725, by Rev. Sam[ue]ll Russell	3	57
Elisabeth, w. of Rich[ar]d, d. Aug. 25, 1758	3	167
Elisabeth, d. Joseph & Elisabeth, b. July 12, 1759	3	158
Elisabeth, m. Russell **BARKER,** b. of Branford, Sept. 8, 1779	3	301
Elizabeth, Jr., d. May 26, 1800, in her 65th y.	3	391
Francis Elisur, s. [Samuel & Susan], b. Nov. 25, 1840	TM3	238
George, [s. John & Lucretia G.], b. Jan. 23, 1839	TM3	236
Hannah, d. Joseph & Elizabeth, b. Feb. 9, 1754	3	141
Hannah, m. Farrington **HARRISON,** b. of Branford, Sept. 29, 1772, by Philemon Robbins	3	376
Harry, d. Mar. 22, 1849, ae 38 y.	TM3	308
Jeremiah, s. Joseph & Mercy, b. May 10, 1782	3	270
John, s. Rich[a]rd & Elisabeth, b. Aug. 7, 1710	3	33
John, m. Elisabeth **HARRISON,** d. of Jno., b. of Branford, Feb. 6, 1752, by Rev. Philemon Robbins	3	125
John, s. Joseph & Elisabeth, b. Feb. 11, 1762	3	178
John, m. Anne **BLACISTON,** b. of Branford, Dec. 16, 1781, by Samuel Eells	3	276
John, s. John A., b. Sept. 1, 1810	TM3	236
John, m. Lucretia G. **GOODNOUGH,** Sept. 25, 1838	TM3	159
John Augustus, s. John & Anne, b. Aug. 21, 1783	3	276
John Augustus, m. Statira **JOHNSON,** b. of Branford, Dec. 9, 1841, by Rev. Timothy P. Gillett	TM3	153
John Chestor, s. Joseph & Mercy, b. Aug. 22, 1785	3	314
Joseph, s. Rich[ar]d & Elisabeth, b. Feb. 3, 1715/6	3	39
Joseph, m. Elizabeth **HOW,** b. of Branford, Dec. 19, 1751, by Nath[anie]ll Harrison, J. P.	3	141

	Vol.	Page

WILFORD, WILLFORD, (cont.)

	Vol.	Page
Joseph, s. Joseph & Elizabeth, b. May 26, 1755	3	141
Joseph, d. Sept. 8, 1770, ae 55	3	200
Joseph, m. Mercy **BARKER**, b. of Branford, Dec. 30, 1778, by Philemon Robbins	3	266
Julia, d. Aug. 3, 1849, ae 42 y.	TM3	308
Lydia, m. Joseph **LINSL[E]Y**, b. of Branford, May 27, 1733, by Rev. Jonath[a]n Mer[r]ick	3	76
Lydia, see Mrs. Lydia **TOPPING**	2	343
Mary, m. Caleb **FRISBIE**, b. of Branford, Apr. 7, 1737, by Rev. Jonathan Mer[r]ick	3	114
Mary Ann, [d. John & Lucretia G.], b. Apr. 20, 1845	TM3	236
Rebecca, d. Joseph & Elisabeth, b. Apr. 5, 1757	3	145
Rebecca, d. Joseph & Elisabeth, d. June 2, 1764, in the 8th y. of her age	3	183
Rebecca, d. Joseph & Elisabeth, b. Oct. 12, 1765	3	200
Rebecca, m. Warham **WILLIAMS**, Jr., b. of Branford, Feb. 17, 1786, by Jason Atwater	3	254
Richard, late of London, free cit[i]zen & salter, d. Oct. 24, 1734, in the 81st y. of his age	3	80
Richard, d. Mar. 12, 1737/8	3	92
Sally, d. John & Anne, b. Feb. 24, 1782; d. June 24, 1782	3	276
Samuel, d. Joseph & Mercy, b. Feb. 17, 1780	3	269
Samuel, of Branford, m. Susan **COOK**, b. of Branford, Oct. 27, 1839	TM3	159
Samuel Augustus, s. [Samuel & Susan], b. Mar. 15, 1844	TM3	238
Sarah, d. Richard & Elisabeth, b. May 25, 1718	3	96
Sarah, m. Ebenezer **LINSL[E]Y**, b. of Branford, Dec. 10, 1734, by Rev. Philemon Robbiins	3	81
Susan, d. Mar. 29, 1849, ae 42 y.	TM3	308
----, child of John & Loretta, b. Apr. 19, 1848	TM3	239
----, d. Samuel, b. May [ ], 1851	TM3	244
WILKINSON, WILKENSON, Hannah, of Milford, m. John **HOWD**, of Branford, some time in the year 1705 or 1706, by Sam[ue]ll Eells, J. P.	3	197
Mary, m. William **LUDDINTON**, b. of Branford, Apr. 17, 1760, by Jonathan Merrick	3	160
Thankfull, of Milford, m. Nathan[ie]ll **HARRISON**, Jr., [of Branford], Apr. 18, 1717, by Sam[ue]ll Eells	3	41
WILLARD, Lois, of East Guilford, m. Oliver **LANFARE**, Jr., of Branford, June 5, 1808	3	396
WILLIAMS, Abigail, d. Rev. Warham & Anne, b. June 13, 1767	3	191
Abigail, d. Rev. Warham & Anne, d. Mar. 24, 1768	3	192
Abigail, d. Rev. Warham & Anne, b. Jan. 2, 1769	3	196
Abigail, m. Stephen **MALTBY**, b. of Branford, Sept. 27, 1788	3	268
Anne, d. Rev. Warham & Anne, b. Feb. 17, 1761	3	176
Anne, w. of Rev. Warham, d. Mar. 25, 1776, in the 43rd y. of her age	3	261

	Vol.	Page
WILLIAMS, (cont.)		
Anne, Mrs., m. Rev. Jason **ATWATER**, b. of Branford, Dec.		
7, 1784, by Warham Williams	3	312
Anne, m. Rev. Jason **ATWATER**, Dec. 7, 1784	3	400
Anne, d. Warham, Jr. & Rebecca, b. Feb. 22, 1787	3	254
Aurelia, d. Stephen & Eunice, b. Aug. 16, 1780	3	291
Charles M., [s. Samuel N. & Amy], b. Aug. 19, 1817	3	418
Dani[e]ll, s. Richard, b. Apr. 15, [16]57	1	172
Davenport, s. Rev. Warham & Anne, b. Jan. 6, 1759	3	158
Davenport, of Branford, m. Mary **ATWATER**, of Hamden,		
Feb. 5, 1789, by Joshua Perry, in Hamden	3	260
Eliza A., m. Joseph **GOODRICH**, b. of Branford, Aug. 2,		
1826, by Rev. Timothy P. Gillett	3	342
Eliza Adeline, [d. Samuel N. & Amy], b. Jan. 25, 1805,		
in New Haven	3	418
Eunice, d. Rev. Warham & Anne, b. Mar. 8, 1771	3	203
Eunice, d. Stephen & Eunice, b. Feb. 16, 1779	3	291
Hannah, of Kelinworth, m. John **ROSE**, Jr., of Branford,		
Dec. 9, 1702	2	344
Hannah, of Wallingford, m. William **BARTHOLOMEW**, Jr.,		
of Branford, Dec. 7, 1726, by Theophilus Yale, J. P.	3	63
Hannah, m. Josiah **TALMAGE**, b. of Branford, July [ ], 1748,		
by Jon[a]th[an] Merrick	3	160
Harry, of Wallingford, m. Rebecca **TODD**, of Northford,		
Dec. 24, [1820], by Origen P. Holcomb	3	412
Henry A., [s. Samuel N. & Amy], b. Dec. 11, 1799	3	418
Irene Almira, [d. Samuel N. & Amy], b. Jan. 28, 1803	3	418
Irene Almira, m. John **BARKER**, b. of Branford, Mar. 31,		
1833, by Rev. Timothy P. Gillett	3	359
James Murry, [s. Samuel N. & Amy], b. Aug. 8, 1811, in		
New Haven	3	418
John N., [s. Samuel N. & Amy], b. May 24, 1809, in New		
Haven	3	418
Jonathan Law, s. Rev. Warham & Anne, b. Nov. 17, 1757	3	146
Jonathan Law, s. Stephen & Eunice, b. Mar. 16, 1784	3	291
Julius, m. Amelia P. **BARKER**, Sept. 26, 1847, by Rev. F.		
Miller	TM3	161
Lucretia J., of Branford, m. Calvin **DOWNS**, of Millford,		
June 24, 1827, by Rev. Timothy P. Gillett	3	345
Lucretia Jenet, [d. Samuel N. & Amy], b. July 8, 1807,		
in New Haven	3	418
Lucy, d. Rev. Warham & Anne, b. Feb. 13, 1765	3	191
Lucy, m. Elihu **FOOT**, b. of Branford, Nov. 11, 1789	3	267
Lydia, of Wallingford, m. James **MALTBY**, of Branford,		
Mar. 21, 1819	3	419
Mary, d. Davenport & Mary, b. May 12, 1792	3	260
Mary Ann, [d. Samuel N. & Amy], b. July 11, 1814, in		
New Milford	3	418

	Vol.	Page
WILLIAMS, (cont.)		
Mary S., m. William C. **SCARRITT**, b. of Branford, Jan. 9,		
1848, by Rev. A. C. Wheat	TM3	161
Samuell, s. Richard, b. Sept. 3, [1655]	1	172
Sam[ue]ll Hall, s. Rev. Warham & Anne, b. Mar. 22, 1756	3	146
Samuel N., b. Feb. 5, 1776, in Susquehanhah, N. Y. ; m.		
Amy **MOULTHROP**, June 7, 1799	3	418
Sarah, d. Rev. Wareham & Anne, b. Feb. 9, 1776	3	261
Sophia, d. Davenport & Mary, b. Aug. 29, 1790	3	260
Stephen, s. Warham & Anne, b. Dec. 30, 1754	3	146
Stephen, m. Eunice **TAINTOR**, b. of Branford, Jan. 23, 1778,		
by Warham Williams	3	291
Stephen, Jr., s. Stephen & Eunice, b. Jan. 13, 1787	3	315
Warham, of Branford, m. Mrs. Ann **HALL**, of Wallingford,		
Nov. 30, 1752, by Rev. Sam[ue]ll Hall	3	133
Warham, s. Warham & Ann, b. Aug. 27, 1753	3	133
Warham, Jr., m. Rebecca **WILLFORD**, b. of Branford, Feb.		
17, 1786, by Jason Atwater	3	254
William Augustus, s. Rev. Warham & Anne, b. Feb. 10, 1763	3	179
William N., [s. Samuel N. & Amy], b. Apr. 9, 1801	3	418
----, d. Dwight & Sarah A., b. May 12, 1851	TM3	243
WILLIAMSON, Richard, s. Richard & Mary, b. May [ ], 1851	TM3	245
WING, Zebulun, s. Judah & Hannah, b. Jan. 30, 1724/5	3	115
WOLCOTT, WOOLCOT, WOLCUT, Jeremiah, of New Haven,		
m.Sarah **GOODSELL**, of Branford, Apr. 13, 1758, by		
Jonathan Merrick	3	163
Jeremiah, m. Sarah **GOODSELL**, Apr. 13, 1758, by		
Jon[a]th[an] Mer[r]ick	3	193
Lucretia, of Branford, m. Bedford **MOWRY**, of Pittsburg,		
Penn., [Feb.] 18, [1822], by Rev. Origen P. Holcomb	3	418
Martha Davenport, d. Jeremiah & Sarah, b. Aug. 18, 1762	3	193
Sarah, d. Jeremiah & Sarah, b. May 5, 1767	3	193
Sarah, m. Dr. Ranson Byrom **HARLOW**, Nov. 18, 1775, by		
Josiah Rogers, J. P.	3	261
Thomas Goodsell, s. Jeremiah & Sarah, b. Aug. 16, 1764	3	193
WOODCOCK, Barnabas, s. Barnabas & Elisabeth, b. Nov. 13, 1739	3	93
WOODHULL, Ellen S., d. John F. & Sarah, b. July 19, 1848	TM3	240
John F., m. Sarah F. **SQUIRE**, July 26, 1847, by Rev.		
Frederick Miller	TM3	161
WOODRUFF, Flora, of Worthington, m. Samuel **BALDWIN**, of		
Branford, Nov. 28, 1799	3	396
WOODWARD, Sarah, of New Haven, m. Samuel **PAGE**, Jr., of		
Branford, Apr. 3, 1766, by Jon[a]th[an] Merrick	3	193
WOOSTER, Mary, of Stratford, m. David **HAR[R]ISON**, of		
Branford, Jan. 1, 1728/9, by Rev. Jedidiah Mills	3	65
WRIGHT, RIGHT, Elizabeth, m. Benjamin **BARTHOLOMEW**, b.		
of Branford, Feb. 2, 1749, by Rev. Philemon Robbins	3	148
Hannah, of Glausenbury, m. John **SWAIN**, of Branford, Oct.		

	Vol.	Page
WRIGHT, RIGHT, (cont.)		
17, 1721, by Rev. Mr. Stephens, at Glausenbury	3	48
Harriet, of North Branford, m. Nelson **POND**, Apr. 23, 1849,		
by Rev. Mr. Chase	TM3	164
YALE, Harriet, Mrs., of Meriden, m. Leonard **SMITH**, of Branford,		
Oct. 19, 1845, by Rev. A. C. Wheat	TM3	158
Phebe, m. Jerome **BLACKSTONE**, b. of Branford, May 11,		
1845, by Rev. A. C. Wheat	TM3	158
YOUNG, John, formerly of Exeter, Mass., m. Lydia **PAMERLE**, of		
Branford, Feb. 3, 1725/6, by Rev. Sam[ue]ll Russell	3	59
John, d. Oct. 8, 1726	3	59
NO SURNAME,		
Abigail, d. Coole & Elisabeth, b. Aug. 15, 1754	3	182
Bridget, ae 22, m. Thomas **O'BRIEN**, ae 24, July 30, 1851	TM3	169
John, s. John & Hannah, b. Apr. 16, 1707	3	31
John W., s. John & Lucretia, b. Jan. 31, 1850	TM3	244
Michal, d. Coole & Elisabeth, b. Aug. [2]5, 1756	3	182
Tyrus, s. Coole & Elisabeth, b. Oct. 25, 1760	3	182
----, s. d. Aug. 12, 1850	TM3	310
----, child d. Sept. 29, 1850 ae 10 wk.	TM3	309

BRIDGEPORT VITAL RECORDS
1821 - 1854

BALDWIN, (cont.)

William W., m. Elizabeth Ann **HURLBURT**, Nov. 17, [1845], by Rev.
S. B. Brittain   62

BANCROFT, Elizabeth, m. Stephen **GAY**, June [ ], 1846, by Rev. Gurdon S.
Coit   74

BANIGAN, James, m. Jane **CALIGAN**, Mar. 3, [1851], by Rev. Michael
Lynch. Witnesses: John McCann, Elizabeth Calagan   108

BANKS, Barzillai, m. Sarah A. **STRATTON**, Oct. 25, 1842, by Rev. Gurdon
S. Coit   55

Charles S., m. Harriet **SHERWOOD**, Nov. 12, 1850, by Rev. Gurdon S.
Coit   104

Emily B., m. Isaac L. **BARTLETT**, May 25, 1846, by Rev. Gurdon S.
Coit   74

BARLOW, Talcot, m. Emeline **GRAY**, b. of Bridgeport, May 23, 1847, by
Rev. Benjamin S. J. Page   75

BARNES, Bridget, m. Walter **CLARY**, Sept. 14, [1851], by Rev. Michael
Lynch. Witnesses: Daniel Langan, Nelly Ennis   110

John, m. Margaret **FAGAN**, June 30, 1851, by Rev. Michael Lynch.
Witnesses: Francis Fagan, Ann Nolan   110

BARNEY, Catharine, m. John **BETTSBOROUGH**, Jan. 8, 1843, by Rev.
Gurdon S. Coit   55

BARNUM, Adelia M., of Bridgeport, m. Preston M. **CARY**, of Weston, Nov.
13, 1842, by Rev. John H. Hunter   47

John F., m. Sarah H. **BROTHERTON**, Sept. 21, 1843, by Rev. J.
Leonard Gilder   49

Lebbeus, of Bethel, m. Mary **HINE**, of Bridgeport, May 30, 1852, by
Rev. Nathaniel Hewit   114

Sarah, of New Town, m. George B. **SMITH**, of Bridgeport, July 2,
1836, by Rev. Nathaniel Ruggles   13

W. S., of New Haven, m. Abigail **PLUMB**, of Bridgeport, Nov. 5, 1849,
by Moses Ballou   92

BARTLETT, Adaline, m. George M. **HUBBELL**, b. of Bridgeport, Sept. 11,
1848, by Rev. Benjamin S. J. Page   86

Annyette, of Bridgeport, m. Robert **SIMPSON**, of Newark, N. J., Apr.
2, 1837, by Rev. Charles F. Pelton   20

Isaac L., m. Emily B. **BANKS**, May 25, 1846, by Rev. Gurdon S. Coit   74

Louisa, of Bridgeport, m. Isaac **NICHOLS**, of New Town, Mar. 20,
1838, by [Rev. John Woodbridge]   29

BASSETT, Caroline, m. Joseph **HAMPTON**, July 4, 1835, by Rev. C. F.
Pelton   10

Mary Clinton, of Bridgeport, m. Barzillai Foote **POND**, of New York,
June 14, 1849, by Rev. Benjamin S. J. Page   90

BATCHELOR, John, m. Mary Augusta **HALL**, b. of Bridgeport, June 29,
1845, by Rev. J. H. Perry   60

Mary, m. John **JAMES**, b. of Bridgeport, Dec. 28, 1845, by Rev. James
H. Perry   61

BATES, Charles, of New York, m. Ann **COLLINS**, of Bridgeport, May 11,
1837, by Rev. Nath[anie]l Hewitt   25

Page

BATES, (cont.)

Sarah Ann, m. William **PATTERSON**, b. of Bridgeport, Sept. 28, 1846,
by Rev. Nathaniel Hewit — 73

BEACH, Caroline S., m. William E. **KEELER**, b. of Bridgeport, Dec. 25,
1843, by Rev. John H. Hunter — 54

Elizabeth, m. Elijah **SHERMAN**, b. of Bridgeport, Nov. 18, 1849, by
Moses Ballou — 94

Horatio N., of Stratfield, m. Harriet M. **PRINDLE**, of Bridgeport,
May 8, 1849, by Rev. Lorenzo T. Bennett, of Guilford — 89

James W., m. Laura Jane **SILLIMAN**, b. of Bridgeport, [Mar. 17, 1849],
by Rev. Cryus Silliman — 94

John F., m. Sarah **PORTER**, Nov. 4, 1843, by Rev. Gurdon S. Coit — 56

John H., m. Mary A. **STRATTON**, Oct. 10, 1847, by Rev. Gurdon S.
Coit — 82

Louisa, of Trumbull, m. Charles N. **FAIRCHILD**, of Bridgeport, Sept.
27, 1841, by Rev. John H. Hunter — 43

Mary S., m. Charles **EDWARDS**, b. of Bridgeport, Feb. 28, 1840, by
Rev. John H. Hunter — 36

Philo, of Trumbull, m. Susan J. **CURTIS**, of Bridgeport, Jan. 12, 1848,
by Rev. Nath[anie]l Hewit — 90

Starr, m. Catharine Ann **BOOTH**, Nov. 28, 1833, by Rev. Gurdon S. Coit — 2

BEALS, Caroline S., m. William **LEIGH**, [Mar. 3, 1851], by Rev. Gurdon S.
Coit — 105

BEARDSLEY, BEARDSLEE, [see also **BEASLEY**,], Abijah, m. Abby G.
SUMMERS, b. of Bridgeport, Jan. 28, 1849, by Rev. Benjamin S. J.
Page — 87

Amanda, of Bridgeport, m. James H. **TRUELUCK**, of Georgia, Oct. 4,
1837, by Rev. Nath[anie]l Hewett — 25

George, m. Sarah **MONROE**, b. of Bridgeport, Oct. 26, 1834, by Rev.
John Blatchford — 22

James H., of New York, m. Elizabeth **EASTMAN**, of Bridgeport, Mar.
31, 1851, by Rev. Benj[amin] S. J. Page — 106

Mary Ann, of Stratford, m. Henry **JUDSON**, of Bridgeport, May 26,
1844, by Rev. Nathaniel Hewit — 63

Ransom B., m. Rebecca L. **BURTON**, b. of Fairfield, Nov. 29, 1848,
by Rev. Nath[anie]l Hewit — 91

Sarah E., Mrs., m. Lewis G. **PRINDLE**, b. of Bridgeport, Sept. 19,
1847, by Rev. William Reid — 76

Thomas, m. Ianthia **BURR**, (Ethiopes), Oct. 3, 1832, by [Rev. John
Blatchford] — 3

BEASIN, Ann, m. Edward **HAUGHNEY**, Oct. 12, 1851, by Rev. Michael
Lynch. Witnesses: Patrick Ward & Mary Braley — 111

BEASLEY, [see also **BEARDSLEY**], Frances E., m. George J. **HOYT**, b. of
Bridgeport, Sept. 30, 1850, by Rev. J. B. Stratton — 100

BEAVENS, Mary J., m. Rasom D. **CURTIS**, b. of Bridgeport, Oct. 17, 1848,
by Rev. Moses Ballow — 88

BECK Margaret, m. Andrew **BRIDTHE**, Sept. 22, [1850], by Rev. Michael
Lynch. Witnesses: Franz Abet, Mary Bridthe — 103

Page

BECK, (cont.)

Maria, m. Daniel H. **STERLING**, b. of Bridgeport, Dec. 7, 1842, by
Rev. John H. Hunter   48

BEE, Bridget, m. Thomas **BEE**, June 15, 1851, by Rev. Michael Lynch.
Witnesses: Dominick Bell, Ruth Bee   110

Thomas, m. Bridget **BEE**, June 15, 1851, by Rev. Michael Lynch.
Whitnesses: Dominick Bell, Ruth Bee   110

BEEBE, BEEBEE, Jane S., m. Charles A. **KIRTLAND**, Nov. 20, 1850, by
Rev. Gurdon S. Coit   104

William J., m. Elizabeth **HINMAN**, Dec. 5, 1838, by [Rev. G. S. Coit] 30

BEECHER, Harriet, Mrs. of Woodbridge, m. Aaron **FAIRCHILD**, Nov. 6,
1836, at Stratford, by Rev. Gurdon S. Coit   16

BEEKER, Margarite A., m. Thomas M. **EMMENUEL**, Oct. 13, 1852, by Rev.
Gurdon S. Coit   116

BEERS, Alexander S., m. Catharine Ann **SCHANK**, Oct. 14, 1849, by Rev.
Gurdon S. Coit   104

Joseph H., of New York, m. Harriet **NASH**, of Bridgeport, Jan. 13,
1847, by Rev. Nath[anie]l Hewit   90

Sarah, m. Stephen **TROWBRIDGE**, May 6, 1848, by Rev. Gurdon S.
Coit   92

BEGLEY, BEGLY, James, m. Catharine **DOOLAN**, Mar. 2, [1851], by Rev.
Michael Lynch. Witnesses: Charles Carty, Bridget Doolan   107

William W., m. Hannah M. **WOODBRIDGE**, Oct. 24, 1837, by Rev. J.
W. LeFevre   24

BELDEN, Henry, of Laparte, Ind., m. Sophronia **EASLAND**, of Stockbridge,
Mass., June 13, 1852, by Rev. Benj[amin] S. J. Page   113

BENEDICT, Jesse W., of New York City, m. Ann **COLEMAN**, of Bridgeport,
July 3, 1833, by Nathaniel Hewit   1

John N., of Milwaukee, Wis., m. Sophia E. **HARTWELL**, of Bridgeport,
Aug. 22, 1850, by Rev. Benj[amin] S. J. Page   99

Mary E., m. Martin **GIBBS**, Aug. 3, 1845, by Rev. Gurdon S. Coit   64

Seth, m. Mary **MILLS**, Sept. 21, 1853, by Rev. Gurdon S. Coit   116

Thaddeus, m. Harriette **BALDWIN**, Mar. 23, 1834, by Rev. Gurdon S.
Coit   5

Thomas, m. Sarah **PECK**, b. of Bridgeport, Nov. 26, 1836, by Rev.
Charles F. Pelton   16

BENHAM, Clarissa S., m. Theron **TOWNER**, b. of New Haven, Sept. 22,
1847, by Rev. Benj[ami]n S. J. Page   76

BENJAMIN, Susan M., m. Lyman W. **SEELEY**, b. of Bridgeport, Apr. 22,
1844, by Rev. John H. Hunter   56

BENNETT, Austin G., of Roxbury, m. Julia Ann **LEININGSTEIN**, of
Bridgeport, May 23, 1851, by Nathaniel Hewit, V. D. M.   109

John, of Athens, N. Y., m. Phebe **NORTHROP**, of Bridgeport, May 15,
1849, by Rev. Nath[anie]l Hewit   91

Johnson F., m. Jerusha **MIDDLEBROOK**, Nov. 24, 1841, by Rev. G. S.
Coit   44

Sarah E., m. William **BROWN**, Oct. 29, 1837, by Rev. J. W. LeFevre   23

BENSON, Esther C., m. Obadiah **JENNINGS**, b. of Fairfield, July 14, 1831,

Page

BENSON, (cont.)

by [Rev. John Blatchford]   3

BETTS, Ann, m. Henry **WOLCOTT**, of Schenectady, N. Y., Sept. 23, 1832,

by [Rev. John Blatchford]   3

Lucy, m. Nelson C. **NICHOLS**, b. of Bridgeport, Apr. 26, 1850, by Rev.

Benj[amin] S. J. Page   96

Philander, of Danbury, m. Antoinette **GIBSONSON** [sic], Jan. 10, 1834,

by Rev. John Blatchford   21

BETTSBOROUGH, John, m. Catharine **BARNEY**, Jan. 8, 1843, by Rev.

Gurden S. Coit   55

BIBBINS, Caroline, m. William **HODGE**, Oct. 17, 1841, by Rev. N. Ruggles   43

Henry, of Fairfield, m. Mary **NASH**, of Bridgeport, Nov. 27, 1832,

by Nathaniel Hewit   2

BILLINGS, J. W., m. Mary **STRATTON**, Dec. 9, 1850, by Rev. Gurdon S.

Coit   105

John H., of New York, m. Julia A. **HUBBELL**, of Bridgeport, Dec. 24,

1844, by Rev. John H. Hunter   59

BIRDSEYE, Ezekiel, of New York, m. Mary Emily **RIPPEN**, of Bridgeport,

July 17, 1834, by Rev. John Blatchford   21

BISHOP, Isabella C., m. Milton H. **COOKE**, May 4, 1852, by Rev. Gurdon S.

Coit   115

Julia P., m. Horace **NICHOLS**, b. of Bridgeport, Oct. 28, 1850, by

Rev. Nathaniel Hewitt   101

Payton R., m. Mary **JONES**, b. of Bridgeport, Feb. 17, 1836, by Rev.

Nath[anie]l Hewitt   18

William D., m. Julia Ann **TOMLINSON**, Oct. 21, 1850, by Rev. Gurdon

S. Coit   104

BLACK, Jane Rebecca, m. Henry **MAY**, b. of Bridgeport, Dec. 31, 1848, by

Rev. William Reid   97

Mary, m. John N. A. **LEWIS**, July 3, 1837, by [Rev. Gurdon S. Coit]   26

BLACKESLEE, [see under **BLAKESLEE**]

BLAKEMAN, BLACKMAN, BLACKEMAN, Celia F., m. William E.

WARD, Jan. 3, 1847, by Rev. Gurdon S. Coit   74

Charles, m. Mary Louisa **CRAIG**, b. of Bridgeport, Oct. 7, 1847, by

Rev. Heman Bangs   77

Frances A., m. Ja[me]s E. **CURTIS**, June 9, 1844, by Rev. Gurdon S.

Coit   64

Harriet M., m. William H. **GOULD**, b. of Bridgeport, June 2, 1842,

by Rev. S. C. Perry   47

Henry, m. Sarah E. **WHITNEY**, June 30, 1846, by Rev. William Reid   70

Joseph Sherman, of Fairfield, m. Elizabeth Hannah **JOHNSON**, of Easton,

Feb. 18, 1849, by William Reid   98

Laura, of Fairfield, m. John **HERTON**, of Bridgeport, Oct. 2, 1836,

by Charles F. Pelton   15

Lewis, m. Sarah M. **WEBB**, Jan. 22, 1843, by Rev. W[illia]m W. Smith   53

Lucinda, m. Aaron **BULKLEY**, of Weston, Nov. 20, 1831, by [Rev. John

Blatchford]   3

Mary E., m. Richard **FOX**, Dec. 24, 1843, by Rev. Gurdon S. Coit   56

BLAKEMAN, BLACKMAN, BLACKEMAN, (cont.)
  Mary E., m. Marquis D. L. **HALL**, b. of Fairfield, May 31, 1844,
    by Rev. J. L. Gilder   57
  Olive, of Bridgeport, m. Charles H. **GILBERT**, of Monroe, July 3,
    1841, by Rev. John H. Hunter   42
  Susan, m. Reuben A. **LOCKWOOD**, b. of Bridgeport, Mar. 12, 1848, by
    Rev. W[illia]m Reid   86
[BLAKESLEE], BLACKESLEE, Mary C., m. Samuel F. **MARSTON**, b. of
  New Burgh St., New York, Nov. 29, 1838, by Rev. Daniel Smith   29
BLOOM, Joseph, m. Adeline **DEMING**, Aug. 12, 1835, by Charles F. Pelton   10
BOARDMAN, Samuel, m. Delia A. **WAKELEE**, Oct. 25, 1846, by Rev.
  Gurdon S. Coit   74
BODWELL, Benjamin H., of New York, m. Rebecca B. **JUDSON**, of
  Huntington, May 13, 1838, by Rev. Gurdon S. Coit   27
BOLLEN, Eliza Ann, m. Joseph **LUTZ**, b. of Bridgeport, Nov. 13, 1841, by
  Rev. Nathaniel Hewitt   52
BOLLES, Julia, m. John **TULLER**, Jr., b. of Bridgeport, July 5, 1847, by
  Rev. Joseph Turner (colored)   78
BONTON*, George C., m. Ellen **PERRY**, b. of Bridgeport, Nov. 24, 1847, by
  Rev. G. S. Gilbert   *(BOUTON (?)   80
BOOTH, BOOTHE, Catharine, m. Richard **CALAGAN**, May 4, [1851], by
  Rev. Michael Lynch. Witnesses: John McCann, Elizabeth Calagan   108
  Catharine Ann, m. Starr **BEACH**, Nov. 28, 1833, by Rev. Gurdon S. Coit   2
  Catharine E., of Stratford, m. George B. **AMBLER**, of Trumbull, Nov.
    16, 1845, by Rev. S. B. Brittain   62
  Charles C., m. Emily **GREGORY**, b. of Bridgeport, Nov. 2, 1834, by
    Rev. Gurdon S. Coit   7
  Harriet, m. Henry **HUBBELL**, b. of Bridgeport, Jan. 14, 1849, by Rev.
    Moses Ballow   89
  Isaac E., of Trumbull, m. Emma A. **MORGAN**, of Bridgeport, Aug. 11,
    1844, by Rev. S. B. Brittain   57
  John, m. Mary **STERLING**, b. of Trumbull, Jan. 7, 1841, by Rev.
    Nathaniel Hewitt   50
  Marshall P., m. Jeannetta H. **LEWIS**, Dec. 28, [1847], by Rev.
    Gurdon S. Coit   82
  Mary Ann, of Bridgeport, m. Barzillai **GRAY**, of Easton, Nov. 25,
    1845, by Rev. James H. Perry   61
  Minerva, m. Harvey **TREAT**, Nov. 21, [1847], by Rev. Gurdon S. Coit   82
  Otis, of Savannah Ga., m. Sarah C. **WHITING**, of Bridgeport, Aug.
    25, 1836, by Rev. Gurdon S. Coit   14
  Philo Treat, of Trumbull, m. Miranda **HUBBELL**, of Huntington, May
    20, 1841, by Rev. Gurdon S. Coit   41
  Sarah M., m. George **PETERS**, Oct. 7, 1845, by Rev. Gurdon S. Coit   64
  William D., of New York, m. Eliza J. **HUBBELL**, of Bridgeport, Nov.
    12, 1851, by Rev. Benj[amin] S. J. Page   110
BOSIEE (?), Amelia E., m. Samuel b. **HURD**, b. of Bridgeport, [Aug.] 26,
  [1849], by Rev. M. Ballou   92
BOSTWICK, Clare M., m. Henry W. **HUBBELL**, Mar. 31, 1836, by Rev.

Page

BRESLOW, Mary, m. Christopher **HOPE**, June 30, 1844, by Rev. Michael
    Lynch. Witnesses: Burt Hope, Jullia Killian   65
BREWER, Maria, of Danbury, m. Thomas **BURTON**, of Bridgeport, Jan. 31,
    1836, by Rev. John Blatchford   22
BRIDGE, Hannah, m. Samuel **DAILEY**, Apr. 13, 1843, by Rev. Gurdon S.
    Coit   55
BRIDTHE, Andrew, m. Margaret **BECK**, Sept. 22, [1850], by Rev. Michael
    Lynch. Witnesses: Franz Abet, Mary Bridthe   103
BROADSTREET, Thomas, m. Silvia Ann **PARKER**, (colored), Aug. 28,
    1842, by Rev. Gurdon S. Coit   55
BROOKS, Abby Ann, m. Rodney **CURTIS**, Dec. 11, 1836, by Rev. Gurdon S.
    Coit   17
    Caroline V., m. Charles Sidney J. **GOODRICH**, Oct. 16, 1839, by Rev.
        Gurdon S. Coit   31
    Emmeline A., m. Charles F. **STERLING**, May 8, 1837, by [Rev. Gurdon
        S. Coit]   26
    Harriet, J., m. William H. **NOBLE**, Oct. 16, 1839, by Rev. Gurdon S.
        Coit   31
    Henry, m. Emily A. **COOK**, June 21, 1843, by Rev. Gurdon S. Coit   56
    James, m. Phebe D. **BURRETT**, b. of Bridgeport, Sept. 25, 1836, by
        Rev. Gurdon S. Coit   15
    Joseph W., of Bridgeport, m. Eunice **HALL**, of Fairfield, Feb. 26,
        1852, by Rev. Benj[amin] S. J. Page   112
    Maria L., m. Frederic **REID**, June 1, 1848, by Rev. Gurdon S. Coit   92
    Matilda, m. Frideric **FRY**, [, 1848], by Rev. Gurdon S. Coit   92
    Sarah, of Bridgeport, m. George W. **COE**, of Derby, Dec. 20, 1846,
        by Rev. J. H. Perry   73
    Thomas, m. Harriet **NAUGHER**, Feb. 10, 1849, by Rev. Gurdon S. Coit   92
    William, of New London, m. Mary E. **FANTON**, of Bridgeport, May 22,
        1838, by Rev. John Woodbridge   29
    ----, m. Richard **GORHAM**, b. of Stratford, June [ ], 1832, by
        [Rev. John Blatchford]   3
BROTHERINGTON, Henry, m. Sally Ann **JENNINGS**, June 28, 1840, by
    Rev. Gurdon S. Coit   36
BROTHERTON, Francis Ann, of Bridgeport, m. George **TURNER**, of
    Trumbull, July 21, 1850, by Rev. William Reid   99
    Louisa M., of New York, m. Oscar B. **NICHOLS**, of Bridgeport, Mar.
        7, 1847, by Rev. William Reid   75
    Sarah H., m. John F. **BARNUM**, Sept. 21, 1843, by Rev. J. Leonard
        Gilder   49
BROWN, Adelia A., of Bridgeport, m. Birdsey **WAKELEE**, of Huntington,
    Oct. 8, 1842, by Rev. Nathaniel Hewitt   52
    Elizabeth m, Henry **JONES**, Oct. 19, 1846, by Rev. Gurdon S. Coit   74
    Horace H., m. Maria **WHITNEY**, b. of Bridgeport, May 18, 1836, by
        Rev. Nath[anie]l Hewitt   19
    Mary E., of Bridgeport, m. Andrew J. **FOOT**, of Newtown, Sept. 22,
        1834, by Rev. Davis Stocking   6
    Sarah Ann, m. George G. **WHEELER**, b. of Bridgeport, Oct. 4, 1835, by

Page

BROWN, (cont.)

Rev. Nath[anie]l Hewit   17

Susan W., m. Stephen **SHERWOOD**, b. of Bridgeport, Dec. 25, 1842,
by Rev. John H. Hunter   48

William, m. Sarah E. **BENNETT**, Oct. 29, 1837, by Rev. J. W. LeFevre   23

BROWNSON, Hannah, of Bridgeport, m. Jonathan **STEARNES**, of New York,
Nov. 12, 1850, by Rev. Benj[amin] S. J. Page   101

BRYAN, George H., of Orange, m. Julia A. **ALLING**, of Twenesburgh, O.,
Nov. 23, 1847, by Rev. William Reid   80

BUCKINGHAM, Henry, m. Abby O. **CURTIS**, May 5, 1853, by Rev. Gurdon
S. Coit   116

John Albert, m. Georgianna Augusta **NICHOLS**, Oct. 31, 1850, by Rev.
Henry W. Bellows, of New York City   102

Mary, m. Judson S. **GARLICK**, b. of Milford, Dec. 24, 1848, by Rev.
Moses Ballow   88

Moses T., m. Mary Ann **SMITH**, Dec. 12, 1836, by Rev. Gurdon S. Coit   17

BUDAN, John D., of Germany, m. Louisa Jane **FRENCH**, of Bridgeport, Nov.
25, [1845], by Rev. S. B. Brittain   62

BULKELEY, BULKLEY, Aaron, of Weston, m. Lucinda **BLAKEMAN**, Nov.
20, 1831, by [Rev. John Blatchford]   3

Sally Ann, of Whitesborough, N. Y., m. Joseph **WAKEMAN**, of Fairfield,
May 11, 1834, by Rev. Nathaniel Ruggles   5

BULYER, Rose, m. Lewis **HENINGER** (Germans), Nov. 22, 1852, by Rev.
Nathaniel Hewit   114

BUNNEL, William R., m. Cornelia **STERLING**, b. of Bridgeport, Jan. 24,
1838, by [Rev. John Woodbridge]   29

BURGESS, Charles, m. Jennette **HURLBERT**, Aug. 2, 1840, by Rev. J. M.
Pease   40

James, m. Margery **McDONALD**, b. of Bridgeport, Sept. 20, 1846, by
Rev. J. Hazard Perry   71

Robert S., m. Mary A. **HOLMES**, Jan. 5, 1845, by Rev. Gurdon S. Coit   64

BURNS, BURN, BURNE, Mary, m. Thomas **CARLEY**, June 21, 1846, by
Rev. Michael Lynch. Witnesses: Michael Murphy, Bridget O'Hara   69

Michael, m. Ellen **O'DONNELL**, Apr. 18, 1847, by Rev. Michael Lynch.
Witnesses: Thomas Lillias, Ellen Burk   75

Nicholas, m. Mary **KEAH**, May 15, 1848, by Rev. Michael Lynch.
Witnesses: Patrick Cain, Anna Casady   83

Richard, m. Catharine **LEARY**, Oct. 14, 1849, by Rev. Michael Lynch.
Witnesses: John Fox, Riss Gill   93

Tho[ma]s., m. Jane **QUIGLEY**, Jan. 12, 1852, by Rev. Michael Lynch.
Witnesses: Barnard Judge, Ann Smyth   112

BURR, BURRS, Ann Maria, of Fairfield, m. Albert **HALL**, of New York, Feb.
25, 1840, by Rev. G. S. Coit   33

Elizabeth, of Fairfield, m. Alexander **HAMILTON**, of Bridgeport,
Sept. 21, 1836, by Rev. Gurdon S. Coit   15

Ianthia, m. Thomas **BEARDSLEY** (Ethiopes), Oct. 3, 1832, by [Rev.
John Blatchford]   3

John, m. Lucy **CURTIS**, b. of Bridgeport, Mar. 16, 1836, by Rev.

Page

CAREY, CARY, (cont.)

Preston M., of Weston, m. Adelia M. **BARNUM**, of Bridgeport, Nov.
13, 1842, by Rev. John H. Hunter ... 47

CARISLE, Eleanor Forester, m. Gurdon Saltonstall **COIT**, b. of Bridgeport,
Feb. 1, 1838, by Rev. Thomas W. Coit, in St. John's Church ... 26

CARLEY, Thomas, m. Mary **BURNE**, June 21, 1846, by Rev. Michael Lynch.
Witnesses: Michael Murphy, Bridget O'Hara ... 69

CARR, Dabney, of St. Louis, Mo., m. Mary E. **DYER**, of Bridgeport, June
29, 1852, by Rev. Benj[amin] S. J. Page ... 113

Eliza, of Bridgeport, m. Edward **HAWLEY**, of Newtown, May 10, 1846
by Rev. William Reid ... 70

CARRIER, Elizabeth E., of Bridgeport, m. Joshua H. **SKINNER**, of Albany,
N Y., Nov. 27, 1844, by Rev. Nathaniel Hewit ... 63

Susan, m. Stiles **HALL**, b. of Bridgeport, Oct. 1, 1848, by Rev.
Nath[anie]l Hewit ... 91

CARROLL, Bryant B., m. Sarah J. **JENNINGS**, b. of Bridgeport, Oct. 11,
1841, by Rev Nathaniel Hewitt ... 52

Mary, m. John **QUIN**, Aug. 23, [1846], by Rev. Michael Lynch.
Witnesses: Lawrence Melvihel, Bridget McCormuck ... 72

CARTON, Bridget, m. Richard **HUGHES**, Oct. 21, 1849, by Rev. Michael
Lynch. Witnesses: Lewis Money, Maria Jackwis ... 93

CASEY, James, m. Mary **HURLEY**, Jan. 20, 1845, by Rev. Michael Lynch.
Witnesses: Michael Gready, Bridgett Lillias ... 66

Mary, m. Pat[ric]k **O'DONNELL**, July 9, 1843, by [Rev. Michael Lynch].
Witnesses: Edw[ar]d Casey, Ellen Burke ... 65

Thomas, m. Mary **HAYESE**, Oct. 22, 1840, by Rev. Michael Lynch.
Witnesses: Michael Cready, Mary Hurley ... 65

CASSIDY, Ann, m. Peter **CLABBY**, Apr. 27, [1851], by Rev. Michael Lynch.
Witnesses: Pat Burns, Rose Cassidy ... 108

CENTER, Abby Louisa, m. Alfred **COOK**, June 21, 1842, by Rev. Gurdon S.
Coit ... 55

CHAMBERLAIN, John, of Hartford, m. Almira E. **WINTUBLE**, of New York
City, Mar. 31, 1850, by Rev. William Reid ... 98

Maria, m. George **WATKINS**, b. of Bridgeport, June 2, 1839, by Rev.
Daniel Smith ... 30

Wyllys, of New Milford, m. Caroline **HALL**, of Bridgeport, May 4,
1835, by Rev. David Stocking ... 9

CHAPMAN, J. P., of New Haven, m. Rachel J. **HARTWELL**, of Bridgeport,
Apr. 24, 1844, by Rev. John H. Hunter ... 57

CHARLES, Robert, m. Louisa **HURLBURT**, Dec. 22, [1845], by Rev. S. B.
Brittain ... 62

CHARY, Michael, m. Bridget **SWORDS**, Feb. 22, [1852], by Rev. Michael
Lynch. Witnesses: Richard Swords. Bridget Malone ... 112

CHATFIELD, Burton L., m. Fanny J. **HATCH**, b. of Bridgeport, Nov. 26,
1840, by Rev. John H. Hunter ... 39

Duine, of Oxford, m. Jane **STEVENS**, of Bridgeport, Jan. 8, 1834,
by Rev. Gurdon S. Coit ... 4

Henry W., m. Susan W. **KIPPUN**, b. of Bridgeport, Sept. 20, 1842, by

Page

CHATFIELD (cont.)

Rev.John H. Hunter   47

Mary A., m. Joseph **DENISER**, Nov. 29, 1851, by Rev. Michael Lynch.
   Witnesses: John O'Shane, Mary A. Arnold   111

Nancy, wid., m. Lewis **KIRTLAND**, b. of Bridgeport, Dec. 17, 1840,
   by Benjamin S. Smith, J. P.   39

CHEENEY, Samuel M., m. Sarah G. **HATCH**, b. of Bridgeport, Feb. 23, 1849,
   by Rev. Benj[amin], S. J. Page   88

CHILD, John F., of Tarrytown, N. Y., m. Abigail **SHEPARD**, of Bridgeport,
   May 14, 1849, by Rev. Nath[anie]l Hewit   91

CHITLER, Johnson R., of New York, m. Samantha **BURRS**, of Bridgeport,
   Apr. 6, 1835, by Rev. John Blatchford   22

CHRISTIE, Margaret, m. Joseph **ROBERTS**, b. of Bridgeport, June 4, 1834,
   by Rev. John Blatchford   21

CLABBY, Mary, m. Michael **RIELLY**, Nov. 13, 1843, by [Rev. Michael
   Lynch]. Witnesses: John Cole, Bridget Canton   65

Peter, m. Ann **CASSIDY**, Apr. 27, [1851], by Rev. Michael Lynch.
   Witnesses: Pat Burns, Rose Cassidy   108

CLARK, CLARKE, Andrew, m. Harriet **NICHOLS**, June 10, 1844, by Rev.
   Gurdon S. Coit   64

Catharine, m. Edward **TUITE***, Sept. 6, [1846], by Rev. Michael Lynch.
   Witnesses: Barnard Kelley, Ann Clark *(TAITE?)   72

Comfort, of Bridgeport, m. Edward **COLLINS**, of New Haven, Jan. 20,
   1840, by Rev. Daniel Smith   35

Elisha, m. Allice **LEWIS**, Nov. 16, 1836, by Rev. Gurdon S. Coit   16

Elizabeth, m. Michael **BOWDREN**, b. of Bridgeport, Oct. 1, 1839, by
   Rev. Daniel Smith   30

Elizabeth, m. Michael **BOWDREN**, b. of Bridgeport, Oct. 1, 1839, by
   Rev. Daniel Smith   32

Emily R., m. Thomas H. **WEBB**, Dec. 9, 1831, by [Rev. John Blatchford]   3

J. F., m. August **WILDNER**, Apr. 14, 1850, by Rev. Gurdon S. Coit   104

John, m. Elizabeth **KIRTLAND**, b. of New York, Apr. 12, 1851, by
   Rev. Benj[amin] S. J. Page   106

Patrick, m. Margaret **MURPHY**, Mar. 5, 1848, by Rev. Michael Lynch.
   Witnesses: Pat Holland, Susan McEvay   81

Sarah A., m. Julius B. **HAWLEY**, Oct. 10, 1844, by Rev. Gurdon S. Coit   64

Sarah C., of New York, m. Tolman C. **PERRY**, of Bridgeport, Oct. 2,
   1851, in New York City, by Rev. Nathaniel Hewit   114

CLARY, Walter, m. Bridget **BARNES**, Sept. 14, [1851], by Rev . Michael
   Lynch. Witnesses: Daniel Langan, Nelly Ennis   110

CLINTON, Richard, m. Mary **MULLEDY**, May 17, 1847, by Rev. Michael
   Lynch. Witnesses: John Coyle, Anne Mulledy   78

COE, George W., of Derby, m. Sarah **BROOKS**, of Bridgeport, Dec. 20, 1846,
   by Rev. J. H. Perry   73

COFFEE, Mary, m. Edward **GIBBIN**, Oct. 5, 1851, by Rev. Michael Lynch.
   Witnesses: Owen Roch, Rose McCabe   111

COIT, Gurdon Saltonstall, m. Eleanor Forester **CARLISLE**, b. of Bridgeport,
   Feb. 1, 1838, by Rev. Thomas W. Coit, in St. John's Church   26

Page

COLEMAN, Ann, of Bridgeport, m. Jesse W. BENEDICT, of New York City,
July 3, 1833, by Nathaniel Hewit 1
Johanna, m. Thomas WALSH, Sept. 3, 1848, by Rev. Michael Lynch.
Witnesses: Garrett Cotter, Catharine Reilly 86
COLEY, Levi, m. Emmeline HALL, of Danbury, Nov. 10, 1833, by Rev. John
Blatchford 21
COLLINS, Ann, of Bridgeport, m. Charles BATES, of New York, May 11,
1837, by Rev. Nath[anie]l Hewitt 25
Edward. of New Haven, m. Comfort CLARKE, of Bridgeport, Jan. 20,
1840, by Rev. Daniel Smith 35
COLOGAN, Eliza, m. Patrick MONAHAN, Feb. 11, [1852], by Rev. Michael
Lynch. Witnesses: Thomas Noonan, Catharine Donohoe 112
COMMELLEY, Ellen, m. Dan[ie]l LYNCII, July 28, 1844, by Rev. Michael
Lynch. Witnesses: Dan[ie]l Ward, Mary Alexander 65
CONDON, Mich[ae]l, m. Margaret WALSH, Oct. 18, 1843, by [Rev. Michael
Lynch]. Witnesses: Tho[ma]s Casey, Bridget Condon 65
CONKLIN, Virginia H., of Bridgeport, m Stephen J. ALLEN, of Westport,
Nov. 2, 1851, by Rev. Benj[amin], S. J. Page 110
CONLEY, Laura J., of New Canaan, m. Henry E. HOUGH, of Bridgeport,
June 8, 1846, by Rev. James H. Perry 68
Rosanna, m. Patrick OWENS, Feb. 3, 1850, by Rev. Michael Lynch.
Witnesses: Thomas Walsh, Mary Armstrong 95
Sarah, m. Samuel William HOUGH, Jan. 5, 1840, by Gurdon S. Coit 33
CONNEFORD, Margaret, m. Michael CUSAR, Sept. 8, 1845, by Rev. Michael
Lynch. Witnesses: John Masterson, Bridget Reilly 66
CONNELL, Margaret C., m. William HURELY, May 5, [1851], by Rev.
Michael Lynch. Witnesses: John Mahoney, Elizabeth Roach 108
Michael, m. Margarett REILLY, Nov. 8, [1847], by Rev. Michael Lynch,
Witnesses: Richard Fitzgibbon, Mary Reilly 79
CONNERS, CONNOR, Allice, m. Timothy O'CONNELL, Feb. 6, 1848, by
Rev. Michael Lynch. Witnesses: Pat Reilly, Catharine Russell 81
Ann, m. Ja[me]s CROWLEY, Feb. 19, 1844, by Rev. Michael Lynch.
Witnesses: Nicholas Crowley, Mary Crowley 65
Charles, m. Anna McKUIRNAN, Mar. 5, 1848, by Rev. Michael Lynch.
Witnesses: Edward Baughney, Jane McKuirnan 81
Eliza, m. John LAWRENCE, Nov. 24, 1847, by Rev. Michael Lynch.
Witnesses: W[illia]m Wallace, Mary Connors 80
John, m. Johannah SWEENEY, May 18, [1851], by Rev. Michael Lynch.
Witnesses: Dan[ie]l Mallehill, Margaret Sullivan 108
Patrick, m. Bridget PURDON, Feb. 5, 1849, by Michael Lynch.
Witnesses: John O'Brien, Catharine Donohoe 87
Patrick, m. Ann SHEA, Oct. 5, 1851, by Rev. Michael Lynch.
Witnesses: Patrick Burk, Margaret Crosby 111
CONRAD, Peter, m. Elizabeth A. FRENCH, Apr. 25, 1843, by Rev. W[illia]m
W. Smith 53
COOK, COOKE, Alfred, m. Abby Louisa CENTER, June 21, 1842, by Rev.
Gurdon S. Coit 55
Ellen, m. John N. DEMING, b. of Bridgeport, Feb. 19, 1839, by

Page

COOK, COOKE, (cont.)

Rev. Daniel Smith   29

Emily A., m. Henry **BROOKS**, June 21, 1843, by Rev. Gurdon S. Coit   56

Mary E., m. Edward **TOMKINS**, Oct. 17, 1838, by [Rev. Gurdon S. Coit]   28

Milton H., m. Isabella C. **BISHOP**, May 4, 1852, by Rev. Gurdon S. Coit   115

COOKLEY, John Joseph, of New York City, m. Sarah Jane **PEPPER**, of

Brooklyn, N. Y., Jan. 26, 1854, by Joshua B. Ferris, J. P.   117

COONEY, Catharine, m. John **REILLY**, May 7, 1844, by Rev. Michael

Lynch. Witnesses: Edw[ar]d Maguire, Mary Killey   65

CORBESON, CORBERSON, Alfred B., m. Clarissa W. **HUBBELL**, b. of

Bridgeport, Dec. 23, 1850, by Rev. Benj[amin] S. J. Page   103

John G., m. Elizabeth **HODGES**, Oct. 12, 1842, by Rev. Gurdon S. Coit   55

CORCORAN, Michael, m. Mary Ann **McMANUS**, Jan. 8, 1846, by Rev.

Michael Lynch. Witnesses: James Banigan, Eliza Cleary   66

CORNBY, Peter, m. Bridget **MULLEN**, Nov. 26, 1849, by Rev. Michael

Lynch. Witnesses: Michael Grant, Mary A. McPherson   95

CORZIAIE, Catharine, m. Hugh **GOODMAN**, Jan. 19, 1845, by Rev. Michael

Lynch. Witnesses: Michael Brown, Margaret O'Neal   66

COSTELO, Martin, m. Rose **SWORDS**, Jan. 25, 1852, by Rev. Michael

Lynch. Witnesses: Michael Mounts, Catharine Leonies   112

COSTER, John, m. Hannah A. **LOYD**, Sept. 16, 1837, by Rev. John

Woodbridge   24

Richard, m. Sarah Ann **WILLIAMS**, Oct. 30, 1843, by Rev. W[illia]m

H. Smith   54

COUNTIER, Susan, m. Benjamin B. **MILLS**, b. of Bridgeport, Nov. 3, 1839,

by Rev. Daniel Smith   32

COX, Angeline R., m. Tho[ma]s **LEWIS**, Mar. 28, 1844, by Rev. Gurdon S.

Coit   64

Bridget, m. Tho[ma]s **O'ROURKE**, May 28, 1848, by Rev. Michael

Lynch. Witnesses: W[illia]m McCormuck, Ann McCormuck   84

CRAFFT, Abby Jane, of Bridgeport, m. John Henry **TRIPLER**, of New York,

July 29, 1846, by Rev. J. H. Perry   71

CRAIG, Mary Louisa, m. Charles **BLAKEMAN**, b. of Bridgeport, Oct. 7,

1847, by Rev. Heman Bangs   77

CRANE, Abigail, of Bridgeport, m. William B. **DOUGLASS**, of Newark, N. J.,

Oct. 12, 1834, by Rev. Davis Stocking   7

Cornelia, of New York, m. James **RUSSELL**, July 13, 1832, by [Rev.

John Blatchford]   3

CRAWFORD, George, m. Jeannetta **PECK**, Nov. 1, 1832, by [Rev. John

Blatchford]   3

Jennette, m. George **CURTIS**, Nov. 24, 1836, by Rev. G. S. Coit   16

William, m. Mrs. Charlotte **EVERETT**, May 25, 1851, by Rev. J. J.

Lewis   107

CROCKER, Edward, m. Polly Ann **SHERWOOD**, Apr. 30, 1835, by Rev. G.

S. Coit   9

CROFUT, CROFOOT, Benedict C., m. Eliza **ROCKWELL**, June 10, 1838,

by [Rev. Gurdon S. Coit]   28

Emily F., m. George **GOULDING**, May 8, 1842, by Rev. Gurdon S.

Page

CROFUT, CROFOOT, (cont.)

Coit 55

Lydia, m. Charles **SHERMAN**, b. of Bridgeport, Apr. 12, 1835, by
Rev. G. S. Coit 8

Nathan B., of New Fairfield, m. Julia **HAWLEY**, of Bridgeport, Mar.
4, 1846, by Rev. J. H. Perry 68

CROSBY, CROSSBY, James, m. Catharine **DOODLE**, Nov. 19, 1849, by
Rev. Michael Lynch. Witnesses: Nicholas Vary, Winefred Egan 94

Mary, of Bridgeport, m. Samuel **DECKER**, of Cortland, N. Y., Oct.
27, 1839, by Rev. Nathaniel Hewitt 51

Mary, of Bridgeport, m. Eleazer **VAN KEERIN**, of New York, Dec. 7,
1841, by Rev. John H. Hunter 45

Mercy, m. Thomas **MORRIS**, Feb. 4, 1838, in Philadelphia, by [Rev,
Gurdon S. Coit] 26

CROWENBURGER, Joseph, of Allsetts, Germany, m. Hannah B. **PEASE**, of
Bridgeport, Apr. 5, 1835, by Rev. John Blatchford 22

CROWLEY, Ja[me]s, m. Ann **CONNERS**, Feb. 19, 1844, by Rev. Michael
Lynch. Witnesses: Nicholas Crowley, Mary Crowley 65

Mary, m. Henry **FREEMAN**, June 27, [1847], by Rev. Michael Lynch.
Witnesses: James Crowley, Ann Rowe 78

Nicholas, m. Elizabeth **KENNA**, June 19, 1848, by Rev. Michael Lynch.
Witnesses: Nicholas Norris, Margarette Taraffe 84

CULL, John, m. Ellen **HERBERT**, June 18, 1846, by Rev. Michael Lynch.
Witnesses: Patrick Morisey, Bridget Liles 69

CULLAM, Julia, m. Mich[ae]l **KILLIAN**, Jan. 22, 1844, by [Rev. Michael
Lynch.] Witnesses: Patrick Duffy, Julia Killian 65

CULLANE, Mary, m. James **WARD**, Apr. 21, 1840, by Rev. Gurdon S. Coit 34

CUMMINGS, CUMMINS, John, m. Margaret **MONAHAN**, Sept. 22, [1850],
by Rev. Michael Lynch. Witnesses: James Bigley, Sarah Cummins 103

John, m. Elizabeth **DALY**, Aug. 14, 1851, by Rev. Michael Lynch.
Witnesses: Thomas Lyon, Mary Heruty 110

CUNNINGHAM, Thomas, of Greensboro, Ga., m. Mary **ROSENDE**, of
Columbus, Ga., Oct. 9, 1839, by Rev. Daniel Smith 32

CURTIS, Abby O., m. Henry **BUCKINGHAM**, May 5, 1853, by Rev. Gurdon
S. Coit 116

Abner, of Sherman, Can.*, m. Ann Maria **HAWLEY**, of Bridgeport,
June 21, 1837, by Rev. John Woodbridge *(Con[necticut]?) 24

Albert, of Stratford, m. Anna G. **GORHAM**, of Bridgeport, Sept. 26,
1840, by Rev. Nathaniel Hewitt 50

C., m. William H. **THOMPSON**, Nov. 23, 1848, by Rev. Gurdon S. Coit 92

Comfort, m. Victor **MAGNE**, Nov. 1, 1849, by Rev. Gurdon S. Coit 104

David C., m. Jane B. **SMITH**, May 18, 1834, by Rev. Gurdon S. Coit 6

Elijah, m. Elizabeth J. **HUBBELL**, [Oct.] 29, [1847], by Rev. Gurdon
S. Coit 82

Eliza J., m. Joseph C. **LEWIS**, Dec. 31, 1843, by Rev. Gurdon S. Coit 56

Ezra B., of St. Louis, Mo., m. Susan E. **HUBBELL**, of Bridgeport,
Oct. 8, 1840, by Rev. John H. Hunter 37

Frederick S., m. Elizabeth **KNAPP**, Sept. 26, 1837, by Rev. John

Page

CURTIS, (cont.)

Woodbridge ... 24

George, m. Jennette **CRAWFORD,** Nov. 24, 1836, by Rev. G. S. Coit ... 16

George S., m. Sarah A. **MIDDLEBROOK,** Mar. 8, 1843, by Rev. Gurdon S. Coit ... 55

Harriet, m. Charles C. **NOBLE,** June [ ], 1835, by B. G. Noble ... 11

Ja[me]s E., m. Frances A. **BLACKMAN,** June 9, 1844, by Rev. Gurdon S. Coit ... 64

Levi, m. Mary C. **HULL,** Dec. 11, 1838, by Rev. G. S. Coit ... 30

Lewis B., m. Harriet E. **JOHNSON,** Nov. 11, 1844, by Rev. Gurdon S. Coit ... 64

Lucy, m. John **BURR,** b. of Bridgeport, Mar. 16, 1836, by Rev. John Blatchford ... 22

Rasom D., m. Mary J. **BEAVENS,** b. of Bridgeport, Oct. 17, 1848, by Rev. Moses Ballow ... 88

Rodney, m. Abby Ann **BROOKS,** Dec. 11, 1836, by Rev. Gurdon S. Coit ... 17

Rodney, m. Lucy **BURR,** b. of Bridgeport, Dec. 28, 1845, by John H. Hunter ... 67

Russell T., m. Maria L. **HUBBELL,** b. of Bridgeport, Nov. 1, 1847, by Rev. Nath[anie]l Hewit ... 90

Ruth Ann, of Bridgeport, m. Ali **ANDREWS,** of Meredin, Mar. 3, 1840, by Rev. Gurdon S. Coit ... 33

Stiles, m. James (?) **WHITING,** Sept. 23, 1838, by [Rev. Gurdon S. Coit] (Both male names) ... 28

Susan, of Trumbull, m. Daniel **STRATTON,** of Bridgeport, May 29, 1839, by Rev. Daniel Smith ... 30

Susan J., of Bridgeport, m. Philo **BEACH,** of Trumbull, Jan. 12, 1848, by Rev. Nath[anie]l Hewit ... 90

Thaddeus, m. Delia **PERRY,** Apr. 16, 1843, by Rev. Gurdon S. Coit ... 55

Wooster, m. Mary **WRIGHT,** Nov. 25, 1838, by [Rev. G. S. Coit] ... 30

CUSAR, Michael, m. Margaret **CONNEFORD,** Sept. 8, 1845, by Rev. Michael Lynch. Witnesses: John Masterson, Bridget Rielly ... 66

DALEY, DAILEY, DALY, Anna, m. Michael **HIGGINS,** May 7, 1848, by Rev. Michael Lynch. Witnesses: John Daugherty, Bridget Higgins ... 83

Catharine, m. Dan[ie]l **QUINLARAN,** June 11, 1848, by Rev. Michael Lynch. Witnesses: James Carmoney, Ellen Tooley ... 84

Elizabeth, m. John **CUMMINGS,** Aug. 14, 1851, by Rev. Michael Lynch. Witnesses: Thomas Lyon, Mary Heruty ... 110

Margaret, of Bridgeport, m. John **HODGDON,** of North Ray, Me., Feb. 24, 1852, by Rev. Benj[amin] S. J. Page ... 112

Samuel, m. Hannah **BRIDGE,** Apr. 13, 1843, by Rev. Gurdon S. Coit ... 55

DANAKER, Christian Augustus, of Philadelphia, m. Evanna **SEGER,** of Bridgeport, Oct. 8, 1840, by Rev. Stephen A. Medley, of Philadelphia ... 37

DANIELS, Mahlon, m. Alice **JACKSON,** Apr. 20, 1851, by Rev. Gurdon S. Coit ... 115

DANTON, Barnard, m. Mary **DANTON,** May 19, 1846, by Rev. Michael Lynch. Witnesses: Christopher Hope, Bridget Breslin ... 69

Page

DANTON, (cont.)

Mary, m. Barnard **DANTON**, May 19, 1846, by Rev. Michael Lynch.
Witnesses: Christopher Hope, Bridget Breslin   69

DANVILLE, Hiram, m. Abigail L. **MILLS**, June 23, 1839, by Rev. G. S. Coit   31

DARENGEN, Mary, m. John T. **SHULTZ**, May 16, 1852, by Rev. Gurdon S.
Coit   115

DARROW, Edmund, of New York, m. Susan Ellen **HUBBELL**, Oct. 3, 1832,
by [Rev. John Blatchford]   3

Mary Francis, m. Samuel **WILMOTT**, Sept. 8, 1834, by Rev. G. S. Coit   6

Rosella, of Bridgeport, m. Samuel E. **SPROULS**, of Charleston, S. C.,
Oct. 1, 1835, by Rev. Gurdon S. Coit   11

DASKAM, James, m. Emmeline **SHERMAN**, Nov. 25, 1841, by Rev. G. S.
Coit   44

DATON, Daniel C., of New Milford, m. Susan C. **DAVIS**, of Bridgeport,
[Jan.] 15, [1837], by Rev. F. Hitchcock   20

DAUGHERTY, Elizabeth, m. John **SMYTH**, Feb. 20, 1848, by Rev. Michael
Lynch. Witnesses. Thomas Flynn, Mary Flynn   81

Julia Ann, m. Henry George **CARLSON**, Jan 1, 1850, by Rev. William
Reid   98

DAVIS, Caroline, m. J. W. **STEWART**, Aug. 21, 1843, by Rev. Gurdon S.
Coit   56

Mary Anne, m. Gilson **LANDON**, Oct. 31, 1843, by Rev. Gurdon S. Coit   56

Susan, m. Thomas **JACKSON** (colored), Mar. 29, 1835, by Rev. Gurdon
S. Coit   8

Susan C., of Bridgeport, m. Daniel C. **DATON**, of New Milford, [Jan.]
15, [1837], by Rev. F. Hitchcock   20

DAVISON, Edward, m. Betsey **SCOVILLE**, Sept. 1, 1850, by Rev. Gurdon S.
Coit   104

DAY, Daniel J., of Apalachachola, Fla., m. Emily E. **JONES**, of Bridgeport,
Oct. 30, 1850, by Rev. Benj[amin] S. J. Page   101

DAYTON, Betsey, m. Edward **HUBBELL**, b. of Bridgeport, Oct. 13, 1847,
by Rev. Benj[amin] S. J. Page   77

DEALORN, Ann, m. Edward **MOLOY**, July 5, 1846, by Rev. Michael Lynch.
Witnesses: Richard Hanan, Margaret O'Neil   72

DEAN, William H., m. Mary J. **MARSH**, b. of Bridgeport, Mar. 10, 1851,
by J. B. Stratton   106

DECKER, Samuel, of Cortland, N. Y., m. Mary **CROSSBY**, of Bridgeport,
Oct. 27, 1839, by Rev. Nathaniel Hewitt   51

DeFOREST, Benjamin C., m. Maria L. **CANFIELD**, b. of Bridgeport, Oct. 17,
1843, by Rev. Nathaniel Hewitt   52

Charles, m. Maria **HOPKINS**, b. of Bridgeport, Oct. 5, 1842, by Rev.
Nathaniel Hewitt   52

Elizabeth, of Bridgeport, m. Frederic S. **HAWLEY**, of San Francisco.,
Cal., Jan. 30, 1851, by Nathaniel Hewit, V. D. M.   109

Hannah M., m. Frederick A. **NORTON**, b. of Fairfield, July 7, 1844,
by Rev. J. L. Gilder   58

Louisa, of Bridgeport, m. Samuel **WOODRUFF**, of Albany, Oct. 25,
1836, by Rev. Nath[anie]l Hewitt   19

Page

EASTMAN, (cont.)

York, Mar. 31, 1851, by Rev. Benj[amin] S. J. Page   106

ECKENSPERGEN, Rosia, m. John **SHETTENHELEN**, b. of Bridgeport, Feb.
6, 1851, by Nathaniel Hewit, V. D. M.   109

EDWARDS, Benj[amin], m. Esther **MALLETT**, Oct. 10, 1842, by Rev.
Gurdon S. Coit   55

Charles, m. Mary S. **BEACH**, b. of Bridgeport, Feb. 28, 1840, by
Rev. John H. Hunter   36

Daniel, of Trumbull, m. Rebecca **SEELEY**, of Bridgeport, June 25,
1850, by Rev. Benj[amin], S. J. Page   96

Isaac S., of Trumbull, m. Delia M. **O'CAINE**, of Stratford, Nov. 26,
1844, by Rev. Nathaniel Hewit   63

John S., of Trumbull, m. Rebecca Ann **LEWES**, of New York, July 3,
1834, by Rev. John Blatchford   21

Sally P., of Trumbull, m. Isaac G. **SMITH**, of Weston, Nov. 29,
1832, by [Rev. John Blatchford]   3

Sarah A., m. Lauren **NICHOLS**, May 7, [1847], by Rev. Gurdon S. Coit   82

Susan, of Stratford, m. Anson M. **LOCKWOOD**, of Weston, Mar. 30,
1834, by Rev. John Tackaberry   5

Susan, m. Jabez **SUMMERS**, b. of Bridgeport, Oct. 1, 1843, by Rev.
John H. Hunter   49

Susan A., of Trumbull, m. Elbert **HAWLEY**, of Monroe, Nov. 17, 1833,
by Rev. John Blatchford   21

Sylvia E., m. Samuell **MALLETT**, June 6, 1847, by Rev. Gurdon S. Coit   82

ELLOITT, Sophia W., of Bridgeport, m. John F. **NORTON**, of Bridgewater,
Mass. (Rev.), Dec. 31, 1850, by Nathaniel Hewit, V. D. M.   109

William, m. Eleanor **ROBERTSON**, June 5, 1842, by Rev. Gurdon S.
Coit   55

ELLISON, Margaret, m. William H. **PEET**, Dec. 24, 1846, by Rev. Gurdon S.
Coit   74

William C., of New York, m. Eliza C. **STERLING**, of Bridgeport, May
8, 1843, by Rev. John H. Hunter   48

ELLSWORTH, Pinckney W., of Hartford, m. Julia M. **STERLING**, of
Bridgeport, Oct. 10, 1842, by Rev. Nathaniel Hewitt   52

EMLY, George, of Binghampton, N. Y., m. Abby Jane **WELLS**, of Fairfield,
Apr. 30, 1837, by Rev. Charles F. Pelton   21

EMMENUEL, Thomas M., m. Margarite A. **BEEKER**, Oct. 13, 1852, by Rev.
Gurdon S. Coit   116

ENGELHURST, Charles, of Minssenburgh, Germany, m. Eliza D. **CAMP**, of
New York, June 30, 1850, by Rev. Benj[amin] S. J. Page   97

EVERETT, Charlotte, Mrs., m. William **CRAWFORD**, May 25, 1851, by
Rev. J. J. Lewis   107

FAGAN, Margaret, m. John **BARNES**, June 30, 1851, by Rev. Michael Lynch.
Witnesses: Francis Fagan, Ann Nolan   110

FAHEY, Ann, m. John **REILLY**, Nov. 2, [1846], by Rev. Michael Lynch.
Witnesses: John Masterson, Catharine Farrell   72

FAIRCHILD, Aaron, m. Mrs. Harriet **BEECHER**, of Woodbridge, Nov. 6,
1836, at Stratford, by Rev. Gurdon S. Coit   16

Page

FRENCH, (cont.)

Elizabeth, m. William **HAYES**, b. of Bridgeport, May 5, 1834, by
    Rev. John Blatchford   21

Elizabeth A., m. Peter **CONRAD**, Apr. 25, 1843, by Rev. W[illia]m
    W. Smith   53

Elizabeth J., of Bridgeport, m. James W. **GRAY**, of Norwalk, Apr.
    20, 1849, by Rev. Benjamin S. J. Page (Perhaps Apr. 16)   89

George, m. Jane **RAYMOND**, Mar. 1, [1848], by Gurdon S. Coit   82

Henry N., m. Harriet **BRADLEY**, b. of Bridgeport, Mar. 10, 1841, by
    Rev. John H. Hunter   40

John, Jr., m. Hannah M. **HULL**, b. of Bridgeport, May 29, 1836, by
    Rev. Charles F. Pelton   13

Louisa Jane, of Bridgeport, m. John D. **BUDAN**, of Germany, Nov. 25,
    [1845], by Rev. S. B. Brittain   62

Maria S., m. Jared **PAGE**, Jan. 1, 1837, by Rev. Charles F. Pelton   19

Mary E., of Bridgeport, m. Charles E. **GODFREY**, of Fairfield, May
    8, 1851, by Rev. J. B. Stratton   107

Mary W., m. Philo **GREGORY**, Oct. 21, 1833, by Gurdon S. Coit   1

FRIES, [see also **FRY**], Catharine, m. Cha[rle]s **SCHELESEY**, Oct. 14, 1851,
    by Rev. Gurdon S. Coit   115

FROST, Catharine, m. Godfrey **NEEL**, June 20, 1853, by Rev. Gurdon S. Coit   116

FRY, [see also **FRIES**], Frederic, m. Matilda **BROOKS**, [, 1848], by Rev.
    Gurdon S. Coit   92

FULLER, Amos, m. Emily F. **WHEELER**, b. of Bridgeport, Apr. 15, 1852,
    by Rev. Benj[amin] S. J. Page   113

George A., m. Huldah A. **MILLS**, Feb. 20, 1850, by Rev. Gurdon S. Coit   104

FURLONG, John, m. Catharine **McAULIFFE**, Jan. 12, 1846, by Rev. Michael
    Lynch. Witnesses: Phil McCormuck, Julia Studley   67

GAFNEY, Andrew, m. Ann **DUNNE**, June 22, 1851, by Rev. Michael Lynch.
    Witnesses: Patrick Dunne, Margaret Dunne   110

Edw[ar]d, m. Ellen **DUNN**, June 8, [1851], by Rev. Michael Lynch.
    Witnesses: Patrick Dunn, Ann Dunn   108

GAINER, Michael, m. Mary **GARRIGAN**, Apr. 7, [1850], by Rev. Michael
    Lynch. Witnesses: Thomas Nevin, Mary Ward   102

GAINS, Ann A., m. Elijah **SAVAGE**, Oct. 13, 1852, at Stratford, by Rev.
    Leonard Collins   113

GAINY, Mary, m. Patrick **KENEDY**, June 14, 1846, by Rev. Michael Lynch.
    Witnesses: Bernard Kenedy, Bridget Russell   69

GARDNER, Robert, m. Mary Jane **KENEDY**, b. of Bridgeport, July 1, 1844,
    by Rev. Nathaniel Hewit   63

GARLICK, Judson S., m. Mary **BUCKINGHAM**, b. of Milford, Dec. 24,
    1848, by Rev. Moses Ballow   88

GARRIGAN, Mary, m. Michael **GAINER**, Apr. 7, [1850], by Rev. Michael
    Lynch. Witnesses: Thomas Nevin, Mary Ward   102

GAY, Stephen, m. Elizabeth **BANCROFT**, June [ ], 1846, by Rev. Gurdon
    S. Coit   74

GIBBIN, Edward, m. Mary **COFFEE**, Oct. 5, 1851, by Rev. Michael Lynch.
    Witnesses: Owen Roch, Rose McCabe   111

Page

GRIDELY, (cont.)

York, Jan. 29, 1852, by Rev. Benj[amin] S. J. Page   111

GRIFFETH, Mary J., m. Henry **OSBORNE,** Dec. 25, 1842, by Rev. Gurdon
S. Coit   55

GRIFFIN, Mary, of Newtown, m. Theodore **KNAPP,** of Norwalk, May 21,
1848, by Rev. Benj[amin] S. J. Page   83

GUARD, John, m. Eliza **PECAR,** Aug. 9, 1837, by [Rev. Gurdon S. Coit]   26

GUNN, Aaron, m. Mrs. Minerva **TREADWELL,** b. of Bridgeport, Nov. 25,
1848, by Rev. Moses Ballow   88

Eliza Ann, m. Harvey A. **PARSONS,** b. of Bridgeport, Oct. 3, 1836,
by Rev. G. S. Coit   15

Jackson, of Bridgeport, m. Mary Ann **MATHEWS,** of Bridgeport,
formerly of New York City, Oct. 17, 1840, by W[illia]m H. Noble, J.
P.   38

Joseph H., m. Harriet S. **NICHOLS,** Oct. 12, 1837, by Rev. J. W. LeFevre   23

Rebecca, m. Samuel W. **HODGES,** Mar. 25, 1838, by Rev. J. W. Lefevre   27

GURNSEY, Jacob S., of Stratford, m. Caroline M. **PARROTT,** of Bridgeport,
Oct. 26, 1841, by Rev. Salmon C. Perry   43

HACKLEY, Sam[ue]l, m. Isabella **McGREGOR,** Apr. 29, 1851, by Rev.
Gurdon S. Coit   115

HAHNECER, Mary, m. August **MUNDERLICK,** Dec. 9, 1851, by Rev.
Gurdon S. Coit   115

HAIGHT, Harvey H., m. Sarah M. **HUBBELL,** b. of Bridgeport, Mar. 19,
1833, by Nathaniel Hewit   1

Joseph, m. Harriet B. **HULER,** Aug. 11, 1844, by Rev. S. B. Brittain   57

HALE, Robert M., m. Eliza J. **HINMAN,** Oct. 18, 1852, by Rev. Gurdon S.
Coit   116

HALL, Albert, of New York, m. Ann Maria **BURR,** of Fairfield, Feb. 25,
1840, by Rev. G. S. Coit   33

Caroline, of Bridgeport, m. Wyllys **CHAMBERLAIN,** of New Milford,
May 4, 1835, by Rev. David Stocking   9

Emmeline, of Danbury, m. Levi **COLEY,** Nov. 10, 1833, by Rev. John
Blatchford   21

Eunice, of Fairfield, m. Joseph W. **BROOKS,** of Bridgeport, Feb. 26,
1852, by Rev. Benj[amin] S. J. Page   112

Henry, m. Harriet **WHEELER,** Dec. 29, 1840, by Rev. Gurdon S. Coit   39

Josiah B., of Bridgeport, m. Anna **BALDWIN,** of Easton, Mar. 20,
1849, by Rev. Nath[anie]l Hewit   91

Louisa, m. Sam[ue]l **STRATTON,** Jan. 9, 1848, by Rev. Gurdon S. Coit   82

Marquis L. L., m. Mary E. **BLACKMAN,** b. of Fairfield, May 31, 1844,
by Rev. J. L. Gilder   57

Mary Augusta, m. John **BATCHELOR,** b. of Bridgeport, June 29, 1845,
by Rev. J. H. Perry   60

Mary J., of Bridgeport, m. George E. **OGDEN,** of Fairfield, Apr. 1,
1849, by Rev. William Reid   97

Orlando B., m. Laura Ann **WHEELER,** b. of Bridgeport, Sept. 22, 1835,
by Rev. John Blatchford   22

Ormell A., of New York, m. Rebeccah N. **HATCH,** of Bridgeport, July 5,

Page

HAWLEY, (cont.)

Rev. William Reid   70

Elbert, of Monroe, m. Susan A. **EDWARDS,** of Trumbull, Nov. 17, 1833,
    by Rev. John Blatchford   21

Eli C., of Bridgeport, m. Elizabeth P. **PLUMB,** of Trumbull, Feb. 11,
    1842, by Rev. John H. Hunter   46

Eliza F., m. John S. **SMITH,** Sept. 16, 1844, by Rev. Gurdon S. Coit   64

Frederic S., of San Francisco, Cal., m. Elizabeth **DeFOREST,** of
    Bridgeport, Jan. 30, 1851, by Nath[anie]l Hewit, V. D. M.   109

Henrietta S., m. Stiles **JOHNSON,** Nov. 26, 1850, by Rev. Gurdon S.
    Coit   104

Julia, of Bridgeport, m. Nathan B. **CROFOOT,** of New Fairfield, Mar.
    4, 1846, by Rev. J. H. Perry   68

Julius B , m Sarah A. **CLARKE,** Oct. 10, 1844, by Rev. Gurdon S. Coit   64

Matilda, m. Josiah S. **FAYERWEATHER,** b. of Bridgeport, May 29,
    1834, by Rev. Nathaniel Hewitt   6

Starr, m. Sarah Ann **BYAS,** b. of Bridgeport, June 13, 1848, by Rev.
    Benj[amin] S. J. Page   84

Stephen, of New Haven, m. Julia A. **MALLETT,** of Bridgeport, Dec. 1,
    1844, by Rev. Nathaniel Hewit   63

HAYES, HAYESE, Anna, m. James **REY,** Feb. 12, 1850, by Rev. Michael
    Lynch. Witnesses: Thomas Rey, Alice Hayes   95

Mary, m. Thomas **CASEY,** Oct. 22, 1840, by Rev. Michael Lynch.
    Witnesses: Michael Cready, Mary Hurley   65

Thomas, 2nd, m. Sarah J. **MORGAN,** b. of Bridgeport, Oct. 2, 1839,
    by Rev. Daniel Smith   30

Thomas, 2nd, m. Sarah J. **MORGAN,** b. of Bridgeport, Oct. 2, 1839,
    by Rev. Daniel Smith   32

William, m. Elizabeth **FRENCH,** b. of Bridgeport, May 5, 1834, by
    Rev. John Blatchford   21

HEALEY, Michael, m. Eliza **LAWLER,** May 7, 1848, by Rev. Michael
    Lynch. Witnesses: Patrick Rea, Margaret O'Connell   83

HEDDIN, Alexander P., m. Ann Maria **LEWIS,** b. of Bridgeport, Mar. 27,
    1850, by Rev. Benj[amin] S. J. Page   96

HELLEY, Mary Ann, m. Charles Frederick **LUTZ,** May 19, 1846, by Rev.
    Michael Lynch. Witnesses: Patrick Reddy, Mrs. A. Lutzs   69

HENDERER, John C., m. Anna C. **LEWIS,** Nov. 23, 1845, by Rev. Gurdon S.
    Coit   64

HENESEY, Mary, m. Thomas **LYONS,** Feb. 22, [1852], by Rev. Michael
    Lynch. Witnesses: John Cummins, Eliza Daley   112

HENINGER, Lewis, m. Rose **BULYER,** (Germans), Nov. 22, 1852, by Rev.
    Nathaniel Hewit   114

HERBERT, Ellen, m. John **CULL,** June 18, 1846, by Rev. Michael Lynch.
    Witnesses: Patrick Morisey, Bridget Liles   69

HERTLAND, Jane E., m. Alanson **HAWLEY,** Nov. 4, 1846, by Rev. Gurdon
    S. Coit   74

HERTON, John, of Bridgeport, m. Laura **BLAKEMAN,** of Fairfield, Oct. 2,
    1836, by Charles F. Pelton   15

HODGE, (cont.)

        by Rev. Gurdon S. Coit   11

        William, m. Caroline **BIBBINS,** Oct. 17, 1841, by Rev. N. Ruggles   43

HODGER, John, m. Catharine **ANDESS,** Sept. 2, 1852, by Rev. Gurdon S.
        Coit   116

HODGES, Eliza Ann, m. William **WILSON,** Oct. 25, 1837, by Rev. J. W.
        LeFevre   23

        Elizabeth, m. John G. **CORBESON,** Oct. 12, 1842, by Rev. Gurdon S.
        Coit   55

        Emily Austin, m. Charles Ropes **WILLIAMS,** Oct. 23, 1850, by Rev.
        Gurdon S. Coit   104

        Lucinda, m. Rodney A. **BURRETT,** b. of Bridgeport, Aug. 13, 1843,
        by Rev. J. Leonard Gilder   49

        Samuel W., m. Rebecca **GUNN,** Mar. 25, 1838, by Rev. J. W. LeFevre   27

HOLDREGE, Henry, Capt., m. Mrs. Margarite C. **HOLT,** b. of New York
        City, [Sept] 1, [1841], at Black Rock, Fairfield, by Rev. Gurdon S.
        Coit   43

HOLMES, Mary A., m. Robert S. **BURGESS,** Jan. 5, 1845, by Rev. Gurdon S.
        Coit   64

HOLT, Margarite C., Mrs. m. Capt. Henry **HOLDREGE,** b. of New York
        City, [Sept.] 1, [1841], at Black Rock, Fairfield, by Rev. Gurdon S.
        Coit   43

HOPE, Christopher, m. Mary **BRESLOW,** June 30, 1844, by Rev. Michael
        Lynch. Witnesses: Burt Hope, Jullia Killian   65

        Ellen, m. William **MOONEY,** Feb. 8, 1847, by Rev. Michael Lynch.
        Witnesses: Patrick Cain, Anna Casidy   75

HOPKINS, Catherine, m. Michael **MOLOY,** Feb. 16, [1852], by Rev. Michael
        Lynch. Witnesses: Barnard Deogan, Theresa Shannon   112

        Maria, m. Charles **DeFOREST,** b. of Bridgeport, Oct. 5, 1842, by Rev.
        Nathaniel Hewitt   52

HORTON *, Giles G., of Pleasantville, N. Y., m. Virginia Maria
        OLMSTEAD, of Milton, Conn., Dec. 1, 1849, by Rev. William Reid
        *(Perhaps "**HARTOW**")   98

        John B., m. Hannah E. **PORTER,** July 4, 1847, by Rev. Gurdon S.
        Coit   82

HOTCHKISS, Fanny M., m. William S. **HANFORD,** b. of Bridgeport, May
        10, 1847, by Rev. Nath[anie]l Hewit   90

HOUGH, Henry E., of Bridgeport, m. Laura J. **CONLEY,** of New Canaan,
        June 8, 1846, by Rev. James H. Perry   68

        Mary W., m. William J. **SHELTON,** Oct. 25, 1842, by Rev. Gurdon S.
        Coit   55

        Samuel William, m. Sarah **CONLEY,** Jan. 5, 1840, by Gurdon S. Coit   33

HOWECK, Hannah, m. Thomas C. **WAIT,** b. of Bridgeport, July 7, 1834, by
        Rev. John Blatchford   21

HOWIE, Elizabeth, m. Henry **ROBINSON,** of Trumbull, Oct. 4, 1831, by
        [Rev. John Blatchford]   3

HOXSIE, Norton A., m. Caroline B. **WHEELER,** Sept. 5, 1844, by Rev.
        Gurdon S. Coit   64

Page

HUBBELL, (cont.)

Harriet, m. Peter **THORP**, Sept. 25, 1837, by [Rev. Gurdon S. Coit]   26

Henry, m. Harriet **BOOTH**, b. of Bridgeport, Jan. 14, 1849, by Rev.
Moses Ballow   89

Henry W., m. Clare M. **BOSTWICK**, Mar. 31, 1836, by Rev. Gurdon S.
Coit   13

Hepsa, of Monroe, m. Philo **REED**, of Huntington, Oct. 13, 1834, by
Rev. John Blatchford   22

Jane E., of Bridgeport, m. Henry L. W. **BURRETT**, of Chester, N. Y.
Nov. 28, 1844, by Rev. Nathaniel Hewit   63

Jennett, m. George **LEWIS**, b. of Bridgeport, Oct. 31, 1838, by Rev.
Nathaniel Hewitt   50

Julia A., of Bridgeport, m. John H. **BILLINGS**, of New York, Dec.
24, 1844, by Rev. John H. Hunter   59

Julia Ann, m. Joseph **WELLS**, b. of Bridgeport, May 25, 1837, by
Rev. Nath[anie]l Hewitt   25

Maria L., m Russell T. **CURTIS**, b. of Bridgeport, Nov. 1, 1847,
by Rev. Nath[anie]l Hewit   90

Mary, of Stratford, m. W[illia]m **LEWIS**, of Bridgeport, Mar. 8,
1837, by Rev. Nath[anie]l Hewitt   25

Miranda, of Huntington, m. Philo Treat **BOOTHE**, of Trumbull, May
20, 1841, by Rev. Gurdon S. Coit   41

Sarah M., m. Harvey H. **HAIGHT**, b. of Bridgeport, Mar. 19, 1833,
by Nathaniel Hewit   1

Susan E., of Bridgeport, m. Ezra B. **CURTIS**, of St. Louis, Mo.,
Oct. 8, 1840, by Rev. John H. Hunter   37

Susan Ellen, m. Edmund **DARROW**, of New York, Oct. 3, 1832, by
[Rev. John Blatchford]   3

Theodore, m. Jane J. **STRATTON**, Nov. 25, 1850, by Rev. Gurdon S.
Coit   104

William P., m. Mary E. **WIXON**, b. of Bridgeport, [July] 22, [1849],
by M. Ballou   91

HUCHELL, Charlotte, of Loch Hesson, m. Lewis **MENZER**, of Lauterback,
Hesson, Germany, June 30, 1850, by Rev. Benj[amin] S. J. Page   97

HUFF, Marietta C., m. Isaac J. **WELLS**, Mar. 27, 1837, by [Rev. Gurdon S.
Coit]   26

HUGHES, HUGES, Eliza, m. George **WITTSTINE**, Jan. 22, [1837], by Rev.
C. F. Pelton   20

Richard, m. Bridget **CARTON**, Oct. 21, 1849, by Rev. Michael Lynch.
Witnesses: Lewis Money, Maria Jackwis   93

HULER, Harriet B., m. Joseph **HAIGHT**, Aug. 11, 1844, by Rev. S. B.
Brittain   57

HULL, Abigail, m. Morehouse W. **BRADLEY**, b. of Bridgeport, Sept. 20,
1843, by Rev. John H. Hunter   49

David, m. Harriet **VANCE**, Sept. [ ], 1846, by Rev. Gurdon S. Coit   74

Ellenor, m. David **HUBBELL**, b. of Bridgeport, May 15, 1837, by Rev.
Nath[anie]l Hewitt   25

Hannah M., m. John **FRENCH**, Jr., b. of Bridgeport, May 29, 1836,

JACKSON, (cont.)

    Coit   115

    Henry F., of Stratford, m. Mary Ann **WELLES**, of Bridgeport, Feb.
        7, 1836, by Rev. Nath[anie]l Hewitt   18

    Mary, m. Jacob **McEWEN**, b. of Bridgeport, Jan. 30, 1834, by Rev.
        John Tackaberry   4

    Sarah, m. Charles **HUBBELL**, b. of Bridgeport, Oct. 7, 1838, by Rev.
        J. W. LeFevre   27

    Thomas, m. Susan **DAVIS**, (colored), Mar. 29, 1835, by Rev. Gurdon
        S. Coit   8

JAMES, John, m. Mary **BATCHELOR**, b. of Bridgeport, Dec. 28, 1845, by
    Rev. James H. Perry   61

    Maria, m. Simeon **DICKERSON**, b. of Bridgeport, Mar. 1, 1835, by
    Rev. Davis Stocking   8

JENKINS, James, m. Elizabeth **WARD**, July 2, 1851, by Rev. Gurdon S. Coit   115

JENNINGS, James, m. Eliza C. **NICHOLS**, b. of Bridgeport, Jan. 21, 1841,
    by Rev. Nathaniel Hewitt   50

    Mary Ann, m. Stiles **HURD**, Nov. 4, 1835, by Rev. Gurdon S. Coit   11

    Obadiah, m. Esther C. **BENSON**, b. of Fairfield, July 14, 1831,
        by [Rev. John Blatchford]   3

    Sally Ann, m. Henry **BROTHERINGTON**, June 28, 1840, by Rev.
        Gurdon S. Coit   36

    Sarah J., m. Bryant B. **CARROLL**, b. of Bridgeport, Oct. 11, 1841,
        by Rev. Nathaniel Hewitt   52

JEPSON, Mary Ann, m. Thomas **RAWLING**, b. of New Haven, Oct. 4, 1847,
    by Rev. Heman Bangs   77

JESUP, Samuel E., of Stamford, m. Sophia A. **WHEELER**, Nov. 5, 1843, by
    Rev. Gurdon S. Coit   56

JOHNSON, Caroline M., m. Frederick G. **SCHULTZ**, b. of East Bridgeport,
    June 23, 1844, by Rev. Morris D. C. Crawford   59

    Elizabeth Hannah, of Easton, m. Joseph Sherman **BLAKEMAN**, of
        Fairfield, Feb. 18, 1849, by Rev. William Reid   98

    Harriet E., m. Lewis B. **CURTIS**, Nov. 11, 1844, by Rev. Gurdon S. Coit   64

    Mary Ann, m. William R. **HIGBY**, b. of Bridgeport, Sept. 23, 1846,
        by Rev. Nathaniel Hewit   73

    Rebecca E., of Boston, Mass., m. Edward L. **THAYER**, of Mendon,
        Mass., May 8, 1851, by Rev. Moses Ballou   106

    Stiles, m. Henrietta S. **HAWLEY**, Nov. 26, 1850, by Rev. Gurdon S. Coit   104

    W[illia]m Beach, of Bermingham, m. Mabel **PAT**, of Bridgeport, June
        9, 1844, by Rev. J. L. Gilder   57

    W[illiam E., m. Amelia **WILLIAMS**, Sept. 21, 1845, by Rev. Gurdon S.
        Coit   64

    William S., of New York, m. Ann Eliza **NICHOLS**, of Bridgeport, June
        17, 1835, by Rev. Gurdon S. Coit   10

JONES, Anna, m. Charles **WEEKS**, b. of Bridgeport, Oct. 27, 1839, by Rev.
    Nathaniel Hewitt   51

    Emily D., m. Charles M. **SHERWOOD**, b. of Bridgeport, June 28, 1835,
        by Rev. Gurdon S. Coit   10

Page

JONES, (cont.)

Emily E., of Bridgeport, m. Daniel J. **DAY**, of Apalachachola, Fla.,
Oct. 30, 1850, by Rev. Benj[amin] S. J. Page   101

Eunice, m. David **PENDLETON**, b. of Bridgeport, Oct. 7, 1849, by
Rev. Nath[anie]l Hewit   100

Harriet, m. Samuel **GREENMAN**, b. of Bridgeport, Sept. 3, 1845, by
Rev. Nathaniel Hewit   63

Henry, m. Elizabeth **BROWN**, Oct. 19, 1846, by Rev. Gurdon S. Coit   74

James W., m. Rebecca C. **LEIGH**, Nov. 16, 1846, by Rev. Gurdon S.
Coit   74

Mary, m. Payton R. **BISHOP**, b. of Bridgeport, Feb. 17, 1836, by
Rev. Nath[anie]l Hewitt   18

Philip James, m. Isabella **BRADLEY**, Oct. 4, 1846, by Rev. Gurdon S.
Coit   74

Samuel, m. Jane **HARRINGTON**, Mar. 19, 1850, by Rev. Gurdon S. Coit   104

Seth B., m. Sarah E. **WHETTEMORE**, b. of Bridgeport, Oct. 11, 1835,
by Rev. Nath[anie]l Hewitt   17

Susan, of Bridgeport, m. William **TOZAL***, of New York, Feb. 23,
1841, by Rev. Nathaniel Hewitt *(**FOZAL**?)   50

Thomas, m. Sarah **LEWIS**, Oct. 11, [1835], by Rev. Gurdon S. Coit   12

William, of Stratford, m. Catharine **WAY**, of Bridgeport, Mar. 27,
1841, by Rev. Nathaniel Hewitt   50

JORDAN, Stephen, m. Mercy Ann **PLATT**, b. of Bridgeport, Dec. 6, 1840, by
Rev. John H. Hunter   39

JOY, Andrew E., m. Eunice E. **NASH**, b. of Bridgeport, June 28, 1843, by
Rev. Nathaniel Hewitt   52

JUDD, Calvin, of Bridgeport, m. Jane E. **ROOD**, of Milford, Oct. 22, 1848,
by Rev. Willian Reid   97

JUDSON, Ann Eliza, m. James L. **MAYNARD**, b. of Bridgeport, Feb. 15,
1852, by Rev. Benj[amin] S. J. Page   111

Garry, m. Jane **PATCHEN**, b. of Bridgeport, Sept. 28, 1833, by Nathaniel
Hewit   2

Henry, m. Mary Ann **WHITNEY**, b. of Bridgeport, Dec. 10, 1843, by
Rev. Nathaniel Hewitt   53

Henry, of Bridgeport, m. Mary Ann **BEARDSLEY**, of Stratford, May 26,
1844, by Rev. Nathaniel Hewit   63

Jeremiah, m. Ann **LINUS**, Apr. [ ], 1832, by [Rev. John Blatchford]   3

Marcellus J., m. Huldah **MALLETT**, b. of Trumbull, Mar. 15, 1835,
by Rev. Gurdon S. Coit   8

Mary, m. Samuel **HINE**, b. of Bridgeport, Sept. 30, 1841, by Rev.
Nathaniel Hewitt   51

Mary Ann, m. William M. **LIVINGSTONE**, b. of Bridgeport, Aug. 4,
1850, by Rev. J. B. Stratton   99

Rebecca B., of Huntington, m. Benjamin H. **BODWELL**, of New York,
May 13, 1838, by Rev. Gurdon S. Coit   27

JUPE, Francis, m. Mana N. **SHERWOOD**, Aug. 15, 1831, by [Rev. John
Blatchford]   3

KAHN, Jean B., m. Sophia **REDEKOFF**, May 16, 1852, by Rev. Gurdon S.

Page

KILLIAN, (cont.)

    Lynch]. Witnesses: Patrick Duffy, Julia Killian   65

KING, Jane, m. John H. MASON, b. of Springfield, Mass., Aug. 8, 1841,
    by Rev. J. H. Hunter   42

KINGSLEY, John B., m. Mrs. Sarah E. LACEY, b. of Bridgeport, May 7,
    1848, by Rev. W[illia]m Reid   86

KINWORTHY, Betsey, m. Edward HILL, b. of Bridgeport, July 4, 1840,
    by Rev. Daniel Harrington   36

KIPPEN, KIPPUN, Susan W., m. Henry W. CHATFIELD, b. of Bridgeport,
    Sept. 20, 1842, by Rev. John H. Hunter   47

    William F., m. Oliva C. DOANE, b. of Bridgeport, Apr. 19, 1842,
    by Rev. Nathaniel Hewitt   52

KIRTLAND, KERTLAND, Charles A., m. Jane S. BEEBE, Nov. 20, 1850, by
    Rev. Gurdon S. Coit   104

    Elizabeth, m. John CLARK, b. of New York, Apr. 12, 1851, by Rev.
    Benj[amin] S. J. Page   106

    Frederick S., m. Cornelia BURROUGHS, May 28, 1840, by Rev. G. S.
    Coit   34

    Lewis, m. wid. Nancy CHATFIELD, b. of Bridgeport, Dec. 17, 1840,
    by Benjamin S. Smith, J. P.   39

KNAPP, Elizabeth, m. Frederick S. CURTIS, Sept. 26, 1837, by Rev. John
    Woodbridge   24

    Hannah Maria, m. Charles WILLIS, b. of Bridgeport, Dec. 28, 1843,
    by Rev. Nathaniel Hewit   62

    Iverson W., m. Harriet MERWIN, b. of Bridgeport, Jan. 23, 1842,
    by Rev. Nathaniel Hewitt   52

    Lucy A., of Bridgeport, m. Janes ROODYARD, of New york, Mar. 4,
    1850, by Rev. Benjamin S. J. Page   96

    Sarah Jane, m. Charles HAWLEY, Sept. [ ], 1833, by [Rev. John
    Blatchford]   3

    Theodore, of Norwalk, m. Mary GRIFFIN, of Newtown, May 21, 1848,
    by Rev. Benj[amin] S. J. Page   83

[KNOX], [see under NOX]

LACEY, LACE, Betsey A., m. John ATKINSON, Aug. 8, 1838, by [Rev.
    Gurdon S. Coit]   28

    John, of New York, m. Mary Ann WHITEING, of Bridgeport, Apr. 5,
    1835, by Rev. Gurdon S. Coit   8

    Rowland B., m. Jane E. SHERMAN, b. of Bridgeport, Nov. 17, 1841,
    by Rev. John H. Hunter   44

    Sarah E., Mrs., m. John B. KINGSLEY, b. of Bridgeport, May 7,
    1848, by Rev. W[illia]m Reid   86

LAMBERT, James, m. Harriet FANTON, Sept. 22, 1846, by Rev. Gurdon S.
    Coit   74

LAMPSON, Henry, m. Mary A. HAMMOND, b. of Bridgeport, Aug. 18,
    1839, by Rev. Daniel Smith   30

LANDON, Gilson, m. Mary Anne DAVIS, Oct. 31, 1843, by Rev. Gurdon S.
    Coit   56

LANDWIG, Frederick, m. Emily DOWNES, Apr. 27, 1836, by Rev. Birdsey

LEWIS, LEWES, (cont.)

Nathaniel Hewitt   50

George, m. Elizabeth **WATERMAN**, June 16, 1843, by Rev. Gurdon S.
Coit   56

Georgianna G., m. Alfred **ROBBINS**, Sept. [ ], 1850, by Rev. Gurdon
S. Coit   104

Jeannetta H., m. Marshall P. **BOOTH**, Dec. 28, [1847], by Rev. Gurdon
S. Coit   82

John, m. Mary Ann **SNOW**, b. of Bridgeport, June 23, 1850, by Rev.
William Reid   99

John N. A., m. Mary **BLACK**, July 3, 1837, by [Rev. Gurdon S. Coit]   26

Joseph C., m. Eliza J. **CURTIS**, Dec. 31, 1843, by Rev. Gurdon S. Coit   56

Maria, m. Joel **MITCHEL**, b. of Bridgeport, Nov. 8, 1835, by Charles
F. Pelton   12

Maria, m. Dilazon **ADAMS**, b. of Bridgeport, Mar. 24, 1841, by Rev.
John H. Hunter   40

Mary, m. Edwin **WOOD**, Sept. 23, 1845, by Rev. Gurdon S. Coit   64

Rebecca Ann, of New York, m. John S. **EDWARDS**, of Trumbull, July 3,
1834, by Rev. John Blatchford   21

Sarah, m. Thomas **JONES**, Oct. 11, [1835], by Rev. Gurdon S. Coit   12

Sarah J., of Southbury, m. Lewis G. **BRAY**, of Bridgeport, Apr. 4, 1848,
by Rev. Benj[amin] S. J. Page   82

Sarah S., m. W[illia]m H. **HUMB**, Apr. 8, 1853, by Rev. Gurdon S. Coit   116

Susan, m. Edwin **WOOD**, Oct. 25, 1838, [by Rev. Gurdon S. Coit]   28

Tho[ma]s, m. Angeline R. **COX**, Mar. 28, 1844, by Rev. Gurdon S. Coit   64

Tho[ma]s, m. Cornelia **HUBBARD**, Oct. 19, 1845, by Rev. Gurdon S.
Coit   64

W[illia]m, of Bridgeport, m. Mary **HUBBELL**, of Stratford, Mar. 8 ,
1837, by Rev. Nath[anie]l Hewitt   25

William A., m. Mary A. **REILLY**, b. of Bridgeport, Oct. 21, 1850, by
Rev. J. B. Stratton   102

LILLIAS, Bridget, m. William **O'KEEFE**, Feb. 23, 1846, by Rev. Michael
Lynch. Witnesses: Patrick Ray, Ellen Herbert   68

LINDLEY, William, m. Anna **NORTH**, Mar. 20, 1842, by Rev. Gurdon S.
Coit   55

LINEN, Robert, m. Caroline A. **WALKER**, May 25, 1840, by Rev. G. S. Coit   34

[LINES], [see under **LYNES**]

LINUS, Ann, m. Jeremiah **JUDSON**, Apr. [ ], 1832, by [Rev. John Blatchford]   3

LIVINGSTONE, William M., m. Mary Ann **JUDSON**, b. of Bridgeport, Aug.
4, 1850, by Rev. J. B. Stratton   99

[LLOYD], LOYD, LOYED, Eliza, m. Claus **MASAR**, Oct. 8, 1837, by Rev. J.
W. Lefevre   23

Hannah A., m. John **COSTER**, Sept. 16, 1837, by Rev. John Woodbridge   24

Philo, of Norwalk, m. Sarah Ann **DOLBEAR**, Sept. 8, 1833, by [Rev.
John Blatchford]   3

LOCKINGTON, Elizabeth, m. Michael **MULLEN**, July 20, 1848, by Rev.
Michael Lynch. Witnesses: Samuel Swanton, Hannah Covel   86

LOCKWOOD, Anson M., of Weston, m. Susan **EDWARDS**, of Stratford,

LYONS, LYON, (cont.)

    12, 1849, by Rev. Nath[anie]l Hewit   100

    Thomas, m. Mary **HENESEY**, Feb. 22, [1852], by Rev. Michael Lynch.
      Witnesses: John Cummins, Eliza Daley   112

McAULEY, William, m. Julia **MITCHELL**, of Long Island, Sept, 7, 1835, by
    Rev. John Blatchford   22

McAULIFFE, Catharine, m. John **FURLONG**, Jan. 12, 1846, by Rev. Michael
    Lynch. Witnesses: Phil McCormuck, Julia Studley   67

McAVOY, Susannah, m. Thomas **MARTIN**, Sept. 3, 1848, By Rev. Michael
    Lynch. Witnesses: Owen Rock, Mary Burk   87

McCANN, Ann, m. Thomas **REILLY**, July 13, 1845, by Rev. Michael Lynch.
    Witnesses: Thomas Clearly, Mary Calaher   66

    John, m. Rose **FINEGAN**, May 25, [1851], by Rev. Michael Lynch.
      Witnesses: John Burns, Margaret Fagan   108

    Thomas, m. Bridget **REILLY**, Feb. 11, 1850, by Rev. Michael Lynch.
      Witnesses: Matt Cleary, Catharine Booth   95

McCAUL, Mary, m. Martin **QUINTIVAN**, Mar. 3, [1851], by Rev. Michael
    Lynch. Witnesses: Dines Calahan, Bridget Smyth   107

McCORMICK, McCORMUCK, Ann, m. Thomas **MALONE**, Nov. 1, 1848,
    by Rev. Michael Lynch. Witnesses: John Mooney, Ann Doolen   87

    Bridget, m. Thomas **LOFTEUS**, Oct. 4, [1846], by Rev. Michael Lynch.
      Witnesses: John Coyle, Bridget Coffey   72

    John, m. Cath[arine] **REYNOLDS**, Jan. 21, 1844, by [Rev. Michael
      Lynch]. Witnesses: John O'Hallaron, Bridget Rielly   65

    Mary, m. Henry **MANSFIELD**, b. of Bridgeport, June 16, 1842, by James
      Fitch, J. P.   46

McCUE, Bridget, m. John **TULLY**, Sept. 30, [1847], by Rev. Michael Lynch.
    Witnesses: John Colye, Elizabeth Quigley   79

McDONALD,, Margery, m. James **BURGESS**, b. of Bridgeport, Sept. 20,
    1846, by Rev. J. Hazard Perry   71

McEWEN, Harriet A., m. Azel R. **WELLS**, b. of Bridgeport, Feb. 3, 1840,
    by Rev. Daniel Smith   35

    Jacob, m. Mary **JACKSON**, b. of Bridgeport, Jan. 30, 1834, by Rev.
    John Tackaberry   4

McGARRAGAN, Elizabeth, m. Patrick **FLEMING**, Apr. 30, 1848, by Rev.
    Michael Lynch. Witnesses: John Masterton, Bridget O'Neil   83

McGOVERN, James, m. Johanna **CAREY**, Feb. 10, 1850, by Rev. Michael
    Lynch. Witnesses: Peter Carey, Mary Brady   95

MACGOWEN, Jane, m. Phil **O'DONNELL**, Sept. 29, 1845, by Rev. Michael
    Lynch. Witnesses: Laurmna Mulvehell, Bridget Burke   66

McGRATH, Margaret, m. Henry **GRADY**, b. of Norwalk, May 11, 1851, by
    Rev. Moses Ballou   107

McGREGOR, Isabella, m. Sam[ue]l **HACKLEY**, Apr. 29, 1851, by Rev.
    Gurdon S. Coit   115

MACHIN, Mary Ann, m. Michael **MOONEY**, Feb. 23, 1846, by Rev. Michael
    Lynch. Witnesses: James Clabbey, Ann Smyth   68

McINTIRE, Duncan, m. Catharine **ANDERSON**, June 4, 1843, by Rev.
    W[illia]m W. Smith   53

McINTIRE, (cont.)

John, m. Martha **SPARKS,** Dec. 17, 1843, by Rev. W[illia]m H. Smith   54

McKEENAN, Jane, m. Edward **McMULLIN,** June 10, [1850], By Rev.
Michael Lynch. Witnesses: Peter Farrell, Jane McMullin   102

McKENZIE, David, m. Laura **STANDISH,** May 9, 1841, by Rev. J. M. Pease   40

McKUIRNAN, Anna, m. Charles **CONNORS,** Mar. 5, 1848, by Rev. Michael
Lynch. Witnesses: Edward Baughney, Jane McKuirnan   81

McMANUS, Mary Ann, m. Michael **CORCORAN,** Jan. 8, 1846, by Rev.
Michael Lynch. Witnesses: James Banigan, Eliza Cleary   66

McMULLIN, Edward, m. Jane **McKEENAN,** June 10, [1850], by Rev.
Michael Lynch. Witnesses: Peter Farrell, Jane McMullin   102

Margaret, of Bridgeport, m. Charles H. **SPEARS,** of New York, Nov.
12, 1850, by Rev. Benj[amin] S. J. Page   101

Mary Jane, m. Ber[nar]d **FARRELL,** May 11, [1851], by Rev. Michael
Lynch. Witnesses: Patrick Ward, Catharine Braeen   108

McPALLION, Michael, m. Ann **ROCK,** Jan. 20, 1851, by Rev. Michael
Lynch. Witnesses: Thomas Costelo, Honora Rock   107

McSHINE, Ellen, m. Bartholomew **DONAHUE,** Aug. 4, [1847], by Rev.
Michael Lynch. Witnesses: John Fagan, Mary A. Lynch   78

MAGNE, Victor, m. Comfort **CURTIS,** Nov. 1, 1849, by Rev. Gurdon S. Coit   104

MAGUIRE, Edw[ard], m. Margarette **SMYTH,** Sept. 29, 1844, by Rev.
Michael Lynch. Witnesses: John Moor, Margaret Moor   65

Mary, m. John **MOORE,** Oct. 27, 1840, by Rev. Michael Lynch.
Witnesses: Edward Magin, Ann Fobes   65

Patrick, m. Bridget **REED,** Nov. 26, 1849, by Rev. Michael Lynch.
Witnesses: Andrew Keenne, Mary Maguire   94

MAKER, Maria, m. John B. **MERRETT,** Oct. 6, 1847, by Rev. Gurdon S.
Coit   82

MALAPOR, Mary M., m. Rev. William F. **HALSEY,** Nov. 13, 1843, by Rev.
Gurdon S. Coit   56

MALL, Gottlieb, m. Theresa **STILT,** Mar. 20, 1853, by Rev. Gurdon S. Coit   116

MALLARD, William R., of New York, m. Caroline S. **SHENNING,** of
Bridgeport, Nov. 29, 1843, by Rev. John H. Hunter   54

MALLETT, Charity, m. Austin **SHERMAN,** Sept. 17, 1848, by Rev. Gurdon
S. Coit   92

Charles, m. Mary S. **SMITH,** Nov. 25, 1841, by Rev. G. S. Coit   44

Esther, m. Benj[amin] **EDWARDS,** Oct. 10, 1842, by Rev. Gurdon S.
Coit   55

Huldah, m. Marcellus J. **JUDSON,** b. of Trumbull, Mar. 15, 1835, by
Rev. Gurdon S. Coit   8

Julia A., of Bridgeport, m. Stephen **HAWLEY,** of New Haven, Dec. 1,
1844, by Rev. Nathainiel Hewit   63

Louisa, m. Joel **SHELTON,** Apr. 7, 1841, by Rev. Gurdon S. Coit   41

Samuell, m. Sylvia E. **EDWARDS,** June 6, 1847, by [Rev. Gurdon S.
Coit]   82

MALLORY, Harriette A., m. Miles **AMBLER,** Mar. 15, 1840, by Rev. G. S.
Coit   33

MALONE, John, m. Mary **CALLAHER,** June 24, [1850], by Rev. Michael

Page

MALONE, (cont.)

  Lynch. Witnesses: Peter Lynch, Elizabeth Callaher   102

  Thomas, m. Ann **McCORMUCK**, Nov. 1, 1848, by Rev. Michael Lynch.

    Witnesses: John Mooney, Ann Doolen   87

MANSFIELD, Henry, m. Mary **McCORMICK**, b. of Bridgeport, June 16,

  1842, by James Fitch, J. P.   46

MARGARVIN, Thomas G., m. Mary **HARPENTER**, June 6, 1849, by Rev.

  Gurdon S. Coit   92

MARSH, Mary J., m. William H. **DEAN**, b. of Bridgeport, Mar. 10, 1851,

  by J. B. Stratton   106

MARSHALL, Augusta Isabella, of Stratford, m. Charles **YOUNGS**, of

  Bridgeport, Oct. 31, 1839, in Stratford, by Rev. Gurdon S. Coit   31

MARSTON, Samuel F., m. Mary C. **BLACKESLEE**, b. of New Burgh St.,

  New York, Nov. 29, 1838, by Rev. Daniel Smith   29

MARTIN, Thomas, m. Susannah **McAVOY**, Sept. 3, 1848, by Rev. Michael

  Lynch. Witnesses; Owen Rock, Mary Burk   87

MASAR, Claus, m. Eliza **LOYED**, Oct. 8, 1837, by Rev. J. W. LeFevre   23

MASON, John H., m. Jane **KING**, b. of Springfield, Mass., Aug. 8, 1841,

  by Rev. J. H. Hunter   42

MATHEWS, Mary Ann, of Bridgeport, formerly of New York City, m.

  Jackson **GUNN**, of Bridgeport, Oct. 17, 1840, by W[illia]m H.

  Noble, J. P.   38

MAY, Ann, m. George F. **HUMISTON**, b. of Bridgeport, Feb. 10, 1850, by

  Rev. Moses Ballou   94

  Caroline, m. Isaac W. **SHEPARD**, June 22, 1843, by Rev. Gurdon S. Coit   55

  Charles, m. Sarah Jane **CALLOW**, Nov. 21, 1838, by [Rev. G. S. Coit]   30

  Elizabeth Ann, of Bridgeport, m. Peter **HOBART**, of Fairfield, Nov.

    10, 1833, by Gurdon S. Coit   2

  Henry, m. Jane Rebecca **BLACK**, b. of Bridgeport, Dec. 31, 1848, by

    Rev. William Reid   97

  Lucy, m. James **HILL**, b. of Bridgeport, May 14, 1837, by Nath[anie]l

    Hewitt   25

MAYER, Fredericka, m. Peter **MONTEM**, June 18, 1853, by Rev. Gurdon S.

  Coit   116

MAYNARD, James L., m. Ann Eliza **JUDSON**, b. of Bridgeport, Feb. 15,

  1852, by Rev. Benj[amin] S. J. Page   111

MELIN, Eliza, of Bridgeport, m. James B. **SHANNON**, of Quebec, L. C.,

  Dec. 22, 1850, by Nathaniel Hewit, V. D. M.   109

MENZER, Lewis, of Lauterback Hesson, Germany, m. Charlotte **HUCHELL**,

  of Loch Hesson, June 30, 1850, by Rev. Benj[amin] S. J. Page   97

MERRELL, **MERIL**, Charlotte, m. Samuel **HAMMOND**, b. of Bridgeport,

  Oct. 7, 1841, by Rev. John H. Hunter   45

  Clarissa, m. Charles G. **SEELEY**, b. of Bridgeport, June 17, 1841,

    by Rev. John H. Hunter   41

  Maud C., m. Kilcin **THEABALL**(?), Apr. 8, 1852, by Rev. Gurdon S.

    Coit   115

MERRETT, John B., m. Maria **MAKER**, Oct. 6, 1847, by Rev. Gurdon S.

  Coit   82

Page

MERWIN, Caleb T., of Milford, m. Maria H. **WHEELER**, of Bridgeport, Apr.
 20, 1852, by Rev. Benj[amin] S. J. Page 113
 Harriet, m. Iverson W. **KNAPP**, b. of Bridgeport, Jan. 23, 1842, by
  Rev. Nathaniel Hewitt 52
MESEROLE, Cadalina A., m. Curtis **PECK**, b. of Bridgeport, Oct. 21, 1840,
 by Rev. John H. Hunter 38
MEYER, Matelina, m. Christopher F. **KELLIN**, Oct. 31, 1852, by Rev.
 Gurdon S. Coit 116
MIDDLEBROOK, MIDDLEBROOKS, Ann M., m. Lemuel H. **BALDWIN**,
 Feb. 8, 1852, by Rev. Gurdon S. Coit 115
 Jerusha, m. Johnson F. **BENNETT**, Nov. 24, 1841, by Rev. G. S. Coit 44
 Maria, m. George **AUGUR**, Nov. 18, 1838, by Rev. G. S. Coit 28
 Sarah A., m. George S. **CURTIS**, Mar. 8, 1843, by Rev. Gurdon S. Coit 55
 Sarah A., of Bridgeport, m. Daniel S. **GRAY**, of Trumbull, Oct. 26,
  1846, by Rev. J. H. Perry 71
 Stiles M., m. Elizabeth B. **NASH**, b. of Bridgeport, Mar. 24, 1834,
  by Rev. Nath[anie]ll Hewitt 5
 Susan, m. George F. **STEVENSON**, Sept. 25, 1846, by Rev. Gurdon S.
  Coit 74
 ----, m. Russell **GORDON**, b. of Bridgeport, [May 25, 1837], by Rev.
  Nath[anie]l Hewitt 25
MILLER, Fanny, m. William **THOMAS**, b. of Bridgeport, Dec. 25, 1844,
 by Rev. Isaac Park 58
 Sarah, m. Charles **WILCOX**, Dec. 24, 1837, by Rev. J. W. LeFevre 24
 William, of New York, m. Mrs. Maria L. **HUBBARD**, of Bridgeport,
  Oct. 12, 1847, by Rev. William Reid 79
MILLS, Abigail L., m. Hiram **DANVILLE**, June 23, 1839, by Rev. G. S.
 Coit 31
 Benjamin B., m. Susan **COUNTIER**, b. of Bridgeport, Nov. 3, 1839,
  by Rev. Daniel Smith 32
 Caroline, m. Henry G. **STRATTON**, b. of Bridgeport, Feb. 13, 1845,
  by Rev. J. Leonard Gilder 59
 Charles, m. Betsey **ROBERTS**, May 16, 1841, by Rev. J. M. Pease 40
 Charles B., m. Elizabeth F. **MILLS**, Oct. 2, 1842, by Rev. Gurdon S. Coit 55
 David Lewis, m. Mary Jane **RICH**, b. of Bridgeport, July 5, 1840,
  by Rev. Daniel Harrington 37
 Elizabeth, m. Richard E. **STANTON**, Jan. 14, 1849, by Rev. Gurdon S.
  Coit 92
 Elizabeth F., m. Charles B. **MILLS**, Oct. 2, 1842, by Rev. Gurdon S. Coit 55
 Huldah A., m. George A. **FULLER**, Feb. 20, 1850, by Rev. Gurdon S.
  Coit 104
 Jonathan, m. Elizabeth Ann **PEET**, May 12, 1839, by Rev. G. S. Coit 31
 Mary, m. Seth **BENEDICT**, Sept. 21, 1853, by Rev. Gurdon S. Coit 116
 Susan A., m. Charles H. **ROWLAND**, Sept. 21, 1846, by Rev. Gurdon
  S. Coit 74
MITCHELL, MITCHEL, Cha[rle]s, m. Mary Ann **FOOTE**, Feb. 1, 1854, by
 Rev. Gurdon S. Coit 116
 Joel, m. Maria **LEWIS**, b. of Bridgeport, Nov. 8, 1835, by Charles

Page

MORRIS, (cont.)

    Witnesses: Michael Gready, Johanna Hayes   66

    Thomas, m. Mercy **CROSBY,** Feb. 4, 1838, in Philadelphia, by

        [Rev. Gurdon S. Coit]   26

MORSE, Sarah Ann, m. William [ ], May 26, 1843, by Rev. Gurdon S. Coit   55

MUDGES, Rachel, m. Henry **CANTHERA,** Mar. 3, 1851, by Rev. Gurdon S.

    Coit   105

MULCHRUM, Harriet Anna, m. George D. **WILLIAMSON,** May [ ], 1850,

    by Rev. Gurdon S. Coit   104

MULLEDY, Mary, m. Richard **CLINTON,** May 17, 1847, by Rev. Michael

    Lynch. Witnesses; John Coyle, Anne Mulledy   78

MULLEN, Bridget, m. Peter **CORNBY,** Nov. 26, 1849, by Rev. Michael

    Lynch. Witnesses; Michael Grant, Mary A. McPherson   95

    Mary E., m. Thomas **KEER,** Aug. 1, 1853, by Rev. Gurdon S. Coit   116

    Michael, m. Elizabeth **LOCKINGTON,** July 20, 1848, by Rev. Michael

    Lynch. Witnesses: Samuel Swanton, Hannah Covel   86

MUNDERLICK, August, m. Mary **HAHNECER,** Dec. 9, 1851, by Rev.

    Gurdon S. Coit   115

MUNGER, Calvin A., m. Grace L. **STILLMAN,** b. of Bridgeport, Nov. 28,

    1844, by Rev. John H. Hunter   58

MURPHY, Catharine, m. Rich[ard] **WILLIAMS,** Mar. 2, [1851], by Rev.

    Michael Lynch. Witnesses: Patrick Bermingham, Mary Murphy   107

    Hugh, m. Bridget **WHEELER,** Nov. 6, 1848, by Rev. Michael Lynch.

    Witnesses: Andrew Crowley, Eliza Collogan   87

    Margaret, m. Patrick **CLARKE,** Mar. 5, 1848, by Rev. Michael Lynch.

    Witnesses: Pat Holland, Susan McEvay   81

    Michael, m. Margaret **HAVEY,** July 11, 1849, by Rev. Michael Lynch.

    Witnesses: John Masterton, Mary Garragan   88

MURRAY, Thomas, m. Catharine **CALLAGAN,** May 5, [1850], by Rev.

    Michael Lynch. Witnesses: Michael Flynn, Eliza Callagan   102

NARY, Ann, m. Joseph **KENNEY,** Nov. 28, [1850], by Rev. Michael Lynch.

    Witnesses: Patrick Devit, Mary Nary   103

NASH, David H., m. Susan E. **STERLING,** b. of Bridgeport, Jan. 6, 1836,

    by Rev. Nath[anie]l Hewett   18

    Elizabeth B., m. Stiles M. **MIDDLEBROOKS,** b. of Bridgeport, Mar.

    24, 1834, by Rev. Nath[aniel]ll Hewitt   5

    Eunice E., m. Andrew E. **JOY,** b. of Bridgeport, June 28, 1843, by

    Rev. Nathaniel Hewitt   52

    Harriet, of Bridgeport, m. Joseph H. **BEERS,** of New York, Jan. 13,

    1847, by Rev. Nath[anie]l Hewit   90

    Mary, of Bridgeport, m. Henry **BIBBINS,** of Fairfield, Nov. 27, 1832,

    by Nathaniel Hewit   2

    William R., m. Julia C. **PILGRIM,** b. of Bridgeport, Nov. 12, 1843,

    by Rev. Nathaniel Hewitt   53

NATHAN, Jacob, m. Eliza **HUYSER,** Oct. 15, 1850, by Rev. Gurdon S. Coit   104

NAUGHER, Harriet, m. Thomas **BROOKS,** Feb. 10, 1849, by Rev. Gurdon S.

    Coit   92

NEEL, Godfrey, m. Catharine **FROST,** June 20, 1853, by Rev. Gurdon S. Coit   116

Page

NILES, (cont.)

Rev. Benj[amin] S. J. Page   114

NOBLE, Charles C., m. Harriet **CURTISS**, June [ ], 1835, by B. G. Noble   11

Sarah Ann, m. Jacob **WODARD**, of Sherman, Jan. 15, 1843, by Rev.
W[illia]m W. Smith   53

William H., m. Harriet J. **BROOKS**, Oct. 16, 1839, by Rev. Gurdon S.
Coit   31

NORMAN, Phebe, of Bridgeport, m. David **LOCKWOOD**, of Black Rock,
Aug. 30, 1846, by Rev. J. H. Perry   71

NORTH, Anna, m. William **LINDLEY**, Mar. 20, 1842, by Rev. Gurdon S.
Coit   55

NORTHEN, William, m. Sarah **ROBBINS**, Jan. 13, 1850, by Rev. Michael
Lynch. Witnesses: John Coybe, Mary Nary   95

NORTHROP, Phebe, of Bridgeport, m. John **BENNETT**, of Athens, N. Y.,
May 15, 1849, by Rev. Nath[anie]l Hewit   91

NORTON, Frederick A., of Fairfield, m. Hannah M. **DeFOREST**, of Fairfield,
July 7, 1844, by Rev. I. I. Gilder   58

George W., of Washington, Conn., m. Rachel **POWLERSON**, of
Bridgeport, Jan. 4, [1836], by Rev. G. S. Coit   13

John F., Rev. of North Bridgwater, Mass., m. Sophia W. **ELLIOTT**,
of Bridgeport, Dec. 31, 1850, by Nathaniel Hewit, V. D. M.   109

NOX, Mary A., m. Charles B. **HUBBELL**, Jr., b. of Bridgeport, Oct. 21,
1850, by Rev. John H. Hunter   38

OAKLEY, Hezekiah S., m. Mary **PRINDLE**, b. of Bridgeport, Mar. 24, 1850,
by Rev. William Reid   98

Martha Matilda, m. John **FOOTE**, b. of Bridgeport, Sept. 24, 1849,
by Rev. William Reid   98

W. B., m. Ann Eliza **CALLOW**, b. of Bridgeport, Oct. 14, 1841, by
Rev. John H. Hunter   43

O'BRIEN, Bridget, m. Richard **KENAN**, Jan. 14, 1849, by Michael Lynch.
Witnesses; John Sheridan, Hanna Crod   87

O'CAINE, Delia M., of Stratford, m. Isaac S. **EDWARDS**, of Trumbull,
Nov. 26, 1844, by Rev. Nathaniel Hewit   63

O'CONNELL, Owen, m. Jane **GIBSON**, Aug. 2, [1846], by Rev. Michael
Lynch. Witnesses: Michael Grady, Mana Mullen   72

Timothy, m. Allice **CONNORS**, Feb. 6, 1848, by Rev. Michael Lynch.
Witnesses: Pat Reilly, Catharine Russell   81

ODELL, Mary A., m. Levi **PARROTT**, b. of Bridgeport, Apr. 22, 1840, by
Rev. Daniel Smith   35

O'DONNELL, Ellen, m. Michael **BURNS**, Apr. 18, 1847, by Rev. Michael
Lynch. Witnesses; Thomas Lillias, Ellen Burk   75

Pat[ric]k, m. Mary **CASEY**, July 9, 1843, by [Rev. Michael Lynch].
Witnesses; Edw[ar]d Casey, Ellen Burke   65

Phil, m. Ellen **SWEET**, Nov. 11, 1840, by Rev. Michael Lynch.
Witnesses: Edward Casey, Ellen Lakey   66

Phil, m. Jane **MACGOWEN**, Sept. 29, 1845, by Rev. Michael Lynch.
Witnesses: Laurmna Mulvehell, Bridget Burke   66

OGDEN, Emeline, of Greenfield, m. Abel **SHERWOOD**, of Fairfield, Mar. 1,

Page

OGDEN, (cont.)

1832, by [Rev. John Blatchford]					3

George E., of Fairfield, m. Mary J. **HALL**, of Bridgeport, Apr. 1,
1849, by Rev. William Reid					97

O'HALLAM, John, m. Ellen **ALLIN**, Oct. 3, 1845, by Rev. Michael Lynch.
Witnesses: James Morusey, Catharine Daly					66

O'KEEFE, William, m. Bridget **LILLIAS**, Feb. 23, 1846, by Rev. Michael
Lynch. Witnesses: Patrick Ray, Ellen Herbert					68

O'KEILER, Giles, m. [   ], **HALL**, wid. of Bronson, b. of Bridgeport,
Dec. 31, 1835, by Rev. Nath[anie]l Hewitt					18

OLMSTEAD, Charles, m. Elizabeth **WARREN**, b. of Bridgeport, Apr. 7, 1839,
by Rev. Nathaniel Hewitt					51

Elizabeth, of Bridgeport, m. William N. **ATWATER**, of New Haven,
Sept. 27, 1847, by Rev. Nath[anie]l Hewitt					90

George, of Newark, N. J., m. Matilda **NICHOLS**, of Bridgeport, June
8, 1834, by Rev. John Blatchford					21

H. Jr., Rev., m. Emily L. **WHEELER**, Jan. 19, 1845, by Rev. Gurdon
S. Coit					64

Virginia Maria, of Milton, Conn., m. Giles G. **HORTON** *, of
Pleasantville, N. Y., Dec. 1, 1849, by Rev. William Reid   *(Perhaps
"**HARTOW**")					98

O'NEIL, James, m. Ann **CAREY**, June 8, [1851], by Rev. Michael Lynch.
Witnesses: Frances Bell, Jane Carty					108

O'ROURKE, Tho[ma]s, m. Bridget **COX**, May 28, 1848, by Rev. Michael
Lynch. Witnesses: W[illia]m McCormuck, Ann McCormuck					84

OSBORNE, Benjamin H., of Trumbull, m. Mary E. **WHITNEY**, of Bridgeport,
Mar. 2, 1846, by Rev. William Reid					70

Henry, m. Mary J. **GRIFFETH**, Dec. 25, 1842, by Rev. Gurdon S. Coit					55

O'SHANE, John, m. Margaret A. **HEWELD**, Nov. 23, 1851, by Rev. Michael
Lynch. Witnesses: Joseph Deniser, Mary A. Chatfield					111

OVEREND, George, m. Ann **HIRSS**, b. of Yorkshire, England, Oct. 23, 1836,
at Thatcherville, by Rev. Gurdon S. Coit					16

OVERTON, Samuel, m. Debby Ann **STREET**, Sept. 29, 1833, by [Rev. John
Blatchford]					3

OWENS, Patrick, m. Rosanna **CONLEY**, Feb. 3, 1850, by Rev. Michael
Lynch. Witnesses: Thomas Walsh, Mary Armstrong					95

PAGE, Jared, m. Maria S. **FRENCH**, Jan. 1, 1837, by Rev. Charles F. Pelton					19

PALMER, Joseph, m. Jane **ROBERTSON**, Apr. 1, 1840, by Rev. G. S. Coit					33

PARKER, Silvia Ann, m. Thomas **BROADSTREET**, (colored), Aug. 28,
1842, by Rev. Gurdon S. Coit					55

PARROTT, Caroline M., of Bridgeport, m. Jacob S. **GURNSEY**, of Stratford,
Oct. 26, 1841, by Rev. Salmon C. Perry					43

Eleanor M., m. Edwin D. **HURD**, June 27, 1847, by Rev. J. Benjamin
S. Page					76

Eliza, m. John W. **BOUTON**, May 19, 1846, by Rev. Gurdon S. Coit					74

Elizabeth, of Bridgeport, m. Abram F. **THOMPSON**, of New Haven,
Aug. 29, 1847, by Rev. Nath[anie]l Hewit					90

Emily, m. Eliphalet B. **STEVENS**, b. of Bridgeport, July 20, 1842,

Page

PARROTT, (cont.)

    by Rev. Salmon C. Perry   47

    Hannah, of Fairfield, m. Isaac **SCOTT**, of Waterbury, May 26, 1834,

        by Rev. Nathaniel Ruggles   6

    Levi, m. Mary A. **ODELL**, b. of Bridgeport, Apr. 22, 1840, by Rev.

        Daniel Smith   35

    Mary Ann, of Bridgeport, m. [ ] **TAYLOR**, of Danbury, Dec. 31,

        1835, by Rev. John Blatchford   22

    Sarah E., m. Wakeman W. **WELLS**, b. of Bridgeport, Oct, 5, [1845],

        by Rev. J. H. Perry   60

PARSONS, Harvey A., m. Eliza Ann **GUNN**, b. of Bridgeport, Oct. 3, 1836,

    by Rev. G. S. Coit   15

    Martha M., m. Stephen S. **STERLING**, Aug. 13, 1839, by Rev. G. S. Coit   31

PAT, Mabel, of Bridgeport, m. W[illia]m Beach **JOHNSON**, of Bermingham,

    June 9, 1844, by Rev. J. L. Gilder   57

PATCHIN, PATCHEN, David S., m. Julia Angeline **ROSS**, Sept. 20, 1837, by

    Rev. J. W. Lefevre   23

    David S., of Bridgeport, m. Elizabeth **PEET**, of Fairfield, Apr. 24,

        1851, by Rev. Benj[amin] S. J. Page   106

    Jane, m. Garry **JUDSON**, b. of Bridgeport, Sept. 28, 1833, by

        Nathaniel Hewit   2

    Jemantha, m. George **SEELEY**, b. of Bridgeport, Mar. [ ], 1839, by

        Rev. Nathaniel Hewitt   51

PATRICK, Charles, of Milford, m. Susannah **HOYT**, of Norwalk, July 22,

    1850, by Rev. Benj[amin] S. J. Page   97

PATTERSON, William, m. Sarah Ann **BATES**, b. of Bridgeport, Sept. 28,

    1846, by Rev. Nathaniel Hewit   73

PEABODY, Geo[rge] H., of Columbus, Ga., m. Elvira **CANFIELD**, of

    Bridgeport, Nov. 1, 1851, by Rev. Nathaniel Hewit   114

PEASE, Hannah B., of Bridgeport, m. Joseph **CROWENBURGER**, of Allsetts,

    Germany, Apr., 5, 1835, by Rev. John Blatchford   22

PECAR, Eliza, m. John **GUARD**, Aug. 9, 1837, by [Rev. Gurdon S. Coit]   26

PECK, Curtis, m. Hannah M. **ALLEN**, Oct. 10, 1838, by [Rev. Gurdon S.

    Coit]   28

    Curtis, m. Cadalina E. **MESEROLE**, b. of Bridgeport, Oct. 21, 1840,

        by Rev. John H. Hunter   38

    Jeannetta, m. George **CRAWFORD**, Nov. 1, 1832, by [Rev. John

        Blatchford]   3

    Joel C., m. Maria **WHEELER**, b. of Bridgeport, Sept. 17, 1848,

        by Rev. Moses Ballow   88

    Maria, m. Christopher **STRICKEFIELD**, Nov. 3, 1840, by Rev. Michael

        Lynch. Witnesses; Fred Lutz, Mary Peck   66

    Nathan, of Bridgeport, m. Rebecca Ann **WEED**, of Darien, Conn., Oct.

        27, 1835, by Rev. Charles F. Pelton   12

    Richard, m. Mary Ann **SMITH**, Oct. 16, 1842, by Rev. Gurdon S. Coit   55

    Sally, of Newtown, m. Johnathan **RIGGS**, of Fairfield, Feb. 8, 1835,

        by Rev. G. S. Coit   7

    Samuel B., m. Julia A. **FAYERWEATHER**, Jan. 5, 1842, by Rev.

Page

PECK, (cont.)

Page

SCHANK, SCHANCK,(cont.)

Ellen, m. Charles A. **STUDLEY**, Mar. 3, 1851, by Rev. Gurdon S. Coit   105

SCHAUL, Charles, m. Mary **FREECK**, Nov. 14, 1852, by Rev. Gurdon S.

Coit   116

SCHELESEY, Cha[rle]s, m. Catharine **FRIES**, Oct. 14, 1851, by Rev. Gurdon

S. Coit   115

SCHILLINGER, John, of Sag Harbour, L. I., m. Julia Ann **FANTON**, Oct. 9,

1836, by Rev. Gurdon S. Coit   15

SCHMIDT, Mary H., m. Lawrence **ANDERSON**, b. of Bridgeport, Jan. 11,

1847, by Rev. Nath[anie]l Hewit   90

SCHULTZ, Frederick G., m. Caroline M. **JOHNSON**, b. of East Bridgeport,

June 23, 1844, by Rev. Morris D. C. Crawford   59

SCHWOLBACK, Jacob, m. Sally **HULL**, b. of Bridgeport, [Jan.] 20, [1850],

by Rev. Moses Ballou   94

SCOTT, Albert, m. Caroline **SEELEY**, b. of Bridgeport, Oct. 30, 1848, by

Rev. Moses Ballow   88

Isaac, of Waterbury, m. Hannah **PARROTT**, of Fairfield, May 26, 1834,

by Rev. Nathaniel Ruggles   6

John, m. Mary B. **SHERWOOD**, Nov. 4, 1844, by Rev. Gurdon S. Coit   64

Reuben, m. Mary L. **PORTER**, Feb. [ ], 1844, by Rev. Gurdon S. Coit   56

SCOVILLE, Betsey, m. Edward **DAVISON**, Sept. 1, 1850, by Rev. Gurdon S.

Coit   104

SCRIBNER, William, m. Lucinda **WRIGHT**, b. of Westport, May 27, 1837,

by Rev. Nath[anie]l Hewitt   25

SEDAN, William, m. Polly **SEELEY**, Mar. 17, 1849, by Rev. Cyrus Silliman   94

SEEBITTS, John A., m. Louisa **WIGNER**, Feb. 13, 1852, by Rev. Gurdon S.

Coit   115

SEELEY, Caroline, m. Albert **SCOTT**, b. of Bridgeport, Oct. 30, 1848, by

Rev. Moses Ballow   88

Charles G., m. Clarissa **MERRELL**, b. of Bridgeport, June 17, 1841,

by Rev. John H. Hunter   41

Charlotte, m. Ezra C. **PRIME**, Oct. 23, 1845, by Rev. Gurdon S. Coit   64

George, m. Jemantha **PATCHIN**, b. of Bridgeport, Mar. [ ], 1839,

by Rev. Nathaniel Hewitt   51

Lyman W., m. Susan M. **BENJAMIN**, b. of Bridgeport, Apr. 22, 1844,

by Rev. John H. Hunter   56

Mary, of Bridgeport, m. Benajah **PLACE**, of Long Island, Oct. 20,

1833, by Gurdon S. Coit   1

Polly, m. William **SEDAN**, Mar. 17, 1849, by Rev. Cryus Silliman   94

Rebecca, of Bridgeport, m. Daniel **EDWARDS**, of Trumbull, June 25,

1850, by Rev. Bemj[amin] S. J. Page   96

----, m. Jane **TUTTLE**, Dec. 31, 1849, by Rev. Gurdon S. Coit   104

SEGER, Evanna, of Bridgeport, m. Christian Augustus **DANAKER**, of

Philadelphia, Oct. 8, 1840, by Rev. Stephen A. Medley, of

Philadelphia   37

Philip B., m. Sarah J. **TOMLINSON**, Apr. 17, 1848, by Rev. Gurdon

S. Coit   92

SELLECK, Warren M., m. Mary Ann **BAILEY**, b. of Bridgeport, Sept. 9,

Page

SMITH, (cont.)

Gurdon S. Coit 26

Julia Ann, m. James **ROBINSON,** b. of Bridgeport, Sept. 14, 1834, by
Rev. John Blatchford 21

Lewis K., m. Margarette M. **KEMPS,** Nov. 1, 1846, by Rev. Gurdon S.
Coit 74

Mahetable, of Bridgeport, m. Ely **GILMAN,** of Hartford, July 15, 1834,
by Rev. John Blatchford 21

Mary Ann, m. Moses T. **BUCKINGHAM,** Dec. 12, 1836, by Rev.
Gurdon S. Coit 17

Mary Ann, m. Richard **PECK,** Oct. 16, 1842, by Rev. Gurdon S. Coit 55

Mary S., m. Charles **MALLETT,** Nov. 25, 1841, by Rev. G. S. Coit 44

SMYTH,[see also **SMITH**], John, m. Elizabeth **DAUGHERTY,** Feb. 20, 1848,
by Rev. Michael Lynch. Witnesses; Thomas Flynn, Mary Flynn 81

Margarette, m. Edw[ard] **MAGUIRE,** Sept. 29, 1844, by Rev. Michael
Lynch. Witnesses: John Moor, Margaret Moor 65

Patrick, m. Mary **FARELLY,** July 13, 1851, by Rev. Michael Lynch.
Witnesses: Patrick Collins, Ann Smyth 110

SNOW, Mary Ann, m. John **LEWIS,** b. of Bridgeport, June 23, 1850, by Rev.
William Reid 99

SOLLY, Geo[rge], m. Elizabeth **PENFIELD,** Oct. 13, 1847, at Black Rock,
by Rev. Benj[amin] S. J. Page 78

SOWECK, Ann, m. Edmund **GILLINGHANE,** b. of Bridgeport, Feb. 2, 1835,
by Rev. John Blatchford 22

SPARKS, Martha, m. John **McINTIRE,** Dec. 17, 1843, by Rev. W[illia]m H.
Smith 54

SPEARS, SPIERS, Charles H., of New York, m. Margaret **McMULLIN,** of
Bridgeport, Nov. 12, 1850, by Rev. Benj[amin] S. J. Page 101

Mary, of Bridgeport, m. Isaac **LOZIE,** of Belleville, N. J., Oct.
23, 1844, by Rev. J. L. Golden 58

SPELMAN, SPILLMAN, John, m. Catharine **EARLE,** Dec. 25, 1852, by Rev.
Gurdon S. Coit 116

Michael, m. Catharine **HIGGINS,** Feb. 9, [1851], by Rev. Michael Lynch.
Witnesses: Thomas Costelo, Bridget Russell 107

SPENCER, Mary, m. John **LEGO,** May [ ], 1832, by [Rev. John Blatchford] 3

SPERRY, Pearl H., m. Adeline **THOMPSON,** Nov. 23, 1840, by Rev. Gurdon
S. Coit 39

SPIERS, [see under **SPEARS**]

SPINNING, Anna M., m. John F. **WHEATON,** b. of Bridgeport, Oct. 17,
1847, by Rev. Benj[amin] S. J. Page 77

Charles C., m. Caroline M. **SMITH,** b. of Bridgeport, Nov. 13, 1850,
by Rev. Benj[amin] S. J. Page 101

Elizabeth, of Bridgeport, m. Marcus **DOUGLASS,** of Newark, N. J.,
Nov. 21, 1847, by Rev. Benj[amin] S. J. Page 80

SPROULS, Samuel E., of Charleston, S. C., m. Rosella **DARROW,** of
Bridgeport, Oct. 1, 1835, by Rev. Gurdon S. Coit 11

SQUIER, SQUIERS, Louisa, of Danbury, m. George W. **WHITE,** Sept. 10,
1843, by Rev. W[illia]m H. Smith 54

Page

SQUIER, SQUIERS, (cont.)

William, of Weston, m. Sarah J. **FOSTER**, of Bridgeport, May 18,
1836, by Rev. Nath[anie]l Hewitt   18

STANDISH, Laura, m. David **McKENZIE**, May 9, 1841, by Rev. J. M. Pease   40

STANLEY, Phebe, m. Henry M. **HINE**, Dec. 26, 1850, by Rev. David L.
Parmelee   103

Phebe, m. Henry M. **FINN**, b. of Bridgeport, Dec. 26, 1851, by Rev.
Mr. Palmelee, of South Farms, Conn. Witness: Nathaniel Hewit, V.
D. M.   109

STANTON, Richard E., m. Elizabeth **MILLS**, Jan. 14, 1849, by Rev. Gurdon
S. Coit   92

STAPLES, Edward J., m. Charlotte H. **LOUNSBURY**, [Feb.] 17, [1848], by
Rev. Gurdon S. Coit   82

STARR, Thomas, m. Amelia Ann **SIMONS**, Nov. 27, 1836, by Rev. Charles
F. Pelton   16

Timothy, m. Adeline **DEMING**, Sept. 20, 1832, by [Rev. John Blatchford]   3

STEARNES, Jonathan, of New York, m. Hannah **BROWNSON**, of Bridgeport,
Nov. 12, 1850, by Rev. Benj[amin] S. J. Page   101

STERLING, Charles F., m. Emmeline A. **BROOKS**, May 8, 1837, by [Rev.
Gurdon S. Coit]   26

Cornelia, m. William R. **BUNNEL**, b. of Bridgeport, Jan. 24, 1838,
by [Rev. John Woodbridge]   29

Daniel H., m. Maria **BECK**, b. of Bridgeport, Dec. 7, 1842, by Rev.
John H. Hunter   48

Eliza C., of Bridgeport, m. William C. **ELLISON**, of New York, May
8, 1843, by Rev. John H. Hunter   48

Gasford, of Bridgeport, m. Adelia B. **SHERWOOD**, of Weston, Nov. 30,
1834, by Rev. Nath[anie]l Hewitt   17

Julia M., of Bridgeport, m. Pinckney W. **ELLSWORTH**, of Hartford,
Oct. 10, 1842, by Rev. Nathaniel Hewitt   52

Mary, m. John **BOOTH**, b. of Trumbull, Jan. 7, 1841, by Rev. Nathaniel
Hewitt   50

Sarah Caroline, m. Philo C. **CALHOUN**, b. of Bridgeport, Aug. 9,
1837, by Rev. Nath[anie]l Hewitt   25

Stephen S., m. Martha M. **PARSONS**, Aug. 13, 1839, by Rev. G. S. Coit   31

Susan E., m. David H. **NASH**, b. of Bridgeport, Jan. 6, 1836, by
Rev. Nath[anie]l Hewitt   18

STEVENS, Eliphalet B., m. Emily **PARROTT**, b. of Bridgeport, July 20,
1842, by Rev. Salmon C. Perry   47

Henry, m, Henrietta Louisa K. **TREAT**, Apr. 6, 1842, by Rev. Gurdon
S. Coit   55

Jane, of Bridgeport, m. Duine **CHATFIELD**, of Oxford, Jan. 8, 1834,
by Rev. Gurdon S. Coit   4

Lewis, m. Mary **JACKERMAN**, Sept. 20, 1835, by Rev. C. F. Pelton   11

STEVENSON, STEPHENSON, George F., m. Susan **MIDDLEBROOK**, Sept.
25, 1846, by Rev. Gurdon S. Coit   74

William G., m. Lucinda **THOMPSON**, b. of Bridgeport, Aug. 24, 1834,
by Rev. Davis Stocking   6

Page

STEWART, J. W., m. Caroline **DAVIS**, Aug. 21, 1843, by Rev. Gurdon S.
    Coit   56
STILES, Josephine, m. James **SUTHERLAND**, b. of Bridgeport, [July] 15,
    [1849], by Rev. Moses Ballou   91
    Lewis W., of South Britain, m. Angeline **NICHOLS**, of Bridgeport,
      July 9, 1843, by Rev. J. Leonard Gilder   48
STILLMAN, Grace L., m. Calvin A. **MUNGER**, b. of Bridgeport, Nov. 28,
    1844, by Rev. John H. Hunter   58
    Harriet, m. Fenelow **HUBBELL**, b. of Bridgeport, Sept. 12, 1833, by
      [ ] Tacaberry   1
    Isabella, of Bridgeport, m. Hickson **FOWLER**, of Brooklyn, N. Y.,
      Nov. 7, 1849, by Rev. Benjamin S. J. Page   93
    Margarette M., m. Rufus **BURK**, b. of Bridgeport, Oct. 11, 1844, by
      Rev John H. Hunter   58
STILLSON, Levi B., of Trumbull, m. Sally **TYRELL**, of Bridgeport, May
    10, 1840, by Rev. Daniel Smith   35
STILT, Theresa, m. Gottlieb **MALL**, Mar. 20, 1853, by Rev. Gurdon S. Coit   116
STOCKWELL, George, m. Adeline **ALLEN**, b. of Bridgeport, June 14, 1835,
    by Rev. Gurdon S. Coit   9
STODDARD, W[illia]m, of Plymouth, m. Mary A. **PENDLETON**, of
    Stratford, Jan. 23, 1849, by Rev. Moses Ballow, in Stratford   89
STOUT, Benjamin F., of St. Louis, Mo., m. Delia C. **THOMPSON**, of
    Bridgeport, Sept. 17, 1847, by Rev. Benjamin S. J. Page   76
STRATTON, Clarissa, of Bridgeport, m. John B. **SMITH**, of Easton, July 21,
    1846, by Rev. William Reid   70
    Daniel, of Bridgeport, m. Susan **CURTIS**, of Trumbull, May 29, 1839,
      by Rev. Daniel Smith   30
    George S., m. Ann Eliza **WOOLEY**, b. of Bridgeport, May 5, 1844, by
      Rev. Nathaniel Hewit   62
    Henry G., m. Caroline **MILLS**, b. of Bridgeport, Feb. 13, 1845, by
      Rev. J. Leonard Gilder   59
    Jane J., m. Theodore **HUBBELL**, Nov. 25, 1850, by Rev. Gurdon S. Coit   104
    Mahala, of Norwalk, m. Robert **KANE**, of Oxford, Nov. 14, 1847, by
      Rev. William Reid   79
    Mary, m. J. W. **BILLINGS**, Dec. 9, 1850, by Rev. Gurdon S. Coit   105
    Mary A., m. John H. **BEACH**, Oct. 10, 1847, by Rev. Gurdon S. Coit   82
    Mary E., m. W[illia]m Hull **RUSSELL**, Nov. 14, 1853, by Rev. Gurdon
      S. Coit   116
    Sam[ue]l, m. Louisa **HALL**, Jan. 9, 1848, by Rev. Gurdon S. Coit   82
    Sarah A., m. Barzillai **BANKS**, Oct. 25, 1842, by Rev. Gurdon S. Coit   55
    Therasa, m. Sam[ue]l S. **PERRY**, b. of Bridgeport, Nov. 1, 1843, by
      Rev. J. Leonard Gilder   49
STREET, Debby Ann, m. Samuel **OVERTON**, Sept. 29, 1833, by [Rev. John
    Blatchford]   3
STRETING, Cornelius, m. Susan A. **HALL**, b. of Bridgeport, May 12, 1850,
    by Rev. Nath[anie]l Hewit   100
STRICKEFIELD, Christopher, m. Maria **PECK**, Nov. 3, 1840, by Rev.
    Michael Lynch. Witnesses: Fred Lutz, Mary Peck   66

Page

STRONG,Emily, m. L. C. SHEPARD, May 7, 1837, by [Rev. Gurdon S. Coit]   26

STUDLEY, Almira, m. George TREAT, Oct. 15, 1843, by Rev. Gurdon S.
    Coit   56

    Charles A., m. Ellen SCHANCK, Mar. 3, 1851, by Rev. Gurdon S. Coit   105

SUMMERS, Abby G., m. Abijah BEARDSLEE, b. of Bridgeport, Jan. 28,
    1849, by Rev. Benjamin S. J. Page   87

    Eden, of Monroe, m. Louisa A. SHERMAN, of Bridgeport, [Feb.] 13,
    [1848], by Rev. G. S. Gilbert   81

    Eunice Catharine, m. James H. WINTON, b. of Bridgeport, Nov. 23,
    1836, by James H. Linsley   17

    Jabez, m. Susan EDWARDS, b. of Bridgeport, Oct. 1, 1843, by Rev.
    John H. Hunter   49

SUTHERLAND, James, m. Josephine STILES, b. of Bridgeport, [July] 15,
    [1849], by Rev. Moses Ballou   91

SWEENEY, Johanna, m. John CONNER, May 18, [1851], by Rev. Michael
    Lynch. Witnesses; Dan[ie]l Mallehill, Margaret Sullivan   108

SWEET, Ellen, m. Phil O'DONNELL, Nov. 11, 1840, by Rev. Michael
    Lynch. Witnesses: Edward Casey, Ellen Lakey   66

SWORD, SWARDS, Bridget, m. Michael CHARY, Feb. 22, [1852], by Rev.
    Michael Lynch. Witnesses: Richard Swords, Bridget Malone   112

    Margaret, m. Patrick HEWES, June 15, 1851, by Rev. Michael Lynch.
    Witnesses: William Lynch, Bridget Malone   110

    Rose, m. Martin COSTELO, Jan. 25, 1852, by Rev. Michael Lynch.
    Witnesses: Michael Mounts, Catharine Leonies   112

TAAFFE, [see also TUFE], Mary, m. Thomas NEWMAN,, Apr. 8, [1850], by
    Rev. Michael Lynch. Witnesses: Andrew Newman, Catharine Dunn   102

TAYLOR, Ormel P., of Brookfield, Conn., m. Elizabeth HIGGINS, of
    Bridgeport, July 26, 1841, by Rev. Salmon C. Perry   42

    Thomas B., of New Town, m. Elizabeth A. HOYT, of Bridgeport, Oct.
    31, 1839, by Rev. Daniel Smith   32

    Ward, of Bridgeport, m. Eliza S. WELLS, of Fairfield, Jan. 1,
    1837, by Rev. Charles F. Pelton   20

    William, m. Margaret GRAHAM, b. of New York, Aug. 7, 1835,. by
    Rev. John Blatchford   22

    ----, of Danbury, m. Mary Ann PARROTT, of Bridgeport, Dec. 31,
    1835, by Rev. John Blatchford   22

TERRY, Sarah A., of New York, m. Hoel H. BOTSFORD, of Bridgeport,
    Aug. 25, 1851, by Rev. Benj[amin] S. J. Page   109

THATCHER, John C., m. Mary FITCH, Oct. 5, 1837, by [Rev. Gurdon S.
    Coit]   26

THAYER, Edward L., of Mendon, Mass., m. Rebecca E. JOHNSON, of
    Boston, Mass., May 8, 1851, by Rev. Moses Ballou   106

THEABALL (?), Kilcin, m. Maud C. MERIL, Apr. 8, 1852, by Rev. Gurdon
    S. Coit   115

THOMAS, Henry, of Albany, N. J*, m. Lucy W. WATERMAN, of
    Bridgeport, Jan. 24, 1849, by Rev. Nath[anie]l Hewit *(N. Y.?)   91

    Lewis, m. Eliza Ann ROBINSON, June 16, 1838, by [Rev. Gurdon S.
    Coit]   28

Page

TYRELL, Charles H., of Southberry, m. Jane **SHERMAN**, of Redding, June 5,
  1844, by Rev. J. L. Gilder   57
  Sally, of Bridgeport, m. Levi B. **STILLSON**, of Trumbull, May 10,
  1840, by Rev. Daniel Smith   35
TYSON, Arthur B., of New York, m. Mary R. **HATCH**, of Bridgeport, Nov.
  27, 1834, by Rev. Davis Stocking   7
UFFORD, Dixon D., m. Harriet J. **GOULD**, [Nov.] 15, [1835], by Anson
  Rood   12
  Sarah, m. Wheeler V. **NICHOLS**, b. of Bridgeport, May 4, 1835, by
  Rev. John Blatchford   22
VANCE, Harriet, m. David **HULL**, Sept. [ ], 1846, by Rev. Gurdon S. Coit 74
  William S., m. Sarah B. **WELLS**, Feb. 7, 1842, by Rev. Gurdon S. Coit   55
VAN KEERIN, Eleazer, of New York, m. Mary **CROSBY**, of Bridgeport, Dec.
  7, 1841, by Rev. John H. Hunter   45
WAIT, Thomas C., m. Hannah **HOWECK**, b. of Bridgeport, July 7, 1834, by
  Rev. John Blatchford   21
WAKELEE, WAKELEY, Birdsey, of Huntington, m. Adelia A. **BROWN**, of
  Bridgeport, Oct. 8, 1842, by Rev. Nathaniel Hewitt   52
  Delia A., m. Samuel **BOARDMAN**, Oct. 25, 1846, by Rev. Gurdon S.
  Coit   74
  Granville, of Stratford, m. Delia Ann **LEWIS**, of Bridgeport, Apr.
  2, 1834, by Rev. Gurdon S. Coit   5
WAKEMAN, Joseph, of Fairfield, m. Sally Ann **BULKELEY**, of
  Whitesborough, N. Y., May 11, 1834, by Rev. Nathaniel Ruggles   5
WALKER, Caroline A., m. Robert **LINEN**, May 25, 1840, by Rev. G. S. Coit 34
  Isaac B., m. Abby B. **SHERMAN**, Nov. 2, 1834, by B. G. Noble   8
  Sarah, m. Samuel B. **HALL**, b. of Bridgeport, Dec. 25, 1845, by John
  H. Hunter   67
  Sarah E., m. Alfred **GREGORY**, July 12, 1837, by [Rev. Gurdon S. Coit]   26
WALLACE, Uriah, m. Sarah E. **TUTTLE**, b. of Bridgeport, Oct. 25, 1846,
  by Rev. William Reed   72
WALSH, Margaret, m. Mich[ae]l **CONDON**, Oct. 18, 1843, by [Rev. Michael
  Lynch]. Witnesses: Tho[ma]s Casey, Bridget Condon   65
  Thomas, m. Johanna Coleman, Sept. 3, 1848, by Rev. Michael Lynch.
  Witnesses: Garrett Cotter, Catharine Reilly   86
WALTERS, WALTER, Henry, m. Marcella **LANGAN**, Oct. 20, [1850], by
  Rev. Michael Lynch. Witnesses: Daniel Rocke, Mary Gormly   103
  Mary A., m. William R. **DIBBLE**, June 26, 1843, by Rev. Gurdon S. Coit   56
WARD, Cha[rle]s, m. Elizabeth **SMITH**, Nov. 6, 1849, by Rev. Gurdon S. Coit 104
  Daniel, m. Mary Ann **HURR**, Sept. 8, 1845, by Rev. Michael Lynch.
  Witnesses: Patrick Ward, Mary Cleary   66
  Elizabeth, m. James **JENKINS**, July 2, 1851, by Rev. Gurdon S. Coit   115
  James, m. Mary **CULLANE**, Apr. 21, 1840, by Rev. Gurdon S. Coit   34
  John, m. Maretta **HAMLIN**, Sept. 4, 1842, by Rev. Gurdon S. Coit   55
  William E., m. Celia F. **BLAKEMAN**, Jan. 3, 1847, by Rev. Gurdon S.
  Coit   74
WARDEN, Eunice A., m. David **WHEELER**, Sept. 29, 1833, by [Rev. John
  Blatchford]   3

Page

WHITNEY, (cont.)

    Sarah E., m. Henry **BLACKEMAN**, June 30, 1846, by Rev. William Reid   70

[WHITTEMORE], [see under **WHETTEMORE**]

WICKES, WICKS, Chauncey B., of Albany, N. Y., m. Frances **LORD**, of

    Bridgeport, June 26, 1849, by Rev. Nath[anie]l Hewit   100

    Francis, of Bridgeport, m. Ez[r]a **ANDREWS**, of Danbury, May 13,

        1846, by Rev. William Reid   70

WIGNER, Louisa, m. John A. **SEEBITTS**, Feb. 13, 1852, by Rev. Gurdon S.

    Coit   115

WILCOX, Augustus W., m. Harriet N. **BALDWIN**, Jan. 7, 1846, by Rev.

    James H. Perry   62

    Charles, m. Sarah **MILLER**, Dec. 24, 1837, by Rev. J. W. LeFevre   24

WILDER, Almond, m. Susan **GOLBERT**, Mar. 17, 1847, by Rev. Gurdon S.

    Coit   82

WILDNER, August, m. J. F. **CLARKE**, Apr. 14, 1850, by Rev. Gurdon S.

    Coit   104

WILLES, George Augusta, m. Mary Jane **WHEELER**, May 28, 1837, by

    [Rev. Gurdon S. Coit]   26

WILLIAMS, Amelia, m. W[illia]m E. **JOHNSON**, Sept. 21, 1845, by Rev.

    Gurdon S. Coit   64

    Charles Ropes, m. Emily Austin **HODGES**, Oct. 23, 1850, by Rev.

        Gurdon S. Coit   104

    Rich[ard], m. Catharine **MURPHY**, Mar. 2, [1851], by Rev. Michael

        Lynch. Witnesses: Patrick Bermingham, Mary Murphy   107

    Sarah Ann, m. Richard **COSTER**, Oct. 30, 1843, by Rev. W[illia]m H.

        Smith   54

    William H., m. Maria **MERRETT**, Jan. 6, 1847, by Rev. Gurdon S. Coit   74

WILLIAMSON, George D., m. Harriet Anna **MULCHRUM**, May [ ], 1850,

    by Rev. Gurdon S. Coit   104

WILLIS, Charles, m. Hannah Maria **KNAPP**, b. of Bridgeport, Dec. 28, 1843

    by Rev. Nathaniel Hewit   62

WILMOTT, WILLMOT, WILMOT, John W., m. Susan **FOGLE**, b. of

    Bridgeport, May 6, 1845, by Rev. John H. Hunter   59

    Louisa, m. Monson H. **HYDE**, b. of Bridgeport, Sept. 12, 1836, by

        Rev. Gurdon S. Coit   14

    Samuel, m. Mary Francis **DARROW**, Sept. 8, 1834, by Rev. G. S. Coit   6

    Samuel, m. Cornelia **SHERWOOD**, Nov. 7, 1853, by Rev. Gurdon S.

        Coit   116

    Thomas J., m. Louisa **GREGORY**, Oct. 1, 1834, by Rev. G. S. Coit   7

WILSON, WILLSON, Abigail A., of Bridgeport, m. Henry **WILSON**, of

    Fairfield, Apr. 12, 1840, by Rev. Matthew Batchelor   36

    Henry, of Fairfield, m. Abigail A. **WILSON**, of Bridgeport, Apr. 12,

        1840, by Rev. Matthew Batchelor   36

    Isaac, m. Elizabeth **SHEPERD**, b. of Bridgeport, Nov. 17, 1833, by

        Nathaniel Hewitt   2

    Roxanna, m. James **CAREY**, Oct. 24, 1841, by Rev. Gurdon S. Coit   44

    William, m. Eliza Ann **HODGES**, Oct. 25, 1837, by Rev. J. W. LeFevre   23

WINCHELL, James, m. May Jane **BUTLER**, b. of New Haven, Aug. 15,